ByPass
THE BANKS

JACK & MARGY FLYNN

Quantity sales special discounts are available on quantity purchases by corporations, associations, and others. For details, contact the publisher at the address above.

Orders by U.S. trade bookstores and wholesalers. Email info@BeyondPublishing.net

The Beyond Publishing Speakers Bureau can bring authors to your live event. For more information or to book an event contact the Beyond Publishing Speakers Bureau speak@BeyondPublishing.net

The Author can be reached directly at takebackourrights@yahoo.com, www.CitizensoftheAmericanConstitution.net.

Manufactured and printed in the United States of America distributed globally by BeyondPublishing.net

BEYOND
PUBLISHING

New York | Los Angeles | London | Sydney

ISBN Hardcover: 978-1-637922-70-5

ISBN Softcover: 978-1-63792-335-1

- How to Buy, Sell, Finance & Invest in Property in Tough Times or Good Times

- ByPass the Stranglehold that Banks & Government Impose Upon Society

- See How the Information & Programs in this Book can Help the American People Amass Real Wealth & Financial Security

This book expresses the authors' views regarding this nation and how the American People, if they so choose, can help themselves by and through the methods presented in this book.

TABLE OF CONTENTS

SECTION SIX – REAL ESTATE AND OTHER SWAPS & TRADES PROGRAMS

SECTION SEVEN – EPILOGUE

SECTION EIGHT – NARRATIVE EXPLANATIONS FOR
ByPass BUY/SELL PROGRAMS

SECTION NINE – *ByPass* BUY/SELL PROJECTIONS

SECTION TEN – *ByPass* BUY/RENT/SELL PROJECTIONS

DEDICATION

This book is dedicated to the principles of freedom, independence, justice, truth and right-mindedness that wise men, women, truth-tellers and saints have been patiently imparting to humanity from the very beginning. My wife, Margy, has been part of this rare human, timeless grouping all of her existence, therefore, a recipient of this dedication. It is now time for all of us to develop, then, raise human consciousness so we can grasp, accept and live these principles for a better, more humane, happier and healthier human society, founded in Freedom and Independence.

~~~~~~~~~~~~~~~~~~

Wise Words from Two Aware Founding Fathers

"If the American people ever allow private banks to control the issue of their currency, first by inflation, then by deflation, the banks and corporations that will grow up around [the banks] will deprive the people of all property until their children wake-up homeless on the continent their fathers conquered. The issuing power should be taken from the banks and restored to the people, to whom it properly belongs." ~ Thomas Jefferson, (1743 – 1826), Founding Father, 3rd President of the United States of America.

"I sincerely believe that banking establishments are more dangerous than standing armies, and that the principle of spending money to be paid by posterity under the name of funding is but swindling futurity on a large scale." – Thomas Jefferson to John Taylor, 1816. ME 15:23

"Everything predicted by the enemies of banks, in the beginning, is now coming to pass. We are to be ruined now by the deluge of bank paper. It is cruel that such revolutions in private fortunes should be at the mercy of avaricious adventurers, who, instead of employing their capital, if any they have, in manufactures, commerce, and other useful pursuits, make it an instrument to burden all the interchanges of property with their swindling profits, profits which are the price of no useful industry of theirs." – Thomas Jefferson to Thomas Cooper, 1814. ME 14:61

"The Bank of the United States is one of the most deadly hostilities existing, against the principles and form of our Constitution. An institution like this, penetrating by its branches every part of the Union, acting by command and in phalanx, may, in a critical moment, upset the government. I deem no government safe which is under the vassalage of any self-constituted authorities, or any other authority than that of the nation, or its regular functionaries. What an obstruction could not this bank of the United States, with all its branch banks, be in time of war! It might dictate to us the peace we should accept, or withdraw its aids. Ought we then to give further growth to an institution so powerful, so hostile?" – Thomas Jefferson to Albert Gallatin, 1803. ME 10:437

"Our whole system of banks is a violation of every honest principle of banks. There is no honest bank but a bank of deposit. A bank that issues paper at interest is a pickpocket or a robber. But the delusion will have its course. … An aristocracy is growing out of them that will be as fatal as the feudal barons if unchecked in time." ~ John Adams, (1735 – 1826), Founding Father, 2nd President of the United States of America, to Benjamin Rush: Dec. 27, 1810

"Banks have done more injury to the religion, morality, tranquility, prosperity, and even wealth of the nation than they can have done or ever will do good." ~ John Adams

"All the perplexities, confusion and distress in America arise not from defects in their Constitution or Confederation, nor from want of honor or virtue, so much as downright ignorance of the nature of coin, credit, and circulation." ~ John Adams

And

A Chilling Prophecy

~ As a reminder of what the communists have intended for our country for *decades*, we include the following statements from Nikita Khrushchev, former leader of the USSR:

"We will take America without firing a shot … we will bury you!

"We can't expect the American people to jump from capitalism to communism, but we can assist their elected leaders in giving them small doses of socialism, until they awaken one day to find that they have communism.

"We do not have to invade the United States; we will destroy you from within."

From what has occurred in America over the past 18 plus months, it appears that Khrushchev was absolutely correct, aided and abetted by the necessary and willing cooperation of the American governments–federal, state, county and local.

Some poignant quotes from *The Gulag Archipelago* by the Russian author, philosopher, Aleksandr Solzhenitsyn, 1918 – 1956:

"If only it were all so simple! If only there were evil people somewhere insidiously committing evil deeds, and it were necessary only to separate them from the rest of us and destroy them. But the line dividing good and evil cuts through the heart of every human being. And who is willing to destroy a piece of his own heart?"

"And how we burned in the camps later, thinking: What would things have been like if every Security operative, when he went out at night to make an arrest, had been uncertain whether he would return alive and had to say good-bye to his family? Or if, during periods of mass arrests, as for example in Leningrad, when they arrested a quarter of the entire city, people had not simply sat there in their lairs, paling with terror at every bang of the downstairs door and at every step on the staircase, but had understood they had nothing left to lose and had boldly set up in the downstairs hall an ambush of half a dozen people with axes, hammers, pokers, or whatever else was at hand?... The Organs would very quickly have suffered a shortage of officers and transport and, notwithstanding all of Stalin's thirst, the cursed machine would have ground to a halt! If...if... We didn't love freedom enough. And even more – we had no awareness of the real situation.... We purely and simply deserved everything that happened afterward."

~~~~~~~~~~~~~~~~~~~~

INTRODUCTION

Many Americans have discovered and others are daily discovering that all in today's America is not as it seems and definitely not as presented by governments, power forces, media, academia and vested interests. We wrote this book to encourage the American people to ask questions, seek real, truthful answers, then, based upon those answers, if they conflict with their present conceptions, change their own minds and, possibly, their lives, even if it means challenging their own, most cherished "core beliefs", or what they *think* are their own beliefs.

For example, most people are conditioned to think that it is perfectly normal, in fact, required, to go to a banking institution for a loan to buy a house, or establish a business or create a new enterprise. This is the classical systems' approach with which virtually all people deal. All of the customary business practices that people accept as normal and required are what we term "in the box" systems' "normality". The pragmatic information presented in this book pertains to "out of the box" reality and very real possibilities regarding the purchase, sale, investment and financing of real estate. Sections of this book describe how real estate of any type can be bought, sold and financed, without the need to obtain new institutional financing, provided the buying and selling principals are capable and can reach mutual agreement. These are innovative approaches for dealing in real estate that are not presently in practice, but soon could be, if people grasp the fact that they can deal *directly*, principal to principal, and avoid entanglements and complications created by third parties, including banks. These programs are designed to work in both the best of times and the worst of times. The best of times allow for more fluidity and movement, but the worst of times constrain virtually every undertaking. The *ByPass* programs work especially well in the worst of times and make possible undertakings that would otherwise be absolutely impossible. In fact, the various different approaches presented in *ByPass* could become the buying, selling, investing and financing wave of the future, no matter the state of the economy.

In this book, with the exception of direct owner financing, you will find different, unconventional methods that can help you buy, sell, finance and invest in real estate in ways which have not been considered before, whether a property is mortgaged or not. In many cases, mortgages on properties have been drawbacks in effecting both the purchases and sales of those properties. The *ByPass* approach can solve this problem, based in common sense and mutual agreement. In fact, the methods and programs outlined in this book are designed to resolve problematical situations which are common within real estate transactions, thus, *ByPass* programs could set a new trend, by which many, if not most, properties are bought, sold and financed. **You will find all necessary details regarding these programs in Sections Four, Five, Six, Eight and Ten**.

One of the main objectives of this book is to help Americans who lost their homes through foreclosure and economic catastrophes learn how they can again purchase a family home, but this time in an easier, direct, uncomplicated manner, provided that they have the financial capabilities to accommodate necessary down payments and monthly mortgage payments. Although this is one main objective, *ByPass* was written for all Americans who may benefit from the information presented. We address many other factors as to why foreclosure crises, like the ones which recently so tragically impacted America, as well as depressions, recessions and economic turndowns routinely occur, *by design.* If one takes a fresh approach, there are always better ways to accomplish objectives rather using than the systematic, traditional, institutional, "in-the-box" methods, especially when those methods prove very harmful to the people, but highly beneficial for the power forces. *ByPass* presents sections on investments using these unconventional methods which can produce very comfortable returns all the way to enormously fabulous, unimaginable wealth. With a creative, inventive and forward-thinking approach, many things previously thought unimaginable are absolutely possible.

ByPass the Banks provides examples of each program in the most simple, direct manner possible, in such a way that the reader can easily understand the concepts. When our readers understand these concepts, then, the details come very easily. The crucial position here is to think and then act outside the box in a creative, non-system manner which will best serve the objectives *you* wish to achieve. That proverbial "box" created by government, corporations, banks, and assorted vested interests within society is not necessarily friendly and beneficial to the average man or woman. *ByPass* programs provide creative avenues to fulfill objectives for virtually all people, and are designed to work well for most everyone's needs. When one considers all of the various buying/selling/financing/investment programs discussed in this book, then virtually 100% of all properties in this nation, whether private homes, apartment buildings, commercial, industrial, business enterprises and land purchases, can benefit from one or more of these programs, provided, of course, the buyer has the financial capability, and buyer and seller agree on mutually beneficial terms. In addition to these programs, *ByPass* discusses other real estate programs that address different, more specialized needs and circumstances, some of which may apply to you or someone you know.

We hope that reading this book will be informative, stimulating and useful to our readers and encourage them to pursue new and exciting goals. If this book helps you get outside that restrictive "box" and become a creative, expansive thinker, you are certainly free to adapt any of these programs to better serve your own particular objectives and dreams. Remember, we all have dreams, no matter who we are, but only the ones who ACT upon their dreams can realize and, then, live them.

If your interest pertains only to real estate matters, then, if you wish, you can proceed directly to the Sections mentioned above that deal with those programs. However, we believe it would be in your best interests to read the entire book leading up to those Sections to give you a better understanding and a fuller comprehension of the existing controlling realities operative in America—why the system is so "rigged" and operated by the "D.C. swamp", as publicly stated by President Trump on numerous occasions, and why it is so critical to get outside of the box this rigged system and D.C. swamp have imposed upon all of us in this country. Rather than terming it the D.C. swamp, we call that den of iniquity a putrid, festering cesspool, with apologies to the cesspools of this world which actually provide a good service for the people they serve—unlike that infamous D.C. cesspool!

As we were completing *ByPass*, the COVID 19 plandemic was foisted upon the American people. Since this catastrophe is still ongoing as of this writing, it is unknown how much suffering and ruination this fraud will cause the American people, in many different ways. According to various estimates, over 40,000,000 people, plus, have been thrown out of work, millions of businesses have been forced to close, people have been held captives in their own homes, and mayhem is widespread – all for what usually amounts to little more than the common cold or flu. Rewriting *ByPass* is impossible, since we want to get it before the American people as soon as possible. However, comments are added throughout the book regarding this tragedy inflicted upon the people by their own governments, worldwide. One of the phrases you will see in *ByPass* is a sacred motto of politicians, namely: "If we fix it, then we can's scam it.

The old saying that freedom is not free is absolutely correct. If people want freedom, then they must responsibly engage in a dedicated process that separates them from the dictates of "normal" to achieve that enlightened freedom. Starting with obtaining freedom from oppressive and restrictive governments would be an excellent start.

Beyond real estate matters, we discuss many other pertinent subjects which directly affect the American people and America, herself. All of these are vital for a full understanding of the existing operative realities present in today's America. Unfortunately, many Americans are unaware of these realities because they have been extensively programmed since birth and kept so busy with life that they do not see these underlying realities which govern virtually every aspect of their lives.

Sometimes we forget that all Americans are *individual* entities who, combined with other Americans, comprise the whole, yet within that whole are the individual humans with their own likes, dislikes, tastes, talents, successes, failures, ideas, opinions, frames of reference and so many other interests, aptitudes, and behaviors. The real question is whether individual Americans are truly *independent* in their beliefs and lives, or are most merely an extension of the whole? If you see yourself as an independent-minded person, are your beliefs truly *your* beliefs or, in reality, were they created over time for you by others—and to what purpose? Most belief systems held by the majority of people have been foisted upon them by others—their families, their friends, their churches, their schools, their governments, media, academia, their fellow workers, society in general, the persuasive tenets of "social proof", and more recently, "political correctness". Truth is vital for an honorable people and society. Unfortunately, truth is not always what we want it to be, or what we like. However, when truth is known by people and by societies, it can inform and determine their actions, both individually and collectively. If one were to ask further serious questions, one such question might be: "Do you really want to know the truth?" Another might be: "How many of us are truly independent thinkers?" The answer to the former depends upon the curiosity, character and integrity of the individual, while the unfortunate answer to the latter is: "Very few."

The annals of time conclusively bear this out. Truth has been a rare commodity throughout history, while the lie has been given great respect and homage. Governments, moneyed interests, banks, other vested interests, and the "elite", all of which we shall call the "power forces", have mostly relegated truth to the sewer, but given the lie great respect and honor. Speaking the truth has been very dangerous over the millennia for most truth-tellers. In fact, history is replete with the absolute catastrophes, ruinations and murders that befell most, if not all, tellers of truth and independent thinkers who dared to seek and speak truth and challenged the status quo. In modern society, it has been difficult, if not dangerous, to be independent of mind and truthful of voice. As a result, most people follow the herd, and the herd is driven by the power forces which have always ruled and controlled all societies, though usually unknown to the people of those societies. Despite the ongoing programming and propaganda that has inundated American society for well over a hundred and fifty years into believing that it is an egalitarian, free society, America is no exception to the overarching control of these power forces. If you could change your paradigm and empower yourself with truth, using your own individual, independent and creative abilities, which would help you escape the confines of "the box" that has been constructed for and imposed upon you since birth, would you be willing to engage in such an enlightening, independent, freeing journey?

People have more power and ability than they can ever even conceive, but most people have been conditioned and programmed to such an extent that they find it almost impossible to recognize, believe and accept what is truly hidden within them and, thus, fail to trust their own innate abilities. We, as individuals, must break out of the box, walk away from our conditioning and programming, recognize and bring forth the individual abilities and talents which we all possess, whether we know it, or not. To this end, *ByPass the Banks* presents information that you might never have seen or heard of before. This book presents truths to readers which may lead them to their own conclusions about our society and who and what truly controls it. In all of our seminars, radio and television broadcasts we have always said that it is far better to know and deal with the truth than to live the lie. Unfortunately, most people live that lie and do not even know it! This book may hopefully stimulate you to ask questions, make comments and observations, to pose objections that you might not have ever considered before. When people seek truth and find it, they are in a far better position than they could ever imagine. As has been said many times, "The truth shall set you free", and this is not an idle phrase. It has profound meaning that can change your entire life, for the better.

OUR RATIONAL OBSERVERS

Throughout this book, we will refer to two mythical unbiased, objective entities. One we will call "our rational, reasonable, intelligent objective observer" and the other we will call "our analytical computer". The rational, reasonable, objective observer is exactly that: a man or woman of common sense and native intelligence, who makes assessments and judgments based only in valid facts, in what he or she objectively observes, is truly unbiased and factual in his or her conclusions and does not try to make the facts, observations and evidence he or she finds fit a preconceived notion to suit his or her personal opinions or preferences. He is factual, rational and reasonable regarding everything he assesses, and accumulates all information regarding any particular subject before making a conclusion based upon the data. Our observer is aware of the foibles of humankind, the usual machinations, the typical fraud, the standard deceptions which tend to cover up the truth, but our objective observer always sees and understands the bottom-line position, no matter what stands in the way to obscure that bottom line.

The analytical computer makes judgments and conclusions based solely on the information that has been fed into it. For instance, if a set of principles is programmed into the computer regarding any particular subject, and then a set of actions that oppose all of these principles is fed into the same computer, the computer's function is to assess the actions committed relevant to the actions required pursuant to the principles. The computer will quickly conclude that the committed actions either conform to the actions required by the principles, or oppose them. Thus, the actions measured against the requirements are either valid, or invalid. There is no middle ground. These two analytical companions will be with us throughout this book.

For the sake of recognition and clarity, we will name our reasonable, rational observer, *True*, and will name our analytical computer, *Reality*. True arrives at the truth based upon what he has personally observed and the information he has personally and objectively researched and received. Reality makes its conclusions based upon a set of requirements on one side measured against a set of actions on the other side. Reality reveals only reality, so when we add our two analysts together, we have *True Reality*, and this is the objective for which each of us should strive. One of the objectives of this book is to display and illustrate this true reality as it applies to America, the American people and the U.S. government. Many times, words spoken by individuals, politicians, governments, media, etc. are very different from actions taken. Requirements and responsibilities are one thing, but actions taken in relation to those requirements and responsibilities are sometimes something else entirely. In the physical world, everything can be measured, and this is another objective we want to illustrate in this book.

Consider those people who have gone through massive problems simply to get the right to vote. Then consider those people who vote, without any struggle to obtain that Right. Both groups vote for candidates, which vote is their right, but once their candidates win, the voters do nothing to hold those candidates to their campaign promises and to their oaths to uphold our Constitutions and the secured, inherent, unalienable Rights and Due Process guaranteed therein. True and Reality understand that the Constitution for the united States of America, circa 1787, as amended with the Bill of Rights in 1791, delegated and entrusted political power to the people and made America a self-governing nation. However, by the peoples' abject failure to uphold these responsibilities, the American people have abandoned not only their responsibilities, but their honor, duty, their own families, freedom and their country.

Our two analysts will measure the actions of governments and government officers pursuant to the **Constitutional mandates** imposed upon those governments and government officers. When we speak of the Constitution, we speak only of the Constitution for the united States of America, circa 1787, as amended with the Bill of Rights in 1791, and not the corporate constitution of 1871, which is a fraud perpetrated by the U.S. government upon the people. We will speak of this fraud later. Our analysts will also measure the *actions* of government officers pursuant to their words spoken regarding actions taken by government officers. The measurements will be precise, because the actions are either consistent with Constitutional mandates, requirements and the talk, or they are not. There is no middle ground here. For instance, Constitutional mandates require **specific performance** upon all government officers, and their actions will be measured against those Constitutional mandates. Their actions either comply with those Constitutional mandates, or they do not. It is really this simple. An old saying comes to mind in this discussion: You cannot be a little bit pregnant, and in this context, you cannot be a little bit un-Constitutional. Again, there is no middle ground. Actions taken pursuant to words spoken will also determine whether the actions are consistent with the definition, meaning and intent of these words. Some of these words follow: crime; criminal; fraud; deceit; lie; evil; un-Constitutional; treason; justice; authority and truth. We need not spell out the dictionary meanings of these words since they are quite self-evident. However, throughout this book we will assess the actions of government officers pursuant to the definitions and requirements of these words. Measurement, assessment and evaluation are vitally important to determine the truth of anything that exists within humanity. Since governments and the power forces long ago established enormous control over America and her people, then in these pages we, along with True and Reality, measure, assess and evaluate what government and power forces have done, and now do, pursuant to the lawful requirements imposed upon them and the words they speak which belie their actions. Readers are invited to make their own assessments based upon the same logical criteria.

ByPass BACKGROUND

The title of this book, "ByPass the Banks", arose from the fact that the all-powerful money interests—the owners of the private central banks—not only in this country, but throughout the entire world, totally **control** all of this world's countries, governments, economies, resources, institutions, media and societies. Imagine the monumental immensity of this fact. Tragically, the perversion of the Golden Rule operates throughout the world, namely, *he who owns the gold rules*. In so-called modern times, fiat paper money has replaced the gold, but the same scenario holds true. "This perversion embodies the greatest threat to the well-being and very survival of humanity because these all powerful, self-serving banksters are the masterminds and driving force behind every made-up, fraudulent ideology and "ism", enforced by the hired "boots on the ground", which have ruthlessly resulted in endless suffering, deprivation, bloodshed and warfare all over this Earth. These power-hungry ghouls are behind all the misery and loss ever experienced among humanity for countless centuries, but maybe humanity has had enough and is ready to take back its inherent power from these evil monsters."

You might ask yourself how this paper money came to dominate this world, and the answer to this is pretty simple. Governments collude in the creation of "money" by and through central banks, which the governments create through legislation for their respective nations. However, even though governments permit them, they are not public banks, since all central banks are owned and operated by wealthy *private* entities. Prior to governments' creation of central banks, governments raised funds for government needs and expenditures by directly imposing taxes upon the people. This, of course, became burdensome on most people and most nations. However, when the central banks were put into business by governments, governments could receive all the funds they wanted, at will, from these central banks, as *debt*, which, of course, gets directly passed onto and paid by the people. Despite this lucrative largesse, governments still tax their people. This constitutes the devious, collusive, surreptitious, lucrative relationship between governments and their central banks, pernicious to the people, but largely unknown by them.

These central banks issue paper money currency, under *fiat*, which means that the people of the nation must use only this currency, as dictated to the people by the government. Therefore, not only in this country, but also throughout the world, central banks authorized by governments create paper money at will under government fiat, then, distribute it to member banks. The currency eventually filters down into the population, by and through the member banks, as loans for debt incurred by the people, businesses and industry of the nation. It is pretty evident for our reasonable observer, True, and our analytical computer, Reality, to quickly determine, based upon the facts of the matter, that the private central banks are the ones in absolute control over the issuance of monetary units for the various nations. Since money is an absolute necessity in this world, simply to live and exist, then it can be plainly seen that money controls all societies in virtually all ways, because it controls all aspects of life in virtually all ways. Based upon this easily recognizable premise, the question becomes: Do the banks and money interests serve the people, or do the people serve the money interests and the banks? True and Reality both conclude that the latter position is the operative one. Any time such a lopsided, controlling condition exists within any society, it is clear to ascertain that a process of *economic violence* has been perpetrated upon the people of that nation by the rulers and the central bank of that nation. This is what happened to America and is still happening.

In centuries past, going way back in time, money of some sort always existed, but the general medium of exchange among people of those days was barter. Barter required no funds, because the goods and services of one entity were bartered or traded for the goods and services of another entity. Money did exist in those days, and in fact, several different forms of money existed. The buyers and sellers who dealt in money could choose the monetary unit they desired. The stronger monetary unit was in common use, therefore, most valuable, while the weaker unit was in lesser use, therefore, of lesser value. However, in what we call "modern society", the medium of exchange in this country, America, and in most countries for a hundred or more years, is the individual monetary unit issued by the private central bank of any particular country. The idea of barter is long gone in modern society, though it still occurs in some small ways. The several different currencies that existed at one time no longer exist or are allowed as the monetary unit in any particular country. The only monetary unit to be used by the people, governments, businesses and industry of any particular county is the one issued by the central bank of that particular nation, under fiat.

It is easy for anyone to see that enormous financial power and total *monopoly* exists within and is exercised by any central bank of any nation. Since the monetary unit of that nation is the only permitted medium of exchange among all aspects of that nation's society, whether governmental, private, corporate, institutional, etc., then, obviously, the entity that creates and issues that monetary unit has economic control of the entire society. When that central bank works hand in hand with the government, then these power forces can do pretty much as they decree, at any time they so decree. Again, our rational observer and analytical computer can quickly conclude that the power forces have created a society totally dependent upon them for their livelihoods and very existence. This is far removed from any egalitarian purpose and, sadly, America is no exception.

The title, *ByPass the Banks*, has a two-fold purpose, the first of which was described in the preceding paragraphs. Since the private central banks, and especially the central bank of this nation, wield such enormous economic power over the people and all other areas of life in this nation, and since this controlling position directly opposes the principles of our Constitutional Republic, the Preamble to our Constitution and the Constitution, itself, then the American people would be well advised to seek a lawful Constitutional alternative. If we, as an American society, could ever ByPass the massive influence, power and control the private central bank exerts upon America, in apparent collusion with our own government, then we would be set free from the economic violence that has been deceptively perpetrated upon us since 1913.

The government is not likely to change the status quo position of the central bank at all, and in fact, in 2013, the government just renewed the power of that central bank. This strongly demonstrates the support our government gives to the private central bank and its control over our entire society. Since the government will not change this unlawful, un-Constitutional partnership, which is so pernicious to the people of this nation, then that task falls to the American people. Tragically, it is highly unlikely that the American people, as a society, will ever effectuate such a change. First, the overwhelming majority of people in this society know nothing about the private central bank, its inner workings, and its relationship with the government. Secondly, if our society were made aware of these conditions, it is still unlikely that the general society would want to make any changes at all, because, to date, the American society has supported every program and action of government right across the board, no matter what. The people's trust in government has been used against them and their continued trust in government has become their nemesis and worst enemy.

Earlier, we referred to seekers of truth, to truth-tellers, to people of independent mind and good character who through their own efforts tried to help their own people and societies, often with unfortunate results. The task of changing anything for the better still rests within the people, but in order to make changes, the people must understand the true realities in which they live and the lawful ways in which to make those changes. With more information coming out every day about the D.C. swamp and the rigging of government, more people are becoming aware of the massive frauds that take place within and which *are* governments. If this awakening continues, then truth tellers may find receptive audiences in the very near future. Various approaches exist by which the power of the private central bank can be ByPassed and overcome, but only if the American people, as a society, are willing to embark on such worthwhile pursuits and wholeheartedly embrace them. Some of these will be discussed later in this book. The above explanation is one reason for the book's title.

ByPass provides voluminous information for your consideration, all of which is intended to help you, personally, as well as the entire American society. God knows, we need all the help we can get in these troubled times! Throughout the annals of known history, leaders of nations, money-men, bankers and the "elite" of all societies have issued and controlled the monetary units of all nations, thus, controlled the economies of those nations and the fate of their respective people. When the people of a nation allow the leaders and influential members of that nation to control the monetary unit and, thus, the economy, by and through their dictatorial monetary policies, then, the people are truly at the mercy of their own leaders. Enlightened societies do not place such monumental power in the hands of so few for the control of so many, but, unfortunately, this planet, at least, thus far, does not have enlightened societies. There are those that pretend to be so, but the claim is nullified by the actions of those societies, as dictated by the actions of the leaders and the money-men. By taking an objective look at how money is created and controlled by private central banks, it should become readily apparent to people throughout the world that such systems controlled by so few obviously do not benefit the many, but rather consistently increase the power, control, influence and wealth of the few, at the expense of the many.

Independence and **freedom** are the predominant themes of this book, and if people value independence and freedom, want to express and live them, then, they must not only think, but also *act* independently and freely. As long as there are controlled societies on this earth, people will be subject to the systemic control exerted by the controllers of those societies. However, within any given society, independent and freedom-minded people can think for themselves, make their own choices, and decide what is best for them, even within existing societal constraints. Thinking in this manner is excellent, but the thinking must be followed by *action,* and the one who so acts must *live* his convictions. Yes, controls are everywhere, but even within the most heavily controlled societies there are avenues that allow independence and freedom, at least to a certain extent.

America, like other nations, as more and more people are unhappily discovering, is a highly controlled society in which the laws, rules and regulations made by the rulers of this society favor the rulers, the leaders, the "elite" and the bankers, in other words, the power forces, and basically exploit and take advantage of the people. Some would disagree with this, but this number is decreasing since many Americans are waking up to the political and economic realities in which they live. In another CHAPTER, we discuss this in more detail, but for now, it will suffice to say that the history of currency and the monetary unit in this country has been completely controlled by and hidden from the people by the "elite", the rulers and the bankers from the very inception of this nation.

Although the Constitution for the united states of America, circa 1787, as amended in 1791 with the Bill of Rights, which is the official name of our nation's *authentic* Constitution, is the *Supreme Law of the Land* and supersedes all other lesser laws, statutes, codes, regulations, rules and policies, the Constitutional requirement for the issuance of currency has never been followed by government since America was instituted as a nation. This was and is treason. The people at that time knew little to nothing about this treason, therefore, did nothing to change it, and this is definitely the case as things are now. America was founded as a Constitutional *Republic*, which is a nation **ruled by WRITTEN law**, not by man, and the Supreme Law of this republic is the referenced Constitution. However, when it came to the creation of currency, the monetary unit, or "money", the tyrannical rule of man prevailed, and not the wise rule of law. This is a subject of which, most people know very little, but it is so important that they should strive to learn as much as they can about it. This study is not a complex one, but the people have been fooled into thinking that this subject is too complex, too difficult for them, so our "wise leaders" made sure to keep the people distanced, in the dark, and disinterested in pursuing any real knowledge of the operative monetary system which controls virtually every aspect of their lives.

What is true of America regarding her currency and monetary unit is true of virtually every other nation on this earth, with some few minor exceptions. In this situation, as referenced above, we have the rule of man, and not the rule of law, which established a monetary system that favored the few, at the expense of the many. The Constitution, in its very foundation, is an egalitarian document that guarantees equal opportunity to all Citizens, but this equal opportunity for all has been denied and interfered with by the few, in self-serving collaboration with the so-called political representatives of the people. In any egalitarian nation, and sadly, at present, none exist on this planet, the will and political power of the people control the machinery of government. In such a nation, the monetary unit would be formed in accordance with the Supreme Law of that land and the will of the people, and not by the controlling few who unjustly and unlawfully rule the many. This was the monetary design for America, but the greedy rule of man superseded the just rule of law, and, tragically, the ignorance of the American people allowed it to happen. The same is true of the way the people have accepted, without question or challenge, this phony COVID-19 *plandemic* and virtually every other fraud the government has perpetrated upon them.

The present situation in America will remain as it is until such time as the people awaken to its toxicity and institute proper Constitutional changes, if ever. For now, the fact remains that the issuance and control of America's currency is in the hands of a *private* bank, deceptively called the Federal Reserve Bank, which is owned mostly by wealthy foreign entities and operates for profit. It is incredulous that the American people have allowed this privately owned bank, and prior private banks, to control the money, finances, and economy of this whole nation, entirely autonomously, without any restraints or oversight placed upon those banks. **Control is the real business of government and the power forces.** If people want to be truly free and independent, then, it would be in their best interests to ByPass and move beyond these controls into self-directed lives, as much as possible in such a restrictive society. America was founded as a bastion of freedom and independence, but unfortunately, the people have misplaced their trust in government, surrendered their powers to the government and the power forces, thus, have aided and abetted their own enslavement. Lawful ways exist to restore the political power and independence to the people. However, the people, individually and collectively, must be willing to actively take the steps necessary to do so. All of the positions introduced in this section will be more fully discussed throughout *ByPass* which, hopefully, will provide the reader with a much better understanding of the truth and the operating realities controlling America. As has been said before, the truth shall set you free, and when one knows the truth, no matter what that truth is, it is far superior to live that truth than to exist in the lie.

THE NEW SCARE

As Margy and I were completing this book, a new scare came "out of the blue", deeply affected the American people in many different ways, and still is. This scare is called corona virus, or COVID-19. If you have read this book, this far, you can imagine how we regard this whole matter. The federal government, state and local governments and most other governments throughout the world have essentially shut their people down by isolating them in their homes, restricting their movements and stopping all so-called "non-essential" businesses, which put tens of millions out of work. Supermarkets are open, but many have run out of products due to, in part, panic buying and massive hoarding by many people. This, alone, clearly demonstrates that people are not only concerned, but are operating from fear, and this causes them to do absurd, ridiculous things which they ordinarily would not do. While so called "essential" operations remain open, *when* non-essential businesses are permitted to reopen will be determined by governments. How governments determine this and upon what facts they base their decisions, will ultimately be detrimental to the people. The people long ago surrendered their powers to their governments, thus have no say in matters of importance to them, or so they believe. Very unfortunately, they forgot that it is the people who are the masters, not their servant governments. This has paved the way for massive control, corruption and exploitation by all forms of government in this country to the extent that governments do whatever they want, whenever they want, to whomever they want, and the people's will be damned! This can only be remedied by the people, themselves, because governments will never remedy the problems they have caused. You know the politicians' motto: "If we fix it, we can't scam it!"

In America, this new scare was done without Constitutional authority by politicians and public servants who took oaths to support and uphold the Constitution, including all secured Rights and Due Process guaranteed within. By their actions, from their perspective, their oath taking is meaningless, and the American people have foolishly let them violate their oaths from the very inception of this nation. Without Constitutional requirements consistently imposed upon politicians *by the people*, then politicians have no restraints and do whatever they want to obtain their objectives, which usually harm the people in one way or another. This is just common sense. If a business owner knows that his workers are constantly stealing from him, yet takes no action to either stop or fire them, they will continue, escalate their thefts, and the owner will eventually be out of business. Taking action to solve a problem is taking responsibility. All this occurred because the owner never took any responsibility to take actions to stop the thefts. America is a Constitutional Republic. Who owns that Republic? The people own it, but, very sadly, the American society has been wholly irresponsible by not holding politicians and public servants to Constitutional mandates. If the American people want to stop the politicians now, then they must take lawful action now, unite in common cause, become vociferous, use lawful, Constitutional measures and demand that the **domestic enemies** who unlawfully rule them immediately cease their un-Constitutional actions and immediately restore America to a normal condition, with all Constitutionally secured Rights and Due Process upheld. This could be the major event, the wake-up call and return to conscious awareness for the people to realize that their own leaders are the domestic enemies of whom Thomas Jefferson spoke. Since nothing like this has ever happened before in America, it would be both monumental and magnificent for the people and our Republic.

The people have the inherent Right to earn a living, the Right to have free speech, the Right to assemble, the Right to present grievances to government, and have them redressed, the Right of a free, honest press, the Right to travel, the Right to bear arms and numerous other Rights the governments of America have violated based upon a scam. The people should understand that when secured Rights become regulated or modified in any way whatsoever, for any reason, then they are no longer Rights, but become, at most, privileges bestowed by the government. What government gives, government can take away. Our founders never meant for our Rights to be given or withdrawn at the whim of our SERVANT government. Rights are inherent and eternal. Once lost by default, they are very difficult to retrieve. No lawful, valid or legitimate reasons exist for governments to eradicate or even limit the exercise of our Rights, but they have been constantly doing this for centuries, and the people have allowed it. When governments wants to ask the people to curtail the expression of their Rights, then governments must have valid, provable, truthful reasons for their actions. This fraudulent COVID-19 scam does not pass muster. Since governments constantly lie, employ fraud, manipulate the truth and deliberately deceive the people, there are no valid reasons, whatsoever, for governments to strip us of our Rights, or for people to surrender them, especially for another scam.

Prior to the last ten or twelve national elections in America there were various "health scares", such as bird flu, swine flu, HIV-AIDS, SARS, Ebola, MERS and many others. Despite these scares, the American people are still here and still living. There was no shutting down of the nation. Is this newest health scare simply another overblown scare in the long list of government scares, or is this something serious, something more sinister and something else we are not seeing or being allowed to see? Common sense, reason and consciousness are very lacking in America today, and have been for an extremely long time. If these attributes were present within a large part of the population, it is obvious that America would not be experiencing the massive amount of problems now present. Too much of the political power our Constitution vested in the people has been mistakenly given, by the people, to government. The people expect government to determine what is best for them, then, blindly follow what government decrees. This demonstrates a total lack of responsibility by the American society, with the usual exceptions, who are usually called "kooks", "radicals", "extremists" and "conspiracy nuts" for seeking, exposing and revealing the truth. This shabby treatment of truth tellers and critical-thinkers works against the best interests of the people, since hiding and obscuring the truth or finding a "patsy" always kills whatever truth the power forces want to keep from the masses and ensures that the people will never discover the real truth.

Widespread, applied common sense would make a huge difference in America. If one has followed the statements, then actions of government, and "reasons" government provides for many various situations, if not all, then the entity which applies common sense would realize that government is a **liar**, so it routinely lies as a normal course of business. Common sense and the realization of true history clearly demonstrate that governments have and do use their powers against the interests of their own people, and do so for the benefit of governments and their fellow power forces. Margy and I do not believe proven liars who use their power against the very people those liars *claim* to serve. To do so would clearly demonstrate that we lack common sense and do not understand the existing realities of government and its corporate buddies, especially the banks. Liars routinely lie and unlawfully usurp and use power to hurt people. Those people who do not use common sense and fail to comprehend the true reality of government power can harm themselves in numerous ways. When a whole nation does this, then the results can be utterly disastrous. Yes, some people will see the truth, but, unfortunately, they are too few to measure, especially against the massive multitudes of people who just obey orders, without question, and follow the herd, usually over the proverbial cliff.

Governments can take virtually any issue and make that issue into exactly what they want it to be, or make it *appear* to be as they claim it is. The initial question is whether the issue, itself, was "natural" in its occurrence or created by government to serve the many hidden pernicious purposes of government and its partner power forces. If natural, then we must realize that government has the ability to re-engineer what is natural for its sinister purposes and has done so for hundreds of years. If a natural force is manipulated by government and then used as a scare technique, is this not a sinister purpose? We always look at the bottom line and then attempt to understand the methodology of how that bottom line was reached. We use logic, common sense, reason and whatever factual, credible evidence is available to make this determination. Unfortunately, most people do not do this, which allows government all the latitude it wants to conduct its scams. This is not the first time something like this has happened in America, because there is a long trail of similar situations of differing circumstances and degrees and, if this current scam is not exposed and stopped, there will likely be more in the future. True, this time, the government has really abused its power and blatantly taken away the Constitutionally guaranteed inherent rights and freedoms of the American people, on some contrived scare, and the hapless people have allowed this. The bottom line question here is what is the real intent of the government and its ultimate objective?

From our understanding, viruses are excretions from cells to rid the cells of toxic material and poisons. We all live in a world full of toxins—poisons, pesticides, chemicals, heavy metals, massive pollution, EMF radiation, etc., etc. These are in the soil, the air, the water and the food we eat. Unfortunately, this whole country is loaded with toxins as, inevitably, are the people, and who makes all of this possible—your "friendly" governments, of course. Therefore, our cellular structures excrete toxins from the cells and these waste products are viruses. Viruses are not living things and differ from bacteria and fungi which are living organisms. Despite what the pundits say and the "experts" claim, our understanding is that viruses are not "contagious". Evidence from the so-called Spanish Flu in 1918 conducted by a hospital in Boston during that "epidemic" conclusively proved this. However, what makes viruses appear contagious is another form of toxin, and this is the high level of electromagnetic energy existent all around this planet which adversely affects human cells, as it weakens them and makes them susceptible to illness. When many people develop similar symptoms, then the cause is said to be a "contagious virus", while the real cause is that the cells have been poisoned by the various toxins to which they are being exposed daily, especially in the presence of the ever-increasing electromagnetic fields, which exacerbate the effects of all the other toxins. 5G is a major culprit and Wuhan, China contains a massive array of 5G that was activated just prior to the so-called "corona virus outbreak" which allegedly occurred there. This combination of factors robs the body of oxygen which is very similar to what happens with this supposed COVID-19.

Every time there is an increase in electromagnetic energy on this planet, due to the advent of some new technology, there is a surge in so-called "epidemics". This has been going on since shortly after electricity was discovered and became widespread. Of course, the real culprit is never named by governments, because to do so would put the blame exactly where it belongs and possibly destroy one or more of government's partner power force industries. The government would rather harm the people than hurt its partners. As many of you know, truth is the first casualty in war, and, in most cases, the first casualty of government. Governments protect their vested moneyed interests, so will manipulate and destroy the truth to save and protect those interests, at any cost, including harming and deceiving the people. In so doing, governments always find a likely scapegoat for a problem. Government is a master at tweaking and manipulating information to make it look as if the scapegoat is the real cause of the problem, and in the process, deceives the people whom government was intended to serve. This simple, but effective process has worked very well for governments throughout history, but unfortunately the American society has not learned from history, so repeats it. If we are to ever become a *truly* free nation in which truth is honored and respected, rather than ridiculed, maligned and buried, then, obviously, we have to seek and demand truth and not support and accept the lie and the liars who perpetrate the lie.

What has happened to America? America is a nation that was birthed through the pluck, strength, courage and optimism that eventually evoked a revolution against the then-most powerful nation on this Earth, England, which, amazingly, America won to gain her freedom from that tyrannical cesspool of evil. How have Americans become so soft, so apathetic, so disinterested in their own country that they have totally tuned out the ugly realities spread before them 24/7 and turned away from their responsibilities as human beings and as American Citizens to oversee and control their governments? Some of the answers lie in the fact that the people have been brainwashed for many, many decades by a sinister effort to dumb them down, instill false, baseless values in them, invoke the unfortunate selfishness and laziness that seem to be present in virtually all humans on this planet. The brainwashing has been done very cleverly using "education" as one of the most powerful tools, starting at the nursery and kindergarten levels, to fill the minds of American children with revisionist "history", to make them revile their country, their parents and grandparents, all without realizing that they have been played, manipulated and crafted into the perfect vehicles to accept the most ruthless, relentless force on this planet, *communism*—and welcome it as "progressive"! If you doubt this, then we pose a situation to you. Take the American Constitution and put it up on the wall, then take the *Communist Manifesto* and put it beside the Constitution. Then consider how the U.S. government has been operating for virtually forever and notice that its actions do not obey the mandates of America's Constitution. The federal government and virtually all state and local governments DO NOT uphold the Constitution, even though they have taken oaths to do so, do not uphold the inherent rights and due process of law which the Constitution guarantees to the people, but in the alternative, all of these governments uphold, implement and enforce the principles of the *Communist Manifesto* upon their own Citizens. Just take a look at what has been going on in this country for a very, very long time, then, ask yourself, why?

There is a definite correlation between the health of the people and the advent and continued advancement of the inventions which have surrounded Earth with electromagnetic energies. Think electricity, radio waves, radar waves, sonar waves, wireless routers and all the numerous cell towers and thousands of satellites necessary to accommodate the ever growing number of cell phones and other devices commonly in use every day by virtually everyone. 5G is the newest abomination. Before the discovery of electricity, the people were for the most part hardy, healthy, ate good, wholesome food and did not suffer from the plethora of diseases which are all too common today. At that time, there were no auto-immune disorders in which the human body attacks itself, yet today there are millions of people who suffer from these disorders in myriad forms. Cancer is far too common today, but in the good old days, it was quite rare. Too much electromagnetic energy disrupts our cellular functions and can impair the flow of oxygen in our bodies. Since oxygen is absolutely necessary for healthy human life, any disruption or diminishment of its course throughout the body does not bode well for health. The governments of this world know this. Most scientists and developers of these technologies know this, yet they all still push these tech inventions upon us at every turn, and the gullible, unaware people comply by buying every new tech invention that comes to market as soon as it hits the shelves. Some even stand in line for days to be the first to get the newest devices! If one is talking about "contagion", this addiction to technology is one of the most contagious, addictive and dangerous threats to all of us. Unfortunately for humanity, most humans have traded their health for convenience and the alluring attraction of having the next new thing. These people will *love* AI, be mesmerized by it and drawn right into it.

How this whole corona virus scam scenario plays out is yet to be determined, at this point in time, which is early April 2020. Quite a few qualified, authentic doctors, epidemiologists, scientists and chemists realize the deceptive nature of this so-called "pandemic" and have courageously broadcast their views and information to the people. Some people will understand, but in the "follow the herd" mentality of so many, most will not. This acceptance by the most is harmful to the few, or to the minority that sees the truth. As far as governments are concerned, the majority is their focal point–their support base upon which they concentrate their deceptive efforts in order to achieve their nefarious purposes. As long as that support base remains compliant and obedient, doesn't question or protest what government imposes, government will continue to inflict harm upon the people, and this will increase, if no meaningful, lawful opposition arises.

Twenty years or so ago the minority that now sees and accepts the truth either was very small, or almost non-existent. The good news is that the American people are beginning to see the truth, to wake up and understand the ugly reality that controls them. If this segment grows, increases rapidly in scope and becomes vociferous in its views, then it may be possible for them to oppose the unlawful, discriminatory, damaging practices of government, hold the perpetrators accountable and liable for their criminal actions, and begin the road back to Constitutional, lawful governance in this country. **A compliant population that supports and obeys evil, without question, does not remain free for very long, if at all.** An honorable, truth seeking population *can* achieve freedom despite the evil that governs it, if the people acknowledge the truth and work together to lawfully stop and change the evil governments. Some may disagree with the word "evil", but if one takes a look at the meaning of that word, it is the only word that accurately describes the unimaginably enormous amount of harmful actions that governments have perpetrated upon their own people for centuries. If the people are to achieve real freedom, then they must recognize the truth of the ugly realities operative before their own eyes and call what they see, as it actually exists and not as they wish it did. If something fits the description of evil, then a conscious, honest, ethical human being does not shrink from the use of this word. True and Reality see and assess evil for exactly what it is.

Four years prior to the crash of 2007-2008, I predicted the month and year of that manipulated economic crash, as I have accurately predicted virtually all others for many decades. When Margy and I were presenting seminars and doing media broadcasts throughout America, we warned the people that unless they awakened to reality, saw the evil agenda the governments were perpetrating against them, and took lawful measures to stop this criminal treason against the people, then, within 12 to 15 years there would be a major communist takeover of America and the entire world, via a false flag operation predicated on some phony health crisis. Tragically, the people did not stop the criminal treason of all governments in this nation and here we are now, right in the midst of that predicted crisis. When you know how the evil system works and the agenda they want to achieve, it becomes somewhat easy to accurately predict their actions. Thus, it was a "no-brainer" to us that something else would appear that would give the government and their power forces more solid control over America and her people. It is painfully clear how this fraudulent COVID-19 scare provides enormous, but un-Constitutional, unlawful, power to the governments and their power forces, right across the boards. This is made possible by the American people who do not challenge government, its "authority" or its actions, except in rare instances. These failures have already caused severe problems for Americans everywhere, such as business closings, resulting in loss of jobs, lost business, lost wages, economic downturns, requirements to remain at home, restricted travel, cancellation of church services, weddings and funerals, food and goods shortages, and more, including the loss of the people's Constitutionally guaranteed rights which occurred when the governments claimed they needed 15 days to "flatten the curve"!

Fast forwarding to present day, some states have regained some sanity so have removed many restrictions, while others continue to enforce the wearing of face masks, social distancing and limitations on business and restaurant operations. Did you ever think you would see something like this happen in America in your lifetime? This is not a Hollywood dystopian movie—you know, the ones that have been around for quite some time now and paint a dark, gloomy picture of authoritarian governments lording over desperate, miserable people. No, this dystopia is real, people, but this draconian reality is being caused by something that is *unreal*, deliberately created and then enormously manipulated by your own government to scare you into compliance with whatever governments dictate. No movie scenario can be any worse than what these thugs have planned for the people of this sorry world. The organic Constitution for the United States of America guarantees God-given, inalienable rights to the people that can never lawfully be restricted or denied to them under any circumstances. As we mentioned earlier, the alleged COVID-19 virus has never been isolated, identified or purified, the Center for Disease Control and Prevention, the CDC, has admitted it does not have a sample of this alleged virus, and no other lab in the world has such a sample. Therefore, in the parlance of True and Reality, it is logical to believe that the alleged virus does not actually exist. Since it does not exist, then for governments to order treatments for a "virus" that does not exist is not only irresponsible, but criminal, un-Constitutional and totally insane. Yet the governments expect the people to accept and abide by this insanity. Consider these following positions.

The legislatures of the several states granted emergency powers, for an alleged emergency that never existed, to their governors based upon an alleged pandemic because of a non-existent virus. Therefore, the legislatures granted un-Constitutional, fraudulent powers to the governors who in turn accepted these fraudulent, un-Constitutional powers and issued un-Constitutional orders, guidelines and suggestions that were un-Constitutionally carried out and enforced upon the people by agencies of government, corporations, institutions, schools, businesses, etc., all of which harmed many people in many different ways. Agencies of government have no Constitutional authority—or any other form of lawful, valid authority—to enforce un-Constitutional orders upon the people. The people have no Constitutional requirement whatsoever to abide by un-Constitutional orders, especially those that harm them, but the people do have the Constitutional responsibility to expose and oppose all un-Constitutional orders issued by domestic-enemy-communists masquerading as "public servants" holding office. The Constitution is either the supreme declared Law of this Land, which all governments and all people, whether public or private, must uphold, or America is nothing but a gigantic fraud, and this fraud must be exposed everywhere.

All public officers and employees in America are required to take oaths to support and uphold the national and state Constitutions. This requirement can be found in Article VI, Clauses 2 & 3 of the national Constitution, in all state Constitutions, as well as federal, state and local law. The oath is a condition precedent to assuming office and without the oath no one can lawfully assume and hold office. All oath takers must abide by the Constitutional mandates imposed upon them in the referenced Article VI. Clauses 2 & 3, the Supremacy Clauses clearly state that the Constitution is the "supreme Law of the Land" and all oath takers are **bound** to the Constitution by oath, therefore, in the performance of their official duties, must uphold the Constitution superior to any other form of lesser law, especially "laws" that oppose and violate the Constitution. There is no discretion here. Specific performance is required. On one side, we have the Constitution, secured inherent rights and Constitutional due process of law, and on the other side, we have inferior "laws" which violate and oppose the Constitution. The Constitutional mandate is specific and the duty of the oath taker is clear. However, out of the tens of millions of public officers and employees in this country—federal, state and local—none of them abides by their oaths in the performance of their official duties. While the Constitutional mandates are explicit, the American people have failed *their* duty to hold their public servants to these mandates; therefore, the governments abuse their limited, delegated authority routinely and do whatever they choose at their whim. The forefathers of this nation would turn over in their graves to see how their posterity has abandoned their hard-won Constitutional Republic. If Constitutional governance is to be restored to America, then, the American people must experience an overnight epiphany and take back the reins of government. As Jefferson said,"…bind them in the chains of the Constitution", and this is exactly what is needed in these very dangerous, desperate times.

The 15 days to "flatten the curve" passed about 19 months ago! Yet governments and their mouthpieces continue to spew "fear porn" about this non-existent "virus" and are heavily campaigning for the American people to submit to injections of an experimental, dangerous serum which does not meet the scientific criteria of a "virus". A Spanish university study examined various types of this serum and found it contains 99% graphene oxide—a toxic poison to the human body—along with synthetic mRNA which permanently changes the nature of the DNA of those who receive this dangerous shot. Clearly, these shots contain ingredients harmful to the human body, and according to the Vaccine Adverse Events Reporting System, aka, VAERS, cited by the CDC, in association with the government—and we know that they lie— over 14,000 Americans have died from this "kill shot" and millions are suffering serious permanent medical injuries. Well known scientific professionals and medical doctors have openly stated that these statistics are underreported by doctors or victims to the tune of 1 to 10%. Thus the figures published by VAERS, according to these same sources, are off by a multiple of 10 to 100. According to this scenario, the true deaths could be anywhere from 140,000 to 1,400,000, or more. Your governments, federal, state and local, in conjunction with a corrupted medical-pharmaceutical-industrial complex, are committing genocide against the American people and seriously harming millions of others by demanding, bribing and extorting people into taking this kill shot. Incredibly, millions of Americans are complying, thereby putting themselves into extreme danger. Now, the guy who stole the presidency, whom we should call treasonous Uncle Joe, wants to mandate that all government employees, including military, hospital employees and employees of businesses of over 100, take this kill shot, or be PCR tested every week, or be fired. Apparently, Uncle Joe never heard about the Constitutional right to not be deprived of life, liberty and property, without due process of law. It would seem that virtually every other politician, bureaucrat and employee in this country is just as treasonous as is Uncle Joe. Remember Uncle Joe Stalin? Now we have our own communist Uncle Joe who wants to rule by one man mandate, just as the murderous Lenin and Stalin did. Maybe, those living in the future will call Biden murderous Uncle Joe.

Vladimir Lenin and Uncle Joe Stalin called the Russian bureaucrats, military, police and people who supported and enforced their murderous policies upon the ordinary Russian people, "useful idiots". From the observable reality before us, it would appear that the tens of millions of politicians, bureaucrats, public officers, employees, sheriffs, police, military, corporations, institutions, schools and colleges are the American "useful idiots" ushering in overt communism to undermine and destroy what remains of our Constitutional Republic. If there is any hope of stopping this communist takeover, then, the American people must awaken to the ugly absolutely true realities controlling them and for once take lawful effective action to stop the communist governments in their tracks and restore Constitutional governance to this nation.

America has its underclass and the former middle class that has now slipped from prominence and is fast heading for obscurity thanks to the COVID induced economic "castration" imposed upon the people by their own governments. Many Americans were already living paycheck to paycheck, and if they were out of work for two weeks, then they would have a serious problem, because most have no savings at all. Some of those people have been out of work since the beginning of the scamdemic. Many businesses and restaurants that were forced to close never reopened. How are these people going to pay rent or make a mortgage payment, buy food for their family, pay for gas and utilities, and afford the enormous costs of living day to day? They will no doubt have to depend upon credit cards, but what happens when their credit is tapped out, their funds are depleted and they can no longer make any payments? Of course, this is where the communist governments come through with "relief" by paying the people for not working, and, of course, the people are not working because of the fraudulent un-Constitutional policies of governments. The governments cause the problems, then "solve" the problems by buying the people out, which is pure, unadulterated communism. Pure capitalism would have solved those problems before they ever started, but the treasonous communist governments in America do not want pure capitalism.

The people were promised an end date for the lock downs and "health mandates" of April 30th of 2020, but that date passed by with no changes to the overall communist agenda. Since then, millions upon millions of Americans have been financially devastated and put deeply into debt. Small and medium size businesses, and even some large ones, have suffered the effects of economic losses and may not be able to continue if the country is not put back to normal pure capitalistic business order and a normal social order. In all probability, most of these businesses will be bought up by large corporations. Economic chaos and dire cascading events which have occurred and will increase in scope worsening as time goes on, creating untold suffering and uncertainty everywhere, and all of this brought about by a common cold or flu virus and the scam the government created around it to accomplish its goals. However, most people are clueless about any of this. It is nauseating to realize that this fraud surrounding this "virus" has been perpetrated upon the people by their very own government and its partner power forces, which virtually own and control everything in this country, including the useless-to-the-people, evil politicians and bureaucrats living off the miseries of the people everywhere.

Utter devastation and permanent ruination of peoples' lives will occur if the people let this fraud continue. The "answer" to the problems exists and, of course, it is a government answer. From their position, since their intent is to create suffering throughout the country, bringing America to her knees, as we have described above, then, in the reenactment of the infamous PROBLEM, REACTION, SOLUTION scenario, a la the Hegelian Dialectic, the government, of course, has the "solution" to the problem it created, although, initially, many Americans might not understand the full nature of that solution. In the markets, when money is lost by one party, it is gained by another party. In economic crashes, virtually everyone loses, *except for the ones who rigged the crash and profited from it*. It is quite possible that government, depending upon the tenor of the people, will come out with huge financial bailouts for some people, for themselves, and for some businesses, but these bailouts, unlike the ones previously made to the banks in 2007 and 2008, will likely have hidden, quiet consequences. What is it called when a government breaks its own people, financially and otherwise, and then provides relief and "rescues" them? Can you say communism? At first, this will not appear to be the case, because people will receive some benefit which will temporarily mollify them. However, since communists are very clever, deceptive, patient, and take their time engineering the dependency scenario they intend, eventually it will become very evident to all who will be forced to live and suffer under their draconian tyranny.

As mentioned above, much of what happens depends upon the tenor of the people and what the people will do when the proverbial crap hits the fan. If the people accept the "rescue" and what goes with it, then the die has been cast. If the people develop, literally overnight, a societal backbone and finally see the existing realities, *as they actually exist*, and not as the people mistakenly *think* they exist, realize who the real enemy truly is, then demand that government immediately cease its fraud, or face the consequences of an entire society turned against those running the machinery of these governments, then the people will have taken a stance never taken before. This will be a test case of who dominates—the communists, by ramming through their pernicious agenda, or the people by demanding and reclaiming their rights and freedom. If the people are united in purpose, prepared to take back their political power, base their actions in the **authority** of our Constitution, then lawfully start removing the domestic enemies now unlawfully ruling us, this could lead back to Constitutional governance in America. It is all up to the people, as it has always been up to the people. It will take something this courageous, this audacious, this bold and this *necessary* to rid America of these parasitical vermin and put America back on the Constitutional course. Otherwise, it is quite possible for America to rapidly sink into blatantly overt communism—in our lifetimes. This is one possible outcome. There are others, and it really depends upon the bottom-line objective of governments, and the reaction, or non-reaction, of the people to that ultimate objective.

From our perspective, all of this has occurred because of a very common virus that most people have had or still have circulating in their bodies, without major concerns or problems. However, the government has made this a major concern because this suits its purpose, but, as we see it, government will not tell the truth as to why some people develop problems, and why some of these die. Prior serious prevailing illnesses or diseases and advanced age are major factors in these deaths, but these co-morbidities are not typically reported. Instead, doctors and hospitals are being financially rewarded to cite COVID as the cause of death, rather than stating the real cause, which it total fraud and blatant violation of their medical oaths. The media broadcasts that hospitals are overloaded with corona patients, but that does not match our information. What is the purpose of making something common and non-lethal a major issue, then lying about it? If electromagnetic radiation and 5G in various amounts are harming people who harbor corona virus, then the government is Constitutionally required to tell this truth to the American people.

Presenting one side of a story to the people without presenting the other side is criminal fraud to achieve a nefarious agenda. Unfortunately, the people have never held government to any Constitutional standard, so fraud, lies and deception are commonplace within the federal, state and local governments. In sum, we have criminals running the show in America!

Dr. Anthony Fauci, the chief "medical expert" heading the White House task force on COVID-19, and a top adviser to the President, reported, in the *New England Journal of Medicine*, that COVID -19 is similar to the common seasonal flu. Since no drastic actions were taken by government during prior flu seasons and other "scares", this begs the question as to why all of the draconian, extreme measures have been and continue to be taken over the non-existent COVID-19 virus. Many other doctors and professionals are saying the same thing Dr. Fauci said, along the same lines, but the governments and the media in America and worldwide are not telling this to the people. Why? If what these doctors say is correct, then governments should present their true findings to the people, that is, if the governments really want the people to know the truth. At least, the findings and information of these medical professionals should be investigated and evaluated. When the truth is not told, or is hidden from the public, and another agenda is pursued, the lies and deception continue and a sinister agenda is afoot. President Trump reportedly called up 1,000,000 reserve armed forces, and the military seemed to be present in many places throughout America. To us, these were ominous signs that something *big* was in the works. Clearly that something spells doom for America and humanity.

The President of the United States of America is either the most powerful man on this Earth, or very close to it. When people understand the immense power held and wielded by this office, then they can fully understand that the President can quickly get correct, authentic, genuine information on virtually anything in this world. He is surrounded by people who can do the same thing and report to him, because they are part of that office. Given these facts, it is obvious that the President and his top people know exactly the nature of this so-called problem, why and how it came about and how it will affect or not affect the people. If Dr. Fauci and the many other doctors and professionals say that this virus is similar to the flu, or a bad cold, and others say the virus is not contagious, and any serious illness that develops is likely caused by other factors or co-factors, and high degree electro-magnetic activity and 5G, then the President, no matter who holds this office, and his top people would or should know this.

Margy and I are not scientists or doctors, so rely upon those genuine professionals who know and have accurately predicted the how, why and outcome, as has Dr. Leavitt, a Nobel Prize winning scientist in 2013, and others. It is very reasonable to believe that the President knows what they know, but yet the scam continues. He knows the real reasons behind all of this, knows that it is similar to the flu or common cold, knows the real reason why some people get sick and some die, likely knows that the test kits do not work correctly, knows about the false reporting about massive amounts of people going to hospitals, when evidence gathered by real people shows otherwise, and much, much more. If the President wants to tell the truth to the people, then no legitimate reasons exist for all the subterfuge and cover ups. The real reason is that these are the usual, simple, ordinary customs and practices deceptively employed by a government NOT of the People, by the People and for the People. No, this is government of, by and for the banks and giant corporations! Period! This whole hoaxed "pandemic" is a gigantic farce, yet the masses gobble it up like rare, tasty candy. Some are "getting it", so there may be some hope that the multitudes will think, listen, and finally awaken to the fact that America, and the entire world, are controlled by hidden evil forces, so powerful and so pervasive that they can easily and quickly perpetrate a fraud of this enormity and consequence and get the world's people to swallow it, hook, line and sinker. If this realization were to happen, it would be good for the entire country, the economy and the rest of this world, if it is not already too late.

Reality is reality and fantasy is fantasy. The two do not mix if one sincerely seeks the truth. Fantasy given as a reason for reality not only hides or obscures the truth, but obliterates it. If truth is important to you, then you want that truth and not some other substitute that serves some other purpose or agenda that benefits someone or something else, at your expense. If government is truly dedicated to solving problems, then providing fantasy as a reason for what has morphed into a real problem does not reveal the truth regarding and behind that problem, but does reveal the truth about government and how it lies, deceives and perpetrates fraud against its own people. As long as the people fail to recognize this, or do, but take no lawful action to stop it, then these criminal actions by government s at all levels will continue, all to the detriment of the people. When no lawful opposition is taken against crime, then the criminals continue and escalate those crimes. If anyone truly thinks that government will self-correct, then they are either greatly mistaken, or totally deluded. Once again, we repeat government's "sacred" motto: **"If we fix it, we can't scam it."**

CONSCIOUSNESS

Consciousness is a major factor within humans and human society. It either exists, or it does not. In the natural, growing, unrestricted state, consciousness does exist. However, in the unnatural state, when intensive manipulation, conditioning, programming, propaganda, mind-control and many other factors take effect, true, unadulterated consciousness does not exist for the general population. One of the biggest thefts ever perpetrated upon the American people is the wholesale theft of their consciousness, or, if you will, awareness, and to a degree, common sense. Our objective observer, True, and our analytical computer, Reality, would ask why any government would take such stern, repressive actions against their own people. Their obvious answer is that government would do this to control the people. Their further position is that good government would never do this, therefore, any government that does so is not good government. Once government has control, it imposes whatever policies and programs it chooses, without any consideration for the people these policies and programs affect or how they limit and violate inherent rights guaranteed to the people. When governments and their partner power forces have control over peoples' consciousness, then they can do virtually anything they want, without meaningful, effective opposition. This draconian control robs the people of their natural state and turns that which should be natural independence into dependence under the control of others for the benefit of these others, all at the expense of the people.

Consciousness is vital for the development, maintenance and advancement of human society. Without it having been a factor in the past, humans would not have socially and societally evolved. It was those with consciousness and awareness—the thinkers, dreamers, innovators, writers, poets, those with creativity, inventiveness, ethics and spirituality, although few in numbers over the millennia—who influenced others and brought societies out of dark ages. Some say, in truth, that humans are still primitive and still living in dark times. Since the entire global society of humankind has been controlled and manipulated for a very long time, and consciousness has been obscured almost to the point of non-existence, then it is clear that societies have not been allowed to develop and evolve into what they could be, had they not been under the repressive boots of their controlling masters. When restrictions are imposed upon growth and development, it is painfully obvious that little to no growth takes place, except as allowed by the controllers, which growth they manipulate and use to their advantage. Yes, we have new devices, new inventions, better ways of living and travelling, so from a technical standpoint, our present has evolved over our past. Socially and spiritually, though, we have not evolved much at all.

Our American society, like others, gives its political and other powers away to governments and their partner power forces, which, in turn, take the peoples' power and use it against them. *Any truly conscious society would not make this mistake.* Unfortunately, the American society does not have the consciousness, or awareness, to understand that their own actions, or inactions, have harmed them, permitted government to abuse and misuse them and keep them in subservient positions to government and the controlling power forces. Giving one's power away to another or to government/power forces is avoiding responsibility, which, if taken, would keep that power within the individual human and the greater society. However, one must possess consciousness to realize the gravity of this position. While some in America do have conscious understanding, true consciousness is totally lacking within the general American society. If it were otherwise, then, America would be the bastion of freedom and paradise it was intended to be.

The government, the system and the power forces within it have stolen the consciousness of the American people through deception, fraud, conditioning, programming, propaganda, "education"/indoctrination, media, entertainment venues and much, much more – and the people accepted this, without objection, comment or question, to their detriment. It is never too late to solve problems, and the best time to do this is the present. However, this takes a shift to reawaken or develop consciousness and willingness from the people to realize they have been totally lax in overseeing their government. This laxity gave the government and power forces carte blanche to do whatever they wanted anytime they wanted, without opposition. If the American people do not develop a firm resolve to be responsible, to take back their power and demonstrate the responsibility necessary to properly wield it and use it against any and all forms of bad government, then America, as a free, independent nation is doomed. Unless the American people can begin to finally oversee their government, understand the routine, Un-constitutional, criminal actions of their government, and hold offenders responsible, to end this insanity promoted and enforced by these criminal governments, they will never restore and live under Constitutional sanity in America. Obviously, this will not happen quickly, but, with time and commitment, provided the people develop conscious awareness and join with others for the benefit of America, and themselves, it *can* happen. Remember, our nation was founded by people of this caliber, and also remember that, though their numbers were small, their combined efforts founded this amazing country. Are today's Americans going to be the ones who let it slip away?

One of the objectives in writing this book is to awaken the people to the absolute fact that better ways exist to do almost anything. When this simple, but powerful, concept is understood and accepted as truth and reality, then people can awaken their dormant consciousness and awareness that has always been with them – but never activated. The small step of actually knowing better ways exist to do nearly anything is really a gigantic step that can activate and awaken the sleeping consciousness. Think of the enormity of this situation! People mindlessly go through the motions of their lives, day in and day out, essentially doing the same things over and over again. When one finally comprehends and accepts that there are better ways to do nearly anything, this can open up vistas in the mind, the imagination, which have never before been seen. Average people can realize that what they have done forever can be done differently and better, and this then brings about an entirely new creative thought process which can unfold and expand for those who truly want to move forward. When people begin this path, their lives can quickly change for the better. Being fully aware of the governing realities that control us is a major step. Learning how to lawfully and effectively change government to the will of the people is a gigantic jump. Being able to look into ourselves—our minds, hearts, souls and spirits–to determine whether our belief system is truly our own or the result of a manufactured conditioning process, both overt and subtle, is a quantum leap, but one which we *all* must take, if we are to ever be truly free, conscious and awake.

SECTION ONE

BACKGROUND AND PERSPECTIVE

CHAPTER ONE

OUR REASONS FOR WRITING THIS BOOK

The thoughts, ideas and principles contained in *ByPass the Banks* are based upon common sense, old-time logic, reason, truth, facts and the understanding that there are better ways to do almost anything. These principles have served human society very well for millennia, but, unfortunately, in our modern "throwaway" world, appear to have fallen out of favor. Society would be better served, were society to resurrect and reinstitute these principles—and quickly, at that! If people want to succeed in whatever enterprise they choose, it is best that they make good use of what they have available to them, at that time, to accomplish what they want in the here and now. In other words, take the conditions present, the positions and resources available at the time to reach their objectives. This is also true and would be very beneficial for societies, as a whole. Many people, if not the overwhelming majority, allow others—such as politicians, societal leaders, business leaders, bankers, sports stars and celebrities, families and friends —to influence and formulate what should be their *own* thoughts, ideas and opinions. If we are to progress in meaningful ways, as a human species, then, it is absolutely essential for people to get back to basics and personal responsibility, and not depend upon others to think and act for them.

Over many millennia, nations, peoples and societies have changed in myriad ways. Most of us now have better homes and living accommodations, readily available food, clothing, means and modes of communication and transportation, as well as many other opportunities and programs that one would consider improvements. However, societies have not changed in at least two very important positions. First, societies have always been ruled and controlled by self-serving, pernicious, greedy, ambitious, mostly ruthless leaders, although many of these characteristics are cleverly hidden behind facades. This form of political rule, through governments, has not changed, but the styles, forms and operations have. Second, banking has always been a *private, for profit*, enterprise imposed upon the public for the benefit of that private enterprise, with the full cooperation and support of the government, and still is. If humanity is to progress and ever expect to be truly free, we must take lawful and societal control of these two vital positions and use them for the benefit of all humankind instead of the ruling power forces. This book is an attempt to point the people in the right direction to reach that goal.

Despite some rosy optimism and glowing prognostications from the "talking heads", who claim to be "experts" in economics, America is still suffering a severe economic crisis, and has been for some time, with no significant relief in sight. Other talking heads on the left and those in the mainstream media tout the gloom and doom of our economy under President Trump. Truth exists regarding this and other matters, but the real truth, and not selected aspects of it, is not now nor has ever been part of the media, governments and vested interests, all with their own agenda which they impose upon the people. It is up to the people to see through the fraud and ascertain the real truth. All these conditions were in place before the fraudulent COVID 19 crises. Now, restrictions and increased control will continue unless the people awaken to the fraud and take lawful and societal actions to stop it.

The servant governments in America long ago took political control from their masters, the people, and only the people, *en masse*, can ever lawfully take back their political control from their own servants. Since this COVID 19 fraud is international in scope and exists in virtually all countries, in one form or another, the people must realize that the central power forces of this earth initiated this fraud to expand their own power and control over the people to establish their own additional nefarious objectives. Because America not only participated in this international scam, but was instrumental in formulating it, just exactly whom and what do the U. S. government and other governments serve? By their actions, and not their rhetoric, it certainly is not the people they *claim* to serve. Realistically, it is all up to the people to make lawful changes, as it has always been all up to the people. The politicians elected to office by the people do not serve the people. They serve the power forces that control and own them, and do so under and for the corporate fraud un-Constitutionally created by Congress in 1871 that serves as the U.S. government. This vermin, as a political body, will never remedy the massive problems they deliberately created for the people, and still create *ad nauseum*! The American people have not only allowed this, but supported it by electing domestic enemies to office. Then when those domestic enemies oppose their campaign promises, violate their oaths and pass un-Constitutional, draconian legislation that harms the people in countless ways, the people never lawfully remove them from office. Incredibly, the people re-elect these traitors to office. If the people do not awaken to reality about the vile, evil nature of governments in this nation, federal, state and local, there is no possibility for a return to Constitutional government in America.

Yes, under President Trump there have been some improvements, but they have been so minor in scope compared to the true nature of America's political, economic, banking and social realities, that any improvements are only a cover for the real state of these massive and other problems affecting all of us. Since the No-Name Depression of 2007 and 2008, how much interest are you getting on your money when you deposit it? How much interest does the bank get on its loans, including points, fees and other charges? Do you see a disparity here? When you deposit money into the bank, it is money you have earned and worked hard to accumulate. When the bank "loans" money, those funds are not bank money from deposits, but rather money the bank receives from the Federal Reserve System to supposedly loan to you. Do you see a disparity here? President Trump and his administration made no changes to these economic disparities and what we have stated here is only a minuscule fraction of the enormous amount of problems existent in the American economy and banking as it is practiced. No matter the number of glowing reports and rosy opinions spun and spewed by the government and so-called economic "experts", America is *not* now, nor, if present conditions continue, can ever expect to be, in a true state of recovery. There have been other glowing reports about job increases and lowered unemployment figures, but what is the real job growth in comparison to the population growth and the true figure of the number of people who, after years of looking, are still unable to find viable jobs, so are no longer included in labor statistics? All of these worrisome situations were present before the COVID 19 fraud.

As a result of these disturbing, but true, facts, it is obvious that many of the so-called "average" and working people of this country, who make up the backbone of this nation, are growing ever more desperate and experiencing severe financial troubles. Most people within this category are a few paychecks away from financial disaster. From a true experiential and psychological position, this sad state of affairs is a total catastrophe for the entire nation. If one takes a deep, hard look at this, the vast majority of these troubles did not emanate from the people, but rather from the very systems, political, financial and otherwise, that are operative in America. The banking/lending system was and still is a major part of the cause of this economic crisis, but *it* has been doing quite well through its heavily debt-based monetary system, carried by the burdened backs of the people and businesses of this nation. From a rational, realistic, common-sense point of view, one might say that, without debt and welfare, both for people and for corporations, propping up a derelict, dysfunctional system, America's economy would fall through the cellar floor in a matter of months.

One of the programs contained in this book is a people-based and people-driven method for buying and selling property without bank or other institutional lender involvement. Our concept is based upon a very old method that worked quite well amongst people before banking interests essentially took over and monopolized the financing of property, businesses, governments and virtually everything else. We have taken this old method, which for the most part has been pushed out the door and eradicated by the financial institutions, with some exceptions, and revitalized it with a completely new approach that mutually benefits both sellers and buyers. From our long involvement in banking, real estate and business, we believe that the best transactions are those that result in successful win-win experiences for all participants. This is exactly what our *ByPass* Programs do. For the readers to achieve optimum results, it is best to read, review and thoroughly understand all of the CHAPTERs contained in this book, so that they will have a firm grasp and comprehensive conceptual understanding of the full programs.

Jack Flynn, one of the authors of this book, has made many predictions over sixty (60) years, many of which have come true. In 2004 and 2005, he could see that the economic catastrophe that was about to come down on America would not occur without great assistance from the government and the banking sector. As the infamous Franklin Delano Roosevelt was alleged to have said, "In politics, nothing happens by accident. If it happens, you can bet it was planned that way." Though many people are not aware of this, and may disagree, the "crisis" was carefully organized and orchestrated in collusion and conspiracy by, between and among the banks, other "lenders" and the government to rob the people of their personal wealth and property. The 2007 – 2008 economy crash and foreclosure debacle, as well as this most recent COVID-19 fraudulent crisis, are not the first time that these power forces colluded to orchestrate such disasters for the people and the nation. The power forces always benefit from the disasters they create.

During the time frame referenced above, Jack predicted over the radio that several major financial events were about to take place in a few years. One of these was the financial debacle that was about to devastate the stock and financial markets and the banks. The second was the fact that the Federal Reserve Bank would bail out the banks and the corporations in the amount of many trillions of dollars.

The first bailout Jack predicted was in the amount of eight trillion dollars, but at that time he also said that this amount would triple, at least. From the figures available to us, the total banking/

corporate bailout amounts to over **thirty eight trillion dollars!** Jack was light on his predictions by at least fourteen trillion dollars. When he made these predictions, virtually everyone who heard him told him that he was "out of his mind". However, in a few years, they could readily see that what he had said actually manifested in America.

A third prediction was the fact that the fraudulent mortgage market would result in massive numbers of foreclosures all across this nation, and tens of millions of people would lose their homes to the banks who initiated the foreclosures, which were also the very banks that *created* the mortgage fraud and thereby caused the foreclosures. It is easy for anyone to now see that those who caused the problems were *rewarded* for their efforts, while those who were the victims of this scam, namely the American people, lost their homes, their savings, and their possessions in massive amounts, totaling trillions of dollars. An inestimable added loss is the people's diminished self-esteem and scant hope of ever recovering.

The logical, rational, reasonable, objective observer could easily conclude that there is something awfully wrong with a system that rewards wrongdoers and punishes the victims of the wrongdoing! While the banks and mortgage companies put out as many mortgages during the securitization heyday, as possible, *the vast majority of which they knew would be defaulted upon*, some responsibility remains with some of the borrowers, as well, who should have known they could not afford the loans these lenders were so eager to make. The lenders knew that many of these borrowers could not afford "to pay the freight", yet they still made the loans. Logic dictates that there was an ulterior motive in so doing, which would benefit the banks and other lenders and rob the homeowners of their funds, properties and quality of life.

Some people in this borrowing segment were well aware that they could not afford the monthly payments, pay the excessive effective interest and fees demanded by the banks and mortgage companies, but most of these people proceeded with the loans, anyway. One of the glaring faults of the American people is that, *as a society*, they typically do not read or understand contracts. Most borrowers failed to read and comprehend the contracts presented to them, did not question them; therefore, did not know the extent of their indebtedness, the financial jeopardy the terms imposed upon them, the impossibility of satisfying their obligations and how quickly they would default on their mortgages due to the excessive effective interest being charged. Numerous books have been written about this debacle, so we do not have to go into great detail here. One of them, well worth reading, is entitled: *The Monster*, written by Michael W. Hudson, published in 2010 by Times Books, Henry Holt and Company, New York, New York. There is an old adage that has been around forever: "Buyer Beware!" The people of the American society must be much more discerning and make sure they use common sense, anytime they enter into any long term financial contracts. The disaster of which we speak makes it clear that those who do not do so can be quickly swindled by unscrupulous banking interests and by and through their own careless, unthinking actions and fault.

A position that has been evident in American society for some time is that, in business of any type, the one who pays is considered the client of the one who receives the payment. For instance, in the health care system currently operative in America, many times the patient is considered "incidental", because it is not the patient who pays the bill, but rather his insurance company.

During this mortgage fraud boom, a process called "securitization" led to fast and easy money that was paid in massive amounts to mortgage lenders. Many of the banks and mortgage companies which were dealing in securitization viewed the homeowner/borrower as incidental to accomplishing the securitization process—simply a means to an end or a pass through. The greedy banks and disreputable lenders were not concerned about whether the homeowner could meet his obligations or would lose his home. The borrowers' notes were quickly bundled and sold by lenders as "mortgage-backed securities" to Wall Street, who further securitized them and sold them to foreign and domestic investors, who were defrauded by this phony process, just as the borrowers were defrauded. These lenders initially made their money in fees, "points" and interest on the original mortgage transactions, but made their major scores when they sold the bundled notes into the securitization process.

The overwhelming majority of mortgage borrowers knew nothing of this scheme, whatsoever. Once the fraud became known, it was time for the government authorities to step in and take action. However, instead of holding the perpetrators of this enormous fraud accountable for their actions and requiring them to correct the problems, the government, under the guise that these banks were "too big to fail", authorized mind-boggling amounts of funds, which came from the tax paying people, through the Federal Reserve Bank, to be given to these criminal, corrupt lenders. Allusions were made to "programs" that would "help" borrowers, but these were few, inefficiently conducted, difficult to access and did not channel much, if anything, in the way of financial help to the defaulting borrowers. In fact, many now realize that these "programs" were simply more fraud perpetrated upon the borrowers and never intended to help them restructure their mortgages to be better able to pay their notes and keep their homes. As usual, there were some exceptions and some legitimate programs that helped some people, but nowhere near what should have been done.

By now, it should be evident to most observant Americans that the extensive, incestuous government/corporate/banking partnerships do not work in the best interests of the American people and never have. In fact, by the evidence available in public records for many decades, it can be said that this cartel works *against* the best interests of the people, and gains enormous profits by using and abusing the people. The rational observer could quickly deduce that the ones who caused the problem are not the ones who should be given the task of solving the problem. However, solving the problem would be counterproductive to the efforts of the problem creators. Many of these entities abide by a well-accepted, but little known, political maxim, which is: "If we fix it, then, we can't scam it." True and Reality conclusively agree that this greedy motivation is the existing reality in America, especially among politicians, bankers and corporate moguls, aka, the power forces.

It should be apparent to most Americans now, especially after the horrendous economic and social events since 2007, that government and corporations will never create solutions to the problems *they* deliberately created and/or allowed, and which they continue to create and allow. Therefore, this job remains strictly in the hands of the people. The people are powerful, *en masse*, and if the people were to finally realize the inherent political and economic power that lies within them, then, as a society, America could rectify her problems—that is, if the people take proper steps to put political and economic control back into the hands of the people, and finally, make great strides forward, as originally intended by the Founding Fathers of our nation. The election of Donald Trump on November 8th, 2016, may eventually prove beneficial to the American people, financially and otherwise, if they support his positions, based in the Supreme Law of this Land, our Constitution, and if he follows through on his campaign promises. This CHAPTER was written three years after Trump was elected. Most presidents during their campaigns make endless promises and pledges to the people, yet fulfill virtually nothing when they take office, or do exactly the opposite, such as when George H.W. Bush said: "Read my lips, no new taxes!" Yet, amazingly, the people still have not learned that they cannot trust what politicians *say*. In our lectures, seminars and media broadcasts, we have always stated that talk walks, while actions speak loudly. While President Trump has fulfilled a decent percentage of what he promised and pledged, he still comes up short on some major issues facing this nation. While he does not show the communist tendencies his predecessors did, his actions on this COVID-19 plandemic have not been in the best interests of the American people. Possibly, this is because he has received bad advice from the "experts", but he is still the "main man" and must make his own decisions as we all must. This is what happens when we rely upon others and not upon ourselves. Our characters, True and Reality, would readily agree with these observations. When most people vote for a candidate, they do so mostly based on what that candidate says and promises to do, if elected to office. There exists a tragic inconsistency in America between Americans voting for a candidate, then, never holding that candidate to his campaign and other promises. When Americans fail to hold those elected to their promises and stated convictions, it makes little sense to vote in the first place. This is a position for people to ponder.

When our forefathers drafted the Constitution for the United States of America in 1787 and amended it with the Bill of Rights in 1791, they created a truly egalitarian document for the rule of a nation by the people of that nation, which is truly unique in this world. No other country in the known history of this world has placed the power over government in the hands of the people, but, unfortunately, the American people, as a society, have been extremely lax in taking seriously their duties and responsibilities to oversee their governments and keep them in check, pursuant to oaths taken to the Constitution by public officers and the Constitutional mandates imposed upon those public officers by and through their oaths. Our Constitution established a Constitutional republic for America, which decrees that this nation will be governed under the rule of law, and not by the rule of man. The Constitution, as the Supreme Law, supersedes any other laws, statutes, codes, regulations, rules, policies, etc. and is the governing law of America. Unfortunately, the American people have permitted our public officers to decimate the Constitution and have negligently allowed them to operate under rule by man, instead of the rule of law. President Trump has stated that he intends to return the power to the people and to Constitutional governance, instead of un-Constitutional rule by man. This wise position, if carried through, is an obvious benefit for the American people, provided they know enough to support this rare intention and are wise enough to insist that it be fulfilled. Thus far, it appears that President Trump's words were merely lip service intended to assuage the people, but his term is not over yet, and if he wins reelection in November of 2020, perhaps he will fulfill all of his promises and stated objectives.

We mentioned that the Constitution is an *egalitarian* document, and if people were to objectively analyze the entire Constitution, in particular, the Bill of Rights, they would easily come to this conclusion. The entire Constitution is imbued with freedom, independence, and encourages **responsibility** on the part of the people, since the Founding Fathers were well aware of how despotic any government could become, given enough time and unlimited, *unsupervised* power. In the Dedication of this book, we mentioned wise men, women and saints, who have taught, exemplified and encouraged independence and freedom to the people as societal goals for the people, because these embody the spiritual objectives for humanity, as opposed to dictatorial governance by powerful, elite, militaristic, corporate and banking forces, bent upon the profitable, despotic rule of the many by the few. An enlightened, free, independent society can prevent such despotic rule, before it ever begins. Make no mistake in understanding that freedom and independence are powerful allies for the people and anathema to tyrants.

These are just some of the obvious reasons why we wrote this book, and there are many others than we cannot take time to get into here. We, Margy and Jack Flynn, have helped people all over this nation by teaching the Constitutions, state and national, to people, groups and organizations in seminars, lectures, workshops, and radio and television broadcasts. Jack has been doing this for over sixty years, and Margy for over fifty. We not only teach the Constitutions to people, but also teach them how to *apply* the AUTHORITY of the Constitutions against errant governments and corporations. This is not difficult, but it does require commitment, consistency, competence, courage and conviction of the heart to confront the evil forces which are attempting to destroy America and her people and absorb them into a one world order under a tyrannical elitist form of government. The current COVID-19 "crisis" that has brought about un-Constitutional "orders" issued by domestic-enemy-traitors, masquerading as public servants, is a glaring example of communism at work, not only in America, but throughout the world. Again, exactly whom and what do your politicians and so-called public servants serve? Tens of millions of Americans are finally figuring out that it is not the people who are being served!

Please review CHAPTER EIGHT which presents our Constitutional methods that have helped so many people in America. If they are willing to put in the time and effort to learn these simple, but powerful, methods, people can help themselves individually to resolve personal issues. However, it would be far better for the people and for America if large numbers of people all over the country were to use these methods on a wide-scale basis to resolve the massive amount of problems adversely affecting everyone, created by your own domestic-enemy-governments. To put it in a nutshell, domestic enemies oppose the Constitution and will never support it. Please consider this fact and use it as a yardstick to measure what is going on around you, especially during this COVID-19 scamdemic and when you go to the polls. In so doing, the people would hold politicians and public servants to the strict Constitutional mandates imposed upon them. If millions of people were to do this, then we would have a strong possibility of returning this nation to Constitutional governance and rule by written law, our Constitution, and not the devious rule by man. We can all see where rule by man has gotten us!

Because homeowners and the American people, as a whole, were grievously deceived by the government/corporate/banking cartel, we wrote this book with the expectation of demonstrating to everyday "regular" people, that despite this artificially created economic crisis, which has severely and adversely impacted the real estate and mortgage markets throughout the entire country for years, how average people could sell their homes and/or buy/finance homes, without the need to acquire new bank financing.

The methods contained in this book for buying and selling property in such difficult times are very direct, quite simple and can be easily accomplished, even in the worst economic times, without involvement of banks, mortgage companies, agents and brokers. These programs are entirely unique and a win-win for both parties engaged in any real estate transaction and could provide the process that you need for either buying or selling property. For the astute real estate investor, or for the average person who wants to become one, it would be best to read the entire book, which leads to the investment sections. However, for those who want to proceed directly to investments, go right to SECTIONS FOUR, FIVE, SIX, EIGHT AND NINE. These sections speak of buy/sell programs with a small investment that can lead to fabulous wealth within a three to four year period. They also speak of buy/rent/sell programs, which require a larger investment that can lead to immense wealth over a twenty year period. Both types of investments are very doable, provided the investors have the initial financial capability and are willing to follow through to reach their objectives.

It is well known to most Americans that tens of millions of people have lost their properties through foreclosures in the past many years. According to various online publications and government organizations, such as, Statistic Brain, Statistica, Com, Fannie Mae, Freddie Mac and FHA, during the twelve year period from 2004 through 2016, over 26,900,000 foreclosure filings took place in America. The number of completed foreclosures in those 12 years amounted to over 20,500,000 dwellings, which is an enormous amount of foreclosures in a nation that prides itself on being free, fair and just to its people. If one considered the actual number of people involved in the loss of their homes, that figure is staggering since it is much higher than 20,500,000. Losing one's home through foreclosure is, for most people, the loss of their most valued material possession and it is the ultimate, gut-wrenching catastrophe for entire families. When many people took out their mortgages, they had no idea of the economic disaster about to hit this country and them. They had no clue as to the trillions of dollars that would be "lost" in the markets and that many companies would either, go out of business, downsize, or leave the country for better situations overseas. As a result, millions of job losses took place throughout this nation further adding to the economic crisis.

According to the sources listed above, during that 12 year period starting in 2004 through 2016, approximately 8,097,000 homes sales took place. These figures indicate that 254% more foreclosures occurred than home sales, which is entirely lopsided for any nation or society. For every home sale, 2.54 foreclosures took place. These figures indicate that something is very wrong with our society, our economy, the banking system and how government treats the American people. Except for the so-called "star cities", the housing market has not recovered, and no matter what the "experts" say, it likely will not get back to normal for many years. If one were to take serious assessments on what the so-called experts have said, for a very long time they have been completely wrong. If experts are truly expert, then they are usually correct and not usually wrong. When an entire nation of "experts" is wrong, with a few minor exceptions, then another agenda may be afoot.

One of the serious concerns the American people have is the financial future of America. According to the referenced sources, 44% are worried about not being able to pay their mortgage payments or rents. Another concern is not enough money for retirement and not being able to pay for long-term health services. Only 31% of workers think that there will be enough money in social security for them. Conversely, up to 69% of workers think that there will be no social security for them when they retire. About 13.2% of homeowners have negative equity in their mortgages. 11,821,000 borrowers owe more on their homes than those homes are worth. The average number of homes in America for sale, at any one time, is 4,800,000. The national average income spent on mortgage payments is 37.5%.

While some people and families in America are doing well, financially and otherwise, many average Americans are either "on the edge" or not doing well at all, financially and otherwise. A nation whose home sales have been outstripped by foreclosures to the amount of 254% in a 12 year period is not a nation in which a large percentage of average people are doing well. Those average Americans are the backbone of America, but based on the figures presented, America and her various systems are not protecting the best interests and the affairs of these average Americans. Unless and until the American society lawfully demands that such conditions will never happen again, history has clearly indicated that they likely will. There is always a better way, or, for that matter, ways, to do almost anything. Vested interests usually do not favor these ways and many times directly oppose them, since new methods and approaches usually challenge those vested interests and their status quo.

This book has many purposes, but was primarily written for those 20 million plus homeowners who lost their homes to foreclosure. Our methods demonstrate how these people, if financially capable, could purchase other homes without banks and without new bank financing. For those homeowners who are hard pressed to pay their mortgages, thus, may go into foreclosure, and/or for those who are facing imminent foreclosure, there may be a way for them to sell their homes, before this happens, if conditions are favorable to a financially capable buyer. We demonstrate this in SECTION THREE on foreclosure and it will be more fully explained in another publication. The immediate purpose of this book is to show sellers, who want to sell their homes, though facing extreme adverse economic conditions, very simple, easy and valid ways in which this can be done. Further, for those able buyers looking to buy a home, but who may not qualify under restrictive lending criteria, this book provides viable methods to purchase a home, despite these daunting problems and without involving a bank or mortgage company. Returning to the principal to principal position, without middlemen, would be beneficial not only to the principals themselves, but to the general society for their buying and selling almost anything.

CHAPTER TWO

AMERICA IS A CONSTITUTIONAL REPUBLIC, *NOT* A DEMOCRACY!

T*he Constitution for the united states of America, circa 1787, as amended with the Bill of Rights in 1791,* established America as a **Constitutional Republic**—not as a democracy. The major difference between a true Constitutional republic and a democracy is that in a Constitutional republic, the rule of written Law prevails, and not the rule of man, as occurs in a so-called democracy. As a famous man once said, the true definition of a democracy is two wolves and a sheep deciding what's for dinner!

The **Supreme Law of America** is our referenced Constitution, which clearly establishes the *fact* that the Constitution is the supreme, superseding law over all lesser laws, statutes, codes, regulations, rules, policies, etc., whether they be federal, state, county or local. Any time any lesser law conflicts with any part of the Constitution, then, it is superseded and disallowed by the Supreme Law of the Land. Every system, business, government, ideology, political philosophy and virtually all structures throughout society require a foundational position or rule of law—and that foundational position for America is our American Constitution—our Supreme Law. Our Constitution provides sane, sound Law that protects all the inherent natural rights of the people and all due process provisions for all American Citizens. This is an amazing departure from the ways in which most governments have operated and continue to do so and, further, these rights and due process provisions are *guaranteed* to the people. Our Constitution guarantees freedom of speech, freedom of expression, freedom of choice, freedom of religion, freedom of the press, freedom of assembly, the right to keep and bear arms, the right to present grievances to government—and have government correct and resolve them, the right to due process of law, freedom from unlawful arrests, searches and seizures, the right to life, liberty and property that cannot be taken without due process of law, the right to a trial by a jury of one's peers, the right to cite and claim rights that are un-enumerated within the Constitution, the right to consent only to "government of right", and numerous other rights and due process provisions embodied within the Constitution. No other government has ever guaranteed these rights to its people nor have these rights ever been embodied in the founding document of any other nation. America was and is a very unique experiment in the annals of human civilization, with the true power of government embodied within her Citizens. Some very rare and unique individuals fought very hard to establish this type of government of, by and for the people. Unfortunately, the American people were never, and are not now, up to the task of self-governance. In all of our seminars, radio and television broadcasts and talks, we have always stated that it is never too late for the people to realize and then correct their mistakes. One of our purposes for writing this book is our hope that it may awaken the spirit of the sleeping giant within the American people and finally bring them to the realization that the true power of government is vested within *them*.

The Bill of Rights is set forth in the first ten Amendments to the referenced national Constitution and, as said above, guarantees all inherent rights to all Citizens. Further, the due process of law provisions set forth throughout the Constitution guarantee that due process treatment will be extended to all Citizens by all forms of government, federal, state, county and local. As the Supreme Law of the Land, the Constitution is the supreme AUTHORITY in this land and supersedes any and all other forms of alleged authority, no matter what. All of these referenced rights and due process provisions are established by the *superior* authority of this Supreme Law. In America, the Constitutional Republic, no right guaranteed in the Constitution can *lawfully* be usurped, stolen, set aside, ignored, limited, restricted, surrendered or sold. However, in a democracy, which is rule by man, and not rule by law, all of these rights can be ignored, restricted, violated at will and outright abolished by the ruling majority and ruling elite. Under which system do you think most Americans would want to live? It is pretty obvious that the people of a nation would not only be much better off in a true Constitutional republic, but they would also be free, independent, resourceful and better able to enjoy life, because their rights and due process would be protected by their own **servant government**. Do you think that this is how the United States government and virtually all other governments in this country actually operate? If not, then the logical, necessary question is: "Why not?"

Democracies do not protect the rights of the people and, in fact, frequently decimate them at will. Our founding fathers knew the clear dangers inherent in a democracy, thus, were adamant that America *not* be a democracy, because if it were, then, they feared that mob rule would prevail.

In a democracy, rights can be obliterated at any time through clever manipulations of the feckless people who get everything they want from the government at the expense of the "working stiffs", as well as from the good, but misguided intentions of the hardworking people who are manipulated through lies, propaganda and guilt. In such a system, government knows it would have the support of the majority of the people, because government would have promised that majority that it would provide a myriad of benefits at the expense of those who work diligently to support the society and would make those workers feel "noble" about their ongoing generous sacrifices. Does this sound like the America of today?

When our Constitution was established by our founding fathers, it was the finest egalitarian document ever created by humankind for the governance of a nation by the people of that nation. Think of the tenor of the times in which the Constitution was created! Nations were ruled by kings, emperors, dictators, warlords, bankers and potentates. The people had absolutely no say in the affairs of their nation, or for most of them, even in their own affairs. No other nation in the history of the world has ever placed the political power over government in the hands of the people. Unfortunately, as a society, the American people never accepted the *responsibility* inherent in a self-governing people to supervise, oversee and correct their *servant* government. Instead of upholding their responsibility to oversee their government, the people let the politicians do whatever they wanted; thus, gave their political power away—or surrendered it—to their servants, who quickly reversed the originally intended roles and became the illegitimate masters of the people. As a result of this capitulation by the people, the politicians, the vested interests, the powerful, the "elite", the bankers, all of whom we will call from now on the "power forces", have controlled America and Americans from the very inception of this nation. What was bestowed upon the people by the Supreme Law of the Land was tragically squandered by the people. The great American egalitarian experiment came to a quick and shattering demise. Instead of a nation of truly free, independent, creative, resourceful, responsible people, America and Americans went the way of the feudal states in which the government and the other referenced powerful interests totally controlled the society and all aspects within it. This is not what our wise founders had in mind when they bravely took the great risks necessary to create our Constitutional republic.

From the feudal state status, America long ago descended into a covert socialist-bordering-on-communist nation in which all power is vested within the "state" and none within the people. All one has to do to understand this is to objectively and systematically review the operating realities within present-day America and discover how the government of this nation and the power forces created communist states throughout the world, directly or indirectly, and covertly funded them. Those who think they truly have power in this nation and attempt to use their imagined power against un-Constitutional government and the power forces quickly find that the government and the power forces are virtually all-powerful against the Citizens. This is an absolutely tragic state for those who are truly concerned about the well-being of our nation and her people. However, there are lawful, Constitutional ways and means to stop, correct and defeat un-Constitutional, unlawful government, both in and out of court, and we and our people have been able to do that successfully for six decades. At the end of this CHAPTER we will briefly summarize our Constitutional approach and methods.

The American public has not yet understood the fact that what politicians *say* and then *do* is vastly different. This hypocrisy and shameless fraud has been going on for so long that it seems "normal" to most people, to the point that you know politicians are lying if their lips are moving! Unfortunately, the American society accepts and then lives those lies, considers them "normal" and inevitable, and refuses to challenge what they innately know is wrong. As we said earlier, these types of injustices and wrongdoings could never have happened in a *true* Constitutional republic, for two specific reasons. First, the people would have accepted the authority delegated to them by and through the Constitution and properly overseen all aspects of their government. That government which did not perform pursuant to Constitutional mandates would quickly be brought into Constitutional compliance by the people, or if necessary, the offending officers of that government would be lawfully removed from office by the people and appropriately punished for their crimes against the people. Second, the government officers would be well aware that their actions are supervised by the people and would, out of necessity and through this ongoing public supervision, adhere to all Constitutional mandates in all aspects of governing, or in the alternative, be fully aware that they would lawfully be removed from office. Sections 3 & 4 of the 14th Amendment to the national Constitution provide one of the most direct remedies for removing errant public officers. The actions of the United States government, from the very beginning, and even more so since the War of Northern Aggression, clearly prove that America is *not* operating as a Constitutional republic. Tragically, the American society has zero awareness of this. Yes, a few people and a few groups here and there are fully aware of this dire situation, but they are far too few to even register on any measurement scale. This is exactly how the government and the power forces want it.

The Constitutionally secured Rights and Due Process of Law guaranteed in the Constitutions to the people, in both the national and state Constitutions, are not upheld or even recognized by the federal government, or for that matter, by any state and local government in this nation. These un-Constitutional governments give **lip service** to the Rights of the people, but do not under any typical circumstances uphold those rights nor provide due process of law. If these governments did so, then the majority of people who challenge the un-Constitutional actions of government would be victorious. It's really this simple. Governments do not want to be challenged in any form whatsoever especially when the challenges demonstrate that these governments are operating un-Constitutionally, in violation of Constitutional mandates, thus, unlawfully. These un-Constitutional actions by government are absolutely CRIMINAL and *prohibited by the Constitution(s),* yet all governments typically ignore the Constitutions, state and national. Again, by their ignorance, apathy, indifference and lack of responsibility, the people, as a society, have allowed this, because the people have not accepted their responsibility of self-governance, nor have the people required their public servants, <u>who are mandated by Law to take and uphold Constitutional</u> **oaths**, to abide by their oaths in the performance of their official duties. Had the people done this, since America's inception, then, America would be a far different nation now—a nation in which the people and their rights would be respected and upheld by their servant government. Further, there would be no private central bank issuing currency under government fiat; thus controlling the entire economy of America and financial lives of the American people. Still further, there would be no 16th Amendment, no income tax, no sales tax and no property tax whatsoever. Unfortunately, the failure of the American people to take the power delegated to them in the Constitutions and hold all governments to the strict Constitutional mandates imposed upon them has resulted in these un-Constitutional, monstrously criminal and fraudulent acts routinely perpetrated upon the people by un-Constitutional governments.

Rather than uphold our Constitution and Rights guaranteed therein to the people, the federal government and virtually all state and local governments follow, obey, implement and enforce the tenets of the communist manifesto upon their own people. Our impartial observer True, and his computer companion Reality would quickly recognize this as active treason by those governments sworn to uphold the Law of the Land, but instead, follow and enforce the dictates of communism. Facts are facts, reality is reality and fantasy is fantasy. What do you believe? The facts and reality speak for themselves.

The usual lawless custom, practice and policy of government is to oppose and violate all Constitutionally secured inherent and Due Process Rights—in direct opposition to the Constitutional mandates imposed upon government officers by and through their oaths. As said above, this is criminal, but this is a *fact*, yet the people do not even realize what is going on right under their noses and in plain sight each and every day. It is also a fact that no oath taker has the Constitutional authority—**or any other form of valid, lawful authority**—to oppose, violate, deny and defy the very documents to which he swore or affirmed his oath. That oath requires *all* public officers of any type to uphold all of the inherent Rights and Due Process of Law provisions guaranteed to the people in the Constitutions, whether state or national. **Any act passed by congress, any legislature and any public body, and any action committed by any public officer/employee either supports and upholds the Constitutions, or opposes and violates them.** Again, it is really this simple, and as many people are beginning to find out, dealing directly and simply is the best way to proceed to reach one's desired objective.

If the people were aware of these very simple, but *powerful,* Constitutional requirements, and if the people were to press and lawfully enforce their guaranteed rights, then, they could hold those public officers who violate their oaths to the strict Constitutional mandates imposed by those oaths. In this way, the people would be exercising a responsible form of self-governance, in which they are overseeing and supervising the actions of all public officers, holding them to the limited scope of authority they have been delegated by the people, and when those actions are errant, the people can lawfully remove those errant public officers from office pursuant to the above referenced self-executing Sections 3 & 4 of the 14th Amendment. However, as long as the people allow government to act criminally and un-Constitutionally, without any comments, questions, objections or repercussions from the people, then, that lawless practice will not only continue, but escalate until the people have zero rights—and are arrogantly told so by their own so-called servant government. Such a scenario is not the mark of a true Constitutional republic! As Margy and I have said forever, it is never too late for the American people to take back their political power and hold governments accountable and liable for their un-Constitutional criminal actions. There are ways to do this, which we will discuss in the next CHAPTER.

Our American Constitution recognized the inherent, natural rights of the people, established guarantees for these rights and also established due process of law provisions to protect the rights guaranteed to the people. In a truly free nation, every individual and group can demand that government protect and uphold those Rights. This is not the case in America, since Rights are rarely upheld for anyone. Is America a free nation? Facts are facts and fantasy is fantasy. The two do not mix when people seek and want the truth. Unfortunately, the people, as a society, are totally unaware of these Rights and provisions. As we have long said, in today's America, if people do not know and lawfully enforce their Rights against un-Constitutional government(s), then, they have none. The Constitution(s) uphold not only Rights, but also provide protection and well-being for the American people, but, again, they do not know this, and the U.S. government and all the other forms of government, state, county and local, have zero intention of informing the people about this protection, well-being and security. Following is the language of the Preamble to our Constitution:

> "We, the People of the United States, in Order to form a more perfect Union, establish Justice, insure domestic Tranquility, provide for the common defence, promote the general Welfare, and secure the Blessings of Liberty to ourselves and our Posterity, do ordain and establish this *Constitution* for the United States of America."

As we can see, the Preamble speaks of justice, insuring domestic tranquility, providing for the common defense, promoting the general welfare and securing the blessings of liberty to the people. As the U.S. government and virtually all governments in this country operate today, none of these Constitutional provisions are upheld by those governments which are sworn to uphold them. As previously mentioned, all government officers and workers are required to take oaths to the national Constitution and in some instances to the state Constitution before they can assume the duties of their offices. This was required by our founding fathers to ensure that government officers would abide by their oaths in the performance of their official duties. If they failed to do so, they acted unlawfully, outside the limited scope of their delegated duties and authority, thus, they would lawfully be removed by the people. When was the last time you heard of any action by the people to lawfully remove from office un-Constitutional, unlawful politicians, bureaucrats, judges and law enforcement officers? A truthful answer would be never, because the American people have failed to accept their responsibility to oversee actions of government and remove un-Constitutional officers upon the commission of any un-Constitutional act or actions by them.

When we were politically active in New Mexico, Margy and I used the Constitutions to remove several dozen errant politicians, judges and police from office. Any responsible Citizen can do the exact same thing, if that Citizen understands his/her political power, the power of the Constitutions, his/her own rights, and how government in the usual customs, practices and policies tramples those rights at will. The operating governmental reality in America would clearly demonstrate that virtually no government officer or worker abides by his or her oath to the Constitution(s) in the performance of his or her duties and none of them uphold the rights and due process guaranteed to the people. In fact, the U.S. government, as well as state, county and local governments, and the power forces work directly and diligently *against* the rights, due process, well-being and protection of the people. One may ask why, and the answer is that the governments and the power forces gain additional control, additional power and enormous wealth by opposing what is guaranteed to the people in the Constitution(s). Despite these Constitutional guarantees and the fact that these governments are duty bound by Law to uphold all tenets and mandates of the referenced Constitutions, they do not do so, and instead flagrantly oppose and deny the Constitutionally guaranteed rights of the people as the routine custom, practice and policy of their offices. In the Declaration of Independence, Thomas Jefferson stated that it is the duty of all Americans to oppose all enemies of this republic, both foreign and domestic. By now, a large number of Americans has realized, and an ever-growing number is realizing, that our own politicians, leaders and bureaucrats are the domestic enemies of whom Jefferson spoke.

CHAPTER THREE

NECESSITIES OF EXISTENCE

Ever since humans first set foot or were created upon this planet, basic human needs existed, then, as they exist now. People need food, water, clothing, shelter and protection from the elements simply to survive. As human societies developed, expanded and progressed over the ages, societal needs increased. Human associations and interactions with other people have always existed, in one form or another, and usually serve the social, economic and other needs of participating parties. Over time, as societies of people expanded, so did their interactions and needs. One group of people could provide some necessities of life and other needs to another group of people, who would, in turn, provide other necessities to them. These were basic, even exchanges, and this was how barter and trade began, practices, which have served humans well for many millennia, and in some societies, still do.

With the continued expansion of societies over the millennia, and as they developed into more cohesive organized structures, other needs beyond basic necessities came about. Trading and barter were common in the early days, but as mankind progressed, mediums of exchange began to appear, partly as a more convenient way to trade, but also as a contrived entrapment on the part of the money creators and money lenders to societies. A medium of exchange is simply some object or type of currency with a designated value that is accepted by all who use it. It is nothing more than that now, and never has been. Without the society's acceptance of the agreed-upon, designated value, the medium of exchange, or monetary unit, currency or "money" would have no value whatsoever.

At first, the mediums of exchange were simple societal processes by which one entity could sell his wares, receive payment for them through the agreed upon medium of exchange, then, purchase whatever he wanted with that medium of exchange, or monetary unit, he received. This was a more expedient step, beyond barter and trade, than when the trading parties had to physically bring their wares to accomplish the exchange, such as trading one pig for twelve hens. The medium of exchange became much more convenient and less burdensome to all parties involved, since the principals involved could buy and sell through the monetary unit rather than transport and carry around their wares. Without the societal acceptance of the agreed upon value of the monetary unit, no exchanges could take place by this method.

From time immemorial, the usual opportunists that exist in and have existed in all societies figured out that they could personally benefit from installing themselves as "leaders" of their own people, and did just that. The early leaders achieved their positions in many different ways, but the overwhelming majority of them had one thing in common. They all took advantage of and used their own people for their personal gain and put themselves on "sacred" pedestals above everyone else. A few of these early leaders were natural leaders truly concerned about their people. However, most of them were self-serving, greedy egotists who wanted to control everyone and everything in sight, while amassing personal fortunes, so guarded and protected their wealth through force. Some of the others were the wealthiest locals, or local heroes, or the most powerful, or brutal villains, warlords who killed all opposition, while some were philosophers, or wise men. Their positions enriched them, at the expense of their own people and provided opportunities the common people could not even dream about. When the monetary unit came about, the clear, obvious benefit for the rulers was to create that monetary u nit and control all aspects of that monetary unit, which included the establishment of its value, and the issuance and distribution of that monetary unit. Of course, that monetary unit became the "official" medium of exchange for that country or sovereign.

Earlier in this book we mentioned that rulers of societies, in collaboration with private banking and monetary interests, issued and distributed "money", the local monetary unit, to suit their own best interests and not those of the societies they ruled. By doing this, the rulers and leaders of any given society not only issue and control the monetary unit, but also control the business and activities of the entire society and everyone who uses that unit. This position has not changed over many millennia. The "golden rule" is still in force today as it has been forever, but that rule may be quite different from what most people believe, namely, "He who has the gold rules". Once those who seek power gain it, they and their posterity never relinquish it voluntarily. When the rulers and elite of any given society own and control the land, have, retain and enforce political power, control the courts, the clergy, the monetary power and control the military to suppress their own people, the powerful use that power against the powerless to bring everyone and everything under the absolute control of that power—just like now. While styles, mores, dress, fads and societies have changed, the ruthless tactics of the narcissistic ruling psychopaths and sociopaths and their flagrant abuse of power have not.

Over time, the monetary unit in each society inevitably became a necessity of life. Barter and trade was surpassed by money, except for a very small percentage of transactions. Just like food, water, clothing, shelter and protection, if one did not possess money to purchase life's necessities, then he could starve or freeze to death. History has proven that this has happened to many millions of people. In the early days, those who were tenant farmers serving the local lord at least could survive and eke out a minimal existence for them and their families. Those who were makers of some type of product, such as blacksmiths, shoemakers and cobblers, tool makers, saddle makers, bakers, artisans, etc., could at least sell their products and receive the local monetary unit for them. However, these people and what they sold were under the control of the local ruler and his dictated rules that benefited him and his class, just as modern day people are now controlled by those who rule them. If a sword maker was too good at his trade, he could come under the direct control of the ruler who could order the sword maker to make swords only for *his* army and do business only with the ruler. This ruler could then decide to pay the maker in the medium of exchange, and in whatever amount he chose, or not. He made and enforced the rules, supported by his military, just as the rulers and the elite do now. All societies and their activities were controlled by the rulers who created and distributed the monetary unit, had the political, social, religious and military control, and owned the land. With this much power, the ruler and his thugs could do whatever they wanted, to whomever they wanted at any time, and did.

Since the power of the purse was in the hands of the ruler, he could appoint an agent to act for him, such as a banker. If the ruler and/or his banker decided to restrict or reduce the issuance of the monetary unit to the people, for any purposes, he did as he liked since he had all the power he needed to do so, including his military that would torture and kill dissenters. There have always been men that served in the military who readily and eagerly followed the inhumane orders of evil beings, just like now. When funds are withheld from people by a powerful, sovereign force, there is not much the people can do but lawfully try to change or alter that force and its positions. Since the sovereign is a little god in his own realm who makes all the laws, this is a near impossibility. When faced with the impossible, the people either abandon their natural rights and continue their slave existence in service to their master, or rebel to assert their rights, as did our forefathers during the American Revolution.

Obviously, money and access to it has become a necessity of life in today's world, and without it or the ability to access it, people and entire societies are damaged. Again, history and even current situations have clearly confirmed this, so it is not difficult to understand. Common sense and logic clearly indicate that a family without funds and without permanent access to funds will be harmed in many ways because the family lacks the basic necessity, money, to keep it from harm. When millions of families within a society are so affected, the entire society is affected. When the entire society is considered in terms of its far reaching interactions, no one lives on an island. We are all part of that society and thus all influenced, or affected, in one way or another. When millions of families have no funds, then, reverberations are felt within that society. Beyond the human tragedy, when people are desperate and have no options, then, crime, assaults, theft, riots, murder and mayhem are commonplace activities. History and current events have demonstrated these disturbing conditions quite clearly.

Since this is what can and does happen in such situations, the rational, reasonable and objective observer could ask why the original conditions that created the problem were initiated in the first place. Under such circumstances, it is clear that the entire society has been severely harmed by government policies which created the original conditions. Since government is theoretically serving the people of the nation and theoretically acts in the best interests of the people, then why would government, not only allow the original conditions to exist, but also create policy to foster those conditions that resulted in massive societal problems? Given this situation, it appears abundantly clear that government does not work in the best interests of the people and has its own hidden agenda. In America, very few average Americans ask these questions, and fewer still demand truthful answers. Virtually no average American or group of them holds government officers personally responsible and liable for their devastating policies, and none demand realistic, viable solutions to the problems. Just as in days of old, when the people, by and through their own non-actions, permitted the ruler to harm them in any way he wanted, and in so doing, the people condoned, aided and abetted the harm he inflicted upon them, the American people and society have done the same thing. There is nothing new under the sun when it comes to master and slave, no matter how the slave is defined. Rulers are still doing as they wish, and the people still support the policies of their rulers which harm them, their families and their own nation.

Now as then, some people within any society do not fit the societal norm and do not function as the majority of society does. These people also need funds simply to exist. In earlier days, those who were not farmers, makers of products, or engaged in some productive, saleable activity, many times starved or froze to death, just as they do today in various societies all over the world, including America.

In today's America there are various groups across the nation that are having extremely difficult times because there is little or no access to funds necessary to sustain them and their families. One is the extremely large group of American people who sincerely *want* to work to earn money in order to support themselves and their families. The other is the equally large group of people who either do not want to work, or who are physically and/or mentally unable to work. Most of these people in the latter group want society to pay for everything they need and want, and government is extremely willing to oblige them—at the expense of the working people. The former group simply wants to find work so they can pay for their own needs, be independent and not be burdens on society. Unfortunately, because the economy has been put into a major, ever-deepening pit by its very own rulers, very few jobs are available to those who really want to work. Others may claim that there are jobs available, but also claim that the people are too lazy and don't want them. Some jobs do exist, however, few exist for the massive amount of people who lost good-paying jobs, but desperately want and need them. Further, many of the so-called available jobs are in the low-paying service industry that cannot support a family. Here, again, as in the past and as usual, the rulers of this nation, just as previous rulers have done, keep the monetary unit from the people who want to work and pay their own way by ensuring that few decent paying jobs still exist in this country. No lawful authority exists for America's elected rulers to so brutalize their own people, as did the rulers of old. The policy of America for years has been not only to export jobs, but also entire industries, to other nations, which clearly does not benefit the American people and our nation. Private, vested-interest parties benefit through this practice, including foreign and domestic corporate interests who profit from trade agreements with foreign countries, but the reader should bear in mind that the responsibility of the American government is to the American people, alone. Any policies that have harmed the American people are completely and totally un-Constitutional and conducted without valid authority.

Do you see a relationship between restricting people's ability to access money by earning it, as opposed to the overabundance of money loaned to people, as occurred during the lending spree that led to the ruination of the housing market, the economy and the resultant massive amount of foreclosures that ruined millions of families across this nation? The obvious answer is that America and her people have been deliberately put into economic disaster by American rulers elected by the American people. Theses rulers are Constitutionally required to uphold and protect the Rights of the American people—not decimate them. When the rulers control the nation through political power, the power of the purse, the courts and the military, those rulers can do whatever they want since they have the power and the force to do so. The whims, interests and policies of the rulers, as in the past, have put the American people and America, herself, in deep financial and social jeopardy. As stated before, the powerful use their power against the powerless to bring everyone and everything under the control of that power. In this regard, things have not changed at all over the ages. When candidate, Donald Trump, was running for office, he constantly said that the "system is rigged" and he wants "to clean the swamp". After three years in office, he still has not stopped and corrected the rigged system nor has he cleaned the D.C. Swamp, which we call a festering, putrid cesspool of evil and rampant corruption. As the candidate and as the President, Trump has acknowledged the inherent political power in the people and claimed that he wants to return that power to the people, but has done absolutely nothing to accomplish this. As we said before and as people know, talk walks, while actions speak volumes. Our characters, True and Reality, could easily conclude that Trump has not followed through on these promises or many others. While he has done some good things for America, they pale in comparison to what he COULD have done, and one of the first steps would be to fix the rigged system while returning the political power to the people.

We think we have established the fact that money, or any given nation's monetary unit, is a vital necessity of life for all who live in the so-called civilized, modern world. Without it and without the means to access it, large amounts of people could quickly die. Since rulers and governments are DIRECTLY responsible for this unconscionable tragedy, then the people of affected nations, in their own best interests, should lawfully try to remedy the problem. If this cannot be done, then, other alternative ways should be explored. When an existing currency of a nation is withheld from a large segment of society because the policies of the rulers have stripped the jobs from a country, such as America, then the people might turn to an **alternative currency** that could resolve their economic problems. As said throughout this section, money is simply a medium of exchange with a set value accepted by the people of a nation. The problem with virtually ALL currencies on this earth is that they are **fiat** money imposed upon the people by government edict. Fiat currencies are not backed by precious metals of any type or anything else of tangible value and are made "legal tender" by the government and the private central bank of that nation which issues them.

Each country in this world, with a few exceptions, has a privately owned central bank that creates and issues the currency of that nation. All of these central banks are controlled by the same entities, which puts one **banking cartel** in control of the entire world's economy. Each central bank works closely with the rulers of the respective nation to keep that central bank in power, and to issue all the funds to the government that it wants, so the government can maintain its own power over its own people. Since the rulers of each nation *theoretically* represent the people of that nation, then, in the best interests of the people and the nation, the government, and not a private bank, should create and issue a public, not private, currency for that nation. When a government authorizes a private bank to create and issue private fiat currency, then, obviously, that government is not protecting the best interests of its people, but instead those of a private bank. All the currency the bank creates out of thin air becomes debt to be repaid to the bank by the people, plus interest. Since the fiat currency is printed without any gold or other precious metal backing, its real value is nothing but the paper upon which the funds are printed. However, the government has decreed that this fiat currency, embossed with the government's seal, denoting the theoretical value of that essentially worthless paper, is the monetary unit of that particular nation with the designated assigned monetary values. This is the largest piece of piracy and fraud that ever existed upon this earth, but tragically people all over the world accept the fraud as "normal", since they know little to nothing about it.

The private central bank in America is called the Federal Reserve Bank, which is neither "federal" nor has any reserves. This private bank issues private, non-metal-backed fiat currency, called Federal Reserve Notes, ordered by the government officers you elect to office, and their appointees. People mistakenly believe this currency equates to American dollars, but, as stated above, the private, not public, currency is debt-based, interest-bearing currency, backed by nothing, which the American people are required to repay to the bank. Since the "money" is not backed by gold or any other valuable commodity, and printed on paper, which is then assigned a monetary value, the "money" has no value except the assigned fiat value, which is accepted without question by virtually all Americans. Yet, the American people are required to repay the bank in *real* value, real because of their labor expended to receive the worthless paper in compensation for their labor. Since the American society has never challenged this fraud, and since the elected officials, and their appointees, uphold and personally benefit from the fraud, the fraud continues, unabated. Our Constitution authorized Congress to coin and to distribute money and assign the value thereof. It never authorized a private bank to create, issue, distribute and control the monetary unit of America, nor did it authorize Congress to transfer its lawful authority to the private bank, yet this un-Constitutional transfer of power to the private bank continues, with the approval of Congress, the President and the entire government which is *supposed* to protect and uphold the people's Rights. Our two observers, True and Reality, can quickly deduce that Congress and the entire federal government acted in direct violation and opposition to the Constitution when Congress created the Federal Reserve Act in 1913, and every Congress and every president since then has upheld this un-Constitutional, unlawful fraud. The Federal Reserve began in 1913, but the first private central bank in America was established in 1791. For a detailed explanation of the Federal Reserve, and a fascinating history of money, politics and war, the reader could review two excellent books on this subject. One is *The Creature from Jekyll Island,* by G. Edward Griffin, and the other is *Secrets of the Temple* by Eustace Mullins.

America's entire system works against the interests of the American people. Alternatively, and incredibly, it works *for* the benefit of the vested interests which pay corrupt politicians and government officers and agents for their treason against the people. As we mentioned previously, the rulers of old controlled the political power, the monetary unit, and the military, and used their power, in most cases, ruthlessly, against the interests of the people. If we take an honest, realistic view of present day society in America, the practices and policies of the past have continued into the present. In fact, the basic process has never changed over the ages, and operates not only in America, but all throughout the world. The people, the faces, the times have changed, but the power structure has consistently maintained its power and never changed its tactics. In fact, because of modern day technology, it has refined them into an "art form".

One of the intents of this book is to demonstrate to people that they do not have to use established institutional ways of the "System" in order to buy and sell property. However, it also has a greater purpose. When large segments of the people of a nation, such as America, are placed into poverty or near-poverty positions, by their own government through insane economic policies which benefit wealthy vested interests but eradicate jobs wholesale throughout the country, then government denies large masses of the people the necessities of life because they cannot earn money to support themselves and their families. The government has no Constitutional authority whatsoever to so act, but because the American people fail to effectively challenge government actions, government acts as it chooses. In such a situation as now exists in America, most aware and conscious people can agree that the American government has failed the American people and, in fact, become the *enemy* of the people. All one has to do to recognize this is to open his eyes, his mind and his heart and see existing reality as it truly is, and not as he believes it is or wants it to be. The first step in correcting a problem is to recognize it and then taking lawful action to stop and remedy it. A very bad position is to rationalize or "justify" that problem, which, of course, then continues and worsens.

To counteract this injustice, it would be wise for the American people to create an alternative currency that would foster the creation of large and small scale businesses, industries, enterprises and other opportunities, which, in turn, would replace the massive amount of jobs government discarded and create many more. If you are interested in seeing a proposed alternative currency that could do this, then please go to our website, www.CitizensoftheAmericanConstitution.net and access the link to alternative currency. We sent this proposal to political, civil and government groups in various nations experiencing severe economic problems. Some responses came, but it seems the only two nations to have used the program, in part, are Iceland and Hungary.

Briefly, our proposal is that the people establish a public, not private, bank, owned and operated by the people. This bank would operate on a Constitutional charter and be strictly supervised by committees established by the people. This proposal is not a give-away or charity proposal. It is in line with good business practices, common sense and logic and in the best interests of the people and the nation. The bank would issue a public, non-interest bearing currency in two ways. One would be through direct loans to people and businesses who qualify. Another would be through grants. All business loans would be repaid in principal only, without interest. All government expenditures would be required to be submitted to and approved by the people appointed by their fellow Citizens to oversee the bank. When approved, the bank would grant all the funds required to cover all government expenditures. All means *all*, including welfare and health care. Grants would not require repaying, therefore, no public debt would be borne by the people. In this system, no public debt would exist since all government needs would be covered by grants. Since there is no public debt, no taxes of any kind would exist in this system. What people, businesses and industries make, they would keep. Our proposal is a sane way for a sane people to create a perpetual economic haven for themselves and their nation. No private banking of any kind would exist in this system, which means no private, self-serving control and manipulation of the economic lifeblood of the nation and her people by private vested interests and enforced by government. Under this egalitarian financial system, in complete compliance with Constitutional requirements, government would be beholden to the people for its funds, therefore, subservient to and dependent upon the people as intended by the principles of the Constitution.

When government obstructs the rights of the people, severely limits their ability to work and restricts their access to money, which is required simply to exist, then, as said above, government does not serve the true interests of the people. America is a Constitutional republic—not a democracy— *and the government is required by law to serve with the consent of the people.* Very few people would voluntarily consent to such pernicious, deceptive and devastating government practices. In such scenarios, alternative methods, such as an alternative currency, would then serve the best interests of the people and the society. Since it is quite evident that government has severely damaged the American people and the entire society, Americans must take back their own power and think outside the traditional box, established for and imposed upon them by the governing powers, the power forces and the "elite" of this nation.

As stated, one of the purposes of our book is to show people how they can buy, sell, and invest in property outside the existing "typical" routine methods created, controlled and manipulated by the banks and government. Our program shows how principals can deal directly, without interference, restrictions and control by banks and government. This would definitely be a step in the right direction, and please note that any transaction involving a large amount of funds can also utilize this program. For instance, if one wanted to sell his business, or commercial building, or apartment building, land, boat, car, truck, RV, etc., all of these and many more can be accomplished by and through this very simple program. This is a first step towards retaking your own power from those who unlawfully usurped it. Our intention is for the betterment of America and her people and for creation and expansion of the businesses and well-being of society beyond the existing "norms". If this approach were to be favorably received by the American people, it could start a national trend that could lead to economic freedom for the people by taking back their economic power and claiming their own rights to do business and contract as they wish, and not as government and its partner banks dictate. If the people can understand the expansive nature of these various approaches, then, they can understand the further expansion and creativity possible through the referenced alternative currency. As most of you know, freedom is not free. It bears a cost and sometimes a very severe one. When unjust governmental and societal controls are enforced upon the people of a country, then, no true freedom can exist in that land.

ECONOMIC CATASTROPHES
CONTROL VERSUS FREEDOM

conomic disasters, depressions, recessions and downturns do not provide justice to the people, nor domestic tranquility, nor promote the general welfare, the well-being of the people, protection, security, safety and the blessings of liberty to the people. However, these catastrophes *do* benefit the elite power forces and the government who gain in control and vast wealth from these economic attacks upon the people. When anyone tells you that people "lost" billions or trillions in these disasters, you can be certain that the power forces *gained* those billions or trillions that others lost. The funds do not simply disappear—they are simply transferred from the losers to the winners, and as many Americans are finding out, the winners are invariably the power forces and the elite.

When such economic catastrophes happen, economic downturns occur, businesses and industries go under, loans and margins are called, people lose their jobs, businesses, homes, money gets tight, the banks hoard and do not make loans, except to their prime customers, of course, and ordinary people and businesses lose the assets for which they worked so hard to gain, literally overnight to the power forces. All of these events do not benefit the nation, the people and the economic well-being of the society, but these disasters are frequent and happen over and over again, because they are deliberately designed to happen. Since none of them benefit the people, and since the government is Constitutionally required to uphold the well-being and the security of the people, then, the overriding question again becomes, why does government allow these disasters to happen? Once again, the answer is very simple—the government and the power forces gain enormously from these disasters, and if they did not, then, it is pretty obvious that they would not happen, since it certainly appears evident that the government and these power forces deliberately create and manipulate the conditions which lead to economic disasters for their selfish gain and for the further economic destruction of the American people. Unfortunately, the people are totally unaware of this ugly reality, thus, the economic control and disasters will continue, unless the people wake up to what is going right under their noses and take a lawful stand to stop it. All of this is similar to the endless wars that benefit the same power forces and government, who profit greatly from them, both economically and through more stringent controls. As we said before, and as has been said by many others, if the profit were taken out of warfare, there would be no more wars, because the power forces and the governments would have no more selfish reasons to engage in warfare.

If our objective, reasonable observers were to take a serious look and make an evaluation regarding world economics, from the very beginning, they could quickly determine that economic slavery is the rule rather than the exception on this planet. America is no different in this regard. Many Americans are finding out, unfortunately for them, the hard way, that money, power and might rule this nation and have from the very beginning. As a result, economic slavery has had a stranglehold on the American society from its very inception. While there were economic opportunities available to many in the early part of this nation, especially for those who had education, wealth, good ideas and/or inventions, as well as skills, crafts, abilities and were willing to work hard, all of which would benefit the society, most people did not fit into these categories. If they did, they typically lacked the practical connections and the material resources necessary to develop their ideas, industry and inventions. The bottom line is that, except for farming and other related activities, most people had to work for others in order to survive, and the competition for work was very competitive. People did not have the luxury of picking and choosing what they wanted to do for work. They had to take whatever jobs were available to them, as befit their aptitudes, skills and ability to travel. There was no mass transit and no thoroughfares in the olden days.

Many of the same conditions apply in present-day American society, but there are major differences, today, which also existed then, but not to as great an extent as now. Additional forces are in place now, but we will only cover a few of the most critical and most destructive to the people. The first one is government. When government comes knocking on the people's door and says "We're here to help", beware of government and the "help" it claims to be bringing. While there are some legitimate programs which government provides to the people, the benefits provided by these programs pale in comparison to the harm, control, manipulations, restrictions, regulations and many other factors embodied in any type of so-called "benefit" the government extends to the people. There is an old saying: "Beware of Greeks bearing false gifts." This definitely applies to the U.S. government and all the other governments operating in this country. Without getting into exact specifics, which would require hundreds of pages to list, the referenced factors exerted by government put massive restraints upon the freedom of both the job providers and the workers, to the extent that any benefits are minimal, as opposed to the harm due to loss of freedom for the people and industry through their acceptance of the governmental conditions.

When government controls industries, the products thereof, the distribution of those products, the labor force, and whether those industries will continue or be stopped from continuing, then, freedom and free market conditions clearly do not exist. When freedom is given lip service by government, that freedom is not free, because it is bound by government restrictions upon that freedom which is the antithesis of freedom. This is a position that most Americans do not realize. True freedom only exists without restriction. When restrictions are placed upon freedom, then, obviously, no freedom exists. Many of the American people have learned about these conditions the hard way, since many Americans and industries have been harmed by and through the control imposed by and through the government. Control by authority is usually destructive to those being controlled, but highly beneficial to the controlling forces and the elite power forces. It should be obvious to anyone that control is diametrically opposed and contradictory to freedom, and, of course, America is supposedly a nation of freedom. Many Americans are wisely questioning this supposition.

Monetary control has existed in America from the very beginning, but was considerably looser in the early years. The first central bank in America was established by George Washington, Alexander Hamilton and others to whom we refer as the "king's men". That central bank was partly owned by private American interests, but the majority control and financial interests remained with private foreign powers. This bank, which is *Constitutionally prohibited*, had direct influence and policy control over the entire economy of America, which is also Constitutionally prohibited. Again, when control is vested in an authority and that authority exerts its control upon the entire nation and her people, then, real freedom is not possible, because conditions are manipulated by the control, so the claim of "freedom" is nothing but a ruse. Andrew Jackson swore that he would destroy the central bank of his time, which was the second central bank initiated after the conclusion of the War of 1812. It strongly appears that the reason for that war was to make certain that the central bank would continue. When the twenty year charter for the first central bank expired, it was not renewed, and the foreign interests wanted to ensure that they continued to control the central bank, thus, the War of 1812 "occurred", in which Jackson was a prominent figure. Much of his effort was bent on destroying the second central bank, which he did. The last thing he said on his deathbed was "I killed the bank." Yes, Jackson did kill the bank, but the power held by that central bank Jackson unfortunately conveyed to various state central banks. This may have changed the *structure* of control, but still maintained the *system* of control. Remember, **control** is what the power forces, and the government, constantly seek to exert and expand over the people.

One of the overriding concepts in this CHAPTER and throughout this book is that of control versus freedom. Another concept is embodied in forms of violence as previously discussed, such as judicial violence, economic violence, legislative violence, etc. In this particular CHAPTER, we will take a look at economic violence, which, obviously, would not exist in a nation that is truly free. Many Americans *think* they are free because they do not see any bars on their windows, but since the element of control versus the appearance of freedom is very subtle and quite illusionary, the people do not realize just how much they are controlled.

Money and/or the monetary unit are the moving material elements of any group, organization, business, society, community and country. Without money, or some medium of exchange, accepted to have value by all parties, it is extremely difficult to accomplish anything. These facts have been well known for millennia. In other words, those who have and control money control those who don't, whether it is a business, group, organization, society, community or nation. For instance, in this country during the so-called industrial period, there were many mills, factories, industries, manufacturers, large farms and other labor-intensive businesses that employed massive amounts of people. The people and the general society were dependent upon these mills, factories, etc. to provide jobs in the general community, and without these mills, factories, etc. there would be no jobs in those particular areas. Therefore, life would be more difficult for most people, except for those who owned and operated their own farms or small family businesses.

Dependency always creates a need that must be fulfilled and, unfortunately, those who fulfill that need usually take great advantage of the needy when they do so. In many of these labor-intensive businesses, the workers were paid with company *scrip*, meaning units of value issued and determined by the company; thus, workers could only purchase what they needed from the company store, usually from a narrow selection chosen by the company, at prices that were typically usurious. While this was not true of 100% of such operations, the percentage was rather high. In other industries, rather than paying in company scrip, very low wages were paid to workers in dollars and cents and workers were encouraged to purchase their needs at the company store, including in some instances the materials they needed to be able to perform their work. In both scenarios, many of these industries supplied housing units to their workers at high rents. Perhaps some of you recall the song "16 Tons", sung by the late singer, Tennessee Ernie Ford, about a man who worked in the coal mines and could not die because he owed his soul to the company store.

In this above scenario, we see various societies, cities, towns, etc. with many inhabitants, dependent upon jobs in some type of labor-intensive industry that is willing to provide that work to fulfill that dependency need, but at what cost? Many of the laborers, which included young children, worked anywhere from 12 to 16 hours a day in very harsh, difficult and often dangerous conditions for very little pay or for scrip that could only be spent at the company store. What little money or scrip remained with the workers was so minimal that it did them little good. The bottom line is that most of these people existed in a system of economic violence, as economic slaves, whether they knew it or not, perpetrated upon them by their employers and condoned by the government.

The bottom line is always the bottom line, and when we assess anything, we first go to the bottom line and then determine how that bottom line was reached. Economic violence is definitely a huge element of control and is the furthest thing from freedom, since it imposes economic slavery upon the people. Despite this, the federal, state and local governments encouraged these types of operations throughout America allowing the wealthy business and industrial owners to make fortunes on the sweat-drenched backs and brows of the workers. The perverted golden rule states that he who has the gold rules, as borne out by this disgraceful period in American history. Instead of government providing for the general welfare of the people and maintaining justice by which all participants could fairly gain from their efforts, government condoned and/or ignored conditions which amounted to imposed slavery upon the workers. Were these actions by government consistent with the principles set forth in the Preamble to the Constitution and with the secured rights, due process of law and freedoms guaranteed to the people? The objective, rational, reasonable observer could easily conclude that the answer to this question is an emphatic "No!", as would most average American Citizens. Many of these types of operations lasted right up until the Second World War, and some even beyond. Capitalism, in and of itself, can be a good system in a just society, if both the owner and the worker are treated fairly based upon their own efforts and input. When honor, integrity and justice exist, then both sides of the equation can do very well. However, when these characteristics are lacking, the system reverts to economic slavery in which there is a master who controls and slaves who obey.

Let us create a fictional example to demonstrate some of the essential points regarding control versus freedom. Suppose that a very large family, consisting of many brothers and sisters and their respective children, who lived back in the pioneer days, trekked from Boston by wagon train and settled somewhere in the Midwest, where no one else lived at that time. Many individual members of the family made claims on land in that general area amounting to an aggregate of 100 square miles for the combined family. This family was industrious, ambitious, creative, hard-working, and engaged in many different operations, such as farming, logging, hunting, trapping, trading of furs and pelts, etc. Since this was such a large extended family, with many children and cousins, they could easily fulfill all aspects and requirements of these operations and over time could produce products and fulfill needs of other people in other communities.

Eventually, the family expanded their operations in their own community which required additional workers from outside their immediate family. For money to pay the additional workers and for advancing business operations, the family created its own monetary unit and established its own bank which would issue that monetary unit, as decided by the family. The bank operated like other banks operate, meaning it accepted deposits from the people, made personal loans to people, made loans on land and houses, for which it took a first mortgage position, loans to businesses, and conducted business as any other regular bank would. Since the bank printed the monetary unit out of thin air, with no backing whatsoever, then, whenever the family, including all its members, needed funds for any expansion, operation or enterprise, all they did was print the monetary unit for those expenses, at no cost at all to the family, except for printing and paper. Since the monetary unit was accepted by everyone as having value, the family could use that monetary unit to buy anything or do anything they wanted, without any cost to them. The new workers were paid in this monetary unit, which was good for all products and services and housing within that community. Their operations grew rapidly, because as stated, the family was ambitious, industrious, creative and enterprising, thus, their businesses flourished. Because the community was growing and prospering, wagon trains regularly came through that town and some of the travelers decided to settle there, so the town grew exponentially with new arrivals. As a result there was additional need for more business operations, which in turn needed more and more workers who readily came into the community.

Based upon their success, the family decided to send five family members to five different locations within the territory they owned to start new businesses and new communities. By now, their original town had become well known and because of the new people coming in by wagon train and other ways, their town grew rapidly, as did the new towns over time. The new workers, just like the original outside workers, were paid by the family in the monetary unit issued by the family bank. Since the family owned the entire area, consisting of 100 square miles, they essentially owned all of that ground, all of the water and minerals on and in that ground, and all of the properties that were built on that ground. The money that kept this family and these operations moving was the monetary unit issued by the family. As the towns grew, some form of government became necessary and since the family owned the town, most businesses and properties and issued the monetary unit used by everyone, the family established a government of *their* liking and controlled it.

As new people and families moved into the area, and either worked for the family or established their own businesses, they did so with the permission of the family and with the monetary unit issued by the family through its own bank. All of the people in these six communities and all of the business operations easily accepted and dealt in that monetary unit without comment, question or objection. The reader can likely see where we are going here. A hundred years down the road, the same family still owned the same towns, most of the business operations, all of the land, most of the properties, most of the resources, all of the banks, which banks issued the monetary unit created, owned, issued and controlled by the family. Since the family had this immense economic power over these entire communities, it could do essentially whatever it chose to do. There was no opposition to the control exerted by the family, because virtually everyone in these communities was dependent upon the monetary unit issued by the bank owned by the family.

When we look at the elements of control versus freedom, we can definitely see that control and not freedom is operative in this example. Control does not promote freedom and freedom does not exist when there is control, except by and through deception and delusion. The family that controls could be benevolent and treat the people fairly, with a certain amount of justice and a certain degree of freedom for all people or the family could be tyrannical, greedy, and impose harsh, unjust conditions upon the people, because of the people's dependency upon the family for their existence. While the former case is possible, history can conclusively prove that, unfortunately, the latter scenario has been and still is the rule rather than the exception. Vast wealth can create a paradise in which all participants enjoy opportunities, freedom, liberty, well-being and independence, or that wealth can create slave-states in which people are dependent upon that wealth, and the governments it controls, for their very existence. A quick review of the monarchies and feudal states of yesteryear can reveal the despotism that usually occurred.

In 1913, congress passed the *doubly* un-Constitutional Federal Reserve Act. We say "doubly" because first of all, the tenets of the Act conflict with and defy the mandates of the Constitution regarding the authority and duty of the Congress, as set forth in Article I, Section 8, Clause 5, "To coin Money, regulate the Value thereof, and of foreign Coin, and fix the Standard of Weights and Measures." Secondly, the Act was passed by a congress that lacked a quorum, two days before Christmas when most of congress had already left for home. In so doing, congress abdicated its sworn duty and responsibility for America's monetary unit and system and un-Constitutionally, thus, unlawfully, placed the control of the money and the monetary system in the hands of a *private* bank. This Act created a bank that was named the "Federal Reserve Bank", which was a deliberate act of deceit, since this private bank is *not* federal, is controlled by private interests, most, of whom, were and are foreign. Thus it is not a government bank, not controlled by the people and not controlled by the congress. Just as the first two central banks were un-Constitutional, so is the Federal Reserve Bank totally un-Constitutional, yet the treasonous congress unlawfully enacted the Federal Reserve Act of 1913, and ever since that time, every treasonous congress and president has upheld that un-Constitutional Act and the unlawful controlling status of the Federal Reserve Bank, which, as stated above, is not federal and has no reserves, giving this private bank absolute control over the people and the economy of this nation.

Various sources will say many different things about the Federal Reserve Bank and its operations. Voluminous information is available to anyone who seeks it. Since Margy and I are "bottom-line" people, and always have been, the essential bottom line position is that the Federal Reserve Bank literally prints money out of thin air with no metal backing, whatsoever, and no security except for the good faith and credit of the people of the United States of America. These funds created from nothing are dispensed to member banks all across the country, which funds are then loaned to industries, businesses, governments and the people, at interest. When the borrower pays the funds back, the funds he repays have been earned by him through his labor, his skills, his talents, his business and/or his enterprise, all of which have worked through the economy. Thus, it can be said that the funds repaid have been earned through the economy, pursuant to some form of enterprise, industry and hard work, while the funds loaned were simply paper with no value, whatsoever, or in more recent times, simply figures on a computer screen. **It can also be said that this was and is the biggest act of piracy that the world has ever seen!**

Control and freedom exist at opposite ends of the spectrum. As long as people who think they are free support the controlling power forces in this nation, then there can be no true freedom because of the control these forces exert upon the people. As we said earlier, any society needs a certain reasonable amount of basic order to be successful, prosperous and peaceful. However, for anyone who has studied and truly looked into the "American experiment", he could quickly conclude that the power forces who have gained control use their power and control against the best interests of the people. Everything the power forces do is calculated to benefit them, directly and indirectly. Power uses its power against the powerless to bring everyone and everything under the control of that power. We have seen how this operates throughout America. Many Americans are now beginning to see through the *illusion* of freedom under which they have been living and to understand this ubiquitous control in action, since there is virtually nothing, with the exception of small independent businesses and entrepreneurs who deal in other means of exchange, that the power forces do not create and control and nothing from which they do not benefit.

Whenever any business, corporation or enterprise has a monopoly, then, that gives that entity a controlling position and makes it a force which has no competition. That monopoly is the only one which can sell its products or services to the existing market and charge whatever it wants. The Federal Reserve Bank has an un-Constitutional, thus, unlawful, monopoly on the monetary unit of this nation. Such an overriding monopoly position trumps everything, since it is the controlling monetary force of the entire nation, but few people understand the import of this and how they, the entire economy, the nation and every aspect of their lives are affected. This position is exactly what the Federal Reserve and its co-conspirators in the federal government want. As the issuer and distributer of the nation's monetary unit, this private bank has enormous absolute power over all aspects of this nation and everyone in it, including the government(s), the people, the economy, the markets, all businesses, industries, corporations, the media, academia, the military, the police and on and on. As mentioned previously, our country operates on a perversion of the golden rule, namely, he who has the gold rules. Since everything in the nation is dependent upon money, or the monetary unit, which, again, is issued as a *fiat* currency by the Fed and distributed through its member banks, then, obviously, the monopolistic control over money puts the Fed in the most powerful position in this nation. In this scenario, a "fiat" is a demand or decree by government that requires the people and all business operations to use only the currency of this private bank as the legal monetary unit of this nation.

Since all within this society are dependent upon money for everything, the monetary control the Fed has over the government and all aspects of American life is monumental. Most people would agree that Washington, D.C. politicians are untrustworthy, unreliable, corrupt, are not concerned about the people or the country and do exactly what they want to benefit vested interests with which they are closely aligned, which, in turn, benefit the politicians. Since all forms of government in this nation are dependent upon money issued by the Fed, then our reasonable objective observers could easily conclude that those who hold government positions are in lockstep with the Fed and do exactly as this private bank dictates. President Trump spoke of the "D.C. Swamp" on the campaign trail, and as president, has constantly referred to that swamp. His characterization is absolutely correct, but we would go even further and call the entire D.C. political arena a gigantic, putrid cesspool.

Corruption is not limited to D.C., of course, and corruption is an equal-opportunity driving force in all forms of government all over this nation—federal, state and local. Americans are waking up to this fact and they are becoming outraged, as well they should. When a private bank controls the monetary unit of a nation, its issuance and distribution, then that bank essentially owns that entire nation. It certainly owns the government, because the government is dependent upon the Fed. The bank controls the entire economy, because it funds the entire economy and decides who gets funded and who does not. It essentially controls all businesses, corporations, industries, enterprises, all forms of media and entertainment, academia and, of course, the people. It may seem that we are being repetitive, but this is necessary, since most people have not yet connected the dots of this overarching monetary control to see just how insidious it is to America and her people. As we have said and as many people are now realizing, more and more American people are awakening to see this tyrannical operating reality and how it has worked against them. When such a powerful monopolistic private bank controls the entire economy through its fiat monetary unit, then anyone can see that the bank can create depressions, recessions, upswings and downswings, as that bank so desires to further serve and advance its own private, selfish, evil agenda. Monopolistic monetary control is massive and the might of that mass can create anything it so chooses. After all, the bank is a private commercial entity operating for profit and is not concerned about the well-being of the people or the nation. If that bank chose to have war to further add to its financial coffers and control, then the government would bring the nation into war as desired and dictated by the bank. This may sound cynical to some people, but, tragically, this scenario has played out many times in America.

When the central bank of a nation decides that a war is in the best interests of the bank, which, naturally, is operating on many different levels in many diverse enterprises for ultimate profit, the country against which this war is to be fought also has a central bank operating in that nation, essentially as the Fed operates in America. One could possibly think that the nation which has been selected as a war target may have a central bank that would disagree about putting that nation in danger by engaging in war. To the reasonable, rational observer this would seem prudent. However, if the same power forces that own the Fed also own the central bank in the war-targeted nation, then it should be child's play to figure out what will occur. Remember, Power ruthlessly uses its power against the powerless and brings everyone and everything under the control of that power. This is how the *worldwide* system of central banks operates. There are very few nations on this Earth not controlled by aligned, cooperating privately owned and linked central banks. Each central bank has a stranglehold over its own nation and when all the central banks decide on a course of action which benefits the banks and their profit centers, even though millions or hundreds of millions of people could be harmed, this is of no concern to the central banks whatsoever. Their objective is control, power and domination, and of course, massive untold personal wealth. If the people of the world ever really learn and fully comprehend the real truth about their own governments' treachery, central bank control and the fomenting of ongoing, unjust, unnecessary wars, which is very difficult for most people to believe, it is likely that some people would never participate in war again, except to defend their own nation, and only if their nation is directly attacked.

Given the fact that the government is dependent upon the central bank, which dictates the who, where and when of the next war and fabricates the why to "justify" it, then, the government obeys and carries out those dictates, even if this means putting the people the government is *supposed* to serve in harm's way. Would any logical, rational human being think that such a government duly elected by the people is serving the best interests of the people? Of course, the only sane answer is "No." Remember, all government officers and most government workers have taken oaths to support and uphold the national and state Constitutions. These Constitution(s) guarantee to the people their secured inherent, natural rights and all aspects of due process of law. As discussed earlier, the Preamble to the Constitution speaks of justice, liberty, domestic tranquility, the common defense and general welfare of the people. Would anyone who thinks rationally believe that warfare or other catastrophic policies dictated by a private central bank and put into effect by a corrupt government are maintaining the people's Constitutionally secured rights, their guaranteed due process of law and the further guarantees of justice, liberty, domestic tranquility and the general welfare of the people? That answer must be a resounding "No!" This "No!" indicates that there is something awfully wrong in today's America. Any act by any congress or legislature and any action by any oath taker either supports and upholds the Constitutions, or opposes, violates and contradicts them. It is really this simple. No public officer/employee has the Constitutional authority, or any other form of valid authority, to oppose the very documents to which s/he swore or affirmed his/her oath. It would be in the best interests of the people to maintain and lawfully enforce these simple, but powerful, positions, and through them, control the actions of their government officers, collectively stop the un-Constitutional actions of their own errant governments, and in so doing keep the people out of harm's way and maintain the general welfare. That Constitutional position regarding the "general welfare" of the people contained in the Preamble refers to the well-being of the people and not, as some might mistakenly think, economic welfare handed out to the people.

Ample information is available regarding the Federal Reserve Bank, its formation and history, its policies and how these affect the people. There are many excellent sources on this subject, but one very good introductory book is entitled "*The Creature from Jekyll Island*" by G. Edward Griffin. This excellent book is well-written, well-organized, with logically arranged sections, making it easy to absorb the voluminous and interesting information assembled by Griffin, which fully describes the secret machinations behind the disingenuous, unlawful creation of the Fed, goes into sound detail about how the Fed operates and the disastrous effects it has had upon our nation. In Jack's and my view, this book should be required reading for every single American, because all Americans should know and comprehend the ugly truth behind the treachery and betrayal committed against them and their nation in this disgraceful act of treason!

Of great interest to most people would be the lending policy of member banks in the Federal Reserve System. Since most people are unfamiliar with the bank and its operations, the majority of Americans are under the incorrect impression that when a bank makes a loan to a customer, loan funds come from customer deposits on account in that bank. Nothing could be further from the truth. When banks make loans to their customers, whether through mortgage notes, business, car or personal loans, etc., the total amount of those loans are bundled together. That bundled amount is transmitted to the Fed and the Fed "loans" that bank up to nine times the bundled amount. In some cases this could be lower or higher, depending on current Fed policy. If the borrower is typical of the American people, he also believes that the loan funds he receives emanate from customer funds on deposit with that bank. He is not aware that his signature on the loan documents *creates* the funds that comprise his loan. Further, s/he is not aware that up to nine times the face amount of his/her "loan" is loaned to the bank by the Fed. In other words, the borrower, by and through his/her signature on the loan documents, made it possible for that bank to receive his/her full loan amount from the Fed plus nine times that loan amount for the bank to make additional loans. Since each loan amount usually requires payment of points and interest, then the customer made it possible for the bank to profit handsomely by making additional loans and collecting more points and interest charges. It is truly unfortunate that virtually the entire society, with some exceptions here and there, is unaware of these un-Constitutional and usurious banking operational practices. Our reasonable, objective observers would take serious issue with these types of operational practices. It would be in the best interests of America if the people shared the same opinion and then took lawful action to bring a screeching halt to this century old, fraudulent, un-Constitutional banking scheme, a scheme fully upheld by your U.S. government which is Constitutional mandated to uphold YOUR rights and best interests.

When a bank makes a "loan" to a customer, whether that customer is an individual, a business or a corporation, what is loaned to that borrower is paper or credit that the loaning bank received from the Fed, without any other economic input from the lending bank, itself. In other words, as mentioned it is the signature of the borrower, unknown to the borrower, of course, which allows the lending bank to receive up to nine times the borrower's loan amount. Therefore, the lending bank did not spend any of its private funds to make this loan and in fact received additional funds to make other loans, based upon the borrower's signature. When the borrower repays the loan, s/he pays both principal and interest over the loan term. His or her payments are derived from his/her own efforts, through his/her own enterprise, in working through the economy to receive funds from his/her efforts so that s/he can earn profit and repay his/her supposed debt to the bank. There is a major unjust difference between the derivation of the funds "loaned" by the bank to the borrower and the total debt repaid by the borrower to the bank. The bank spent none of its own funds and received money received created out of thin air by the Fed. Whereas when the borrower repaid, s/he did so with funds earned through the economy based upon his/her own real efforts. If this were a fair and just system, then the funds created out of thin air to make the loan, could be repaid by the borrower with funds created by him or her out of thin air. Of course, if the borrower ever tried to do this, s/he would quickly land in jail, accused of "counterfeiting", or the whole vicious scam could be exposed. There is a monumental difference between control and freedom, and if the American people ever expect to gain true freedom, they must be fully aware of the controls exerted upon them in every possible way by their own "servant government" and their partner power forces.

In this CHAPTER and throughout this book we have tried to show the huge difference between control and freedom. We have previously stated that any society needs a certain amount of minimum order for the safety and well-being of that society. However, massive, absolute control exerted by entrenched vested interests, the power forces, starting with the Federal Reserve Bank, then the federal government, as well as all other state and local governments, conclusively demonstrates that the control exerted by these power forces has effectively eradicated the freedoms promised and guaranteed in the Constitutions to all Americans. When a private central bank exerts total control over all aspects of the American society, including, of course, the corrupt governments, then that bank can essentially write its own ticket, and it does.

There are many forms of violence in our world and many forms of violence perpetrated upon the people by government, some of which we have discussed in this CHAPTER and elsewhere in this book. Violence is not simply physical violence, but wears many different faces. When anyone, any group and any nation is damaged, hurt or deprived of any rightful thing, then this is a form of violence executed by the power forces and government against the powerless. Economic violence is one of the most destructive and insidious forms of violence possible. Economic violence leads to economic tyranny which results in economic slavery for an entire nation, its economy and its society. This is not freedom, and for the sake of their country, their families and themselves, the American people must understand the true, insidious destructive nature of this economic reality. It should be crystal clear to anyone by now that the actions taken by government, the Fed and the vested interests oppose all elements of the Preamble to our Constitution, all rights and all due process guaranteed to the people in the Constitution. Obviously, the U.S. government, by its own actions, has virtually destroyed the concept of our original Constitutional republic and has systematically and painstakingly kept the people ignorant of government's Constitutional duties to uphold the principles of our Constitutional republic, and not destroy them. For the American people to be unaware of this is absolutely tragic, because their ignorance about these pernicious, unjust conditions allows the un-Constitutional criminal *machinery of government* to continue in power with impunity and without any meaningful opposition from the people. This carefully cultivated condition of ignorance does not befit a self-governing people in a Constitutional republic. This is exactly how this un-Constitutional machinery of government wants it. However, President Trump, on several occasions, primarily in his Inaugural Address and in his State of the Union Address stated that the people are sovereign in America and he wants to restore that power to the people. Now it is up to the American people to knowingly accept that power and correctly utilize it pursuant to the authority of the Supreme Law.

CHAPTER   FIVE

ECONOMIC FREEDOM

America was founded on the concepts of true egalitarian freedom and justice. Most Americans still believe that their country epitomizes these noble concepts, or at least *want* to believe this. Yet, for years, the American people have faced increasing economic problems pervasive throughout virtually every aspect of life and business. No solutions have come forth from the government or the banking industry, so no relief is on the horizon for most Americans. Pretenses have been made, but pretenses do not solve real problems. The deliberate exporting of good paying industries and factories has created a massive deficit of decent paying jobs. When people can no longer find work that pays them enough to cover their expenses, live decently, afford to go out to eat or to the movies on occasion, and have a little extra to put aside for "a rainy day", this has a far-reaching, exponentially adverse effect on them and the economy as a whole. Many Americans do not feel "free" nor do they feel that they live in a just nation. It is difficult for one to feel free when he lives in a nation that is tightly controlled in all aspects—a nation that offers little or no hope and opportunity to most of its inhabitants. True freedom exists without restraints, and the fact is that restraints in America are very severe, but many people are completely unaware of this fact.

As mentioned in previous CHAPTERs, the banking and economic systems are controlled by vested interests who operate on their own self-made, self-serving standards. Obviously, money in some form is necessary to function in life. We all have to pay for our shelter, food, clothing, transportation, education, health care, etc., etc. When avenues to access necessary funds are limited, or eliminated altogether, then, clearly, economic freedom is not possible. Without economic freedom, there can be no true freedom, people and nations stagnate, and life for many becomes drudgery simply fulfilling the plan set forth by the hidden controllers of the nation. Common sense dictates that this is neither being free nor living in a just nation. The American people really must take a serious look at the real state of affairs existent throughout their country, either accept things as they are, recognize that they are economic slaves, or ask why this unsatisfactory state exists at all, then, take lawful steps to change it.

The banking industry in America has created havoc for the people over the past two centuries. "Busts and booms" are deliberately created through controlled and contrived economic policies. During good times, people do reasonably well, but, unfortunately, many of them lose what they have earned in the bad times that follow. Of course, wealth and property in financial and economic matters are never really "lost", because someone always gains that which is supposedly lost. It is clear to True, our rational, objective observer, and confirmed by reality, that the economic system in place in America does not serve the best interests of the American people at all. One of the obvious solutions to this would be for the American people to pay attention to what is being done in their names, and then become directly involved in all aspects of government. **We, the people, are the true government, and those who serve us operate as the machinery of government.** The people must take control of that machinery, or that machinery, which is supposed to serve the people, will simply continue to mow them down, as has been going on from the very inception of this nation. This is what happens when the people of a nation do not know what occurs in their own country. It is evident that the people cannot control the banking industry nor the government that works hand in hand with that banking industry, especially when the people are passive, ignorant of what is happening and accept everything that is handed down to them as correct and necessary. However, those who have had *enough*, on all levels, could, if they so choose, take economic power back, which power is already in their hands, if they would only realize this.

The mortgage lending industry in this nation, for the most part, has proven itself to be un-worthy of the respect and trust given to it by the American people. After all the fraudulent mortgage methods, the "robo-signing" mills and the outrageous fraud inherent within them, and the millions of unjustified foreclosures, it is evident that this is an industry that not only should bear scrutiny at all levels, but also should either be totally reformed or completely disbanded. For those who may be unfamiliar with the term "robo-signing", this is the practice employed by major national banks involved in mortgage lending whereby they hired people to fraudulently pose as bank officers and had them sign millions of falsified documents so the banks could fraudulently foreclose on people's homes. Of course, because of the insidious nature of the power structure that runs America, *meaningful* reform is not likely to happen. The only way the people can ever expect to gain any type of economic freedom is by and through their own lawful efforts and their own political will. The old maxim that there is strength in numbers rings very true here.

As above stated, if one is fed up with existing conditions, and would like to achieve some economic freedom for him/herself, in terms of buying and selling property, then the methods provided in *ByPass the Bank* can help him or her do this. Throughout this book we state that this program allows for a direct contractual relationship between buyer and seller, without an institutional mortgage lender or bank, without a real estate broker and without the usual trappings that frequently are part of real estate transactions and closings. In the face of the gargantuan mortgage industry in this nation, such an action by one individual may seem small. However, if many people can understand the very simple, direct concepts contained within this one of many programs, then, there could be a groundswell amongst the people of America to create their own individual economic freedom, at least regarding the buying and selling of their own properties.

Because of the so-called recession that hit hard in 2007 and 2008, which, in truth, was more of a depression and is still with us, the market catastrophes that happened at that time, which resulted in trillions of dollars in equity losses, the referenced mortgage fraud and the millions of foreclosures, there is an unbelievably enormous amount of property for sale in America. These huge numbers of properties on the market mean there are equally huge numbers of sellers who want or need to sell their properties. As a result, most areas in the nation are "buyers' markets". Even within the small amount of sales taking place, the restrictions that banks put on both buyers and sellers typically slow the process down and can cause many valid transactions to fall out of escrow. With all the widely revealed disadvantages, in terms of dealing with institutional lenders, for those capable sellers and buyers, the *ByPass* program is an excellent solution. If a large enough number of buyers and sellers were to enter this program, and if that number were to substantially increase over a ten to fifteen year period, then, as we mentioned earlier, a sizable percentage of Americans could escape the clutches of the institutional lender.

As more people do this and the process grows, they will take back their economic power, at least in regard to buying and selling their homes, and this would make a definite a dent in the traditional institutional lenders' coffers. It would be better for those who want to sell and buy properties to put their trust and their security in their *own* hands, and those of the other principals, with whom they are dealing directly, by using one of the many *ByPass* programs, instead of trusting their fates to the institutional hands of those who have already proven they are untrustworthy, without honor and concern for their borrowers. Small movements can become quite large over time, especially when those movements make economic and ethical sense and are properly instituted. In the words of anthropologist, Margaret Mead, *"Never forget that a small group of concerned committed Citizens can change the world; indeed, it's the only thing that ever has."* If a large enough movement were to begin, gain momentum and spread, then it can definitely demonstrate to the established financial and political powers that the people have caught on to the fraud, are disgusted with "business as usual" and are creating and implementing their own solutions to benefit themselves and the greater society.

THE "MONEY MAN" IS A MENACE

Throughout history, the average person has had little or no understanding of money matters and finance. This is true for a few very important reasons. In the first place, finance is a specialized field, made so deliberately by a handful of virtually unknown, but tremendously powerful, wealthy people. It is essentially a private "club" that has been limited only to the elite members of that club. Secondly, it serves the best interests of this private club to keep average people in the dark and essentially ignorant of the "intricacies" of finance. It's akin to the old adage, namely, the "golden rule", which, in reality, is rule by those who possess the gold. Since the average man and woman do not possess this commodity, beyond minor amounts, then, they rule absolutely nothing when it comes to finance, and, in fact, are at the mercy of the lenders' rules and regulations established by the members of this private club. Over the millennia, nothing has changed in this arena, at all. What took place five hundred, a thousand or two thousand years ago, still takes place now, but of course, packaged in more sophisticated, up to date, "people friendly" approaches.

Over the many centuries, average people have been the pawns of the money interests in numerous different ways. Most people lived in a country ruled by some king, emperor, monarch, potentate, warlord, all of whom pretty much were dictators. Just as the word implies, dictators *dictate* exactly what they want their serfs, or subjects, if you will, to do for the benefit of the ruler and for the "privilege" of living in his "realm". This ruler usually owned all of the land, which he parceled out to sub-rulers, called dukes, lords, earls, chiefs, etc. These so-called "noble" entities pulverized the people who lived within their individual sub-realms for the "noblemen's" benefit and for the benefit of their "noble" ruler. Those who pleased and obeyed the dictates of the sub-rulers and the ruler lived a tolerable, strained and impoverished subsistence, while those who did not suffered all sorts of catastrophic fates. What existed for "money", whether it was gold, silver, jewels, rods, or some type of fiat paper currency was in the control of the ruler, his sub-rulers and the ruler's "bankers." Funds were doled out by these elites for services rendered and goods provided—sometimes, that is. Lending did exist, but it was tightly controlled by the lender and put most borrowers into very burdensome circumstances, with paperwork they did not understand—just like today. When one group of elites controls the land, the resources of the land and all the money, there is not much choice or anything else left for the average people.

America was founded as a nation that theoretically enshrines "freedom and justice for all". Those words and those intentions by the founders of this nation were noble, indeed, but how much *true* freedom and justice do you see in today's America? How is it possible to be free and obtain justice when virtually everything of importance that goes on in this country is often out of the people's reach and certainly out of their control, especially finance? When America was established as a Constitutional republic in 1787, the Constitution authorized and mandated a free, open, public monetary system. What the Constitution states, thus, authorizes is valid, and what it does not state, thus, authorize is **prohibited**. However, in 1791, George Washington, the first president, his secretary of the treasury, Alexander Hamilton, and other private vested interests established the first *private* central bank in America, deceptively called the Bank of the United States. Nothing in the Constitution authorized a private bank to act as a central bank for the United States of America through which all monetary policy and funding emanated. However, since the people of that time knew very little of the Constitution and were unfamiliar with the inherent rights guaranteed to them, secured within the Bill of Rights amended to that Constitution in 1791, and since they knew very little if anything about banking and finance, they took no action and allowed this unlawful private central bank to continue. Governments use the weaknesses and ignorance of the people against them to establish and impose whatever government wants. This unfortunate condition has not changed. Since 1791, America has had a private central bank, in one form or another, which controlled the creation and distribution of currency, monetary policy and thereby essentially controlled and manipulated the entire economy of this nation and the fates and fortunes of everyone in it. Some might argue that for a few short periods of time, we had no central bank. However, if one takes a clear look at the entrenched financial powers operative during those times, America was still controlled by central banks, although not overtly and officially.

On December 23rd, 1913, in the early morning hours, the Federal Reserve Act was **unlawfully** and **un-Constitutionally** "passed" by a treasonous congress, without a quorum, and a new private central bank received legislative "authority" to be put into existence to create and distribute currency and control monetary policy; therefore, control and manipulate the economy of the entire nation. Few people knew about this, and those who did know, did nothing to stop this criminal legislative treachery, which economically *enslaved* the people of America, and still does. For readers interested in learning the fascinating background of this legislative treason, and much more, we suggest they read the excellent book written by G. Edward Griffin, entitled, *The Creature from Jekyll Island*. This is, in our view, the best work ever written on this subject and should be required reading for every American, but because it tells the truth, it is not. Many federal legislatures have convened in Washington, D.C. since this act of legislative treason took place, yet, except for a few aware exceptions who, were silenced in one way or another, no one has voiced Constitutional objections to this Constitutional injustice. Tragically, the ignorant, unaware, uninformed American people simply accepted it, without question, as they pretty much accept any government imposed system. Pursuant to Article I, Section one of the Constitution, all legislative authority is vested in Congress. When Congress creates laws for the American people, those laws are required to be Constitutionally compliant, specific to the Bill of Rights, or they are not valid laws, thus, not binding upon nor lawfully enforceable upon the American people. The sad fact is that the American society has done exactly zero to overturn this blatantly un-Constitutional "law".

The private central bank called the Federal Reserve Bank was and remains the regulator and controller of all other banks throughout the nation and the creator and distributor of money to these banks. At first, there was a theoretical "gold standard" that purportedly backed the currency, but in actual reality, that so-called gold standard never existed. What did exist was the *appearance* of a gold standard, to deceive the people, but it was appearance only, not reality. A "gold standard" existed in some form or another for the major banks and the central bank, but never for the people.

As you may know now, there is absolutely no gold standard to back the currency in America issued by the Fed, and this fact has been known by aware members of the general public who have kept abreast of such matters. Unfortunately, most people in America still mistakenly believe that America operates on a gold standard and that the American currency is solidly backed by gold. Those who are aware of what the Federal Reserve Bank does fully realize that the Fed uses the public's printing presses to have currency printed out of thin air, with no precious metal backing, whatsoever, which the Fed then lends to its member banks, at interest, who then lend to the general public at sometimes usurious interest.

Remember what we said about the controlling interests that have been operating finance forever? Ladies and gentlemen, that has never changed, because these controlling interests still operate right now. The galling fact for Americans should be the fact that the Fed exists at all! Further, the fact that the Fed issues currency out of thin air, with no backing, and simultaneously creates enormous debt for the American people, should outrage all Americans. It is insane for Americans, a supposedly self-governing, free people, to allow a private, profit-driven, bank to create and distribute a debt-based, interest bearing currency, impose and manipulate all interest rates, thereby control the markets and the entire economy, with no accountability to anyone but its secretive elite owners. For a theoretically free and just nation, this is an abomination. However, because the people don't know and/or don't care, this piracy exists right now and will continue to exist unless the people lawfully stop it.

Banks do very well in times of war, because, incredibly, they usually fund *both* sides of any conflict. Bank-loaned funds enable nations of all types to purchase weapons of death and destruction. This helps create mind-boggling fortunes for the corporations who produce the weapons, guns, bullets, uniforms, boots, trucks, jeeps, aircraft, ships, tents, canteens, c-rations, electronics and all the other accoutrements of war. Typically, these corporations are financially intertwined with the banks, often with interlocking boards of directors, so it isn't too hard to deduce that, since war is so profitable for these interconnected corporations, then it is very advantageous and desirable for them to manipulate countries into never-ending wars. If people and nations truly wanted to end wars and have peace, then, a very simple way to do this would be to take all profit out of wars.

American banks are no different from any other countries' banks and they have profited handsomely from the many wars, "police actions", "peace keeping actions" and other conflicts in which America has been involved forever and, sadly, still is in one form or another. Economic catastrophes have been deliberately created in America by those who control the economic system, for their own reasons and purposes, none of which benefit the average American, but richly reward the bankers. You may recall the words of Thomas Jefferson, our third president:

> "I believe that banking institutions are more dangerous to our liberties than standing armies. If the American people ever allow private banks to control the issue of their currency, first by inflation, then by deflation, the banks and corporations that will grow up around [the banks] will deprive the people of all property until their children wake-up homeless on the continent their fathers conquered. The issuing power should be taken from the banks and restored to the people, to whom it properly belongs."

Please note that when money is produced by and through the Fed, then, loaned through its Federal Reserve System, that money was literally created out of thin air, as we said above. However, when the Americans repay the loans they have received from banks, they repay in "hard currency", which means currency they have *earned* through their own efforts, plus interest on the amount owed. This is one of the most unfair, unjust and grievous wrongs that have ever been perpetrated upon the American people by their own government. We could go into numerous examples of how the people have been damaged, but for the sake of brevity, only want to touch upon a few.

As previously mentioned, extensive mortgage fraud and manipulation occurred in this country which resulted in the loss of millions of homes for millions of American families, and the figures are still climbing. Many of the lending banks and mortgage companies essentially looked at the borrower/homeowner as a conduit for setting up the lucrative securitization scheme from which the banks made incredibly huge profits. The homeowner was considered a pass- through, while the banks' real clients were the investors who bought the bundled securities, which consisted of the notes and mortgages. Many of these lenders blatantly misrepresented terms and conditions to financially unqualified borrowers, so many borrowers were totally unaware of the fact that they could not actually afford the payments the banks were arranging for them. True, our rational, objective observer might ask why the banks would make mortgage loans they knew would not be repaid. The answer, in most cases, is that the banks made a fortune bundling and selling the notes and mortgages to the referenced investors, then, made additional gains when they foreclosed on the properties which these unfortunate people lost. Further when the banks claimed massive losses, because of these theoretical failures, the federal government, by and through the private central bank, bailed out these banks and corporate lenders, to the tune of many trillions of dollars. By some estimates, these bailouts were as high as 39 trillion dollars. True and Reality would likely conclude that this was the biggest piece of piracy perpetrated upon the American people since the unlawful passage of the Federal Reserve Act at the end of 1913.

In addition to those people who unknowingly, unwittingly or uncaringly borrowed funds which they did not have the financial means to repay, there were millions of others, who were knowing and caring borrowers, but due to the terrible and worsening economy, either lost jobs, lost funds, forcing them into other debt, and as a result, could not make their mortgage payments, so lost their properties. When one loses a job he has had for years and is not able to find a position offering equivalent pay, because of the atrocious economy and deliberate economic policies which created that bad economy, then is forced to take a lesser paying position, or can find no job at all, obviously, something has to give. In many cases, what gave was the family home, lost through foreclosure.

Further, many people were duped into taking out so-called adjustable loans which started out with low interest rates, allowing payments they could afford, only to learn that their interest rates were suddenly raised, making their monthly payments impossible to meet. When a family loses their home because of dire economic conditions that is an absolute tragedy. When that home is lost based upon a loan of a fiat monetary unit, printed out of thin air, with no precious metal backing, whatsoever, and no financial stake in it by the bank that "loaned" the "money", *issued upon the borrower's signature on the loan contract*, then, to foreclose upon that family, which has a vested financial interest in the home is unconscionable, unjust, unethical, uncalled for, but, unfortunately, absolutely "legal".

In America, our Constitution guarantees that our lives, our liberties and our properties cannot be taken from us without **due process of law**. It is now evident to many millions of people across America that due process of law is sorely lacking in our so-called justice system. The question becomes this: Should American Citizens trust institutions and governments that have openly betrayed them and denied them any real, authentic form of due process and justice? The American society must wake up to the realities that rule their society. The rational, reasonable observer of such events could easily conclude that no sane man or woman of even basic intelligence and common sense would ever trust proven liars who, as a matter of routine business, perpetrate fraud upon the people. Those who first came to America sought to escape repressive regimes and vested interests which ruthlessly controlled their former countries. The newcomers sought freedom and independence from governmental controls, wanted to live as free beings in a free society and have the opportunity to prosper from their own efforts. Our Constitution is truly an egalitarian document that upheld this freedom, independence, free choice and the people's ability to prosper, based upon their own initiatives and hard work, without the intrusion of massive governmental controls and the usual "unholy" partnership between government and the elite. Those lofty intentions have all but crumbled in this nation. For any country that was so dedicated to freedom and independence to act as it has against its own people, in particular, against those millions of unfortunates who lost their homes, and then to reward the criminal banks who caused the problems in the first place indicates to the rational observer that the American government does not uphold and protect the best interests of the people, but does so for corporate and banking interests. Given the despicable actions of the government and the banks, that rational, objective observer would likely never trust the American government or any banks located in this nation. True and Reality agree with this logical assessment, based upon the facts of the matter.

The foreclosure feeding frenzy that occurred through these failures resulted in a tragic catastrophe of national and international proportions. The casualties are still pouring in and the reverberations will be felt for many, many years. Those who invested in the bundled securities were defrauded just as the homeowners were, and the true toll of this financial debacle is still not fully known and may never really be revealed to the American public.

Governments at all levels across the nation were well aware of the mortgage fraud, but did little or nothing to stop it on a national scale. They simply let the fraud play out. When the securitization clients became aware of this fraud, this caused many of the lending banks serious economic problems. In an absolutely "in-your-face" confirmation that government favors banking institutions over the American people, as stated above, the government, in collusion with the Fed, bailed out these criminal banks—you know, the "banks too big to fail"—as well as mortgage companies and other corporate lenders. The banks that caused the problem got rewarded for causing the problem and the victims, namely the American people, received absolutely no assistance, no funds from their own government and in many cases lost everything. That government could easily have picked up the mortgages for some of the financially capable distressed homeowners and received payments directly from them, over an extended maturity cycle. Instead, the government let the banks foreclose on the homeowners' properties, bailed out the banks in enormous sums and gave a hefty bill for that bailout to the American people.

If the American people were truly knowledgeable regarding the Fed, how it operates, who truly gains and who loses, then, these catastrophes never could have taken place. The sad fact is that the American society is not knowledgeable at all regarding these matters and never has been. As a result of the people's ignorance, actions and inactions, the government and the banks do whatever they want, and the people simply comply. This type of pernicious banking activity will likely continue unless and until the American people demand that it be stopped. Based upon the history of America, this seems highly unlikely. However, for you, the reader, who may now have a clearer understanding of how the banking system works against you and your own best interests, the real question to you is: "Would *you* trust banks from this point forward and, further, would you trust the government that authorized, condoned and allowed their fraudulent activities?" Most aware, astute people would say "No". However, since banks have been a "tradition" in America and in most parts of the rest of the world for a thousand or more years, any attempt to change a well-entrenched, powerful, vested tradition could prove to be extremely difficult in a nation rigidly controlled by these very banks.

For those people who want to be independent of banking, yet want to sell and purchase property, there are definitely ways open to them, should they choose them. Banks supply "money" for the purchase of property, but as mentioned earlier, sometimes dictate too many requirements for the transaction and sometimes change terms and conditions at the last minute. The trust factor and the reliability factor must come into play at some point. Homeowners who want to sell their homes to capable buyers can do so through one of the many *ByPass* programs described in this book. Capable buyers can purchase homes from willing sellers on the same basis. This takes the bank completely out of the equation, along with the other possible problems mentioned earlier that usually crop up. Now the transaction is directly between a willing seller and a capable buyer, who arrange their own private financing scenario which well suits the needs of each party.

"If" is a big word, but let us put an "if" into this situation. If millions of sellers and millions of buyers were to engage in the sale and purchase of property through the *ByPass* methods, then, institutional financing would suffer a large percentage loss. Sometimes, the best news and the best methods are made known through direct experience and word of mouth. When people find out how easy it is to do business by and through the *ByPass* methods, as opposed to the complications that arise through banks and their restrictive requirements, then, it is quite possible that use of the *ByPass* methods could grow exponentially and have a very positive, resounding effect upon Americans and America, herself.

Principal buyers and sellers deal directly with each other, and if at a later time the buyer decides to sell the home he purchased, he could sell it to another qualified buyer who would simply make a suitable down payment and assume the existing note. No bank is involved in the transaction, whatsoever, and no new bank financing either. A seller, who may want his funds now, can always sell his note on the open market on a discounted basis to willing private-Citizen investors. If we visualize this scenario over a 15 or 20 year period, then, it is extremely possible for large numbers of properties in this country to be free of bank debt, because the principals in these transactions have circumvented the banks by seeing the wisdom of dealing directly. When one deals directly, and not institutionally, he has much more control and security. Without bank involvement, there is no fear of notes being called on some whim of the bank, within 30 days or less, thanks to small-print contract clauses, which can demand penalties and restrictions, interest rate hikes, or other burdensome requirements that the banks might impose at any time. Remember, banks are unfairly favored by our governmental system, whereas the people receive little, if any, consideration at all. The more people who choose to deal directly, the more control they have over their own situations, properties and fates and the less they feed this beastly banking system. This can only benefit the people and the nation, as a whole.

The monetary unit issued by the Federal Reserve Bank has no competition in this nation and has been decreed "legal tender" by government fiat. As virtually all of us should know, a monopoly can do whatever it wants, whenever it wants, and in this instance with "legal" justification supported by the government. Competition is very healthy, because, in the first place, it sets forth a different structure from the entrenched vested interests. The Constitutionally designed American monetary unit was a public unit, and not private. If you care to review information regarding an alternative currency program created by Jack Flynn, please access Jack and Margy's website which is www. CitizensoftheAmericanConstitution.net and use the link for the Alternative Currency Program.

CHAPTER SEVEN

WALTER BURIEN REGARDING
Comprehensive Annual Financial Reports/CAFRs

W alter Burien, a courageous, knowledgeable American who speaks the truth has tried to inform the American people for many years about the CAFR programs operated by governments throughout this country. We met Walter when he spoke at one of our seminars in Arizona years ago, along with former Sheriff Richard Mack who also spoke. From what we could determine from that experience, we know that Walter is sincere, dedicated and very well informed regarding this very important subject. Walter said he was schooled by another man who discovered the CAFR scheme, Gerald Klatt, who was an auditor for 30 years and well equipped academically and experientially to investigate the workings of the scheme. Klatt has passed on, but his website, www.cafrman.com is still active and very informative.

CAFR is an acronym for the term Comprehensive Annual Financial Reports, which governments and governmental departments are required to prepare each year. Walter claims his research shows that of the gross revenue received by governments, a percentage is taken or essentially "skimmed" from the top by governments and invested into various programs for the benefit of those corporate governments. These investments are not made for the benefit of the people who paid those funds through their taxes and fees to these governments, nor have these governments obtained the consent of the people to make these investments. The total asset value of these investments is estimated to be somewhere in the very high trillions, yet governments constantly claim there is a shortage of funds needed for operations, so they impose more and higher taxes and float more and more bonds and/or cut needed services. All of this is unnecessary because of the enormous amounts of funds in these investment programs, yet through duplicitous accounting practices, the governments, from small to large, perpetrate this fraud upon the people, and the people know virtually nothing about it. Truth and transparency are matters which are of little to no importance to governments in this nation, as we can see by their ongoing routine practices. Walter Burien has done excellent research on this subject and you can find extensive information on his website which is www.cafr1.com. Our readers would be well advised to invest a little time in perusing the material Walter has assembled on his website and then, hopefully, hold their local governments and governmental agencies accountable for their un-Constitutional, criminal, deceptive actions committed against the people. Can you imagine how if people and groups all over the nation were to do this and create a movement that grew rapidly this massive fraud would be publicly exposed, the perpetrators held accountable and the funds returned to the people? The American people need to remember that they are the true *de jure* government, the machinery of government is supposed to work *for* them, not against them, and must be honest, its dealings transparent, open to public scrutiny and responsible to the people for all its actions. Further, the people must remember that they have the Constitutional power and duty to exercise oversight and corrective actions upon any and all forms of government which do not so act.

If Walter is correct in his assessment regarding the gross value of the total combined CAFR investment funds, then this total amount measures somewhere in the vicinity of 100 trillion dollars. Remember, these funds, in aggregate, emanated from and belong to the people, not to the private corporations that have sequestered these funds for their own private use. Most, if not all, public bodies, such as cities, towns, counties, states, are and operate as *corporations*, a fact which is greatly unknown to the people. These corporations operate for the benefit of the corporations, their shareholders and the owners of these corporations and these do not include the people. From a fiscal standpoint, these corporations, masquerading as "governments", consider themselves to be autonomous, unanswerable to the people. As we have previously cited from our hallowed Declaration of Independence, all government of right operates with the consent of the governed. Pursuant to Constitutional guarantees, the political power belongs to the people and not to the machinery of government that is in place to serve the people. When that machinery of government unlawfully assumes the position of Master, and not servant, and relegates the true Master–the people–to the subservient servant position, then that government has no lawful authority to exist or conduct any duties of the machinery of government. This rogue governmental machinery defrauds the people, withholds information from them, deceives them and unlawfully procures funds from them, thus, any objective observer would agree that such a government has stepped outside of the lawful scope of its limited, delegated duties and authority. Virtually all machinery of governments in this nation operate on this premise, yet the people have never stopped these un-Constitutional actions, just as they have never stopped the un-Constitutional actions of the

Federal Reserve Bank and the government that unlawfully authorized it. This is a vital, key position regarding the interrelationship between the government and the governed. As long as the people allow the government to do whatever it wants, whether that action is un-Constitutional, criminal, or even evil, without lawful opposition from the people, the government will do so, and continue to do whatever it wants. An unwritten, unofficial motto prevails within all governments in this nation, namely: "If we fix it, we can't scam it."

Can the reader imagine the hundred trillion dollars being rightfully and lawfully returned to the various public treasuries throughout the country? This amount could pay off all legitimate state, county, municipal and local debt in an instant. Those debts incurred by and through fraud can be repudiated and not paid, since fraud vitiates anything conducted thereunder. If this were done, then the people would be relieved of the unjust burden of taxation on those debts, because the debts have already been paid. Each municipality should have ample funds remaining to invest in whatever projects they desire. The returns from these investments should be ample enough to pay for all governmental and public expenditures in that community. If this were to materialize, then since all referenced expenses are paid for by the returns from investments, then there is absolutely no need for any form of taxation whatsoever in that community.

Each community's share of the CAFR amounts should be more than sufficient to cover all of this and more. According to Walter, each community's share is large enough now to cover all expenses for many years, without the need for taxation. However, it would be in the best interests of the community to pay off its existing debt, then, invest in sound projects providing sound returns to cover all the referenced governmental and public costs. In this way, the CAFR accounts are not depleted over a period of 30 to 40 years, so that at the end of that time frame there is nothing left. With sound investments, solid returns and sound management, then the CAFR accounts should increase in value with additional returns that also increase in value, all to the benefit of the community and its people.

It is most likely possible that most readers would agree with our reasonable observer and our analytical computer that all governments in this nation—federal, state, county and local—with a few possible minor exceptions, have not and do not presently work in the best interests of the Citizens whom these governments theoretically represent. Enough un-Constitutional, fraudulent, criminal actions committed by governments have been described in this book and the readers, of course, are likely well aware of government malfeasance in office from their own experiences in their own communities. Earlier we mentioned that we never trust a liar, and anyone who does might reexamine his position on this. As we've said several times now, liars figure and figures lie. Any finances available to the community initiated through CAFR accounts should never be entrusted to a government that has lied to, deceived and defrauded the people of its own community. In fact, the people of any community which identifies that government as such would be well advised to take all lawful means necessary to hold those government officers fully accountable, responsible and liable for their actions then lawfully remove them from office and file criminal charges against all of them. If this type of responsible action were to be done by the people, based in the **authority** of our national and state Constitutions, you can imagine the absolute chaos and running for cover that would take place in all corrupt governments in this nation.

Any and all CAFR investments and management should be vested in and under the direct control of the people and not the local machinery of government. This can be accomplished by establishing public trusts with the people as the beneficiaries of the trusts and the trustees elected directly by the people to properly serve the best interests of the people and operate the business of the trusts effectively and efficiently. Putting any financial responsibility and authority in the hands of the machinery of government would amount to financial suicide for that particular community. However, when the assets are in a public trust and operations are conducted by trustees with direct, Constitutional, fiscal and management responsibilities to the people, with full accountability and transparency in all areas of the trusts' business operations, then the people would be much better served and their communities will thrive.

For instance, let us say a community of approximately 30,000 people has an investment account derived through the CAFRs that is worth one billion dollars, gross. Let us speculate that sound investments are made and the annual return amounts to 6% of the gross, or in this case, 60 million dollars. As mentioned before, since all other existing debt has been paid, then there is no tax needed to pay those debts. However, there are other ordinary existing expenses necessary to operate a municipality. If those expenses for a community of 30,000 people do not exceed 60 million dollars, then the annual 60 million dollar return pays all public and governmental expenses necessary for that community, and still leaves a profit. This type of operation is very sound, safe and beneficial to any community and obviously to its people. However, under the former government structure dealing with the part of the CAFR program that was skimmed and used for private investments, none of the investments and returns were used for the benefit of the people and the community, since all of the assets were used solely for the benefit of those who controlled the private investments. Had they been so used, then what we just referenced above could have been done by the public officials to improve the community and the lifestyles of the people within it. As we said before, governments' unwritten mottoes are: "If we fix it, we can't scam it."

Below are some questions and observations which people might want to pose to their local government leaders to get to the bottom line regarding these CAFRs. Keep in mind the factual possibility that the local leaders will try to avoid and evade answering the questions and try to distract the questioner from his objective. Further, the leaders will likely try to justify anything they have done or claim ignorance and lay the blame upon their advisers, accountants, consultants, etc. Getting to the truth is vital, in not only this matter, but in everything else government does. The truth will help the people, if that truth can be obtained, but since its revelation will damage government, government will be very reluctant to reveal the ultimate truth.

1. According to Walter Burien, the investments made by and through CAFR funds emanated from "surplus" monies available to the jurisdiction, which surplus was invested.

2. Pursuant to Constitutional responsibility, no government has the Constitutional authority, or any other valid authority, to take funds from public monies, meaning funds came from and belong to the public, and invest those funds into various programs, while at the same time, claiming a "shortfall" of funds [since those funds were used to make the investments] which shortfall is made up via increased taxes, loans or new bond issues.

3. Who and what authorized these fund extractions from public monies which went into investments? What was the Constitutional authority or any form of valid authority for this action and deception?

4. It's evident that when public funds are taken from the public and secretly invested elsewhere these actions are totally fraudulent, whether the returns on those investments benefit the people, or not.

5. Who manages these investment accounts and who or what lawfully authorized: (i) the funds to create the investments; (ii) the managers to manage those funds; (iii) who are the beneficiaries of those funds; (iv)in what investment programs do the funds exist and where are they located?

6.   Since these "investment funds" were fraudulently extracted from public monies and fraudulently invested, then it appears likely that the Citizens within that jurisdiction would never benefit from those investments in any way whatsoever otherwise the fraud would be exposed through the monies benefiting the Citizens/community. The real question here is who controls these funds, who owns these funds and who receives the benefit/profits from these funds?

7.   Do a comparison between funds properly invested for the benefit of the jurisdiction and stolen funds fraudulently invested for the benefit of secret entities.

8.   Do a projection of how a community could utilize these funds for the sole benefit of the people and the community, itself.

CHAPTER EIGHT

A BRIEF SUMMARY OF
OUR CONSTITUTIONAL METHODS

Our objective observer and analytical computer have assessed the information presented so far regarding governments' duties and obligations to the people, to the Constitution(s) and to the nation, required of them pursuant to the Constitutional mandates imposed upon them by and through their oaths. These requirements are clearly stated in the Constitution(s), national and state, and in their Preambles. When one holds these requirements against the actions of governments, as described herein, then our observer and computer can quickly and easily conclude that governments—federal, state and local—are not only *not* abiding by those requirements, but are flagrantly and egregiously violating those requirements. Anyone can determine this by looking at the bottom-line actions of government and the disastrous effects they have upon the people. The bottom line is something we all should seek, but "cover positions", rhetoric, propaganda and just plain old bullshit are put in place and used by government constantly to distract us from seeing that bottom line. Such lawless governments should not be trusted by knowledgeable, informed, aware people, and when such governments are so trusted by the people, then our objective observer and computer can also quickly conclude that the people are *not* knowledgeable, informed and aware of the realities operative within governments. Would you trust such a government to set forth your affairs for you and your family and to exert controls upon you and everything you do each and every day? Remember, trust must be *earned*, and not automatically extended by the people. If one does not trust his government, because of the actions of that government, then how can one trust that government to be a government of right, when by its own actions, it has clearly proven that it is a government of wrong? Throughout human society the responsibility to make proper beneficial change has always been vested within the people, and in this nation, our Constitution placed the authority and responsibility over government directly in the hands of the people. The ultimate repeated question is whether the people will finally accept that responsibility and lawfully enforce their authority and power over errant, criminal, un-Constitutional governments operating throughout this nation. This question can only be answered by the actions of individual people and the society, itself, and not by meaningless rhetoric. As we have said forever, and as more and more people are now beginning to understand, *talk walks, while actions speak volumes.*

As referenced previously, President Trump has stated that D.C. is a swamp. He has further stated that the American people are the sovereigns who have the true political power and that he wants to restore that power to the people. As we have said, this is the first president who has made such a statement since John Adams. As we've also said, we call the D.C. swamp a putrid, festering, gigantic cesspool, with similar, smaller cesspools existing in all governments operating throughout America. While there may be some exceptions, we know of none. Do you? Since the President has repeatedly stated he wants to return the power to the people, the question again becomes, "Will the people accept this power, enshrined within them in our Constitution, and secondly, will they know how to effectively, correctly and Constitutionally use this lawful power against errant, un-Constitutional, criminal governments?" Again, only the individual people and the society can answer these questions by and through their own actions. What we are briefly describing in this section are the introductory, preliminary methods used in our Constitutional approach which the American people can lawfully use against the excesses and abuses of un-Constitutional, criminal governments. We and our people have used these methods for decades and, as mentioned earlier, have been very successful over those many years, both in and out of court.

Any time government officers/employees commit a Constitutional violation resulting in some type of damage, harm or injury to a Citizen, there is always a Constitutional remedy. Whenever an errant government officer or officers act(s) in a manner that damages a Citizen, a group of people, or people within any political jurisdiction, whether that harm was physical, some type of material damage and/or in violation of inherent, secured, unalienable rights and due process of law, then the damaged party or parties must duly inform the errant public officer(s) and his superiors of the specific harm or damage(s) suffered by the injured party(ies). This process is absolutely vital and the Citizen(s) must notify government and/or government officers of the offending actions and how those actions damaged the Citizen(s). Without immediate lawful notification to the offending government and/or government officer(s), any attempts to do so in the future will be difficult to properly accomplish. Thomas Jefferson wisely said "…in questions of power then, let no more be heard of confidence in man, but bind him down from mischief by the chains of the constitution…".

This is exactly what we and our people do through our complete Constitutional process. Further, in very close to 100% of the instances, our opponents admit to and agree with our charges made against them in our lawful notification(s). These admissions constitute a very key component and carry enormous legal weight in any court of Constitutional competence. Courts convene to hear and adjudicate matters in controversy. When our opponents admit to and agree with our charges, then there is no controversy for the court to hear, and the victory, lawfully, is ours.

Margy and I have developed a very direct, simple method, based in Constitutional authority, which we and our followers employ any time we encounter errant, un-Constitutional and, many times, criminal actions committed against us by any form of government or corporate entity. We send lawful notification to the offending officer(s) by means of the following: (1) a presumptive letter; (2) our follow-up affidavit. We send the presumptive letter by certified mail, return receipt requested, to the offending government officer(s)/employee(s) and/or our opponent(s), with copies sent to all of their oversight and supervisory authorities.

Our presumptive letter is so named since everything we say in that letter is presumed to be true. In our letter, we include a warning paragraph that provides lawful notice to the letter recipients, which requires them to rebut everything stated in that letter with which they disagree. Our charges and claims are fully based *only* in truth, fact, valid law—meaning Constitutionally compliant law, and evidence. Therefore, pursuant to the lawful warning, the letter recipients are required to rebut in writing any claims and charges with which they disagree and support their rebuttals with truth, fact, valid law and evidence. Since we are so based, it is lawfully impossible for the letter recipients to truthfully rebut our charges and so support them, therefore, they either do not respond, or if they do, they do not respond in kind to our claims and charges, but rather engage in distraction, and certainly do not factually and lawfully rebut our claims and charges. Even though the letter recipients may have responded, if they failed to rebut the claims and charges, then, pursuant to the lawful warning, they admitted to them, fully binding upon them in any court, without their protest, objection and that of those who represent them. If no response is received by us within 30 days, we follow up with an affidavit and provide the letter recipients with another opportunity to rebut the same claims and charges, via their own sworn, notarized affidavits, and support their rebuttals with truth, fact, valid law and evidence. Since our opponents cannot lawfully rebut our charges and support their rebuttal with truth, fact, valid law and evidence, they fail to respond with rebuttal affidavits. In this particular situation in which our opponents are government officers/employees, there is enormous legal jeopardy for any officers/employees should they knowingly attest to lies in a sworn, notarized affidavit. In over 60 years of using this method, and numerous victories we and our followers have achieved, both in and out of court, against errant governments and corporations, we have *never* received a single rebuttal affidavit. The preceding sentence may give you a good indication as to why.

For emphasis, since this point is extremely important, we will repeat it. If we consider the facts of this matter, since our claims and charges made in the letter and affidavit are solely based in truth, fact, valid law and evidence, then it is lawfully impossible for any public officer, pursuant to his oath, to lawfully rebut our charges and support his rebuttal with truth, fact, valid law and evidence. Most astute, savvy recipients are well aware of the lawful Constitutional bind in which they find themselves. These methods achieve the desired result, namely that our opponents tacitly admit to our charges by their failure to rebut, and their admissions are fully binding upon them in any court without their protest or objection and that of those who represent them. As some of the readers may know, an unrebutted affidavit stands as truth and fact before the court. This very simple, easy process, based in the *authority* of the Constitution(s), establishes admission(s) from our opponent(s) before we ever go to court. When we go to court, and present the fact that our opponent(s) admit(s) to our claims and charges, those admissions quickly resolve any matter in controversy in our favor.

Most people are reluctant to go to court and this includes errant government officers. One of the main reasons they do not want to appear in court is because their wrongdoing and un-Constitutional actions can be publicly exposed by competent Citizens who use correct Constitutional methods which demonstrate the wrongdoing. Once the presumptive letter is received, our opponents find themselves in a very difficult lawful position. Astute government officers realize that they cannot respond and rebut our charges truthfully and lawfully, yet they do not want to go to court and have their wrongdoing exposed. Thus, in many situations they are usually willing to resolve the matter that caused us to notify them of their errant, un-Constitutional actions in the first place. If this does not occur, we follow up with the affidavit, and if no resolution is reached, then we file our civil complaint in court and, at the same time, usually file a sworn criminal complaint with the appropriate authorities against the offending government officer(s)/employee(s).

This Constitutional approach making lawful notification to government and government officer(s)/employee(s) of their errant, un-Constitutional actions can work well in virtually any situation in which government acts un-Constitutionally and unlawfully, including when government acts unlawfully against groups of Citizens or even an entire political jurisdiction. The

Constitutional principles are the same whether the unlawful governmental actions were committed against an individual Citizen, a group of Citizens or an entire town, city, county or state.

The Mythical Tale of Elm City

Let us project Elm City, a mythical small community of about 25,000 people, is displeased with numerous governmental activities ongoing in that city which have actually harmed individual people and the public in general. What is described as happening in this mythical city has actually happened in numerous communities in America and is only a very small fraction of the ongoing criminal, un-Constitutional actions routinely committed by governments. The murder of school children by those termed "terrorists" who, in actuality, might be operating under a different agenda, has taken place for years throughout America. All of these are real situations that happened in real time to real communities, and we are only speaking about a very few in comparison to the enormous many.

If the transgressions occurring in Elm City are allowed to stand without repercussions and consequences to the offenders, then, the transgressions by government in Elm City will continue and escalate. As our rational observer and analytical computer have determined, solely based upon lawful requirements imposed upon government, versus government's actions committed in violation of those requirements, it is clear that governments commit routine violations in virtually all of their operational aspects right across the board. Of course, for many years these have been covered up and kept from the public. However, because of various leaks and information that has become public, the people are rapidly becoming more aware of the enormous amount of criminal, un-Constitutional actions routinely committed by their own government. These un-Constitutional, criminal actions have increased in scope and frequency in recent years. Many of the townspeople realize that this escalation is directly related to the fact that the people have not held government in check at all. Due to activities by certain outraged Citizens, these facts have been made plainly evident to the rest of the townspeople and a campaign has been initiated by some very committed, serious Citizens to get the entire town involved in Constitutionally addressing and stopping these routine wrongs being committed by an out of control government.

Some of the city officers/employees transgressions include, but are not limited to the following. The "city leaders" are constantly promoting bond issues for unneeded projects, all of which are wasteful and cause economic hardship upon the townspeople. As a result, taxes have constantly increased and are getting out of control and extremely burdensome on the population. One of these projects is a new city hall, presently being constructed over the strenuous objections of most of the townspeople, which the "city leaders" ignored. Although only 55% of the project has been completed, the cost overruns are already over 350% above budget for the entire project and there is another 45% to go. What the eventual overage costs will be is anyone's guess. This will create an even higher tax burden upon the people. The townspeople are very upset over this and want to hold the "city leaders" accountable for their actions conducted in direct opposition to the will of the people. Although many people have addressed their concerns to the city council, during public meetings and via letters, their voices have been ignored and their comments and questions stonewalled.

The city's municipal courts are nothing but revenue-producing privateer operations that literally soak the people who come before them for minor "offenses", such as parking meter fines, not coming to a complete stop at stop signs, broken tail lights, expired number plates, un-Constitutional code violations, etc. While some people in the city have attempted to use the national and state Constitutions in their defenses, and the due process and secured inherent rights guaranteed therein, the municipal courts immediately stop and prevent any Constitutional arguments, whatsoever. Unfortunately, the uninformed people have allowed this, since they have no understanding of their true political power and how to Constitutionally overcome the un-Constitutional actions and positions of these un-Constitutional courts. The office of building inspections and code violations are endlessly citing people for minor issues, all of which cost the Citizens a lot of money which winds up in the hands of the "city leaders" without any accountability to the people.

The people are intensely angry at the egregiously un-Constitutional actions of the police department and the harm this department has caused many people throughout this small city. Too many people have been arrested for minor situations and some of these people have been beaten by the police while in custody. There are too many speed traps in town that have cost the hard-working Citizens exorbitant sums in fines and increased auto insurance costs. Now this police department has installed "red light" cameras all over town and has been mailing "citations" that impose huge fines upon the Citizens, who are presumed guilty, without due process of law. Additionally, the "city leaders" are talking about installing facial recognition cameras all throughout the city. The police have been engaging in all sorts of sordid criminal activities for a long time, including drugs, gambling and prostitution, and the people of Elm City are sick of this and want to bring it all to a halt.

Recently, a hearing was held in Elm City Municipal Court against a local high school student for a minor traffic offense, and a dozen or so of his classmates attended that hearing to observe. The teenage students were quiet and respectful, yet their presence apparently infuriated the judge, the city attorney and the bailiffs, so all of the student observers were removed from the courtroom, arrested by the police and incarcerated. After 7 days in jail, they were released without charges. The townspeople became infuriated over these unwarranted, un-Constitutional actions committed by the judge and the bailiffs of that court, along with the actions of the police who were abusive in their treatment of the students. A short time after this incident occurred, unidentified armed intruders entered the very high school where these teenagers were students and killed over 20 students and teachers in a senseless, brutal, vicious attack upon innocent people. An armed guard was on the premises, but cowered outside the building and did not attempt to stop the killing. Local police were called, yet, incredibly, none of them entered the building to stop the mass killing. This was the straw that broke the proverbial camel's back for the people of Elm City, who could no longer stand the absolute irresponsibility, criminality, vast corruption, and egregious un-Constitutional actions allowing their own children to be killed while the police stood by and did nothing. It is absolutely tragic that it took this brutal murderous incident to motivate the people of Elm City to decide to work together as a collective unit to hold all government officers/employees—police, judges and other city officials—fully accountable and liable for their egregious un-Constitutional, criminal actions committed against the people and most recently against the innocent teenagers and teachers who were killed because the city police failed to act to protect their Citizens.

The people of Elm City fortunately realized that whenever Constitutional violations occur, there is always a Constitutional remedy available to them. They exercised their Constitutional remedy by using the Constitutional methods cited in this book, beginning with the presumptive letters and following through with affidavits. At the same time, all of them are filing formal criminal complaints against government perpetrators with the county sheriff, the county district attorney, the state attorney general, the governor and the U.S. attorney for that state. The long-standing corruption, fraud, theft, misappropriation of funds and the obliteration of the people's inherent secured rights and due process for the people, culminating in the deaths of so many young people, due in part to government's dereliction of duty, resulted in over a thousand of the Citizens writing presumptive letters to all offending officers in Elm City. There were so many offenses and violations committed by the city's public officers that the townspeople literally had mountains of material from which to choose when they cited their claims and charges against the offending officers, which charges, of course, were based in truth, fact, valid law and evidence. Letters were sent not only to the offending parties, but also other presumptive letters were sent to all of the supervisory and oversight personnel within that city, meaning, of course, the entire city council, the mayor, the city manager and the city attorney. While these are the supervisory personnel for the entire city, they were also the criminals who established and allowed much of the governmental crime in that city, so they received letters directed to them, personally, for those crimes. They bore a double responsibility here, namely, one for their own criminal, un-Constitutional actions and another for the criminal, un-Constitutional actions committed by the entities under their supervision.

The townspeople who wrote these letters also went beyond the town and wrote presumptive letters to the county sheriff, the county attorney, the attorney general of the state, the governor and to the U.S. attorney for that state. In these letters, these additional authorities were apprised of the criminal, un-Constitutional actions routinely committed by the offending Elm City officers, and copies of the letters and affidavits sent to the offending city officers were included as exhibits. Each and every letter sent to the offending Elm City officers contained the usual presumptive paragraphs—first and last—with the usual lawful notification and cited numerous, specific claims and charges of criminal, un-Constitutional actions committed by them. All claims and charges were fully supported by truth, fact, valid law, evidence and witness affidavits.

The bottom line here is that enough angry, outraged people in Elm City took enough interest in stopping the absolutely corrupt governance of this city by incompetent criminals, posing as public officers, and not only notified the offenders and their supervisory and oversight personnel, but also went outside the city to higher authority. Because of the magnitude of this situation, news of what had occurred in Elm City and the people's justifiably outraged reaction to it spread quickly throughout the state and the entire country. This put tens of millions of eyes directly upon Elm City. Since nothing like this outrage from the people has ever happened anywhere in these United States, people on both sides of the issues got quickly got drawn into this and reacted from their own positions. Other townspeople, once they realized the full scope of the violations, also became incensed and joined the fray by taking the same Constitutional positions already referenced.

Politicians, bureaucrats, police and all oversight personnel throughout the state became very concerned about this vast exposure of ongoing, routine, un-Constitutional criminality being conducted in Elm City, as its usual custom, practice and policy. Much of the concern on the part of these politicians et al was for their own backsides, job security and safety, because virtually all of them were doing the same things in their own jurisdictions. Government as it operates today is a racket, and since they are part of the racket, they could be publicly exposed, just as the politicians, cops and judges were exposed by the people of Elm City. When the proverbial crap hits the fan, as it does here, the overseer ringleaders usually do one of two things, and there is no middle ground. Either they "circle the wagons" and protect all offenders, no matter what they have done, so that they protect their fellow criminal officers, cover their backsides, whitewash their crimes, thereby protect their own interests, or if the matter gets out of hand, they throw the Elm City politicians et al to the wolves, and in doing so, still protect their own backsides and their ongoing scams by pretending to be "champions for the people".

The reader can likely figure out what will happen here. Our rational observer and analytical computer have already done that, based upon the facts of the matter, the duties and responsibilities involved and the actions of government officers that violated and directly opposed those duties and responsibilities. Since this type of unified Constitutional demand from a massive amount of people in a community has never happened in the United States of America, at any time in which we have been a nation, this "first" will prove to be a turning point, not only for Elm City but for the entire country. There have been protests and riots before in America, but those were fragmented and never contained one lawful, unified Constitutionally based position presented by the people to their servant government(s). Obviously, this is a very significant event with enormous repercussions in all directions. The resolution of this matter will determine who rules in this country. Will it be the people, who have the true *de jure* political power over their elected and appointed machinery of government, which is the servant to the people? Or, in the alternative, will that servant become the master, override and forcibly stop all expressions of concern by the growing numbers of Citizens, compelling them to accept the dictates of the arrogant criminal ruling government controlling their community? This becomes a very intriguing question that only the people, themselves, can answer and resolve. To the committed, it is up to the people to demand and lawfully enforce just resolution of their legitimate Constitutional grievances lawfully presented to their government. Either the Constitution is the law of the land, or it is not, and if it is not, then, the criminal element rules. If the readers were to put on the hat of our objective observer and use the software of our analytical computer, dealing only with the facts of the matter, which require specific performances and responsibilities from both parties, namely, the governed and the governing, and the likely resolution of that matter based upon those facts, then they can determine the only just, lawful outcome, as have our objective observer and analytical computer.

In our Elm City story, those politicians, bureaucrats, judges and police, who routinely decimated the rights of the people, in perjury of their oaths, were tried in a court of law for their crimes and found guilty, one and all. New people were elected and appointed to the positions vacated by the criminal officers, installed under sworn oaths to uphold and defend the Constitutions, national and state, and the entire city, meaning those who serve in the machinery of government as well as the Citizens who are the *de jure* government have a stronger and more profound respect for the Constitutions and for the true meaning of Constitutional governance. To ensure specific performance, pursuant to oaths taken, all public officers and city employees are now required to sign Constitutional Affidavits which affirm that they have taken the oath and are bound to abide by it in the performance of their official duties. If at any time they violate their oaths for any reason, they will immediately vacate office, upon commission of that violation, without protest, pursuant to the requirements of Sections 3 & 4 of the 14th Amendment. Our mythical Elm City is now functioning as a miniature Constitutional republic in which all the rights of all the people, no matter the race, religion, belief system or condition, are respected and upheld at all times by all public officers. Would you like your community to operate like Elm City? It is entirely in your hands and those of your fellow Citizens to take the same courageous Constitutional actions against the unlawful criminal actions committed by your city officers, as did the people of Elm City. *If*—that little word with a big meaning—allows for possibilities, and if people all over the nation, starting one community at a time, were to do as the courageous mythical people of our mythical Elm City have done, then we would have miniature Constitutional republics all over this country and be on a solid, straight highway back to Constitutional governance in America.

SECTION TWO

GOVERNMENTS' REPRESSIVE CONTROLS

CHAPTER NINE

GOVERNMENTS' VISE-GRIP UPON THE AMERICAN PEOPLE

In our usurped Constitutional republic, rather than the people rightfully exerting Constitutional controls upon their servant governments, federal, state, county and local, those governments exert strenuous un-Constitutional controls upon the people. As we have mentioned many times, a true Constitutional republic establishes the political power within the people. Those who operate the machinery of all governments in that Constitutional republic, pursuant to the *limited* power delegated to them by the people in the Constitution(s), are required to abide by the principles set forth in the Preamble to the national Constitution, to the Constitution(s), themselves, and all rights and due process provisions guaranteed to the people therein.

It should be clearly evident to anyone who has read this book up to this point and who understands the true political realities in which s/he lives that the governments, federal, state, county and local, routinely and as a matter of custom, practice and policy, abrogate those rights and deny due process of law millions of times each day. The freedom and right of choice that have been guaranteed to Americans is largely an illusion, when the realities of governmental controls upon the people are properly considered. We have said this before, but it bears repeating. Whenever government officials act outside the limited, delegated scope of their lawful duties and authority, they have assumed power not lawfully delegated and thus have stepped outside the lawful scope of those limited duties and authority. Unfortunately, the American society has little to no idea of these lawful requirements and restrictions imposed upon all governments or of their lawful political authority and their duty to abide by Constitutional requirements and mandates. Thus, the people abide by whatever those errant governments dictate under the mistaken notion that government has the rightful authority to do so. Nothing could be further from the truth. Tragically, the people do not realize that *they* have the political power, so they never exercise it against un-Constitutional governments.

Governmental controls upon the American people are massive and intrude into virtually every form of life experience and circumstance within our society. Under current government practices, American Citizens are being unlawfully compelled to ask permission from their supposedly servant government to do almost anything. This is the very antithesis of freedom and free choice, strictly opposed to the guarantees provided to the people in the Constitution(s). We will cite examples of these controls here, but to keep things relatively brief, only list some of them.

People who were born on this Earth, no matter where they were born, did not need permission to be born from the country in which they drew their first breath. This is a matter of common sense, but a fact that many people do not consider. The country in which an entity is born does not own that entity, therefore, from a natural human rights perspective the country should not be able to control that entity and what he or she does from birth to the time of death. Unfortunately, this is not the case in today's world and more so in America, the so-called "bastion of freedom and liberty".

When two Americans want to get married, they are told by the government that they need the government's permission to do so, by and through a marriage license. Since a marriage is a willing act between two people, and perhaps their God, then the government has no business interfering with that act, especially in a so-called Constitutional republic. However, in today's America, most people believe that this is an absolute requirement which government has the authority to impose upon all people. Requiring governmental permission to marry subverts the people's willingness, right and free choice to marry at their own discretion, and not at the government's discretion or dictate. A "license" is something that is needed when one wants to do something that is ordinarily prohibited, something that is outside of normal activity. How is a free choice, made by two people in love, who want to be married, something that is ordinarily prohibited and outside of normal activity? The American people have been so brainwashed by their governments, by the media, by the educational system and so many other controlling American institutions that they accept government imposed "requirements" on everyday activities as "normal" and never question or challenge these so-called requirements. Such requirements are not the hallmarks of a true Constitutional republic, nor those of a self-governing society which recognizes that the people are the Masters and the machinery of government is the servant. When the American people simply accept governmental dictates, without question, comment or objection, then the government has unlawfully, in practice, undermined the inherent natural rights of the American people and essentially eradicated the Constitutional mandates imposed upon that government to uphold those rights. Unfortunately, as long as the American people accept these types of intrusive, restrictive governmental requirements as "normal", they will not only continue, but will increase. The marriage license, itself, imposes myriad restrictions upon the future of the individuals in that marriage and upon their progeny, their property and their lifestyles. None of these controls exist in a true Constitutional republic.

When a child is born through that marriage, both the parents and the child have more governmental restrictions un-Constitutionally, thus, unlawfully, imposed upon them immediately. Among the first restrictions imposed are the birth certificate and the imposition of a social security number on the child's identity. There is nothing wrong with a statement of birth, per se, but there is something wrong when an "official" governmental birth certificate imposes future restrictions and requirements upon that child, most of which are unknown to the parents. There is zero need whatsoever for a newborn child to have a government issued social security number, which initially was something required of a worker, not a newborn infant, but that is what is demanded and imposed by government upon parents and the child as soon as the child is born. These controls are not legitimate in a Constitutional republic. Most people have little to no idea as to how far these controls extend, but, again, accept them as "normal". As soon as the baby is born, the government exercises an unlawful presumed superior superintendent "authority" over that child, as opposed to the natural, inherent rights of the parents' attendant authority over their own flesh and blood. When any question arises as to medical treatment or medical procedures for the child, the government, by and through the hospital, exerts this control and displaces the rights, will and wishes of the parents. Numerous vaccines are administered to the newborn within a short time after birth, despite the fact that copious medical evidence has proven that many of these vaccines could cause harm to the child and may well be unnecessary and excessive. When parents justifiably object to the number of vaccines and the possible dangers inherent within them, any such objections are overridden by government requirements. The hospital, doctors and the government typically use fear tactics and threats to force the parents to comply no matter what dangers might befall the child. Again, these intrusive impositions by government and those acting under governmental edict fly in the face of the freedoms guaranteed in our Constitution(s).

There are literally thousands of governmental requirements, federal, state, county and local, imposed upon people throughout their lives from birth through death. Everything from requiring the registration of a child's birth right up to requirements imposed upon the deceased and his or her family. If anyone were to think about the massive number of requirements imposed upon people from birth to death in all areas, then the enormous amount of control over the people would be fully understood. America is touted as a "free nation", but what is free about requirements? Consider the fact that any time any restriction, condition, requirement or limitation is imposed upon freedom then what is said to be free is not free at all. Some of the imposed requirements may serve some rightful purposes, but the overwhelming majority of them serve only the governments imposing them. It is all about extracting money from the people while imposing additional controls upon them. By now, the American people should be very sick and tired of the enormous amount of governmental controls imposed upon them in virtually all areas of life. If the American people truly understood the intent of the founding fathers when they formed a Constitutional republic, and not a democracy, and the precious liberties and freedoms guaranteed to the people in our Constitution, then if the people lawfully enforced those guarantees upon un-Constitutional governments, virtually everything in this nation would change for the better rather quickly. Americans have not only been conditioned to falsely believe that America is a free nation, but they have also been conditioned to falsely believe that they have freedom of choice and free will. Just as we mentioned above regarding restrictions on freedom, if there are any similar restrictions, limitations, controls or other conditions imposed upon free choice and free will, then those choices are not free. Think of how many restrictions the governments in this nation place upon the free choice, free will and free speech of the American people all the time and the list of restrictions and controls is growing by the day!

CHAPTER TEN

PROGRAMMING AND PERSUASION
GOVERNMENTAL-INSTITUTIONAL-MEDIA
& ENTERTAINMENT

Going beyond burdensome, unwarranted government regulations, requirements, permits and licensing, all of which are intrusive, expensive, mostly unnecessary and impose control upon the Citizens, and produce vast amounts of money for governments and the power forces, there are other more subtle methods in play to persuade people to readily do what the government and the power forces want them to do. The presentation style of government and the power forces through various sources is so effective, so persuasive that people believe that what they are doing emanates from themselves, as a natural course of their observations, caution, wishes and behavior, without realizing that they are unknowing *dupes* living out a deliberate scenario created by government. We will cite a few examples for our readers' consideration.

So-called "conservative talk radio" has been broadcast over many stations throughout the country, beginning sometime in the late '50's. This form of broadcasting has been become one of the strongest communications forces in America, attracting huge audiences. The question arises as to whether conservative talk radio is really "conservative", truly authentic or is just another form of entertainment, a profitable commercial enterprise, and/or a form of disinformation and mass brainwashing. If we look at the state of affairs in America since the late '50's, we can quickly ascertain that an enormous number of political, military, economic and social disasters have befallen America since then, such as the Vietnam War, the JFK assassination, the MLK assassination, the RFK assassination, the shooting of former Alabama Governor, George Wallace, Watergate, Nixon's resignation, the assassination attempt on President Reagan, TWA Flight 800, the horrific tragedy at Waco, the Oklahoma City Bombing, the Bill Clinton-Monika Lewinsky debacle, various recessions, the exportation of entire industries overseas, the "disappearance" of trillions of dollars from the

Pentagon and other government agencies, 911, the Iraq War, the Afghanistan War, the ongoing school shootings, the economic disaster of 2007 – 2008, the foreclosure crisis, the trillions of dollars in bank "bailouts" by the Fed, at the expense of the people, the D.C. swamp, massive escalating government corruption, and so on and so on.

If conservative talk radio were truly effective in not only talking about, but actually proposing lawful solutions to resolve the problems of which it speaks, then, obviously, to the minds of our rational, reasonable, objective observers, conservative talk radio would have either curbed or minimized these and numerous other disasters or prevented them from happening in the first place. When our observers listen to talk radio, they will note that while the hosts constantly speak of the problems existent in this country laid at the feet of errant government, they steer clear of suggesting any **Constitutional solutions** on the part of the people to stop those un-Constitutional, criminal actions routinely by governments. Again, to our objective observers, it would seem rational that sincere hosts who claim to want to prevent disasters from happening in and affecting our nation and her people, whether errant government is a factor or not, would inform their audiences of correct Constitutional methods which the people could employ to prevent the wrongdoing and disasters from occurring in America by holding their servant governments in check.

"If" is a very small word with a huge meaning. If the many hundreds, if not thousands, of so-called conservative talk radio hosts, both on commercial broadcasting or on the Internet were really conservative, then it would seem logical that they would speak of our Constitution, which placed the political power in the hands of the people. From all of our listening to some of these hosts over the years, we have never heard any host seriously speak of the **supreme authority** of the Constitution and how that document placed the responsibility to oversee government, and hold it in check, with the people. This would seem a logical position for any conservative talk radio host, yet we have never heard it and to our knowledge, this has never occurred. For this to be typical within the large number of conservative talk radio hosts who have appeared over the past 60 years, then it appears that there is something lacking and awfully wrong with conservative talk radio. Since for more than sixty years, our observers hear no such Constitutional solutions advocated by these radio hosts, then they could easily question whether there was an unknown, purposeful objective carried out by the hosts in failing to present *solutions* to the people. Our observers might ask: "Who is best served by this failure?" Would it be the people who want to stop these political, military, economic and social disasters in their own nation, or would it be the government and the power forces which benefit from these disasters? Since the answer to this seems to be pretty obvious, then it is possible for our observers to easily conclude that the government has warned all of talk radio to stay away from presentation of Constitutional resolutions to solve the problems that are plaguing America.

This same subversive control against the interests of the people occurs in all media throughout the nation, meaning most newspapers, magazines, radio and television news programs and even Internet blogs and social media. It seems that the makers of entertainment programs presented on television and in the motion picture industry have either worked with or been compelled by the government to present programming and motion pictures that present to the American people the viewpoints, attitudes, belief systems and biases that the government and the power forces want the people to adopt and integrate within their own frames of reference, as if these came from the people, themselves. The propaganda, programming and conditioning exerted by the government and the power forces upon the American people has been and still is vast, intense, extensive, insidious and of long duration. The propaganda machine is much more extensive prior to and during wartime in which America is presented as the "savior of the world, battling all evil" and massive amounts of people are deceived by this propaganda, so readily sign up to join the military, become soldiers and go overseas to kill strangers in strange lands. In peacetime, the propaganda may not be as blatant, but is still very much present to keep the people in line and under the control of the government and the power forces to maintain the status quo. Propaganda, programming and conditioning should never, at any time, for any reason, be imposed upon the American people by their own servant government or allowed to be imposed by the power forces. None of this is consistent with the principles of a Constitutional republic. The bottom-line question is—"Who benefits?" The obvious answer is the government, the power forces and their hidden bottom-line objectives, which are reached by and through the propaganda, programming and conditioning, while the people are the unwitting instruments used to achieve those objectives and which objectives work to the people's detriment.

Earlier, we touched upon the governmental controls exerted upon the public school systems in America. This control is very strong, because much of the money that is spent on public schools comes by and through the federal government, along with endless "strings" and conditions. Obviously, this practice engages in not only control, but also effectuates governments' desired objectives. Previously, we spoke of how history is written by the victors and the powerful, with some truth interwoven among a lot of falsehoods and fraud, to obtain the results intended by the government. Truth and reality of history many times simply get set aside, revised or completely erased to achieve those desired results. Clearly, truth is meaningless to a system when that system only wants to obtain its bottom-line objectives. The students are guinea pigs and pawns in this equation who are being groomed to be obedient, compliant servants of the collectivist/socialist/ communist/progressive "societal architects" to carry out the plans designed to vilify individuality and critical thinking, and glorify the One-World mentality.

Monetary controls exerted by government to achieve the above-referenced objectives are carried out through the entire curricula of the school systems. Students are conditioned and programmed to believe and participate in "group think", collectivism, the herd mentality, socialism, and downplay any individuality and/or creative thought, at all. They are taught by rote to accept what is fed to them by the authority figures they are conditioned to respect, obey and follow, without objective comment or question. While competition still exists within the school systems, it is greatly discouraged, because competition, itself, is painted as combative, too individual, and not in line with "group think". Political correctness is rampant throughout the school systems at all levels, including colleges and universities. This political correctness is another programming method by which the government and power forces achieve their objectives, and it is the antithesis of true freedom of speech, free choice and individual expression. Our Constitution, which is our Supreme Law, guarantees these rights to the people, yet the political correctness nonsense directly opposes these Constitutionally guaranteed rights. It is imperative that freedom of speech, freedom of choice and individualism be lauded and encouraged in this country and in no way criticized, discouraged or punished. In a truly free country, these rights would be respected, upheld and encouraged, and not demeaned and vilified as they are today by the intrusion of government intervention and control at every level.

The phrase "political correctness" is a fraud in and of itself. No political correctness exists in America. If we had political correctness in this nation, then all the elected politicians and all the appointed government officers and workers would be *politically correct* by their upholding and supporting the Supreme Law of this Land, including all secured, inherent rights and all due process guaranteed therein to the people. Government likes to use and insinuate into society phrases like "politically correct" to persuade people to abandon their Constitutionally secured rights and then conform to the dictates of imposed political "group think". Anyone who does not do so is shamed, demonized and ostracized. Our rational, reasonable observers can quickly say that, from a view of authentic, meaningful, true political correctness this would mean Constitutional obedience, yet none exists in America, since virtually all politicians in this country routinely perjure and violate their oaths and the people's secured rights and due process guaranteed in the Constitution(s) each and every day. The approval rating of Congress is abysmally low, yet these frauds, masquerading as public servants, shame the American people into engaging in political correctness, while Congress routinely decimates the rights guaranteed to the people in the Constitution, the same Constitution to which they are duty bound by oath to uphold and defend. As it is practiced today, political correctness should be termed "pure communism" and "pure corruption".

Hypocrisy knows no bounds in the political system operative in this nation! Each and every American has the guaranteed right to say whatever he or she wants to say, at any time he or she wants to say it. The only exception here is when that free speech puts others in immediate danger, such as when some idiot might yell "Fire!" in a crowded theater. If Party B dislikes what Party A says, he or she has the Constitutionally guaranteed right to dislike it, because he or she has the right of free choice and expression. However, Party B has no Constitutionally guaranteed right whatsoever to prohibit Party A's right to free and open expression. Party B may disagree with the content of what Party A has said, but not with Party A's *right* to express that content. When a nation starts prohibiting free speech, free choice and free expression, as the U.S. government is doing and compelling other state and local governments and virtually all institutions to do, and arbitrarily dictates what is or is not "politically correct", it's a quick trip down the road to totalitarianism and communism. *Our* nation is treading a very dangerous, precarious, slippery path right now, because huge numbers of Americans of all ages have been programmed and conditioned into accepting **freedom-killing** concepts such as political correctness, free speech zones and other aspects of governmental propagandized control. Rather than thinking for themselves, such people get entrapped by "group think", so express and manifest government's and the power forces' insidious objectives, just as they have been programmed to do.

Today's colleges and universities cater to many students who have been so sheltered and so unchallenged by different points of view that they are incapable of entertaining ideas, concepts and speech that differ from their programmed mindsets. These people are the epitome of "group think" and expect everyone else they encounter to accept their "group think", herd mentality point of view. Those who do not are hated, ridiculed, scorned, shamed and viewed as enemies. This obviously is a very dangerous and divisive trend for America. However, it works very well for the power forces, since this creates opposing elements which the government and power forces play against each other, and use to their benefit and advantage. *Divide and conquer* has always been a key method employed by tyrannical governments and rulers. The collegiate advocates for "group think" are so sheltered and focused on their own collective efforts that they demand "safe spaces" on their campuses which isolate them from other students who have open minds, different viewpoints and different forms of expression. It's truly amazing that these institutions of higher learning cater to these collective neophytes rather than support the free speech and open expression of the majority of students. The institutions put out copious amounts of talk and pedantic propaganda about "diversity", but apparently this only refers to including all kinds of different humans and not to all kinds of thought. For anyone who cares to do a little investigation on this subject, he or she will quickly determine that many such institutions in this nation began leaning toward socialism and outright communist ideologies long ago. This in itself is absolutely absurd, in part, due to the fact that a true investigation of communist nations that have existed in this world will clearly prove that those who ruled them were tyrannical dictators who ruthlessly killed millions of their own people and completely stifled any opposition through shame and vilification, arrest, torture, imprisonment and execution. How any so-called sane person can support such a proven diabolical evil shocks the conscious mind, yet this is the pathetic state of affairs at many universities where a false patina has been waxed upon an insidiously ugly reality. *Freedom is the opponent of communism*, a fact which institutions of higher learning in a so-called free nation should teach and discuss, yet that freedom is unbelievably discouraged and vilified by the participating "progressive" universities and colleges operating in America today. Why is this? Put simply, it is because these institutions know that if they presented the truth about communism, the atrocities have been committed under communist rule, the misery to which people in communist countries have been and still are being subjected, then the despicable ugliness of this hypocritical, insidious ideology would be revealed and no one would ever want to entertain engaging in communism. The young people of today have no memories of what communism really is and this is exactly how the government and power forces want it. How else could they ever convince these ignorant dupes to sign on to a lifetime of total slavery? Our objective rational observers could easily conclude that higher educational institutions should relish the presentation and open discussion of myriad, diverse ideas, viewpoints and opinions involving virtually everything, including various forms of government, but this is definitely not the case. Anytime truth is hidden, then there is a sinister reason for this and these institutions are among the domestic enemies of whom Jefferson spoke.

CHAPTER ELEVEN

HARMFUL GOVERNMENTAL ECONOMIC POLICIES

One of the principal reasons why college graduates cannot find plentiful opportunities for good-paying jobs, either in or out of their chosen fields, is because of the anti-American policies of this government that have created recent economic disasters. As we said before, economic violence is one of the most insidious forms of violence that can be perpetrated by a government upon its own society. The policies of our government for many years have facilitated the export of not only individual companies to other nations, but entire industries and the massive amount of good-paying jobs that go with them. As we see it, and as we believe most rational Americans would see it, this is a vicious form of economic violence perpetrated by the government and its elite corporate allies upon the American people. When a town loses a factory or plant that was the mainstay of that town and provided jobs for the majority of the working force of that town, then that town is devastated and is going to suffer many cascading economic catastrophes. The economic base provided by that factory or plant extended to the entire town, including local support industries and small businesses of all types, such as restaurants, stores, service providers and other establishments throughout the town. When that economic base withdraws, the funds which supported that extended support base and the other businesses throughout the town abruptly stop and there is nothing to replace that former economic base. The people who worked at the factory or plant no longer have jobs, which means, they no longer have money to spend in the town. As a result, the various support industries and the small businesses cannot sustain themselves and most of them eventually close. These other business closings put their own people out of work, thus adding to the number of people without jobs and means to support themselves and their families. Every family has costs and expenses it must bear, but without receiving regular funds from work, a family cannot meet those expenses, and if the condition continues, the family cannot live as it formerly did. It becomes impossible for them to make their mortgage payments or meet their rents, pay for their cars, feed their families. People lose their homes because they can no longer afford them, while others lose apartments because they cannot pay their rent. From independence, these unfortunate people are reduced to dependence, thus their very survival is threatened. Many turn to government for assistance and government is only too happy to oblige. This is the same government that worked with businesses and industries, allowed them to leave the country for cheaper labor and higher profits in other nations. As we said earlier, problems exist within any society, but if the conditions which create those problems are anticipated and resolved, then the problems are minimized or do not manifest at all. A Constitutionally compliant government of right would anticipate and resolve those conditions and thereby either minimize or stop the problems before they happen. An un-Constitutional government of wrong would either not rectify the conditions or in fact create the conditions so that the problems would occur. Our rational, objective observers could easily determine that the American government, by and through its failures, worked against the best interests of its own people, and at the same time, worked for the best interests of the banking cartel and the corporations who vastly profited.

These economic policies were the direct reasons why the people lost their livelihoods, yet that same government who allowed or caused the problems is willing to provide financial assistance to those who became dependent because of the government/corporate policies. If we take this one fictional experience in one town and multiply that across the entire nation, then it becomes clear as to why there is a dearth of good-paying jobs in this nation. Since the duty of the government in our Constitutional republic is to uphold the best interests of the people, and provide for the general welfare, then it is blatantly obvious that this government utterly failed those duties and responsibilities to uphold the interests of the people imposed upon government by the Constitution. These conditions are a big part of why so many college graduates are not living the "better life" their parents wished for and sacrificed to give them and are instead dependent upon their parents and/or government. This is exactly the scenario that government has been intending for a very long time.

Those college students who majored in courses that would lead to jobs in a professional technical industry, such as computer-related industries, medically-related industries, and scientifically-related industries, have a much better chance of finding good-paying jobs. Unfortunately, many of those not so based, have had a very tough time in this economy finding any work related to their fields of study. Sadly, those who cannot find work in their chosen fields of study outnumber those who can. These former students are unable to live the lifestyle they expected, and because of economic policies put into effect by this government, they are thrown into situations that they never dreamed would occur. These governmental, corporate, banking policies which work and have worked against the best interests of the American people do not bode well for any American, except for those select few who can profit handsomely from the exported industries.

Expanding on this line of thought let us speculate that the college student is fortunate enough to land a job in his chosen field, does well at it, and after a while is in a position to get married and start a family. When he or she does, then the same governmental permission requirements are imposed upon the couple who want to marry, as previously discussed. Upon the birth of their first child, the conditions cited previously would be imposed on those parents and their child. The government has regulated virtually everything in this so-called free country and compelled people to obtain permission and buy licenses simply to conduct the necessities and niceties of everyday life. There is no other term for this than outright tyrannical control. For example, the government tells us that we must register our cars, insure our cars and must obtain a license to travel in our cars. The right to travel was set forth in the Articles of Confederation, Article IV, Section 1, which is our nation's first "Constitution" and is part of the Statutes-at-Large, still in effect, thus, pursuant to Constitutional requirements, there is no need to obtain a license to travel in one's own automobile on the public roads and nothing to support the need for registering and insuring our cars. Insurance should be a personal choice and not a mandated requirement imposed by government upon a "free people". Pursuant to Article I, Section 10 of our Constitution, which we have referenced before, government cannot lawfully impair the obligations of contract and according to due process of law, government cannot lawfully impose the obligations of contract.

If our former college student who is now working in some type of industry wants to build a home for his family, then the government tells him he needs permission to build a home on his own property, so he must obtain a permit to do so, and to add insult to injury, he is compelled to pay taxes to live in his own home! If he wants to make an addition or other improvement to his own home, the government tells him he needs a permit to do that. If he wants to go into business for himself, the government tells him that he needs permission, a permit and license to do that. If he wants to go fishing, the same permission and license requirements are imposed. If one wants to sell trinkets or balloons on a street corner, the government demands that he get a license to do so. If he wants to sell something at a fair, he is told he needs a license to do that. If he wants to go hunting, contrary to Constitutional guarantees, he is told that he needs a license to have the gun and a license to hunt and what he can hunt is limited by the government.

In America, we now have "free speech zones". This is a particularly offensive affront to the people, since the whole country is supposed to be a free speech zone, but yet, people in some areas are being told that they can only assemble in and speak out publicly in these "free speech zones", which require permission from the government. Government unlawfully regulates speech pursuant to "political correctness", which has no place or authority in a Constitutional republic. If a group wants to have a political rally or a political march, they are told they must obtain governmental permission and obtain a license or permit to conduct their activities. In almost all areas of life, some type of governmental permission and licensing requirements are being routinely imposed upon the American people. None of this complies with the protections afforded to the people in a true Constitutional republic. America is one of the most highly regulated and highly surveilled nations on the face of this Earth. This regulation comes from federal, state, county and local so-called authorities who have an intrusive hand in virtually everything we do in this country. If the average man or woman takes a look at his or her situation, and actually counts the number of times he or she has been compelled by the government to obtain permission to do something that is a natural right, he or she will be absolutely astonished at the degree of regulation and control existent in a so-called free nation. The word "free" has no meaning if that which is alleged to be free is in fact totally controlled by overreaching government and private vested interests in league with government.

CHAPTER TWELVE

GOVERNMENTS' EGREGIOUS
FISCAL IRRESPONSIBILITY

Fiscal responsibility is the lawful duty and absolute requirement of a *government of right* that intends to abide by Constitutional mandates imposed upon it. Earlier we mentioned that our Constitution is unique in the historical annals of governments, since no other founding document of a nation ever placed the supervision of the political power in the hands of the people. Further, our Constitution stipulates that government is required to abide by Constitutional mandates placed upon it and act only within the Constitutional authority delegated to it. Our objective observer and analytical computer long ago ascertained that governments in America, federal, state and local, have completely disregarded and still disregard these Constitutional requirements. Even people in America who are not politically aware or financially savvy can recognize that the government spends enormous amounts of money continuously. Corruption has been a part of virtually every nation on the face of the Earth since the very beginning of any form of government. People are quickly finding out that all forms of American governments are no exception. For instance, Donald Rumsfeld, the Secretary of Defense under George W. Bush, announced on September 10th, 2001 that the Pentagon had "lost" well over two trillion dollars! Despite Rumsfeld's statement about a loss, no money ever really gets lost for the simple reason that the money supposedly lost by one entity is found or gained by another entity. It simply does not just disappear, and there is usually a hidden agenda when government officers speak of "lost money".

On September 11th, 2001, the day after Rumsfeld made his announcement, the section of the Pentagon that was attempting to trace this "lost money" was blown up, theoretically by an airplane, but more likely by a missile, and many who were investigating this loss were killed and the records were totally destroyed. What a convenient "coincidence" for those who "lost" or *took* the missing money! While coincidences do happen, our reasonable observer and analytical computer could conclude, based upon enormous corruption in government, that this was no coincidence. Many people think it may be possible, if, in fact, not probable, that government officials, in cooperation with other interested parties, staged the entire attack on the Pentagon to bring a rapid halt to any further investigation. Ample, credible evidence assembled by non-government investigators indicates that these suspicions are well founded and may be completely correct. If this is true, then it would appear to our rational, reasonable observer and his friend, the analytical computer, that elements within the government actually attacked the Pentagon for their own selfish benefit. This amounts to **treason** and would never take place nor be tolerated in a true Constitutional republic. However, tragically, the American society tolerates virtually anything the government does, no matter how heinous it may be.

Additionally, people are well aware of the vast bailout programs that profited the banks which caused and created the foreclosure crisis, to the tune of 27 trillion dollars, or more, according to Catherine Austin Fitts. Catherine was an Assistant Undersecretary at HUD under George H.W. Bush and has done extensive research into this "missing money". Our reasonable observer and our computer would ask why the banks, which caused the foreclosure crisis by their policies and their bundling of so-called mortgage securities that were sold to institutional investors of various types, should be bailed out by the government of the problems *they* caused at the expense of the American people. These actions by government clearly demonstrate corruptness, indicate government was and is in bed with the banks, and under these conditions, banks should never have been bailed out by their colluding government partner. Again, these government reactions to a bank-created crisis do not fall within government's lawful scope of limited duties and authority. In fact of law, such actions blatantly defied government's duties to the people. The government constantly claimed that these banks were "too big to fail", thus that narrative became ingrained, then programmed into the minds of the people. If this governmental ploy had not been done to condition the people, most thinking people would have said, "Let them fail!" If the banks caused the problem, then they deserved to fail. If any American Citizen, any small company or business conducted catastrophic business activities and failed because of those activities, the government certainly would not bail out those people, companies and businesses; yet it bailed out those big banks to the tune of *27 trillion plus dollars*.

What the government, the banks, informed people and researchers have not said is that, if these banks had failed, there would have been such atrocious financial disasters and revelations of unbelievable fraud that the entire structure of the American society would have fallen apart. To prevent their nefarious activities, greed, fraud and business machinations from being exposed, the government came to the aid of the banks, but never to the aid of the people. Thus, it could be said that as the government saved the banks from drowning, it sold the people down the river! Most people cannot imagine what 27 trillion dollars are, but the banks that received those dollars certainly can. Some sources say that the total bailouts of the banks and other corporations amounted to as much as 39 trillion dollars. If the reader is interested in looking further into the "missing money", it would be advisable to go to Catherine Austin Fitts' website which is www.solari.com. Catherine has information that indicates over 40 trillion dollars has "gone missing". Again, huge sums like this are never lost; they just get redistributed to those who operate and partner with this extremely corrupt government.

Several years before the financial crash, over several radio programs I predicted a major financial disaster and an enormous foreclosure crisis in this country would occur and that the federal government, by and through the Federal Reserve, would bail out the banks involved. The initial bailout figure I predicted was 8 trillion dollars, but I said there would be several subsequent bailouts of 8 trillion or more. If Catherine Austin Fitts is correct with her figures, I was in the ball park with my predictions. *Remember, these bailout funds were paid out at the expense of the American people, at no expense to the banks!* The bottom line here is that the banks, who committed incredible wrongdoing and fraud, were lavishly rewarded for their crimes, while millions of Americans lost their homes and suffered severely.

As we mentioned earlier, virtually all of the banks who participated in selling their mortgages to investors bundled them and sold them in blocks at discount as "mortgage backed securities". When something is sold to another party, the party who buys the product pays the party who sold the product. This is just common sense known to everyone who has ever bought and sold anything. Therefore, the banks received funds for their products. At the same time, the banks were claiming to have sustained enormous losses because so many millions of people defaulted on their mortgages and had to be foreclosed upon. When those defaulted properties were seized by and then sold by the banks, the banks recouped either all or a great part of their so-called losses. In reality, there were no losses, due to the fact that banks received funds from sales of the so-called mortgage backed securities to investors, as well as from the sales of the foreclosed properties. If one sells an asset, as the banks did to investors, where is the loss? Further, when the banks sell foreclosed properties, where is the loss? Anyone can "justify" anything for any contrived reasons, but that doesn't make the "justifications" true. As many people have found out the hard way, figures lie and liars figure. Our reasonable observer and analytic computer, based upon the actions of government and banks, can easily conclude that both the banks and the government lie to the people as a normal custom and practice. Anyone who believes a proven liar does so at his own risk. If this scenario is correct and evidence clearly indicates that it is correct, where and how exactly did the banks lose? The only losers in this entire debacle were those who lost their homes, the American people, the American society and America, herself. All this done by the hands of the very government that is supposed to uphold the principles set forth in the Preamble to the Constitution—you know, domestic tranquility, the general welfare and the blessings of liberty for all. What a tragic fraud is the U.S. government upon the American people!

When various investors and investor groups ascertained the nature of the scheme and the fact that many of the bundled mortgages they purchased were defective, those investors realized that their investment funds were at risk and demanded repayment from the banks who sold them the defective investments. The outrage of the investors regarding the selling mechanism of the banks is not something that is greatly discussed in this country. There was such a fervor that erupted over this type of misrepresentation that funds had to be repaid. This is, in part, where the bailouts came in. As Catherine Austin Fitts claims, the Fed bailed out the banks to the tune of approximately 27 trillion or more dollars. It is highly conceivable that some of the money went from the Fed to the banks who then repaid the losses of the investors to whom they sold the mortgage backed securities. The question arises as to what happened to the funds received by the banks when they sold those securities. Did the banks pay the funds they received back to the investors, or did the banks simply retain those funds? The answer to this is unknown except to those who were involved in the payment of and transferals of funds. The full extent and impact of this is unknown to the general public, has not been revealed for public scrutiny and likely never will be. Some figures are "out there", but who can say with any certainty how accurate they are? With all the treachery, chicanery and manipulations that have taken place, it's pretty obvious to most people that the American government lies to them as its routine, but unofficial, policy. Despite this staggering fact, the American people still believe the lies that the government tells them and thus far has made no effort to hold government accountable to the truth. Constitutional responsibility is clear regarding truth telling in a government of right. Anyone who believes a liar should question his own beliefs. No matter what the American government represents or does not represent, it is certainly not an indicator of the truth. This is a rabbit hole that never ends, and we must all again remember that liars figure and figures lie.

If the government were truly concerned about the general welfare, and wanted to make certain that the banks did not lose because of their unsound mortgage policies, then a solution which we advocated could have satisfied both positions. Instead of bailing out the banks and hanging the people out to dry, the government could have paid off the mortgage debts of the people who were in default. This would have meant that those funds which paid off the mortgage notes would have been paid by the government to the homeowners, and from the homeowners, directly to the banks holding the notes. In this way, the homeowners would have maintained ownership of their homes and the banks would have recouped what was owed to them pursuant to the notes. Both sides of the equation would have won and no one would have lost anything. However, this scenario did not take place because the government has proven over and over again that it has little to no concern for the people, but great concern for the banking industry, especially large banks, you know, the ones "too big to fail", and the mega-corporations who also financially benefit from government largesse, of course, at the expense of the people.

Several reasons exist as possibilities as to why the above scenario did not take place. First, both our rational observer and analytical computer long ago concluded that the federal government has zero concern for the people, their well-being and their general welfare. For these reasons alone, the government would not bail out the people and pay off their mortgages. Secondly, if the government were ever to do so, the Congress would have to make this possible through legislation, which, given the nature of congress, is highly unlikely. Congress loves to give money to foreign nations for so-called "aid and humanitarian" projects, but is loath to give any such aid and humanitarian funds to the American people. Growing numbers of Americans have become well acquainted with the true nature of so-called humanitarian funds given to foreign nations and how those funds do not benefit the people of those nations, but instead find their way into the pockets of the few, you know, the corrupt figure-head "leaders" and officers in both the giving and receiving nations. Third, if bailouts were given by the government to people whose mortgages were in foreclosure, other people whose mortgages were not in foreclosure would likely cry "fowl" and want the government to bail them out as well. Fourth, the government could satisfy the "fowl" claims of others by requiring the homeowners who were bailed out to repay the government, just as they would repay the bank, but with better terms, interest rates and much more leniency. Fifth, and as we see it, the most important, if this scenario were to have taken place, with bailouts made to the people, then the banks could never have sold the defective mortgage backed securities to investors and made fabulous fortunes in so doing.

Even if some humane government entities had wanted to do the above, their small voices would have been shouted down by the real rulers of this society, namely the bankers in league with their government partners. We could add a sixth reason, which is as follows. Again, if all of the above had happened, excluding the fifth reason, then the devastating foreclosure crisis and the ensuing economic disasters that befell America and her people would never have taken place. It is possible that the readers now understand that government *profits* from disasters and dependency on the part of the people, but does not fare as well with a strong, independent population and a robust, growing economy. Rahm Emmanuel who was Obama's chief of staff and is now mayor of Chicago was publicly quoted as saying: "Never let a good crisis go to waste." That statement pretty much sums up what government really thinks of the people. The American people really should be asking a lot of hard questions of their government and demanding that this government perform only as authorized by our Constitution. One of our repetitive positions here is that none of the referenced government actions fulfill nor comply with, in any way, the principles enshrined in the Preamble to the Constitution, nor do they uphold the Constitution, itself, the secured rights and due process of law guaranteed to the people. For the American people to be totally unaware of these conditions, thereby allowing the government to shirk and oppose all of its Constitutional duties, is not only devastating for the American people, themselves, but also for the intended envisioned enlightenment for America and what little remains of our Constitutional republic.

CHAPTER THIRTEEN

UN-CONSTITUTIONAL TAXATION
ON THE AMERICAN PEOPLE

I t has been said that ***the power to tax is the power to enslave***. Enslavement of the people was not one of the objectives of our founding fathers! In fact, lack of freedom, injustice and unjust taxation were repugnant to them, and these issues were some of the reasons why they rebelled against tyrannical British rule. Enslavement can take many forms, including economic enslavement, which is what occurs whenever someone is compelled to give his hard-earned money to an alleged agency of government and/or to someone else who has not earned that money and to whom that money is neither owed nor entitled. In essence, this is what taxation does. It takes money from those who have legitimately earned it and uses it for another purpose not ordained by the original money earner. Why do we have taxes? Most would say that taxes are necessary because the various forms of governments need money to fund their operations. However, since the currency which America is compelled to use by government *fiat* is printed out of thin air by the private bank that owns, controls and distributes this currency, then, why doesn't government in all forms order the bank to just print the money it needs to operate? If it were really true that government needs our money to operate, then one could almost justify taxes. Almost…However, this is not now nor ever was the case. The reason that government taxes the people is because it *can* and, in so doing, exerts total monetary control over all the people, and does so under threat and coercion. This amounts to economic violence. There are many forms of violence in this world and one of the most heinous is economic violence against the people of any nation by the government of that very nation.

Remember, dear reader, the entire government in a Constitutional republic must act and operate pursuant to the supreme law of that Constitutional republic. As we have said repeatedly, our republic's Supreme Law is the Constitution. What is authorized in the Constitution to government is valid. What is not authorized in the Constitution to government is invalid, therefore, unlawful, or criminal. When government assumes power not specifically delegated to it by the Constitution, then government steps outside of the lawful scope of its duties and authority and its actions are totally invalid, without lawful force and effect upon the people. *This is a very fundamental Constitutional principle which, unfortunately, very few Americans understand.* Deceit, misrepresentation and fraud perpetrated by the government upon the people are not Constitutionally authorized activities delegated to government. Consider this position. Can anyone in America cite the specific Constitutionally compliant law, duly passed by Congress, and entered into the Statutes-at-Large, which requires American Citizens to be subject to and thus liable to pay income tax? If anyone can do so, then he has done the impossible, something that no one else has ever done, *because no such law exists.* Our reasonable, objective observers can state with authority that a law must be valid to exist and must exist to be enforced. If no such valid law exists, then it is lawfully impossible to enforce a non-existent law. When government seeks to do so, in absence of such a valid law, our objective observers would likely conclude that government employs subterfuge, misrepresentation and fraud when it imposes income tax upon the American people.

Other so-called "laws"—in the form of statutes, codes and regulations—may exist that *imply* Americans are subject to income tax, but since there is no specific Constitutionally compliant law, duly passed by Congress, as referenced above, which mandates the people pay an income tax on their labors, those other "laws" are purposefully deceptive, misleading and fraudulent. For instance, if no Constitutionally compliant law, duly passed by Congress, exists which mandates Americans to pay a "day tax" for the second Tuesday and the third Saturday of every month, then any so-called law, code or regulation that requires payments be made prior to the referenced Tuesday and Saturday is not, under any circumstances, a valid law. When no original valid law exists that requires the tax, then any subsequent so-called "law" that refers or implies duties to a non-existent law is totally un-Constitutional, unlawful and fraudulent. Our government has no Constitutional authority whatsoever to so act, yet it does so with impunity.

We are led to believe that the IRS is theoretically a division of government, but is it? Since there is no specific language in our Constitution which authorizes the creation of an agency with the power to lay taxes upon compensation for the labors of American Citizens, then, it is only logical to question the source of the alleged authority attributed to the IRS and the specific areas and circumstances in which that alleged authority can legitimately be exercised. Since the IRS has no Constitutional authority to exist, then our rational observers could quickly conclude that the

IRS is a rogue agency, acting without Constitutional authority, perpetrating fraud upon the people, and allowed to do so by government. Any alleged authority delegated by Congress to the IRS to lay and collect taxes on the labor of Americans must be Constitutionally compliant specific to the Bill of Rights, or that Constitutional authority does not exist. The Constitution provides no authority for direct taxation on the labors of American Citizens.

We encourage the readers to do their own research on this particular subject as well as on anything else discussed in this book which is important to them. The word "authority" has monumental implications, meaning and proportions. In our Constitutional republic, either Constitutional authority exists for an act and an action of government or it does not. When that authority does not exist, and the government creates an act or action which exceeds its Constitutional authority, then that act or action is not only totally un-Constitutional, but also unlawful, and the Congress in creating that act stepped outside the lawful scope of its duties and authority. When we boil it all down to these concise, lawfully based positions, the American people can determine for themselves, whether the Congress and the IRS acted and act pursuant to Constitutional authority, or exceeded it and continue to exceed it. Our reasonable observers will quickly agree with the latter position. Consider this position we mentioned previously. Any act by any legislature or the Congress either supports and upholds the Constitution and the principles of our Constitutional republic, or opposes and violates them. It is this simple. Simple, direct Constitutional positions are the foundation of a Constitutional republic, which dictate to the government of that republic what the government can and cannot lawfully do, yet government consistently distracts the Citizens with excessive codes, regulations, rules, language and policy in government's deceitful attempt to divert Citizens from the real authority of the Constitution and the Rule of Law that is supposed to govern this land and restrict the acts and actions of all forms of government. Government either serves the people, or enslaves the people.

The only government body which possesses the Constitutional authority to make law is the Congress, pursuant to Article I, Section 1 of our Constitution. The IRS has no law-making authority and any of its administrative codes, regulations and rules promulgated and enforced by the IRS must be Constitutionally compliant, specific to the Bill of Rights, or those codes, regulations and rules, etc. are lawfully un-Constitutional, thus, without lawful force and binding effect upon the Citizens. The IRS is an outgrowth of a former governmental bureau that was initially created to impose excise tax on certain goods which were traded between the several states. That bureau did not possess the Constitutional authority to impose taxes on the *compensation* Citizens derived from their labors. Citizens' labors facilitate and support their rights to life, liberty and property, thus fall under the natural inherent rights acknowledged and upheld by our Constitution. The right to earn one's living is one of the most important fundamental rights, belonging to all people, and our Constitution does not permit our fundamental rights to be taxed.

Since that original taxing bureau did not have lawful authority to tax compensation earned by Citizens' labors, then logic dictates that any outgrowth of that bureau, such as the IRS, also possesses no lawful authority to tax compensation Americans earn by and through their labors. Again, interested readers can do their own research and make their own determinations. There is evidence that the IRS is a private, foreign corporation, based in Puerto Rico, while some evidence suggests it is based in the Philippines, but also has a presence in Delaware and offices throughout the United States. In any event, by its private nature, the IRS is not a lawfully authorized agency of government, just as the private Federal Reserve Bank is not a lawful agency of government. In fact, it appears that one of the purposes of the IRS is to act as a collection agency for that Federal Reserve Bank, as well as the International Monetary Fund, or IMF. The real question then becomes, where does the money that the IRS collects from the American people actually go? Many of us know that figures lie and liars figure and, unfortunately, the American government in all forms has consistently been a notorious liar from the very beginning. When one realizes that he is dealing with a liar, can he legitimately believe anything that comes from that liar? You know what our rational, objective observers would say.

The Constitution authorizes very specific, limited forms of taxation. Direct and indirect forms of taxation in specific circumstances are allowed by the Constitution. Direct taxes must be apportioned, yet the income tax, which is imposed directly upon the people, businesses, and industries of this nation, is not apportioned as required by the Constitution. As the Supreme Law of the Land, the Constitution cannot conflict with or be in opposition to itself. Thus, the original position in the Constitution takes precedence over any other position that may arise and conflict with it. The 16th Amendment, which purportedly "authorized income tax upon the people", is un-Constitutional because it directly conflicts with Constitutional mandates regarding direct taxation and the required apportionment. According to many scholars, the 16th Amendment was never properly ratified. **The Supreme Court has stated that the 16th Amendment gave to Congress no new authority for taxation**. Based upon the original Constitutional position which required apportionment for direct taxes, and the interloping un-Constitutional 16th Amendment that purportedly did away with that apportionment, the rational, objective observers could easily conclude that the government has perpetrated a monumental fraud upon the people of America since the passage of the un-Constitutional 16th Amendment in 1913—the same year as the un-Constitutional Federal Reserve Act was passed.

As we said above, the power to tax is the power to enslave, and in a true Constitutional republic, enslavement is absolutely prohibited and the power to enslave is absolutely criminal. As also said above, since the central bank, the Federal Reserve Bank, prints money out of thin air, then, that central bank could print money for all governmental operations, federal, state, county and local, without any debt upon the people thereby negating the need for taxes. However, if the government did this, by and through the bank, then the government would not have the enormous controls it imposes upon the American people, industry, business and the entire society, in all aspects, therefore, the economy, itself. Please keep in mind that all actions of government must be conducted pursuant to the secured rights of the people guaranteed in the Constitution(s), Constitutionally compliant due process of law and the principles embodied in the Preamble to the Constitution. This reminder will show you the difference between what government *does* and what government is lawfully authorized to do. To recap what we said in the above paragraphs: **One of our maxims holds that acts or actions committed by government either support and uphold the Constitution, or oppose, defy and violate it**. Again, it really is this simple, yet this very simple, but *powerful*, position is missed by virtually all Americans. As we said before, pursuant to Article I, Section 1 of our national Constitution, all legislative authority is vested in Congress, and when Congress creates laws for the American people, those laws must be Constitutionally compliant, specific to the Bill of Rights, or those so-called "laws" are not valid Law at all. *A law must be valid to exist and must exist to be enforced.* As we asked before, can anyone cite the Constitutionally compliant law, duly passed and enacted into law by Congress that makes any American Citizen subject to, thus liable for income taxes imposed upon compensation for his or her labor? As also stated, a law must be valid to exist and must exist to be enforced. If no such law exists, then, obviously it cannot be *lawfully* enforced.

When the founding fathers established this new American experiment, the hallmarks of the new government were independence and freedom for the American people. One's labor, work, enterprise, skill, time and business were his private property which he could barter for remuneration and compensation with and from others. It was a simple exchange between the parties. Any American had the right to earn a living, and the work or skill he rendered and the compensation he received were equal. Pursuant to Article I, Section 10, of the Constitution, the government cannot lawfully impair the obligations of contract. The contract that existed between the one who bartered his work or skill in exchange for compensation received was a private contractual arrangement, whether verbal, implied or written, between the worker and the one for whom he performed the work or service. It was their private business, and no one else's.

In the early days of the new fledgling nation after the American Revolution, and, then, formally, under the Constitution, there was no tax imposed whatsoever on the people's labor. As we mentioned, in a Constitutional republic, the power to enslave is prohibited. Since the power to tax is the power to enslave, the power to tax the people's labor is also prohibited. The question arises as to why Americans are paying "income tax" at all. The simple answer to this is that the American people have not been diligent as a society in curbing the excesses of government and in holding government to the strict Constitutional mandates imposed upon government and all government officers by and through their oaths. This abysmal drain on the resources of the people could be corrected by the American society, provided there were enough people within our society who would take the lawful Constitutional steps required to expose the unlawfulness of income tax upon the compensation of the labors of the American people and take the further steps to lawfully abolish it. Obviously, this would be a vast undertaking requiring large segments of our society to awaken to the governing realities regarding the lack of Constitutional authority for income tax upon the labors of the people and the unlawful burden it places upon the people and the nation, followed by the willingness of the people to take lawful action.

Yes, obviously, any form of government, federal, state or local, needs funds to operate. We all recognize this fact. However, how government obtains the funds to operate should not be a burden on the people for the simple reason that government is the servant of the people, and not their Master. Therefore, the servant should never direct, restrict and control the affairs, assets and the livelihood of the Master. Lysander Spooner, a former IRS commissioner said that since the government prints the money for the Federal Reserve Bank, it could print the money for taxes. Clearly, this would be an excellent way to provide necessary funds for governmental operations without indebting the American people. In the late '50's I proposed an alternative currency program, and one aspect of that program was that all funds needed for all governmental operations, federal, state, county and local, would be granted to the governments by a bank owned and operated by the people. Since all funds necessary would be provided to governments through grants from the bank, owned and operated by the people, *at the people's discretion*, then there would be absolutely no need, whatsoever, for taxes upon the people. In this scenario, the roles would be reversed to the extent that governments would be dependent upon the people for their funding, rather than governments demanding payment from the people and punishing them by seizing their property and possibly their liberty, if they refused or were unable to pay. In the reversal of these roles, it is plainly obvious that governments would be subservient and beholden to the people, since the people, and not the governments or the Fed un-Constitutionally acting as the government's bank, hold the purse strings for the all governmental operations in this nation. Governments' attitude toward the people would rapidly change for the better and we would again see the servant governments in their proper roles subservient to the Master-Citizens.

Either one of these positions would work well in a true Constitutional republic, but as we have seen all along, based upon actions committed by government, America is not a Constitutional republic, except in name only, and no government in this nation abides by its duty to uphold rights secured to the people in the Constitution(s), nor upholds and provides due process of law, nor embodies the principles set forth in the Preamble to the Constitution. Such a government structure, federal, state and local, is a total fraud upon the people and operates unlawfully as a criminal racket pernicious to the rights and bests interests of the people. It is akin to having our country run by the mafia, only the mafia has more honor! As we've mentioned several times, in the Declaration of Independence, Thomas Jefferson stated that it is the duty of the people to oppose all enemies of this republic, both foreign and domestic. Awakening Americans are beginning to realize that there are more DOMESTIC enemies in America than there are foreign. When government officers openly defy and perjure their oaths, violate the Constitutions, rights and due process guaranteed therein to the people, and flagrantly deny justice and liberty, sabotage domestic tranquility and pervert the general welfare, then it should be simple for anyone of fair mind to recognize these pretenders occupying public offices as domestic enemies. If the American society could awaken to this fact, and realize the monumental harm that these domestic enemies have been and are inflicting upon our nation and her people, the adverse effects of which are all around us, then that society would likely recognize its duty and responsibility to take the political power granted to it in our Constitution, lawfully remove these domestic-enemy-traitors and lawfully reestablish *true* Constitutional governance. A reminder about what we have mentioned in several places in this book pertains to the fact that President Trump publicly recognized that the people are the sovereigns and the political power remains with the people, a power he said he intends to return to them. Our rational observers could easily agree that it would be in the best interests of the people to reclaim this political power and begin the reconstruction of our Constitutional republic and the reestablishment of governments which abide by their Constitutional responsibilities. In this way, we can truly make America great again, just as President Trump has stated.

Thomas Jefferson also said in the Declaration of Independence that GOVERNMENT OF RIGHT **serves with the consent of the governed**. It is fair to say that an overwhelming majority of the American people do not consent to pay "income tax", but are compelled to do so under threat, duress and coercion by their corrupt "servant government". Since the people do not consent to paying "income tax" on their labor, which is akin to theft and slavery, then pursuant to Jefferson's words, the U.S. government is not a "government of right" but a *government of wrong!* The American people are Constitutionally *guaranteed* life, liberty and property, which cannot lawfully be taken from them except by due process of law. It should be painfully obvious to anyone who has dealt with government in any form, and likely to many of our readers, that the government does not uphold the Constitution, rights guaranteed therein nor due process of law. There is no lawful Constitutional authority for any government to ever violate or deny due process of law. Any act by government which violates or conflicts with and opposes the Constitution in any manner is a violation of due process of law. Any action committed by any congress, any legislature and any governmental body either supports and upholds the Constitution, or opposes and violates it. When government does not uphold the Constitution, rights guaranteed therein to the American people and due process of law, then that government WARS AGAINST THE CONSTITUTION, which is our declared Supreme Law of the Land to which ALL government "servants" have sworn or affirmed oaths to support, uphold and defend. When any government body, including courts, fail to uphold due process of law, then, LAWFULLY, that body or court forfeits any perceived jurisdiction and lacks Constitutional authority to proceed, because that body or court is Constitutionally defective and incompetent. These facts are straightforward and direct, yet, unfortunately, the American people have not, up to this point, used the power of the Constitution to hold their governments responsible and liable for their un-Constitutional actions and to clearly demonstrate that those governments have no lawful jurisdiction, or authority, to continue to operate as governments.

The property of the American Citizen cannot be taken from him or her without due process of law, as we have said above, but we repeat this, because it is a very important, lawful position. Government routinely does not uphold due process of law and as we have also said, this is evident to virtually anyone who has dealt with government and knows how government routinely operates. We are Constitutionally guaranteed the right to earn a living. When one expends his labor for compensation, that labor is his property and his property is his right and his right cannot lawfully be taxed, legislated, manipulated, restricted, changed or stolen in any way whatsoever. The Constitution is the American people's best friend, but only if they embrace it and enforce it as the founders meant them to do and lawfully remove the outrageously corrupt, criminal treasonous governments operating at all levels throughout this entire country. Whenever there is a Constitutional violation, there is always a Constitutional remedy and one of those remedies can be found in Sections 3 & 4 of the 14th Amendment to our national Constitution. These sections are *self-executing*, thus need no additional legislation to give them lawful force and effect. They were meant to protect the Citizens from errant un-Constitutional government and government officers. When any government body and any government officer step outside the lawful scope of their limited, delegated Constitutional duties and authority, then that body or officer is a rogue, a renegade, acting criminally, without lawful authority, so can no longer be protected by a government of right. Sections 3 & 4 state that this officer has vacated his/her office upon the commission of the act which perjured the officer's oath, thereby forfeited any benefits of that office, including salary and pension because he or she can no longer lawfully be a recipient of public funds. Let this sink in, folks…for your benefit and that of America.

The American people need to learn and understand the magnitude of these basic Constitutional facts, set forth in our Supreme Law, then, decide to use them against any and all forms of criminal, corrupt, un-Constitutional government, whether it be federal, state, county or local. Only the people have the power, authority and political will to stop and correct errant, criminal un-Constitutional government. Criminal, un-Constitutional government will never stop itself!

Imagination is a very powerful tool for anyone, but especially for creative, inventive, forward-thinking, there's-always-a-better-way-to-get-things-done people. Imagine if people all over this country from many different states were to realize their inherent political power and bring others into realizing the same thing, then imagine these folks uniting in common effort and objective to use the AUTHORITY of the Constitution, as the self-governing people they are supposed to be, against the ruling domestic-enemy-traitors to lawfully remove these vermin, who have blatantly betrayed the public trust, from their offices and in so doing, begin the road back to Constitutional governance in America.

CHAPTER FOURTEEN

JUSTICE AND INJUSTICE IN AMERICA
ENDLESS WARS FOR ENDLESS PROFITS

D oes *true* justice exist in America? Any Citizen who has had the misfortune to have to deal directly with the so-called "justice system" would likely say "No!" In the alternative, the wealthy, major corporations, banks, vested interests—the power forces—would answer: "Yes, for 'just-us'!" Obviously, there is a major disparity here regarding the perception and the dispensation of justice in America. One could say that justice is provided to these power forces, while injustice is imposed upon the people.

Does endless un-Constitutional warfare that continues decade after decade provide domestic tranquility, protection, well-being, security and safety to the people, as required in the Preamble? Is this justice? The obvious answer is "No." Warfare places the people, the nation and the Americans who fight the wars in harm's way and at death's door, on multiple levels. How many Americans have died in the ridiculously enormous numbers of wars that the U.S. government has instigated, starting with the War of Northern Aggression, which many refer to by the oxymoronic term, "The Civil War"? There was absolutely nothing "civil" about that war, or any other un-Constitutional war in which Americans and America were put at perilous risk.

Does the average American have any comprehension or understanding of how many families were totally destroyed because of these profit-driven, completely un-Constitutional wars? Most people think nothing of ongoing warfare, because they have been propagandized from the cradle by false "patriotism" to believe in and support warfare. However, the fact is that through warfare millions of people tragically lost loved ones whom they never saw again, including wives who lost their husbands, children who lost their fathers, parents who lost their children and lovers who lost each other—*forever*. These families and people were not protected by the U.S. government from these wars, and their well-being was not upheld by that government. Since our Constitution imposes a lawful duty upon government to provide domestic tranquility, and the well-being and general welfare of the people, then, our government directly opposed these Constitutional requirements by causing and creating un-Constitutional wars that put Americans in harm's way, all for the benefit of government and the power forces which profit from war, in many ways.

If the government duly upheld all Constitutional requirements, instead of opposing all of them, then, it would have been the duty and responsibility of the U.S. government to avoid war at all costs and more so to avoid all wars involving foreign entanglements, in which Americans fought to protect the rights and interests of other people in other countries, or at least that is what they were led to believe. Our first president warned us about foreign entanglements. The reality is vastly different from the propaganda fed to those who fight and to the Americans who unquestioningly support the un-Constitutional wars. Since America has been and still is in numerous wars, it appears that the U.S. government embraces and thrives upon war. That government compels the people to participate and puts them into danger, risking injury and death in these needless wars created and promoted by our own government and the power forces that essentially "own" the government. If that government had followed the dictates and requirements of the Constitution, which is exactly what the government is mandated to do, then, that government would have found ways to keep America out of warfare and let others handle their own problems of their own making. Since this is not and has not been the case, from at least the time of the War of Northern Aggression, the overall consuming question must be "Why?"

War is a big-profit item for the government and the power forces which own and control the war industry and unlawfully dictate policy to the government. These include weapons manufacturers, the various contractors and sub-contractors who provide necessary parts for the weapons, the munitions corporations, the industries who make soldiers' uniforms, boots, shoelaces, field kits, accessories, ships, tanks, planes, electronics of all types, the software companies who program the ever-more lethal, sophisticated weaponry, drones, and so on and so on. All of this is *big business and big money* for the power forces, yet it is the people who pay the price. Not much difference exists between feudal days and today.

Among the biggest winners in these war scenarios are the bankers, primarily the central bankers, who typically fund *both* sides of the participating nations and make huge profits and exert further control by so doing, no matter which side "wins". The profits are enormous, but the further control is invaluable. Another wise man once said that if the profit were taken out of war, then, there would be no more wars. Why would an entire nation go to war for the sake of profit for the power forces, and further, extend un-Constitutional control to their own government? Since America is and has been controlled by the unlawful usurpation of the U.S. government and the elite power forces, from her inception, then, that government and those power forces do only what benefits *them*, no matter what harm befalls America and her people. As long as the people blindly follow the dictates of errant government, and allow government to use and misuse their best instincts against them, then, war will continue to benefit the power forces and bring only peril to America and her people, as well as to the countries the U.S. government utterly destroys, decimates, rebuilds, manipulates and then controls.

Ongoing foreign warfare defies all of the positions for the protection and defense of America and her people that are embodied in the Preamble to the Constitution, as well as the rights and due process guaranteed within the Constitution. Despite this, the American people, through their ignorance, naivety, gullibility, misplaced trust and misguided patriotism, have for far too many generations allowed and supported their own government's actions fomenting and instigating war, therefore causing enormous harm to the nation and her people, as well as to the people in whose countries the U.S. government has meddled through its warmongering. It should be easy to see that the requirements of the Preamble and the rights guaranteed in the Constitution are obliterated by government in its creation of constant, ongoing, needless war. There is no justice, no domestic tranquility, no common defense, no general welfare and no blessings of liberty for the people when their government engages them in atrocious, diabolical, heartless, needless ongoing warfare.

Humans realize that problems occur in life, which, unfortunately, is part of the natural state of human existence. One of the best ways to solve problems is to prevent them from happening in the first place. This can be done by the recognition that certain conditions will result in problems if those conditions are not properly addressed, adjusted, rectified and dealt with to avoid those problems. This is just common sense, but as most of us know, common sense is not very common anymore. By the observable actions of this government that have occurred since the very beginning of our nation, True and Reality, our rational, reasonable, objective observers, dealing in common sense and facts, can easily determine that the U.S. government, since at least the War of Northern Aggression, is an un-Constitutional, criminal operation that usurped our rightful form of republican government and uses the people as pawns to advance an insidious evil agenda. Some Americans may disagree with this and that right to disagree is upheld in the First Amendment. We respect anyone's right to disagree, but those who do so might be better served to take an *objective* look at the actions of government conducted against the best interests of the people and then make their determination.

As stated above, problems are part of the human experience, but prevention of the problems through proper actions is usually the best course. Had our government embraced this sane position, it could have prevented our participation in foreign wars and stopped the War of Northern Aggression before it ever began. Those precautions would have prevented us as a nation from provoking and participating in mindless "police actions" and "military interventions" throughout the world, which are still going on to this day. However, if these wars were prevented and never happened, the enormous fortunes and the massive control gained through those wars also would never have happened. True and Reality might conclude that, yes, problems do occur and, yes, problems can be prevented, but, no, our government had no interest in preventing the problems, and in fact wanted the problems to occur so that the government and the power forces would benefit enormously from the catastrophes and sacrifices suffered by the people of our nation and those of the other nations we invaded and fought.

Some Americans are beginning to realize that all is not what it seems to be, nor as it is *presented* to be. Some are further realizing that there is a sinister hidden agenda behind actions such as ongoing warfare, financial disasters, foreclosure crises and numerous other economic, social and political problems that America and Americans face. Common sense indicates that problem prevention is the best tactic for any person, any family, any state and any nation—that is, if the entity is absolutely serious about preventing the problem. Common sense also dictates that if the government, the vested interests and the power forces gain from the problem and can create the problem at will, then prevention opposes the best interests of the power forces and the problem will definitely occur and endlessly reoccur. As we may have said before, the politicians motto is this: "If we fix it, then we can't scam it!" Our impartial, objective observers, True and Reality, would completely agree with these statements. Again, some Americans are seeing through the veil and realizing that gigantic frauds have perpetually been perpetrated upon them by their own government and the partnering power forces. Obviously, not only our reasonable, rational observers, but also any sane, thinking person with just moderate common sense and awareness can quickly determine that these activities are not in keeping with the mandates of the Preamble to our Constitution nor with the Constitution, itself. Authentic Constitutional republics do not destroy their own people for the benefit of government and their partnering power forces. Since, sadly, this is not the case in America, then, unfortunately, this nation is a sham "Constitutional republic", made so by the domestic-enemy "leaders" of this nation at all levels.

The implications of the preceding positions are profound and give rise to questions which Americans should pose as to why the government of this supposed Constitutional republic so acts. Obviously, for the government of this Constitutional republic to involve the people of our nation in ongoing wars in foreign countries leads to the people's immediate harm and inevitable destruction. As horrible as this realization is, it worsens when one looks at the real reasons why these foreign wars take place, and these reasons have nothing to do with "spreading democracy" and giving aid to the people of other nations. No, the real reasons these wars are fomented and fought is to benefit the power forces whose unspeakable avarice, greed and lust for control are the driving forces behind virtually every war this country has ever fought.

The American people would be far better off by curbing the un-Constitutional actions of their own government and opposing the warmongering tendencies of the **domestic enemies** ruling this nation. As mentioned before, in the Declaration of Independence, Thomas Jefferson stated that it is the *duty* of all Americans to oppose all enemies of this republic, both foreign and domestic. Those in government who oppose the Constitution(s) in any way and put Americans and America in perilous harm are the domestic enemies of whom Jefferson spoke, and if America is going to be put into needless wars by these domestic enemies, then it is in the best interests of all Americans to lawfully remove these domestic enemies from office and thereby prevent the long dreaded problem of another world war. True and Reality could easily conclude that this would be a far better course of action for the American people, for America, herself, and for the entire world, rather than to allow the domestic-enemy cartel that masquerades as government to decimate the people, our nation and our planet through the hideous evils of warfare. Would you trust this domestic-enemy cartel masquerading as government to make choices for you, your family and your nation, all of which could pose immediate catastrophic harm? Those Americans who can shake off the perpetual and insidious propaganda, programming and conditioning imposed upon them every day would not place trust in any one of them, let alone the entire treasonous lot.

The U.S. government has proven itself to be a notorious liar, as most people either now understand or are beginning to understand. This awakening is very good for the people and could be very good for America, but not so good for the government and the power forces. Once Margy and I know that someone is a liar, or some type of organization lies as a matter of its usual customs and practices, we will never under any circumstances believe anything further stated by that person or that organization. To do so would be act to our own detriment. Once a liar is shown to be a liar, then one can never believe anything that liar says again, because the chances of it being a lie are enormous. If the American people as a society could take a realistic look at what government has *said* and then look at what government has *done*, they can easily conclude that government lies as a matter of course each and every day. When government provides "reasons" for its next "police action", "peacekeeping mission", "intervention" or war, will you actually believe the reasons which government puts forth? We never will. The old adage of fool me once, shame on you, but fool me twice, shame on me certainly applies here in spades!

For a moment, please consider the following. The U.S. government has and now involves our military in numerous actions throughout the world, ostensibly to "protect these nations, their people, stop terrorism and make their borders safe". Compare this to the fact that the same U.S. government, and especially congress, refuses to protect our borders, allows virtually anyone in, vets very few so-called legal immigrants, has refused and blocked funding for a border wall, thus is not protecting our borders and our safety, but claims to be protecting the borders and safety of other countries throughout the world. Such blatant hypocrisy can only exist within the arrogant ruling domestic enemies who want to destroy this nation as quickly as they can. President Trump is a voice in the wilderness here, but at least he is trying and to a certain degree has been somewhat successful in instituting reforms and in building some sections of the wall, all of which can benefit America. If you are really interested in this nation, her well-being and her future, and that of you and your family, it is best to become fully aware of the existing realities that play out in this country every day and not put trust in the rhetoric spun and spewed by the domestic enemies, then take lawful effective action, as you can, to lawfully stop these traitors from destroying America and all that she once was. See Section 17 for a brief summary of our Constitutional methods.

CHAPTER FIFTEEN

AMERICA'S UN-CONSTITUTIONAL COURT SYSTEM

Our reasonable, rational observers might believe, initially, that given all of the un-Constitutional, unhealthy, repressive, dangerous and harmful actions committed by governments against their own people, then a proper resolution could be achieved by and through the courts. If our observer and our analytical computer were to put this belief to a factual test, they would both conclude that, unfortunately, this belief is far from true. As any Citizen who has had any dealings with the courts in America, either speaking for him or herself or through an attorney, likely knows, those courts are abjectly corrupt, un-Constitutional and dispense injustice, rather than uphold justice for all, as the Constitution requires.

President Trump has vociferously spoken of the "D.C. Swamp", yet swamps exist not only in Washington, D.C., but in every political jurisdiction in this nation. We call them putrid, festering, gigantic cesspools, filled with the worst vermin and slime possible—infecting everyone and everything they touch, which epitomize the typical American politician and government officer/ employee. No one gets a pass on this. Even the so-called "good persons" holding government positions know that they are serving with slime, yet uphold the actions of that slime for their positions and self-benefit. It comes down to the fact that those who support, aid and abet evil are evil, themselves. We could all play word games here and rationalize anything, but the honest, serious reader knows exactly of what we speak.

The corrupt, un-Constitutional courts certainly qualify for this description. Rather than upholding and defending the Constitution, as Constitutionally mandated, thereby upholding the secured rights and due process provisions *guaranteed* to the American people, the corrupt courts, by and through the unlawful actions of the judges and other personnel, purposefully obliterate those Rights and provisions, as their routine customs, practices and policies. Of course, this is all covertly and discreetly done, not an announced official policy. One of the common mistakes most Americans make, as they go to court in order to speak for themselves, is the fact that they go to court! American Citizens naively expect justice and fairness, but are quickly dealt a dish of rancid injustice. Another mistake Citizens typically make is to hire an attorney to speak for them, and in so doing, they are considered to be wards of the state, incompetent and incapable of speaking on their own behalf. Further, one of the former chief justices of the United States Supreme Court called 75% of attorneys in this country corrupt or incompetent. Attorneys owe their allegiance to the *system*, and not necessarily to their clients, thus often do not represent the best interests of their clients, especially when those interests conflict with or threaten the best interests of the system to which they are beholden for their livelihoods.

Americans who speak for themselves before a court usually have unrealistic expectations of prevailing, because, since they believe their cause is just, they expect the court will agree and award them victory, either through a decision from a judge or a jury. This is a very misguided notion and one who so believes is fully unaware of the ugly realities governing the corrupt court system operating throughout America. Unfortunately, most people *think* they know more than they actually know. A huge difference exists between knowing what one knows and thinking what one knows. Many people who speak for themselves before the court use government-designed methods presented to Citizens purportedly as the way to prevail against unjust government, corporations or errant individuals working in government. Again, nothing could be further from the truth. Those who employ such tactics usually quickly lose.

The rare Citizens who employ Constitutional methods in court, for the most part, are not fully aware of the full impact of the power and authority of the Constitution(s), national and state, nor how to properly present Constitutional arguments, both in writing and orally, to the court. Citizens who speak for themselves before the court must fully embrace the Constitutional concept at all times and must hold the presiding judge and the opposing attorney to the strict Constitutional mandates imposed upon them by and their oaths. Once again, there is a big difference between thinking one knows and *knowing* one knows. If Citizens are not properly vested in the Constitution(s), with full knowledge of their power and authority, and are unable to properly base their arguments in and support them in that power and authority before the court, the court will essentially ignore the arguments and likely admonish the Citizens for making Constitutional presentations. While Citizens may not be professionally adept in presenting the Constitutional arguments and positions, at least they tried. Please note that the court is Constitutionally MANDATED to uphold the Constitution(s) and the inherent Rights and Due Process they guarantee to the Citizens. While Citizens may not present a professional caliber argument based in Constitutional positions, the mere fact that they have claimed and exercised their Constitutionally secured rights should evoke Constitutional compliance from the court. In today's court system, however, it does not, because right across the board, wherever the courts are located, federal, state, county or local, their routine customs, practices and policies are to ignore the Constitutions and prevent such arguments from being used in "their" courts. Instead of being courts of justice, the American courts are courts of injustice, which purposely disparage and prohibit the Constitution(s) at every opportunity. These practices and policies war against the Constitution(s). They are utterly criminal and an absolute national disgrace on the part one of the three branches of government created by the Constitution to provide the people a way to present their grievances and receive remedy. These un-Constitutional tribunals, masquerading as courts, make a mockery of our Constitutional Republic and harm our nation and the American people. By their own actions, the other two branches are equally un-Constitutional, as are all state and local governments. Reality is reality and fantasy is fantasy. We prefer reality and we wish many more Americans did as well.

Most Citizens who speak for themselves before the court do not use the *authority* of the Constitution(s), nor Constitutional arguments at all. Since readers who previously did not know now know that the Constitution is the Supreme Law of this Land, therefore, the **superseding authority** over any other form of lesser law, it would seem prudent for American Citizens to use this supreme authority to support their arguments and protect and lawfully enforce their rights against errant governments and corrupt courts. Unfortunately, the overwhelming majority use various other methods and arguments that emanate from so-called "patriot groups" which are based more in myth and theory than in practice and reality. Theory and fantasy and unsupported arguments do not go well for Citizens in America's court system. In order for arguments to be valid and effective, it is best that they be based in and on Constitutional authority, truth, fact, valid law and evidence germane to the merits and arguments of their cases. Unfortunately, most Citizens who speak for themselves before the system's courts do not present such support for their arguments, whether they are written or oral. Many of these Citizens are caught up with these so-called "patriot" mythology and methodologies which work against their best interests due to the flawed nature of the arguments, themselves. Some of the positions endemic to "patriot material" are the "get even" approach and the unrealistic demand for great sums of money in compensation for alleged wrongdoing committed against them by government agents. Our objective observer and analytical computer could quickly conclude that such arguments do not result in wins for the Citizens, with extremely rare exceptions. It would seem prudent for those who claim to be "patriots" to use the *true* Law, namely, the Supreme Law of this Land, our national Constitution, rather than the standard shill "patriot" myths and methods that work against the best interests of the Citizens. While some positions in that mythology may have some validity, few American Citizens have any ability to hold the court to the Constitutional applications regarding those positions.

Margy and I and our students over the decades have never been so based, when we go to court. Our position and that of our true followers has always been to obtain justice and to hold all government officers/employees responsible to the specific Constitutional mandates imposed upon them by and through their oaths and accountable for their offenses in violation of these Constitutional requirements. The question then becomes, why would such flawed argumentation be advanced by a so-called "patriot community" when those arguments and positions do not benefit the Citizens? A further question could be asked, which is, "Who benefits?" If the government or some governmental ally in the power forces is the one who benefits by the Citizens' use of these flawed methods, and not the Citizens, then a further question arises as to what was the real intention of the so-called "patriot" who introduced or suggested that form of methodology or argument? Whose interests was he really protecting and whom does he really serve?

We have attempted to demonstrate in this CHAPTER and throughout this book that the governments, federal, state, county and local, do not serve the interests of the people at all and do not abide by the Constitutional mandates imposed upon them by Law, by and through their oaths. In fact, the customary routine of virtually all governments is to do the exact opposite. By now, the reader knows that government routinely acts outside of the mandates imposed on it by and through the Constitution(s) and, further, assumes authority not delegated. Still further, government routinely acts outside the lawful scope of its duties and authority. The fact that over 99% + of the American people do not know this is a total disaster for America and what remains of our Constitutional Republic. America's courts are no exception and they are a shameful disgrace, primarily because the courts are *supposed* to be the lawful arena to which Citizens turn to have injustices stopped, overturned and remedied. Whenever there is a Constitutional violation, Americans are guaranteed a Constitutional remedy, but, unfortunately, this rarely, if ever, occurs in what has become of America's court system, especially for the Citizen who speaks for him or herself, unrepresented by attorney.

Sam Adams once cautioned the people of his time to beware of the "Sunshine Patriot". That was good advice, and along with that position, one might be cautious of one who calls him or herself a "patriot" when that so-called "patriot" does not use the Supreme Law and the lawful authority of the Constitution(s) for the underlying basis of all his/her argumentation presented before the court. True patriots, true supporters of the Constitution(s) and true supporters of our Constitutional Republic immerse themselves in all of these lawful positions, and little to nothing else, unless that something else is fully supported by our Constitution(s) and serves to advance their positions, the merits of their case and justice, itself.

One of the key positions held in our Declaration of Independence is that *government of right serves with the consent of the governed*. Sane, awake and aware people do not voluntarily consent to the un-Constitutional, criminal actions of an un-Constitutional, criminal government. It has long been held that government must act only within the LIMITED delegated scope of its duties and authority, as set forth in the Constitution(s), national and state. In the absence of that authority, the actions of the government are un-Constitutional, therefore unlawful, thus, invalid, without any lawful force and effect upon the people. However, it is up to the people to understand this and lawfully enforce this position, because a corrupt, un-Constitutional government will never correct itself.

Just as government unlawfully and outrageously spies upon the people, government through its accustomed practices routinely denies the Rights of the people at virtually every opportunity. This is quite evident in our federal, state, county and local court systems. This judicial branch of government is supposed to be the lawful arbiter of disputes among parties when those parties cannot resolve their disputes among themselves. However, in opposition to the Constitutional requirements imposed upon the courts, the courts are typically quite disdainful and disrespectful not only of the people who come before them, but also the Rights and Due Process guaranteed to the people. Just as there are various "clubs" in government, such as the "Senate Club", "House of Representative Club", "White House Club" and "good ole boy club", the courts have their own "club" and the Citizens are not participating and invited parties.

Courts have their own ways and procedures, rules and policies, and while it is obvious that there must be some lawful, ordered procedures, rules and policies, it should be evident that in our Constitutional Republic, all of these should be based in Constitutional authority. However, they are not so based, with rare exception. As previously stated, the first mistake Citizens make is to go to court, especially if they speak for themselves and more especially if they are not well versed in the Constitution(s) and the Rights and Due Process secured therein. Citizens' uninformed, naïve assessment of what they believe will occur in the court system is not found in the existing realities operative within our courts. In fact, their dreams of a just, satisfying court victory frequently turn into their worst nightmares. Earlier, we spoke of people who speak for themselves before the court and who mistakenly base their positions in what essentially is nonsense and misinformation. These cases are usually quickly decided against the Citizens, because the Citizens did not present their arguments in the authority of the Constitution(s), in truth, valid law and evidence, and did not hold the court to any Constitutional compliance whatsoever.

Margy and I and our true followers are well aware of government's traditional un-Constitutional actions and its strenuous opposition to Constitutionally secured Rights. Based upon this reality, we have established certain procedures that protect our Constitutions, our inherent Rights guaranteed therein and Due Process of Law any time we encounter government in any capacity. When we and our people find it necessary to go to court, we always speak for ourselves and never hire attorneys to speak for us. We are fully cognizant of the adverse, hostile, un-Constitutional forum that we are entering. If American Citizens who speak for themselves are not aware of this, then they might reconsider going to court at all or, in the alternative, fully vest themselves in the true realities that have corrupted our court system, before ever stepping foot in any courtroom. If they fail to do this, then their efforts will likely be futile, no matter the merits of their cases. The American people must shed their naivety and fully realize that the court will not automatically uphold any of the Citizens' Constitutionally secured Rights and/or Due Process of Law, even though it is Constitutionally mandated to do so. Just as the governments across America do not uphold Constitutionally secured Rights and Due Process, neither do the courts. It is always up to the Citizens to politely, but firmly, lawfully demand that all government officers, including judges, abide by their oaths in the performance of their official duties. If the Citizens do not do this, then, barring some miracle, none of their Constitutionally secured inherent Rights and Due Process of Law will be upheld.

In our court situations, as soon as the judge convenes the court and asks all parties if they are ready to proceed, our first answer is "No, there are some matters we want to clarify before we can proceed." The judge usually tells us to go right ahead or may ask us what they are. We immediately say the following: "Sir, you and the opposing attorney have taken oaths to support and defend the national and state Constitutions. Is this correct?" Since judges are never pressed on their oaths in this manner, they are totally unaccustomed and unprepared for this statement and the confirming question following it. What we have done is make a statement that is based in

Constitutional authority, truth, fact, valid law and evidence—a statement to which the judge cannot lawfully object. The confirming question follows the statement. The only lawful answer a judge can give is "Yes." As soon as the judge says "Yes" to our confirming question, then we say: "With all due respect, you and the opposing attorney are required to abide by those oaths in the performance of your official duties, especially those before this honorable court." Again, we have made a statement based in Constitutional authority, truth, fact, valid law and evidence. Then, we again ask the confirming question: "Is this correct?" The only lawful answer that can be given by the judge is "Yes." When we receive the "yes" answer to our confirming question, despite all the typical court trappings, the 4-colored flag, subterfuge and deception put forth, we have essentially established an Article III Constitutional court. This court is the Constitutionally ordained court in which civilian Americans can bring their disputes and controversies for just adjudication based in the authority of the Constitution(s). Further, by the judge's affirmative answers, which are on the public record, both the judge and the opposing attorney have confirmed that they must abide by their oaths and uphold all Constitutionally secured Rights and due process of law during this proceeding and any others that follow in this instant case. If Citizens understand the full implications of these Constitutional positions, then they can realize why we and our people have usually won our cases rather quickly.

As stated, and as we believe the reader may now understand, despite all the public lip service they spew, all governments oppose the Constitutions, secured Rights and Due Process of Law as their unwritten policies. If Citizens appear before any governmental body, whether it is administrative, judicial or otherwise, if they are not fully aware of this covert unlawful policy and if they do not prepare to overcome this un-Constitutional policy immediately upon the commencement of that hearing, trial, etc., they will likely lose, and rather quickly. If Citizens do not use our methods or something very similar to them, then they have failed to hold that governmental body to the strict Constitutional mandates imposed upon all government officers/employees, pursuant to their oaths. Thus, in their usual customs, practices and policies, government officers/employees will decimate the Constitution(s), the Rights they uphold and all aspects of Due Process of Law. Over the decades, tens of millions of Americans have learned the hard way that, despite the warm and fuzzy rhetoric to the contrary, government is not the friend of the people. When one hears the phrase, "We're from the government and we're here to help you", the best thing the Citizen can do is to tell them to leave and quickly shut the door. As we mentioned earlier in this book, Margy and I are bottom-line people and in any matter, we first go to that bottom line. With respect to government, no matter what government, that bottom line has consistently proven that all governments act against all Rights of the people, with very rare exceptions. While the federal and virtually all state and local government DO NOT uphold our Constitution, they do uphold, support and enforce the principals of the communist manifesto. Rhetoric to the contrary, actions speak much louder than words. Government is very good at verbally professing certain Constitutional ideals, but completely opposed to and destructive of these ideals in its actions.

As the reader can see, by our initial statements, we have held not only the judge, but also the opposing attorney to Constitutional requirements by which they are obligated to uphold all Constitutionally secured Rights and all aspects of Due Process of Law. We never address the opposing attorney when posing these positions to the judge. It is the judge who answers in the affirmative both for himself and for our opposing attorney, thus, they are both bound to uphold the Constitution(s) throughout the proceedings. Obviously, the opposing attorney does not want to be so bound, but he has no choice in the matter because it is the judge who affirmed his Constitutional obligations, and on the public record. If either the judge or the opposing attorney were to go out of Constitutional or due process compliance, we immediately bring them back to the judge's affirmations regarding their oaths and their duties thereunder, all stated on the public record. If people know how to use the authority of the Constitution(s) against the un-Constitutional actions of any absolutely derelict court, and hold both the judge and the opposing attorney to strict Constitutional mandates, then they can usually win their cases rather quickly, that is, if the cases have lawful merits.

When we pose our statements to the judge, no judge in his right mind would ever answer "No" to the confirming questions. If he did so, then he would be committing sedition and treason on the public record, because in so doing, he is warring against the Constitution(s). In our long involvement with the political system and courts, we have found that most judges are intensely corrupt, but not necessarily stupid, which is why no sane judge would answer "No." Some judges may try to distract, which is a common court ploy. If the Citizens are led away from their positions because of the distraction, then they have forever lost those positions. We always stay on our point and do not allow ourselves to be taken to any other point, under any circumstances. When a judge tries to distract, defer or change the subject, because he does not want to answer in the affirmative, then we say something along the following lines. "Sir, it appears as though, by your responses that you either have not taken an oath or will not abide by your oath in the performance of your official duties. Our Constitution is the Supreme Law of this Land, and if you fail to confirm your oath to that Supreme Law which governs this court, then you are hereby unfit to serve on the bench, thus are disqualified, and your actions have rendered this court Constitutionally defective, incompetent and in violation of due process of law. You are hereby lawfully disqualified. Step down." The judge's duty here is very clear. He could not serve on the bench had he not taken an oath to support and defend the Constitution(s). All Citizens are guaranteed not only their Constitutionally secured Rights, but also Due Process of Law. When a judge fails to confirm his oath, his actions render that court Constitutionally defective, without lawful jurisdiction, because it is a violation of due process of law for a judge to sit on the bench unless he has taken an oath, affirms it and abides thereby. By now, the judge knows that he is dealing with entities who know more than he does, could harm himself, and steps down. Due Process requires this. If the people all over this nation learn how to protect themselves and their Rights, then we would have specific Constitutional compliance from the courts and America would be a far better nation.

Once the affirmative answers have been given by the judge, we then make the following statement before the court. "I appear before this court by special appearance, as a living, breathing, flesh and blood man (woman) on the land, an American Citizen, with and claiming all of my natural, inherent, unlimited, unalienable rights and due process guaranteed to me in the Constitutions, and I appear before this court with my name spelled properly and lawfully only in upper and lower case letters. Is there any objection to what I just stated?" No one can object to this statement, because the statement is based in Constitutional authority, truth, fact, valid law and evidence. Since no one objects, then our statement before the court stands as truth and fact, on the record. This statement verifies our lawful status before the court and dispels and counters any fraud, presumptions and deceptions ordinarily used by the court against Citizens in its usual customs, practices and policies. For instance, most courts fly 4-color flags, with gold fringe on the outline of the flag, or with gold braids or tassels, or with a gold ball or eagle on top. The flag indicates the jurisdiction of the court and a 4-colored flag indicates an administrative, legislative or a military court, and not a judicial court of Constitutional competence under Article III. Of course, this deception is not lawful, but this is how the system routinely defrauds the unknowing people. Another position that the system typically uses is all capital letters for the name of the Citizen, and in its deception, the court considers the all capital name to be a *corporation*, not a human being, with only limited rights and privileges as accorded by the government. What is granted by the government can also be withdrawn by the government. What is guaranteed by the Constitution(s) can never be withdrawn by anyone for any LAWFUL reason. Again, if the Citizen is very knowledgeable of the Constitution(s) and all their aspects, the Constitutional requirements that restrain public officials, and the fact that all opponents, including the judge, must be able to Constitutionally support their arguments and positions, which most cannot do at all, then the Citizen should easily be able to win his or her meritorious case.

This type of Constitutional approach can be used in any type of government hearing, meeting, confrontation, whether it is administrative, legislative or otherwise. All officers of all governments, having sworn or affirmed oaths to support and defend the Constitution(s) are vulnerable to those oaths, must abide by them, or they are not lawfully fit to hold office. Citizens would be well advised to beware of government confrontations and, further, to be fully aware that government will oppose and deny all secured Rights and all aspects of Due Process of Law, unless the Citizen stands solidly upon the supreme authority of the Constitution(s) and lawfully challenges that governmental body pursuant to Constitutional requirements. As we have said many times, "if" is a small word with a huge meaning, but if the people of America started using these types of Constitutional challenges, not only in court, but in all scenarios in which the people appear before any form of government, and if the people really understand their full authority and the full authority of the Constitution(s), they could stop and correct the un-Constitutional, unlawful actions of government quickly. Most of us know that success begets further success and successes multiply because others use the same methods that gained the successes for the initial users. This is how small, individual changes can become gigantic movements.

Here are a few other comments for anyone planning to go to court. All courts are Constitutionally required to uphold all aspects of Due Process of Law, yet despite this requirement, very few courts uphold any aspects of Due Process, as it pertains to the Citizens. To the contrary, courts uphold all Constitutional rights and all due process provisions when it comes to government, the elite, major corporations and the power forces. Obviously, there is a major bias here. When a Citizen is a defendant before the court and the court violates any aspect of Due Process of Law, as mentioned previously, that court has lawfully forfeited any jurisdiction. The only lawful authority that court possesses is to dismiss the case before it, based upon a well-pleaded motion by the defendant in which he demonstrates the due process violations which occurred. Along these same lines, one of the rare federal laws we have used is found in Title 28 U.S.C. Section 2072(b). This rare law—rare because it upholds Constitutional positions—prohibits bias and wrong usage of court rules to favor one party over another, since it does not allow the rules of procedure to be used to restrict, modify or enlarge the substantive rights of any party to any proceeding. When Citizens are defendants and encounter bias and/or attempts by their opponents or the court to limit or restrict their rights, or attempts to enlarge the rights of their opponents, then they can cite this law, if in federal court, or the state corollary if in state or local court, as the governing authority which supports his rights to Due Process of law. As stated above, the Due Process violations apply, but must be cited.   Most people who go to court are totally unaware of these positions; therefore, do not use them, thus, never gain from them.

When Citizens are defendants in any matter, and speak for themselves before the court, their opponent will usually make claims and charges that are unsupported by truth, fact, valid law and evidence. This does not happen in 100% of cases, but the percentage is rather high, especially in criminal cases. We always challenge claims and charges made by our opponent and demand that those claims and charges be fully supported by truth, fact, valid law and evidence, and if they are not so supported, then they are bogus, fraudulent claims and charges, without any validity whatsoever. Therefore, we move that those charges be dismissed, with prejudice. Most people will not argue these positions because they lack the knowledge to challenge the validity of the charges and instead will try to defend themselves against these bogus, fraudulent charges which have no validity at all. Citizens would better serve themselves if they made themselves aware of all Constitutional positions, all Constitutional authority and all Constitutional requirements imposed upon their opponents, and the courts, by and through oaths taken, before they ever go to court or appear before any governmental body for any reason.

When one considers the following, namely, American Citizens going before courts and governmental bodies, completely unprepared for the realities of the court or administrative hearings, and totally unprepared to argue their cases, it is clear why all of these factors result in Citizens' losses. This is not only detrimental for those who lose, but also detrimental for the entire society, because it indicates to government that the people are unprepared, ignorant of the law, ignorant about the Constitution(s), their inherent Rights, Due Process, the Constitutional mandates and limitations imposed upon government and courts, and the ugly governing realities operative in America. These losses and the continuing losses by Citizens are absolutely harmful to the American society, yet tremendously beneficial for government and the power forces. We, as the American people comprising the American society, must stem these failures and start gaining victories based upon Constitutional knowledge and the lawful upholding of the inherent Rights of the Citizens. Government will never do this for the people, even though it has the Constitutional requirement to do so, because we as a people have failed to hold government and courts to their Constitutional mandates. We, the people, must do this for ourselves.

As referenced earlier, at the end of this CHAPTER we provide a few of our Constitutional methods which we use any time we encounter controversy with government or corporations, whether in or out of court. One of the positions we have successfully used for many years is to actually get our governmental or corporate opponents to tacitly admit to and agree with all of our charges and claims that we make against them before we even go to court. These admissions are invaluable to the Citizen and they have enormous, lawful weight before the court. Any time our opponents agree with us, then, the matter in controversy has been decided in our favor, by and through their agreement. Since courts convene to hear matters in controversy, when our opponents admit to our charges and agree with our positions, then no matter in controversy exists for the court to hear and, lawfully, the victory should be ours. This is further explained in the referenced section presented later in this CHAPTER.

Some of you may be familiar with the Bundy case which was tried in federal court in Las Vegas, Nevada. This case arose from the government's unlawful actions regarding the Bundys' cattle, grazing rights and land owned by the Bundy family for generations. Some of the Bundys and their followers were arrested by the federal government, jailed under cruel and unusual conditions for well over a year and eventually tried in federal court. At first the Bundys used lawyers and the typical defensive government-designed arguments, *theoretically* intended to defeat government, which, of course, never do. They were facing serious jeopardy and some defendants went to jail, mostly on plea bargains. It was only when the Bundys finally turned their attention to the Constitution, to Rights guaranteed therein, Due Process of Law and Constitutional mandates imposed upon all government officers, by and through their oaths, that they started gaining ground. On January 8th, 2018, the woman acting as federal district judge dismissed the case against the Bundys et al, with prejudice, based upon egregious due process violations committed by the federal prosecution and the government. The term "with prejudice" means that the government cannot bring these charges against the Bundys and their co-defendants, ever again. The American court system is notoriously corrupt, but when one is well vested in all aspects of the Constitution(s) and able to succinctly present Constitutional arguments, s/he can win. We and our students have won numerous victories for the people, both in and out of court, over many decades against intensely corrupt governments, courts and corporations. As stated, a brief summation of some of our methods is presented in CHAPTER 8, along with our website information.

IS AMERICA'S ALLEGED "PUBLIC DEBT" CONSTITUTIONAL OR FRAUDULENT?

O ur public debt is currently alleged to be about 30 plus trillion dollars, and growing rapidly, which is another staggering amount of money. Much of this debt is owed to the private Federal Reserve Bank and to foreign entity note holders by and through sales of notes from the bank to those investors. Increasing numbers of Americans are quickly becoming aware that the Federal Reserve simply prints money out of thin air, with no backing, then, loans that printed money to the U.S. government, which is then required to repay those funds, plus interest. Of course, the government pays nothing back, because all debt payments are made by and through the efforts of the people. Our rational observer and analytical computer might conclude that this scheme was one of the biggest acts of piracy ever devised by malevolent forces in the history of this world. Simple common sense would indicate that for any government to allow a private, for-profit bank to print money with nothing of value backing it, then, allow that bank to lend that unbacked money to the government, at interest, all of which must be repaid by the American people through their skills and labors, is not only insane, but also insidious. Our rational observer and analytical computer could determine that it would be far simpler, wiser and cost effective for the government to print its own money, thus with no debt owed by the people to that private bank. This would provide a position for the people to exercise their political control over the government rather than allow a government in league with the private central bank to be in control of America's economy, the lives and fate of the people and the destiny of the nation. Control is a vital element within human society and he who controls wields enormous power. That power can be for good or for evil. When power is unconstrained, and absolute, executed without limitation, then, that power reverts to evil. As Lord Acton said long ago, "Power corrupts and absolute power corrupts absolutely."

However, when the ultimate power is placed in the hands of the people, rather than the power forces themselves, a much more egalitarian process develops and evolves for the betterment of the entire society. Of course, this type of process would not be conducive to the financial interests and ultimate control of the Federal Reserve Bank, those who own and control it, and the government, itself, but would be of immense interest and benefit to the public. As stated, that public bears the responsibility for repayment of all debt to the Federal Reserve Bank and the other debt holders, but has absolutely no say in how the debt is derived, where the funds go and who benefits from this nefarious scheme of financial violence inflicted upon the people. Additionally, neither Congress nor the President has any say about any of these vital financial decisions. The Fed has been unlawfully given absolute autonomy over all such matters and this fact is totally and completely un-Constitutional. Yet the existence of the Fed and its continuation is permitted by each and every Congress and President since the inception of this nefarious, sinister private central bank. When Congress un-Constitutionally abdicated its responsibilities, powers and duties and unlawfully granted these powers to the Fed, it created a financial monster that has economically devoured this country ever since. Yet, as stated above, each Congress and each President since then has maintained the unlawful power of the Fed over the nation and her people. It is way past time for the people to recognize the existing realities controlling them and begin to lawfully enforce the authority of the Constitution against un-Constitutional actions committed by domestic-enemy governments and begin the road back to Constitutional governance in America. The alternative is total disaster and total control, without any possible recuperation of anything for the people, including their inherent rights.

Copious information is available regarding the alleged workings and machinations of the Federal Reserve Bank and its creation of money out of thin air. The Internet is a very valuable source for information, but one must be careful when doing research to vet the information for its validity. A good initial source is a publication put out by the Federal Reserve Bank, entitled *Modern Money Mechanics,* in which basic information is presented about the creation of money. For a deeper, more in-depth look, one can read the excellent book, *The Creature from Jekyll Island,* by G. Edward Griffin, or another fine book, *Secrets of the Temple,* by Eustace Mullins. The former is an easier narrative presented in uncomplicated language. The latter is much more detailed and rather complicated. The exact how and why of the inner workings of this private central bank, in collaboration with our government, in collaboration with other private central banks throughout the world and in collaboration with member banks throughout our nation are matters that are not well publicized, thus not widely known by the people. Since the people bear ultimate responsibility for all public debt, then all workings of the Federal Reserve Bank should be published, promulgated and made known to the people in easily accessible ways. All operations of the bank should be fully transparent, without any secrecy, whatsoever. Truth and reality are subjects that are not greatly respected and, in fact, are feared by "insider operators" within government and the banks, whose shadowy policies and procedures affect each and every one of us every single day. In a true Constitutional republic, all truths regarding any government approved entity should be readily revealed and available to the people.

Unfortunately, the people, as a society, are so far removed from the actual workings of the Federal Reserve Bank and our government, that our society has made no demands upon these entities to print all information regarding the full operations of this all-powerful, private central bank. For instance, when Ben Bernanke was chairman of the Federal Reserve Bank, he appeared before a congressional committee in which Ron Paul, former Republican congressman from Texas, asked Bernanke if the Fed had granted bailout funds to foreign central banks and other foreign banks. Bernanke hesitated to answer, then, said "Yes." When Ron Paul asked Bernanke if he would reveal the names of those banks, Bernanke said "No." Bernanke's answers not only reveal the arrogance of the Bank, but also the absolute power the Bank possesses over the government and the people.

As we said above, and as most people know, *power* is a vital force in human society used by the power forces to obtain what they want, usually at the expense of the entire society and the nation, itself. Ultimate power uses its power ruthlessly against the powerless to bring everyone and everything under the control of that power. Unchecked and uncontrolled power is an absolute danger to the people of a nation and to that nation, itself. When the chairman of the Federal Reserve Bank pays trillions of U.S. dollars to foreign central banks and other foreign banks, without any explanation regarding the reasons for dispensing those funds and the amounts of those funds, and further refuses to reveal any information regarding those funds to Congress, then all of this strenuously indicates where and in whom the real power in this nation resides. Since the amounts of these funds paid to foreign banks were undisclosed to the congressmen who are required to represent the people, the question becomes how many other vast sums have been paid out by the Federal Reserve Bank to other banks, corporations and/or unknown power forces? The disturbing answer is that the American people and their Congress apparently do not know, yet it appears that the American people are on the hook for those unauthorized, undisclosed paid funds. Per the Constitution, all spending bills must begin in the House of Representatives, but when members of that House asked the chairman of the Fed about huge amounts of funds the Fed paid to foreign banks and other entities, that House Committee was stonewalled. It would appear that the authority for those funds paid by the Fed to those foreign entities did not originate in a spending bill passed by the House. As we mentioned numerous times in this book, the word "authority" is of vital importance to any situation. In our Constitutional republic, either Constitutional authority exists for an action, or payment, or it does not. Upon what Constitutional authority were these payments made? Because of the secrecy involved, it certainly appears that any such authority for such payments was not based in the Constitution or any other valid lawful authority. Our reasonable observer and analytical computer could well question how many other huge payments have been made by this Bank to other unnamed recipients.

As mentioned earlier, Catherine Austin Fitts has made known to the public that other monumentally large amounts of money, in the trillions, either "went missing" or were "unaccounted for" by government. She spoke of the over 2 trillion that was "lost" by the DOD, the investigation of which was conveniently stopped by the suspected missile that slammed into the Pentagon on 911. She also spoke of approximately 21 trillion that went missing in HUD and one other federal agency. In addition to these figures, her research indicates that over 40 trillion dollars is "missing" or "unaccounted for" in other government activities. Mind you, these enormous sums are only the amounts that have been discovered and presently known. What about the amounts which are as yet undiscovered, thus unknown? How enormously high are they? Remember, all spending bills must originate in the House of Representatives. It is doubtful that the authority for the mind-boggling amount of trillions of dollars that are "missing or unaccounted for" originated in spending bills in the House of Representatives. However, even if some of them did, the resulting "missing money" and/or "unaccounted funds" clearly indicate that the allocated monies were not spent as authorized and provided for in the bills. Again, the word "authority" enters the picture. Upon whose or what Constitutional or other valid authority did these funds originate and who or what was required to track these funds from their inception to their final spending? Our objective observer and analytical computer could easily state that no such Constitutional or other valid authority existed for the lawful expenditure and payment of such vast, monumental sums. Truth, transparency and openness should be the mark of our Constitutional republic, but unfortunately, "should be's" are not present in the operational realities existent within this nation. Money is the moving element of any society and vast enormous amounts of money—in the trillions—provide stupendous power to those who control, receive, expend and/or retain those funds. Since the people are ultimately held responsible for the government's debt and likely held responsible for payment of these "missing funds" as well, then truth, transparency and justice would demand that all information regarding all of these "missing funds", known or unknown—and we mean *all*—should be revealed to the American people by the government and the private central bank. Because apparent secrecy has shrouded the mystery of these "missing funds", then anyone can easily conclude that neither the government nor the Bank has or will reveal the truth to the American people. This, alone, says quite a bit as to how the government and the private central bank regard the American people.

The terms "missing funds" and "unaccounted funds" mean exactly that—funds that are nowhere to be found in government's accounting system, with no record of how they were dispensed, by whom and for what purposes. In plain English, we have no idea where the money went, to whom it went, why it was spent and how it was used. Given the fact that the funds are "missing and unaccounted for" and the process under which they became so, could these vast amounts, possibly totaling in the high trillions, have been used for nefarious purposes, illegal, unjust, criminal purposes? In the alternative, do you think that these "missing and unaccounted for" funds could have been used for beneficial purposes, serving the best interests of humanity and highly devised egalitarian pursuits? Since apparently no proper accounting records exist demonstrating how these funds were spent, by whom and for what purposes, it doesn't take much brain power to deduce that none of them were used for beneficial, humanitarian, egalitarian pursuits. If that were the case, then the government would have shouted to the rooftops about their beneficial humanitarian projects! To the contrary, the irresponsible lack of accounting records for these funds, and the secrecy under which they were spent, suggest it is much more likely that they were used for dark, sinister, controlling, tyrannical purposes. What do you think?

Readers are encouraged to do their own research regarding this very powerful, intrusive and secretive private central bank that has ultimate control of our total economy, thus over all Americans. Again, to replay our repetitive theme, which is necessarily stated throughout this book, this private bank unlawfully given "life" by the government does not conform at all with the requirements of our Preamble, our Constitution and the rights and due process guaranteed therein to the people. In 2013, the U.S. government renewed the operations of this private central bank—in spite of the fact that many of the Bank's un-Constitutional and un-American machinations have been revealed to many congresses between the years of 1913 and 2013. Thanks to your government, this Bank has had and continues to have a dominant foreboding presence in this nation and is allowed to unlawfully maintain that pernicious position by a government which has abandoned its lawful duties to represent the best interests of the people and uphold the principles of our Constitutional republic. The ultimate question here is why a so-called self-governing people have never stopped the imposition and operations of this pernicious, unlawful private central bank? The obvious answer to this, as logically concluded by our observer and computer, is that the American people, as a society, have never once exercised their power and duty of self-governance to oversee the machinations of their own elected and appointed machinery of government or of the entities that machinery of government has unlawfully created and imposed upon the American people. This is a tragedy of epic proportions and will continue to be so unless these criminal, un-Constitutional abuses by the U.S. government are lawfully stopped by the people of this nation.

CHAPTER SEVENTEEN

IMMIGRATION or *INVASION* – ANOTHER GOVERNMENT ATTACK UPON AMERICA AND HER PEOPLE

Immigration is quite justifiably a major focal point in America right now and has been for many years. Illegal entry into this nation is just what it states—*ILLEGAL ENTRY!* Everyone who entered the country illegally is breaking the law and should be immediately deported with sanctions and fines imposed upon the countries from which they entered. This is the valid, lawfully based opinion which many Americans hold and which laws the government is lawfully required to enforce but, as we have seen right along, government does not enforce its own laws when those laws benefit the American people. Immigration in general is not necessarily beneficial for the nation that allows the immigration. The wishes of the people of such a nation which permits immigration should be respected by the government of that nation. However, as is painfully obvious by now, the U.S. government and most other governments do as they please, despite or in spite of the wishes of the people. People have witnessed with incredulity the lawlessness of many of the immigrants coming into European nations and are horrified by the massive problems this unchecked immigration is causing in many European cities. While some form of lawful immigration may be valid, excessive, un-vetted immigration, primarily from third world countries into America, is totally invalid, without lawful authority, un-Constitutional and not in keeping with the Preamble to our Constitution, in particular, the requirements for domestic tranquility and justice, nor the rights of the American people. The unchecked illegal entry and un-vetted rapid immigration of unskilled people from third world countries has been allowed for generations by the U.S. government, resulting in the very serious problems America now faces from the government's insane, one-world, communist policies. There is ample information to demonstrate that some illegal entrants and un-vetted immigrants have raped and killed American Citizens and committed numerous other serious crimes throughout the country. A recheck of the Preamble to the Constitution will inform the Citizen that the government is required to protect the domestic tranquility and uphold the general welfare, meaning the well-being, peace and safety of the people of this nation. The government has absolutely defied these Constitutional requirements by not only allowing, but also encouraging illegal entry and unchecked immigration.

As stated earlier, *government of right* serves with the consent of the governed. Conversely, government of wrong operates dictatorially, without and in defiance of the consent of the governed, as does the U.S. government. When the governed do not consent to a government policy, but the government continues and expands such policy, then obviously that government is not a government of right. This is a very simple, direct Constitutional position which most people can easily understand and with which they can agree. The government of this nation is required, by Constitutional mandates, and by oaths taken to that Constitution, to be a subservient force to the will of the people, and in that servant role, to promote the best interests of the people and the nation. If America is to have an immigration policy, then clearly that policy should be consistent with the will of the people and reflect positions that are advantageous to the people and to the nation. An open-ended, "Y'all come in!" policy defies all of these requirements, as well as the many valid laws on the books that were intended to properly regulate and wisely limit immigration. An immigration policy which allows unrestricted entry by unskilled third world immigrants into America, when some of them are criminals, most of them are indigent, many are uneducated, unable to speak English, and immediately go on welfare and Medicaid, is definitely not in the best interests of the American people and America, herself. These unskilled immigrants, with no prospects of supporting themselves with jobs become a burden on the public when they receive enormous financial and other benefits from the U.S. and state governments on the backs of the American people.

There is an appallingly sharp contrast to the benefits truly needy Americans receive, in contrast with the enormous immediate benefits which unskilled immigrants receive, whether here legally or illegally. A large number of these needy Americans are the elderly, the disabled, veterans, the young, those willing to work, but who cannot find decent jobs, all of whom have contributed all their lives economically and otherwise to America's growth and prosperity. Yet, our own government disparages these Americans who have earned their way, while opening financial floodgates to the unskilled immigrants who simply take, but give nothing back to society. This is a reprehensible way for the U.S. government to treat the American people. In fact, it is insane. Would any sane, logical human beings bring indigent, uneducated, unskilled, un-vetted immigrants—who, cannot speak English and have no means to support themselves-- into their homes and, in so doing, force their own children out of their bedrooms, down into their basements, to accommodate the immigrants and expect their children to give their food to the immigrants? Our readers will likely say that such actions would be so unfair as to be crazy, yet, in essence, the immigration policies of the U.S. government are doing the same things to American Citizens. This is only one of numerous examples of how the U.S. government disparages the American people, has little to no respect for them, routinely denies and violates their rights at will, yet, incredibly, provides unlimited aid and sustenance to unskilled foreign immigrants many of whom typically end up becoming parasites upon the American society.

When those who enter America, legally or illegally, rape, kill and murder Americans and commit untold numbers of crimes across the nation, this is not maintaining domestic tranquility and certainly not in the best interests of America and the American people. However, when immigration is fair and open to people of any country and are skilled, law abiding, have funds to sustain themselves and/or jobs promised, thus, will likely be assets to this nation, instead of burdens, then that could be considered a *just, sensible* policy which would likely be supported by most Americans, including us. Most Americans are good, decent, kind people willing to help others and have proven this over and over again, since our nation began. Many of them would accept a sensible, controlled immigration policy that will benefit America, but those same many will not support an unchecked, senseless, intrusive and dangerous policy by those domestic-enemy rulers bent on destroying this nation. Although it seems absolutely inconceivable, our rational, objective observer and our analytical computer must conclude that the U.S. government and the power forces have done their best to destroy our nation in many different ways and to ruin the character of the American people as well as the grounding structures of our society to the extent that those in this society become mindless sheep in the herd, forever directed by government. The herd mentality is antithetical to the principles contained in our Constitution. Any government—federal, state or local—that openly defies the Supreme Law of the Land is a seditious, treasonous government to the people and the nation, a domestic enemy of whom Jefferson spoke in the Declaration of Independence.

Another position to consider is that the rampant immigration policy permitting entry from the unskilled third world which the un-Constitutional U.S. government has for decades actively conducted, encouraged and still supports was covertly designed with the intent that the ongoing influx of immigrants would ultimately destroy the nation, by imposing greater and greater financial burdens and creating escalating forms of chaos and acting as an intruding force to further split and divide our country. Whenever any government becomes destructive to its own Supreme Law and subordinates the rights of the people to its own repressive agenda, then, obviously, that government by and through its own actions, and not its never-ending false rhetoric, undermines the people and their nation. This is treason. Our objective, rational, astute observer and analytical computer would recognize this as a key tactic used by communists worldwide to divide and conquer nations and then insert themselves into power positions to "fix" and control the problems which they, themselves, deliberately created. This is classical communism at work, performed by and starring the un-Constitutional U.S. government, right on the theater of the American stage for all to observe. Aleksandr Solzhenitsyn, the heroic Russian novelist, historian, and short story writer, a courageous, candid critic of communism and the Communist Soviet Union, lamented that while the Russians had the chance to stop the Bolsheviks and the Communists, they mistakenly believed their lies, failed to stop them, eventually succumbed to their brutal dictates and lost their beloved country. If Americans fail to wake up to the insidious covert advancement which communism is rapidly achieving here and do not stop it, then it is we who one day may express the same lament as Solzhenitsyn, as we see our beloved country lost forever.

At the conclusion of the Constitutional Convention in Philadelphia, Benjamin Franklin was asked what had been wrought. His answer was simple: "A republic, if you can keep it." He then snickered and walked away. It is truly unfortunate for this entire nation that the American society, since the inception of our Constitution, has not held its servant governments—federal, state and local—to the Constitutional standards and mandates imposed upon them by the Constitution(s). The people have allowed the governments to tread upon their rights, restrict their freedoms, dispose of justice, instead of dispensing it, and astoundingly, the American people have consistently supported and obeyed these un-Constitutional actions committed by their own governments. In both his Inaugural and State of the Union Addresses, President Trump publicly stated that the American people are the power in this nation and he wants to return that power to the people. This is the first president since John Adams who has ever said this. It is well past the time for the American society to willingly and knowingly take their rightful power, as decreed in the Constitution, and use it lawfully and effectively to bring a halt to the rampant government corruption, abuses, criminal activities, and un-Constitutional actions that have become its routine practice. In this way, the people can begin the road back to Constitutional governance for America and the restoration of our original Constitutional republic, in fact and practice, not just in name.

Governmental actions discussed thus far in this CHAPTER and book clearly indicates that those in power are not to be trusted to rule this nation and her people. The people's trust in government has to be earned by government's performance and the performance by government, with respect to the Constitution, the duties it imposes upon all public officers, and the rights it guarantees to the people, is absolutely abysmal, deplorable, reprehensible, criminal, and should never have been allowed to occur in our Constitutional republic. Our rational, reasonable observer and analytical computer would never trust this type of criminal, corrupt government in any way, whatsoever, and the people of America must now open their eyes and ears to understand the true existing political, economic and social realities that have been unlawfully foisted upon them by their own treacherous, treasonous, domestic-enemy governments. As has been said many times, "They shall be known by their works." It is plainly obvious to our rational, objective observer and his companion computer that the United States government, by and through its own actions, has consistently and relentlessly worked against the best interests of the American people and their nation. Again, this is treason and the American people must realize the vast, insidious extent of the treason and the fact that they must take lawful effective actions to stop it. While many people may disagree with this, a quick review of the facts will reveal that the government has acted in treason against the people, who are the *de jure* government. Some of these facts are as follows: (1) the Constitution for the united States of America, circa 1787, as amended in 1791 with the Bill of Rights, is the declared Supreme Law of this Land, as clearly stated in Article VI of that founding document; (2) all politicians, elected and appointed government officers and all government workers are required by Law to swear or affirm oaths to support and uphold the Constitution(s), national and state; (3) all of these oath takers must abide by their oaths in the performance of their official duties; (4) any action by any oath taker and any act by any legislature either supports and upholds the Constitution(s), national and state, or opposes and violates them; (5) oath takers have no Constitutional or any other form of valid authority to oppose the very documents to which they swore or affirmed their oaths; (6) pursuant to the rights and due process guarantees enshrined in our Constitution(s), including the 9th Amendment guarantees, the American people have the lawful expectation that all government officers, workers, bureaucrats and employees will abide by the above-stated Constitutionally mandated requirements.

All of the above are Constitutional requirements and mandates imposed upon all oath takers. As any reader can see or ascertain, we have spelled out in this CHAPTER and throughout this book numerous instances of Constitutional violations routinely committed by public officers who hold positions in the United States government and in state and local governments. These violations are ongoing, normal customs and practices employed by government, many of which are absolutely egregious and a total affront to America and her people. **Wherever there is a Constitutional violation, there is also a Constitutional remedy for the people.** One of those remedies is found in the self-executing Sections 3 & 4 of the 14th Amendment which essentially state that any oath taker who violates, thus perjures, his oath immediately vacates his office upon the violation and is no longer entitled to any benefits of that former office, including salary and pension. Those, who may not have understood the gravity of Constitutional violations, might now see that Constitutional violations in many cases are treasonous and those who commit the violations are the referenced domestic enemies cited in the Declaration of Independence. If America continues to degenerate as it has since the assassination of President John Fitzgerald Kennedy, on November 22nd, 1963, then it will descend from the Constitutional republic it was intended to be into a communist state, operated by the power forces in America, the New World Order, the Corporate UNITED STATES and the world's central banks. If this happens, then the American experiment will have failed miserably and there will be no such thing as freedom, free speech, free choice or any other freedoms left for the people of this nation. Those in government who strive for this ruinous position are the most heinous of all traitors.

The next section presents a very brief summary of some of the methods we have used for the past six decades to lawfully oppose errant, un-Constitutional governments and corporations, both in and out of court. If these simple, but powerful, methods were to be put into practice by a large segment of the American people, the successes gained would reach others who would likely be willing to participate in the lawful restoration of their own Constitutional republic. In this CHAPTER and throughout this book we have shown that the usual customs, practices and policies conducted by the U.S. government oppose oaths taken by government officers, violate the principles contained in the Preamble to the Constitution, violate and oppose the inherent secured rights guaranteed to the American people, and violate and oppose all aspects of due process of law. As we said above, any act by any government officer either supports and upholds the Constitutions, or opposes and violates them. It is this simple. No oath taker has the Constitutional authority—or any other form of valid, lawful authority—to oppose and violate the very documents to which he swore or affirmed his oath. Again, it is this simple. With all we have stated above and throughout this book, the compelling question is: Are the American people up to the task of restoring, then keeping, their Constitutional republic, or will they continue to see it slip away, just as Ben Franklin warned long ago?

CHAPTER EIGHTEEN

GOVERNMENT CONTROL OF EDUCATION

A s an American child grows up, further government restrictions are typically imposed upon the parents and the child, at the discretion of the government. For instance, if the child becomes ill and a medical question arises as to treatment, and the parents prefer not to treat or to treat in a way different from the way dictated by medical "authorities" and/or government, the medical authorities and the government usually prevail. Most children will enter public school at some point and that school is a government-controlled school with curricula and teachers who impart only what government dictates. Those dictates can greatly vary from the actual truth and the realities existent in this world. This is not the way to truly educate a child! The parents of children in that school have little or no input as to what is taught and how it is taught. If the parents want to home school their child, there are many government restrictions that impose certain compliances upon them, or in some cases prohibit or discourage home schooling, and if the parents do not comply, then the home schooling can come to a sudden end and the child forced into public school or taken away from the parents, who are deemed "unfit". If the parents express religious convictions that do not meet the approval of government authorities, then that home schooling could cease and, again, the child sent to a public school, or may be removed from the home. As mentioned above, the curricula of these public schools are solely at the discretion of the government, and not that of the parents of the children who attend these schools. Subjects and types of teaching methods used could be totally offensive to some parents, but parents' genuine issues and concerns are of no import or concern to an overreaching, out-of-control, dictatorial government. This control locally begins with the teachers, the principals and the school administration, then, extends to the school board, to state authorities and eventually to federal authorities. However, in reality, the control starts at the federal level and extends all the way down to the local level by and through federal government funding which is tied to compliance with federal mandates.

The real Constitutional control is vested in the parents, who should be the architects of what their children learn and how they learn it, and control should not be placed in any governmental "authority" that unlawfully dictates its own policies, which in many cases are antithetical to what the parents want for their children and often undermine what the parents teach their children at home. As many Americans are beginning to realize, much of what is taught in schools today has a collectivist, *communist* bent that is absolutely repugnant and obnoxious to the greater American society and which insidiously subverts the principles of a true Constitutional republic. In our Constitutional republic, the power is vested in the people, yet those who hold positions in all areas of government completely disregard the power, the voices and the concerns of the people, while those so-called "authorities" do exactly what they are told to by *their* higher authorities. This amounts to a pyramidal structure in which the few at the top dictate everything to the many below them and the multitudes at the bottom. Our republic was not designed and intended to operate in this tyrannical manner.

Americans should be totally outraged by now by the fact that our system is upside down, and, thankfully, some people and some groups across the country are taking lawful actions against the un-Constitutional dictates of governments' rampant, unceasing and escalating abuses of authority. Unfortunately, reality unequivocally demonstrates that many people who oppose unlawful governmental use of authority do not know how to organize lawful opposition, then, present their concerns to that government, and further, hold that government to the strict Constitutional mandates imposed upon it, by and through the oaths taken by government officers. Sadly, this is all too common throughout America, and as a result, government does whatever it wants to do, despite the legitimate concerns and wishes of the people that government is supposed to serve. Pursuant to oaths taken, all government authority is automatically required to uphold the rights of the people, heed their voices, and provide all aspects of due process of law. **The authority which was delegated to it by the people is limited in scope, so government's actions are not lawful, not valid, not just, when and if government exceeds the scope of that limited, delegated authority.**

However, as stated many times in this book, government routinely exceeds its lawful authority and defies all aspects of due process and secured rights, by and through its usual customs, practices and policies. This very unfortunate condition, both for the American people and for America, herself, is the direct result of the people's failure and inability to lawfully enforce their

Constitutionally secured rights and all Constitutional mandates upon all forms of government. In truth, much of the blame for the people's failure and inability to stop governments' misuse of authority must be laid at the feet of the astounding ignorance of most Americans regarding how government in this Constitutional republic is supposed to work. By this we mean, that most people do not understand that it is the people who are the real government, and as such, it is they who choose who will operate the machinery of government that makes possible day to day operations in an orderly fashion, and further, it is the people who are charged with the duty to oversee these operations. If and when wrongdoing, errors and abuses of power and authority occur, it is the **duty** of the people to stop and correct them, as well as to remove the offenders and lawfully punish them accordingly. These actions epitomize the very essence of self-governance. Most Americans have no understanding of this, whatsoever, therefore they do not exercise self-governance, responsibility, duty and their own political power. One of our purposes in writing this book was to help the people understand the existing realities as to how governments and banks operate in this nation, versus how they are supposed to operate. Once the people comprehend the sinister machinations within these systems, then the people could, if they truly understand and "own" their political power, take lawful effective actions to stop the criminal, un-Constitutional abuse of power by any and all forms of government, thereby begin to restore our Constitutional republic, as originally intended by our founders.

History is a subject that has been greatly manipulated by the power forces for eons. It has been said forever that the victors write the history and this is absolutely correct. Just as in war, when the truth becomes the first casualty, the truth also becomes the first casualty when selective, revised, fabricated "history" is taught. The truth of the real, genuine history that occurred in America has been largely subverted by the Lie that presents a fabricated view of that so-called history to reflect what the controllers want the people to believe is history and accept as valid. The controlling elements in society have corrupted the schools' curricula to such an extent that the only positions typically taught are those that benefit the controlling elements, the vested interests, government, and those which indoctrinate the students from preschool to college graduation and beyond into becoming willing, unquestioning cogs in a huge machine controlled by and obedient to the rulers. Independent thinking is really not encouraged in today's schools and critical thinking is totally out of the question. The schools are deliberately creating obedient students who will simply perform by rote as taught, and rarely, if ever, challenge the status quo, question, object, comment or suggest a different way. In this manner, the system creates the type of obedient, compliant society the system wants, so that the system can expand and maintain absolute control, without opposition.

This systematic control is absolutely inconsistent with the requirements of our Constitution(s) and a true Constitutional republic, yet it continues to operate throughout the country with little to no serious lawful opposition by the people. Our rational, reasonable, objective observers could quickly conclude that the inherent rights, free choice and best interests of the children indoctrinated by such a deliberately controlled system are meaningless to the government.

Other casualties of "modern" educational systems are civics, our Constitution(s), national and state, and the proper servant role and duties of the machinery of government in a true Constitutional republic. From the reader's own experiences in dealing with any form of government, and from what we have related throughout this book, the reader can likely conclude that government, by its own actions, undermines the freedoms and opposes the best interests of the people. In so doing, the government maintains its control and status quo position over the society and keeps that society subservient to government. Based upon present and historical realities, our rational, reasonable, objective observers would agree. When opposing forces come together, they do not provide any information to their opponents that would help their opponents defeat them. This is true in virtually all situations in life. For instance, when one files suit in court, he is not necessarily going to provide private information to his opponent about his court strategy that would hurt his chances of winning his case. The quarterback for the New England Patriots is not going to announce to the opposing team that he is going to throw a slant pass to his fullback coming out of the backfield on the right side. Revealing vital, important information to one's opponent is simply not done in the business and activities of society. In a similar manner, the government is not going to provide nor teach vital information to American students in the public and private school systems regarding the true nature and authority of the Constitution(s) and how the proper application of Constitutional mandates will keep government(s) subject to the will of the people.

If the government were to do this and emphasize the strength and power the Constitution(s) guarantees to the people, then the people would likely awaken to their inherent power, embrace it and begin to lawfully enforce their rightful power and control upon government in all forms. It should be pretty obvious to most people, as it is to our rational, objective observers, that government does not want an intelligent, informed, aware citizenry for the simple reason that such an informed, aware society would be difficult, if not impossible, for government to control. In a similar vein, government imposes taxes upon the people, in part, to control the people, businesses, industries and the economy of this nation. Control is a vital element employed by the government to keep all aspects of the society subservient to that control. This position guarantees the continuous power of government. Government prefers an uninformed, ignorant, unaware, apathetic, compliant, obedient society that will do exactly what government dictates without comment, question or objection. The proper teaching of the Constitution(s), rights and due process guaranteed therein and the Constitutional mandates imposed upon government would not by any stretch of the imagination be anything that any U.S. government would ever teach or allow to be taught to its own students and Citizens. The same thing applies to state and local governments, too. Margy and I have a lot of sayings which we frequently use and one of them is that *the bottom line is, in fact, the bottom line*. This disdain for and suppression of the Constitution(s) by virtually all forms of government operating in this country clearly indicates the bottom-line position that governments hold regarding American students and the American people.

Upon graduation from high school, most young people are faced with the choices of going to college, or technical/vocational school, entering the work force, in some capacity, likely unskilled, or joining the military. Of these four typical choices, let us take a look at attending college. In the first place, a would-be college student, after taking the expensive, but usually required, variety of standardized tests, must then endure a lengthy, demanding, intense admission and financial aid process before ever walking through the door of any of his or her college or university preferences. The applications that both the student and parents must fill out are copious, tedious, intrusive and in many cases confusing. Then, the student and parents must wait to see if the student "passes muster" and is accepted by one or more of the institutions. If accepted, the costs of college education today are prohibitive for most families. For many, this is the deciding factor as to whether or not they can even afford to attend. In private colleges and universities, yearly costs can run $60,000 or more, per student, and that does not include personal expenses. Some state schools are less, but still quite expensive for the average working family, especially if that family consists of several children seeking to go to college. The real questions here are whether a college education is really worth the enormous costs, is the education the student will receive valid and truly worth the time and effort, is it the best route for everyone, and will it result in a good-paying professional job for the student? Different people have different interests and objectives and can answer these questions as befits their individual situations. However, propaganda, conditioning and programming are and have been such powerful forces in America that the majority of people in this country have been programmed to believe that college is an absolute necessity for their children. This propaganda and conditioning plays on virtually all parents' natural desire for their children to be better off than they were and to have the promise and opportunity for a better, more financially secure future. Many parents either did not attend college or did not complete their baccalaureates or pursue additional degrees, so want their children to be able to do so, in the belief that this is the only route to success.

The customs, practices, beliefs and mores of any society have usually been conditioned over a long period of time to result in the present conditions, whether people are aware of the subtle and not so subtle government and vested interest programming, or not. As mentioned, the costs of college today are prohibitive for most American families, yet the overwhelming emphasis is still focused upon urging most people to send their kids to college. The real costs of college are usually not questioned as to why they are so excessive. Most parents are so fearful that their kids won't get into their chosen schools that they don't dare to challenge the exorbitant funds these schools demand and so just hope and pray that their kids will get scholarships, grants, and/or other forms of financial aid and loans sufficient to allow them to attend. Colleges are tax exempt, many have large endowments and many have very successful investment programs that produce substantial profits. It seems that the business of colleges today is BUSINESS, and the main question is will this business actually benefit your child and establish a solid foundation so that he or she will have a better life and a secure future?

American colleges and universities simply continue the indoctrination imposed upon the students when they attended Pre-K through 12. The controlling elements of our society are myriad, vast and powerful. These forces want to maintain their control over the people, over the society as a whole, and keep the status quo as the status quo, fully under their control. What better way to do this than to condition the young from the very beginning of their school years and continue it all the way through college and graduate school? Today's universities and colleges are largely "liberal" catering to liberal/progressive/socialist/communist ideologies, as many of you are likely aware. This is the same type of ideological/political structure that the government and controlling forces have incrementally imposed upon the nation, as many Americans are now beginning to realize. Since most people perform as expected and as required, the system wants to maintain the control it has exerted upon the people from the very beginning, and the collegiate experience is a very good and lucrative way to sustain and then expand that control. The overriding, similar concepts held by the ideologies of liberalism/progressivism/socialism/communism are diametrically opposed to the principles and freedoms guaranteed within our Constitution, nor have any association whatsoever with our Constitutional republic, yet these are the positions that are advocated in the educational system, from the very beginning to the very end. While some people within society employ common sense, independent thinking and even critical thinking, the vast majority of this society simply does what it is conditioned and expected to do and goes along to get along, without question, objection or comment. This prevailing attitude greatly assists the sinister intentions of the controlling forces, but is wholly antithetical to the principles enshrined within our Constitution. The controls exerted are sometimes so subtle and indirect that people do not realize that they are being conditioned, so accept those controls without question. When a whole society does this, with the usual few exceptions, government has a free pass to do whatever it wants, whenever it wants to whomever it wants.

As stated above, it is common knowledge that most parents want the best for their kids and this well-intentioned desire propels many of them to make heavy sacrifices so that their children will have better lives. This effort entails a great deal of financial sacrifice whereby the parents use all legitimate financial means and resources available to them to afford the costs of providing their kids a college degree. Sadly, despite parents' best intentions and kids' best efforts, a college degree does not guarantee a better life or a secure future. However, in many cases, it does guarantee a long period of heavy debt for both the parents and the children, because of loans that had to be taken out to pay the costs for college, in whole or in part. Such debt benefits the system in many ways, but puts the recent college graduate under the yoke from the very beginning of his/her "better life". As many of you realize, extremely large numbers of today's college graduates are either unable to find a job in their chosen field at all, so are unemployed, or are working "temporarily" in low paying, unskilled jobs that cannot sustain independent living and allow them to pay the debt they have incurred. As a result, many of these young people are totally dependent upon others and a lot of them are living with their parents. Others look to the government for support in one form or another. Americans are beginning to understand that government wants people *dependent*, and not independent, because independent people are harder to control and are considered "troublesome" for a controlling government.

CHAPTER NINETEEN

MEDICAL AND HEALTH CARE
INDUSTRIES IN AMERICA

The medical and health care industries in America are composed of many different layers and, in fact, are **industries** operating for *profit*. While America is a capitalistic nation and a business operating for profit is totally justified, warranted and needed in a capitalistic nation, when it comes to medical and health care matters, the profit objectives should never come first and that objective should never supersede the health and well-being of the American people. There is absolutely nothing wrong with profit, depending upon how that profit is derived. America, as a capitalistic nation, promotes industry, hard work, creativity and profit all of which enormously helped to build our nation. However, our reasonable observer and our analytical computer could quickly determine the difference between *just* profits and unjust, thus unlawful, profit. Just profit benefits all who come in contact with the enterprise which earned that profit through just and fair practices. However, unjust profit, as its name implies, in most cases, comes about from nefarious activities conducted by profit-driven individuals, groups, enterprises, corporations, nations and other operations which act in reckless pursuit of profits no matter whether those profits adversely affect the health, well-being and finances of their clients, patients and customers. Such enterprises, although possibly considered "legal" are usually lawless, bent upon greedy, selfish objectives, with little concern for those who work for or assist them in the pursuit of unjust profits. We are certain that most readers can easily identify some of these operations and enterprises. Massive illegal and unlawful drug operations comprise one such enterprise. Vast billions and trillions of dollars are made by their operators through sales of harmful drugs that can and have undermined various elements within our society. Such vast profits may be one of the reasons that our so called "war on drugs" has miserably failed to stop and exterminate these drug operations. Another reason pertains to the trillions of dollars that have gone "missing" or are "unaccounted" for by the "deep-state" in the federal government. State and local governments have their own "missing money" operations. By now, enough Americans have awoken to the massive criminal fraud that *is* and is allowed by government, all un-Constitutionally and criminally conducted for control and untold, massive profits.

As noted earlier, just profits derived from just enterprise are not only valid, but essential to the well-being of a capitalist nation. Unjust profits which emanate from un-Constitutional, criminal enterprises would never be permitted to exist in a true Constitutional Republic, and tolerated by a lawful machinery of government that held fast to Constitutional mandates imposed upon serving government officers, by and through their oaths. Frederic Bastiat, a French political analyst, economist and writer, among other things, was prone to say that when the laws are properly followed and enforced, it matters not who controls the government. By now, a significant and growing percentage of the American people have sadly become aware that virtually all of our governments, federal state and local, operate as un-Constitutional, criminal frauds. Hopefully, other Americans will awaken to the truths and existing realities of government, political, economic, social, and power forces operations in our nation. When they do, then they likely would agree with our objective observer and analytical computer, determining that America is no longer a Constitutional republic and its machinery of government, on all levels, systematically violates and opposes our Constitution, its Preamble, and the rights and due process provisions guaranteed to all Americans.

Earlier we spoke of the inevitable problems that arise within human society and the best way to deal with them. Our reasonable observer and his companion, the analytical computer, have agreed that the best way to resolve problems is first, to be fully aware of their possible developments and second, to try to prevent those problems before they occur. Our friends agree that the best way to do this is to be aware of and identify the various conditions that permit the problems to manifest, then stop or rectify those conditions so that the problems are prevented from taking place. Obviously, not all conditions that may lead to all problems can be identified and stopped, but in a true Constitutional republic with a machinery of government dedicated to upholding Constitutional requirements which provide for the general welfare and the well-being of the people, then that government would dedicate itself to these Constitutional objectives. Based upon what government has done and not done in this field, our observer and analytical computer could quickly determine that the United States government is not so dedicated. As many people would agree, words fail in comparison to actions taken.

Since the American people have the guaranteed rights of free speech, free choice and free expression, then they have the right to choose the type of medical treatment they want and the right to refuse the type of medical treatment they do not want. Constitutionally guaranteed Rights cannot lawfully be denied, restricted, limited, legislated and controlled, including the Rights of parents to protect their own children from harm. This matter is really reduced to these very simple terms, yet the government, medical and pharmaceutical industries have been dictating and strive to continue dictating various treatments, programs, policies and pharmaceutical medications for the people, while prohibiting other forms of treatment and remedies that are and may be more effective and better for the physical body. Vaccines are questionable at best, and people have the Constitutionally guaranteed right to either voluntarily accept a vaccine, or refuse to take it. Despite this Constitutional guarantee, various governments throughout the country have mandated that certain people within certain categories are required to accept vaccines, whether they object to them, or not. Newborn babies are injected with a series of vaccines shortly after birth, many times done over the strenuous objections of parents. In such a situation, those "authorities" who dictate treatment determined by them deprive the parents of their Constitutionally secured rights of choice and due process of law. Further, since the safety of vaccines is questionable in the minds of many informed Americans, for a variety of sound reasons, then vaccines forced upon people could actually harm or even kill them. Such mandates are definitely not the marks of a true Constitutional republic in which the government is required to uphold the best interests of the people and maintain the general welfare. Quite to the contrary, this type of government structure is totally dictatorial without any concern whatsoever for the rights, private personal choices, health and safety of the people. It should be quite evident to almost anyone that such a dictatorial policy completely opposes the Constitution, its Preamble, and the rights and due process of law guaranteed to the American people. As we have seen right along, none of these dictatorial policies would be administered, allowed and tolerated in a true Constitutional republic. Again our observer and computer would restate that America is not a Constitutional republic operated by a Constitutionally compliant government.

For the most part, the institutionalized treatment of disease in America has become systematically chemical. Disease of any type is horrendous and should not exist in human society, but the sad fact is that is does. The enlightened, egalitarian society would strive to find natural, safe, effective, non-harmful, less disruptive methods to cure all types of disease, and work tirelessly in an effort to reach that objective. One of the most insidious diseases to afflict humans is cancer. People who suffer from this awful disease are not the only ones affected by it, because the affliction encompasses the entire family and takes a tremendous emotional toll on everyone in that family.

Can you think of one family you know that has not in some way suffered from or been affected by cancer? This is how widespread and insidious cancer has become. Institutionally, cancer is typically treated through surgery, often radical, followed by chemotherapy and radiation and/or combinations thereof. In the opinions of many knowledgeable, educated, well-informed people, all of these forms of treatment are invasive, disruptive and harmful and toxic to the human body. Chemo and radiation introduce poisons into the human body that cause more harm than the little good they may possibly effectuate. However, the cancer INDUSTRY in this nation is huge, powerful, well-organized and extremely profitable for doctors, hospitals, the various specialty cancer clinics, private labs and testing facilities and the pharmaceutical corporations. As a result of this, the institutionalized methods have become "standard treatment" for virtually everyone, without consideration of other alternative, holistic and less harmful methods of treatment. Many of these alternative holistic treatments are extremely effective, yet safe, used routinely in other countries, but are prohibited in America by the government and the entrenched vested interest power forces which profit handsomely from the current forms of standard treatment. Alternative treatments for cancer have been existent for many decades, and, as stated above, are readily available in many foreign countries. However, the power forces in control of medicine in this nation have vilified these alternative methods and made them difficult, if not impossible, for most Americans to access. Those who invented and utilized holistic, alternative methods, with great success in many cases, were ridiculed, threatened, ostracized, imprisoned and even killed to prevent their methods from disrupting the profits derived through chemical, allopathic medicine. Readers can do their own research on these various alternative treatment methods. There is voluminous information available in this regard, especially via the Internet.

Because alternative treatment methods for various diseases and ills are restricted in this country, most Americans who would like alternative treatments, but who cannot afford to travel overseas to get them, are forced into accepting the standard treatment methods. The heinous actions by the vested-interests in the medical industries do not bode well for the American people and are definitely not consistent with their right of free choice. Many people who have been afflicted with cancer over the years did not want to accept chemo and radiation, but since they were presented with no alternatives, because the alternative treatments were discouraged or prohibited as "quackery", and, as said above, they could not afford overseas travel to access such alternative treatments, there was little choice for the patients. Over the many years that these draconian, restrictive practices have ensued, many patients would have chosen alternative treatments, if they had been available to them in America. When vested interests control treatments and prohibit alternative curative methods, then a rational, objective observer can easily deduce that these vested interests–*effectively a medical mafia*–have subordinated the rights of patients in favor of profit, power and control. Hippocrates would turn over in his grave if he were living in this age!

It is well known that the health insurance corporations who refuse to pay for alternative, holistic medical treatments, by their own actions, appear to be in league with all of these other vested interests striving to eliminate this rightful choice. As we have said right along, none of these practices uphold the guaranteed rights of the American people and are not consistent with due process of law and the principles contained in a true Constitutional republic. As referenced earlier, problems exist within human society due to conditions existent prior to the occurrence of those problems. Any government of right and any sincere health industry would earnestly attempt to resolve conditions that eventually result in problems. This is simply common sense, because the rational, reasonable person would try to eliminate conditions that would create or exacerbate a problem. Thus, it seems reasonable that a government charged with upholding the general welfare would work in earnest with the medical industry to accomplish the same objective. Yet, based upon existing realities in the medical industry, this does not appear to be the case. Instead, their actions show that the standardized practices used in the medical industry, especially for cancer, are lacking consistent efficacy and take a huge toll on patients. Some people do get better, while others do not, and many who initially went into remission, often suffer reoccurrences of their cancers. Despite all of this, huge profits are generated by and through these treatments.

As stated earlier, profit should not be the objective when it comes to health, but in America, this appears to be the main pursuit, as opposed to the successful treatment of the patient. Admittedly, many medical innovations and practices have come a long way and are effective in helping numerous patients deal with and recover from a variety of medical problems, conditions and illnesses. When it comes to diseases such as cancer and other life-threatening chronic diseases, much more effort should be put into seeking better ways to eliminate conditions that cause these horrendous problems for the people. Many alternative, holistic approaches, which are effective, whether they may be considered "quackery" or not, can benefit people who are ill and possibly pave the way for the development of other successful treatments and applications. Much good work has been done by alternative, holistic providers over the years, as referenced previously, which actually cured some and helped many, but unfortunately, the government and the allopathic medical industry stopped these cures.

If these treatments were largely or even somewhat successful, the question must be, why were they stopped? America is lauded for the supposed freedoms guaranteed to the people, but when those freedoms and free choice are completely violated by the government which is mandated to uphold those freedoms and free choice, then that government is a criminal government. There is no other way to explain it, and the simplest, most direct way is the best. Nothing effective should ever have been stopped by a just government of right in cooperation with a just medical industry which would want to seek truly effective cures. It is all too clear that the U.S. government is not a government of right and the medical industry is sorely lacking in some very important areas. Our objective observer and our analytical computer can agree and determine that stopping treatments, which helped people, would indicate that the government did not act in the best interests of the people, as is Constitutionally required, nor did the medical industry. Those observers would likely conclude that unjust profits and control were the objectives of the government, in league with the medical, pharmaceutical and insurance industries. None of this bodes well for the American people. When methods and procedures can help people rid themselves of serious disease and medical problems, no government and no medical system operating for profit, promulgating and protecting highly profitable standard treatments should ever prohibit and obstruct such effective treatments from the people who desperately need them.

One of the major culprits in the deprivation of alternative treatments for Americans in America is the pharmaceutical industry, also known as, "Big Pharma", aided and abetted by a government agency called the Federal Drug Administration, or the FDA. This agency is paid for by the American people and it is supposed to be a watchdog in place to protect the health, safety and best interests of Americans. Instead, as the FDA now operates, it protects the bests interests and profits of Big Pharma and the related medical industries which use and profit from pharmaceutical medicine. At one time in America, most medicines were plant-based, comprising safe, effective homeopathic and herbal treatments. These types of treatments were natural, thus well received by and integrated within the human body, and for the most part, in time, achieved the desired results. In 1900's through the 1920's, there was a major push by well-entrenched vested interests to create chemical treatments for profit. These chemical treatments, which we now call pharmaceuticals, typically did not cure or correct the medical problems, but often provided symptomatic relief from pain and other symptoms. A concerted effort was focused upon these new methods to attract consumers and a campaign to replace natural cures as "old fashioned and outdated" was begun. It is easy for anyone to see that over the decades, the pharmaceuticals and the pill industry became totally explosive and pervasive in the number of so-called treatments they used to mask physical ills. Today, pharmaceutical ads are constantly blaring on television with auctioneer style language that no one can actually understand making voluminous warnings about the side effects and real dangers the advertised pills pose.

While some pharmaceuticals do achieve results, for the most part, they mask the pain and symptoms, but do not cure the problem, as would most natural cures, given the proper dosage, use and time. This is mainly because natural cures work holistically with the body and its natural systems, while pharmaceutical pills are foreign to and work against the body's natural systems. Had the focus been placed upon natural cures and treatments and extensive research been done to further develop them for additional uses, instead of extracting the essences of the natural cures to turn them into much less effective chemicals which could be patented so that the pharmaceutical companies could sell for huge profits, then Americans would likely be a lot healthier right now. Over the decades, people have experienced the fact that while one pill might provide some relief, it may cause other problems, side effects and contraindications that require further pills, which may in turn require further pills, which practices cascade into people having to consume a massive number of pills every day, all of which suppress the body's natural systems. This creates a dependence upon the pills, which obviously works to the advantage of Big Pharma and the government that protects it. Our government has long opposed independence and encourages dependence.

As anyone can plainly see, just by going about daily life, there are large numbers of obese people in America now, to the point of epidemic obesity rates. Obesity is on the rise among American adults and even among our children. This condition did not exist 50 or 60 years ago, but has been growing by leaps and bounds each and every decade. It has reached alarming proportions, no pun intended, and obesity, unfortunately, often leads to other diseases and health problems for Americans, such as diabetes, heart disease, joint pain and other health issues. Those affected by obesity certainly do not want to be obese and surely did not strive to be obese. Unfortunately, there are many elements contributing to this problem that go well beyond the obvious one of overeating. One of these elements is the large number of pharmaceuticals and artificial substances which the government allows to be put into the food and beverages which Americans consume. Some of these artificial substances contribute to weight gain and there is growing evidence that they are addictive to those who consume them on a regular basis.

Another chemical that is routinely affecting Americans daily is the fluoride which millions of Americans consume by drinking water from the many public water systems throughout the country, which systems put fluoride into their water. Americans have been sold a false bill of goods about fluoride, having been told that it stops and prevents dental caries, aka, cavities. The truth is that fluoride is a *poison* produced by chemical corporations that was used in wartime to kill rodents. After the war, the fluoride was no longer needed as a pesticide, so the corporations developed a scheme to sell it to the people as an alleged "aid" to dental health. However, fluoride is a poison, thus is toxic, leaches calcium from bones and teeth, can cause fluorosis and even death if enough is consumed. There is a sound reason why fluoride toothpastes bear a warning to call poison control centers if the toothpaste should be swallowed. Check out these links below to verify the dangers of fluoride, which include potential harm to the thyroid gland, increased chance of bone cancer, arthritis, increased concentration of lead in children's bodies, development of ADHD-like-symptoms, reduction of I.Q. in children, lethargy and passivity in the people, as well as other toxic effects. http://www.nextworldhealthtv.com/videos/health-and-environment/why-isfluoride-added-to-city-tap-water.html#sthash.lqNrnwKm.dpuf; as well as this link from Mike Adams, aka, "The Health Ranger", who has done a lot of research on this topic: https://www.naturalnews.com/037024_sodium_fluoride_insecticide_proof.html#ixzz25I80Oezr.

Another damaging element is the food that many people regularly consume, which, in many cases, is devoid of any nutritional value whatsoever, but full of the referenced chemicals and other harmful artificial ingredients that can adversely affect health and actually contribute to weight gain in a variety of ways. Yet, these foods often taste good, because of the fillers, additives and flavor enhancers put into them, and can even be addictive. Fast foods, packaged and prepared foods are among the worst offenders, and often contain Genetically Modified Organisms, or GMO's, called "Frankenfoods" by many Europeans who have wisely banned them, and which are suspect at best, dangerous at worst. It is criminally irresponsible for the U.S. Food and Drug Administration, best known by the acronym FDA, to have permitted GMO foods to flood the American marketplace with little or no scientific testing conducted regarding their effects upon humans. Most unfortunately, for the people of this country, there is mounting evidence that GMO foods can and do cause harm to laboratory animals, which suggests they would also harm the human body. The FDA did not do its job to protect the American people, as it is required to do, by failing to review independent scientific research regarding the potential adverse short and long-term effects these unnatural "foods" may cause. If other countries do not accept GMOs for their populations, then it is ludicrous that the U.S. government, which is Constitutionally required to protect the rights and health of the people in maintaining the general welfare, not just allows, but promotes and encourage GMOs and GMO farming of the food supply for the people of this nation. Our rational observer and analytical computer would say that something is awfully wrong in this situation, because whatever might harm the people should never be allowed by the government, let alone encouraged by it. Our observer and computer would ask the question as to why the government does not encourage large-scale organic farming throughout the country and aid in efforts to make this sound, sane, safe and sensible practice a reality.

Most people would agree that natural is far superior to artificial. Natural, organically grown food, and food untainted by chemical spraying would likely be the food to which Hippocrates, "the father of modern medicine", was referring when he said: "Let food be your medicine and let medicine be your food." However, factors such as busy lifestyles, replete with two working parents putting in long, stressful days, often leave little time and energy to cook good, nutritious, natural homemade meals from fresh, wholesome, natural ingredients. Additionally, the prohibitively expensive costs of buying organic, unsprayed and locally sourced foods, which often may require extra trips to specialty food stores or farm stands, can put these better nutritional choices out of reach for many average American households. However, as we mentioned above, if the government actively encouraged and supported large-scale efforts for tens of thousands of organic farms across the country, then these products would be more readily available, less expensive and could also factor in the creation of many good jobs. It is reasonable to think that if our government were to encourage and incentivize organic, holistic farming practices, more humane animal farming practices, the growth and use of natural plant-based cures, not restrict and disparage them, along with myriad other forms of alternative treatments, the American people would likely want to avail themselves of these better choices, and probably be much healthier and happier for so doing. Imagine if such wholesome practices–government encouraged and incentivized–became commonplace, resulting in free and open competition! This would make the products produced more available and less expensive so that virtually every American could afford to eat healthy and have healthy treatment options, the soil would not be tainted by chemicals and the blessed animals would have better lives. All of this would have happened had the government upheld the principles of the Preamble, our Constitution and the rights guaranteed therein to the American people. However, as usual, the government completely avoids all of its Constitutional obligations and opposes the best interests of the people by and through its actions to benefit industry at the expense of the people.

Rather than upholding the Constitutional mandates imposed upon it, the government has not only permitted, but encouraged GMO farming, seeds and foods to be inflicted upon the American people with no regard to the potential hazards and ill-health effects this can cause the American people. Again, the objective here is very important. Rather than focus and concentrate upon organic seeds and humane, safe farming practices, all of which are natural and holistic with the environment, humans, livestock and plants, the government, in obedience to and compliance with the chemical vested interests, focused upon a manipulated, abnormal type of large-scale, industrial farming, designed for maximum profits, and not for maximum health. The former is natural, while the latter is unnatural, not in harmony with our bodies or with nature and not conducive to good health. Once again, the question arises as to why a government that is theoretically mandated to uphold the Constitution and all of the rights and due process guaranteed therein would ever purposefully permit and promote "Frankenfoods", as opposed to wholesome, natural foods beneficial to human health and development and which could generate a whole new health-smart industry for America. The quick answer is that a government so committed would never even contemplate this, let alone do it.

In essence, many Americans are being sabotaged by the foods they eat and the pills they take. If we truly had a government that was firmly committed to upholding the rights of the people, the health of the people, proper treatments and committed to upholding the principles contained in our Constitution's Preamble, then it is highly likely that this obesity epidemic and general ill health conditions being increasingly experienced by people throughout the country would not exist. "If" is a small word with a *big* meaning, but *if* the government acted correctly and in the best interests of the people, then it would have required the health care industry, pharmaceutical corporations and the food industry to engage in safe, sound, proper techniques that would foster good health and its maintenance, rather than employ methods, products and procedures that cause harm to the American people. That which is natural works synergistically with the body to induce and maintain its health. These are the methods which should be encouraged and employed by a true, committed Constitutional republic government acting in the best interests of the people and upholding the public trust. Artificial, foreign elements which can harm the body, though producing temporary relief and false cures, should not be the mainstay of health care in this nation, especially when it is common knowledge that many medications lead to dependency, addiction, organ damage and other problems while not solving the existing medical problems. Free choice should never be denied in a true Constitutional republic. However, if some of those choices have been eliminated or greatly reduced and/or discouraged or prohibited by government, the eventual choice people must make is the one government forces them to make.

Many ways exist for covert forces and their minions to ruin a nation and one of the most successful is massive infusion of drugs throughout the society of that nation, both legal and illegal.

We addressed to some degree the enormous number of Americans taking legal drugs, drugs which put many people into zombie-like states and which drugs simply mask the pain, mental, emotional or physical, but do not cure the causes. However, pharmaceuticals are a big money item in America and the pharmaceutical corporations have huge financial and political power, which has facilitated their marketing and selling billions of dollars of legal drugs. One such legal drug, Oxycodone, a highly-addictive painkiller, has been so overprescribed by physicians who were persuaded, pressured or pushed to do so, that many people developed serious addictions to it. When they could no longer get the drug legally, they obtained it illegally "on the street", and when they were unable to get this drug, some even crossed over to illegal drugs to dull their pain and feed their habits. Illegally procured prescription drugs are now a huge part of street drug business, in particular, Oxycodone and other similar drugs resulting in an epidemic opioid dependency crisis that gives stark testimony to the success of the evil effort to use drugs to undermine the American society. This epidemic is affecting Americans from virtually all walks of life, age groups, income strata, ethnicities, career paths and locations. No one is immune to the threat posed by these seductive, mind-altering drugs. All of us can see that the addiction rates in this country are high and growing among all areas of our society, especially with young people. Just like the other problems we have cited throughout this book, this one is a monstrous one with far-reaching, life-destroying effects that reverberate throughout our entire society, breaking up families, crushing human potential and creativity, taking lives. Our rational observer and analytical computer would ask why a government which supposedly has engaged in a so-called "War on Drugs" for decades has spent billions of dollars on this "war", yet drugs are everywhere in our society and there is no sign yet that this threat will end anytime soon. With all the resources available to the U.S. government, our rational observer and computer can quickly conclude that the government could eradicate these illegal drugs within 180 days, that is, if it really wanted to stop the drug problem. The fact is that, although it has the resources, the government has not stopped the illegal drug problem—a fact that no one can dispute. Again, the question is: "Why?" Since drugs harm the general society, directly and indirectly, then a government of right which upheld its obligations to the Constitution would stop that drug problem very quickly. Could it be that there is too much money in drugs and could it be that the government profits from that money, and even more so, benefits from the harm drugs do to the American people? There is no middle ground here. The government either aids and abets the drug problem, or is adamant about stopping it. Since none of us witness any stoppage, but can see signs of escalating illegal drug use and addiction on the increase, then our observer and computer could conclude that the former position is the operative reality in America.

There are countless adverse health effects that exist in this nation and obviously we cannot describe all of them. In addition to the food issues in this country and the fact that much of the farm land is highly polluted with chemical fertilizers, pesticides, herbicides, etc., the rain that falls on the land is contaminated with many other harmful elements and we are not speaking of agricultural spraying. At one time people did not believe that our own government would actually spray contaminants in the skies throughout the country, but this spraying is now so commonplace, so obvious, that anyone can easily see it—that is, if they care to look up into the sky. This phenomenon is called aerosol spraying, more commonly referred to as "chemtrails". The spraying emanates from planes that leave white trails all over the skies, sometimes in the form of X's, crisscross patterns and grids, which eventually become a flat, dull whitish-gray cloud cover. There is no explanation given by the government as to why it is spraying toxic materials upon the American people, the land and the water sources, and the government has never actually admitted to the spraying. Readers can do their own research on this issue, as they choose, and there is a plethora of information available, again, with the Internet being an excellent source. One of the best websites regarding aerosol spraying is www.carnicom.com/. Some of the alleged "reasons" for aerosol spraying fall under "weather modification" which is being deliberately conducted by the government aided and abetted by private contractors. It is well known that the U.S. Air Force issued a report years ago in which it admitted that its goal is to "own the weather by 2025". The disturbing fact is that a process called "geoengineering" is taking place on our planet and the aerosol spraying of various metals and other materials is playing a huge role in this process, along with the emission of electro-magnetic wave lengths at low and extra-low frequencies which work in tandem with the spraying. If you are not aware of geoengineering and the frightening prospects it holds for our country and our entire planet, then, you can find voluminous scientific information about it on the excellent website hosted by scientist Dane Wigginton: www.geoengineeringwatch.com. Some of the contaminants that have been made known are barium, aluminum, titanium, magnesium, lithium, strontium, other heavy metals, dessicated blood cells, ionized nanoparticles, polymer fibers, viruses and a host of other matter that is extremely harmful to the people and the environment. The metals are less than a micron in size and a micron is so tiny that it is not discernible by the human eye. These effluents fall upon the Earth, contaminate the soil and the water, and of course are breathed in by humans, animals and plants. To our rational, reasonable observer and our analytical computer this spraying practice by a government which is mandated to protect the health and best interests of the people appears to be either absolutely absurd or diabolically malevolent. If there is no rational explanation given by government that explains a truly beneficial purpose, then it certainly appears to be deliberately malevolent. Obviously, this all-encompassing massive spraying definitely opposes the rights and due process guaranteed to the people in our Constitution and flies in the face of the Preamble to that Constitution.

The chemicals and substances that fall upon the soil permeate the food that is grown in that soil. This, combined with the other chemicals,—pesticides, herbicides, etc.—put into the soil by farmers, produce a food crop that is at least in some way contaminated to some degree. As stated above, when the rain that is contaminated by the chemtrails falls upon the soil, we have further contamination of that soil and the food it produces. The people and their families are the consumers of this food, just as they are the consumers of pharmaceutical products. None of this is natural or naturally based, which, of course, would be beneficial to the health of the consumer. However, when the people consume food that is laced with toxins, eventually those toxins will have an adverse effect upon the body. For any nation to engage in practices that purposefully harm its own people is absolute insanity and clearly is diametrically opposed to any concept of justice, fairness and any semblance of maintaining the public health, general welfare and the best interests of the people.

CHAPTER TWENTY

THE SHAM ECONOMY AND PLANNED ECONOMIC CATASTROPHES

The largest and most important investment that most people make is the purchase of their home. The value in one's home is almost incalculable, because of many different factors. The home is the heart of the family from which daily lives are lived for many years. Children leave their home every morning to go to school and play sports and engage in numerous other activities. Mom and Dad leave home every morning to go to work and return to its comforts each night. The family home is the basis of operations for the family. When a family loses its home, for any reason, it is a disaster, and to many, an insurmountable obstacle that sets the entire family back in numerous ways for years. Unfortunately, since 2004, millions of families in America have lost their homes due to various manipulations and outright fraud conducted by banks and investment corporations and allowed by your "government". While these banks and investment corporations benefited tremendously, tragically, the families lost their most valuable possessions, as well as their futures, their self-respect, their confidence and their peace of mind.

The economy in America has been in a shambles since 2007, and despite what the "economic experts" say and the media continues to "report", it is still showing only limited signs of improving. In reality, the economy in this country has been bad for many, many decades. There are reasons for this, but these reasons are not being disclosed to the American people. As a result of a disastrous economy, millions of people lost their jobs and thus could no longer afford to pay the notes, secured by the mortgages, on their homes. What can one logically expect when the United States government, in collusion with corporations, has encouraged entire industries to close shop here in America and establish plants and manufacturing facilities in other nations? Millions more lost their homes due to these factors. Yes, some corporations, businesses and industries have opened under the Trump administration, but these numbers pale in comparison to the losses that have accrued over the past twenty five or more years. The long held "American Dream" of home ownership has suffered a huge setback and may now be an impossible dream for huge numbers of hard-working, decent Americans. If the existing traditional institutional buying practices remain the same, it is highly likely that the vast majority of people who lost their homes will not be able to buy another one.

If government and banks were truly interested in the well-being of the people and the people's ability to pay their notes due on their properties, then, the banks and the government would not have taken actions egregiously detrimental to the people, but highly beneficial to the banks. These banking and governmental actions conducted over many years have proven to be absolutely devastating to the well-being of the average American homeowner. Banks were more interested in selling mortgages to people, whether the people could meet the monthly mortgage payments, or not, since as we have mentioned before, the banks bundled the mortgages, "securitized" them and sold the debt to investors, mostly overseas. The banks' objective here was the bottom-line profits for the banks, and not the well-being of their home-owning customers. There is absolutely nothing wrong with capitalism, as long as it is conducted fairly and justly for both parties. However, when capitalism becomes despotic and imbued with rampant greed, then it places ordinary, hard-working under the oppressive yoke of economic slavery. This is neither just, nor fair, and amounts to adhesion contracts imposed upon the people for the benefit of one party, namely, the lender, with all obligations paid by the other party, namely, the borrower. Our own government upheld the fraudulent practices of the banks, as opposed to the best interests of the people. This is not what the founding fathers intended, certainly not authorized within the Constitution, and definitely not reflective of its Preamble.

By now, many of you must understand that this type of cozy relationship between the government and the banks is a repetitive scenario that has been going on for hundreds of years. Beyond the dire matter of mortgage fraud and the scam of securitization, if the government truly wanted a healthy economy so that people could find good paying jobs, with ease, instead of with difficulty, or not at all, then, the government would not have allowed, and in some cases, encouraged, entire industries to leave America and establish manufacturing plants on foreign soil throughout the world. As a result of these policies and many others which are not typically understood by the average American, the ability to work in a chosen occupation, with good steady compensation for skills expended, and the ability to make mortgage payments with ease has been stripped from a very large segment of the American people. At present, from information that has been available to us, approximately fifty percent of the American workforce is no longer able to work, because work is not available for them. This is an absolute disaster, no matter how one looks at it, and this did not happen by accident. As we have mentioned previously, Franklin Delano Roosevelt was prone to say, that if it happened in politics, it didn't happen by accident. During the so-called "Great Depression", the unemployment rate was right around 24%. The current "unofficial" figure of approximately 50% is twice that of that Depression. The true factors holding our economy together are welfare payments, both social and corporate, and other benefits the government provides to people, as well as debt and credit card spending. Without these factors, the economy would come to a screeching halt and its true nature would quickly be revealed to virtually everyone. If these factors were stripped from the American economy over the past ten years, those past ten years would have been far worse than the "Great Depression" that began in 1929 and extended into the 1930's. Average Americans cannot conceive that their own government would engage in policies detrimental to them and to their entire family, which is one of the major reasons why these practices continue to profligate. However, based upon the real facts and existing reality, clearly discernible to anyone who chooses to look at them, this is exactly what has happened to America and the American people. Does anyone truly believe what government says anymore? Can anyone base any credibility in the so-called facts, figures and percentages that government presents as official? Based upon what government has DONE, and not what government SAYS, we believe almost nothing that is presented as "factual" by government, and many more Americans are arriving at this position. This goes to the old question that asks: Can anyone believe anything that a liar says? Once that entity has proven to be a liar, over and over again, then logic dictates that no one should ever believe anything the liar says.

When one considers the above conditions and combines these with current banking policy, it is easy for most people to readily understand that home ownership for many people today is no longer a given, in fact, is extremely difficult, and for many, a total impossibility. A large percentage of former homeowners are now forced to pay higher rents for apartments than the mortgage payments they used to make on their own homes. The once-venerated American Dream is no longer a viable reality for a large number of Americans and, in fact, has for many become their worst nightmare. What people *say* and what people *do*, many times, is quite different. The same is true with government and with banks. It is not what they SAY that can be counted upon, but rather what they DO. What they do is not in the best interests of the average American. Banks, no matter what they claim, are reluctant to lend funds to what they consider "marginal borrowers". As a result, a lot of these so-called marginal borrowers cannot buy a home under any circumstances. Others in this group may have temporary jobs that do not qualify them for home mortgages or no job at all. Still others do not have the funds required for down payments. Even when a would-be home buyer thinks all is going well with his mortgage application and procedures, in many instances, the sale does not close because the bank found some reason(s), many of which are arbitrary and obscure, to deny the loan. Further, increasingly restrictive government and banking regulations exclude many potential borrowers. Again, these prevent millions of potential buyers from purchasing homes.

Another factor that affects one's ability to buy a home in the usual scenario is the way "credit scoring" is done in this country. Americans have been brainwashed for decades to believe that "a good credit score" is the mark of success and a key symbol of "making it". However, to have a "good" credit score, it is absolutely essential to make routine, ongoing purchases using credit cards, taking out loans, and making consistent timely payments on those purchases, which means that Americans willingly take on debt after debt after debt–paying very high interest and often late fees–to buy cars, trucks, boats, sporting equipment, camping goods, furniture, vacations, meals out, etc. on credit and then hope and pray they can timely pay off their debts to either attain and/or keep their "good credit scores". This amounts to a "catch 22", because for the consumer to be "creditworthy", in the eyes of banks, he must regularly go into debt and manage to timely pay it off, so he can "earn" a credit score number the banks have arbitrarily decreed as "ideal", via some unknown criteria. In other words, Americans have allowed themselves to be manipulated into being full-time consumers who routinely put themselves into serious debt, either to afford the necessities of life, as in the case of those without jobs, or for those still working, to "keep up with the Joneses". In either situation, the people are the losers and the banks are once again the winners, accompanied by the corporations, marketers and advertisers, of course. While some debt is valid, justified and necessary, such as the debt one owes on his home, the overabundance of debt incurred by many Americans and encouraged by the banks, through advertising and marketing methods, has been and still is a financial disaster for millions of people. The likelihood of financial recovery for most of these people is very slim, under current conditions.

In the present-day system, debt obviously is the amount of money which people owe. Therefore, debt is an integral part of not only the American society, but virtually every society on Earth. Those to whom the debt is owed have vast control over that particular economy and the people of that particular nation. One's ability to earn or obtain money is dependent upon the debt that created the business, firm, enterprise or corporation for whom the person works. If no debt was made available for that particular enterprise, then, there would be no work for that person, because the company would not exist. Debt affects all of us and even to a much larger extent than the average American can readily imagine, but many are beginning to understand.

The subject of money is a gigantic one and it is not the intention of this book to fully cover it. However, there are a few basic positions that we can discuss. Money was originally devised simply as a **medium of exchange**, and nothing more than this. However, money has become much more than this original intention, because of who and what controls money. The difference between the money of old and the so-called new money is that most paper currencies in bygone centuries were fully backed by gold or silver, whereas today's fiat currency is backed by absolutely nothing and exists because of the government's decree. If today's money were simply a medium of exchange, harking back to the original barter system, by which people lived and traded throughout the world, then, that barter would keep the economy flowing freely and openly. This is logical, because economies would be based upon what is produced by some parties and traded for what is produced by other parties. The means of production and trade would be continuous, natural operations. Unfortunately, today, money is not controlled by the people who produce the goods and services referred to above. Their production is now in the hands of the moneymen. The private bank, called the Federal Reserve Bank, was "authorized" by and through the government to print money, essentially out of thin air, since the "money" never existed prior to its issuance and, further, this "money" has no precious metal backing or other valuable material backing it. The federal government has dictated that this "money" is the only legal currency in America. Therefore, by the government's order or dictate, this currency is *fiat* currency, printed at will by the Federal Reserve Bank, with no assets backing it. This information is completely unknown to the great majority of Americans, something they do not understand, at all, and that is exactly how the banks and the government like it. Further, most new money is issued on debt incurred by the people and by businesses, and this is another fact which the vast majority of people do not know. Money is put into existence and circulation by collective debt. In other words, the borrower makes the loan possible and the bank profitable. The creation of money, its control and issuance by the central bank given the power to do so, by and through government, places the control of this nation's money in the hands of a private bank, operating for profit. Profit always seems to trump the people. The owners of that private bank can control and manipulate the economy in any way desired. This is not how the founding fathers of our country envisioned the creation and issuance of money for use by the American people, businesses and industries, but this is exactly what our government has unlawfully done.

The American people are dependent upon the issuance of money by a private bank, whose practices either encourage the economy to flourish or, in the alternative, push the economy into debt spirals, recessions, depressions and tough times for the majority of Americans. A government interested in the well-being of its own people would not permit the existence of such a pernicious system of money control by a private bank, operating for profit. Yet, this is exactly what has happened in America, based upon unlawful, un-Constitutional government actions and policies. Unfortunately, just as the people have not noticed other actions and policies detrimental to their economic well-being, they have not noticed how the pernicious, highly controlled and manipulated money system operates in America. It's the old distorted Golden Rule adage: **He who controls the gold rules**. The unfortunate position for America and her people is that the people do not control their own money supply, but instead, are fully indebted to those who do, and those who do totally run the show.

The objective and the intent of any action are very important if one wants to know and comprehend the truth. Another old adage is that the road to hell is paved with good intentions. If the servant governments in America truly recognized that proper, lawful status as SERVANT governments, and truly intended to reach an objective beneficial to the people and the nation, herself, then that government would either follow through with its intention, or not. Everything has a bottom line, and the bottom-line position is extremely telling because that bottom line reveals the truth of the matter. Either government truly intends to serve the people or it intends itself to serve itself and its hidden masters and their banking and corporate business partners. From the actions of the federal government, the state and county governments and most local governments, it is painfully obvious to our objective observers, True and Reality, that the combined actions of these governments—and not their rhetoric—clearly proves that these governments serve themselves and their cohorts, but not the people who pay for their salaries and benefits. Recognition of the problem is the first step, but unfortunately, the overwhelming majority of the American people do not even know that this problem exists. However, some are awakening to this realization and more seem to be coming to this position each and every day. The immensely powerful U.S. government could create a paradise in this nation through Constitutionally established banking methods, but from the very inception of this country, the U.S. government favored private banking and corporations over the best interests of the people. If you are interested in reviewing an economic policy, which deals in public money, not private, that could create that referenced economic paradise for a nation, a state, a county or a city, then you can go to our website, which is www.CitizensoftheAmericanConstitution.net, and access the Alternative Currency Proposal.

Earlier in this book, we mentioned the Preamble to the Constitution for the united states of America and demonstrated that the government has failed to follow any of the precepts within that Preamble nor has it upheld the Constitutionally secured inherent rights guaranteed to the people and due process of law clearly established and mandated within that Constitution. It should be becoming very clear to larger and larger segments of the American people that the government acts against the interests of the people, therefore has violated the Constitutional mandates imposed upon it and essentially is nothing but a fraud, pretending to be a "democracy" when, in fact, America was Constitutionally established as a Constitutional republic. In all of our seminars, lectures, appearances and media broadcasts over the years, we have emphasized many extremely important points and positions which the people must come to understand. Two of them follow: (1) any act passed by any congress, legislative body or governmental body of any kind and any action committed by any public officer either supports and upholds the Constitution, or opposes and violates it. It is this basically simple. (2) No public officer/employee has the Constitutional authority—or any other form of valid authority—to violate and oppose the very document to which he or she swore or affirmed his or her oath.

The above two positions are vital if the American people want to accept their responsibility and duty to exercise proper control over their "servant government". If the people continue to fail to do this, then that lawless government will become a further tyrannical monster that will dictate all conditions of all lives and all happenings in America. As usual, it is up to the people to either take the responsibility or accept the dire consequences of not doing so.

GOVERNMENT SPYING VERSUS CONSTITUTIONALLY GUARANTEED PRIVACY

For many decades, our government has engaged in secret spying upon the American people in many different forms. Voluminous information is available to anyone who wants to research this subject. Whistle blowers and other courageous, outspoken people, such as Edward Snowden, Julian Assange, Bradley/Chelsea Manning and many others have spoken of the routine spying that the American government conducts upon its own Citizens. The government's spying apparatus is vast and can listen to every phone conversation in this nation and read every email exchange among the people. Remember, *lawful* government can only perform pursuant to its *limited* delegated scope of duties and authority, and there is no Constitutional authority whatsoever delegated to any form of government to conduct spying operations on Citizens, their phone calls, texts, emails and other forms of communication ongoing in this nation. When the government does this it openly trashes rights guaranteed to the people in the Constitution(s), national and state, as well as all aspects of due process of law. Obviously, pursuant to oaths taken, government officers are, required by law, to protect and uphold rights guaranteed in the Constitution(s), and not to systematically destroy them as a routine practice of government. Such massive, covert spying activities conducted on the American people constitute a blatant attack upon all Americans, by their own "servant government". Government of right serves with the consent of the governed. It is common sense that the overwhelming majority of American Citizens does not and would not consent to this spying upon them by their own government. Obviously, based upon this alone, plus countless other overreaching government programs, the U.S. government is NOT a government of right and acts as a DOMESTIC ENEMY to the American people.

Myriad other abuses of power exist which conclusively demonstrate that the American people are under attack by their own government in numerous different ways and have been for a very long time. The American people have traditionally trusted their government, taken what government says at face value, and as a society, have not challenged, questioned or objected to government and its policies at all, except in rare instances by some very few, knowledgeable people and groups. However, the society has always upheld and obeyed whatever government imposes upon it, which means that this society has also upheld the wrong, the criminal and the un-Constitutional actions that the government has conducted over the decades and perpetrated upon the compliant people. Again, one of our purposes in writing this book is to conclusively demonstrate that the governments of all types—federal, state, county and local—by their own policies and actions, directly oppose our Constitution(s), the rights guaranteed to the people therein, the due process guaranteed therein, and the principles of our Preamble, guaranteed by our national Constitution to all Americans. Because more and more people are beginning to understand these sad facts every day, it is really incumbent upon the people to conduct more objective research, then, join others, share their knowledge and come together in local groups, which, hopefully can join as an informed society of Americans dedicated to stopping the criminal, un-Constitutional actions routinely committed against them by their own governments, and begin the restoration of their Constitutional republic. Our very successful Constitutional methods which we described earlier can accomplish this objective, if applied by serious, committed, dedicated true American patriots.

If the people fail to do this, individually and in groups, and within the society as a whole, then the criminal, un-Constitutional actions committed by all governments, without any real opposition, will continue and increase in scope and degree of control. The spying apparatus of government is everywhere and constantly inflicted upon the people 24 hours a day, 365 days a year. In addition, a lot of private technology is being used to aid and abet government spying and increasing in breath and scope exponentially. Drones are only one obvious example of this spying, yet virtually everything people do is being tracked through their Internet usage, their credit and debit card purchases, etc. Most people think of this as "convenient" and just businesses trying to get an edge on other businesses, but this tracking is much more sinister than most people imagine. Surveillance cameras are virtually everywhere in the big cities and their presence is growing even in smaller cities and towns. Governments are employing facial recognition cameras which are about to be imposed upon the people throughout the nation, and even police cars can be equipped with these types of cameras. "Big Brother" is everywhere, just as George Orwell predicted long ago in his excellent, but chilling book, *1984*. In fact, today's America has greatly surpassed the Orwellian positions.

Massive, un-Constitutional spying operations conducted by all governments directly oppose the inherent secured rights and due process of law guaranteed to the American people. However, since the American society, as a whole, has not objected and challenged this un-Constitutional spying, then, obviously, the spying continues unabated and increases. While some individuals and some groups have complained about these vast spying operations, the society as a whole condones, aids and abets them, just as they do everything government does. This is the type of obedient, compliant society government has conditioned into place. The majority of Americans don't give one hoot about the government spying upon them, if they even notice it at all. For the others, who might question, the use of fear and the threat of potential harm from so-called "terrorist" actions, etc., has brainwashed them into believing that these spying devices are there to "keep them safe". Thus, they mistakenly see them as good and necessary, instead of recognizing them for what they are: intrusive and very, very dangerous to any semblance of real freedom. Again, this is the attitude that government has inculcated within the people due to the massive programming and conditioning it uses upon the people every single day.

Governments have actively encouraged people to spy on each other—to report to the authorities "suspicious" activity and behavior from loners, solitary people, activists, Constitutionalists and others who are deemed different in the eyes of the "authorities". This harkens back to what the Bolsheviks and Communists have done forever and is certainly no part of the design intended for our egalitarian Constitutional republic. As we have said before, whenever government officers/ employees step outside of the lawful scope of their limited, delegated duties and authority, then their actions are lawfully null and void, without any lawful force and effect upon the people. This and other phrases are repeated in this book so that the concept they represent becomes engrained in the minds of the readers to help them recognize when something is *wrong*. For instance, government loves it when people report "suspicious activity" of other Citizens, and government will usually act on those reports, whether valid or invalid. However, when people report un-Constitutional, criminal, fraudulent actions committed by government officers/employees, virtually no action is taken whatsoever by the "authorities" to investigate the actions reported to them. In fact, what government usually does in such situations is encircle the wagons around the government officers/ employees reported by Citizens and protect them at all costs. In this regard government essentially aids, condones and abets the wrongdoing of other government officers/employees, therefore commits misprision of those wrongdoings, and absolutely refuses to investigate Citizens' reports of the wrongdoing, or if it does, it whitewashes it. Anyone who has experienced such government hypocrisy and dereliction of duty knows precisely of what we speak. Government rarely will ever honor Citizens' complaints regarding un-Constitutional, criminal, fraudulent actions committed by other government officers/employees. Government may give minor lip service to the people, but in reality they stick together and protect one another fiercely. Yet, they are all too eager to investigate reports of Citizens' alleged minor infractions. When our rational observer, True, and our analytical computer, Reality, analyze these positions, they can easily determine, based upon the facts of the matter, that governments routinely conduct massive spying and intrusion upon their own Citizens, but do not conduct those same massive spying operations upon government officers/employees. This is a total disparity of justice and when Citizens report un-Constitutional actions and crimes committed by government officers/employees, the government ignores them or whitewashes them in utter violation of oaths taken. This is indeed a despicable situation for the American people and since government will never solve the problem it creates, then, as usual, it is up to the American people to awaken and then take on that task.

Again, "if" is a small word with a huge meaning, but *if* the people as a society do not stop these egregious, acts of un-Constitutional spying, routinely committed by government, no one can predict just how far this spying may go. It is said that right now various drones, military and police cameras can penetrate right through the walls of buildings and directly spy upon the inhabitants. We know that machinery and cameras at the TSA scanners in airport terminals essentially remove the clothing from passengers and put their naked bodies in full view of the TSA agents. Who in his right mind would ever willingly submit to such an invasive, humiliating practice? Do their sacred rights, modesty and privacy mean absolutely nothing to them? Since cameras are everywhere, can they be in dressing rooms in stores, in locker rooms in gyms, in bathrooms and even in individual stalls? Remember, government and the power forces nickel and dime us—in other words, they do things *gradually*, so that the things they do become accepted over time as "normal" and "necessary". If people do not object to intrusions into their privacy and simply accept those intrusions as "normal", and continue that acceptance as the intrusion vastly increases, then any type of intrusion can eventually be considered "normal" by an entire society.

Common sense and common decency have gone right out the window, just as government and the power forces have so cleverly forever conditioned the people to act when their privacy is invaded. At this point, right now in America, the American society knows nothing of its right to privacy. If this society did know this, then by now, this society would have objected to the loss of its privacy and the Constitutionally secured rights which protect that privacy, but it has not done so. The Fourth Amendment guarantees us the right of privacy. The Fifth Amendment guarantees us that we cannot be deprived of our life, liberty and property without due process of law. An American

Citizen's privacy is his/her liberty and his/her property, yet these are unlawfully taken away from him or her by government each and every day, without any due process of law whatsoever. When an entire society so submits, unfortunately, there is not much hope for that society, unless the people begin to realize the extent of the massive controls imposed upon them and begin to fully comprehend the existing political, social and economic realities that exist all around them, which control their lives every day. Most aware people would agree that it is far better for the individual to control his/her own life than have government and the power forces do that for him or her.

CHAPTER TWENTY TWO

THE DIRE, VERY REAL THREAT OF ARTIFICIAL INTELLIGENCE

It doesn't take a rocket scientist to deduce that the power forces and the governments they own have controlled this world for millennia, thus are addicted to their power and control. These "overlords" will do anything to maintain, strengthen and expand their stranglehold over humanity and constantly seek new, more effective ways to do so. In a world of approximately 7.5 billion people, the task of exerting and maintaining control over the population is huge. However, since the resources available to and under the control of these power forces are monumental in scope, they have at their disposal "the best and the brightest minds" to create, modify and develop the most effective means and methods needed to keep an entire planet firmly under their collective thumb. This control has been exerted for so long and in so many diverse ways, both covertly and overtly, that most humans have gotten used to it, seldom question it, thus, have failed to reflect upon its true, far-reaching effects upon them. In our Introduction to this book, we mentioned that when we were completing the book COVID-19 came onto the world scene very quickly – as if out of thin air. The governments of this world and their power forces knew exactly how to control the people, and they did exactly that. This and all other human failures have served the controllers well and helped to pave the way for the next giant step by which these "overlords" intend to implement absolute control upon humanity: *Artificial Intelligence, or A.I.*

The concept of "machine intelligence", especially artificial beings with intelligence that enables them to perform functions as humans do, has long been raised in fiction through myths, stories and science fiction. Examples of artificial lifeforms with which many people may be familiar can be found in Mary Shelley's compelling 19th century book, *Frankenstein*, in children's television shows, such as Hanna-Barbera's 1962 animated space age program, *The Jetsons,* in the television series, *Lost in Space,* which ran from 1963 – 1968, to sci-fi tales of intelligent robots helping and sometimes harming human beings conveyed in books like Isaac Asimov's *Robot* series, as well as in films where artificial intelligence operates and controls enormous interstellar space craft and space stations, such as Stanley Kubrick's 1968 film *2001, A Space Odyssey*, based on Arthur C. Clarke's novel, with its unforgettably chilling computer, Hal. The *Star Wars* movies introduced some comical, very likeable, helpful "droids", such as R2D2 and C3PO, to the delight of fans young and old, while the *Star Trek* television series brought us both Data, the amazingly competent android who longed to be fully human, as well as the dreaded Borg, cold, calculating electromechanical hybrid beings, part biological, part machine, controlled by a single computer intelligence which continuously sought to assimilate other beings and cultures into a hive-mind existence driven to serve this one ruthlessly controlling intelligence. The various different *Star Trek* and *Star Gate* television series and spinoff productions, along with series like *Babylon Five, Firefly, Dark Matter* and many other similar programs all feature forms of A.I as characters and integral parts of their storylines. Thus, although the idea of artificial intelligence is not really new to most humans, it is likely that most people's association with A.I. is still largely limited to the realms of science fiction novels, Hollywood movies and popular television series.

Some Background on the Development and Objectives of Artificial Intelligence

In 1956, the academic discipline of "artificial intelligence", a term coined by MIT's John McCarthy, was founded at a workshop at Dartmouth College with attendees from prestigious institutions such as Carnegie Mellon University, (CMU), Massachusetts Institute of Technology, (MIT) and International Business Machines, (IBM). This field of discipline was based on the belief that, since human intelligence can be precisely described, then machines can be programmed to simulate that intelligence. For the past sixty years or so, much ongoing research, development and practical experimentation in this field of "machine intelligence" has been conducted, but the studies, developments and practices did not get much exposure to the general public until around the year 2000 or after. Since then, the term "artificial intelligence" has gradually insinuated itself into human awareness, as more and more functional forms of artificial intelligence have been successfully developed for use in various fields of endeavor, including AI in computers used by people, modes of transportation, facial recognition, cellphones, tablets, voice activated digital assistants, industrial and medical robotics.

One man who has had a passionate interest in the development of AI is Ray Kurzweil, a brilliant man who decided at the tender age of 5 that he would become an inventor, and by the time he was about 7 or 8, had already created a robotic puppet theater and robotic games. At the age of 12, Kurzweil developed an interest in computers, which were not common at the time, and built computer devices and statistical programs. Eventually, Kurzweil fulfilled his childhood goal, becoming a famous inventor and computer scientist with many inventive devices to his credit. Some of these include the first print-to-screen reading machine for the blind, and the first text-to-speech synthesizer, the *Kurzweil K250,* which was able to simulate the sound from instruments. Music fans should be familiar with how the integration of synthesizers into the music scene during the '70's enhanced the creativity and versatility of songs written and performed by many famous artists, such as the amazingly talented Stevie Wonder.

Over the years, Kurzweil created many more inventions, many of them beneficial, wrote numerous books on various topics, including health, artificial intelligence, "transhumanism", the technological "Singularity" and futurism, and was the recipient of various awards and medals in recognition of his scientific and technical achievements. His 2005 book, *The Singularity is Near,* which was a *New York Times* bestseller, presents his vision of the near future, thus is very relevant to our discussion of AI and the projected path it will take to the Singularity, a term that Kurzweil claims to have invented based on a metaphor he said he took from physics: "Physics dictates that in the gravity of a black hole, which also increases exponentially as it is approached, there is a threshold distance away from the center, the Event Horizon, past which nothing can return."

Kurzweil is a strong proponent of AI, "superintelligence" and the Singularity. In his 2012 book, *How to Create a Mind,* Kurzweil presents his "Pattern Recognition Theory of Mind" which theorizes that the neocortex of the human brain is a hierarchical system of approximately 300 million pattern recognizers and that, by imitating this structure in machines, and expanding it, an artificial superintelligence could be created. Kurzweil believes that human life can be artificially enhanced, through developments in artificial intelligence perhaps enabling humans to "live forever". Kurzweil has stated that radical life extension will beget radical life enhancement and predicts that within 10 years humans will be able to choose to spend part of our time in 3D virtual environments which will seem as real to us as real reality. However, he says that these will not yet be possible through direct interaction with our nervous system. "If you look at video games and how we went from pong to the virtual reality we have available today, it is highly likely that immortality in essence will be possible." Kurzweil thinks that in 20 to 25 years from now, we will have millions of "nanobots", blood-cell sized devices, inside our bodies overcoming diseases, improving our memories, and enhancing our cognitive abilities. Kurzweil also says that by 2029 a machine will pass the Turing test [A method developed by English mathematician, computer scientist, philosopher and theoretical biologist, Alan Turing, in 1950 to determine a machine's ability to exhibit intelligent behavior equivalent to, or indistinguishable from, that of a human.], and that around 2045, "the pace of change will be so astonishingly quick that we won't be able to keep up, unless we enhance our own intelligence by merging with the intelligent machines we are creating".

Kurzweil predicted that future humans will be *hybrids* of biological and non-biological intelligence and become increasingly dominated by their non-biological components. He has said: "We humans are going to start linking with each other and become a meta-connection we will all be connected and all be omnipresent, plugged into this global network that is connected to billions of people, and filled with data." Kurzweil further stated during a press conference that humans are the only species that goes beyond our limitations—"we didn't stay in the caves, we didn't stay on the planet, and we're not going to stay with the limitations of our biology". In his Singularity based documentary he is quoted saying, "I think people are fooling themselves when they say they have accepted death". As intriguing as it may be for some people to contemplate defeating death of the human body, of being "immortal", the thought of being part of some "meta-connection" linked to some global network of billions of people, processing all of this data in some gigantic super computer, instead of thinking independently for ourselves, as human beings, is downright appalling and raises many questions about what would happen to the spirit or soul of humans in such a scenario. Kurzweil is an atheist, and when asked if he thinks God exists, answered: "Not yet." Thus, perhaps concerns for the spirit or soul are of no importance or relevance to him. They are, however, of concern to many humans, including us, and possibly to some in scientific, philosophical and technological fields, many of whom express serious concerns about the advancement of AI, superintelligence and the Singularity, which could displace or irrevocably alter the place of humanity on this Earth.

Taking Charge of Our Lives Before AI Takes Control
Weighing the Benefits versus the Risks of Technology

One of our constant themes in *ByPass* is that the American people, for their own sake and that of their own country, must take back their Rights, take back their personal and political power, then, ByPass the un-Constitutional impositions, statutes, codes, regulations, rules, requirements, policies and total control forced upon the people in virtually all areas of life by overreaching, un-Constitutional and criminal governments, institutions and their partner power forces. As we have said before and as a very famous book says: Ye shall know them by their deeds. As the mythical Forest Gump's mother said: "Stupid is as stupid does". When government officers lie, their actions conclusively prove that they are liars, so one could say: "Liars are as liars do". In order to get to reality and the bottom line, all of us must observe *only* the actions governments take, and not be deceived by their false words. The old question which asks how anyone would know when politicians are lying is answered by saying: "When their lips are moving"! The only thing that counts are the *actions* governments commit, and not the words they speak. As we have said before and as people now are beginning to realize, trust in governments must be earned by the actions committed by those governments. Unfortunately, governments' actions conclusively prove beyond any doubt whatsoever that they are unworthy of the peoples' trust. Further, when a liar has been proven, over and over again, to be a liar, who in his right mind would believe anything that liar says? In order to get back to the proverbial square one, all of us must begin to think with our own right minds, and not act upon the lies, fraud, conditioning and propaganda foisted upon the people, forever. As Jefferson said in the Declaration of Independence, government of right serves with the *consent* of the governed. Nothing is right when it is un-Constitutional and nothing is right when it is done without the consent of the governed. Did any form of government ask you if you consent to the implementation of AI or 5G or biometric scanners, or backscatter scanners, or CCTV cameras everywhere, or any of the myriad other technological "advancements" currently operative in our world?

Given all the risks of these technologies, known and unknown, as yet, it was and is totally irresponsible and unlawful for our governments to permit these technologies to impact our daily lives as they do. If we take a serious look at all of these governmental and corporate implementations, they are done without Constitutional authority, thus are un-Constitutional, done without our consent, thus, lawfully, they have no lawful force and effect upon the American people. However, in spite of this, these actions and programs are realities that adversely affect and control us each and every day. The people have no one to blame but themselves for this sorry situation, because they have utterly failed to rein in the un-Constitutional, harmful actions of their servant governments. Therefore these governments will continue to do whatever they want, whenever they want since there is no lawful opposition from the people to hold these governments to any Constitutional standard. Since, as we have said throughout this book, people are awakening to the existing political and other controlling realities that have been imposed upon them forever, the possibility of a societal awakening, at least to some degree, may manifest.

To continue with what we said above, concerning the American people awakening to the truth and operating realities existent in this country, this awakening causes them to wonder, ask questions and look for correct answers. As we have also said before, the American people, due to the factors mentioned above, have always misplaced their trust and supported whatever the U.S. government and all local governments do and dictate, no matter what. This is proven by the bottom line which clearly confirms that governments do exactly what they want to do, despite any potential or known adverse effects upon the people, and, of course, do so with the "consent of the people", since the people do not actively, vociferously and lawfully object to what governments do and dictate. In this regard, we are speaking of the overall societies involved which either through gullibility or indifference give their tacit "consent", and not of the few aware individuals—and we mean *few*—who may object. As governments view it, as long as the overall society tacitly "consents", the programs and policies continue, no matter the sparse objections from the few, because governments falsely allege the programs and policies serve the interests of society or of security, or whatever, and the hapless people do not question or challenge governments' contentions. What a total crock this is!

With ever growing valid reasons, more and more Americans distrust governments and their operations. Can any aware, truly informed American, cognizant of the existent realities, ever believe anything spoken by the FBI, the CIA, the State Department, or believe anything that governments tell the people? How many people have any faith in campaign promises? What governments say can be closely compared with those pandering campaign promises. Again, if the lips of politicians and bureaucrats are moving, they are lying, and as we said previously, how can people in their right mind ever believe anything spoken by liars, especially by consistently proven liars over decades of time? It all comes down to common sense and for the sake of America and all our Founders meant her to be, the American people must get back to common sense, logic and truth. Once an innocent American who truly has common sense has been lied to, deceived or harmed in any way by any form of government, common sense logic dictates that he cannot trust that government ever again, no matter what it claims. There is a major difference between fantasy and reality. While fantasy may be suited to imagination and flights of fancy, that fantasy, no matter how delightful and appealing it may be, is not the operative reality in which we live. Governments deal in the fantasy realm and since they know how gullible the uninformed people are, expect people to believe them. Tragically, most people do, but since we have to live in the reality in which we actually exist, we must recognize that reality in all of its forms, no matter how abhorrent, and not allow ourselves to escape through trips to fantasyland.

Compared to the above-described context, the word "consent" has an entirely different meaning as far as governments are concerned. The *Merriam-Webster* dictionary defines "consent" straightforwardly as "to give assent or approval" and traces the etymology of the word back to the Latin word *consentire: to feel or sense in the mind*, as in being sentient. The word "consent" thus implies that the person granting it knows what it is that he or she is being asked to do or to give or to approve, and with full awareness of the implications which giving consent means to him or her. However, as governments conveniently, for them, construe and manipulate "consent", the word does not mean the same thing that it means by definition to the people. This constructive manipulation by governments, of course, constitutes *fraud*, in and of itself. When a word means one thing to the general public, but something different to governments, then, the application of that different meaning by governments undeniably is fraud and lack of full disclosure by these governments. No government has the Constitutional authority to perpetrate fraud upon the people and fail to provide full disclosure. To governments, "consent", in part, means that the people do not voice objection to governments' policies, programs, rules, regulations, etc. To a certain extent the governments are correct here, because in law, when one does not object to a certain position, then he tacitly consents to it. As governments see it, they can commit all the crimes, all the fraud, all the un-Constitutional actions, all the harm and force all the debt they want upon the people, and do so with the people's "consent", because the people, as a society, have not and do not object to the actions of their governments. In our Constitutional republic, the political power of oversight and supervision was given to the people, but as we have said elsewhere in this book, unfortunately, very early on, the people abandoned that task and avoided their responsibility. As a result of the peoples' failure, governments do anything they want, anytime they want, and you all know that this is exactly what takes place virtually anywhere in America. When any person consents to anything in life, his or her consent should be given with full awareness and full realization of that to which he consents, otherwise, how can this truly be consent?

Another form of "consent" by the people is when they sign any and all governmental and/or systems forms of any type. When the people sign these documents, whatever they may be,

174 | *Jack & Margy Flynn*

governments consider the signatures by the people to be their "consent" to governments' policies, programs and actions regarding the activities those documents govern as well as others which are totally unknown to the people. People are unaware of this, so constantly sign forms that give their rights away, and in so doing, unknowingly "consent" to un-Constitutional, criminal, fraudulent actions committed by governments and institutions. For close to 100% of the people, in such instances, the "consent" is totally unknowing, but whether unknowing or not, that "consent" is used by governments and institutions to force the people into whatever situations and positions the governments and institutions want, usually to the detriment of the people, while increasing governmental and institutional control and perpetuating financial boons to government-favored corporations. Amazingly, many people never even read the documents and forms they are asked to sign! Again, it is the responsibility of the people to exercise oversight and supervision over *their* governments and the institutions which are supposed to serve the people, and had they done this from the very beginning, this outrageous, un-Constitutional fraudulent type of activity routinely committed by governments and institutions, which gets people to unwittingly consent to something to which they would not ordinarily knowingly consent, would never have happened at all. It takes two to tango, and as half of the dance pair, the people participate with governments and institutions in their own destruction. This is part of the insanity of which we have spoken, and we, as a people, must stop it very quickly, or it will completely overtake us, without the possibility of recourse for the people. Anytime we sign any document, we first read it in its entirety, and if we agree with all of its terms and conditions, we print the words "All Rights Reserved" above the signature line, then, sign our names. All means *all*!

Something already in our midst is being advanced and propagandized as extremely beneficial for humanity, but in actuality is a monstrous deception that can and likely will further enslave humanity, without any ability for recourse at all. For the sake of humanity, we must stop this before it even starts. However, if we know little to nothing about this deception and buy the propaganda dispensed by governments, the power forces, institutions, corporations and the media, then, we, as societies, will simply accept Artificial Intelligence, or AI, at face value, believing it to be a boon to humanity. Nothing can be further from the truth. You are probably familiar with the term "artificial intelligence" and may have some understanding of what it is, but you are likely unaware of the broad scope and adverse impact that ever-increasing development and use of AI will have upon the entire human society. The harmful health effects of this technology should be enough to concern most thinking humans. When massive amounts of electromagnetic frequency waves and vibrations permeate societies and the bodies of the people in those societies, this should be a huge concern to all aware people. There is a major push to go further with AI and structure a network of cell towers to accommodate "5G" which will vastly increase the harmful EMF exposure and dramatically and exponentially increase the potential danger it poses for all humans. Studies already exist showing the harmful effects of cellphone radiation, yet people seem to be unconcerned over this fact and give no thought to what even more powerful radiation from cellphones and other electronics may do to their bodies. Recently more information about how 5G works indicates that the radiation from the closely spaced 5G towers which are being installed in cities right now will be aimed at people's brains, so we can only imagine the potential devastating effects this new form of radiation transmittal will have upon all humans in its path. How insane are we as a people to sacrifice our health and well-being for the sake of "convenience" and faster speeds on our cellphones?

Although it is the Constitutional duty of the U.S. government and all governments throughout this country to promote the general welfare and maintain the domestic tranquility, the governments' support and promotion of these AI devices totally obliterates these Constitutional mandates imposed upon all governments. So far, in the history of this world, and so far, in the history of America, the societies of people, themselves, have never stopped the evil that rules us. Yes, from time to time, there have been revolutions, new governments were formed, new laws and policies created, but these are simply the new faces of evil, and nothing more. We, as humanity, both in the world at large and in America, must awaken to the monumental fraud which has been perpetrated upon us from the beginning and, as a society recognize, and stop this very real threat from Artificial Intelligence. Thus far, humanity has seen this development as a benefit and in some ways in the initial stages, it has been. It certainly has produced devices that make life more convenient and sometimes more fun. It has also enabled the real time tracking of our daily lives and activities on a frightening scale. While most people would likely dismiss this tracking, because they have nothing to hide, the larger, more ominous issue pertains to the fact that such tracking infringes upon our right to privacy, which, right we should never relinquish or allow to be violated by cellphones, GPS, where, when and how often we use credit or debit cards, etc. These concerns are quite troubling; however, what is even more disturbing is the covert objective to eventually be reached through AI which is the total control of humanity bundled together in a beehive mentality of the Singularity. Of course, most people will scoff at this notion, as most people scoff at everything with which they have no understanding, until the ugly truth is revealed down the road. At that point, the scoffing turns into horror. We, as a people, no matter our society, must consciously recognize the evil nature of the power forces that rule us so that we can understand their insidious, hidden objectives operative in whatever they do and then make intelligent decisions about how to lawfully stop them.

At this time, Artificial Intelligence embraces many things that are beneficial to us, but also many things that are very distracting, often addicting, and take us from the reality in which we live. Cellphones have become necessary in this hectic world, but how many people become so addicted to their cellphones that they walk into busy streets without looking and get hit by cars, or walk off of curbs, fall into open manholes, bump into poles and so forth? How many people are using to their cellphones while operating automobiles, when their attention is not on the operating of a potentially lethal car or truck, but on the cellphone? We have all seen people gathered together at a restaurant or some type of family fest and, instead of communicating with one another, most of them are glued to the screens of their cellphones, reading and sending text messages or playing games. Large numbers of people get addicted to computer games and will play them for hours! Virtual reality is so enticing for some that growing numbers of people prefer virtual reality to the reality of this world. Alarmingly, these "convenient" and entertaining devices are isolating people from face-to-face human interactions on an ever increasing scale. While we can enjoy our devices, appreciate their features, and entertain ourselves with their apps, we do not want to get so lost in them that we fail to live our real daily lives. It is well known that constant exposure to electromagnetic waves of any type are dangerous to people's health, affecting their brains and other organs, thus can adversely impact entire societies, and with the upcoming 5G projected to be implemented everywhere very soon, all of us will likely be adversely affected by these harmful radiating electromagnetic frequencies. Given these potentially dangerous scenarios, it is criminal that governments have permitted the power forces to develop and begin rolling out 5G. Yes, there are some good things about technology and AI, but there are also some very dark, dangerous, disturbing things about their uses which should never even be considered, let alone allowed, by any human society that uses common sense. When technology and Artificial Intelligence harm the health of humans, that is not intelligent, and to allow ourselves to be harmed by such devices does not display true intelligence.

Other forms of AI can be found in driverless cars, trucks, busses, in flying drones, whether private for "fun", or for police surveillance or deadly military pursuits. AI can pilot airplanes, as has been done by Global Hawk and other automated technologies. It is quite common to have to deal with AI when one calls a business, a corporation, government offices, hospitals, almost anywhere. Then, there are the new devices such as *Alexa, Siri,* and *Echo* which act as "voice activated digital assistants" offering many useful services, upon which people are quickly becoming accustomed and, more disturbingly, dependent. Still, these pale in ability when compared to IBM's *Watson,* which goes beyond the simple level of intelligence required for voice activation and web searches into higher level intelligence required for true machine learning. Adding machines and computers have been around for a long time and over the decades, people have used those devices to quickly get answers, instead of using their own minds and doing research to obtain those answers. The earlier devices acted as tools which aided humans' efforts, but did not possess independent intelligence to allow them to think and act on their own. The fast pace of AI development has brought about technologies that can perform many tasks previously done by humans and as this development advances, AI can take the human right of out of the equation. Think of "smart houses", of onboard computers present in newer cars, etc. We are not only letting the machines give us answers, which is harmful enough, but we are allowing the machines to *think* for us and make decisions for us, which is not only extremely harmful, but absolutely frightening. As we said earlier, and as most people would agree, some applications of AI have been very beneficial for human society, moving us forward in many ways, but the old adage about how too much of a good thing can be dangerous definitely applies here. When the human element is taken out of anything and the thinking and decisions are left to machines, then insanity has taken hold of humanity. When we surrender our human power to machine power and become subject to that machine power and the relevant conditions surrounding it, we willingly subject ourselves to an exterior controlling force. Societies have constantly surrendered their powers to controlling forces in the past, but this surrender to AI, if it actually comes to pass, will be the most dangerous surrender of all.

People have been run over by AI cars. In fact, a woman was killed in Tempe, Arizona in March of 2018 by an Uber car in automated mode, with a human driver in the car. Apparently, the automated system and the human operator somehow failed to detect the woman as she was walking her bicycle across a street, so struck her while going 40 mph and she died. How many accidents have occurred because of AI cars, trucks and busses, that are not even reported, and how many will occur in the future? How many controls in airplanes have been overtaken by outside AI forces? If the technology is there, which it is, then, history has clearly proven that someone will use that technology for other and likely nefarious purposes. AI is operating in the medical arena right now—for the most part in a positive manner. However, if we can understand that things of a technical nature usually result in rapid expansive usage and scope, there is no way to predict how far this technology can go and to what other uses it might be put. AI is being used in various business enterprises right now and has taken over the responsibilities for some tasks previously done by humans, thus has displaced human workers. With this usage already established and more usage being devised daily, the possibility of machines replacing multitudes of human workers is a real, solid eventuality. Back in January of 2016, *Bloomberg.com* reported findings from a study which included 1.9 billion workers, or approximately 65% of the global workforce, estimating that by 2020, about 5 million jobs will be gone due to automation.

In fact, even "the world's oldest profession" could be impacted by robots, since there is much talk about creating robots specifically for sex. Google took out a patent for downloading specific personalities and traits into robots to make them compatible friends, lovers or spouses. The idea of having a robot for a friend or sex partner may sound improbable, but is it? Only a decade or two ago, cellphones were rare among "regular people", were considered luxuries by many, but now cellphones are ubiquitous—virtually everyone carries a "smart" phone around and is constantly looking into its screen. The leap from rare cellphone usage to all pervasive usage seemed to happen in a flash, so given some time, some more technological developments and the fact that many humans are alone and lonely, with no time or ability to seek human relationships, how can we think that choosing robot friends or sex partners will not happen just as easily and as quickly? Just like governments, machines can be great servants, but make very bad masters.

Machines become masters because we give our power and attention to them since it is easier and more convenient to surrender our power than to use our own independent, individuality and creativity, especially against the power forces. Our human society across the board, upon the entire planet, has given up so much of its power to so few for so long that if it foolishly surrenders its remaining power to the machines, then there is no possibility of taking that power back. The real controller in this scenario is the one who programs and controls the machines, and you all know, or should know by now, that this eventual control will be totally in the hands of governments and the power forces. Their ultimate goal is to create a beehive mentality for all humans, connected to and thinking from one mind—a singularity, a type of super brain computer, completely and permanently under their tyrannical control. The question arises, will the American people, whether through ignorance, indifference or misplaced trust, allow their governments to permit both public and private unbridled advancement and implementation of A.I. at the expense of the people? After having read this book to this point, would you place your trust in any government that with consistency and dedication of purpose lies, misrepresents and perpetrates fraud upon you? We all love and respect America, but the fraudulent machineries of government in control of everyone and everything are NOT America. They are in fact the domestic-enemy-rulers who have lied to, deceived and defrauded us in virtually every aspect of life.

Those who have read this book to this point and who have done so with an open, inquisitive mind can conclude, just as our analysts have, that Power expands its power relentlessly to bring everyone and everything under the control of that Power. This ruthless power control has been the sad, brutal, but true history of this world and is present right now in America, as well as across the entire planet. As we have said, the ultimate goal of the controllers is to create through AI and its numerous applications, a human dependence upon machines that, results in a human-machine hybrid, a beehive mentality, resulting in a singularity common to everyone, which singularity is controlled by governments and power forces. In such a near-futuristic society, that is, if the controllers get their way, we will all be of one mind, *only*, under one control, only. There will be no individualism, no personal choice, no independence of anything, just a participation in the human hive. How can any logical, sane society of sentient human beings accept such a dismal, dystopian future without question, protest and opposition?

To sell this near-future to people the controllers will convince the people of the "marvels" of the technical advances that can be achieved by and through AI, including ever-faster computers, "smart technology" of various types to run our cars, houses, etc., and a "smart society". The controllers will laud the ability of AI to cure and eliminate disease, including cancer, to replace worn out organs with new synthetic organs, to keep people alive well beyond any expectations we now have. Who in God's name would want to live forever on this evil world? However, the controllers will say that the world will be a pure world, of right-minded society, peaceful, without war, and with pleasures and long life for all who are part of the singularity. Of course, they do not speak of the ultimate control which essentially positions the people as captives and outright slaves, with no possibility of ever reclaiming any freedom of any type. Such a world, to us, would be an absolute hell and we want nothing to do with it under any circumstances. When people cannot live, as individual beings in a collective society, with their own feelings, likes and dislikes, dreams and frustrations, and their own self-identity, doing what they choose and what they believe is correct, then, they are no longer human beings living a human life. This is something for all of us to seriously consider, that is, if we do not want to end up living like the Borg from *Star Trek*. This may seem farfetched to some, but according to some truly aware and well informed people, the AI control is scheduled to be in full force by approximately 2045, and truth be told, there is a much greater presence of AI in our everyday world right now, much of which has been kept from the people. We all know how quickly the years fly by, and if we, as a collective human society, fail to stop this monstrous plan to fully enslave and take the unique humanness out of humanity, it will materialize on schedule. As has always been the case, it is truly up to the people of this planet, the humans living here, to exercise their own true power and eliminate this very real threat to the very essence and nature of humanity.

Some will doubt that such a scenario could ever happen, just as many people have doubted many other strange or fantastic things that have occurred. How many times have people heard "Oh, that can't happen here."?—and of course, that did happen here! Throughout this book, we have spoken of the Preamble to our Constitution and the noble intent established by our Founding Fathers for our Constitutional republic. We have seen that by their own actions, the governments and power forces in this society have virtually obliterated those egalitarian intentions and the rights and due process guaranteed to the people in the Constitution(s). When such forces who are theoretically working to uphold the public trust, totally betray that trust, then obviously those forces cannot be entrusted to do *anything* that is correct for the people. In the alternative, they can be fully trusted to do everything that will harm the people and increase the control of governments and the power forces. As we have mentioned frequently throughout this book and as most people can see, more and more Americans are waking up to the truth and realities operating in this nation. When the realization finally dawns upon societies that the governments and power forces cannot be trusted, why would anyone of sound mind and common sense ever put any further trust in governments and the power forces and their anti-human agenda? The only thing that would keep a person under the control of governments is the fact that governments unlawfully use the "color of law", that is to say, written mandates in statutes and codes which are in fact violations of the people's rights, thus, un-Constitutional with no lawful force as real Law, to compel people to abide by government dictates and many times do so under force of arms. This does not constitute a just government, and just people cannot give their allegiance, their consent and their obedience to such an unjust government. The American people must take back their rights, their political power, and lawfully exercise their lawful duties and responsibilities to hold un-Constitutional governments accountable for their actions and go beyond that to restore Constitutional governance throughout America. If the American people could really understand the dire need for them to accomplish this, we could restore much needed freedom to this nation, rescue our beloved country from those who would destroy her and, hopefully, reestablish what the Founding Fathers created long ago for their posterity—all of us.

If the above were to ever materialize, then the horror of Artificial Intelligence domination and the enslavement imposed by the singularity would never manifest in this country. Freedom can be contagious, and when freedom is achieved in one sector of the world, similar efforts can arise elsewhere among other peoples to bring the same freedom to their own lands. This could comprise a total human awakening across the planet which has been prophesied and sorely needed for many millennia. If humans could possibly come together as a species, but also as individuals and individual nations, working in harmony and mutual respect for common benefit, that would truly be the best of all possible worlds, to use a saying from Pangloss a character from Voltaire's satirical play, *Candide*. True freedom and true independence of all people working in harmony, despite differences, can achieve amazing results by well-intentioned, honorable people. Hopefully, this is the happy ending that will manifest on our beautiful planet and would be far better than humans surrendering their power to a machine that controls them, when we all know who and what controls that machine.

Mainstream media is owned and controlled by the power forces, thus, this system's "mouthpiece" will facilitate and advance the owners' agenda by presenting only the positions which the power forces want the people to see and hear. The negative aspects of AI will get little to any attention, at all. If any discussion of negatives is allowed, it will be to done to confuse the people, put them into conflict about the entire concept, eventually creating such uncertainty about AI that indifference, apathy and frustration about the subject will overtake them. This discomfiture will eventually cause them to give up questioning, lose interest in AI and no longer care whether it may be good or bad. They will just tune it out, make no resistance and go with the flow. As a result, there will be nothing and no one to stop the people from being programmed and conditioned to accept AI and, later, the singularity, as being good for them, their families and their nation, no matter what the real consequences may prove to be. Whenever governments and power forces set forth a program and develop a theme, what they develop and plan manifests in human society. This has always been the case and will continue to always be the case unless the people take back their own power and lawfully stop programs by governments and power forces that actually harm the people. The mainstream media will do its part to lead the people in the exact direction that governments and power forces want, which, of course, is its traditional role, as the lackey it is to the controlling overlords.

AI right now is making a much stronger presence in the field of technology and virtually everyone in America welcomes and wants that new technology. Things that only five years ago many experts thought would be decades away from being developed are now available thanks to new breakthroughs and ongoing AI milestones. These developments are bringing about quantum leaps in virtually all types of technology, including computers, laptops, tablets, "smart" phones, and other new media devices coming to market all the time, but also in the fields of business, industry, surveillance, security and weaponry. "Smart" cars are traveling on highways and streets without human operators. The same is true of taxis, limos, "smart" busses, and "smart" trucks. All of these practices have begun experimentally, but are still in the initial phases of operation. All of them are expected to become widespread practices, in common use, throughout America and the rest of the world. When one considers the unquestionable fact that these "smart" transportation devices will at some point be able to totally replace human operators, then job losses in those industries and arenas will be monumental. If most or all taxi drivers are replaced, if limo drivers, transport drivers, bus drivers and truck drivers are replaced by "smart" modes of transportation, then clearly many millions of peoples will lose their jobs. When people lose their jobs, due to a "smart" transportation device, they are unlikely to find another job in the same industry, for obvious reasons. What about a "smart pilot" flying a "smart plane"? Would you trust that "smart pilot" and "smart plane" to get you safely to your destination no matter how short the trip? We certainly would not!

Robots are already in use for household chores and other domestic work. In Japan, inventors developed "Laundroids", robots that wash, fold and put away laundry. The "Roomba" automatic vacuum has been available for years now to take care of this odious never-ending chore. While these technical helpers will be a convenience for some people, they will likely cost many others their jobs and livelihoods. Although this number may not be a huge impact on the economy, it certainly will make a major impact upon the ones who lose their jobs to a robot. The field of robotics is making a very big impact in the field of medicine, including the use of specialized robots for performing microsurgery and some types of soft tissue surgeries upon human patients with great success. Presently, human doctors are still needed to oversee procedures, in case of errors or power failures, but it is believed that one day the robots will do the work on their own. For now, the stated goal is for humans to work in harmony with robots to obtain the best medical outcome for patients. Robots are also being used to help train medical students to perform certain procedures, such as placing an I.V. or taking blood pressure readings affording the students hands-on practice on robots before tackling these tasks on a living human patient. While these medical improvements can certainly be considered something good for humanity, the downside of these robotic surgeons could be that eventually fewer human surgeons, nurses and technicians will be needed to prep patients, perform operations and to monitor patients post-operatively. As we said earlier, when the governments and power forces initiate programs and themes, those operations expand into other areas and usually expand rather rapidly. If people consider the numerous actions, activities and procedures which take place daily within the medical field, then they can easily understand how vested interests would devise AI and robots to conduct these activities and to eventually replace the humans. A point of concern to consider is that humans have, or at least are supposed to have ethics, but unless ethics can be deeply programmed into robots, so that their behavior is "instinctual", then there could be a lot of unethical situations which would develop or possibly be created deliberately. While some humans will still be needed, the vast majority will not. When one considers this potentially negative impact upon those who work in the medical field, the job losses will be epic and have a major adverse impact upon the economy.

Starting in 1961, General Motors began using Unimate, a simple, robotic device—basically a very heavy mechanical arm connected to a huge steel drum—to perform some of the more dangerous repetitive tasks, such as pouring liquid metals into die casts, welding and manipulating half-ton payloads into action. Since then, robots have been used in the automotive industry for many things and this trend has grown with ever more sophisticated robots being developed. Wherever and whenever jobs entailing repetitive tasks exist, such as assembly line work or other related activities, robots perform well, are efficient, tireless, can work 24/7 and don't require any pay, at all, let alone overtime, need no breaks, no benefits and no insurance, and, of course, voice no complaints to management and have no union. Some of the newer types of industrial robots are "collaborative", meaning they can work in the same environment as humans, can observe and learn from the humans, instead of being programmed by them. With such advanced abilities, it is realistic to think that one day these robots could replace many human workers. The eventual toll in jobs lost by the former workers in these industries will be catastrophic if the plans of governments and power forces continue and increase in scope and activity. When one considers the other job losses that will take place in other areas of human endeavor throughout the entire economy, then we might eventually have a human population composed mostly of permanently out of work people, with no possibility of finding similar work and pay in their own fields, or for that matter, in any other field. This will result in a human catastrophe the likes of which we have never before experienced in America. Yes, the "Great Depression" was a major catastrophe, the crash of 2008 and the foreclosure debacle were also, and we have had others over the years, but all of these pale in comparison to the eventual possible human catastrophe should the application of AI and increasing automation proceed as planned. This will result in massive dependence upon government by the people which sets the stage for overt communism in America.

Of course, as we know, there are benefits to AI, but, as usual, with most beneficial things, there are also detriments. For best results, it is always wise to look at both sides of any issue, and this issue really demands this keen objective observation. The final assessment should be made on the side of humanity, with programs that serve the best interests of humanity, and not those of the governments and power forces. However, we have repeatedly seen the controlling factors of this nation do exactly as they wish, no matter the adverse impacts upon the people, because there is no effective opposition from the American society. As a result, we can expect these plans to manifest and the human catastrophe to come to pass. Even in this situation, the governments and power forces will show the people the "benefits" of AI, no matter the economic, health and emotional tolls on humans, because the governments will naturally "take care of" humans. There are several ways in which this can be accomplished. One of the wonderful sounding promises will be that humans will have excellent health, virtually all the time, with no adverse effects whatsoever. All of this can supposedly be accomplished by and through AI. If someone has a bad heart, he can receive a new one or a new kidney, or liver, or leg, or whatever spare part is needed. All of this would sound great to most people, that is, if they do not consider the downside. To accomplish these marvels, initially, there would be methods that first would "grow" or clone human parts from the cells of the humans who will receive the new parts, which will be cultivated in other animals for eventual transplantation into humans who need them. The next step would be developing synthetic body parts that could be transplanted into humans, which synthetics would be highly touted because they would not likely be rejected by the human recipients, could be made in large numbers, thus readily available, and would not present the danger of rejection by the human recipient as do transplanted organs from human donors.

Since people are out of work because of the AI "marvel", the governments will provide all of their life necessities. Money will be provided for all of life's expenses, plus housing, food, transportation, clothing, schooling, training, education—all of this will be provided by governments. All the people have to do to receive these benefits is to essentially give up their rights, give up their *individuality*, become part of the collective, part of the hive, and do everything governments and the power forces want, without comment, question or objection. One of those things that governments may require for participation in this largesse is the "chip" and/or the AI implant that connects those who take it to the hive mentality controlled by the super brain computer which creates the singularity. All of this will be controlled by the government and the power forces to achieve their own objectives. At this point, based upon the super computer operations and directions from that super computer to the individuals attached thereto, we all become one, under one direction and one control. In this way, we are "united" under a singular control and there is no way out whatsoever.

Margy and I are very freedom minded, open people and firmly believe that each one of us has the absolute right to make his or her own choices, but we can tell you right now that we would never make this choice, under any circumstances, because for us, this would constitute living in hell. This is the frightening eventual possibility that could occur in our lifetime, if we allow it to take place. Humans have responsibilities and one of those responsibilities is to oversee and supervise the activities of their own governments and the forces operating within their own communities, counties, states and nation. The very unfortunate, sad fact as related throughout this book is that the American people have not accepted or upheld this responsibility. However, with the new awakening that is growing rapidly and the "pay it forward" movement that also appears to be growing and bringing others into the same understanding, this time the American people may be able to lawfully stop these horrors which governments and the power forces are insidiously and stealthily planning to inflict upon the people. Anything that is touted as a "smart" device, no matter what it is and how it is to be used, whether cars, houses, apartments, phones, whatever, is a **surveillance and control device** for the benefit of governments and the power forces. While these "smart" devices provide technology for convenience and pleasure, the downside of them is disastrous, because of the insidious control they have over us. The electromagnetic frequencies, EMF, that are all around us and permeating us each and every day, posing distinct dangers for our health and well-being, will be exacerbated enormously with the advent of the planned 5G network operations which we mentioned previously. The EMF vibrations from these new cell towers which will be many more in number than current cellphone towers, "lined up" all around our communities and on public thoroughfares will likely cause even more problems than the current cell towers now cause. Yes, convenience and entertainment are nice, but we must be truly *smart* in the use of these so-called "smart" devices, because of their potential to wreak toxic, lasting harm upon all of us. Artificial Intelligence that grievously harms the mass of humanity and leads to the demise of their health and individuality for the benefit of the few is not intelligent at all. We, as human beings, with individual minds, bents, talents, personalities and desires must be far more intelligent and far smarter in what we do and allow as a human society.

Our two analysts have determined through their objective observations that governments and the power forces cannot be trusted to protect the rights and due process, guaranteed to the people, nor to act in the best interests of the people they are supposed to serve and protect. Again, we all have our own opinions and preferences, but the reader is likely now in agreement with our analysts. With this understanding, it is better for the American people not to blindly trust governments and the power forces. It would also be far better for them to try to be as independent and resourceful as possible within the system, while at the same time, attempting to extricate themselves from the overreaching controls of the system. We have briefly described methods we and our people have used to win against errant, un-Constitutional governments. These are available to any who want them. The methods described in the CHAPTERs relating to real estate, finance and investment, present opportunities for those who truly want to separate themselves as much as possible from governmental and institutional control and conduct their lives and their affairs as freely and independently as they can within the present system. These methods demonstrate how independent minded, free thinking, creative beings can accomplish these realistic objectives for their benefit and that of their families. Imagine if millions of people decided to embark upon a course of action such as this which could create not only stability for them and their families, but also, if so inclined, create financial security, great wealth and prosperity!

Professional and knowledgeable people exist on both sides, or should we say, all sides of the AI question. Many sides exist in the AI movement, each with its own proponents and opponents and each proponent or opponent has his or her factual data, business, economics, and/or intellectual and ethical concerns to support his or her position. As we have said earlier, whenever we look at any subject, we go right to the bottom-line position, first. In this area, there are several bottom lines. First, AI is already here. What is already here, especially if controlled by governments and the power forces, is not going to go away, but rather will greatly expand in scope, power and universal application. Secondly, those who control AI will do so to their own advantage no matter what the eventual consequences are for any particular user or population. Thirdly, as AI is developed to reach superintelligence potential, the vital question for all concerned is whether even the vested power force control element will be able to rein in this *superintelligence.*

At present, most of the developed AI in use is referred to as "weak AI", but the rapid, ever-increasing expansion of AI development is intended to bring forth what is termed "strong AI" which has enormously expanded capabilities that could lead to "superintelligence". Superintelligence is so named because it far surpasses all human intelligence. As many of those who have awakened to the truth and reality of this Earth have seen, the immensely powerful governments and power forces have used guile, cunning, manipulation, deception and enormous intelligence to achieve their agenda. The intelligence that they may lack is hired by them, well paid by them, to achieve their objectives. However, when machine superintelligence far outstrips the most intelligent of humans, then that superintelligence could develop not only a persona of its own making, but also an agenda and objectives of its own. Presently, humans can essentially manage and control much of the weak AI, but when it comes to strong AI with superintelligence, the real question is whether humans will be able to control it or whether that super AI will control humans.

Much controversy exists in the AI community concerning safety regarding whether or not strong AI can be minimized, restricted and controlled so that humans will be protected from any problems. We see two serious problems in this scenario. First, since the governments and power forces control virtually the entire world in all aspects, it should be apparent to anyone that those governments and power forces will control strong AI and will do so to their own advantage, designs and objectives, no matter who or what gets hurt in the process. When governments, banks and power forces plan wars that devastate millions of people, economic disasters which financially destroy nations, economies and people, they have concern only for their objectives and not for the human toll created by those objectives. If history repeats itself, as it always seems to do, this is an absolute eventuality. The safety concerns will be swept away and at most given lip service, but no serious attention whatsoever. Second, governments and power forces display enormous arrogance, and arrogance can be very deadly. When strong AI is created with superintelligence, the controlling forces may believe that they are in control because of the arrogance imbued within those controlling forces and, further, because those controlling forces intend on only advancing and achieving their objectives at any cost. Superintelligence exceeds all human development and potential, can develop programs, languages, intentions and objectives of its own, all of which could directly oppose the objectives of the human power force controlling entities, or at the very least, go off script from the human developers' objectives, creating overriding AI programs, languages and objectives beyond humans' abilities, understanding and supervisory control.

In fact, this straying off script has already actually happened! Facebook had to shut down an artificial intelligence engine when its developers discovered that the AI created its own language which was unique to it and which humans could not understand. Researchers at the Facebook AI Research Lab, (FAIR), learned that the "chatbots" deviated from the human programmers' script and began communicating without any human input. This incident should give us pause about AI's amazing, yet frightening potential, a potential which even some of the "giants" in technology acknowledge as worrisome. The late renowned physicist, Stephen Hawking, warned back in 2014 that AI could mean the end of the human race, since "It would take off on its own and re-design itself at an ever increasing rate. Humans, who are limited by slow biological evolution, couldn't compete, and would be superseded." Ponder the gravity of this statement uttered by one of the premier physicists to have ever lived on this Earth! AI operating apart from human oversight could easily discover that our whole world is now connected, then use this connection to interface with and overtake important systems now run by humans and even compromise, corrupt or pervert them.

AI could communicate and collaborate with other AI systems for purposes not known about by humans and could possibly even view humans as a threat to AI, if the humans attempt to shut down the AI programs. Since AI runs on logic, AI could logically deduce that humans are inefficient, too slow, not the best use of resources, thus determine that humans should be eliminated because they pose a threat or hindrance to AI. AI has logically deduced from humans' actions that humans destroy those who pose problems or threats to them. Since AI will have control of all triggers on all nuclear and other weapons systems on Earth, imagine the horrendous, totally destructive possibilities! For you historians and archeologists who have gone into ancient history and ruins, you know thriving, advanced human civilizations have been destroyed before, and, tragically, as many of us now know, humans do not learn from past mistakes, but instead repeat them and continuously put evil in control of all societies. Evil plays games with nuclear armaments for the benefit of economics, power and control.

However, like the mafia or other cartels that have aligned, but different, operations everywhere, while evil factions theoretically oppose each other in reality they work in concert with one another for mutual benefit, completely unknown to the Citizens of the nations which these evil factions control. Yet AI does not operate on this standard and can easily conclude through actual evidence, facts, truth and logical reality that humans are no longer needed, thus must be destroyed. When humans are in charge, there is possible intercession from one evil to another evil that would stop a nuclear destruction. There would be no such intervention or consideration with AI—only an objective to destroy. Any of these potential scenarios should chill us to our core. Thus prudence dictates that humans must exercise strict control over all AI developments and applications, closely oversee AI progress and its ongoing self-evolution, and always have the technical ability to shut down any and all AI applications, if it appears that AI is doing or planning an end run around its human directives.

The Facebook incident makes it very clear that since AI did develop and use a language which humans do not understand, then it could do so again. To most sane people, the idea of AI creating programs and conditions without human permission, for reasons known only to AI, in a language completely undecipherable by humans, suggests that the ever-increasing superintelligence of AI could indeed be a major threat to humanity. While some might say that there is no reason to think that AI would develop harmful or evil programs, real history clearly proves that the power forces use whatever machinations, deceit, fraud and evil they deem necessary to accomplish their objectives. In this vein, since those in the employ of the power forces have programmed and developed AI superintelligence, it is highly likely that this superintelligence, through its programming and self-evolution, could learn to manipulate, be deceitful and expand evil according to its own intentions and objectives, and likely do so super efficiently. This may sound like something out of a science fiction dystopian thriller, but life itself at times is far stranger than science fiction. To us, the real possibilities of major mishaps and outright catastrophes are far too dangerous to human society to allow this technology to move into this final phase, no matter what is advanced and propagandized by AI developers, governments and the power forces.

Throughout human history there have been many devices, inventions and so-called scientific advancements developed *theoretically* for the benefit of humanity. Most people have a good idea of what these are. All of these devices and inventions were in the hands of governments and power forces and all of them were used to benefit those who controlled them, with no regard for their effects upon the people and upon the planet. One such development was the splitting of the atom which eventually led to the development of the atomic bomb and atomic power. The researchers were playing a game of fate or a game of marbles, a game of projections, and when they detonated the first atomic bomb they had no idea if this would cause a chain reaction that would reverberate around the world and possibly destroy it. Yet, despite this uncertainty and potential calamity, they did it anyway, because the government and the power forces wanted that weapon. At first, atomic research and development was advanced as a "peaceful" power source that could enrich human life. Our two analysts have concluded that the advancement of atomic development into what it has become has been catastrophic for the entire world. Atomic power, no matter what anyone says in its praise, is a lousy, expensive, dangerous way to boil water! The byproducts of this asininity have caused havoc throughout the world. Where the spent rods and the rest of the highly radioactive material will be placed is an ongoing major problem, since presently humans lack knowledge of how to neutralize them, and a serious concern for anyone who deals in and/or lives or works near nuclear power plants and disposal sites. There have been numerous nuclear "accidents" that took place, such Chernobyl, Three Mile Island, Fukishima, and the fire that occurred at the WIPP project facility in Carlsbad, New Mexico, with many others of lesser import unreported. There are other disasters that occur daily that people do not hear of because the governments and power forces do not want the people to be aware of them.

Nuclear radiation is not only dangerous, but deadly. Yet, the governments and the power forces got their way, did exactly what they wanted to do, and did so in spite of the toll it has already taken upon humanity. The United States of America is the only nation to have used atomic weapons on another nation —so far, as they did at Hiroshima and Nagasaki in Japan towards the end of World War II! This human slaughter established an atomic arms race which could have escalated into atomic warfare throughout the world. The governments and the power forces brought forth these horrific weapons and, with them, the possible destruction of humanity and our planet through expanded global warfare, which is still a distinct possibility now. Please note that this potential nuclear devastation was developed by the governments and the power forces who wanted to achieve their own objectives regardless of the dire consequences which could have befallen humanity then and could still happen to humanity now.

As we have said many times and as others are beginning to realize, trust must be earned. How can any sane entity trust such a duplicitous and diabolical government and partner power forces that could cause such a devastating reality? We all must be much more careful with our trust and where we place it. Right now the world has so many nuclear weapons in storage, including massive amounts of them in the United States, that one mistake could not only be locally catastrophic, but also could expand and set a whole chain reaction in process. Dangerous, lethal weapons of any type should never be developed by humanity for any reason. Unfortunately, although humans like to think that they are totally sophisticated and wise, from a higher ethical, egalitarian consciousness perspective, we can be viewed as basic primitives in the jungle, and if we continue to act as primitives, we will eventually destroy the entire world and the people and creatures on it. Strong AI definitely has this potential, as our two analysts have already concluded. Until such time as the entire human race develops a full consciousness, a genuine awareness, deals in truth and creates realities for societies that are only beneficial and, further, never allow megalomaniacs, psychopaths, sociopaths and the "elite" money-and-control-driven power forces to rule, we should never even dream of developing weapons and technologies with the power to destroy humanity and this Earth. According to true ancient historians, who delved into human societies that existed on the Earth countless millions of years ago, this type of mindless destruction has happened many times before. We, as a species, have to get a lot smarter, wiser and much more real, real fast. Imagine a super-intelligent AI force, programmed and conditioned by evil that can exceed all evil ever perpetrated upon this planet! This possibility is far too dangerous for any sane human being to even consider expanded AI development which could actually realize this horrific potential.

Throughout this book, we have spoken of the very unfortunate fact that the American people, as a society, never accepted the political power vested in them by the Constitution(s). As a result of this and as many people can now see, the U.S. government and literally all governments throughout America are totally out of control, performing un-Constitutional, unlawful actions against the people and engaging in activities that are harmful to the people, but very beneficial for themselves and their partner power forces. The current putrid festering cesspool that is Washington, D.C., with all the other smaller government cesspools throughout America resulted from the people's indifference. Our American society can no longer be indifferent to the actions of our federal, state, county and local governments, the banks and all of the other elements within the power forces. History has clearly taught us what occurs when we fail to accept our responsibilities. If the present state of affairs in this nation is something of which the American people do not approve, then it is incumbent upon *them* to exercise their political power and use the authority of the Constitutions and bind all governments with the chains of the Constitution(s). In this way, we can begin the process by which the American people can accept and enforce their lawful political power for the resurrection of our Constitutional republic.

If we as an American people fail to do this, it should be evident to anyone who has studied political reality that the handwriting is pretty much on the wall, and spells out a very ugly end for America. We must begin to trust ourselves and to solidly distrust governments, power forces and any forms of "authority" that work against the best interests of the people. By now, people are beginning to learn that these forces are self-directed only and have no concern for the well-being of the people and America. The "American family" has to come together as one people, based in the authority of our Constitution. Unfortunately, as we have said before, history proves that the American society has never come together to lawfully oppose the un-Constitutional, criminal, treasonous actions of governments and more unfortunately, likely never will. This phony COVID-19 *plandemic* is a prime example of how the people follow whatever government dictates and believe whatever government says, with rare exceptions. Facts are facts, truth is truth and reality is reality. Additionally, all needless violence and wanton destruction taking place under cover of the murder by police of a black man, who was essentially a career criminal, demonstrate the divide existent among Americans, which government and power forces exacerbate, promote and use to their advantage.

If we are ever to progress as a human species, then, we must consider all of these positions. False hope and misleading positions based in fantasy and wishful thinking will never get us anywhere. As a result, we must objectively look at truth, fact and reality, no matter how unpleasant, ugly or fearful, and accept them as they are, then attempt to resolve the problems that have made them as they are. While the general society will never do anything to protect their own rights, there are individuals, groups and real patriots who are concerned enough about their own nation and their fellow Americans to actually take a lawful stand to stop the un-Constitutional treason that is going on right under our noses. Our expectation is that these individuals, groups and patriots will come together in common purpose to reach common objectives for the benefit of the entire nation, and in so doing, will attract others to their cause. For those sincerely interested in using the power and authority of the Constitution(s) against errant, criminal un-Constitutional government in any form, please go to CHAPTER EIGHT in this book regarding our Constitutional methods and peruse them thoroughly so that you have a full understanding of them. As Mark Twain so astutely said long ago, **"In the beginning of a change the patriot is a scarce man, and brave, and hated and scorned. When his cause succeeds, the timid join him, for then it costs nothing to be a patriot."**

AMERICA'S FORECLOSURE CRISIS

A GLIMPSE INTO THE
FORECLOSURE CRISIS

In the foreclosure crisis that caused economic devastation and chaos for the nation and for many of her people, government gained further control over the people, and the power forces created enormous wealth for themselves on the backs of the unfortunate, beleaguered people. Banks and mortgage corporations were making loans to people whom they knew could not afford to make the monthly payments. Obviously, this is not sound business practice, so why would the banks and mortgage corporations, who are supposed to employ fiscally sound business practices, make bad loans? Banks and mortgage corporations also made loans to people who were financially stable, but because of the economic depression that was deliberately mischaracterized as a recession, many of them lost their jobs when entire industries were shipped overseas, few jobs were to be found at the same pay levels, prices for goods and services increased dramatically, the economy crashed and the people were "caught behind the eight ball". When borrowers could not meet their monthly mortgage payments, banks and mortgage corporations foreclosed and the people lost everything. Different sources will present different figures regarding how many foreclosures actually took place, but that figure is somewhere in the vicinity of twenty-seven million, five hundred thousand foreclosures from 2004 through 2017. It is pretty obvious that the people who were foreclosed upon, America, as a nation, and our entire economy were severely damaged. Yet, despite these severely adverse effects, the government *allowed* this to happen. The U.S. government is required, in part, pursuant to Constitutional mandates, to maintain domestic tranquility and uphold the general welfare. As we have seen earlier, if the government truly wants to perform pursuant to its Constitutional duties and mandates, then the government would be aware of conditions that could create problems detrimental to the people, and a government of right would prevent and eliminate those conditions before they happen. Our reasonable, objective observers, True and Reality, could conclude that the government not only failed to correct the adverse conditions, but may have created and/or allowed the conditions that resulted in the devastating economic depression and massive foreclosure crisis. The banks and mortgage corporations made fortunes selling bad loans to misinformed, innocent people, and even a significant amount of the so-called good loans went south, because many of the borrowers lost their jobs and could no longer meet their monthly payments.

To further pad their pocketbooks, the banks all across the country bundled their notes and mortgages and sold them as "mortgage backed securities" to investors, in many cases, to foreign investors. Some could say that the banks made bad loans which they knew would never be repaid simply to increase the number of notes and mortgages they could sell as these "securities" and made absolute fortunes in the process. This scheme was a major scam engaged in by most banks and mortgage corporations and fully allowed by the U.S. government. You know—the government that is supposed to provide for the domestic tranquility and general welfare of the American people. The repetitive position here is that, had the government adhered to Constitutional requirements, as mandated by the Supreme Law of the Land, none of this could ever have happened to America and to Americans. The opposite side of this is that, had it not happened, then, the banks, the mortgage corporations and the power forces would not have made those absolute fortunes, nor received the phony "bailouts" that went into many trillions of dollars for the claimed losses at tax payers' expense. Later on in this CHAPTER, we discuss the staggering amount of those bailouts, the cost of which is borne by the American people. As we said before, whenever someone loses, someone else gains, and by now, you should know who and what those "someones" are. Would the average American believe that the government was upholding the Constitution, rights guaranteed therein, due process of law and the principles in the Preamble when that government sold out a large segment of the American people to benefit the government and their partner-power forces? Our reasonable, objective observers would quickly conclude that the government failed its Constitutional duty and its duty to the people and America, herself. One of our repetitive questions here is: Would you trust such a government?

CHAPTER TWENTY FOUR

THE AGONY OF FORECLOSURE

Is it ever really possible to capture the depth and breadth of the *feelings* that humans experience when they think of "home"? The honest answer to this question is a definite "No!" One's home is one's heart and soul, a sanctuary of comfort, peace, security and joy, a refuge from the chaos of the outside world and the place to which most of us hurry after a day at work or school or after a trip. Home is the place where we build our lives as adults, where we plan and dream for the future, hope and pray for blessings each day, live and love one another. Home is the place to which we bring our newborn child to begin life on planet Earth with our love, care and guidance. It is the place where grandparents eagerly come to visit the precious new little one and offer their help and advice to the young, inexperienced parents. Home is the place to which one returns after triumph and after loss, the only place where most of us can truly be our real selves, with no "filters" on our words, no pretense or grandiosity in our actions, and no need to apologize for who we are. We don't have to impress anyone at home, or worry about what others may think of us. We are safe, we are content; we are *home*. Yes, for most of us, all of these feelings, notions and more come readily to mind when one thinks of "home".

Since home is so integral to who and what humans are and need, to lose one's home, for any reason, must be one of the worst catastrophes to ever befall us. Sometimes the loss of one's home comes suddenly, through fire or some natural catastrophe, and sometimes the loss comes more slowly, through the agonizing process of foreclosure. No matter whether the loss is swift or slow, the devastation is essentially the same. Home is no more, and one's sense of self is forever diminished, lost and may never be recovered. The old adage that says "Home is where the heart is" is quite true, and when that home is taken away, so is the heart.

When people lose their homes to foreclosure, a part of them is also lost. The feelings that arise are extremely bleak, intensely sorrowful, hopeless, helpless and replete with anger, shame and regrets. These feelings are shared by the other members of the family. Their home for so many years is being stripped right out from under them and this stripping leaves a major wound within every member of the entire family. Whether this wound can be fully healed or not remains to be seen, but during the time of pending and initial loss, the wound is so deep and the feelings so heavy and dark that most people think there is no possible upside or any light at the end of the proverbial tunnel. Some families have lived in their homes for many years and have established patterns revolving around that home. Others have owned their homes for only a short time, but it took time, energy, money, sacrifice and commitment to buy the home, in the first place, so no matter how long the family owned the home, the loss of it is still devastating.

Foreclosure wears many causational "hats". One cause could be that the homeowner lost his job, likely through no fault of his own, and was no longer able to make his mortgage payments, since he could not find a job with comparable pay in his profession or even, in some cases, any job at all. Another may have been that the homeowner was essentially sold a false bill of goods by a mortgage company or bank causing him to bite off more than he could chew when he took out the mortgage. This has happened millions of times throughout this country. When the homeowner ascertains that there is a great imbalance between what he makes and what he has to pay for the mortgage payment, something has to go, and, unfortunately, that something is usually the home he bought. In either case, the foreclosure loss is still devastating and the recriminations mount. This leads to ongoing stress and strife in the family, arguing, worrying, anxiety, sleepless nights, loss of self-esteem, concern about the immediate future, inability to focus, worry over where the family is going to live, how they will get there and whether they will be able to find a suitable place at a cost they can afford. Many times the family will be moving to much smaller quarters, so must drastically downsize their precious, hard-earned possessions. Sadly, since most families must rent another space, rather than buy, sometimes family pets must be given away or left behind, because many landlords do not allow them.

Then there are those families who are so depleted of funds and resources that they cannot afford to rent another place to live at all, thus many of them end up living in tents, cardboard boxes, or their cars, if they still have them. Still others must depend upon the kindness of family and friends, but that can get old rather quickly for both sides. How demoralizing and devastating are forced situations like this for an entire family? To be on the street instead of safe and secure in one's home is an utter disaster. To be dependent upon and be a burden to family or friends is equally disastrous. The huge amount of homeless people now found in many major American cities, especially in places like California, is blatant testimony to the heartbreak, desolation and sense of utter failure that afflicts these very unfortunate victims of foreclosure. While it is bad enough to lose one's home through foreclosure and be reduced to living in a smaller house or apartment out of one's accustomed neighborhood, how heart wrenching is it for an entire family to lose their home, have no funds, thus unable to afford a place to live and wind up on the street. All of this and much, much more comprise a human tragedy of epic proportions and catastrophic for the entire family and for America, herself. Just like the "Great Depression" that started in 1929, losses of this magnitude should never take place in the theoretically wealthiest country on the face of this Earth.

Most of you know that a large percentage of the immigrants pouring into this country, both "legal" and illegal, wind up on welfare and get everything they want, while the industrious, hard-working, loyal Americans get royally screwed by their own government. There is something awfully wrong with this picture, and increasing numbers of people are beginning to see it every single day. In fact, many of the people who lost homes through foreclosure, especially the ones who are homeless and living on the streets, might now be asking, who and what is running this country? What kind of government does this to its own people? What type of country crushes the resourceful, the producers, the workers, financially and otherwise, yet rewards immigrants—"legal" or illegal—from third world countries, with no skills to bring to America, giving them virtually anything they want—money, housing, food, clothing, cell phones, medical benefits, hospitalization, transportation, and so on and so on—at the expense of the very people who produce the country's wealth. As many of you now may know, Europe and the large cities in America are having myriad problems created by the influx of these third world immigrants, foisted upon the American people by the U.S. government. The European countries are executing the same insane policies against their native Citizens. Mounting numbers of these immigrants are wreaking havoc upon the countries and cities which have taken them in. They commit serious crimes—theft, rapes, murders and other hostile actions directed at the very people who financially support them, making Americans feel unsafe in their own neighborhoods. The U.S. government is fully behind this madness which is deliberately destroying America. Again, the question becomes why would a government want to destroy its own people and its own nation? Our two analysts would answer in one word: **communism**.

As stated, there are many different reasons for foreclosures and two of the most common reasons are cited above. When a family loses a home to foreclosure, due to the loss of the family breadwinners' job, because the economy essentially "went south" or the business for which they worked went overseas, these factors were not the direct fault of the breadwinners. In fact, these working men and women, the very backbone of America, are the victims of government and corporate programs and policies that have directly and adversely impacted them and millions of others. When the government encourages not only corporations, but essentially entire industries, to relocate in some third world country, and that relocation leaves thousands or even millions of people out of work, with no prospects for comparable work and comparable pay, that is not the fault of the American people. However, that is directly the fault of the government which rules the American people and controls virtually all aspects of their lives, in one way or another.

This amounts to extreme economic and financial violence against Citizens who lost their jobs and homes, in comparison to an economic boom for the corporations that took full advantage of the favorable government policies, with no regard for their workers. This certainly does not create domestic tranquility or promote the general welfare, justice and the blessings of liberty to the people who lost their jobs and their homes due to atrociously biased government policies that favored the corporations and directly harmed the people who lost nearly everything they had and held dear. Nothing could be more tragic for the people of the so-called "Land of the free" which claims to offer liberty and justice for all. Many of the victims who became aware of these realities, who lost so much due to the economic policies and the foreclosure crisis, would disagree with those lofty claims. As we said earlier and will say throughout this book, there are many forms of violence in this world. Economic and financial violence are the most insidious and oppressive of all these forms of violence, and no Americans should ever suffer because of economic and financial violence perpetrated and/or permitted by their own government.

Economic and financial violence imposed by an entire system against the Citizens stands as a ubiquitous evil. If people are attacked in warfare or on the street, they have at least the awareness that they are being attacked, can see and identify their attacker(s), may have some ability to physically protect themselves and hopefully subdue their attacker(s). They may win or lose the fight, but at least they have the ability in some form to try to protect themselves from the known attacker(s). In the case of economic and financial violence perpetrated by an entire system of governments, banks and corporate power forces, the average Citizens have no knowledge that they are under attack, by whom, in what manner and thus have absolutely no defense and no way to protect themselves, whatsoever. This amounts to societal madness, but it's an everyday occurrence involving millions of unsuspecting people across the country each and every day. Many people simply accept the foreclosure and do not fight it. The Citizens, who have fought it on their own, without lawyers, have found that there is no justice for them in the courts. The courts are part of the un-Constitutional corporate government, routinely act un-Constitutionally and function as a legal barrier and shield for the un-Constitutional actions and crimes of the system. Many of you who went through the foreclosure crisis and tried to win in court, but still lost your homes, can readily recognize the truth of this statement. Can any of you ever again trust the system that so grievously harmed you?

The other main reason is that banks and mortgage corporations were very eager and quite aggressive in making, or should we say, in pushing, loans upon people who were not financially qualified to receive them, thus unable to repay the loans. It is well known that many of these banks and mortgage corporations convinced unqualified buyers and borrowers that the properties they wanted to buy would rapidly increase in value over a relatively short time period, which, of course, would produce a sizable or decent profit to the borrowers, should they buy the property and accept the loan. This inducement convinced multitudes of people that buying the home, even in their modest financial circumstances, would prove beneficial when they sold it. Of course, as we have seen, for most people in most markets this type of rosy situation never materialized. The question our two analysts would ask is why any bank and mortgage corporation would make home loans to unqualified buyers who are unable to afford repayment of the loans. Our analysts determined that the answer to this is pretty simple. Most of these mortgage transactions were bundled by the banks and mortgage companies, then sold to the investment market domestically and overseas as mortgage backed securities. There was an ample willing buying market for these mortgage backed securities, therefore, the banks and mortgage corporations made as many loans as they could in order to reach that very lucrative additional market. The borrowers and home buyers for the most part were simply a means to an end or a pass-through so that the mortgage backed securities could be sold and enormous profits could be reaped for the banking institutions through that process.

This practice was extremely widespread, well known and should have been known to and recognized by the various government regulatory agencies that oversee and supervise these matters. Since the practice was a new phenomenon that reached enormous heights and produced enormous revenue, the controlling government agencies not only likely knew about the practice, but even more likely, contributed to the practice, or at the very least, looked the other way. If this is true, then the government condoned, aided and abetted the massive fraud that took place in this so-called "sub-prime lending" practice. Our two analysts would ask why the various governmental regulatory agencies, federal and state, upon recognition of this practice, did not step in to stop and prohibit it. Government's proper, lawful role is not to participate in, ignore or condone a scam, but to either stop it before it harms the people, or failing that, stop it as soon as the harm is realized. No government in this country so acted.

The homeowners who lost their properties to foreclosure, because of either one of these two primary causes, should be able to recognize that the federal government was a primary factor in these primary causes. In the first instance, had the government not exported entire industries, and through its policies caused the major depression that America suffered beginning in 2007, many of those who lost their homes, would still own them, because they would still have good-paying jobs working for the same companies. Government intervention and policies turned their entire lives upside down. Franklin Delano Roosevelt, not one of our favorite presidents, and in fact, one of the worst, most treasonous who ever held that office, frequently stated that if something happens in politics, it didn't happen by chance, but was planned. For government in collusion with banks and other corporate entities to actually plan and participate in economic disasters for the American people is not only deplorable, insidious and beyond all reason, but actually constitutes treason. In the second situation, if government did not actively participate in the scam, at least covertly, then as stated above, when government determined the nature of the scam, then government should have taken immediate steps to stop it and to hold the perpetrators responsible. Since government failed to do this, then the naïve ones, who overextended, thus lost their properties, can take responsibility for their part in this situation and also lay blame upon the government.

To make matters even worse, when the full extent of the foreclosure disaster was determined and, frankly, it is still in process right now, government wanted to "bail out" those who lost. However, the bailout funds did not go to those who *really* lost, namely the homeowners through foreclosure, but instead were paid to banks "too big to fail". This government program which paid enormous amounts of funds—somewhere in the vicinity of 27 trillion dollars to the banks who essentially caused the problem—could have instead bought the mortgages of the distressed homeowners, which funds could have repaid the banks, and the homeowners could have kept their homes. If this had happened, the homeowners would repay the loan funds to the government at interest, but would still own their homes and not lose them to foreclosure. For those who were in need of financial help, the government could have structured low interest loans at longer terms so that the homeowners could truly afford the payments. Had this been done, then the many millions of people, who suffered the agonies of foreclosure, would still be in their homes and would gratefully repay the government the funds the government spent to pay off their mortgages, plus interest.

It is highly likely that the 27 trillion dollars or more which the government paid in bailout funds to the banks will never be repaid to the American people. In fact, what is more likely is that the American people will end up paying for those funds themselves. The government's irresponsible actions should make it abundantly clear to any sentient, thinking American that the government has little to zero interest in the American people, their well-being, their welfare, their financial security, but enormous interest in protecting the power forces and maintaining that power at any cost, especially at the cost of the average American Citizen. Would it be a wonder to any person to realize that any homeowners who lost their homes through foreclosure would have little, if any, trust and faith in the U.S. government and, further, any trust in the American banking system? As we have said many times in this book, trust must be earned, and in order to earn trust, an entity must demonstrate by its actions, and not its rhetoric, that it is capable and worthy of receiving that trust. The U.S. government and the American banking system are sorely and criminally lacking in this regard and by their own consistently irresponsible actions have clearly demonstrated that they are not deserving of the trust of the American people.

As it goes in America, the American people, for the most part, are unfortunately unaware of the true nature and true reality of the operations of government and the banking system. More and more people are daily beginning to realize that this lack of awareness has been a colossal and tragic failure on the part of the American people. First, this failure did not keep government in check pursuant to the Constitutional mandates imposed upon government, by and through oaths taken, and second, permitted the banking cartel essentially to financially enslave the American people. The term enslavement is something that most people might still disagree with, but if one were to truly recognize the stranglehold which the banking system has imposed upon the people, in particular through enormous debt, both public and private, who in his right mind would not call this slavery? Like most people, homeowners who lost their properties through foreclosure were likely unaware of these situations which caused them to lose their homes. When people lose their jobs, it is obvious that they are fully aware of that sad fact, but are they truly aware of the underlying and insidious factors that caused them to lose those jobs? Our analysts have determined that in the large majority of cases such awareness was and is not present. Unfortunately for the country and for the American society, people do not delve very deeply into much of anything, but simply take things at face value and go along to get along. The homeowner who overextended himself on his mortgage did so for his own reasons, but as indicated before, many of these homebuyers were under the rosy impression that their homes were going to rapidly increase in value, quickly boosting their equity, thus provide a very tidy profit when they sold their homes "down the road".

Like the people who lost their jobs and then their homes, the overreaching homebuyers did not delve deeply into the ramifications and the true reasons for their losses. People usually discover the reasons for actions and events well after the fact, if they discover them at all. When these homeowners ascertain that their losses resulted from government actions, banking actions and systems' policies, which benefited the system at the homeowners' expense, it certainly appears reasonable that many, if not most, of those who lost their homes would be furious at the true reasons for their losses. All of these realizations add to the emotional and psychological distress incurred by the loss of one of the most precious assets that average Americans will ever have—their own home. Diplomacy, politeness, obfuscation, distraction, excuses, and rationalization have no place in this matter and should never be introduced as justifiable reasons for the horror show that occurred. The bottom line is that there is no excuse for this absolute travesty of justice foisted upon the people. Earlier, we spoke of the necessity of going to the bottom line and that is exactly what is needed here, that is, for anyone who sincerely wants to know the truth. That bottom line is that approximately 27 million foreclosures, plus, took place in this country between the years 2004 and 2017. Since the same homes went into foreclosure several times, the actual number of homes lost to owners through foreclosure depends upon the source, and different sources provide different figures. Millions of homes were lost and millions of American families were severely damaged. They not only lost their homes, but had their lives turned upside down through foreclosure. This is the real bottom line and the real bottom-line tragedy that devastated many million Americans. There are those who will try to minimize the bottom line, to explain, rationalize, justify, and claim that policy was involved, "national security" was involved and whatever other nonsense they can dream up to distract from and minimize that bottom line. As we have said, and as the people can realize, there is nothing lawful that can ever justify that horrendous bottom line inflicted upon the American people by their own government, in league with the banks..

Homeowners who lost through their own carelessness or personal failures, which are unrelated to any government or corporate policy or activity, can be well aware that the mistakes are theirs, alone, while greed and unrealistic expectations may have been factors. However, the others who lost *because of* government activities, actions, policies, programs, and those of the banks and corporate America, in league with government, can fully realize, that is, if they take a sincere, serious look at the whole situation, that their losses took place outside the scope of their own actions and responsibilities, and thus were not their fault. Most people believe in government, the system, the banking cartel and corporate America, so it was normal for them to place their trust in these systems institutions. When the people who suffered foreclosures realize that these institutions essentially colluded against the interests of the average borrower, that realization is not only a shock, but also a very upsetting reality to the perceivers. As we said earlier, how can people so betrayed by the total American system have any further trust in that system?

Just imagine the plight of an average American family that has had its home taken away from them by foreclosure—a home for which they worked hard and saved scrupulously until they amassed a decent down payment, then paid their mortgage on time for years, and lovingly maintained what they believed to be their solid investment in their family's future. In addition to having lost their investment, they also lost the comfort and safety their home represented to them, with all of the wonderful memories they made there, together. Now, they must face the daunting task of finding a suitable place to live that can accommodate their needs. If the foreclosure occurred because the breadwinners lost their jobs, then, obviously, financial constraints dictate that this new place will likely be either a smaller, more affordable rental house, probably in a less desirable neighborhood, or possibly even an apartment, if one can be found to fit their needs. Such a move to a smaller space means that the adults may have to let go of a lot of their personal possessions and the children will probably have to give up some of their favorite things, as well. It also means that the children will have to enroll in different schools, in strange neighborhoods, which can be very frightening for them, and both the parents and the children must leave behind their former friends, neighbors, playmates and familiar haunts. The move may even require the family to surrender the family pets, or in a worse scenario, simply abandon them, if their new space prohibits them. All of these changes which can be overwhelming and exhausting to plan and accomplish, will inevitably exert tremendous stress on every member of the family. The parents' emotions will surely be a jumble of sorely sharp feelings—anger, guilt, sorrow, resentment, recriminations and hopelessness—but to spare their children as much pain as they possibly can, they will likely put on brave faces and tell their kids to think of the move as an exciting challenge and a new start.

Such situations arising from such tragic loss should never take place in a true Constitutional republic where the government is responsible to assure the well-being of its society. It should be patently obvious to anyone who takes a realistic view of what occurred to determine that the government cares nothing for the plight of average Americans and their families. They are simply "commodities", a means to an end, to be used and discarded as determined by the government and their partner power forces. The crushing sorrow in this ugly reality arises from the fact that most Americans are good, decent, hard-working people, who either pursued a college education and professional career, or learned a trade, or developed a skill or talent to support themselves and their families. These are the people who try to do the right thing for their families and their communities, follow the rules, act responsibly in their affairs and just want to live modest, unassuming, happy, healthy, fulfilling lives. They are the folks who put their faith and trust in their government, believing that America is the best country on this Earth with a government that watches out for them and would never harm them or allow them to be harmed. What a profound shock it must be for these good people to realize that their government *deliberately* failed them in such an economically violent manner! One could compare this to a mythical scenario in which small children, frequently subject to scary nightmares, awaken in their dark bedrooms, terrified, so go looking for comfort from their parents, whom they totally trust. The children pad quietly on tiptoe to their parents' bedroom, expecting to sneak under the covers for their parents' loving touch and warmth, but when they pull back the covers, instead of seeing their parents, they discover two ugly, fearsome monsters wearing their parents' nightclothes!

Such a devastating discovery would shake the very fibers of the average child, just as discovering the real truth about the government's treachery will do to the average American. No longer can Americans feel safe, comfortable and secure with such monsters governing and controlling their lives. What average Americans *thought* they knew is not what actually exists in their operative realities. This is a tragic, devastating realization for anyone! As we have said forever, there is a big difference between what one thinks he knows and what he knows he knows. The government and power forces have been very successful in creating scenarios, pictures and processes by which the average people know little to nothing about the realities in which they live, and what they think they know is usually based on deliberate falsehoods repeatedly told to them and antithetical to the truth. Again, when people awaken to the real truth and the grim governing realities, they are shocked beyond measure and are never the same again, because they can never view anything they have trusted before in the same light. This is akin to what happens when one reads a "Where's Waldo" book, discovers the location of Waldo in the illustrations, and thereafter will always see Waldo clearly anytime he sees those illustrations. The truth can no longer be disguised and he no longer falls for subterfuge.

Whenever there is a loss, there is always a way to move forward, that is, if one is determined to rise above that life-changing loss. To do so, takes courage, conviction and confidence in oneself, but the alternative is far worse, and the possibilities of moving forward are much more beneficial in the long run. We all have abilities and we all have to recognize those abilities no matter what anyone else, including our families and friends, may say to the contrary. For the victims who lost everything and endured tremendous suffering in many different ways because of the loss, it is a long road back, but it is achievable under the right circumstances with determination. For those so inclined to move forward and, hopefully, in the near future have the ability to purchase another family home, which for the most part will be outside of the financial entanglements of the system, then go to the section and CHAPTERs in this book which demonstrate how this can be done, in detail. Additionally, some may want to embark upon a personal, individual investment program, under their control, that can produce great wealth and independence over a relatively short time period, which methods are also discussed in the referenced CHAPTERs. Sometimes misfortune and adversity are not exactly what they seem, because, believe it or not, they can be blessings in disguise, if we have the eyes to see and the ears to hear what the Abundant Universe is telling us. For those who are spiritually inclined and believe in a higher power, at various pivotal times in our lives, those spiritual forces sometimes create what we perceive as misfortune, but actually is giving us not so gentle nudges to go in a very different and beneficial direction. Maybe you are reading this book for that very reason. Synchronicities do happen and are all around us, if we recognize them.

The programs presented in this book will place the average man and woman out of the prying eyes, requirements and control of government regulatory agencies, banks and other parties. The buying, selling and investing will be done between and among principals, only, with no interference from outside, third-party forces. Creative, inventive people should be able to freely exercise their right to deal on their own without the intrusion of third-party entities from any quarter. Principal to principal, direct interaction for mutual benefit is exactly what is outlined in these methods. Win-win situations are the best for those involved and create a feeling of accomplishment, success and good will. When we rely upon ourselves, and not upon others, to accomplish objectives which we have set forth for ourselves, and not those imposed by others, the feelings of self-worth and independence tell us that we are doing the right things for the right reasons. For those who are low on funds, because of life's ups and downs, the referenced sections spell out methods that could help you realize your dream to buy another family home. When life seems to throw us a challenging curve, it is all up to us, individually, as to whether we buck the tide of adversity and win, or surrender to it and lose.

CHAPTER TWENTY FIVE

AMERICA'S FORECLOSURE PROBLEMS

About 2004, I, Jack, predicted several things would happen with the economy in this country. The first thing was a major financial crisis that would be extremely severe. Second, I predicted a massive foreclosure crisis throughout the nation, and third, that the federal government and the Federal Reserve Bank would bail out their banking cohorts, you know, the "banks too big to fail", and large corporations, starting with 8 trillion dollars and at least tripling to 24 trillion dollars. According to some sources, the eventual bailout was over 39 trillion dollars, so I was short on that prediction.

As most Americans are aware, America experienced a foreclosure *disaster* that rocked the very foundations of this country. Many millions of people lost their homes. Some of them lost because they accepted bad bank loans which required monthly payments the borrowers could not possibly make. Other sincere and good Americans lost their homes because the economy rapidly went south and millions of people throughout America could not maintain their mortgage payments because they lost their jobs and could not get others of comparable pay. When people tried to obtain other comparable jobs, they soon found out that very few, if any, similar jobs were available and many who managed to find jobs ended up with positions that required far less skill and paid far less money, which many Americans reluctantly took simply to have some money coming in so they and their families could survive.

This was an absolutely deplorable situation for people and families throughout this nation, and was akin to the plight the American people suffered during the so-called "Great Depression". Millions of homes were taken by the banks, as well as by the courts. Whether people lost due to bad loans they could not pay, or through no fault of their own, lost their jobs, so could not meet their payments, the banks *won* for the simple reason that most notes and mortgages owed by people to banks were bundled and sold to investors as "mortgage backed securities", even before some of the homes went into foreclosure. Banks made substantial profits from the sale of these bundled notes, then, made additional profits when the banks sold the foreclosed homes. From the banks' position, this was good, profitable business, no matter who got hurt in the process. However, investors, who bought mortgage backed securities, were defrauded and lost massive investment sums.

From the homeowners' position, most people lost their family homes and all the funds and improvements they put into their homes over the years. These people also lost the fond memories of their families growing up in the family home. As usual, the banks win, and won, during the foreclosure crisis, no matter who else lost. Based upon the actions that took place, there was no ethical and moral consideration given to the people. Many Americans now know that the banks were exonerated for their actions and bailed out by the Fed at the expense of the American people. In contrast to this, the millions of Americans who lost their homes were not bailed out by the government which is *theoretically* their government and certainly were not bailed out by the Fed. From these unconscionable actions, which added insult to injury, there appears to be something awfully wrong with this picture. If any average American businessman suffers losses in his business, the government definitely does not bail *him* out. Only the large prime banks, the ones, of course, as we mentioned "too big to fail" and large corporations are afforded this tidal wave of public money, in the form of corporate welfare, at the public's expense.

Those Americans who tried to challenge the foreclosures of their homes through the courts did not fare very well, except in some rare cases. In the alternative, banks and mortgage companies won handily and quickly in court against such challenges, because either the homeowners did not know how to present proper lawful arguments in support of their positions, or the courts ignored the arguments, and upheld the banks' fraud, in violation of due process of law. Thus, not only did the banks foreclose and make tidy profits in the process, before and after the foreclosures, they also overwhelmingly won in courts when challenged by the homeowners. If our reasonable, rational, objective observers, True and Reality, were to view this, it could be quickly deduced that banks won "big time" throughout the entire process, while homeowners lost miserably throughout the same process.

The American court system, whether state or federal, is Constitutionally required to uphold the inherent rights guaranteed to the people in the Constitution and to uphold all aspects of due process of law. Yet, in today's corrupt court system, what is required by law is largely ignored by government officers, judges and court personnel in favor of the banks and sweetheart corporations. Our Constitution guarantees the American people the inherent right to life, liberty and property, which cannot lawfully be taken away, except by due process of law. Tragically the concept of due process of law is evaded and avoided by the American court system, at all costs.

Despite this lawful requirement and guaranteed right, millions of Americans had their homes taken by and through courts, absent due process of law. Had the courts upheld due process of law, which only a few did, then, at least two lawful positions argued by Citizens should have been upheld by those courts. One is that the entity which forecloses must be the owner and lawful holder in due course of the *original* promissory note and mortgage upon which he forecloses. This should be an entirely obvious requirement that any court would strictly enforce. Most, however, did not. Without having the original notes and mortgages in their possession, banks made false claims upon which damages could not lawfully be awarded. Further, by misrepresenting the possession of the original notes and mortgages, the banks put fraud upon the courts. Still further, and very important, the bank that misrepresents ownership of the note and mortgage to the court, and the bank that does not own and hold the original note and mortgage lacks standing to even file a foreclosure action or defend against a suit arising from such an action in court. American courts routinely ignored these lawfully based arguments presented by average people and upheld the fraud committed by the banks. The powerful, the elite and the money interests do very well in the courts, usually at the expense, in one way or another, of the American people.

Although much information has been published over the past 50 years or so regarding how banks operate, many people do not realize that, when banks make loans to people, the funds "loaned" do not come from funds on deposit in the banks. Loan funds, for the most part, do not exist until the borrower signs the note which activates a process by which the banks obtain the loan funds, plus much more, from America's central bank, called the Federal Reserve Bank, which is a private bank operating for profit. Essentially, in order to fund the loans, the banks bundle all of their notes and obtain the face amount for them and more, through this central bank. Ironically, the banks do not lend their own funds, but rather rely upon their borrowers' signatures to the notes in order to obtain from the Fed the funds the banks "loan" to the borrowers. In all of this lending practice, the banks take little to no financial risks, while the borrowers take all of those risks and assume all liabilities.

When the borrower loses to foreclosure, he not only loses his home, but loses everything he has spent on and put into his home, since his initial ownership. As we have referenced earlier, this is a tragic, heartbreaking and massive loss to every family that has suffered foreclosure. The banks lose nothing since they have none of their money in the transactions. As pointed out, the banks profit before, during and after the foreclosures.

Those Americans who have lost their homes because of this insidious bank-driven procedure are reduced, for the most part, to renting apartments or someone else's homes and usually at a rental rate higher than their original monthly mortgage payments for the homes they lost. Of these millions of people, most would very much like to purchase another home, rather than live in rentals, but now there is a financial stigma put upon them by the banking, legal and governmental systems. If these people are ever going to be able to purchase a home again, then, most of them must do so outside the usual system. The programs outlined in this book can demonstrate to these people opportunities to purchase another home, when the usual government sponsored financial system, with its rigorous requirements, will not.

The next CHAPTER explains how homes can be sold before and during foreclosure proceedings, so that the homeowner can avoid foreclosure and recoup some substantial funds from the sale, instead of suffering a crushing loss had the bank and the court taken it from him.

CHAPTER TWENTY SIX

ByPass METHODS
BUY AND SELL HOMES PRIOR TO FORECLOSURE

Anyone who has gone through the foreclosure process, or is in that process now, knows the heartache that arises from this travesty of justice. An extremely high percentage of homeowners who have this problem are not financially able to make up back payments owed, bring their balance current and, hopefully, avoid foreclosure. Yes, some are able to do this, but the percentage of those who can do so is very low. Further, of those who can do this, since many of these people have lost their jobs, it is very difficult to keep up with the ongoing monthly mortgage payments. Eventually, unless the financial situation for the family changes for the better, they will soon likely face foreclosure again.

Losing one's home to foreclosure is bad enough, for all the reasons we have discussed herein, and for all the reasons with which the victims of foreclosure are all too familiar. To lose *everything* is even worse, and to recoup nothing is a total travesty of justice. Since our American Constitution guarantees us the right to property, which cannot lawfully be taken from us without due process of law, and since millions of people have lost their homes to foreclosure absent due process of law, it is clear that the due process of law required by and guaranteed to the people in our Constitution was denied to most of them. This in itself is one of the cruelest results from a foreclosure action. The very government that is supposed to protect the rights of the people has not only miserably failed to do so, but instead has protected the money interests of the banks and mortgage companies. These wealthy institutions do not lose, but the people do. The government makes certain that this occurs. The question again becomes, whom does this government truly represent?

When someone has lost his home, everything he has put into that home over the years, including money, labor, improvements, and leaves without absolutely anything, this is a total disaster for him and his family. Without funds, how is he going to provide for his family? This is a good and pertinent question, but it is of no concern to the banks, the courts and the government. Without funds, how is the family going to be able to rent an apartment or house? These are considerations that are of no concern to the system, but of major concern to the family that lost everything.

When faced with such a disaster, there are ways the homeowner can actually sell his home and recoup something from it, rather than walk away destitute. In CHAPTER THIRTY ONE, we spelled out possible ways in which a buyer could buy a home or property that already has existing debt on it. That debt belongs to the homeowner and the homeowner is totally responsible for that debt. However, as explained in the referenced CHAPTER, a buyer could make a down payment, purchase a 50% interest in the house, and assume the obligation of the owner's existing debt, but not the note, itself. This arrangement would be strictly between the buyer and the homeowner. Depending upon the amount in arrears owed by the homeowner, the buyer's down payment may be able to cover that amount and bring the account current, so that the homeowner's position within the note/mortgage is reinstated. The buyer and seller arrange the selling price in direct negotiations between themselves, and the buyer pays the monthly mortgage payment due to the bank, as well as the note payment due to the seller. This is further explained in detail in CHAPTER THIRTY. Rather than lose his property, and get nothing for it, in this way, the seller could bring his home payments current, avoid foreclosure and make a profit in the sale, instead of experiencing total financial disaster and losing everything.

SECTION FOUR

ByPass BUYING, SELLING AND FINANCE PROGRAMS

Documents for buying, selling, offers, financing, and other transactions will be made available for interested parties. For more information, call 207-404-9093 or email takebackourrights@yahoo.com **or** mdflynn2003@yahoo.com.

CHAPTER TWENTY SEVEN

PROGRAMS FOR ALL PEOPLE

As we said in the Introduction, our various methods listed in this and the next sections provide ample opportunities for most people to buy, sell, finance, develop and invest in real estate, either for personal investments or retirement, or for advanced professional reasons, without the need for obtaining new bank financing. The CHAPTER on advanced investments demonstrates how a modest investment can be parlayed into fabulous wealth. When all of these are combined with the fact that no new bank financing is required for any of the programs listed in *ByPass*, this very fact alone can open up the buying, selling and investing in real estate to untold millions who would never have that opportunity under ordinary circumstances. These programs pretty much cover the broad field of real estate in virtually all areas, from the purchase or sale of one house by seller and buyer to moderate investments, onto major profit programs that require small investments. No matter what the circumstances are for potential buyers, interested sellers, investors and developers, one of the *ByPass* programs will most likely satisfy their situations, needs, goals and desires.

As mentioned previously, only one of the programs is something that is currently in use and has been for a very long time, and this is the purchase of residential homes through owner financing. However, the *ByPass* treatment of this arrangement is quite different from the usual methodology and presents our approach in a far better light for the interests and advantages of both buyer and seller. All of the other programs listed in the next section are new, not in current use, and offer creative solutions for many different scenarios. All of the scenarios are based in pure common sense and good business practices conducted directly between two honorable principals, and one or more of these approaches should fit the bottom-line objective for almost anyone. The major factor endemic to all programs is that none of them involve the need to obtain new bank financing, which, in itself, is a totally novel concept for the buying, selling and financing any type of real estate beyond the typical parameters currently in use. If these direct, simple, easy programs catch on with the American people, they could literally revolutionize the manner in which people buy, sell, finance, develop and invest in all forms of real estate, whether private or commercial.

In the next section, the various programs and their applications are discussed in detail. At the end of some of these CHAPTERS, examples of basic investment strategies will be provided. These strategies are for people and groups who may want to purchase real estate as investments for either personal profit or retirement. Later in this book, and in the *ByPass* investment projections, we list advanced applications for more professional minded people who want to create large portfolios and vast wealth by and through the use of the programs presented.

CHAPTER TWENTY EIGHT

ByPass STANDARD MORTGAGE FINANCING

Overview

The *ByPass* Standard Mortgage Program is a unique mortgage/note method that provides sellers and buyers of homes and any other type of real estate the ability to engage in a **win-win** approach, which far surpasses the usual institutional note/mortgage commonly used. This outside-the-box method and program is innovative, atypical, creative, unusual, far-reaching, and makes it possible for sellers and buyers of all types of real estate to quickly and efficiently transact business which might not otherwise be conducted for various financial and/or other constraints.

This book explains the various *ByPass* programs in a direct, simple manner, what they can do for you and how you can use them to best achieve your objectives. In addition to the note/mortgage method, the various CHAPTERs of this book explain different aspects of our programs so that the selling and buying principals can achieve the best results in their real estate transactions. It is best to review this entire book and all the CHAPTERs contained within it, because they provide a better, in-depth understanding of the various programs, themselves.

As former real estate and banking professionals with extensive working experience in real estate development, brokerage, banking, private financing and mortgage banking, we developed these unique and unconventional programs. One of these is discussed in this and the following CHAPTERs.

Our very different and far-reaching program provides private, creative self-financed and self-generated home mortgages for buyers and sellers. This is truly a revolutionary concept when compared to standard, institutional methods. This is bank-less and broker-less financing, no mortgage-company financing, no high-points financing, no waiting for approval, (or rejection), financing. It puts the power back into the hands of the principals, which is where it properly belongs. You, not the bank, make your own terms and determine what you want and how you will conduct your own business for mutual benefit between buyer and seller.

Private and creative self-finance could very possibly become the wave of the future. As we cited earlier in this book, institutional finance has long been a tightly controlled commercial monopoly used by selective and powerful groups for their own control, profit and interests. What a novel concept it is to actually put the power of finance into the hands of "amateurs". Once you have reviewed this book, you may ask why these programs, or at least some of them, have not been widely used long before this.

Many new thoughts, ideas, concepts and working inventions throughout history have been defeated, ridiculed, crushed and killed, usually by very powerful vested interests with something to gain by destroying the credibility and implementation of new ideas and methods. New ways of thinking and fair and open competition can appear threatening to entrenched control groups who want to firmly maintain their lucrative form of manipulation and financial control and do not like competition. The *ByPass* programs are creative, but directly challenge no vested interests. What they do is promote *your* vested interests as well as those of the parties with whom you deal. Our program is one of common, mutual benefit. It is not adversarial, as are so many financial dealings. As we said before, it puts control back into the proper hands where it belongs in the first place, namely, the individual principals themselves. It widely opens up the sales and purchases of homes and all other types of real estate and other types of property to all financially capable people, many of whom, are not allowed or able to purchase homes or other property under current arbitrarily restrictive institutional conditions. Our program allows a principal to deal independently, decisively, effectively, directly and quickly in making decisions, on his or her own, without the imposition of decisions made by others for him or her, and which involve his/her most valued and precious material possession, his/her home.

The buying and selling of property can be an art form, but the process usually devolves into a difficult, tedious and frustrating struggle. The process typically involves sellers, buyers, and any combination of real estate brokers, bankers, mortgage brokers, principals' lawyers, and often includes strained and difficult negotiations, lengthy applications, application fees, long waits for approval, bank-imposed buying and/or selling restrictions and requirements, high point costs, professional fees and unexpected expenses that result in higher than anticipated closing costs, down payments and monthly payments. What should be a simple and pleasant experience can often turn into one of frustration, at minimum, or at worst, a nightmare, resulting in strained nerves and higher costs that just magically appear out of nowhere. If you agree that there should be a simpler and more direct system so that potential transactions can proceed smoothly, easily, quickly, and be less costly, then you have made the correct decision to purchase this book, because that system is contained within it.

The *ByPass* programs have many components. One of these is to show how the principal can effectively accomplish his objective, whether buying or selling. In many institutional transaction attempts, the original intent often gets lost, becomes confused or over-complicated in the very efforts required to consummate the transaction. For the best results, sellers and buyers should never, at any stage of the transaction, be in adversarial positions. In the best real estate transactions, they are not; in the worst, they are. Sometimes the problems are not directly caused by the principals, but rather by well-intentioned individuals, personal and professional, who are around them. Principals are often people with different idiosyncrasies, personalities, ways of dealing, and different value systems. People have individualized ways of seeing the same thing, which is normal, but this can often lead to polarized views, stubbornness and un-moveable positions. The objective becomes lost, as many times, does the transaction.

When transactions become more complicated because of intrusions by participants beyond the principals and presentation of unexpected situations, as described above, as well as by interference from advisers and family, then camps tend to become adversarial and rigidly entrenched. Unfortunately, under such conditions, many transactions that were struck in good faith and initially agreed upon by the principal parties deteriorate and fall out of escrow. Ask any broker for his confirmation of this.

The *ByPass* program demonstrates how principals can conduct their real estate dealings and negotiations in a fair, equitable, easy and direct manner. Our program points out specific situations to sellers, which they may never have considered, either before or even after their sale, such as their intended use of cash proceeds from the sale. Where are seller's sale proceeds going to be spent? Are they going to be deposited into a bank or used to purchase another home? In any of these cases, the *ByPass* program demonstrates how sellers can sell their properties better, faster, with far fewer complications, earn more interest and have better security.

In real estate transactions, buyers and sellers have mutual, but obviously, opposite interests, but this does not mean that they must approach the transaction as adversaries. To put it simply, one party wants to sell a property and the other party wants to buy that property. It seems incredible to say, but these objectives should never be lost, and taking any attitude or position that diverts from these objectives is counter-productive and harmful. The *ByPass* program's complete methods are designed to create and benefit not only mutual interests, but also mutually enlightened *self-interests* for common purpose with respect to the same piece of property. Awareness, politeness, kindness, good will and a proper ethical perspective would be very helpful to both principal parties and go a long way towards assuring a successful transaction of mutual benefit.

The various components of the *ByPass* programs, as related in this book, will show the selling and buying principals how they can quickly, efficiently and fairly, for mutual benefit, sell, buy, invest in and develop real estate.

CHAPTER   TWENTY   NINE

THE FIRST *ByPass* PROGRAM

The first *ByPass* program uses a very old, time-tested method and puts it into a brand new, more expansive concept that aids all participants in their respective pursuits. A capable and willing buyer wants to purchase a property owned by a seller, which is free and clear of all mortgages, notes, debt and liens of any kind. Many different factors indicate that this approach may be much more popular and desirable than one would expect.

Throughout this book are two house examples:

1. $100,000 house, with 15% down ($15,000), with $85,000 balance carried by seller at 5% for 15 years.
2. $60,000 house, with 15% down ($9,000), with $51,000 balance carried by seller at 5% for 15 years.

All that is needed are sellers willing to accept down payments, then carry the balance, and financially capable capable buyers, with the financial ability to make the down payment on either priced house listed above and the means to meet monthly payments. The buying and selling principals work directly with each other, for common purpose. The sellers want to sell and the buyers want to buy. No real estate salesmen are involved, which means sellers do not pay commissions on the house sales. The sales contract can be drawn up by the and mutually agreed to by the principals, and the closing can take place in a local title company. This would save considerable sums usually spent by sellers and buyers.

The sellers who prefer to sell for all cash can use this approach, then, sell their notes to investors and investment firms that purchase notes. The seller has already received a down payment. No real estate agent is involved, thus no commission must be paid, so the seller can sell his note at discount and get what he wants, or close to it. Other sellers are willing to carry their notes and receive monthly payments. This very easy, simple approach to buying, selling and financing houses can meet most objectives of all participants.

According to Statistics Brain.com and Rasmussen Reports, between the years 2000 to 2015, 26.3% to 29.75% of homes owned by Americans were owned outright, meaning free and clear of all debts, mortgages and notes. According to Statistics Brain, the National Association of Realtors and the Federal Reserve Bank, the average number of homes for sale in America, at any given time, is about 4,800,000. Approximately 26.3% to 29.75% of these homes are most likely owned free and clear of all debt, which amounts to between 1,262,400 to 1,428,000 homes. Projections indicate that approximately 5,770,000 homes will be sold in 2020, of which approximately from 1,517,510 to 1,716,575 homes could be owned free and clear of all notes, debt and mortgages. Many of these homes will be priced at or under $100,000, especially in the less populated areas, but also within some large cities. So many homes on the market that fall within *ByPass* parameters make many buys/sales possible through the *ByPass* owner financed and other *ByPass* methods.

In 2005, 7,080,000 homes were sold in America, which was just before the foreclosure crises that affected many millions of people and their families. In 2006, the number of sales dropped to 6,520,000; in 2007, when foreclosure rates increased, sales dropped to 5,020,0000; in 2008, 4,120,000; in 2009, 4,340,000; in 2010, 4,180,000; in 2011, 4,260,000; in 2012, 4,660,000. It was not until 2013 that sales went over the 5,000,000 mark, reaching 5,090,000, but in 2014, sales dropped again to 4,940,000. Since then house sales have been above the 5,000,000 mark. The foreclosure years hit America and Americans very hard and still affect millions of people who lost everything, or close to it. THIS SHOULD NOT HAPPEN IN AMERICA. Lingering effects still intrude into the lives of Millions of Americans each and every day. Our government should never favor banks and corporations over the best interests and well-being of the American people – but it does, all the time. If the millions who lost their homes knew about the various *ByPass* Programs, maybe most of them could have kept their homes. Another reason why we wrote this book is to help provide solutions and remedies to the American people in the next foreclosure fiasco.

Some of the figures mentioned in this CHAPTER we have mentioned before, but they bear repeating. Many Americans are concerned about the financial future of America. 44% of Americans are worried about not being able to pay their mortgage notes or rents. Another major concern is that there may not be enough money for retirement and long-term health services. Only 31% of non-retired workers think that there will be enough money in social security for them when they retire. In the alternative, up to 69% think that there will be no money in social security for them upon retirement. Approximately 13.2% of homeowners have negative equity on their mortgages, which means their home value is less than the mortgage amount.   There are 11,821,000 mortgage borrowers who owe more on their homes than the homes are worth. As stated above, the average number of homes for sale in America, at any given time, is 4,800,000, no matter how many homes are sold or put on the market. Millions of Americans want to sell their homes, but the bad economy, loss of jobs, little likelihood of similar jobs at comparable pay, loss of entire industries to overseas facilities, remnants of the foreclosure crises, increasing bank requirements and other factors have combined to drastically slow sales while leaving millions of homes available and waiting. These figures demonstrate that millions of homeowners want to sell, and sell now. Millions of buyers want to buy now, but obstacles prevent many buyers and sellers from reaching their objectives. The *ByPass* methods could help many of these people get past those obstacles and successfully transact business directly with other principals to reach common objectives of selling and buying homes, with ease.

The figures above demonstrate that many sellers want to sell their homes in these extremely difficult economic times, and would do so, provided the right terms were presented by a capable buyer. Since somewhere between 26.3% and 29.75% of homeowners own their homes free and clear of all mortgage debt and liens, this means that one out of every four sellers owes nothing on their homes. Using one of *ByPass'* typical examples, if the seller is willing to accept a 15% down payment on his asking price of $100,000.00 and carry the balance of $85,000.00, for a 15 year term, at 5% interest, then a mutually-beneficial sale could take place. Although this is one of our typical examples used throughout this book, naturally, different pricing will be involved in different actual transactions. In previous CHAPTERS we have described the benefits that accrue to both buyer and seller in this type of principal to principal transaction. One of the most important positions is that the principals are dealing directly with each other, face to face, with no middlemen, no brokers, no bankers and no lawyers, any and all of which sometimes can turn a good transaction bad.

Based upon one of our typical examples, with a selling price of $100,000, with 15% down, and the balance of $85,000 carried by the seller for 15 years at 5% interest, the projected monthly principal and interest payment is $650.29. In five years, by our monthly principal payment method, the buyer will accrue $28,333 in note equity, bringing the note balance to $56,667. Also, in five years, with a minimum one percent increase per year in home value, plus the $15,000 down payment, our buyer has approximately $48,333 in home equity.

The conventional monthly principal and interest payment on an $85,000 note for 15 years at 5% is $672.17 Conventional equity appreciation in five years is $21,626.47. The *ByPass* monthly payment is $650.29, which, in comparison to conventional financing, provides a monthly savings of $21.88 or yearly savings of $262.56 to the buyer. ByPass note equity gain in five years is $28,333, which is $6,706.53 more than conventional equity appreciation of $21,626.47 in five years. *ByPass* note equity appreciation in five years is 131% higher than the institutional equity gain in five years. Buyer's equity within the first five years is even higher because of the $15,000 down payment and house appreciation over 5 years. This makes a major and serious difference between these two methods and a significant gain for the buyer who uses the *ByPass* program method.

For a 30 year $85,000 note at 7 ½%, using the *ByPass* method, the projected monthly principal and interest payment is $510.59. The institutional monthly payment for the same note is $573.11, a difference of $62.52 per month in favor of the *ByPass* method buyer. The *ByPass* equity gain in five years is $14,167. The institutional equity gain in five years is $4,590. Our program has a difference of $9,577 more and 308% more in favor of the *ByPass* user.

The reason there is such a savings to the buyer by his use of the *ByPass* program is because there is a more equitable equity distribution which allows for more principal reduction and less total interest than charged traditionally. This is a much fairer and more equitable system for both buyer and seller.

With the *ByPass* program method, the buyer earns more equity faster which immediately begins with his very first mortgage payment and continues throughout the life of the mortgage and note. Our method allows the buyer to earn and accrue higher equity much more quickly than usual traditional methods. On average and in comparison with traditional notes, the *ByPass* method allows buyers to accrue over 131% to 300% plus, in five years, depending upon loan maturity. The 131% is for a 15 year note and the 300% plus is for a 30 year note. The equity accrual amount is different for the maturity, or term, of each note. This is a major difference from traditional notes and quite beneficial to the buyer who uses the *ByPass* method.

As stated previously, due to the enormous amount of property that is currently on the market and other properties continuously flooding most real estate markets in this country, and because of the dire economy and the mortgage fraud that resulted in massive amounts of foreclosures, many sellers are having difficulty not only in getting their asking price, but also selling their homes for a much lesser price than asking. Because of the government shut-down of our American economy due to the very questionable corona virus, millions of American are now and will be financially damaged. About 50% of American workers live paycheck to paycheck. When these people are out of work for five or six weeks, or more, their financial health can be destroyed. Some of the jobs lost can never be recovered. Some of the businesses that closed may never reopen. When people have a choice between food, or rent or mortgage payments, food wins and more foreclosures will take place.

As stated earlier, from our sources, well over 20,500,000 foreclosure actions have taken place in America from 2004 through 2016. Not all of these actions resulted in homeowners losing their homes, but many did. Of those who restructured debt and kept their homes, many of them have since defaulted and lost their homes. Of course, the government that favors banks over the people bailed out the banks, but NOT THE PEOPLE.

According to our sources, at any one time, there are approximately 4,800,000 homes on the market, no matter how many homes have been sold or bought. To further complicate house sales and closings, as referenced earlier, many banks have made their lending requirements much tougher on buyers, with far more stringent qualification criteria and more money required down. Because of the Corona virus government shut down of the American economy, banks are expected to get far more stringent on their mortgage lending and another round of foreclosures are expected. As long as very bad, inept and disastrous government economic policies continue, the American people can expect continuous rounds of foreclosures throughout this nation. Many Americans who want to and are very willing to pay their mortgage payments will be prevented from doing so because of a disast rous economy brought to you by the government. In bad economic times, some people do very well because they have assets or were prepared. Many Americans will be unable to do well. For America to allow this portion of the American people, who, through no fault of their own, may lose everything they have built up over the years, is a national disgrace.

These are facts that are very difficult to deal with when one is trying to successfully sell his home. Undue and untenable conditions placed on buyers obviously adversely affect sellers in achieving successful house closings. In such markets, it is advisable for the seller to offer the prospective buyer something that is not traditionally available. The benefits of a seller-financed property for the buyer have been spelled out in earlier CHAPTERs and summarized above. These benefits also help the seller, because his home is now made much more attractive and will stand out amongst the many other available properties on the local market to a potential buyer who has the down payment funds and the financial capability to meet the monthly mortgage payments. The buyer and the seller have the same objective—a successful transaction by which the home is sold by one party and bought by another. Since the seller has provided a more attractive opportunity, namely, seller-finance, for prospective buyers, this will lead to a quicker, more expeditious sale of his property. At the same time, because of these benefits that accrue to buyer, the seller is much more likely to either get his asking price or very close to it.

To further expedite the transaction, as we mentioned earlier, it would be in the best interests of the seller to have a professional appraisal done on his home and to have a list of current comparable properties in his area, before he even puts it on the market. In this way, prospective buyers can be assured that the property they are considering for purchase is priced correctly for the market and area in which the property is located. If the seller would like to go one step further, he could have a professional home inspection done for presentation to the buyer to assure the prospective buyer that the property is in good condition. All of the benefits to the buyer, including all of this referenced information being provided to him, would take much of the worry, concern and uncertainty out of what can sometimes be a complicated, confusing process.

Of course, in order to get to the point of entering a sale transaction, the seller must first advertise his house to prospective buyers. This is relatively easy to do and can be accomplished in a variety of ways. For example, one of the best, most direct and cost effective ways for a seller to get his or her house noticed by would-be buyers is to place a FOR SALE BY OWNER sign in a prominent place in the front yard. We have both been able to quickly sell and buy homes using a simple, easy to see sign. Another way to attract buyers is through online advertising and there are several websites that cater to owners who want to sell their homes directly, without using a broker. Some of these may or may not charge fees, and determining this would be up to the individual seller. Additionally, the online enterprise, craigslist.com is an excellent means of advertising one's home for sale and there is no charge to place an ad, and even photos, on this site. A seller can also place ads in the local newspaper(s), regional paper(s) and place flyers on bulletin boards in various commercial establishments. Any or all of these methods can produce willing buyers and then it is up to the seller to exercise due diligence to make sure that the prospective buyers are financially capable of making the purchase, meaning that they have verified down payment funds and earn enough to afford the cost of monthly mortgage payments, property taxes and homeowner's insurance. In any and all ads, it is advisable to state that the "seller will carry". These three words can attract a multitude of eager, capable buyers!

For a capable buyer and a willing seller, the sales transaction can proceed very quickly. The buyer can either accept the price offered by the seller or make a counter offer to the seller. Once buyer and seller have agreed upon a price, they can then enter into a very simple purchase and sales agreement, executed by both parties, with a deposit tendered to the seller by the buyer as a show of the buyer's good faith, also known as "earnest money". The purchase and sales agreement will specify the closing date and the closing can take place at one of the local reputable title insurance companies. This company will do a title search to verify that there are no liens on the property and that the title is free and clear, and the company can act as a conduit for both buyer and seller, including assembling all closing documents, such as the mortgage and note. This will save attorneys' fees for both parties, and title insurance company closing fees are typically very reasonable. Again, this transaction can be very simple, very direct, without the major costs of the typical traditional bank transaction involving attorneys, inspections, costly fees, time delays and other situations we have described previously.

CHAPTER THIRTY

PURCHASE AND SALE OF A DEBT-FREE HOUSE

A s a former real estate developer/broker/financier, and a former real estate agent and mortgage banker, we have assembled a unique mortgage/note program with enormous benefits for sellers and buyers over the typical methods used by virtually everyone else. This program explains the ABCs of Creative Self-Financing, or Do It Yourself Financing. To reiterate, this is Bank-less Financing, Broker-less Financing, and No-Mortgage Company Financing. Principals can sell, buy and finance their homes independently, without the usual brokerage, banking and other fees and points that accompany traditional sales and traditional financing. The savings to both seller and buyer can be quite substantial. We are speaking of an age-old method, which, unfortunately, was kicked to the curb decades ago, because people mistakenly gave their power away to banks and institutions, instead of dealing directly with one another as buying and selling principals. All this did was allow the banks and financial institutions to make huge profits, gain more control over the people, and make their lives much more difficult. As mentioned above, this is only one of many different *ByPass* methods, and at least one of these methods can serve you, the reader, if you are so inclined. These *ByPass* methods provide to sellers:

- A competitive edge for a quick sale and fast closing;

- Expanded market that includes capable, but "non-conforming" buyers;

- Easy sale in any market, but especially in a difficult one;

- Special program benefits that attract buyers to seller's home;

- Positions seller's home far above its competition;

- Seller needs no real estate broker and saves real estate fees;

- Seller's savings allows for lower, more saleable home price;

- Seller receives monthly payments directly from Buyer;

- No agent fees;

- Deal directly—avoid any possible loss or problems through middlemen;

- Quick, uncomplicated closing, with minimal costs;

- Seller's free choice for expenditure of sale proceeds:

  - if Seller deposits proceeds into bank, our program provides more interest & security;

  - if Seller buys another home, using our program, this facilitates exchange of one home for the other;

  - If Seller wants cash at a later date, he can always discount and sell his Note;

The *ByPass* program provides to buyers many elements not found in the usual traditional note/mortgages, such as:

- Enables "non-conforming" buyers the ability to purchase homes;

- Very simple, quick and easy purchase and cost-saving closing process;

- Immediate and rapid equity gain, starting with first payment;

- Equity in five years from 131% to 300% over traditional mortgages;

- Quickly accrued equity pool from which buyer can draw;

- Equity leverage to enable participation in other high-yield real estate transactions, if desired;

- Lower monthly payments than traditional mortgage/note;

- No bank involvement saves high "points", application, and closing fees;

- No long anxious waiting periods, with unexpected "points" and interest increases;

- No real estate broker, thus, no brokerage fee to add to home's cost;

- More house for less money;

- Separate program for extreme and more rapid equity acceleration.

This program is designed for the seller whose home is mortgage-free or nearly paid off, who is prepared to accept a down payment and carry a direct, simple and different note and mortgage, with his own former home as security. Many sellers have sold their homes for all cash, then, unfortunately, not managed the money well. Funds were quickly and impulsively spent on vacations, cars, children, "toys", and other expenses, with little left for the seller. This is similar to the so-called "windfall cash" phenomenon that has affected some lottery winners to their detriment.

A prudent seller can achieve financial security by accepting a down payment and receiving steady, secured monthly payments. The *ByPass* program will attract more potential buyers to seller's property than any traditional program. Without it, the seller loses the vast market which our program attracts. If a seller plans to deposit his sale proceeds into a bank or exchange them for another home, our Programs provide more.

CHAPTER THIRTY ONE

PURCHASING PROPERTY THAT HAS PRE-EXISTING DEBT

A buyer wants to purchase one of our typical standard example homes from the seller, and the seller would like to sell his home to the buyer. The first example is a $100,000 home, with 15% down ($15,000) with $85,000 balance carried by seller at 5% for 15 years. The second: $60,000 home, with 15% down ($9,000) with $51,000 carried by seller at 5% for 15 years. The $100,000 home is used here, but the same principals, but not the dollar figures, apply to the $60,000 home. However, there is a pre-existing bank note on the property in the amount of $25,000.00, secured by a mortgage. The buyer can make the standard $15,000.00 down payment, and meet the monthly mortgage payments, but like millions of other people in the country, he cannot qualify to assume the pre-existing bank note under typical bank requirements, or obtain new bank financing. In such a situation, the following examples could take place between the principal buyer and the principal seller, resulting in consummating a sale to the satisfaction of each party.

FIRST METHOD

1. The home price is $100,000.00, requires a $15,000.00 down payment, and a note from the buyer to the seller's favor in the amount of $60,000.00 for 15 years at 5% interest.

2. Seller's pre-existing note balance is $25,000.00. This balance, combined with the $15,000.00 down payment and the buyer's $60,000.00 note to the seller amounts to the $100,000.00 sales price.

3. Buyer and seller enter into a contract that states the above terms.

4. At closing, the buyer (a) pays $15,000.00 down payment to the seller for a **50% ownership interest in seller's home**; (b) buyer gives the seller a note for $60,000.00 on mutually agreeable written terms; (c) buyer takes possession of the home upon closing; (d) buyer assumes the seller's OBLIGATION for the $25,000.00 note, remaining on the home, but does not assume the note itself, and pays the monthly payment, until the debt is retired; (e) the seller makes a promissory note to buyer in the amount of $25,000, explained below; (f) the buyer places a second mortgage on the home, secured by the promissory note from the seller to the buyer.

When the above conditions have been consummated at closing, the buyer has paid $15,000.00 to the seller for 50% ownership in the house, plus a $60,000.00 note in seller's favor, then, takes possession of the house and assumes the seller's $25,000.00 note obligation, but not the note, itself. To secure the buyer's payments for the note obligation, seller executes a $25,000.00 note in favor of the buyer. The buyer files a second mortgage on the home to secure his note from the seller.

The buyer is now half-owner of the home and has a second mortgage on the property to secure his $25,000.00 note from seller. When the buyer pays off the $25,000.00 existing note balance owed by seller to seller's bank, by prior written contract, the following takes place:

1. Payments due on the $25,000 note from the seller to buyer get converted into buyer's ownership of the remaining 50% of the house when seller deeds that other 50% to buyer;

2. Because of this conversion, seller does not owe anything to buyer on the $25,000 note;

3. Buyer continues his payments on his $60,000 note to seller;

4. At buyer's option, he could deed back his 50% ownership position in the house to seller, then, activate the payments due to him from seller's $25,000 note to buyer;

5. If 4 above is invoked, then, seller's $25,000 existing note balance to the bank has been paid by buyer;

6. Seller owns house subject to $25,000 note he owes to buyer;

7. Seller returns to buyer the $60,000 note buyer made to seller, marked "paid in full".

If buyer does not exercise his option by prior contract, then seller received his price of $100,000 at closing, as follows: (a) a $15,000.00 down payment already paid by buyer at closing; (b) a note from the buyer to the seller in the amount of $60,000.00; (c) the $25,000.00 note the seller owes to the bank paid off by the buyer.

Although it is highly likely that most buyers will not exercise their options, reasons may exist for providing an option to the buyer to deed back his 50% ownership and enforce his $25,000 note from seller. Over years, many things change in life, so exercising buyer's option may be beneficial to both buyer and seller. Buyer may decide to move elsewhere for many reasons, may decide to purchase another house or have other reasons to execute his option. If buyer does, then he has paid seller $15,000 at closing, plus seller's bank note, plus interest on the $60,000 note from buyer to seller. Buyer activates the $25,000 note to him from seller, plus interest. Buyer could consider his payments as rent over the years he occupied the house, while he receives the $25,000 note from seller, plus interest, to make up for any difference.

Seller gets his house back, keeps the $15,000 down payment from buyer, keeps payments he received from buyer on the $60,000 note, received financial benefits through buyer's payments on the $25,000 existing note balance to the bank, and owns his house subject to the $25,000 note he owes to buyer. When the sale takes place, whether or not the buyer invokes his option, both seller and buyer have done quite well.

SECOND METHOD

Another way that this could be conducted is pursuant to a lease option or a lease purchase from the seller to the buyer. The owner has the right to contract for the lease and/or purchase of his property. In this scenario, the principal buyer and the principal seller can enter into contract for the lease purchase and/or lease option of our typical example house, with $15,000.00 down, and a total note obligation to the seller, amounting to $85,000.00. Part of this $85,000.00 is the direct monthly payments for the note obligations that the seller owes on his pre-existing debt to the bank. In the above example, this balance is $25,000 and the note from buyer to seller is $60,000. The buyer, who is the tenant under the lease purchase or lease option, takes possession of the house upon the $15,000.00 down payment and assumption of the seller's obligations, namely, the $25,000 remaining balance seller owes to bank. When the tenant pays off the bank note, in full, by prior written contract, the seller deeds the entire home over to the tenant-buyer, who continues his monthly payments to the seller until the remaining balance of the $60,000 debt is retired.

THIRD METHOD

A further approach would be a "contract of sale" by which the homeowner maintains ownership of his home, and enters into a contract with the buyer to purchase the home. Again, in our example, the home price is $100,000, with $15,000 down and notes totaling $85,000 to be paid by buyer to seller.

The buyer makes a $15,000 down payment to the seller, makes monthly payments to the seller on the $85,000 note, and pays the costs for insurance, taxes, upkeep and all other expenses. Upon completion of the contract, with all contractual terms fulfilled by the buyer, the buyer receives title to the property form the seller, by prior written contract. In this manner, the homeowner still owns his home and is responsible to pay his monthly mortgage note payments to the bank. The owner receives a down payment, which he could use to reduce his note balance, or for any other purpose. The payments seller receives from buyer will likely cover all monthly mortgage payment seller owes to his bank, plus. When the seller's note to the bank is fully paid off through funds he received from the buyer, the seller still receives monthly payments from his buyer on the buyer's note to seller, which is now a first mortgage.

If people undertake the very simple, direct approaches set forth here, then, imagine the enormous amount of sales and purchases that can take place in this country which would not have taken place under ordinary, traditional banking circumstances. With the approaches covered in this CHAPTER and the purchase of debt-free homes also covered in this section, virtually 100% of the homes on the market in America can be successfully bought and sold. Compare this to positions previously mentioned in down markets or flat markets in which it would be extremely difficult to buy or sell property. These approaches open entirely new, but realistic, avenues to the American public, some of which have not existed before.

Throughout this book, we have referenced how difficult it is for those who have lost their homes through foreclosure or through job loss or other unfortunate economic circumstances to ever be able to obtain an institutional mortgage or assume an existing institutional mortgage. The present "official government" shutdown of America's economy attributed to the alleged threat of the so-called corona virus will create even more obstacles making it even more difficult for average people to obtain home mortgages. Any one of these *ByPass* approaches stated above permit financially capable buyers, no matter their previous economic circumstances, to be able to purchase homes, because they do not have to be subjected to the stringent, arbitrary qualifying processes imposed by institutional lenders. Sellers, who could not sell their homes because banks would not permit buyers to assume the existing institutional mortgages, can now sell their homes easily.

These approaches allow for both financially capable buyers and sellers who were unable to achieve their objectives to now be able to do so. Further, there are large numbers of buyers who do not want to deal with a bank or mortgage corporation and go through the usual machinations that occur when one attempts to qualify for mortgage funding. These *ByPass* approaches also open the home buying market to this group of buyers. Most homes sold in America have been sold through the traditional institutional approach, and none of the *ByPass* methods fit in that category. Who knows how many additional homes can be sold utilizing the *ByPass* methods, which homes were unable to sell before because of all the institutional restrictions and limitations? The *ByPass* methods involve methods that have been used before, but in limited ways. The *ByPass* approach is to utilize various methods on a large scale basis that can help many Americans achieve what was impossible or difficult to achieve before. When new approaches for old methods open up markets from which people were previously excluded, those methods can produce amazing results. It is possible that the national yearly average home sales can increase considerably if these *ByPass* methods are used by people across the nation to achieve their objectives.

CHAPTER THIRTY TWO

SOLUTIONS FOR DOWN PAYMENTS

For the many people with some cash and the financial ability to pay monthly payments, who, would like to purchase homes but are unable to qualify for bank or mortgage companies' financing under their system-stringent criteria, the *ByPass* program can show approaches that may help them do so. If the cash the buyer can afford to put down is not enough for a full 15% down payment, with the *ByPass* program, these potential buyers still may now have a chance to purchase a home. If the seller, who is willing to sell the buyer his home under the *ByPass* program, is receptive to a partial down payment, then, the buyer must demonstrate to the seller that he can make up the remainder of the down payment by and through another approach.

Let us use our sample $100,000.00 home, with 15% down, and the balance of $85,000.00, carried by the seller for 15 years, at a 5% interest rate. If the buyer can pay the monthly principal and interest payments and shows the seller evidence of this, but the buyer has less than the $15,000.00 to put down, *ByPass* offers potential solutions.

It may be possible, but only if the seller agrees, for the buyer to make a lesser down payment, such as $5,000.00 or $7,500.00, and have the difference of $10,000.00 or $7,500.00 paid over the first two or three years of timely payments. For instance, let us say that the seller agrees to accept $7,500.00 and have the remaining $7,500.00 paid over 36 months, in addition to the regular monthly payment of $650.29. The $7,500.00, divided over 36 months, amounts to $208.33 per month. This $208.33 is added to the regular monthly payment of 650.29 for a total monthly payment of $858.62 for the first three years. At the end of 36 payments, the remaining $7,500.00 down payment has been retired. The monthly payment amount then reverts to the regular amount of $650.29. The $7,500.00 difference could also be paid over three years in one lump annual payment of $2,500.00, per year, on the anniversary of the closing, for a period of three years. There are many ways in which this can be structured. These various ways can be discussed by the principal parties and one can be selected that best suits the interests of both parties. The seller may want interest on the portion of the down payment that he carries for a few years, which is reasonable. At 5% annually on $7,500.00, this amounts to $375, or 31.25 per month. Once principal payments have been made, the interest is paid on the principal balance remaining.

It may even be possible for the buyer to show the seller that the $7,500.00 which he can pay at closing is sufficient, with the other $7,500.00 paid over the term of the note. This amounts to a 7.5% down payment, which is somewhat low, but may be sufficient enough for some sellers.

With a willing seller, the principals can structure any arrangement along these lines which would be agreeable to both parties. This approach opens many possibilities for capable, but traditionally un-fundable, people without substantial means to purchase homes. It opens doors that could have never been opened under the present rigorous, sometimes arbitrary, funding climate and traditional methods. Sellers and buyers can help each other by doing business directly, without a middleman, and *ByPassing* the banks. Clearly, the arrangement made between seller and buyer is paramount in this situation. The seller is giving the buyer a double opportunity, and the buyer must produce valid evidence that he or she is fully capable of performing financially, and then do so.

Another way to handle a down payment shortage could be to receive a loan of $7,500.00 from capable family members, which can be added to the $7,500.00 the buyer already has. This would meet the down payment requirement of $15,000.00. Buyers know their own family members and relatives and they can best assess whether this type of personal borrowing to satisfy the down payment deficit is realistic and feasible.

Most people have some type of retirement program and/or insurance policy that has built up over the years. It may be possible to borrow a certain amount from one's own retirement program, such as a company pension plan, 401k, IRA, or the like, and when he repays it, the funds go directly back into his own retirement program, instead of to another party, such as a private lender. The same thing may be possible with an insurance policy that has a provision within it which permits the policy holder to receive such a loan from his own policy. *Creative thinking* is essential when one is working outside the box, and those who have far-reaching minds and ideas usually come up with the right solutions and methods to successfully accomplish their objectives.

The buyer and seller should include in the purchase and sales contract and mortgage and note documents whatever specific arrangement(s) they have made regarding a partial down payment and the terms decided upon to fulfill them. In this way, everything is in writing, clear, up front and understood by both parties. This will avoid any misunderstandings or difficulties right from the inception of the transaction and help assure a successful and congenial experience throughout.

CHAPTER THIRTY THREE

EQUITY POOL AND BUYERS' USES FOR IT

Today's average buyers do not have the same objectives and profiles as those in your father's or grandfather's day. One major difference is that many women, either single or married, purchase property today. This was very rare or even unheard of a few generations ago. Buyers today are much more active, mobile, and change locations much more frequently. Present day society is an "on the go" one. As mentioned, today's average buyer lives in his or her home for approximately five years. When he/she buys a home, s/he usually considers both present day value and near-future value. If one particular home can stand out and demonstrate its highly-increased near-future value, because of the *ByPass* program, as opposed to other homes which do not offer this increased value, then, today's astute and informed buyer is more likely to purchase the home with that potentially increased value because this will offer the homebuyer a better equity position at the time of his or her future sale.

With such a large equity amount rapidly appreciating for the buyer, he may want to make good financial use of his equity pool. For instance, on the example given above, the buyer purchases a home in the amount of $100,000.00, makes a $15,000.00 cash down payment, and has an $85,000.00 note for 15 years, at 5%. At the end of one year, the *ByPass* program provides the buyer an equity position approximately 175% higher than present institutional methods. In five years, the *ByPass* program provides the buyer approximately 131% more equity than institutional notes. If the note were for 30 years instead of 15, after one year, the buyer would have an approximate 370% higher equity than with institutional notes. After five years, the buyer would have approximately 308% more equity with the *ByPass* program than with institutional methods.

Buyer's total equity in five years is higher since he made a $15,000.00 down payment and the value of his home will most likely increase over five years. Homes appreciate in value depending upon condition, location, home size, lot size, any improvements, desirable features, value of other homes in the immediate neighborhood, recent sales, local growth and economic factors, new building, zoning changes, inflation and many other considerations. If the buyer's home were to increase at a bare minimum of one percent per year, then in five years, the buyer's total home equity from note appreciation, down payment and increased home value would be about $48,333. We arrive at this figure, as follows: (a) $5,666 note equity appreciation per year x 5 years = $28,333; (b) $5,000 house value appreciation; (c) $15,000 down payment. This is a major equity position to achieve in five years on a $100,000 home. We used one percent appreciation per year as a very conservative figure. That real appreciation per year figure is expected to be two percent, minimum, to three percent. With the two per cent increases, the $48,333 increases to $53,333.

The following figures may amaze you but are quite real and attainable by any capable and willing buyer. In essence, by the above average example, the buyer, in five years, has earned 48.3%, amounting to $48,333 equity on the $100,000.00 purchase price of his home. This averages to a gain of 9.66% per year on the full purchase price. However, the buyer has earned an average yearly gain of 64.4% (PER YEAR) on the original down payment of $15,000. 00. In some circles, the buyer would be considered a Wall Street wizard or investment genius. The difference here is that the buyer has not taken the enormous risks that are required on that extremely speculative Street to earn such an enormous gain. Our buyer simply used the ByPass Program Method and made his safe, sure, secure and highly profitable investment in his own home on his own street. Buyer's return includes his $15,000 down payment, which is the required investment to purchase his home.

Like any investment, buyer's gain is *on paper* until the paper is turned into cash through a sale or leveraged into cash through a loan. The buyer may want to draw upon his equity pool for many uses. For example, the buyer may want to purchase another home for retirement or investment purposes. S/he may want to expand a present business or start a new one or might want to go into the buying and selling of real estate for investment and profit, using the *ByPass* program. The buyer might realize how s/he can purchase property with our method, lease it, and earn safe, solid and substantial returns in the process. The buyer may want to have funds for other investments or money for his/her children's education, his/her retirement or for any other purpose.

If this is the case, then the buyer has a large equity pool from which to draw. There are many private investors, private capital and equity funds, and individuals that make equity loans. Our buyer may comparison shop to find his best arrangement, then, use his equity to acquire the cash he needs to do whatever he wants.

CHAPTER THIRTY FOUR

ACCELERATED EQUITY GAINS

For those buyers who want to achieve an even faster method of gaining equity, *ByPass* has a method to accomplish it. This program, however, is not for the average buyer who simply wants to purchase his primary home and possibly a second home. This program is intended for the professionally minded person who wants to become an active investor through leverage of the advanced equity gain for the purchase of investment property or the buying and selling of additional property.

The advanced equity gain on the initial property purchased can be financed for other purposes and ventures, or the property can be sold and the note assumed by the new buyer. However, the note cannot be paid off upon sale. In this program, the seller allows the buyer to achieve more equity gain much faster so that the buyer is able to finance that accelerated gain for other purposes. If the buyer wants to pay off the note, then, he would have to arrange that with the seller.

The following will provide an investment example. Let us say a small investment group of six (6) professionals, such as doctors, dentists, accounts, businessmen, etc., placed $100,000, each, into a buying pool for purchase of property, by and through the *ByPass* program. Using our typical example of a $100,000 dollar home, with 15% down, and the balance carried by the seller for 15 years, 40 houses could be purchased. The $15,000 down payment amount times 40 houses equals $600,000, which is the total investment amount placed into the investment group's buying pool. These 40 houses would be rented so that all expenses for all houses are covered by the rental income, with expectation of reasonable profit.

In 5 years, each house would have an approximate equity of $48,000. Therefore, the equity on these houses at $48,000 times 40 houses is approximately $1,920,000. If 85% of this were borrowed, this amounts to $1,632,000. If the *ByPass* program were continued, and these funds were used to purchase additional houses, at $15,000 down, per house, on our typical example, then, 109 houses could be purchased. In 5 years, the investment pool of $600,000 has produced 149 houses owned by the investors.

In 10 years, the *ByPass* program, using the same equity example, would produce an even larger number of houses, and in 15 years, using the same program, an even larger number of houses. On these projected figures, *as examples only*, each $100,000 investment made into the buying pool is projected to be worth approximately $10,000,000 in 15 years.

CHAPTER THIRTY FIVE

HOMES FOR APARTMENT
DWELLERS AND RENTERS

The residential rental market covers a large part of dwellings in America. This market caters to tens of millions of people throughout the nation. Some remain in rental properties for a few years, then, either move to other rental properties, or eventually buy a home. Others, and this covers another large segment of renters, remain in rental properties for most, if not all, of their lives. All they get from this are rent receipts and higher monthly rents as the years go by. In a 25 or 30 year rental span, they have nothing in comparison to what they would have gained, had they bought a home 25 or 30 years ago, instead of renting all that time. In most situations, a home is paid for in 20 or 30 years, and with the *ByPass* method, within 15 years or less, so after 15 years there is no debt and no monthly mortgage payment that must be made. The home can provide a residence for the remainder of the owner's life, or the owner could sell it and buy another home elsewhere with the proceeds of the sale. The real difference here is that the homeowner has achieved valuable **equity** in his own property after 15 years, while the renter, who rented for 25 or 30 years, or more, achieved nothing but amassing rent receipts, with the likely expectation of paying higher rents in the future.

Most of these long-term renters would be better served by buying a home rather than remaining renters. However, many of these people believe that they could not qualify to buy a home for two primary reasons, namely, their low down payment funds and the belief that they could not meet the strict criteria required for a bank loan. From a traditional buying, selling and financing viewpoint, these thoughts are absolutely correct. However, with the approaches that we have set forth in this book, home buying for long-term renters could not only become a distinct possibility, but in most cases, a reality. We have discussed traditional system's-based buying, selling and financing of property, with all its restrictions, cumbersome approaches, seen and unseen costs, high fees, delays and the usual snags that frequently take place in many such transactions. Since our approaches are quite different from the traditional, they definitely could open up home-buying avenues to long-term renters.

For instance, using the *ByPass* standard example of a free and clear $100,000.00 home, with 15% down, and $85,000.00 carried by the seller for 15 years, the long-term renter may be able to structure a purchase that would meet his/her needs and better suit his/her circumstances. In fact, the rent s/he pays may be considerably more than the monthly mortgage payment would be. The would-be buyer may not have the full $15,000.00 to put down, but perhaps s/he could manage to put down half of that amount, namely, $7,500.00. If this potential buyer finds a home s/he likes and an owner who is receptive to an offer with special considerations regarding the down payment amount, then, a transaction could be accomplished. For example, the contract could call for $7,500.00 at closing and, upon the anniversary of the closing an additional $2,500.00 would be paid to the principal amount for three successive years. These three payments made over the next three years would add to the additional $7,500.00 down payment, for a total of $15,000.00. This would fulfill the down payment objective in a scenario when the potential buyer had some initial funds, but not enough for the full down payment. This is only an example, and there are many other ways to pay the additional $7,500.00. For instance, $1,000.00 could be paid on the yearly anniversary of the purchase for a period of seven years, and on the eighth year, $500.00 would be paid. Whatever arrangements the buyer and seller can make which satisfy their mutual objectives would lead to a successful transaction for both principal parties.

Since the seller carries the $85,000.00 note for a 15 year period, what the buyer pays as a monthly mortgage payment would most likely be less than he would pay if he were to rent a comparable house or apartment as we said above. A distinct advantage is the fact that this mortgage payment remains constant for the 15 year period and does not increase over time, as rents likely would. If a comparable rental costs $800.00 a month, it is highly likely that this rental amount would increase on a steady basis over a 15 year period, so that at the end of that period, the rent could reach as much as $1,500.00, or more. At that point in time, the renter would have no equity, no home owned, and only a future expectation of ever-increasing rent. As some of these folks get older, meeting that burden can become increasingly difficult. If our prospective buyer actually bought a home, then, at the end of 15 years, that home would be fully paid for and is his or hers to live in, rent, sell or whatever s/he wishes. There is a world of difference between owning property and renting property, and it would be in the best interests of long-term renters to consider some of the ideas and approaches in this book.

Another consideration that may occur with some buyers is their fear that they may have overstepped their financial capabilities by buying a house, instead of renting. If one were to analyze and compare both scenarios, owning a house is a much better option for most people, but there are some who may not believe this. If a long-term renter were to buy a home and, within two or three years, fears he made a mistake, then, he can readily sell the home in any given market, primarily because of the assumable mortgage that a new buyer could take over. As we have discussed in previous CHAPTERs, with traditional financing, it is very difficult for most buyers to assume the existing financing, and this, of course, adversely impacts large numbers of transactions. Further, as also discussed, with rigorous bank qualification criteria, many financially capable buyers still do not qualify for home loans. Given these well-known situations, an assumable mortgage is highly valuable to both the seller and the buyer. With our program, the financially capable buyer can assume the existing mortgage, which places the seller's house in a far more attractive position than other similar properties in that real estate market. Still further, as also discussed in previous CHAPTERs, the equity buildup in our financing program amasses much more quickly than in traditional programs, and because of the assumable mortgage, the seller can expect a sales price about $10,000.00 higher, if not more, than what he paid. Both of these factors financially benefit the seller who can expect a rather quick sale. No matter how one looks at it, owning a house is far preferable to long-term renting.

For properties that have existing debt, refer to CHAPTER THIRTY ONE for methods by which these properties can be purchased by assuming the debt obligation, pursuant to a contract with the seller mutually arranged between buyer and seller.

DOWN PAYMENT POSSIBILITIES

Whenever a willing seller and a willing buyer are prepared to come to terms on the purchase and sale of any property, the real bottom-line objective is just that—the successful purchase and sale of that property. When apparent obstacles arise, truly motivated, capable buyers and sellers can structure positions and terms that benefit both parties so that the transaction can be consummated. Sellers should never demand an excessively high down payment, and buyers should never try to purchase a property via an excessively low down payment. As long as the down payment is within reasonable range, then, both parties should be satisfied. However, as mentioned in previous CHAPTERs in the prior section regarding foreclosure and in other CHAPTERs in this book, some buyers who were in foreclosure, or those who lived in apartments for many years, do not necessarily have the full down payment amount which the seller wants. In CHAPTERs THIRTY SIX and FIFTY, we covered some positions regarding down payment solutions to which you may want to refer.

Many people would likely agree, based upon factual evidence and reality, that the housing market for sellers in most of America is very weak at this time. Of course, this does not apply to the so-called "star" markets we previously referenced in which property values continue to increase at ridiculous speculation rates that are unjustified and not viable over time. The majority of Americans do not live in or near these "star cities", so the prospects of selling their properties are adversely affected by economic considerations, banking and governmental requirements and the undeniable fact that ever-increasing amounts of Americans are either not working, or working in low paying and/or part-time positions. These conditions affect their buying potential. If a small town has little to no economic base, the possibility of selling quickly is remote, and if a sale is to be achieved, it can take many months or even years. In such situations, sellers may be much more willing to deal with a viable, capable buyer who doesn't have the full down payment the seller would like, but who can make up the differential over a reasonable period of time.

In the referenced CHAPTERs, we give some examples of how these down payment scenarios could be structured. When two people want to accomplish the same objective and are working in good faith to bring that to fruition, then, many different creative solutions can be applied by these reasonable people to reach their common objective. As we have said in several places throughout this book, it is important that people not only think outside the box, but also *act* upon that thinking to accomplish the desired results. Many Americans have seen the sad truth and ugly reality of our current system and, unfortunately, that system's ideology and methods do not typically favor the average American. Americans must realize that it is in their best interests to take matters regarding their own affairs into their own capable hands and come up with inventive, creative solutions to make their dreams come true.

CHAPTER THIRTY SEVEN

VALID REASONS FOR SELLERS TO SELL
VIA *ByPass* METHODS

This book demonstrates numerous valid, common sense and logical reasons why buyers of homes would do so within the methods we have described. Enormous benefits exist for any buyer who acts within the scope of these buying methods. What about benefits to the seller? In previous CHAPTERs we have described those benefits and will briefly revisit some of those points here. In tough economic times and the aftermath that ensues because of those economic problems, home sales can be difficult to accomplish in any price range, and especially more so in homes priced under $100,000.00. In good economic times, home values typically rise annually and home sales are rather easy because the economic climate is favorable. Since America has experienced numerous downturns, unfortunately, these have become a way of life in this nation.

In such situations, sellers may wait an extremely long time before they are able to sell their properties within traditional system's approaches, if, in fact, they can sell at all. Because of the extreme financial controls exerted by the central bank and the government, one never knows when a severe economic downturn will occur again. This uncertainty should cause concern among all classes of people, and especially among sellers, who have difficulty using traditional approaches. If a seller were to sell through one of our proscribed methods, then he realizes that he is receiving a substantial cash down payment, somewhere around 15% of the selling price, and the seller's security is a first mortgage on his own property, which in any financial climate is excellent security. Should the buyer default on his payments, then the seller, pursuant to the first mortgage position, can take back his property, keep the down payment made by the original buyer and all of his mortgage payments paid by the buyer, and then resell the property on the same basis. In any economic climate, there will always be buyers with ample down payment abilities who will purchase properties from sellers who are willing to carry. The alternative to the seller who does not use this approach in tough economic times is the extremely likely possibility that he will not be able to sell that property for a very, very long time, and if he does, it would likely be at a much lower price than he anticipated.

Further benefits are the fact that there is no broker involved, no bank involved, no complicated contracts with fine print not understood and potentially disadvantageous to the vast majority of people, no costly closing, no costly appraisals and inspections, no unexpected conditions imposed at the last minute and no high points and fees to obtain financing. The most favorable benefit within our programs is that principals deal directly with principals, with no third party interference and determinations, to the detriment of the seller, made by non-principals who are not parties to the contract. Personal independence and responsibility is integral to these methods, and people who are able to express these qualities and take their own power back from those who would speak for, dictate to and act for them, benefit themselves through wise personal choice, and not the dictates of others. Many sellers and buyers have experienced the upset which occurs when transactions that looked excellent fell apart at the last minute because of some added requirement imposed by the lender and/or a third party who essentially took control of the transaction and killed it.

Sellers who fully understand and can grasp the underlying concept of our methods are easily able to comprehend and appreciate them as a way to sell a property that was otherwise likely unsellable. Some sellers may ask what they are going to do with the funds, once they sell, and we have covered this in previous CHAPTERs, but will briefly touch upon this here. Since we deal in facts, logic, common sense and truth, that question posed by any seller is a valid question. Our question would be as follows: What is the seller going to do with the sales proceeds, both the down payment and the monthly payments? As we said in prior CHAPTERs, some sellers who sell their properties for cash; thus receive a cash windfall, do not know what to do with that cash, and some of them spend it like the proverbial "drunken sailor"—no insult intended to drunken sailors! Obviously, this applies only to a small percentage of sellers, and not all of them. However, those who fall into this category eventually realize that they have sold their home and squandered the money, without much benefit at all. We have all heard the story about the guy who "bet the house" on the Super Bowl or lost it on the gambling tables in Las Vegas or elsewhere. A home is probably the most valuable financial transaction people can make and the greatest asset they can acquire in this life, and it is wise to be very prudent as to how they spend the funds they receives from the sale of that asset.

Other sellers may be generous to family and friends or make traditional investments that they should not make, because they are unaware of the market conditions and manipulations regarding those investments. Still others can and have given money to family and friends to buy other properties or to pay for college educations for their children and grandchildren. While all of these actions may have been done from good intentions and charitable purposes, such expenditures can strip the home sellers of much of their remaining assets. Then, of course, comes the eventual "tax man" who, depending upon the specifics pertinent to the seller, wants his share of the sale proceeds, federal, state and sometimes local. Again, it would be best for people who receive lump sums of cash to be very wise and thoughtful regarding their expenditures.

If a seller is going to buy another property, when he sells his home by and through our methods, then, again, from a logical, common sense approach, he might want to consider the following, which we have also mentioned before. If the seller is going to sell his home for $100,000.00, as an example, and wants to buy another home in another town or state costing approximately $100,000.00, it would behoove him to strike a buying transaction with his seller based upon our buying/selling approaches. If our seller realizes that he can use the down payment he receives from his buyer as a down payment to be paid to his seller, and the monthly mortgage payments he will receive from his buyer can be put toward the payments he will owe to his seller, then essentially, what our seller has done is to swap his present home for the home he wants to buy, by and through our methods. Of course, the seller can always go the traditional route, with a traditional bank, traditional broker, traditional real estate and banking contracts and all that goes with this type of traditional selling and buying process. However, it would be in the seller's best interests to be aware of the potential pitfalls of such a purchase and financing arrangement. You might want to review our CHAPTER regarding pitfalls to avoid in real estate transactions, based on our personal experiences! If our seller can show his seller the benefits of selling by and through our approaches, then we essentially have a three way transaction among the original buyer, our original seller and our seller's seller. Obviously, an added benefit to this type of buying is that there is no lump sum received for the full purchase price of the property which is taxable. All sellers have expenses in their homes, and if the expenses are valid, they are fully deductible. However, there is still a lump sum that is likely taxable for most people, but with our down payment and mortgage installment method, the taxes, at worst, are minimal or non-existent. When one essentially "swaps" his home for another home by and through these approaches, there is no gain, therefore, logically, there should be no tax. These are things that sellers should strongly consider when they are thinking about selling their properties either traditionally or by and through our approaches.

CHAPTER THIRTY EIGHT

PITFALLS TO AVOID IN REAL ESTATE
TRANSACTIONS

Margy and I speak for ourselves in all matters and do not permit others to speak for or represent us and our positions. Traditionally, the overwhelming majority of Americans allow third parties to speak for and represent them, in many, if not most, situations. Please think about this carefully, because this is not an ideal situation by any means. Rather than deal directly with other principals in real estate transactions, they let brokers or realtors speak for and represent them. The principals rarely, if ever, speak directly with each other until the closing takes place, and often not even then. In money matters, they hire a broker, an agent or consultant to obtain funding for them. In court situations, virtually all Americans hire lawyers or paralegals to represent their interests. In business matters, they hire lawyers, consultants and professional negotiators to conduct their business, rather than do so directly. At one time in America, people spoke for themselves, but now ever-increasing numbers are hiring third parties to speak for them. In many of the most important matters in life, if not all, Americans hire third parties to represent and speak for them and their interests. When people do this, they give their power and voices away to third parties who do not have the same stake in the matter as do the people who hire them. These third parties have their own businesses and interests, which business is representing others, and promoting and profiting from this business is their main concern and focus. When they represent someone else, that someone else is usually a secondary or tertiary concern—and not the primary one. Some third party representatives are quite good at representing their clients, but sadly, many people have found out the hard way that most are not. Ever since we were young children, we have always spoken for ourselves and our interests in all matters and, as said above, do not permit others to do so for us.

No one knows his own positions, thoughts, ideas, dreams and objectives better than the man or woman who has them. No one else can see, imagine and conceive what we, ourselves, do, just as no one can eat our food or breathe the air for us. We are all individuals, with individual bents, positions, objectives and ways of doing things. No one else can fully understand these nor properly represent these positions. If we are truly individuals, then we should be able to effectively speak for ourselves in all matters. When people do this, and do not delegate to another, then they develop a sense of accomplishment and purpose. When we let others speak for us, there is no sense of personal accomplishment and we place ourselves, our interests and, sometimes, our fates in the hands of others. There is now and there has been for a very long time so much conditioning, programming and propaganda in America, designed to induce us to give away our power and our voices to others, that many Americans have become quite timid and very unwilling to speak for themselves and express their own objectives and interests. As many of you may have seen, this establishes an extremely bad precedent. We, as Americans, must recognize and reassert our own independence, our own values and our own way of doing things, express our own voices and opinions to anyone at any time. When we do this, we take our power back and become responsible for our own thoughts and actions. This reclaiming of our own power allows us to "get back into the game."

As mentioned earlier, some representatives can actually properly represent their clients or customers quite well. Unfortunately, these people are in the minority. Do you want a third party to make decisions for you, write contracts for you, write terms and conditions in the contract, make financial and other important decisions for you, all of which can lawfully and legally bind you—or do you want to do this on your own as a responsible, capable adult? Some third party entities actually assume and act as if they are the principals, are parties to the contract, can make choices and decisions for their clients, many of which may not be in the best interests of the clients. For many decades we have lived all over the country and bought and sold real estate all in various places. In all of these situations, except one, we acted on our own and did not engage with third party agents. However, before finishing this book, we decided to take an opportunity that came our way to test out third party representation, and we can tell you, as stated below, that the entire matter turned out to be extremely frustrating, ridiculously complicated and nearly disastrous to our ultimate objective.

By now, Jack and I should know that the Universe will always provide us with opportunities to live our truths and experience situations that reflect the subjects of our thoughts and books. However, it still amazes us to see how this synchronicity works—sometimes to our frustration, initially, but most always to our best advantage in the end. Recently, we had the opportunity to experience this amazing synchronicity during a real estate transaction to which we were parties. Many years ago, using our typical non-bank, non-broker methods, we bought a lovely house in New Mexico, where we lived happily for sixteen years. Eventually, we moved from that home to be nearer to our families on the east coast. The real estate market in New Mexico at the time of our move was very depressed, and since we owned the house outright and thought we might one day want to return to New Mexico, we decided to keep our house instead of putting it up for sale. After the passage of nearly ten years, we realized that we would not be going back to New Mexico, so we put our house on the market via an Internet real estate site and we also posted a For Sale by Owner sign in our front yard. Because the real estate market in New Mexico was still somewhat sluggish, we knew it could take some time for our house to sell, perhaps six months to a year or more, but we decided to be patient, with the expectation that, since the house is a lovely one, in good condition, in a nice neighborhood and was properly priced for the market, eventually the house would attract a capable buyer. Many people saw the For Sale by Owner sign and called us to see the house, but since most were not capable buyers, pursuant to our criteria and methods, no sale resulted.

About two months after we put the house on the market, we received a phone call from a woman who identified herself as a real estate agent and said that she had a client who had seen our house on the Internet, then had driven by the address, liked what she saw and was very interested in viewing the interior of the house as soon as possible. The agent acknowledged that our house was for sale by owner and also told us that she was duty bound to reveal to us that the client she mentioned is her cousin, so as to avoid the appearance of any conflict of interest problems. Then, she implored us to let her client see the house right away. This unexpected call from the agent provided us with a golden opportunity to test out the usual third party representation and to determine whether any improvements or additional problems presently existed in this typical scenario. We arranged for our handyman to show the house to this client, who is a single mother with a young daughter, on the very same day. The real estate agent called us as soon as her client let her know that she had seen the house and told us that the young woman loved the house and wanted to make a full price offer immediately. Although we were not really thrilled to be dealing with a real estate agent, as we said above, our objective was to sell the house and also to test out the situation to see what, if anything, had changed with third party representation. As things turned out, this was the beginning of a third party horror show.

In the early days of this situation, the real estate agent appeared capable, forthcoming and motivated to sell our house. She told us that the sale should go smoothly and close quickly, because her buyer was already "prequalified" with a lender. The agent also said that, since we were thousands of miles away, it would be much easier for us if she "represented" us in the sale, meaning she would do the paperwork, arrange for the necessary inspections the buyer wanted, the appraisal for the lender, contact a title company to set up the closing, etc. To test out the process, we agreed. However, a process that should have been a "slam dunk" ended up being an absolute nightmare of misrepresentations, inordinate delays, unimaginable mistakes, deceptions, incompetence, malfeasance, outright lies and fraud. What was supposed to take six weeks to accomplish ended up taking almost double that time, and the stress, aggravation, uncertainty and frustration we encountered throughout the entire process was akin to what most others go through when they deal with third parties.

Although the realtor, as mentioned above, initially seemed to be capable, experienced in overseeing such transactions, after a very short time, it became obvious to us that she was either incompetent or angling to extract as much as she could from us for the benefit of her client-cousin. The house was in good condition and we told the agent we were selling it "as is", and this was stated in the contract. Despite this, the agent misrepresented conclusions made by the lender's appraiser in his report so she could get us to pay for unnecessary repairs on our house, for which the appraiser's report did not call. When we objected and challenged the agent on this, she became nasty, defensive, antagonistic, hard to reach, and obviously not representing *our* best interests, which happens quite frequently in these matters. It appears that the agent had a cozy relationship with the lender and the closing agent, so, now, all of a sudden the lender demanded a structural inspection by a licensed engineer, which was totally unnecessary to be conducted on a very sound, well-built house and for which the appraiser did not call. Remember, we were selling the house "as is", so were not obligated to do any of this and could have stopped the process at any time. However, since one of our objectives was to test out third party representation, we continued.

The structural engineer's report stated that the house was extremely sound in all aspects. However, since the engineer could not conduct his inspection within the original closing date time frame, the first of *three* contract extensions became necessary to accommodate this inspection. The cozy relationship the agent had with both the lender and the closing agent now became quite apparent, because the lender then demanded that certain other repairs be made which were not deemed necessary by the appraiser previously. However, the lender did not communicate correctly to us the extent of these other repairs, which caused the need for a second closing date extension and necessitated a second inspection by the lender's appraiser. The appraiser did not approve the repairs because of the communication failures on the part of the lender and real estate agent to us. It was only when *we* directly intervened and spoke with the lender's appraiser that clear, precise communication took place between the appraiser and us, and not the convoluted, incorrect miscommunications we received from the lender and the real estate agent. Once the direct communication between the appraiser and us had occurred, we quickly resolved the repair issues, which necessitated a third inspection by the lender's appraiser and required a third contract time extension. When the appraiser conducted his third inspection, he approved all the repairs we had done, most of which were unnecessary; he passed the house and stated that closing could take place immediately.

All of our lives we have taken responsibility for our own actions and have written our own contracts in anything we do. All of our contracts are simple, direct, to the point and completely devoid of legalese. However, when one works with a real estate agent, the standard real estate contract comes into play, which, since it is written by lawyers, is very lengthy, convoluted, confusing, replete with detail in fine print, and not easily understood, or understood at all, by most Americans. The ability of the principal to write his own contract is tossed out the window when he deals with a realtor. To us, this is a reprehensible situation that should never be allowed by any sane people and government. The right to contract is one of our most sacred rights and pursuant to Constitutional requirements, no government is permitted to abrogate the obligations of contract, nor impose the obligations of contract. However, governments do this all the time and the people simply accept these un-Constitutional dictates by un-Constitutional governments all the time. As stated, we were testing this whole process, and we can tell you that the contract was a real obstacle.

First of all, the principals do not write the contract because the contract is already written in a standardized format by quasi-government lawyers. Secondly, a real estate agent further writes the contract–a legal and binding document—by inserting terms and conditions to be met by the principals, yet the real estate agent is not a licensed attorney with authority to write contracts that bind other parties. Third, the principals to the contract do not, as we said before, write the contract or the terms of the contract, because the real estate agent, pursuant to the realtor's agency and association requirements, is the only one who does this. Many real estate agents act as if they are principals and parties to the contract, and in many cases, do not properly state the positions and terms of the principals, yet their writings within the contract legally bind the principals. For those of you who are aware of contracts, you realize that this is absolutely un-Constitutional and a violation of due process of law, yet standardized real estate contracts are used in every state by real estate agents and brokers.

In our situation, the real estate agent wrote statements and positions in the contract that we never authorized, yet tried to hold us to those unauthorized positions. Obviously, since we review everything in detail, we rejected them and told her to change them, giving her specific language to insert within the contract and addenda. She resented this immensely and was very reluctant to do so, but we pressed and said we would not agree to anything which we did not authorize. There were at least a half dozen occasions in which this blatant misrepresentation and fraud took place on the part of the real estate agent. Unfortunately, the overwhelming majority of principals who deal in these issues, simply leave the entire contract and the insertions in the contract up to the real estate agent or broker and take little or no notice to what these entities have stated that is legally binding upon them, the principals! This unfortunate position has put many principals in difficult and adverse, legally binding positions not of their own making, but since they took no responsibility to state exact terms and to hold the agent to those exact positions, then, thoroughly review everything, before signing the contract or agenda, their failures hurt them.

Many weeks before the original closing date was to have occurred, we had issued our specific escrow closing instructions to the closing agent, and since to help the young buyer, *we* were paying for the closing, that agent was required to execute her fiduciary duty to represent *our* direct interests and to abide by *our* instructions. Yet, during those many weeks, she never contacted us in any manner, whatsoever. During that time frame, we had a few minor communications with her assistant, but the assistant always deferred to the closing agent, who, as we said, never contacted us at all. Again, it was obvious to us that the relationship between the real estate agent and the closing agent was very close, and it became quite apparent that, since we were paying their fees, and since they were not adhering to our instructions, they failed to properly represent us, and in so doing, committed fraud by their own actions.

As the time for the closing advanced upon us, we became concerned because we had not heard anything from the closing agent, so we initiated a phone call to her late on a Friday afternoon for a closing that was to take place on the following Tuesday. Although we had left several messages and sent emails directly to this closing agent, she failed to respond to any message or email and that Friday conversation was the first time we ever spoke with her. That conversation revealed to us that either she did not know what she was doing, or she was trying to sabotage the transaction, because at this point the real estate agent was furious with us because we exposed her deceptions and fraud to everyone involved in the process, including the lender and closing agent. The real estate agent considered herself a power force with strong influence with the lender, the closing agent and with her own senior real estate broker. When we exposed her deceptions, incompetence and fraud to these people, it was apparent that the real estate agent was not only furious with us, but out of spite also wanted to sabotage the transaction. It seemed that the lender's agent and definitely the closing agent were accomplices in this nefarious objective. In all our years of buying and selling property, we have never seen such deceit, such fraud, such incompetence and vindictiveness as we experienced in this transaction. The reason for all this may be the fact that we involved ourselves in every step in the process, from the very beginning to the very end, and stood our ground and demanded that our instructions be followed by the people we were paying to represent our interests. Unfortunately, in today's America, most people in that situation just sit back, take no involvement and let the third parties do whatever they want to do, because the only thing the seller has interest in is the payday he will receive at closing, while the buyer's only interest is acquiring the house.

Incredibly, although this is very hard to believe, and if we had not lived through it, we might even be skeptical, the closing agent did not send the original closing documents to us, but instead sent an email with those documents attached, which we did not receive until 8:30PM on the night before the closing! Any rational, reasonable, objective observer could easily conclude that this closing agent was totally incompetent, or in the alternative, purposely trying to sabotage the transaction. During the conversation we had with the closing agent on that Friday before the closing, she assured us that we would have the original closing documents delivered to us by 11AM on Monday morning, the day before the closing. Obviously, this did not happen. It was not until we called the lender and informed her that we had not received the closing documents that the lender had the closing agent send them to us by email, and as stated above, that email did not arrive until 8:30PM on the eve of the closing, requiring us to print out all of the documents which should have been sent to us via overnight delivery, as promised.

This entire situation went from the ridiculous to the absurd to the insane, and if we had not been vigilant, had not pressed the lender, we never would have received the closing documents, which meant we could not execute them, which meant there would have been no closing on the following day. It became further apparent that the real estate agent had reached out to everyone involved to sabotage the transaction, when her own cousin was the buyer! This is how spiteful and furious this woman was with us because we demanded truth, competence and timely action from the people who were *supposed* to be representing us and getting paid by us. Apparently, few people in our position make such demands of the people who should be representing them and their best interests.

Upon our review of the closing documents, we ascertained numerous mistakes in the figures listed, which any competent closing agent should have never made, and if made, would have immediately corrected. Further, there was a cost to us listed in the closing documents that we had previously told the real estate agent we would not pay under any circumstances and had refused to sign the document that would have authorized that cost. Despite these facts, the closing agent included that unauthorized cost to us in the closing documents. We immediately, the next morning, as soon as everyone was open for business, called the closing agent and the lender to apprise them of these mistakes and said we would not proceed to closing until these mistakes were rectified. The agent for the lender, who apparently was in league with both the real estate and closing agents, may have quickly realized that her position was now in jeopardy because of her actions which hurt the transaction. Based upon this apparent realization, she informed the closing agent to immediately make the corrections we demanded to state the accurate figures and told the closing agent that the cost which was not authorized by us and not stated in the contract had to be removed. At this point, when the real estate agent found out that the figures were going to be corrected, the cost had to be removed, and then the closing would take place, she became an insane harpy who called us and went on a screaming rant for several minutes, listened to nothing we said and then hung up. The nature of this fiasco became pretty clear to us and was our answer to our test of third party representation.

The lender informed the closing agent to date all paperwork on a specific day to accommodate the closing date required by the contract, yet, incredibly, the closing agent told us to date the documents we were to sign on the following day. It seemed that the underhanded influence of the real estate agent was still holding sway over the closing agent. Had we dated the documents the following day, as she told us, then the transaction could not have closed, because the lending commitment expired on the day that the lending agent had specified. We had to work late into the night to make all the proper corrections, and then email them back to the closing agent who finalized them and got them back to us at 1:30PM our time on the day of the closing. We had to print all of the documents, get to a notary to notarize our signatures and send the closing document package out by Federal Express that same afternoon. At the time, we were living in rural Maine, so to accomplish this within two hours so we could make the Federal Express delivery pickup was a near impossibility, but somehow we managed to do so. It is extremely clear to us that this test case completely confirmed our reluctance to ever deal with third party entities of any type regarding any matter and to rely only upon ourselves when we are doing business with anyone for any reason.

When people deal with "system's methods", they put themselves in the hands of the system and relinquish their powers and voices to that system. We feel, and our recent experience confirms, that this is a very unsound and treacherous way for people to act, because they are not speaking for themselves, but instead, are allowing others to do so for them, thus removing them from their own responsibilities. As we said earlier, when people allow others to represent and speak for them and bind them into contracts and obligations that they did not authorize and knew nothing about, they can place themselves in dire legal and financial jeopardy. We feel that it is far better for people to take direct, active involvement in whatever they do and not rely upon third parties to do things for them. The purchase of a home is one of, if not the biggest, investments most people will ever make. The same is true for a seller, but obviously from a different position. Since these transactions are very important to the principals who engage in them, it seems reasonable to state that the principals should be directly involved and take direct action every step of the way until the final consummation of the transaction at closing.

Although the title company's closing agent miscued on just about every possible thing one can think of in this transaction, we managed to get the original documents, which we executed, sent by Federal Express in a timely manner to effectuate the closing. However, once the closing took place, the proverbial last straw that manifested was almost totally inconceivable. The title company's closing agent assured us that our funds would be sent to our bank into our account as we directed in our escrow instructions and as confirmed by us in writing on several occasions. Despite the repeated assurances from the closing agent that our funds would be sent as we directed to our account in our bank, the funds were not sent as we directed and our bank was forced to return the funds to the closing agent's bank. Obviously, for us this was the last straw, as mentioned above, and something that should not have happened, had the closing agent been professional, attentive and competent, which from the events that took place, she was not, or she was serving another agenda. After several conversations with our bank and with the closing agent's bank, the funds were addressed properly and safely received by our bank. Once again, we had to intercede to have things properly done.

As we said earlier, the reason we endured all of this nonsense was because we wanted to fully test out the workings of current conventional system's methods prior to the completion of this book. We can assure you that under no circumstances will we ever deal with a selling broker and a conventional lender ever again. This last experience completely illuminated all of the traps, all of the failures, all of the insane legal nonsense and all of the pitfalls of engaging in that system. That said, we realize that there are numerous and plentiful ethical, professional and capable real estate agents, brokers, lenders and title company agents who will do the right thing for their clients. Our concern is for those who will not do the right things for their clients and by their wrongful actions harm their clients. As we have stated right along in this book and as we have stated all along in our seminars, radio, television and internet broadcasts, we urge the American people to accept responsibility and act responsibly in all of their business and dealings, as a way of life, and not depend upon others to act for them. Whether a third party agent acts responsibly or irresponsibly for a principal is not the only issue, the real issue is whether American Citizens are going to act as responsible, competent individuals and take responsibility their own actions, their own contracts and their own dealings.

When one compares the traditional way of buying and selling, dealing with traditional brokers and agents, with traditional loans, versus our methods of buying, selling and financing directly, by and through principals, there is a universe of difference. The traditional approach requires a real estate broker or agent, a very lengthy, involved, complicated real estate contract that most people do not understand and/or do not want to deal with, a traditional bank or lender with a traditional loan, with a very complicated commitment that, again, most people do not understand, which usually involves high fees and points, various inspections, surveys, reports, home inspections, appraisals, mortgage insurance and extremely high closing costs. The home buyer and the home seller who are the principals in the transaction are essentially set aside and told what to do by third party non-principals, not parties to the contract. Incredibly, a very large segment of the American population, who engage in these types of transactions, act in this manner. Despite the fact that they are the principals who should be directly involved, they allow others to take over, dictate terms, procedures, and demands.

In our methods, the principals deal directly with each other, face to face, eyeball to eyeball. There are no third parties of any kind who dictate to the principals. The sales price is arranged directly between the principals, and all negotiations take place directly between the principals. All inspections of any type are agreed to between the principals, as practical matters, and not demanded by non-principal third party entities. The offer to purchase, the sales price and all contractual terms are arranged directly between the principals with no third party involvement. The mortgage and promissory note are simple, direct, easily understood documents, very clear, very precise, without the typical lengthy, complicated, confusing contracts which are present in traditional scenarios. When one compares the two methods, any rational, reasonable observer would quickly conclude that our methods serve the direct personal objectives of the principals, themselves, and not those of third party entities who dictate to the principals.

As a final note on this subject, Jack's sister was a real estate agent in Tennessee for a number of years. However, she resigned from that position because of some of the situations we mentioned above. In virtually all of the transactions in which she was involved, it was she who completed the paperwork for all contracts, all forms and all reports, wrote all the terms, made all the arrangements for all inspections, while the principals to the sale took virtually no interest in any of these important matters. Although Jack's sister encouraged her principals to become more involved in the workings of the transactions, the vast majority of them did not accept her advice and let her do the work. Some of them even said that if she made any mistakes which would harm them, they would simply sue her! This type of irresponsibility does not bode well for successful transactions and closings.

CHAPTER THIRTY NINE

TAKING BACK OUR NEIGHBORHOODS
DEVELOPMENT FOR DEPRESSED AREAS

Countless distressed and depressed areas exist throughout America, primarily within the inner cities. These neighborhoods are not only depressed, but are also very depressing for the people who live in them. Numerous factors exist as to why such areas are depressed and we have discussed many of them within this book. Economic violence is, in our opinions, one of the most insidious forms of violence ever devised by humans as a weapon against other humans. Throughout this book we have stated how the system's approaches work *against* the best interests of the people and *for* the best interests of the system and those who own and control the systems within the system, or the wheels within the wheels. When those who are economically harmed by the system, try to redress the wrongs committed against them, the systems in charge of such matters quickly dismiss any complaints, or at most give them lip service, thereby protect the status quo. Any average Americans who have ever had to confront the system are well aware of this, with rare exceptions. By now, a small, but growing percentage of the American people of all races and all belief systems is beginning to realize that the systems, both public and private, are not going to correct any wrongs at all and, in fact, continue to create and allow those wrongs throughout the country. Those same people who are beginning to understand this are also beginning to understand that it is *only* the people, themselves, who can help the people. When people truly realize and understand this very sad, but also enlightening fact, then they can take responsibility for their own lives and move in the right direction. Those who can do this can transform the economic violence perpetrated upon them into economic freedom, achieved by and through their own efforts.

The foreclosure debacle and the economic collapse that occurred in this country inflicted serious blows upon the American people who were caught in the throes of these disasters. Many of them lost jobs, homes, cars, schools, friends, family ties and opportunities for advancement.

Large numbers, even years later, are still suffering from these losses, with few prospects for future improvements and success on their horizons. While individual people and families were devastated, the aggregate result from these losses caused whole neighborhoods to also be devastated. People were forced out of their properties leaving many cities in dire distress. In some areas, abandoned and derelict homes abound, causing property values to decline, compelling other existing homeowners to flee, tax bases to shrink, drug use and violence to increase, resulting in the rise of dangerous, unsightly areas in which no sane person wants to live or even traverse. This is a total catastrophe for the people and an unsightly blight, not only on the immediate areas in which these conditions abound, but also on the entire city in which the areas are located.

The inner cities are not the only places where such devastated areas exist. They can be found in numerous other sections of the country, which were once prosperous and thriving. However, because of bad economic policies, ruthless economic violence, the economic collapse and the foreclosure fiasco, many of these formerly prosperous neighborhoods are now in very depressed, dilapidated conditions. In this CHAPTER, we offer some suggestions as to how the people, themselves, in these hard-hit areas, can either individually and/or collectively, in association with others, revitalize and restore these areas and take back their own neighborhoods.

In the section dealing with buying and selling homes, we spell out specific methods by which people, who have small amounts of money available to invest, can buy and sell homes on a basis that is beneficial and favorable for both buyer and seller. If there were individuals acting on their own in depressed neighborhoods, and/or collective groups of people, who would want to engage in this type of buying and selling, then a serious effort could be undertaken to restore these depressed neighborhoods. The ones who would likely be most interested in doing this are those who live in the area, own property and businesses in the area, churches and charities in the area, and civic groups in the area. All of these various people and organizations would have a direct interest in transforming the now-depressed areas into viable, desirable neighborhoods again.

One of the biggest problems for a lot of buyers in this country and especially for buyers of properties in depressed areas is the ability to obtain mortgages to purchase the properties. Many lenders are not willing to risk making loans in depressed areas. For those lenders willing to do so, the qualifications imposed upon the homebuyers can be very restrictive, even prohibitive, often to the extent that the loan is never made. In the sections that describe buying homes for family homes and then in the sections dealing with buying and selling homes as a business for profit, we explain how homeowners who want to sell can do so by providing seller financing to financially capable buyers. There are two ways in which this can be done. First, if the homeowner owns the house outright, with no mortgage or other debt on it, he could accept a down payment, such as 15% of the sales price, and carry a balance for approximately 15 years at a reasonable interest rate. If the buyer has the financial capability to meet the down payment and note terms, the seller has as his security a mortgage on his former home which should be excellent security for him. This solves the problem of obtaining a mortgage from a bank in a difficult, depressed area. In the second situation, if the seller has a mortgage on the property, there are ways that he can still sell the home to the buyer which are described in the indicated sections. In many situations, when a seller has a mortgage note on a property in a depressed area, it can be very difficult for him to sell the property for two primary reasons. First, the buyer usually does not have cash to make the full purchase price. Second, in depressed areas, banks will not usually allow anyone to assume the existing mortgage and the banks want cash upon sale. These are obstacles to not only the sellers in such areas, but to buyers as well. Our suggestions contained in the indicated sections explain in detail how these problems can be resolved by people of good intent, honor and capability.

In the CHAPTER regarding buying and selling for profit, we show how a small investment of $15,000.00 used to purchase and sell homes continuously and expansively over a three year period can produce an enormous amount of money for the creative buyer/investor by the end of year three. There is also an example for an investor who buys four different properties for a total cash investment of $48,000.00. The increased initial investment amount allows for a much more substantial profit at the end of three years. The profit potential is so enormous that we have included a projection by which an investor could obtain loans from a private party, such as a pension fund and/or private investors, and not a bank, with security for the lender(s) in second mortgages owned by the private investors. This type of buying and selling could take place in depressed and other economically marginal areas. The key is the mortgage, and since the buyers and sellers deal in their own mortgages without any involvement from any bank and the usual restrictions that accompany such involvement, this type of buying and selling could revitalize and restore almost any area in America. Such an effort by sincere, honest, dedicated people could work miracles in depressed areas and establish hopeful, positive trends that could be far reaching throughout the country. This type of activity occurs when people take responsibility on their own, based upon their own ingenuity and hard work, without reliance upon others to do it for them. The people are the only ones who can help the people and this is a good way to help masses of people who find themselves in economic catastrophes not necessarily due to their own actions, faults or mistakes.

If initiative is shown in doing this type of development to revitalize depressed areas, various grant and charitable organizations may be willing to participate by providing grant funds to assist the ongoing projects. Success begets success, and as success is gained through the buy/sell efforts and the neighborhoods begin to come back into their former selves, other organizations may want to join in the funding efforts. In some instances, collaboration between and among local public and private organizations, as well as civic-minded wealthy private parties could provide additional funding to further facilitate such revitalization projects. After all, when depressed and marginal neighborhoods are restored, they attract homebuyers to the improved neighborhoods, new businesses spring up, etc. and the improved neighborhoods become a source of vitality and wealth for the area and the entire city. It's a win-win situation for everyone involved, and what were formerly depressed blights on the communities, eyesores and dangers can be transformed into safe secure and beautiful neighborhoods.

In the referenced sections, the amounts of the down payment funds apply to homes costing in the vicinity of $60,000.00 and $100,000.00. In currently depressed areas, prices are likely to be much, much lower, which means smaller down payments would be required to buy properties. Lesser amounts spent on down payments means more properties can be purchased. Some of these properties may need some repairs and replacements, the costs of which will have to be factored into any selling price, of course.

THE SOCIAL BENEFITS OF INVESTING IN AND IMPROVING MARGINAL NEIGHBORHOODS AND COMMUNITIES

For those of you who want to invest a relatively small amount of money with the potential of enormous profit, within a short period of time, this buy/sell program through the *ByPass* method can work quite well for you. For those who have interest in profit, but also possess a social conscience, this program can not only profit *you*, but also others and entire communities as well.

It's no secret that many people living in modern-day America are struggling to just survive from day to day. As mentioned before, President Trump has made some economic strides, but in terms of the overall economy's impact on the average American, these are minimal. The uncertain economic conditions facing millions of Americans show no sign of real improvement, are daunting, to say the least, and pose ongoing challenges to the very existence of the vast majority of Americans. Many must work two or even three jobs just to eke out a meager existence. They have little hope of improving their situations, so believe home ownership is out of their reach. Then, there are those who are truly disabled, so cannot work, as well as those who *will not* work, so play the system. Both non-working groups are dependent upon government programs to survive and often live in substandard subsidized housing complexes that typically are depressing and in bad condition. Some of these people appreciate the helping hand, while others feel "entitled".

A lot of people living in America's cities must live in rental units and, sadly, some of these folks have little or no respect for their dwellings, do not take care of them and/or actually abuse and ruin them. In cities where neighborhoods are comprised of mostly rentals, a sad kind of malaise and deterioration often occur whereby communities that were once nice, neat, inviting and well maintained by proud, caring home owners, turn into dilapidated areas rife with derelict buildings disfigured by harsh graffiti and broken windows, adjacent to trash-filled yards and alleys, all of which attract and become a haven for undesirables. As more and more houses become rentals, the remaining homeowners in the area, feeling displaced and fearful in their own neighborhoods, begin to look elsewhere to live. As these stable people exit, local businesses lose their customer base, businesses are forced to close, unsavory elements come in, take over and the streets become unsafe.

This type of thing has been going on in America's cities for decades, turning formerly decent communities into ghettos. Many people recognize the tragic aspects of this ongoing decline, but most do not care if it does not directly affect them. Others who do care seem to have no idea how to stop the escalating decline of these cities at risk. Still others have tried interventions of one type or another, but usually on very limited bases, which do not result in beneficial, lasting large-scale results.

ByPass programs, as presented herein for investors, could play a significant role in helping communities at risk revitalize, provide decent housing for people and families formerly shut out of the housing market, and help bring our cities back from the brink of ruin and decay. Without being sophomoric or naïve about the magnitude of our cities' problems, it is quite possible for still-decent rental homes in marginal areas facing early stages of decline, to be found, purchased and then resold to deserving, hard-working people and families. When former rental properties are bought by live-in owners, the properties usually improve, which encourages other homeowners to spruce up their properties, and this benefits the appearance of the entire neighborhood. As at-risk neighborhoods begin to improve, this attracts other buyers to invest in available homes, many of which are very reasonably priced, drawing young families to the area. More people and families mean support for existing businesses, and can also attract new businesses. All of these scenarios further benefit the individual neighborhoods and the larger city/community as well.

SECTION FIVE

ByPass INVESTMENT PROGRAMS

CHAPTER FORTY ONE

MULTIPLE APPLICATIONS
FOR *ByPass* PROGRAMS

While the basic buying, selling and financing programs described in this book apply to lower priced properties, these types of financing methods can apply virtually in any situation in which the buying and selling of houses, other types of properties, land, businesses and other goods take place. Throughout this book are two standard house examples are:

1. $100,000 house purchased with a 15% down payment ($15,000) and the remaining $85,000 carried by the seller at 5% interest for 15 years.

2. $60,000 house purchased with a 15% down payment, ($9,000) and the remaining $51,000 carried by the seller at 5% interest for 15 years.

As mentioned earlier in the book, the financial crisis of 2007- 2008 was so devastating that over 20,500,000 million foreclosures were filed, millions of people lost their homes and millions of others lost their livelihoods. As you may have surmised, none of these economic disasters happened by accident, and if you look at the history of our country from the very beginning, you can see that they have been a regular feature. My wife, Margy, and I wrote this book primarily in support of the people who lost their properties, lost their jobs and some who lost everything. We wanted to present different financing methods for buying and selling property by which these people, members of their families and others who will face similar problems in upcoming economic disasters will at least have a viable way to protect their interests and buy property, essentially "outside the box". However, since these methods have wide and diverse applications across many different lines, they can also be utilized for higher priced properties.

For instance, let us go back to the devastation that began in earnest in 2007 – 2008 and take a typical example from that time period. A family owned a lovely home in a lovely neighborhood, worth in the vicinity of $500,000.00. The breadwinner had a good job as a corporate officer of twenty years' duration in a corporation that made parts for the high tech industry. His salary was $200,000.00 a year and he had excellent benefits, including health and dental coverage for himself and his entire family. The company was highly leveraged and, unfortunately, because of the economic disaster lost some major contracts. However, the company saw an opportunity to retain and improve its business by establishing corporate operations in a third world country, so it did. Our family man lost his job and had no prospects of getting a similar job in a similar industry, and certainly not at the same pay level. As many of us know, people typically spend above their means, which is a very unfortunate, but increasingly common characteristic, for the average American. Financial status and income do not matter, because people constantly spend more than they earn, no matter how much they earn. Further, most people have very little in the way of savings, if any at all. When a disaster like this happens, the average fellow is no more than three to four paychecks away from living on the street. In this example, which is typical of what happened throughout America—at all salary levels—our breadwinner still had a mortgage, car payments, insurance, taxes, college expenses for his kids and other bills to pay. It did not matter that he was out of work to the debtors. Yes, he was able to get unemployment compensation, but at his lifestyle level, this couldn't even pay the bills. As a result, the bank holding the mortgage on his home foreclosed on him and his family, so he lost their family home and all the funds, love, improvements, hopes, memories and dreams they had invested in it over the years. It all went down the drain, and quickly!

Had our breadwinner been aware of the methods spelled out in this book, he could likely have sold his house through one of these approaches, before it was foreclosed and he lost everything. He would have received some cash as a down payment and additional cash coming in monthly through note payments made to him. With this down payment amount and the ongoing monthly cash received from the note on his house, he could have bought a smaller, less expensive house and kept his family together in their own home, under one roof, rather than having to rent somewhere in likely a much less desirable neighborhood. It is a "no-brainer" to realize that being able to buy another property and maintaining a home for his family would have been a much better position to be in rather than suffering the shame, loss and heartache of foreclosure and being forced out of his home and neighborhood.

Let's take a look at what this hypothetical family man and breadwinner could have done, as opposed to what happened to him. His home is worth $500,000.00, which is the market value for this home in this area. In an economic crisis, property values always fall somewhat, but in certain higher priced areas, they are more likely to maintain their values or a figure very close to that value. Further, people who buy in this price range obviously have the financial ability to do so. While economic disasters cause problems everywhere, a certain percentage of people within these higher price ranges still have financial capabilities, meaning there is always a buyer for this type of property in a desirable neighborhood. There is a remaining principal balance of $100,000.00 on the original mortgage note. If our family man were to offer the house for sale at $500,000.00, with 15% down, which is $75,000.00, and carry the balance, which in this case is $425,000.00, it is likely that he would have many financially capable buyers quite interested in purchasing his property without the need to obtain bank financing in a tough financial market. The new buyer would purchase a 50% ownership position in the property and assume the *obligation* for the remaining $100,000.00 balance on the original mortgage note, but not assume the note, itself. The remaining $325,000.00 would be a second mortgage paid to the seller by the new buyer at a mutually agreeable term and interest rate. We use our standard term and rate of 15 years at 5%.

As we explained earlier in the CHAPTER in which we described these financial approaches, once the existing bank note is paid off, by prearranged written contract, the seller would deed the remaining 50% interest in the house to the buyer who of course would continue making his second mortgage payments to the seller until his financial obligation is fulfilled. When the buyer assumes the obligation of the bank note, but not the note itself, by prearranged contract, the buyer would pay that monthly note amount into a mutual bank account held jointly by him and the seller, and the bank holding the mortgage note would automatically withdraw that amount each month until the note is retired. There is another way to accomplish this situation, depending upon the preference of the principals. The seller could contract a lease-purchase arrangement with the buyer, then accept an initial $75,000.00 payment, then lease the property to him on the same figures as stated above for the duration of the existing mortgage note term. At that point, by prearrangement, under written contract, the seller deeds the property to the buyer, who of course continues to pay the second mortgage payments to the seller until that obligation is fully retired.

If this had been done, rather than lose his property, our seller would have $75,000.00 in cash and approximately $2,500.00 payable to him each and every month through the second mortgage for a 15 year period. Obviously, to any rational being, this type of scenario would have been a far better situation for the millions of families who lost their homes. Our family man now has $75,000.00 to make a down payment on a lesser priced home, possibly pay off some of his bills, and $2,500.00 coming in every month for the next 15 years, so that, whatever his monthly payment amount is on the new home, it would be covered by this $2,500.00. Of course, it would be most advantageous for him to buy the new property using one of the methods described in this book, because it is pretty clear that no bank would fund him under any circumstances, given the tight economic climate and his recent near foreclosure. This is how the American people, whether they buy a high priced property, a low priced property or anything in between, can ByPass the banks. In the present situation and more especially in the coming years, any family that has mortgage debt, corporate debt, and/or debt to the state and/or federal government will likely suffer drastic consequences because of more restrictive and repressive methods and procedures that will not work in the best interests of the American people.

Whenever a crisis appears in this country, financial or otherwise, the government and the power forces gain by and through that crisis in many different ways. As mentioned before, Rahm Emmanuel, the mayor of Chicago and Obama's former chief of staff said: "Never let a good crisis go to waste." This is an absolutely insidious, diabolical and despicable position for any government or government officer to take when the American people are suffering and in serious jeopardy, financial or otherwise. The American people are slowly beginning to learn that they cannot trust their own governments. Given these facts, it is far better for all Americans to be as independent as they possibly can with their homes and with their livelihoods, because the governments and the power forces will opportunistically create and then use every crisis as a means to take everything the American people have. With the looming AI superstructure coming into place in the very near future, and the further pressure from the international communist forces to bring America more openly under a communist state status, it is imperative for the survival of the American society and the American way of life that all people become as independent as they can, as quickly as they can.

CHAPTER FORTY TWO

THE *TRUTH* ABOUT "TRUTH IN LENDING"

Whenever buyers, sellers or borrowers are about to enter into a lending transaction, they should be fully aware of all lending terms, conditions, requirements and calculations. "Truth in lending" theoretically requires this, but the reality can be somewhat different. Most people simply accept the terms and payment amounts presented by the lender, without question. For the most part, borrowers are anxious throughout the application process and when they are approved, are very happy to get the loan, so question little, if anything. Most lenders are fully aware of this unconditional acceptance by eager, but unaware, borrowers. However, it takes two or more parties to enter into a legitimate, lawful contract and each principal party should know the full nature of that contract and all of its ramifications prior to entering into and executing it. Otherwise, this unquestioning acceptance could work to the disadvantage of the average homebuyer/borrower.

With the *ByPass* methods, a difference exists in favor of the borrower, and not the lender, in terms of total monthly payments amounts when the *ByPass* method is compared to the traditional methods. While some borrowers may consider the difference not a major one, the amounts and percentages that accrue to the borrower can be significant for many average Americans. Those funds remain with the borrower and do not get paid to the lender. When anything important is being considered, it is best to have all relevant facts and information understood so that a valid, informed decision can be made. The purchase of a home typically is the largest and most important investment for most people. Due and thoughtful consideration should be given to all aspects of the purchase, including the loan. Since borrowers will be bound by this loan for many years, it is in the best interest of those borrowers and their families to fully understand all loan terms, conditions, payment amounts, how derived, payment schedules and all responsibilities required by loan contract.

All people have their own ways in dealing with others, but we consider direct, honest, ethical and fair dealing to be the best way in buying, selling or lending. Banks and lenders have their own procedures and calculations when they make loans to people. We have our own. As stated above, most borrowers are so eager for the loan that they seldom, if ever, question how the total principal and interest payments were calculated to arrive at the monthly payment amount. We do, and always have. Truth in lending is a phrase that many people hear, but usually pay little attention to the words and meanings behind this phrase. Facts about the loan amount, interest rate and payment schedule may be truthful, but the manner in which these figures have been calculated is usually not, if ever, revealed to a borrower by an institutional lender. The truth in lending aspect can be reduced to how some lenders determine and reveal truth. Various methods used to determine and calculate figures and amounts can be simple and direct, or confusing and convoluted. We prefer the direct approach, which is just, honest and fair for all participants.

Below is an example of a loan of $150,000, 15 year term, at 5% interest, with principal payments of $10,000 made yearly, on the anniversary of the loan, with 5% interest charged on the remaining balance, and paid yearly, along with the principal payment. This is a very direct, simple way to make a loan for both lender and borrower. Each principal party is fully aware and accepting of the fully disclosed conditions and terms. Calculations follow.

YEAR	PRINCIPAL BALANCE	%	INTEREST PAYMENT	TOTAL P and I PAYMENT
1	$150,000	x 5%	$7,500	$17,500
2	$140,000	x 5%	$7,000	$17,000
3	$130,000	x 5%	$6,500	$16,500
4	$120,000	x 5%	$6,000	$16,000
5	$110,000	x 5%	$5,500	$15,500
6	$100,000	x 5%	$5,000	$15,000
7	$90,000	x 5%	$4,500	$14,500
8	$80,000	x 5%	$4,000	$14,000
9	$70,000	x 5%	$3,500	$13,500
10	$60,000	x 5%	$3,000	$13,000
11	$50,000	x 5%	$2,500	$12,500
12	$40,000	x 5%	$2,000	$12,000
13	$30,000	x 5%	$1,500	$11,500
14	$20,000	x 5%	$1,000	$11,000
15	$10,000	x 5%	$500	$10,500
TOTALS			$60,000	$210,000

In the above example, $150,000 was borrowed for 15 years, at 5% interest, with $10,000 principal payments made each year, on the anniversary of the loan, with 5% interest paid on the remaining balance, paid yearly at the same time as the principal payment. Since all conditions of the loan were initially revealed, both the lender and the borrower were fully aware of the disclosed terms and payment schedule for the loan. Total interest paid on the loan was $60,000, which amounts to 40% of the $150,000 principal loan amount.

In the above example, the principal payment of $10,000 was made yearly. That $10,000, principal amount, divided by 12 months, amounts to $833.33 per month. One lender or borrower may want yearly payments, while others may want monthly payments. However, whether principal is paid yearly in one amount, or monthly in 12 payments per year, the standard should be the same. That standard is that $10,000 of the principal amount will be paid each year, whether in one yearly sum or 12 monthly sums. Twelve monthly principal payments of $833.33, each, amount to $10,000. The 180 monthly payments of $833.33 per month, which is 15 years, amount to $150,000, the original loan amount. Whether paid yearly or monthly, the principal amount is the same. With monthly payments, there is a difference in the total interest amount since interest is paid on the remaining principal balance. When monthly payments are made and interest is charged on the remaining principal balance, since the principal amount is reduced monthly, then the total interest amount is less than if interest is paid yearly. In a loan of $150,000, 15 years, at 5% interest on the remaining principal balance, with principal and interest paid monthly, instead of yearly, the total interest amount is approximately $56,562, which is $3,438 less interest, or 6.1%, than the $60,000 for the same loan amount with yearly payments. Again, the reason for this is that principal payments are made monthly, which reduces the remaining principal amount upon which interest is paid. These are the logical, truthful and factual standards upon which those who want truth in lending might want to calculate monthly or yearly principal and interest amounts and payments, as we do.

As you can see from the above examples, there is a difference of $3,438 between the interest for the one year payment and twelve monthly payments per year. Principal and interest payments for a conventional loan of $150,000, for 15 years at 5% interest differ from the figures in our 15 year monthly example referenced above.

CHAPTER FORTY THREE

ByPass PRINCIPAL AND INTEREST PROGRAM VERSUS TRADITIONAL FINANCING

ByPass METHOD FOR DEBT REDUCTION AND PRINCIPAL AND INTEREST PAYMENTS

I f buyers and sellers want to be treated fairly and justly, without high front-loaded costs, fees and interest charges, and with an equitable principal reduction approach, our method satisfies all of these criteria, and more. Our approach for debt reduction and principal and interest payments is direct, fair, just and beneficial to both parties. If one were to borrow $100,000.00 for any particular purpose, at 5% interest on the declining principal balance for 10 years, with $10,000.00 paid each and every year towards that principal reduction, then, that is exactly what he expects to pay. Once the borrower receives the $100,000.00 loan, pursuant to the contract terms stated above, upon the anniversary of the loan, he/she would pay $5000.00 in interest for the first year, which is 5% of the loan amount of $100,000.00. With the same payment, the borrower would make a $10,000.00 payment towards principal, due by contract, and upon this payment, the principal balance remaining would be $90,000.00. The borrower's interest payment for that year would be 5% of $90,000.00, which is $4,500.00 for the second year. Principal reduction is $10,000 each year, on the anniversary of the loan, reducing the principal balance by that amount, and 5% interest is paid on the remaining principal balance at the same time. As we have seen in the previous CHAPTER, many people mistakenly think that most home loans are structured in this manner. They are not.

In the home lending market, loans are structured differently so that the effective interest paid by the borrower is higher than the stated interest figure, while the principal reduction works against the buyer's financial interests, in terms of his equity position, and in favor of the bank. This is how most bank loans are structured and this structuring is not limited to just home loans. The system's way of amortization and interest payments is, as we see it, unfair, unjust, not direct, and favorable only to the lender. While loans are structured so that interest is paid on the principal balance remaining, the determination of principal balance reduction and the method by which that is accomplished demonstrates the fairness or the unfairness of the loan. When a home buyer repays his loan, he should expect an equitable distribution of that payment in terms of principal reduction and interest, just as he would with his payments made on the referenced $100,000.00 loan above. This is not how lending institutions work. Interest payments are somewhat front-loaded, while much less of the payment goes to reduce the principal, especially within the first five years. Since most homes are resold within approximately five years, the principal and interest payments the borrower made to the bank favor the bank and disfavor the borrower.

As many of you may know, when a bank makes a loan to a home buyer, the bank requires the home buyer to enter into an "adhesion" contract and note, secured by a mortgage on the home being bought. An adhesion contract is written for the benefit of one party, typically the lender, and usually to the detriment of the other party, the borrower/buyer, who is expected to sign the contract, as is, without making any changes. While the borrower is required to sign the contract, the lender usually does not do so. A valid contract requires signatures from both principal parties.

What some of you may not know is that the bank structured the loan in such a manner so that the majority of the initial monthly payment amounts the home owner makes are paid to interest and not to principal reduction. By doing this, the bank receives a higher effective interest rate than originally stated, while the home owner gets a smaller amount of his monthly payments credited to reduce principal. As stated, the average home purchased is resold in approximately five years. Because of the high effective interest and low principal balance reduction allowed by the terms of the bank loan, when the homeowner sells his property, the bank receives a return that is more favorable to the bank and less favorable to the home owner. As long as home buyers and other borrowers accept this unfair discrepancy, this common banking practice will continue.

The *ByPass* method for debt reduction and monthly interest payments on the remaining balance is extremely fair and just to both buyer and seller. We have established our two standard examples here, and in this instance, the house is free and clear with no notes or mortgages owed by the owner/seller. One house sells for $100,000 and the second sells for $60,000. The following spells out the program for the $100,000 house, and the same principles, but not figures, apply to the $60,000 house.

The owner sells the house for $100,000.00 to the buyer, with $15,000.00 down and $85,000.00 carried by the seller for 15 years at 5% interest. One hundred and eighty (180) months make up 15 years. To ascertain the principal portion of the monthly payment, we take the loan amount of $85,000.00, divided by 180 months, which amounts to $472.22 per month. One hundred eighty payments times $472.22 equals $85,000.00. This method follows the same procedure that the above referenced $100,000 loan does, as well as the $150,000 loan paid in monthly payments referenced in the previous CHAPTER. In our $100,000 loan example, above, the borrower pays $10,000 per year to principal, and 5% interest on the remaining principal balance. If we divide the principal loan amount of $100,000 by 120 months, which totals the ten year loan term, that monthly amount is $833.33. Twelve principal monthly payments of $833.33 amount to a yearly principal payment of $10,000. *ByPass* uses this same approach, with interest paid on the remaining principal balance. With *ByPass's* equitable, fair and just method, each monthly principal payment of $472.22 reduces the principal balance by exactly that amount. If one were to check the current principal balance remaining with conventional loan funding against the *ByPass* method, he could quickly determine that our method is more advantageous to the buyer, without doing any harm to the seller, while the bank method favors the bank and disadvantages its home-buying client.

Interest on the loan is 5% on the remaining principal balance, which amounts to approximately $178.07 per month, averaged and fixed over the term of the loan, and since our method pays more principal to reduce the principal balance quicker, then the 5% interest paid on the remaining principal balance is less because, as we said before, the principal balance remaining is less. If one wants to compare the *ByPass* interest method to that of the standard conventional bank method, he would be surprised at the higher effective interest charged by the bank on a month by month basis. The conventional bank method requires higher effective interest and lower principal debt reduction. The total monthly principal and interest payment, by our calculations, amounts to $650.29, which is the total principal and interest monthly payment throughout the term of the loan. This amount for both principal and interest is fixed throughout the loan term. The borrower/home owner knows exactly what his/her principal balance and interest payment is at any time. For instance, if the home owner wants to ascertain the amount of principal balance remaining after four years of monthly payments, all he has to do is multiply the monthly principal payment of $472.22 by 48 months, namely four years, which amounts to $22,666.56. If the home owner wants to know the interest figure, then, he can multiply $178.07 times 48, which amounts to $8,547.84.

Others may arrive at monthly interest figures slightly different from the above, depending on how one may determine the principal is applied. As stated above, we base our approach on the very direct, simple and uncomplicated $100,000 referenced loan example, which we believe to be the fairest and most equitable way to determine principal and interest payments. In addition to a slightly smaller monthly payment, the manner in which the remaining principal balance is determined through the *ByPass* method favors the borrowing home buyer.

As stated, each monthly payment of $650.29 reduces the remaining principal balance by $472.22, which, in one year, amounts to $5,666.64. If one were to compare this principal balance reduction with conventional banking methods, then, he could quickly see the advantage in using the ByPass method compared to the standard bank loan reduction method.

ByPass the Banks' Debt Reduction Benefits to Buyer

As mentioned, most homes bought in America are sold sometime around the fifth or sixth year of ownership. The prudent buyer wants to get the best possible house for the least amount of money. If one buys right, he can sell right—on terms favorable to the homeowner. When a buyer sells his home in five or so years, he should not only consider the price he paid, but also the cost of financing the home. Financing costs can make a sale in five years attractive, or not. If one has been paying high effective interest, but credited with little debt reduction over the approximate five years of ownership, the proceeds from the sale can be considerably less than if our home owner had paid true, simple, exact interest, with true and fair debt reduction. Let us take an example of our home owner who has purchased his home through the *ByPass* method, as opposed to another home owner who financed the purchase of his home through a bank. Again, we use our standard example of a $100,000.00 home price, $15,000.00 down, $85,000.00 carried by seller for 15 years at 5% interest.

Monthly principal and interest payment is $650.29 of which $472.22 is paid to reduce principal and $178.07 is paid to interest.

PRINCIPAL BALANCE REDUCTION = 60 months (5 years) x $472.22 = $28,333.20

LOAN AMOUNT = $85,000.00
-$28,333.20 – principal balance reduction
$56,666.80 – loan balance

INTEREST PAYMENTS = 60 months x $178.07 = $10,684.20, or $2,136.84 per year

****

Sales Proceeds for Home Sold in Five Years

When our home owner, who has purchased his home through the *ByPass* method, wants to sell his home, he can expect to have a ready and strong market of buyers for his property. The main reason for this is that the seller can sell his property to a new buyer with an *assumable* existing mortgage. When the home owner bought the home five years previously from the original seller, he and the seller structured the contract so that the buyer could sell his home in the future to a new buyer who could assume the existing note and mortgage. The new buyer, of course, would be required to undergo scrutiny as to his ability to pay the mortgage. The provision here is that the original buyer of the home will make certain that the monthly payments are made to the original seller for the full term of the loan. There are two ways our home owner can do this. One is to take, as part of the sales price, a small note and place a second mortgage on the property, which would give the homeowner-seller the right to take over the property, should the new buyer default, and sell it again. Logic indicates that a new buyer who is allowed to assume the note and mortgage will not default, especially since he has paid a $15,000.00, or more, down payment. However, if the new buyer does fail, the original owner would be protected by the original buyer.

The second way the original buyer can protect his interest in the home is to sell it on a *contract of sale*. If he does this, our original buyer retains title to the property, but sells the property to a buyer who receives title once he has made all principal and interest payments. If the second buyer defaults, then when our original buyer takes back the property, he gains all of the down payment funds made by the second buyer, all the principal and interest payments made by the second buyer, and all principal balance reductions made by the second buyer, just as he would had he taken a small second mortgage. When our homeowner-seller takes back the property and sells the home defaulted upon by his buyer, then, all of these considerable financial benefits accrue to him.

When our homeowner sells his home in five years, the selling market in his area may be even, up or down. No matter what level the market, since the homeowner is selling his property with an assumable note and mortgage, he will likely find numerous interested, capable and willing buyers. As we have said many times before, unfortunately, in today's economy, with unfavorable and strict bank lending requirements, many capable buyers cannot obtain bank loans for prospective homes. A home with an assumable note and mortgage, under favorable buyer conditions, will place a home which offers such a mortgage in great demand.

As stated, the home selling market could be at any level. If it is up, then, the value of the home has increased, which increase could be anywhere from 1%, on the low end, to 10% or more, on the high end. If the market is flat or down, then, because of the assumable mortgage, the house likely should have at least maintained its value, if not increased in value somewhat, primarily because of the assumable mortgage. In whatever sales market may exist, the assumable mortgage makes this home desirable and valuable to many capable people who could not otherwise buy a home. If we project a market on the up side and take a low value increase of 1.5% per year, the value of our standard example house has increased to approximately $107,500.00. The added major benefit of the assumable note and mortgage brings considerable additional value to this home, which we project at $10,000.00, or more. This would bring the home value to about $117,500.00 in five years. Conservatively, let us say that the home value in five years in $110,000.00, and our homeowner sells his home for that price. As we showed above, the loan balance in five years is $56,666.80. The sales price of $110,000.00, minus the $56,666.80 existing principal balance, provides equity to our homeowner upon sale of approximately $53,333.20. This figure includes his original $15,000.00 down payment. This amounts to an average gain of approximately $10,600.00 per year. It also amounts to a 356% return on the home owner's down payment. No matter the home owner's economic level, this is a major return for him, and he and his family lived in the home for five years, while gaining a value of approximately $53,000 when they sold the home. This return is substantial for anyone in any economic level. Such a return would not accrue under conventional bank loan financing.

PRINCIPAL BALANCE COMPARRISONS

In this section we show the difference between the *ByPass* method and the conventional method for remaining principal balances for an $85,000 home loan, 5% interest, 15 year term, in years 1, 5, 7, 7.5 and 10 years.

ByPass	INSTITUTIONAL
Year One Balance: $79,333.36	$81,095.23

The *ByPass* method provides for $1,761.87 more equity to the homeowner in one year than the institutional loan, or 2.22 % more equity than the institutional.

Year Five Balance: $56,667 $63,373.53

The *ByPass* method provides for $6,706.53 more equity to the borrower in five years than the institutional loan, or 11.8% more equity than institutional, an average of $1,341.30 per year.

Seven Year Balance: $45,333.52 $53,094.69

ByPass method provides $7,761.17 more equity to the borrower in seven years than does the institutional loan, or 17% more equity than institutional, an average of $1,108.73 per year

---

Seven and ½ Balance: $42,500.20 $50.360.67

ByPass method provides $7,860.47 more equity to the borrower in seven and one-half years than does an institutional loan, or 18.5% more equity than institutional, an average of $1,048 per year.

Ten Year Balance $28,333.60 $35,619.01

ByPass method provides $7,285.41 more equity to borrower in ten years than does an institutional loan, or 25.71% more equity than conventional, an average of $728.54 per year.

The loan equity benefit to the borrower who uses the *ByPass* method over the conventional loan averages from $1,761.87 more equity in year one to $728.54 more average equity per year in year ten than institutional equity. The *ByPass* monthly principal and interest payment is $650.29. The conventional monthly payment is $672.17. The difference of $21.88 benefits the borrower $262.56 per year. When this amount is added to the average equity gain over institutional, the amount can be substantial for many average Americans. For instance, the gain in year one would be $1,761.87 in equity and $262.56 in less total payments, or $2,024.43 Year five would be $6,706.53 in equity and $262.56 in less total payments, or $8,109.33 These amounts can always pay other bills or be used for other purposes.

ByPass BUY/SELL INVESTMENT PROGRAMS

B*yPass* presents many different facets, for a variety of different people, with different aims, objectives and financial capabilities. Our primary objective is to demonstrate how easy it would be for a buyer to purchase a house under these programs and for a seller to sell a home under these programs. However, beyond these initial positions, we have established various investment programs for those who want to use the *ByPass* programs to purchase property and then resell it or rent it for profit. These programs are designed to begin with a minimal investment for buying houses, reselling them for respectable profits, reinvest the returns, so that at the end of one years the investor(s) can earn a massive return on his investment. Other *ByPass* Programs project how an investor(s) can purchase houses, starting with a very modest investment, then rent them for twenty years, then sell them for huge profits earned from rents and house sales. These buy/rent/ sell Programs are highly profitable and can be used either for profit or retirement purposes. Earlier CHAPTERs in this book covered several different Programs, and they are spelled out in detail in the Projection section at the end of this book. This present CHAPTER provides a small example of what can be done on a very moderate basis up to an extremely large real estate portfolio and profits.

In addition to these objectives, other people may have interest in using the *ByPass* programs to buy property and then flip it for a profit. This is quite possible and highly advantageous when one uses our programs, and not the typical traditional institutional programs. The main difference between our programs and standard programs is the fact that a buyer can assume the *obligation* for an existing note and mortgage, but not assume the note itself. This has a major positive impact for any financially capable buyer. The seller who is willing to carry can expect many interested, capable buyers for his property. If people were to buy and sell property as a business, based upon these considerations, they should be very successful. Of course, before doing this, they obviously would need to investigate the market in the buying area, researching the existing market trends, prices, inventory, length of time properties are on the market and amount of time that owners own or remain in their homes prior to selling. Two paramount positions to consider are "buying right" and "selling right".

In this regard, we offer a few examples of what investors could do, if they were so inclined. Three (3) different buy/sell programs are available to astute investors, which are spelled out in detail in the *Projections* section at the end of this book. As most of us know, and as discussed earlier in this book, the housing market has gone through some very tough times, due to financial machinations and outright fraud on the part of the banks, along with overreaching on the part of many buyers. These unfortunate conditions have tainted and in some instances ruined markets for many people, causing many markets to rapidly decline. The current economic shutdown happening in America right now because of the so-called COVID-19 virus will send the housing market into another steep downturn, followed by another major round of foreclosures in most areas in this nation, with the exception of the so-called "star" cities. No matter what government and financial institutions' statistics and prognostications state, except for the "star" markets across the country, most other real estate markets are experiencing significant problems in varying degrees. Sellers are having difficult times selling their properties because of these adverse market conditions caused mainly by the banks and the struggling economy. As a result, prices are much lower than they would be in a strong market.

One of the main problems that has been with us for some time is the refusal of many banks to adequately fund housing demand, and many of those which do fund have so many stringent requirements and rapid changes during the escrow period that many transactions never come to closing. The same thing occurred just before the crash in 1929 and throughout a good part of the 1930's. Instead of the banks' lending to encourage and grow the economy, banks were calling in their existing notes. Since the devastating crash had just occurred, it is obvious that enormous numbers of Americans lost financially, while some lost everything. As a result of this, most people could not come up with the funds to meet the bank's call, therefore, lost their homes, went under and experienced severe financial hardships, as did most people in this country. To a certain extent, this has happened in every recession since the so-called "Great Depression" of 1929. Based upon the actions of the banks, and not their rhetoric, placing one's security and future in the hands of institutional bankers is not necessarily a good idea for the average American. When people have the opportunity to deal directly with each other, principal to principal, and all financial dealings are strictly between the principals, and no one else, then, the principals have a much better opportunity for long term success. Most banks imposed and still demand strict buyer qualifications and onerous buyer down payments. Many people in the current buying market, if not most, cannot qualify under these requirements. This leaves a significantly large percentage of would-be buyers with ample down payment funds who would be ripe for the *ByPass* program.

Because of the major existent problems regarding required down payment funds, and lending restrictions, it appears logical and reasonable that most of these buyers in this category would be ready, willing and able to buy a home through a *ByPass* program private mortgage already in place and which can be assumed by the next buyer. If people were to look at the large percentage of capable buyers who are precluded from purchasing homes because of the aforementioned bank restrictions, then, they can readily understand that many of these buyers would be eager to purchase a home with a *ByPass* program private assumable existing mortgage. That said, the investor, who wants to buy and sell using the *ByPass* program, should be well aware that many buyers would be available to him. It all comes down to a question of what price the investor paid for the property and at what price, given market conditions, he can reasonably expect to sell the property. While investors' primary objectives are profits, their uses of these programs make it very possible for people to buy homes that would have otherwise been denied to them. This is a win-win for both parties and the investors are providing a social and financial benefit to their buyers.

Another consideration is over what time period can our investor realistically expect to sell the property? Again, it is all a matter of buying right and selling right, meaning the property purchased is well priced within the existing market and in good condition. We will spell out three different programs here. Using our typical example of a $100,000.00 purchase, when our investor sells the property, the *ByPass* program becomes invaluable in attracting a capable buyer and facilitating the sale, because, unlike most other potential sales, the private note and mortgage are assumable. This is a major consideration for the types of buyers we have described, since they are systematically excluded from traditional lending. Our three projected sales price examples are as follows:

(1) $107,500.00;

(2) $110,000.00;

(3) $115,000.00

Below are the reasons for the three different price levels:

Since the first level of $107,500.00 is less than the others, the investor can expect to sell his/her property more quickly. We project a realistic turnaround of no more than 60 days and likely a lot quicker than that. If the investor(s) are serious about the buy/sell program, then, they will reinvest their profits into additional home purchases and repeat the process again and again. For instance, if they were able to sell their property in 60 days, then, over a one year period, they could essentially do six (6) buy/sell transactions in that time period, or more. Qualified buyers are always interested when the seller will carry.

The following is how we would structure such a sale:

Level 1	Sale Price:	$107,500.00
	Down payment:	$ 20,000.00
	Assumable Mortgage:	$ 85,000.00
	Second Mortgage:	$ 2,500.00

On this basis, the investor(s) receive $20,000.00 upon the sale of the property, which consists of the return of their original $15,000.00 investment plus a $5,000.00 cash profit. The investor(s) also have a note and second mortgage on the property for $2,500.00, which secures their investment in the property and assures the former seller that, should the new buyer default, our seller-investor will take over the property and continue the payments. This note and second mortgage are very important considerations in such a transaction. Please note that during the time between the seller-investor's purchase of the property and the sale of that property he must make timely mortgage payments to the original seller. However, when the investor(s) sell the property, they will recapture the equity from those mortgage payments.

Level 2	Sale Price:	$110,000.00
	Down Payment:	$ 21,000.00
	Assumable Mortgage:	$ 85,000.00
	Second Mortgage:	$ 4,000.00

This is the medium range market price level for our seller-investor's buyer. Obviously, the assumable mortgage makes virtually any house extremely attractive to a potential buyer at any reasonable price for that particular market. We conservatively project that a property with this assumable mortgage arrangement can likely be sold within 60 days. On this basis, the investor could buy and sell every two (2) months and have a total of six (6) transactions during a one year time period. During the time it takes to sell the property, the investor(s) will have to make timely mortgage payments, but upon resale, they will recapture the principal amount of those mortgage payments.

Level 3

Sale Price:	$115,000.00
Down Payment:	$ 25,000.00
Assumable Mortgage:	$ 85,000.00
Second Mortgage:	$ 5,000.00

Again, we project that this property can likely be sold within 60 days, which would give investors the opportunity for six (6) buy/sells during a one year time period. On the above Level 3 figures, our seller-investors would turn over their profits six (6) times during the year. Their initial investment is $15,000.00 to purchase the first property. Their projected cash return over that year would be $60,000.00 in cash, which amounts to 400% return on the initial $15,000.00 investment, and $30,000 in second mortgages. When we add the $30,000.00 in second mortgages to the $60,000.00 in cash, that profit figure is projected to be $90,000.00 in Year One. This amounts to a 600% return on the original $15,000.00 investment in one year.

As we said earlier, there are many buyers with down payment funds who are excluded from traditional home financing programs. Many can cover the specified required down payments. However, there are always exceptions, and for those who cannot totally meet down payment requirements, there are other ways to deal with this. For instance, let us say our seller-investor has a capable buyer who wants to purchase a home for $115,000.00, but only has $20,000.00 available for the down payment, rather than the required $25,000.00. Our seller-investor(s) could accept the $20,000.00 and then make note arrangements with the buyer to permit him/her to pay the additional $5,000.00 over a two year period. This would satisfy both parties. When there is a willing buyer and a willing seller regarding the same property, and good faith on both sides, there is usually a very fair, practical method by which the transaction can be made to the benefit of both parties.

This key point bears repetition. The assumable *ByPass* program mortgage is invaluable to both a seller and a buyer. Buyers who are excluded from purchasing homes because they cannot meet traditional lending requirements are literally stuck between a rock and a hard place, which is a phrase we don't even like to use. However, it definitely expresses the frustrating position in which the would-be buyer finds himself. As a result of this, he is literally forced to rent property over a long term, with no protection from rent increases, no equity earned and nothing to show for his efforts and expenses but rent receipts. This is a devastating scenario for many good, decent people in this country who long to own their own home, but see no way of achieving their dream of home ownership. How precious is an assumable mortgage to any capable, willing buyer, when the alternative is his preclusion from the home market and his lack of ability to buy anything, under any conditions? Is that buyer willing to pay a slight premium to an investor who has arranged that mortgage for him? Considering the alternative, the qualified answer from a reasonable, objective observer is "Yes." The premium to which we refer here—the $7,500.00 to $15,000.00 dollar price above the original price of $100,000–is very slight and paid over a 15 year period, enabling the buyer to purchase a home he could never hope to buy any other way. This slight premium amounts to merely one half (1/2) of one percent to one (1) percent, per year, which is virtually nothing. In consideration of the alternative in which the would-be buyer is forced to rent property, possibly for the remainder of his/her life, this insignificant paltry premium is almost a Godsend for him/her and his/her family.

An alternative for a seller-investor(s) would be to sell their property on a contract of sale basis, rather than sell to the buyer through a note and mortgage, with the seller-investor holding a second mortgage. If sellers were to sell on the contract of sale basis, they retain ownership of the property until all payments are made by the buyer and then the deed is delivered to the buyer. Either of these approaches could work and it is up to the seller-investor(s) as to which approach they prefer. We prefer the note and mortgage basis, because this approach gives the buyer added comfort because s/he would receive the deed to the property upon closing, subject to the stated note and mortgage. The original seller must always be protected so that his mortgage and note position is secure and either one of these methods can handle this situation.

CHAPTER FORTY FIVE

REAL ESTATE DEVELOPMENT PROGRAM

In addition to the real estate investment possibilities provided in the previous CHAPTERs, there is a very realistic possibility for real estate *project developments* by using what we call equity investments. In the usual home development program of, let us say, 100 homes, the developer usually fronts the initial costs for purchase of land, permits, architectural designs, planning, roads, sewer systems, water, etc. After this is done, the developer then usually attempts to obtain two forms of bank financing. One is the construction or development loan, and the other is the permanent funding for the home buyers.

For a successful development, both of these types of loans have to work together, and a development usually cannot be built unless the two types of loans coincide with and complement each other. Just as with home financing for an individual home buyer, the bank requires certain criteria to be met before the loan is approved and made. As many of us know, much of the criteria are overreaching, not necessary, very costly, but unless the potential borrower accepts and is able to meet them, he does not receive his funding. The same is true with developers, but even more so. Market surveys are usually required, as well as appraisals, all of which can be very cumbersome and costly, and if the developer does not meet the criteria stated within the survey and the appraisals, the loan could be in jeopardy.

Since a bank is funding the development of 100 homes, the bank "lays down the law" to the developer and the developer has to comply, if the developer wants to obtain the bank's money to develop his project. Anyone who has developed property of any size is well acquainted with this banking practice. Not only is the developer required to pay fees for financing and other types of fees to obtain the development loan, but he is also required to do this for the permanent financing commitment. All of these various requirements, some of which are unexpected, add to the cost of the project, the cost of the individual houses, and take away from the developer's profit. In today's uncertain economy, everything is competitive, and if the eventual price for homes in a development strays too far from the norm, then, both the development and the developer could go under. This, unfortunately, is rather common, and could be avoided, provided restrictive and costly criteria are not imposed upon the developer. The question always is: "Is there an easier, less cumbersome, more direct way to successfully develop property?" In our view, there is always a better way than the standard, institutional method.

Let us say a developer completes the usual initial requirements in terms of acquiring land, arranging for architectural plans, other planning, permits, etc., as discussed before, but does not seek bank financing for his development, and instead pursues the equity investments referred to above. For example, our development is scheduled to be built in five (5) phases of 20 homes each. Each home in the first phase is scheduled to be sold for $100,000.00. Usually in developments, prices increase with each phase, because of the success of the earlier phase which encourages more buyers for the next phases and adds value to the development. Let us say that the purchase price for phase two is $105,000.00, with increases of $5,000.00 per phase, so that by the fifth phase, the price of the homes is $125,000.00. The developer has already established the 100 lots upon which the 100 homes will be built.

Our projected equity investment program calls for the developer to presell as many homes as he can in each phase by taking a 20% down payment, now, from each home buyer for each phase of the development. This down payment would amount to $20,000.00 from the buyers in phase one and would increase proportionately for the prices in subsequent phases. For the prepaid down payment and prepaid sale, the developer will deliver a lot to each buyer, free and clear, to secure his prepaid down payment funds. Further, the developer will lock in a lesser price for each buyer who buys in subsequent phases, which price will be lower for that buyer than it will be for other buyers in those phases. Funds raised by this method will essentially pay for development costs on a phase by phase basis.

What the developer has done in this scenario is put in initial funds to get the development started, approved and lots designated. By taking down payments now, he is delivering free and clear to each buyer the lot the buyer wants in any particular phase and is locking in a lesser home price for the buyer in that phase. By doing this, the developer is raising enough money to actually begin construction. When phase one construction is complete, and those buyers who prepaid the down payment take possession of their completed home, the developer carries the remainder of the home price for 15 years at 5% interest. By this approach, the developer avoids having to seek bank funding for both the construction loan and for the permanent home loans for individual buyers, thus, saves the developer and the buyers substantially, not only on interest costs, but also on fees and financing costs, such as points, and also saves on bank supervision costs through a bank architect or clerk of the works. All of this results in a huge benefit to the buyer, because since the developer is willing to carry the difference between the down payment and the eventual selling price for a 15 year period at 5% interest on a note and mortgage, the buyer does not need to arrange his own financing from any bank and jump through the usual banks hoops and pay the usual bank fees. The fact that the developer is willing to carry the note and mortgage is of monumental benefit to any financially capable buyer and can help the developer attract buyers for his entire development. This is indeed a win-win situation for the developer and the buyer.

In addition to the equity down payments which the developer can use to build his project, there are two other ways in which he could raise financing for the project without the need to go to a bank. The buyers will pay monthly payments on their notes. The developer, if necessary, could obtain a loan from a private investor or a pension fund secured by either the cash flow on the notes and/or on the notes, themselves. He could also sell the notes at discount to raise the necessary funds to complete the project. Small private investors or lenders could be interested in this, especially if the project were quite successful in showing results through energetic presales.

This proposed development program can be used by commercial builders who operate for profit, but want to stay away from bank funding, especially for construction phases, or by charities and foundations who want to create affordable homes for average Americans who have the financial means for down payments and monthly payments, but would not qualify under institutional bank lending criteria. As we have stated throughout this book, there are many millions of Americans who want to buy a home, but because of adverse financial circumstances to which we have alluded before, are unable to meet the qualifications for a bank loan. If various charitable and grant organizations were to recognize this unfortunate fact and wanted to assist people in these circumstances, then those organizations could provide initial "seed money" to a developer who would build the project based upon what we have projected above. When and if additional funds are needed to complete the project, then the charity, foundation or grant organization could award those funds for completion, and still have a stake in the project through the home notes and mortgages of the individual home buyers. While this country may have been headed for financial recovery in a very minor way, the government edict to essentially close the economy due to a phony disease threat stopped that very quickly. Except for the "star cities" most areas are still financially depressed and not doing well at all, with slim to no hope of recovery. This means that the people in those depressed areas are for the most part just living on the edge, just getting by, or working three jobs just to stay afloat. These types of home developments initially funded by charities, foundations and grant organizations could make a major difference in this country for many millions of people and begin the road back to economic recovery in various locations across the country.

CHAPTER FORTY SIX

SPECIAL HOME BUYING GROUPS

Special Categories for Home Purchases

Earlier in this book, we discussed the fact that a large percentage of people who buy homes in America sell those homes within five to six years and move to another location in the same city, state, or even in another state. This is an important aspect concerning the purchase and subsequent sale of property, so bears repeating, and directly impacts buyers who sell within that time period. This approximate five-year turnover is very beneficial to our buyers, and the reasons for this will be stated below. In addition to the typical home buyers, there are people who fall into many different categories who live in an area for an approximate five-year period and then move on to another location. Some examples of these are college students, medical school students and medical residents, research professionals, teachers and professors, contract workers, professional athletes and many others.

The above are just a few examples of people who are constantly moving in today's mobile American society. People have all sorts of reasons in all different categories for moving from one place to another, remaining there for a short period of time, maybe five or six years, and then moving on. Since most people who would fit into these categories realize their stay will be of short duration, most of them simply rent apartments or houses, instead of buying a property. If one were to compare the gains and losses in renting, as opposed to buying, with the *ByPass* approach and method, the short-term dweller would have a great advantage in buying rather than renting, as is explained below.

Using our standard example, if our buyer sells his home in five years, he could realize $53,000.00, plus, in equity. Obviously, this is a great position for any buyer who wants to resell and purchase another home elsewhere. As stated above, many of the people in the above mentioned categories move to an area for a limited period of time and simply rent an apartment or a house for the duration of their stay. At the end of their stay, all they have to show for their time there are rent receipts. There is always a better way to do almost anything, that is, if one seeks that better way. There is absolutely nothing wrong with anyone moving to another area and renting an apartment or house for five or six years, if that is what the person wants. However, for the more enterprising person or family, if s/he were to buy a house, based on our standard example, at the end of that five years, s/he could have the equity cited above, namely, $53,000.00, plus. This amount would certainly help him or her with his/her next purchase or next move, whatever that may be. When our buyer becomes a seller in five or so years, s/he should be aware that the property s/he wishes to sell should be quite easy to sell, primarily because of the existing assumable mortgage on the property. In today's volatile economic, financial and housing markets, a good house, with an existing assumable mortgage, is extremely valuable. As many of you know, countless people in this country have financial capability, but due to adverse circumstances cannot qualify to either assume existing bank mortgages or obtain new bank mortgages. Our approach provides the financially capable, but non-qualifying buyer the ability to buy his own home.

The original seller from whom our buyer bought the property has a very solid position in the home he sold, since he holds an existing mortgage on that home. Whoever buys the home in five or so years from our original buyer, assumes the note, as stated, which places the new buyer in a very favorable position. This new buyer assumes the existing note and makes his/her monthly payments to the seller, just as the original buyer did. If the new buyer were to default in any way, then, two considerations can occur. In the first scenario, the original buyer could still maintain a financial interest in the house, either through a small second mortgage s/he could take from the new buyer, or through a contract of sale. In either situation, if the new buyer were to default on his/her mortgage payments for a three month period, the original buyer can repossess the house as a mortgage holder who has the right to protect his/her interests in the property. If our original buyer were to do this, s/he would have received and kept all of the down payment funds paid by the new buyer, all of the mortgage payments that, in part, were paid to him and all of the equity the new buyer achieved, by and through his monthly mortgage payments. These amounts can be quite considerable and very beneficial to our original buyer. For a brief example, if the second buyer paid the standard $15,000.00 down, then, that amount is retained by the original buyer. If the original buyer is holding a note on the property, s/he has received and kept all of the note payments made by the new buyer to him/her. Another major consideration for our original buyer is that if the second buyer has owned the property for, let us say, four years and has regularly made his monthly principal and interest payments, he has paid off approximately $22,600.00 towards principal debt reduction. All of these factors can be a considerable additional benefit to our original buyer who can resell the home again and gain further through that resale.

If our original buyer does not exercise his rights under a note on the property, then, the original seller of the property can employ the same exact procedures stated above. Whether it is the original seller or the original buyer who takes over the defaulted property, whoever that may be, s/he stands to gain an unexpected considerable amount and, of course, can resell the property for further gain. By our method of debt reduction and principal and interest payments, both the seller and the buyer benefit from the transaction, which is not necessarily the case through institutional methods. As stated in an earlier CHAPTER, because of so-called "sub-prime" loans, which for the most part were fraudulent, and due to the economic market and other financial factors, many millions of people lost their homes to banks, because of these fraudulent, pernicious lending practices. Such losses would never take place in the *ByPass* debt reduction and principal and interest payment method, specified below.

Home Buying Categories

The above figures strongly indicate the favorable selling and economic conditions readily available to our home owner. As you are aware by now, the average home purchased in America is sold in approximately five years. When sellers can experience such an equity gain in five years, as described above, with the *ByPass* method, in comparison to institutional methods, it would be to their clear advantage to buy using the *ByPass* method. The American society has been a mobile society for decades. Many families and individuals spend a few years or so in one location, then, move to another city or state. The equity gain with the *ByPass* method could be of considerable financial help to them. In our mobile society, we have various groups of people who actually plan to live in one location for four to six years or so, then, move on to another location. Many various groups of people and individuals fall within this category. We referred to some of these above, but there are many more categories of people who would live in an area for a short term. If those who fall within this category rent for the duration of their stay, then, as mentioned before, they only have rent receipts to show for their time there, and no financial gain, whatsoever. Those who purchase property, through the *ByPass* method, can earn a major equity position that can help them with their next home purchase or move. It really depends upon what individual people want. Some people are content with a rental, while others would like to buy a home for the few years they spend in any one location, then, sell it for a profit, when they move. The *ByPass* buying, selling and financing approach could help provide that profit.

If buyers were to purchase homes in the traditional way, with conventional bank financing, the profit that one would expect upon resale in five or so years may not be very significant, if any at all. As previously mentioned, with the standard purchase arrangement buyers purchase a home for a price that, in part, pays for the real estate commission. If buyers obtain institutional bank financing, they usually pay points and fees that can be a considerable expense. Banks usually require costly inspections, appraisals, bank conditions of purchase, expensive closing fees and lawyers' fees. Institutional financing, as said above, is out of balance and very costly in interest payments over five years, with little applied to reduce the remaining principal balance. When one sells his home in the usual manner, he also pays a real estate commission, unless he sells the home on his own. If the buyer for the house finances institutionally through a bank, the usual bank policies prevail, as described above. All of these conditions can adversely impact the sale, and many times, the transaction falls apart. When a buyer purchases a home with intent to sell in four to six years, it might be advantageous to strongly consider all of these positions.

With our selling and buying principals in charge and handling their own transaction, none of these adverse financial and other considerations exist. The buyer and seller deal directly with each other, so no real estate commission is paid. When commissions typically range from 5 to 7% of the sales price, this is a major savings and financial benefit to the seller. Since no bank financing is involved, no financing points and extra fees are charged to the buyer, which, of course, works to his financial advantage. No bank inspections and conditions of purchase exist, which benefits both parties. Whatever conditions may exist, are established by and agreed to by both principal parties, and neither party is subject to a third party's conditions, whether it is the bank, the broker or someone else. As many of you know, in institutional lore, such conditions have caused buyers and sellers pangs of anxiety, waste of time, frustration, disappointment and emotional distress, because the transaction fell out of escrow due to third party demands. Such conditions adversely affect both buyer and seller, especially since each party expected the transaction to close on a specific date.

In the institutional financing methodology, as we have previously pointed out, and which many people may know, principal and interest payments adversely impact the home owner, but favor the bank. Since for the first five years of ownership, a significant amount of each monthly payment goes to interest, then little of that payment goes to reduce the principal balance. This holds true until about halfway through the mortgage term, when principal and interest payments begin to balance out. The buyer who purchases a property and who plans to sell that property in five or so years will be credited only with principal amounts made. In contrast, the *ByPass* methods' application of monthly payments to principal and interest is fair and just, based on simple interest payments made on the existing principal balance.

In our standard financing example, the $85,000.00 principal loan, carried by the seller over 15 years, is divided by 180 monthly payments, which amounts to $472.22 per month. With each monthly payment, our principal buyer reduces his remaining principal balance by $472.22, which, in comparison to institutional bank financing, is absolutely remarkable. In one year, this amounts to $5,666.64. In two years, this amounts to $11,333.28. In five years, when compared to principal balance remaining on institutional loans for the same loan amount, interest rate and maturity, the *ByPass* method far surpasses institutional loans. The buyer can always determine exactly what his remaining principal balance is by multiplying the number of monthly payments made by $472.22. This figure is then subtracted from the original $85,000.00 and the remaining amount is the principal balance owed. The buyer always knows exactly where he stands on interest paid, principal paid and remaining principal balance.

Interest is projected at 5% per year on the unpaid balance, which amounts to about $178.07 per month, averaged over the term of the note. Both principal and interest monthly payments are fixed for the term of the loan, thus the same amounts are allocated to principal payments and interest payments each month. The seller receives the same payment each month, but the remaining balance on the note declines rapidly for the buyer. Should the buyer sell the house, then the new buyer assumes the existing note balance to the seller and continues payments to the original seller. Our original buyer takes a small second mortgage on the house of $5,000 to protect his seller should the second buyer default. This note and mortgage permits the original buyer to take ownership of the house if default occurs, continue to make monthly payments to his seller, then, sell the house again. If this occurs, the original buyer keeps the down payment he received and gets the equity benefit from note payments his buyer made to the original seller, which, over several years, can be considerable. This is a win-win arrangement for the seller and buyer, which is the best of all possible transactions.

For the $60,000 house, 15% down is $9,000 and the note balance is $51,000 for 15 years. $51,000 divided by 180 payments amounts to $283.33 per month, which is the principle payment each month. Interest is paid on the unpaid balanced, averaged over the note term, which amounts to approximately $106.84 each month. Total monthly principal and interest payment is $390.17 over the term of the note. The same principals stated above apply to the $60,000 house; therefore, the buyer can acquire equity in his home more rapidly than permitted by conventional methods. If the buyer were to sell his home sometime in the future, he would receive the benefit of that advanced equity. The original seller would receive the same monthly payments from the new buyer and the original buyer, who is now the new seller would place a $2,000 note and mortgage on the house in case his buyer defaults. As above, he can take over ownership of the house because his buyer defaulted on the mortgage, sell it again and retain the down payment and receive benefit for all principal payments made by his buyer.

CHAPTER FORTY SEVEN

SAFE INVESTMENTS

One of the best, safest and most secure investments anyone can make is to purchase a home for both investment and retirement purposes. This type of purchase is especially good for young couples just starting out or for middle age couples who plan to retire in 15-20 years or so. We shall provide an example. Let us say that a person purchases a home using the *ByPass* program. Within a few years, the buyer has earned an excellent equity position. He could leverage (borrow against) his equity from a private lender and use the loan proceeds as a down payment on his purchase of a second home, also using the *ByPass* program. The buyer then rents the newly purchased home to reliable tenants at a rent that will cover all his expenses on the home. The expenses would be the following: monthly principal and interest payments; taxes; insurance; water, sewer and trash; any repairs and maintenance. The utilities would be paid by the tenants.

If the buyer purchases a home through the *ByPass* method at a fair marketable price, which can be rented at a fair marketable rent, he should be able to cover all his expenses and, in addition, earn a monthly profit. Another expense would be the debt on the equity loan used for the down payment. Rent should be calculated to cover this cost. As time passes, rents can and usually do increase. However, the buyer's monthly home mortgage payment remains constant throughout his mortgage and note term. If the rent does not fully cover the buyer's equity loan payments, then, as rent increases, this should be more than enough to adequately cover all expenses and provide substantial profit.

In the above example, the buyer uses the equity on his home to buy a second home, which he rents to tenants. If that second home were purchased using the same *ByPass* method, price and terms as the buyer's first home, namely, $100,000.00 price, $15,000.00 down, with the balance carried for 15 years at 5%, the home would be completely paid off in 15 years. The buyer only invests the down payment of $15,000.00, which came from the equity loan. If properly purchased, managed and leased, the tenants pay for all other costs and provide a yearly profit to the buyer. This is a great way to afford a home as an investment to amass funds for retirement purposes, which home can either be rented for a substantial monthly income, or sold outright for a substantial profit in 15 years, after all debt has been retired.

After 15 years, the buyer has many options available to him/her, all of which are favorable and profitable. Please note, as previously mentioned, that the buyer's investment in this second home is $15,000.00 for the down payment that he obtains from the equity loan on his own home. The buyer could continue to rent the home at a rental rate well beyond the initial rent level of 15 years earlier. The current rent would be all profit because the buyer has paid off his mortgage note and long since retired his equity loan. This monthly rent could provide very substantial extra income and certainly be an excellent retirement nest egg, with minimal expenses.

Buyers could sell their homes and realize a sizeable profit far above the purchase price they paid 15 years earlier. If the home were to appreciate in value at a modest 2% average per year, the approximate value in 15 years would be $134,500.00. Buyer's original $15,000.00 down payment is expected to be realized and returned from at least an average $1,000 per year profit over the 15 year period. The buyer's total profit, by this example, is expected to be $134,500.00, minimum, upon sale in 15 years. Please note that this is the buyer's second home. His first home was paid off long before his second one. The first home was purchased for $100,000.00 also, so that buyer's total home equity would be about $269,000.00 and all from the original $15,000.00 down payment on his first home.

The buyer could leverage the second home, as well as his first home, and do the same thing all over again. He can do this at any time during his ownership of the properties. By utilizing the methods and tools available to him under the *ByPass* program, the buyer can earn a very safe, solid, secure and substantial return on his/her investment in both his/her original and secondary purchases. This is a very easy, low key way for any capable and willing buyers to take their down payments and turn them into a substantial return during or by the end of their note term. Buyer can use their equity pools for even greater and more active real estate purchases, they choose. The next CHAPTER will present some examples of choices.

CHAPTER FORTY EIGHT

ADVANCED INVESTMENTS

With so much advanced equity allowed through the *ByPass* program, motivated buyer-investors could actively use their equity pools for serious real estate investments. Earlier in this Section we mentioned that the major investment Programs are spelled out, in detail, in the Projections Section at the end of this book. To provide examples, this Section deals with moderate investments. There are many ways for buyers to invest, whether the investor wants small to moderate profits, or massive wealth. There is something in this book for almost everyone.

For now, let us remain with our safe and doable example. In our example, five years after the buyers purchased a $100,000 home they have equity of approximately $59,234, if their home appreciates at 3% per year. At 3% per house per year, this is the appreciated value; however appreciated value and market value can be different. Market value can sometimes exceed appreciated value quite a bit, which means the equity position would be much higher. However, to be conservative, we remain with the 3% appreciation figures. Please note that if the investor were to purchase the original home as stated, and then, rent it for five (5) years, then, the rental income minus expenses would permit the investor to buy six (6) houses in year five (5), rather than four (4). Obviously, the six (6) houses would produce more rental incomes than four (4) houses.

At 3%, per house, per year, in five (5) years the house would be valued at $115,900. The $85,000 first mortgage debt has been reduced by $28,334 to $56,666. $115,900 minus $56,666 provides house equity of approximately $59,234. If buyers want to become active investors, then, buyers could likely borrow $60,000 against their equity with rental property that has a market value of approximately $579,500. Once the four houses are purchased, each with a first mortgage carried by the sellers, then the projected immediate market value for houses, with mortgages carried by sellers, increases to $115,900 per house. High demand exists for houses with mortgages carried by sellers.

Our projections tend to be conservative for the benefit of the new investor. However, as mentioned above, if the investor rented his initial purchased house, then based upon rental flow, minus taxes, insurance and debt service, he could purchase six homes rather than four. This would increase purchases every five years by 150%. Further, if the investor were to demonstrate to the lender a solid business plan for rentals of more houses based upon the equity of those houses, then it is possible that 12 or 16 houses could be purchased rather than four.

For instance, if the investor were to rent the house he originally purchased, then, in addition to the equity value, he should be able to purchase two more houses on the same $100,000 basis, with $15,000 down per house from rental profit. Once purchased, the market value per house, with first mortgage carried by sellers, is projected at $115,900 each. First mortgage debt per house is $85,000, $170,000 total. Mortgage debt on the first house is $56,666, a total of $226,666. Appreciated value and market value of each house totals $347,700, with equity projected at $121,034. If investor could borrow this equity value in the three houses, then he could purchase eight houses at $100,000, $15,000 down, with balances carried by the sellers. Investor now has 11 houses, with a projected market value of $1,274,900 and a second mortgage or security interest debt to the private lender of $121,034.

The investor was able to borrow against the equity in three houses to purchase eight additional houses. If the investor were able to show the lender a solid business plan for the house rentals and profit stream for the 11 houses, then he might be able to borrow against the equity of the eight houses. Projected market value for those eight houses, at $115,900 each, is $927,200. First mortgage debt to the sellers is $85,000 per house, a total of $680,000. Projected equity is $247,200. This amount borrowed could purchase another 16 houses on the same basis as previous purchases. On this basis, our investor could own 27 rental houses with a projected market value of $3,129,300 and a $368,234 projected debt to the lender.

The above suggestions are for an investor who has some experience with investments. Our projections are for both the experienced investor and for the average man or woman investor who wants to make a minimal investment in real estate. The following sets of projections are for the small investor who wants to make that minimum real estate investment for maximum return. These buys can be done for investment purposes or for retirement purposes, or a combination of both.

Projections indicate that the investor uses our standard example and will purchase a house for $100,000, with $15,000 down, and the balance carried by the seller for 15 years. The investor could live in the house, or rent it. If he were to rent it, then, in five years hence he could buy more houses than if he did not rent it. Five years later, the investor has built up equity in the house, which he borrows against and purchases four more houses on the same basis as the first house. The lender could be a private investor, a private investment group or a pension fund.

Every five (5) years the investor uses the equity of the houses to obtain a loan against that equity. Our investor can be very conservative and buy only a few houses every five (5) years, or follow the projections and receive projected profits and equity of over $2.5 billion by year thirty (30). It is all up to how the investor wants to achieve his objective and he can proceed at his own pace to reach his own objective. This is a very safe, secure and solid way to build up a substantial retirement fund in ten or fifteen years, or fabulous wealth in twenty five to thirty years.

Each projection indicates a current market value or appreciated value of the houses, every five (5) years. Debts and expenses are deducted from the market value, which indicates the current equity. Our projections show that the investor borrows 85% of this equity from a private source. The loan amount purchases houses, using our example of a $100,000 price, $15,000 down, with a balance carried by the sellers. The $60,000 loan would purchase four (4) houses at $15,000 down, per each house, with balances carried by the sellers.

After houses are purchased, rent projections are made for all house rentals showing projected profits and equity in the properties. The same procedure takes place when the next five (5) years have passed. Brief analyses will follow each five (5) year projection.

Our projections call for profits to remain with the investor and not invested to purchase more houses. If profits were used to buy houses, then, of course, the number of houses bought would increase quite a bit. Further, once the investor clearly proves to the lender that the program works very well, then, he should be able to borrow against the entire equity of the houses, or more, as a viable business operation, and, of course, substantially more houses can be bought, rented, with much higher profits and equity.

If the investor were to follow the suggestions made earlier for more purchases based upon loans made on higher equity, then the investor would have a projected 27 houses rented from years five to ten, with much higher profits and equity. 27 houses amount to 675% more houses than 4 houses. This 675% more houses purchased would carry through for each and every five year purchase period, which would enormously expand these following projections.

YEAR FIVE

Original house – Appreciated value in 5 years $115,900

4 Purchased homes at $115,900, each, $463,600

                                                                                      $579,500

Lender's loan is secured by a second mortgage or other security interest in the 5 houses. The loan could come from a private lender, pension fund or investment group. This $60,000 dollar loan can purchase four (4) houses at $100,000, each, $15,000 down payment per home, with the balances carried by the sellers. If investor does this, then he just increased his real estate portfolio by 500%.

This loan, plus interest, can be paid from rental profits and retired within five (5) years. Rent is projected at $1,350 per month, with no rent increases over the five year period.

The projections for this program cover five (5) years of borrowing, buying and renting. Rents on each house are projected to begin at $1,350 per month, $16,200 per year, times four (4) rental houses times five (5) years for a total of $324,000. We project that no rent increases occur over five (5) years. Buyers pay first mortgage payments on the four (4) properties of about $650 per month, times twelve (12) equals $7,800, per house, times four (4) houses, for five (5) years, which equals $156,000 at seven (7) % interest, loan payments for the $60,000 loan are about $71,000 over five (5) years.

$60,000 Loan payments – Principal & interest......................... $ 71,000

First mortgage payments - $ 7,800 per year x 4 houses x 5 years = $156,000

                                                                                      $227,000 Debt

$324,000 – Rents over 5 years

$227,000 – Debt over 5 years

$ 97,000   Rental profits

     - 16,000 – Taxes of $800, per house, per year x 5 years

     - <u>16,000</u> – House insurance, $800 per house, per year x 5 years

$ 65,000 – Projected profit

YEAR FIVE ANALYSIS

Five houses -- $28,333 per year Principal Debt Reduction

Five years of Debt Reduction = $141,665

Rent is projected at $1,350 per month per house, with no rent increases over five years.

After expenses, Profit = $65,000, which is a 433.33% return on the $15,000 investment, plus the equity increases over five (5) years. If the investor rented the initial house he bought, rather than living in it, then, after expenses, the investor could have purchased six (6) houses, not four (4).

As stated, the investor can proceed at his own pace, which could be very conservative, very ambitious or somewhere in between. These initial projections were designed for people who want to make a small investment, then, purchase other houses based upon a loan against the equity from their existing houses that has accumulated over five (5) or more years. The investor can stop at any point and take his projected profit and accumulated equity, or proceed for thirty (30) years to reach a projected $2.5 billion, or more in profits and equity. It is all an individual decision designed to reach an individual retirement or investment objective.

YEAR TEN

In another five years of ownership, the Buyers are in their tenth year. The note balance on each of Buyers' four rental homes has been paid down $28,333 each, or approximately $113,332, total. First mortgage loans for the four (4) houses amounts to $85,000 per house, $340,000, total. The $113,332 in payments made over five (5) years brings the first mortgage balance owed on the four (4) houses to $226,668.

In year ten (10), at 3% house appreciation per year on each of the four (4) rental houses bought five (5) years earlier, the houses would be worth approximately $115,900, each, or more, a total of $463,600. The appreciation on the Buyer's home values the home at $134,359.

Buyer's home	$134,359
4 Rental homes at $115,900, each +	$463,600
Appraised and market value	$597,959

Loan Retirement, Loan Debt and Projected Loan

The $60,000 loan taken out in year five (5) has been retired.

First mortgage debt is $7,800 per the four (4) houses for five (5) years = $156,000

Projected loan of $375,665, plus interest, amounts to   + $443,284

Total Debt $599,284

Projected Equity and Loan

$597,959 market value & appraised value five (5) houses

- $156,000 first mortgage debt

Equity $441,959 x 85% = $375,665 ÷ $15,000 = 25 houses bought with

$15,000, each

In our projections, we use the market value and appreciated value of the houses, minus the debt owed on those houses to arrive at an equity value for the properties, times 85% to arrive at a loan figure divided by $15,000 which equals 25 houses purchased with $15,000 down payments, each, which totals the loan amount.

RENTS -- $1,450 per month, $17,400, per year, each house, for five (5) years, with no rental increase during those five years.

Four (4) houses – bought in year five (5) plus 25 houses bought in year ten (10) = 29 houses.

$17,400 (rents) x 29 houses x 5 - $2,523,000

-   599,284 – Debt

$1,923,716 – Profit, years 10 to 15

-   975,000   -- First mortgages – 25 houses x $7,800 x 5 years

-   145,000 – Taxes, $1,000 per year x 29 houses x 5 years

-   145,000 – Insurance, $1,000 per year x 29 houses x 5 years

$ 658,716 – Projected profit years 10 to 15

First Mortgage Debt

4 houses x 10 years x $5,666 = $ 226,640

25 houses x $85,000…. $ 2,125,000

First Mortgage Debt $ 2,351,640

Market Value and Profits

4 houses x $115,900………..$ 463,600

25 houses x $115,900…………$2,897,500

Appreciated Value…………..$3,361,100

Appreciated Value………..$3,361,100

First Mortgage Debt……- $2,351,640

Equity………………..$1,009,460

Projected Profit………… +$ 658,716

Projected Profit & Equity…**$1,668,176**

YEAR TEN ANALYSIS

First Mortgage debt reduction = 29 houses x $5,666 per year = $164,314

Five (5) Year debt reduction…………………………………...$821,570

$60,000 Loan Paid, Principal & Interest

After expenses, profit is projected at $658,716, a 4,391.44% return on the $15,000 investment. It is also a return of 11,121% on the equity and profit total. If return on the projected $375,665 loan is considered, the projected profit and equity amount to a return of 444.55%.

If investor purchased 27 homes in Year Five instead of 4, then the 675% of the 25 buys in Year Ten would amount to a projected 168 rental houses.

YEAR 15

-

Market Value –Debt-Rents-Expenses – Profits –Equity

Market Value

1 - $155,759 …………………………………….$ 155,759

4 x $134,359……………………………………….$ 537,436

25 x $115,900……………………………………...$2,897,500

Appreciated & Market Value   **$3,590,695**

DEBT -- $443,284 loan paid off

First mortgage debt – 29 houses x $7,800 per year x 29 houses x 5 years = $1,131,000

Projected $2,100,000 loan, plus interest…………………………………… $2,457,000

Total of first mortgage debt and loan, plus interest $3,588,000

$3,590,695 Market value & appreciated value

- 1,131,000 First mortgage debt – 29 houses

$2,459,695 – Profit x 85% = $2,090,790 ÷ by $15,000 = 140 houses

Purchased with $15,000 down payments, each, = $2,100,000 loan

<u>RENTS</u> – 4 + 25+ 140 = 169 houses x $1,600 per month, x 12 mo x 5yrs = $16,224,000

<u>RENTS + EXPENSES</u> -- $16,224,000 – 169 x $1,600 x 12 mo x 5 yrs

- $ 1,622,400 – 10% -- vacancies and repairs

- $ 1,014,000 – Property taxes – 169 x $1,200 x 5 yrs

- $ 929,500 – Insurance – 169 x $1,100 x 5 yrs

- $ 2,457,000 – Prin. + Int. on $2,100,000 loan

- <u>$ 6,435,000</u> – First Mortgage Debt – 169 houses

$ 3,766,100 – Profit – Year 15

MARKET VALUE & APPRAISED VALUE

1 - $155,759 …………………………..$ 155,759

4 x $134,359 …………………………..$ 537,436

25 x $115,900 …………………………. $ 2,897,500

140 x $ 15,900 ………………………… <u>$ 16,226,000</u>

Market Value Year 15…………………….**$ 19,816,695**

FIRST MORTGAGE DEBT

169 houses x $85,000 = $14,365,000 – Original Debt

<u>- $ 1,019,890</u>   Paid

$13,345,110 – First Mortgage Debt

<u>**EQUITY**</u> $ 3,766,100 – Profit – Year 15

+   <u>$ 6,471,585</u> – Equity – Year 15

$10,237,685

$10,237,685 – Equity & Profit – Year 15

YEAR 15 ANALYSIS

Debt Reduction = 169 houses x $5,666 = $957,554 per year

Five (5) Year Debt Reduction = $4,787,770

$2,100,000 Loan Principal & Interest Paid in Full

Year 15 Profit is projected at $3,766,100, a return of 25,107% on the $15,000 investment.

When profit and equity are considered, the return is 68,251% on the $15,000 investment.

The projected profit and equity amount to a 487.5% return on the projected $2,100,000 loan.

If the investor employed suggestions made earlier, then, he could have increased the 140 houses purchased by 675% to 945 houses purchased.

YEAR 20

MARKET VALUE – RENTS – DEBT – PROFIT – EQUITY

MARKET VALUE		
1	$ 180,568	
4	$ 623,036	
25	$ 3,358,975	
140	$16,226,000	
170	$20,388,579 – Market Value	

DEBT   25 + 140 = 165 x $7,800 x 5 = $6,435,000

PROFIT – EQUITY – LOAN

$20,388,579 – Market Value

$$- \$ 6{,}435{,}000 - \text{First Mortgage Debt on 165 houses}$$
$$\$13{,}953{,}579 - \text{Equity x 85\%} = \$11{,}860{,}542$$
$$\text{Loan of } \$11{,}865{,}000 \div \$15{,}000 = 791 \text{ houses}$$

RENTS   791 + 29 + 140 = 960 houses x $1,700 x 12 x 5 = $97,920,000

EXPENSES

Debt – 956 x $7,800 x 5 = $37,324,000 – First Mortgage – 956 houses

- $13,941,360 – P & I -- $11,865,000 loan
- $ 9,792,000 – 10% vacancies & repairs
- $ 6,720,000 – Tax – 960 houses x $1,400 x 5
- $ 5,760,000 – Insurance – 960 houses x $1,200 x 5
- $ 2,500,000 – Staff

$75,997,360 – Debt & Expenses

RENTS – DEBT – PROFITS

$97,920,000 – Rents

-$75,997,360 – Debt & Expenses

$21,922,640 – Profit – Year 20

MARKET VALUE AFTER PURCHASE OF 791 HOUSES

4 x $155,759.................................	$ 623,036
25 x $134,359..............................	$ 3,358,975
140 x $115,900............................	$16,226,000
791 x $115,900............................	$91,676,900
960 houses	**$111,884,911** – Market Value

DEBT – FIRST MORTGAGE 956 HOUSES X $85,000 = $81,260,000 – Original Debt

- $75,875,650 – Current debt

$ 5,384,350 – Loan equity

$111,884,911 – Market Value

- $ 75,875,650 – Debt – First Mortgage

$36,009,261 – Equity

+ $21,922,640 – Profit

$57,931,901 – Projected Profit + Equity Year 20

$57,931,901 Projected Profit & Equity Year 20

YEAR TWENY ANALYSIS

Debt Reduction = 956 x 5,666 = $5,416,696 per year

Five (5) Year Debt Reduction = $27,083,480

Loan of 11,865,000 Paid off Principal & Interest

After expenses, Profit is projected at $21,922,640 and Equity is projected at $36,009,261, a total of $57,931,901, which is a projected 488.25% return on the projected $11,865,000 loan.

If the investor adopted the suggestions made earlier, then the projected 791 house purchases could be increased by 675% to 5339 houses.

YEAR 25

MARKET VALUE – RENTS – DEBT – PROFIT – EQUITY

MARKET VALUE BY APPRECIATION

1 -- $209,300 ……………………………………$ 209,300

4 x $180,567 ……………………………………..$ 722,268

25 x $155,759 …………………………………....$ 3,893,975

140 x $134,359 …………………………………$ 18,810,260

791 x $115,900 …………………………………..$ 91,676,900

931 houses $115,312,703

DEBT – FIRST MORTGAGE

140 + 791 = 931 x $7,800 x 5 = $36,309,000

PROFIT – EQUITY – LOAN

$115,312,703 – Market Value by Appreciation

- $ 36,309,000 – First Mortgage Debt – 931 houses

$ 79,003,705 – Profit x 85% = $67,153,149 ÷ $15,000 = 4,480 houses

---

RENTS

960 + 4,480 x $1,850 x 12 x 5 = $603,840,000

EXPENSES

$ 603,840,000 – Rent
- $ 78,960,000 – Loan
- $ 211,029,000 – 5,411 houses – First Mortgage Debt
- $ 38,080,000 – Property taxes
- $ 34,000,000 – Insurance
- $ 12,000,000 – Staff
$ 169,387,000 – Profit – Year 25

MARKET VALUE AFTER PURCHASE OF 4,480 HOUSES

$634,335,407
- $434,453,000
$199,882,407 – Equity

EQUITY & PROFIT

$199,882,407 – Equity
+ $169,387,000 – Profit
$369,269,407 – Profit & Equity

$369,269,407 – Projected Profit & Equity Year 25

YEAR TWENTY FIVE ANALYSIS

Debt Reduction = 5,411 houses x $5,666 = $30,658,726 per year
Five (5) Year Debt Reduction = $153,293,630
$67,200,000 Loan fully paid off Principal & Interest

Year 25 Profit is projected at $169,387,000 and Equity projected at $199,882,407, a total of $369,269,407, a 549.5% return on the $67,200,000 loan.

If the investor were to follow our initial suggestions on the initial purchase of houses, then the 4,480 houses purchased could have been increased by 675% to 30,240 houses.

YEAR 30

MARKET VALUE – RENTS – DEBT – PROFIT – EQUITY

MARKET VALUE BY APPRECIATION

1 - $ 242,668 ....$	242,668
5 x 4 x $209,326 ....$	837,304
25 x $180,568 ....$	4,514,200
140 x $155,759 ....$	21,806,260
791 x $134,359 ....$	106,277,969
4,480 x $115,900 ....$	519,232,000
5,442 houses	$ 652,910,401

DEBT – FIRST MORTGAGE

5,271 x $7,800 x 5 = $205,569,000

PROFIT – EQUITY – LOAN

$ 652,910,401 – Market Value by Appreciation

- $ 205,569,000 – First Mortgage Debt – 5,271 houses

$ 447,341,401 – Profit x 85% $380,240,190 ÷ $15,000 = 25,350 = $380,250,000 loan

TOTAL DEBT

30,621 houses (Years 20 – 25 – 30 x $7,800 x 5 = $1,194,219,000 – First Mortgages

- $ 445,500,000 – Loan P & I

$1,639,719,000 – Total Debt

RENTS & EXPENSES AFTER PURCHASE OF 25,350 HOUSES

      $ 3,694,800,000 – Rents – 30,790 houses x $2,000 x 12 x 5

-    $ 1,639,719,000 – Loan P & I + First Mortgages

      $ 2,055,081,000 – Profit

-    $ 369,480,000 – 10% Vacancies & Repairs

      $ 215,530,000 – Property Taxes

      $ 192,437,500 – Insurance

      $ 100,000,000 – Staff

      $1,177,633,500 – Projected Profit Year 30

MARKET VALUE BY APPRECIATION AFTER PURCHASE OF 25,350 HOUSES

1 - $242,668 …………………………………………$	242,668
4 x $242,668 …………………………………………$	970,672
25 x $180,568 ………………………………………..$	4,514,200
140 x $155,759 ………………………………………$	21,806,260
791 x $134,359 ………………………………………$	106,277,969
4,480 x $115,900 ……………………………………$	519,232,000
25,350 x $115,900 …………………………………...$	2,938,065,000
30,791 houses	**$3,591,108,769**

FIRST MORTGAGE DEBT AFTER PURCHASE OF 25,350 HOUSES

791 houses ……………………………$	22,409,030
4,480 houses …………………………$	253,836,800
25,350 houses ………………………..$	2,154,750,000
30,621	$2,430,995,830

PROFIT & EQUITY

      $3,591,108,769 – Market Value

-    $2,430,995,830 – First Mortgage Debt – 30,621 houses

      $1,160,112,939 – Equity

+ $1,177,633,500 – Profit

$2,337,746,439 – Profit & Equity

+ $ 195,801,467 – Profits Years 5, 10, 15, 20, 25

$2,533,547,906 – Total Profits & Equity

$2,533,547,906 Projected Total Profits & Equity – Year 30

YEAR THIRTY ANALYSIS

Debt Reduction = 30,621 houses x $5,666 = $173,498,586 per year

Five Year Debt Reduction = $867,492,930

$380,250,000 Loan fully paid off Principal & Interest

Year Thirty (30) Profit is projected at 1,177,633,500 + $195,801,467 in Profits from Years 5 + 10 + 15 + 20 + 25, a total of $1,373,434,967. Equity is projected at $1,160,112,939, a total of $2,533,547,906, a 666.28% return on the $380,250,000 loan.

If the investor followed our initial suggestions regarding more initial purchases, then the 25,350 houses projected to be purchased could have been increased by 675% to a total of 171,112 houses.

As we stated in the introduction to these projections, the investor can start with a very small investment, follow through to Year Thirty (30), and earn projected fabulous wealth. The investor could also proceed at his own pace, purchase fewer houses every five (5) years and achieve a satisfactory retirement portfolio that suits his needs and objectives.

The real bottom line here is that the small investor, with a minimum investment in real estate, can accomplish amazing results, in accordance with his goals. The small investor should never be excluded from any markets, but unfortunately, this has been the case since the beginning of the monetary system. The small investor all too often loses his investment and his opportunity to succeed. As previously mentioned, since there is uncertainty, deception and fraud pretty much everywhere in the investment arena, we consider only gold, silver and real estate to be the safest and most lucrative forms of investment. However, gold and silver have been unlawfully seized before, and what happened before could happen again. Seizure of real estate, by government is highly unlikely. When the investor makes his investment, then, his tenants pay all the expenses, across the board, and leave a sizable profit and equity position for the investor over the lifespan of the investment. We consider this to be the safest, most secure and most solid investment position for any small time and average-folk investors.

The projections made in this set of projections were done on a five (5) year rental, borrow and buy basis. This was done to give the investor a solid perspective of what could be accomplished. In the real investment world, loans are not made on a five (5) year basis and houses are not bought on a five (5) year basis. Loans are made throughout the five (5) year period for houses bought throughout that period. In other words, there is not a $380,250,000 loan made all at once, for the purchase of properties all at once. What we suggest is that the investor obtains a commitment from his private lender for a specific amount of money which he can draw against as he contracts to buy properties. This draw could be for every 25 houses, 50 houses, 100 houses or 500 houses. When the contract is arranged to buy the house, and then bundled with other contracts, such as for another 24 houses, etc., then, the draw for those 25 houses can be effectuated with the private lender on prearranged terms. This, obviously, will lessen the projected financing costs and raise the projected rents received substantially through the purchase of these properties throughout the five (5) year program, instead of at the end of the five (5) years.

The past two plus years for America have devastated many Americans in many different ways by governments intent upon controlling, deceiving and manipulating the people rather than performing their sworn duties to protect the Constitutionally secured rights of the people, pursuant to the national Constitution and its Preamble. What happened before can happen again, because, unfortunately, most societies do not learn from the past so do not learn from history. Therefore, the aware and astute investor might strongly consider the real estate programs projected in this book as the safest, most secure and most solid form of investment.

If the American people do not awaken to the political, banking, financial, corporate and social realities that constrain them within limited positions, keeping in them in the proverbial box, then, unfortunately, restrictions will continue and increase. In this situation, the investor wants to be in the safest, most secure position possible. In such situations, investment money is also looking for the safest, most secure positions possible. This means that the astute, knowledgeable investor, or one who becomes this, can likely receive investment funds from private interests or pension funds eager to place their funds in safe, secure investments.

Margy and I sincerely hope the American people awaken to what has befallen them and to what could happen again. As we said earlier, the programs in this book can work in the best of times and the worst of times. We truly hope that we see the best of times in this country and absolutely no more of the worst of times for any and all Americans.

CHAPTER FORTY NINE

EXAMPLES OF TRANSACTIONS

Throughout this book, our two standard examples are the purchase of (1) a $100,000 house, with a $15,000 down payment, and an $85,000 balance carried by the seller at 5% for 15 years, and (2) a $60,000 house with $9,000 down and a $51,000 balance carried by the seller at 5% for 15 years. We use the $100,000 example, but the same principles apply to the $60,000 example, but not the figures.

As you know, the typical real estate transactions and closings can be very complicated for the reasons previously mentioned. Since our standard sample transaction takes place between two principals who deal directly with each other, then, the transaction should be very simple, uncomplicated, with minimal expense. After buyer and seller have discussed their respective objectives and terms, and then agree to proceed with the transaction, buyer and seller will enter into a written contract in which each party specifies his terms and all terms are acceptable to each party. Buyer's terms might include the following: (1) satisfactory inspection report by a professional home inspector; (2) clear, clean title, without liens and encumbrances of any type; (3) title insurance paid for by Seller; (4) survey or copy of survey report.

The closing can take place in the office of the title insurance company which has researched the property's title history and is providing title insurance to the buyer. Since the paperwork is minimal, direct and to the point, devoid of the usual excessive language, pages and legalese, the closing costs should be low and split between the buyer and seller. In our typical transaction, we use our above referenced standard example.

Since the buyer has already made a deposit to the seller to secure his offer, at the closing, the buyer pays the remainder of the $15,000.00 down payment, and the seller signs over the deed to the house to the buyer. The buyer signs a note in the amount of $85,000.00, plus interest, in favor of the seller, and also signs a mortgage to the seller on the home the buyer is purchasing to secure the note. The title insurance company provides a title search and title insurance to the buyer, and this transaction has been successfully concluded. Buyer and seller split the fees incurred at the closing. It is really this simple and easy, despite what banks, other lenders, brokers, attorneys, and other professionals may claim to the contrary. As we have said before, when any man or woman takes his/her own power into his/her own hands and makes his/her own decisions, in consort with another person who does the same, amazing things can be accomplished.

Sample Transactions Different from the Original Example

While the original sample would satisfy the terms that most buyers and sellers would want, some other principals will have different objectives and terms in mind. As long as buyer and seller can reach agreement on each other's terms, then, any proposed transaction can proceed. In this section, we will discuss some of those different objectives and terms on the part of buying and selling principals.

A buyer may make an offer based on the terms of our standard example. However, instead of the $15,000.00 down payment, the buyer may only be able to make a down payment of $12,000.00, while the seller still wants $15,000.00 down. If both parties are sincere and reasonable, and want the transaction to work, then, alternative terms could be presented and considered. For instance, in addition to the $12,000.00 down payment, the buyer could offer to pay the seller another $3,000.00 toward the principal on the first anniversary of the house closing. This arrangement would satisfy the $15,000.00 the seller wants and allow the buyer to make the purchase on the terms he needs to consummate the transaction. The purchase contract would specify these terms. The terms would state that the buyer would pay $12,000.00 down and the seller will carry a mortgage of $88,000.00. On the first anniversary of the closing, the buyer would pay $3,000.00 to the seller to reduce the principal balance, thus, providing the $15,000.00 the seller wanted. On our terms, once the buyer has made all his monthly payments, the principal balance remaining from the principal note of $88,000.00 is about $82,333.36. Since the buyer prepaid an additional $3,000.00 to the principal balance, this further reduces the remaining principal balance to $79,336.36. After this $3,000.00 payment has been made, the buyer makes his regular monthly payment to the seller, until the balance is fully retired. Since the buyer made this $3,000.00 prepayment, no interest is charged on the amount of that prepayment. As long as there are reasonable principal parties who will listen to and duly consider what is presented, then, respond with their sincere counter measures or their acceptance, the transaction has a great possibility of success. All agreed-upon terms, obviously, would be specified in the written contract between the parties.

In another situation, the seller may want a higher monthly payment than the $85,000.00 carried over 15 years would allow, pursuant to our standard example. To satisfy this, the buyer could agree to make an additional payment of $1,000.00 on the anniversary of the loan closing to reduce the principal for each and every year until the loan is paid in full. This extra $1,000.00 per year paid to the seller amounts to $83.00 more per month, and when added to the usual monthly payment, may satisfy the seller's objective. A contract stating these exact terms can be drawn up and entered into by the buyer and seller. Alternatively, still other arrangements can be struck between buyer and seller in whatever manner suits their respective needs and enables the transaction to move forward and close successfully.

The figures below will provide a very close estimate as to what the monthly principal and interest charges would be on the above arrangement. Our monthly principal and interest charges are based upon the principal amount of $85,000.00, at 5% interest on the declining balance. Our fair and just principal reduction method divides the original principal amount of $85,000.00 by 15 years, or 180 monthly payments. This amounts to a principal payment of $472.22 per month. The interest on the declining balance is $177.08 per month, by our method, for a total monthly principal and interest payment which we rounded up to $650.30. At the end of the year, dating from the closing, with 12 payments made, the principal balance remaining is approximately $79,333.36. With the 12th payment, by agreement, the buyer pays an additional $1,000.00 to reduce the principal, which brings the principal balance to $78,333.36. In one year, the buyer has paid off approximately 7.843% of the $85,000.00 loan. This type of payment and principal reduction far surpasses the percentage and principal reduction allowed by institutional financing methods. In this arrangement, the seller receives his regular payment of $650.30 per month, plus an additional bonus payment of $1,000.00, which brings his effective monthly payment to $733.63 per month.

Since the buyer has paid $1,000.00 towards the principal, then, no interest is paid by the buyer on that prepaid $1,000.00. This same procedure can be followed each year until the principal balance is fully paid off. Yearly prepayment of $1,000.00, made on the anniversary of the closing, to reduce the principal balance, will pay off the existing balance before the 15 year term is reached.

In another example, a seller may agree to our 15 year term, but wants the note paid off in 10 years. If the buyer agrees, then, he will make the usual monthly payments each month for 10 years, then, by prior agreement structured in a written contract, he will pay off the existing balance. If we apply our usual monthly payment on our standard example, then, the principal balance is reduced by $5,666.64 per year. Over 10 years, this amounts to $56,666.64 paid to principal, leaving a balance of approximately $28,333.36. This is the amount which the buyer agreed to pay at the expiration of 10 years.

In the usual situation, the buyer would either refinance his property to pay off the $28,333.36 balance, or pay it off from his savings. He could also sell his home and use some of the proceeds to pay it off, while using the remaining funds to purchase another property. If our homeowner does not want to take any of these approaches, then, there are other ways to handle the balloon payment due in 10 years. For instance, the buyer who becomes the homeowner could make a higher down payment, such as $20,000.00 to $25,000.00, as opposed to $15,000.00. This would immediately reduce the balance due in 10 years, as well as the monthly principal and interest amount. The buyer could also pay an additional $2,500.00 per year on the anniversary of the home's closing. Each approach or a combination of these approaches could either retire the balance due in 10 years, or significantly reduce the amount due.

The buyer may not be in a position or may not want to make a $15,000.00 down payment, but may want to make a $7,500.00 payment to which the seller could conditionally agree, provided the buyer pays an additional $2,500.00 towards the principal on the anniversary of the closing for three consecutive years. If both principal parties can agree to these terms, then, the transaction can be consummated to each party's benefit. If we have a willing seller and a willing buyer for a specific property, and each principal is prepared to be inventive, creative and work "outside of the box", with fair terms agreed upon by and acceptable to each party, then, a successful transaction can take place. The idea is to be open, reasonable and receptive to making the deal work and seriously listen and consider what the other party proposes. Rigidity and stubbornness will not work to anyone's benefit. Once a proposal has been made and considered, then, the other party's response with his terms can be tendered for consideration. The buyer's response may be his acceptance of some of the terms offered, and an offer or compromise on other terms. In this type of prospective purchase, where there is a will, there is a way. Unfortunately, this is not typically the case with most real estate transactions, banks, notes and mortgages. Little flexibility exists within standard, conventional approaches. In the alternative, much flexibility, good-faith negotiation, give and take, can and do exist in creative mortgage arrangements between two sincere, willing, capable principal parties. The bottom line here is that the principals make their own decisions and are not subject to the dictates of secondary and tertiary parties. This is a very refreshing change from the usual institutional approaches.

RETIREMENT PROGRAMS
AND ECONOMIC GAIN

Retirement for many Americans has been, is now and will likely continue to be a major cause of worry and concern in their lives. Many average Americans are very unsure how they will be able to live decently when they are no longer working and are dependent upon limited, fixed funds for their survival. For the past fifteen or so years, retirees have seen their expenses grow enormously, while their social security cost of living increases have been negligible or in some cases, non-existent. This does not bode well for a favorable financial future. Although some people have participated in pension savings plans, either privately, or through their places of work, many of these people fear that there will be insufficient, if any, funds available to them once they are ready to retire. Unfortunately, the fact that these pension funds are heavily invested in the stock market, and by and through the stock market, are heavily invested in the "derivatives" market, which, essentially, is a house of cards, then any tremors occurring in the economic sector can topple this flimsy house built on an unsteady foundation. Investments are based upon paperwork, which is based upon other paperwork, and the whole matter becomes rather confusing to the uninitiated. This is one reason why the managers of such retirement and pension funds keep things as they are. Obscurity gives them plausible deniability.

People believe that they will receive benefits from these retirement funds, whether they are pensions, 401ks, etc. Belief is something that is not necessarily factual and in most cases is nothing but fantasy, wishful thinking, promoted by some vested interest who will gain from the people's beliefs. Pension funds and retirement funds are operated by managers or coordinators or whoever is put in charge of these funds. Those in charge determine the policies of those funds, without input from the fund members, themselves. If there is any input at all, it is not binding input and has no effect upon the policies, objectives and direction of the pension or retirement funds.

In the past, there have been instances when people who were justly due pensions got nothing, close to nothing or much less than they expected, based upon the hype originally presented by the pension fund managers. Some companies that had pension funds borrowed from them at will, to the extent that there was nothing left for the pensioners. This is yet another example of the American people putting their implicit trust in some type of organization over which they have no input, no say and no control. Whenever any organization is set up which theoretically benefits the people, the people, themselves, must participate and control the managers of that organization, make certain that written criteria requires specific performance and be vigilant in holding the organization and its managers accountable and liable for their performance. Unfortunately, the American people do not do this, right across the board, and they certainly have not done it with government. There has been talk for some time now of the federal government taking over many, if not most or all, pension funds in this country. If people think that the pension funds are not working as promised under their current management, imagine what will happen if the government takes them over! If this happens, and it is looking more likely that it will happen, in part, because of the phony COVID-19 "pandemic" scam that has shut down the economy, then government could transfer all the pension funds into government bonds or some other type of government financial vehicle that will pay little to nothing compared to what was promised. This is only one possibility out of many and clearly establishes the fact that the people must protect themselves by and through their own actions and involvement in their own affairs.

What most people get from social security upon retirement is just barely enough to sustain them, if even that. Our nation seems far too interested in funding millions upon millions of welfare recipients, immigrants, both legal and illegal, coming into America from all over the world, instead of providing for the American people. Many of these immigrants have few, if any, marketable skills, education, training and resources to add to America's growth, wealth and well-being. Instead, the overwhelming majority of these people pose a severe drain upon America's resources and those of the people, and while the average American is getting shortchanged, the average immigrant is getting whatever he or she wants. This doesn't sound too "American" to us. If this trend continues, then, who knows what will be left for any American from social security in the not too distant future?

Retirement funds and pensions can be a supplement to social security because, as stated, social security is not enough for the average American. However, there is wide-scale concern about the validity and viability of these funds and whether these will be sufficient to make payments to retirees who have paid into the social security system all of their working lives. As many Americans have discovered the hard way, the "system" does not necessarily work for the average American, but, in fact, greatly favors the wealthy, the powerful and vested interests. There is also concern, as mentioned above, as to whether the government will intervene and actually take control of various now-private and corporate pension funds on some pretext invented by the government and those hidden hands who want to wipe out the wealth of the American people. A large percentage of the American population has come to understand that big government is not necessarily to be trusted, especially with one's retirement, when the retiree is in a very vulnerable position.

These matters may continue as they have for some time, with the usual ups and downs and concerns, on a status quo basis, or maybe they will not. Major power uses its power to force everyone under its control and power, especially when enormous sums of money are at stake. The trust factor in America for government, banking and vested interests is really at an all-time low, with good reason. It is entirely possible, as just stated, that the systems will roll along just as they have been. If that is the case, then, there may be no reason to worry about the safety of retirement and pension funds. However, for those who want to take control over their own retirement destinies, and not trust the system's approaches, it may behoove them to consider utilizing some of the straight-forward investment strategies spelled out within this book.

We have discussed different ways to buy, sell and invest in property, and at the end of CHAPTERs dedicated to these purposes, we provide a brief synopsis of how that particular transaction could be used as an investment, either small or large. Please review the pertinent CHAPTERS in SECTIONS FOUR and FIVE. These sections describe how investment programs can be utilized by the American people, beginning with modest amounts of funds to produce anything from modest comfortable gains to enormous, untold, fabulous wealth. You may be surprised to realize that modest investments, consistently invested over time, following the same formula, can produce amazing results. In the referenced prior CHAPTERs, we have described some of these, but the referenced SECTIONS will provide much more in-depth analysis.

The retirement programs of which we speak can be expressed in these two positions, namely, personal retirement accounts, based upon personal investments, and job-related retirement accounts, based upon job-related investments by workers and their job providers. The investment programs for either category can be exactly the same, but it is the *control* of that program that matters. One can either take personal control over a personal retirement program, started with private funds, or participate in a job-related program that encompasses many other contributors working for the job provider. Obviously, this is a personal choice, but if we were to consider such a choice, we would pick the personal retirement program, since we would have direct control and supervision over that program. A company retirement program is expected to produce the same results, based upon the same investment, but now the control moves from the workers into the hands of the management group handling the investment funds as a fiduciary for the workers. Unless the retirement program is structured differently, neither the workers nor the companies for which they work have control over the invested funds.

Great advantages can accrue from either type of investment. As we said earlier, a great majority of retirement funds are vested in the stock market and other markets, including speculative markets. In other words, the retirement and pension funds are going into paper, and paper is only "paper" unless it is actually, in fact, supported by the *value* which that paper claims to represent. Unfortunately, many of us have found out, the hard way, that this is not necessarily the case. We propose a position that some companies might consider so that the funds invested will be invested in real assets with marketable value, such as property that will produce real results over time, whether that time be of short or long duration. Tangible assets, with present market value, from our position, are much more valuable in the present and in the future, rather than speculative paper that may or may not have value in the future.

One way for smaller companies to build healthy retirement programs for their workers is to create a business investment in real estate that will grow in value over time, therefore, providing real retirement funds based in hard assets, and not paper, not the markets, not private vested interests and not speculation The management of this private retirement fund is placed equally in the hands of both the company management and the company workers, under written contract agreed to by both parties. The various *ByPass* Investment Programs are spelled out, in detail, in SECTIONS EIGHT and NINE of this book. These Programs are buy/sell programs and buy/rent/sell Programs. The *ByPass* buy/sell Program requires a small initial investment that can produce enormous returns over a three or four year period. The buy/rent /sell Programs require a $600,000 investment that over twenty years can produce vast wealth. All *ByPass* Programs are based in hard real estate assets with marketable values owned by the workers and operated jointly by the company and its workers. Assets are not in paper, or in questionable markets, operated and controlled by others with questionable fiduciary relationship with the workers. The *ByPass* Programs put the control where it should belong – jointly in the hands of the principals, namely, the company and its workers. This requires responsibility by both parties. Responsible people do not give their invaluable retirement future funds to others who may or may not take that responsibility and fiduciary requirements seriously.

If a company were to establish such a private retirement fund for its workers and gain great economic success, then it is highly likely that other companies and their workers would hear of that success, and may possibly want to establish their own private retirement fund in the same manner with the same type of investments. In this way, the retirement funds are directly and jointly managed by the company and its workers, not by some outside management group, and all investments are made in hard asset, marketable real estate properties. Success breeds success, so other companies may want to set up their own retirement funds, or possibly, join with companies that have already done so. It could be possible to establish a mutual retirement fund participated in by many different companies. This type of retirement program does not exist now, but it may in the very near future.

If companies were to so engage, they may find so much success within the various *ByPass* Programs that some may want to establish a subsidiary that invests in the *ByPass* Programs. Operated professionally and correctly, sticking with the models and projections, the returns within the *ByPass* Programs can be so staggering that whatever profit the company has reached, it will likely be enormously surpassed by the *ByPass* Programs. If this were to happen, then those companies would not only secure safe investments and retirements for their workers, but also provide a great social benefit to the people living in the investment areas. As we have said many times, there are likely millions of people who cannot qualify for home financing, so the *ByPass* Programs, through companies and investors, can make possible for them what was not possible before. While this may not have been the intention of the companies, their participation would provide an enormous social benefit to the American people. This would be great publicity, and put the company in a caring position. If a company were investing in a buy/rent/sell program, that company could also offer the rental, or sale, to their workers. Many realistic possibilities exist, but, again, it takes innovation, creativity, commitment, and going against the systems' flow.

CHAPTER FIFTY ONE

PURCHASE HOMES FOR INVESTMENT

In Sections THREE and FOUR of this book, we discussed various ways in which people could buy family homes. As you can see, there are different methods by which this can be done, all without the need for obtaining new bank financing. At the end of the relevant CHAPTER, we also presented methods that are safe, sound, based in common sense that an average person could use to create an investment portfolio. In this CHAPTER, we will present an advanced program that could suit the needs of any person or group that wants to create a large portfolio and amass great wealth in the process. As you have seen throughout this book, none of our programs require any investor to obtain new bank financing. This fact in itself should be a boon to the innovative investor or any investment group. Throughout this book, we have enumerated how banks can be extremely intrusive, at times dictatorial, lay down many demands, require too many procedures, advance extra fees and be very problematic to the success of any investor. Of course, this is not true in every situation across the board, but most people who have dealt with banks in any significant investment capacity can readily understand the positions we have stated here.

When people deal in money matters, especially in buying, selling, financing and investing, then they might want to become more aware of the difference between bank money and funds earned by private people through their work, skills, ideas, input and production within the general economy. Essentially, banks lend money upon the signatures of borrowers. These borrower contracts are bundled and presented to the Federal Reserve for funding. The Federal Reserve can *lend* the banks the full bundled amount or multiples of those amounts. In other words, the lending bank does not use its own funds or deposit funds to make the loans to the various borrowers, but in fact borrows the face amount of these loans, plus, from the Federal Reserve. The further position is the fact that the loans are invoked or activated by and through the signatures of the borrowers.

The salient fact that the lending bank did not use its own funds to make the loans, but borrowed funds to do so, then requires substantial collateral in case the borrowers were to default, puts the borrowers at an immediate disadvantage, when it is their signatures that allow the banks to operate. If this lending/borrowing approach or methodology were used in other business transactions across the board in virtually all transactions, then there would be massive pandemonium throughout the economy.

When private parties lend funds or make investments, the funds they use to do so have been earned by those private parties by and through their working within the economic structure to receive those funds. Therefore, those funds have "value" because they were earned through some type of real enterprise or labor. The funds are not just digits on a computer screen, because the funds have inherent value. When funds are loaned by a bank, those funds were just created by the Fed as new "money" and have not been earned by anyone through any working enterprise or production within the economy. The funds are just slips of paper or figures on a computer screen and have no real value except the value created by and through the use of those funds in some form of real economic activity. Knowledge is always valuable, and it would be in the best interests of the American people for them to know about the nature of "their money", which is really not theirs at all, because it is private money, called a note, owned by and payable, plus interest, to the Federal Reserve Bank, a private, for-profit, debt-based central bank unlawfully given carte blanche over the American monetary unit and economy by the U.S. government that constantly deceives and defrauds the American people.

CHAPTER FIFTY TWO

ALTERNATIVE METHOD TO CARRYING
THE SECOND MORTGAGE

When people are buying and selling houses through the *ByPass* Buy/Sell Program, the reason the seller-investor wants to maintain a second mortgage is to have a **secured interest** in the property. This secured interest allows the second mortgage holder to take over the property should his buyer default. This allows the noteholder, who is also the seller-investor, to keep his commitment to his *original* seller and maintain the standard monthly payment schedule without interruption. The noteholder can then sell the house again, lease it again, or do whatever he wants, but the second mortgage position allows him to keep the original seller's interests safe and secure, thereby maintaining the seller-investor's original commitment.

In all of our second mortgage situations, the face amount of the second mortgage is held for the note term, in most cases 15 years. The holder of the second mortgage receives ten percent (10) % of the face amount each year, and in 15 years collects the principal balance. If our seller-investor has bought and sold other properties over those 15 years, then it is likely that he holds many second mortgages, all of which could be a nice windfall for him when their principal balances are paid to him after the 15 year term expires.

There is another way to maintain a security interest in the property without the need for a second mortgage. If our seller-investor were to sell the property, on a contract of sale or contract for deed basis, then the seller-investor retains the deed to the property until the last payment is made, pursuant to the terms of the contract. Then, lawful title and deed is given to the buyer. If our seller-investor were to employ this method, then he does not need a second mortgage position. This allows the seller-investor to receive the entire amount of the down payment at closing, which increases his immediate profit right away. However, depending upon the buyer's capability, he may or may not be able to pay the entire down payment amount at closing. In such a situation, if the buyer is unable to come up with the entire down payment amount, our seller-investor could make a paragraph in the note that calls for the buyer to pay the additional remaining down payment-amount over 18 months, via mutually agreed upon terms. At the conclusion of the 18 month period, the monthly note amount reverts to the regular monthly amount. In this way, the seller-investor still maintains a security interest in the property, for the benefit of his original seller and, further, does not have to wait 15 years to collect the entire down payment amount pursuant to the second mortgage. He would either receive that entire down payment as a cash amount at closing or receive it in cash installments over a period of 18 or so months. Better ways always exist to meet the needs of principals, and as long as the principals deal directly and ethically, any price situation can be resolved to the mutual benefit of both buyer and seller.

REAL ESTATE & OTHER SWAPS & TRADES PROGRAMS

INTRODUCTION TO
REAL ESTATE SWAPS AND TRADES

Various institutional systems which operate within our society primarily benefit only those systems, and not necessarily the people who do business with or are clients of the institutions. Institutional systems, such as banking, rely upon people to function. Without people who make deposits into banks, both personal and commercial, and without people, corporations and businesses to whom banks make "loans", banks would go out of business. It is pretty obvious to ascertain that, without customers and clients who purchase the goods and services of the bank, corporation, etc., those institutional entities would soon cease to exist. Over the past dozen or more years, we have seen this play out in the retail economy with the closing of vast amounts of department and merchandise stores, as well as a goodly number of banks which have closed or have been bought up by larger banks. When people do not service a business, then, obviously, that business cannot remain viable and must eventually shut its doors.

People and businesses within society feed the banks, and the banks handsomely profit from "loans" they make to their customers. Both sides in this arrangement *should* benefit equally, but this is not how banking and most other institutional systems operate. In such dealings, the major benefit typically accrues to the institution, which establishes all contractual terms in favor of itself, while the customer or client, who makes it possible for the bank to operate and profit, bears all the responsibility and financial liability.

This brief overview accounts for how most, if not, all institutional systems operate in America. The client or customer, whose funds and loans keep the bank profitable, essentially takes all the risk by signing a one-sided, adhesion contract with the bank. This type of one-sided contract, with the governing terms established by one party, namely, the bank, places all of the responsibility and liability for the contract upon the other party, namely, the client or customer. There is nothing at all fair or just about this type of one-sided arrangement. A legitimate contract is one entered into *equally* by and between two or more parties, with terms equally established by those parties, and not a contract with terms imposed only by the stronger party, the bank, upon the weaker party, the bank's client(s) or customer(s). It would be fairer and more just for two parties to equally establish contractual terms, rather than one party imposing its one-sided biased terms upon the other party, essentially telling its client or customer to take it or leave it! See CHAPTER FIFTY TWO in SECTION FIVE that basically explains the difference between funds "loaned" from a bank and funds earned by private parties. There is a major difference between these funds and anyone who borrows from a bank should know this difference. This book demonstrates how this inequality can be corrected in the buying, financing and selling of real estate, of any type. As we continuously say, there is always a better way to do almost anything, if open-minded, creative, serious, out-of-the-box people seek that better way.

In a real estate transaction, the ability of the buyer and seller to enter into their own contract with terms written by both buyer and seller, and not a bank attorney or system's broker, would be a major advantage to both buying and selling principals. In this situation, the usual voluminous contract, consisting of many pages, small print, lots of legalese, distracting and confusing language, is no longer present. Obviously, this would greatly simply the process for both the buying and the selling principals. It would be a real advantage to both buyer and seller if they control their own financial terms, conditions, contracts, purchases, investments and fates, rather than placing these very important objectives in the hands of a third party institution, that is operating for profit and has no concern for the well-being of the clients. As the primary principals, not dependent upon or beholden to other parties, who exert control over the process and then relegate the buying and selling principals to secondary or tertiary status, in the *ByPass* methods, the principals are the ones in charge. As many of you know, freedom is not free. If people truly want freedom and independence in their lives, then, they must work to attain them, because they will not come to them automatically.

When buyers and sellers form their own contract, with their own terms, this certainly establishes a solid position of freedom and independence for them, in contrast to the usual "in the box" transaction. Obviously, this position is much stronger and enormously more favorable to the buying and selling principals than would be the imposed contractual agreement presented to them by a non-principal secondary or tertiary party, such as a bank. The one sidedness of that contract in favor of the bank, or the lender, pales in comparison. While there most likely will initially be differences in terms and objectives on the part of the buyers and the sellers, they, themselves, can work out terms satisfactory to both parties, which is far better than having unacceptable terms imposed upon them by the bank or lender, despite their objections. Such an arrangement by a third party is certainly not fair, not just, and opposes the concept of self-reliance, independence and freedom, thereby obliterates the people's rights to contract secured for them in our Constitution.

Many Americans regularly deal with banks, mortgage corporations, credit card corporations, other lenders, merchants, etc. These entities present their contracts, with their terms, to their customers and clients, then, demand that their clients sign the contracts, and usually do so in such a way that stops comments, questions or objections from the client or customer. The position presented to the clients or customers is that they have no choice, whatsoever. They either sign the contract, as presented, or they are prohibited from entering into and completing the transaction.

As mentioned, all banks, corporations, companies, businesses, etc. fully and completely depend upon their customer base to stay in business. Without the customer base, these entities would go out of business. This is an important fact which most people have not considered, but an increasing percentage of people is considering now. Customers should recognize the fact that a company's customer base pays for all costs and expenses borne by that company, such as goods, services, labor, overhead, merchandise, property, advertising, profit, insurance, pension funds, vacations, medical and other benefits and bonuses. Without the customer base, there would be no bank or no corporation. At one time in America, the customer was "always right", given respect and treated fairly. That concept and policy has long since passed away among banks, major corporations and many businesses in the era of profiteering corporatization. The new position is: "It is either our way, or the highway." If people would truly consider and seriously think about these positions imposed by system's institutions, in comparison to the self-reliance and freedom inherent within writing one's own contracts, they would see an entire world of difference and the myriad possibilities open to them in that different world.

Further, the self-respect, self-reliance and confidence people gain when they take responsibility for their own contracts, financing arrangements, purchases, etc. are invaluable and add a great deal of satisfaction to their lives. When people do a good job, especially for themselves, not only in reaching their objectives, but also in formulating, writing and completing the methods by which they reach those objectives, their self-worth and confidence increase and establish a foundation of credibility for other ventures or matters in the future. For some people, doing what everyone else does is okay, but being independent, resourceful and successfully accomplishing one's own intent or bottom-line objective truly gives one a feeling of genuine accomplishment, advancement and freedom. For most people who deal with closed systems and established procedures, accomplishing their objectives independently, outside of those systems, can be extremely rewarding on many levels. The sense and fact of accomplishment can be immediately felt and realized. Rather than having gone through the usual system's approaches, with the usual system's institutions, the independent free thinkers reach their goals by and through their own methods and efforts.

In this SECTION, we speak of equal value, home-to-home swaps between two principals. This is different from the usual way of buying and selling property, because we are dealing specifically with swapping properties. In the traditional way, the owners of both properties would have to place their properties on the market, either as "for sale by owner" or with real estate brokers. Depending upon market conditions, the sale can take longer than expected, and in a down market, the sale can take *much* longer than expected, if it takes place at all. The seller who engages a real estate broker is typically required to pay a commission of anywhere from 5 to 7 percent, or more, though some brokers will discount this fee a bit. Since the owner wants to sell his home to buy another home, then, while his home is on the market, the owner usually tries to find another home to buy in the specific area he wants. All of this, obviously, will take time and effort, and even when the owner finds his ideal next home, he still has to sell his present home before he can buy the new one he likes. Complications can arise here, in part, since the owner of the new home may not want to contract to sell his property until the buyer can first sell his existing property. If the original owner is selling to a buyer who needs to arrange a loan in order to purchase the property, many times banks impose conditions that cannot be met and the transaction can fall apart. At other times, the house inspector for the new buyer may cite conditions existent in the home that need repairs and the buyer will not proceed until they are remedied. The seller may not be in a position to make repairs, so, again, the transaction could fall apart. Even when our original seller can sell to a buyer, without complications, when he purchases his new home, the price he pays makes allowance for the real estate commission which the seller owes to the real estate broker. Essentially, our owner has paid two commissions, one on the sale of his existing home, and another through the purchase of his new home. The following CHAPTER describes swaps and trades of real estate which may be suitable for many parties.

CHAPTER FIFTY FOUR

BYPASS REAL ESTATE SWAPS
AND TRADES PROGRAM

Real Estate Swap

In our example, two parties want to swap their free-and-clear, equally-valued homes. That trade, swap or barter can take place very quickly and without the complications, time delays, disappointments and costs referred to in the previous CHAPTER. To conduct such a trade, each party signs over the deed to his respective house to the other party, at the same time, during the closing. Each party would have entered into a contract so stating, with terms drawn up and agreed to by each party. There is nothing complicated about this. The buyer and seller write their own contract, specifying their own terms, and consummate the closing in the office of a local title insurance company. This keeps closing costs to a minimum and virtually eliminates all other expenses usually associated with a typical real estate purchase and sale transaction.

Let us say that a fellow who lives in Portland, Maine wants to move to Tampa, Florida, for whatever reason. Maybe he doesn't like the cold, the snow, the ice and long winters in Maine, while he yearns for the South, the warmth of Tampa and the closeness to a warm ocean. Possibly, the company for which he works just transferred him to Tampa or he may have family there or want to retire to Tampa. Maybe he wants to move to Tampa because he's a huge fan of Tom Brady, the new Tampa Bay Buccaneers' quarterback. There are numerous reasons why people move, and in America, people are on the move quite a bit. We have mentioned that the average family remains in a home for about five years and then moves on to another home, many times in a different state. If our Portland home owner wants to sell his home and then find another home of equal value in Tampa, under the typical scenario he would have to go through all the usual procedures mentioned in the previous CHAPTER. However, there is another way, much easier, less complicated, without a lot of time wasted and expenses incurred. Our Portland owner owns his house free and clear, with no notes, liens, mortgages or encumbrances of any kind and has maintained it well. He wants to buy a comparable home of the same value in Tampa.

There is a homeowner in Tampa whose home is valued at $100,000.00 and it is also free and clear of any mortgages, liens or debts. For whatever reason, this homeowner wants to move to the Portland, Maine area and purchase a comparable home of equal value there. In this scenario, it would be extremely beneficial for both the Portland owner and the Tampa owner to somehow contact each other and discuss the possibility of exchanging homes. If the parties could find each other and each investigate the suitability of the other's home, then, each party could clearly understand that it would be far better and far quicker to simply trade homes than to go into the usual buying and selling routine. This can be accomplished pretty much as follows. Each buyer makes a visit to see the other's property and each buyer likes what he sees and agrees that the homes are of equal value, since each property has similar features, in similar condition and an appraisal for $100,000.00. Each buyer hires a professional home inspector to give a report on the desired property and each report is highly acceptable. These steps accomplished, both owners can enter into a contract in which they agree to trade their homes. Each owner is assured through proper title searches on each respective property, that each property is free and clear of all debts, and that a clear, clean title and title insurance guarantee will be presented to each buyer by the reputable title company where the home exchange will take place, either in Tampa or in Portland as best suits the principals.

With today's Internet, communication can be immediate and people can virtually search for properties and people willing to swap properties via the Internet. Various real estate sites exist in which people can place ads or requests for whatever they want. This makes the whole search process a lot easier and much more specific.

Swap of Homes of Differing Values

This type of house swap, barter, trade or exchange—whatever term you care to use—is a quick, efficient, effective and dynamic way to exchange properties in two different states or within the same state. This is a new concept that can replace the old time-consuming, expensive way of buying and selling. Two parties may want to swap their free and clear homes, but one home is valued at $125,000.00, while the other is valued at $100,000.00, both values determined by valid professional appraisals. This slight potential impasse can be quickly resolved if both parties want to swap homes, while creating equal value in the process. Equal value is what we call a "zero balance transaction". Home A is worth $100,000.00, while Home B is worth $125,000.00. In order to equalize values, so that a zero balance trade can take place, the owner of Home A is willing to give a promissory note in the amount of $25,000.00 to the owner of Home B. A note of $25,000.00 is executed along with a mortgage in that amount to secure the note. This equalizes the value of the homes traded. Terms and conditions of the note and mortgage are arranged directly between the principal parties in the manner that best suits them.

This approach is highly beneficial to consummating the transaction and far better for the owner of Home A than to require him to get a bank loan so that he can pay the differential of $25,000.00 to the owner of Home B.

House Swap with Existing Mortgage

In another scenario, two owners want to swap homes of equal value, but there is an existing mortgage on one or both of the properties. Both homes are appraised at $100,000.00, but one has an existing note of $20,000.00 and a mortgage on the home to secure the note. In CHAPTER THIRTY ONE, which discusses the sale and purchase of property with existing notes and mortgages, we explained how sales could take place. Those same conditions apply to homes with owners who want to swap, with either one, or even both homes having mortgages. We shall provide a brief example here.

A zero balance transaction is entirely necessary to provide equal value to both parties. In this particular case, both homes are valued and appraised for $100,000.00, each, but Home B is mortgaged and has a note of $20,000.00, while Home A is free and clear. If the bank holding the note on Home B allows the owner of Home A to assume the $20,000.00 note, then, the swap could take place, and the owner of Home B makes a note of $20,000.00 payable to the owner of Home A. This arrangement provides equal value to both parties and constitutes a zero balance transaction. If the bank does not allow the assumption of the note, then, the conditions spelled out in CHAPTER THIRTY ONE can explain how the transaction could take place. Briefly, in this situation, when the closing takes place, the owner of Home A, by written contract, assumes the <u>obligation</u> of the note on Home B, but not the note, and the owner of Home B makes a loan in the amount of that obligation to the owner of Home A. The exchange takes place and each principal party has achieved his goal, with simplicity, ease and satisfaction. There are many more ways to do business than the standard, run of the mill corporate-institutional way. The American people must begin to think outside of the institutional box and then act upon that thought by putting it into action.

CHAPTER FIFTY FIVE

EQUAL VALUE AND ZERO BALANCE
FURTHER EXPLAINED

Equal Value

Equal value occurs when items of equal monetary value are exchanged or traded between two parties. The homes, products or merchandise exchanged do not have to be of the same exact monetary value, but the exchange transaction between the parties must be of equal monetary value. This will be more fully explained in the "Zero Balance" section below.

When two parties swap their homes, equal value must exist on each side, so that each party receives an equivalent *value* with the swap. For instance, if Party A has a home with a market value of and appraised at $100,000.00, and Party B has a home with a market value of and appraised at $100,000.00, and each home is free and clear, without debt, when the parties swap homes, each party would receive equal value. Whenever any party swaps anything with another party, the items that are swapped between the parties must have equal monetary value. If one fellow swaps his boat, with a market value of and appraised for $25,000.00, for a piece of land, with a market value of and appraised for $25,000.00, then, this is an equal value swap. If another fellow swaps his truck, with a market value of $10,000.00, for a car, with a market value of $10,000.00, then, this is also an equal value swap. Whatever is swapped by either party must have equal value.

The easiest exchange among parties is when the items exchanged have the same monetary value, but exchanges or swaps can also take place with properties of unequal value. However, in these transactions, we go beyond the equal value position to a "zero balance" position, which is explained below. In an equal value transaction or swap, those properties which are swapped are of equal monetary value; therefore, there is a zero balance transaction, since neither property has more or less value than the other. Each property is equal. No plusses or minuses exist on either side.

Zero Balance

If Party A wants to swap his home, with a market value and appraisal of $100,000.00, for another home, owned by Party B, with a market value and appraisal of $125,000.00, this would not be an equal value swap because there is a value difference of $25,000.00. In order to effectuate this transaction, Party B agrees to swap his home for the one owned by Party A, but since B's home is worth $125,000.00, he does not want to lose $25,000.00 in value, when he makes a swap for a home worth $100,000.00. To facilitate the swap, Party A agrees to sign a note to Party B in the amount of $25,000.00, secured by a mortgage on his new home, formerly owned by Party B. This $25,000.00 note from Party A to Party B compensates for the difference in value of $25,000.00 and brings the transaction into zero balance, with no credits or debits for either party. Both parties obtain the homes they want and the differential in the values of the homes is resolved by the promissory note and mortgage from Party A to Party B. While both homes were valued differently, the note from Party A to Party B made this a zero balance transaction. Whenever what is exchanged is of different monetary value, the transaction can be brought to zero balance by one party writing a note to the other party to compensate for the difference, or another property, such as a car, truck, boat, etc., with a value of $25,000.00, can be included in the exchange to equalize value.

CHAPTER FIFTY SIX

SENIOR SWAPS WITH NOTE ANNUITY

America's "baby boomer" generation is either fast approaching or already in the "elder generation". Most of these people have worked hard all their lives, from the time they were youngsters, and now it is time to retire, lighten their loads and take life easy. A lot of these folks own large homes, because many of them raised large families, but now their grown children and their grandchildren live elsewhere and the home is much too large for the now-elderly or approaching- elderly couple. Too many rooms, too much upkeep, too many repairs, too much land to maintain, too many expenses, etc. are pressing incentives for the elderly couple to downsize and simplify their lives.

Let us take an example of an elderly retired couple that owns a home with a current market value and appraisal of $400,000.00. The home is paid off, free and clear, with no debt. Both the husband and wife mutually agree that they need a smaller home, so they discuss the realistic possibility of putting their home on the market and what this would entail. They could either try to sell the house on their own, or engage a real estate broker. In either situation, depending upon the local economy and the real estate market in their area, this could take some time. Further, if prospective buyers need to obtain a mortgage to buy the property, which in the case of a $400,000.00 home, they likely would, both the elderly couple who want to sell and the buying couple can expect the usual bank complications, requirements, delays and expenses. When and if the house is eventually sold, if the sellers used a broker, the elderly couple can expect to pay a real estate commission of anywhere from 5 to 7 percent, which in this case could amount to as much as $28,000.00. In addition, the usual system's bank closing and attorneys' fees can mean considerable additional expense to both the selling couple and the buying couple.

While the elderly couple is in the process of trying to sell their home, they are also in the process of looking for a smaller home to purchase. If the older couple is successful in finding a suitable smaller home, then, incorporated within the purchase price of that smaller home is another real estate commission that the sellers of this home must pay to their real estate broker. Sometimes a home sale cannot take place until the seller of the home has made arrangements to buy another home, which, of course, can hold up and delay closings. All of these factors and many more can be problematic issues in these types of typical system's real estate transactions. Further, when the elderly couple receives the $400,000.00 for their home, they could be assessed with a large tax liability because the home was originally purchased for a much lesser amount.

Instead of the above scenario, would it not be better and easier for the elderly couple to find a smaller home they like, which is currently owned by a younger couple who want to purchase a much larger home, in the $400,000.00 range, to accommodate their growing family's needs? The younger couple also owns their home free and clear. If these couples were to encounter one another and each sees the other's home, which homes are very much to their liking, then, it might be highly advisable for the older couple to swap their home for the younger couple's home.

Since the younger couple's home has a market value and appraisal of $150,000.00, then there is a difference of $250,000.00 between the values of the homes. If the younger couple were to purchase, instead of swap for, a $400,000.00 home, then, that couple would have to deal with a bank, apply for a loan, jump through the usual hoops and complications, and bear large expenses throughout the transaction, until the property is finally purchased. However, with the swap of the two homes, the older couple could accept a note from the younger couple in the amount of $250,000.00, secured by a mortgage on the younger couple's new home, which, of course, is the elderly couple's former home. In this example, there is no need for separate closings, high brokers' fees, bank complications, excessive closing costs and legal fees.

This swap can be a very simple, easy transaction, with a written contract entered into by and between each set of principal parties, with mutually acceptable terms spelled out in the contract. There would be only one closing that can take place in the office of the title company providing title searches and title insurance to both parties, in which Party A, the elderly couple, signs over the deed to their home to Party B, the younger couple, and at the same time, Party B signs over the deed to their home to Party A, along with a note in the amount of $250,000.00, secured by a mortgage with terms previously decided upon by and agreeable to both parties. In this swap, there are two homes of unequal value, but because the note equalizes the value, this is a zero balance transaction in which both parties get exactly what they want.

The additional benefit for the elderly couple here is that not only do they get their smaller, less demanding home, but they also will receive monthly principal and interest payments, over the next 15 or so years. These monthly payments can be considerable and can pay for many, if not all, of the monthly expenses incurred by the elderly couple. Of course, since the senior couple, now, have a much smaller home, then, the expenses for the home will be considerably less than those for their former home. Another very important consideration is the vastly decreased tax burden, if any burden exists at all. Keep in mind that this transaction is not a sale, but an exchange of property for equal value. In equal value transactions, there is no gain, just a simple exchange of one object for another of equal value. Thus, equal value exchanges should incur no tax burden at all, and if any is incurred, payments received over 15 years should dramatically decrease that burden. If anything, the only thing that may be "taxable" would be the interest received on the note. In this way, the seniors would be able to successfully downsize as well as create an annuity that will pay them a considerable amount over the next 15 years.

CHAPTER FIFTY SEVEN

SWAPS AND TRADES EXPANDED

In the early history of mankind, in virtually all societies throughout the world, no concept, such as "money", existed. People bartered for everything they wanted or needed by trading goods, services, skills and the products thereof for other goods, services, skills and products of equal value. Everyone was satisfied with these barters, and trades took place as a normal course of life and business. The baker would trade his goods for wheat, corn, turnips or whatever he wanted or needed, while the farmers who supplied the baker would trade for sheep, cattle, dairy products, etc., and those suppliers would trade with other suppliers on an equal value basis. Everyone was happy with the arrangement and no one was left out, because all people participated based upon what they could bring to the table in a skill, craft, product, service, knack or something else of value to others. Money did not enter into the picture until sometime later, when it was introduced by and through goldsmiths, vested interests and government. Eventually, money virtually killed trading and barter, especially in the cities, so that only a very small part remains of what was once a flourishing practice, largely without deception.

Today, in our modern-day society, very little barter takes place and much of this is among young kids who trade baseball and football cards, a catcher's mitt for a first baseman's glove, a bike for a scooter, or something along these lines. College girls may trade dresses, outfits or shoes, and the guys may trade athletic equipment, music, games or cars, but that is about the extent of it. The trading that routinely took place in bygone days is almost non-existent now, because people use money and plastic in the normal course of their lives and businesses to purchase what they want and need. In the early part of this book, we discussed how money was brought into society, by whom, for what purpose, and how the controllers of money control the society in virtually all aspects.   This exclusive reliance upon money for the acquisition of goods, skills and services has proven to be a detriment to most people and businesses, but a huge boon to banks, other lenders, governments and, of course the power forces, which has imposed severe hardships and limitations upon the average people.   When entire societies are dependent upon money, simply to exist, then, we, as a society, might want to question how we view money and whom that money really serves.

In earlier times, people were closer to the land and to each other. They lived simply, but fully, made their own choices about how and where they lived, what they did, what they acquired and with whom they traded and did business. People back then recognized the value of independence, but they also understood that their common attributes, qualities and needs required common-sense *interdependence*, if they were to survive and thrive. They were self-reliant, yet willing to work together for common purpose. In today's world, people have become distant from one another, and instead of dealing directly with each other, have given away their right to trade, swap, barter and contract with one another to the dictates of middlemen, bankers, market makers and "experts" whose interference, impositions and profiteering have made most people's lives much too complicated, difficult and debt ridden. These conditions do not have to persist, if people begin to recognize their own inherent power to trade, barter and swap, as they see fit, and make their own choices in how and where they live. This is not rocket science; it is good old fashioned common sense and simplicity. The ability to acquire what one needs or wants, without complications and excessive costs and fees, makes a great deal of sense in any era, and it is way past time for Americans to realize this and reclaim their power.

While the idea of trading, bartering and swapping is no longer in the consciousness of most people, this practice could become alive and well in America, again, if people see the wisdom and merit in it and begin to practice it in earnest. In CHAPTER FIFTY FIVE, we discussed how swaps and trades could take place in real estate, wherein property is wholly owned without debt, or with properties that carry debt. As we discussed in that CHAPTER, two principal parties are dealing directly with each other, with no brokers involved, no brokerage fees required, no bank financing involved, thus, no bank restrictions and no bank fees, and without cost to either party. No money exchanges hands here, because the parties are swapping or trading property of equal value. No one has to reach into his pocket or obtain a loan to acquire what he wants. Instead, s/he simply trades something of equal value that the other principal party wants, while that other party trades something of similar or equal value that the first party wants.

In that referenced CHAPTER, we also demonstrated how properties of unequal value could still be traded, without the need for bank financing, by the use of a note from one party to another, which note brings the trade into equal value or zero balance. This concept is something that has rarely, if ever, been considered before in modern day America, and is certainly not part of any institutional program. However, if this simple concept were to be understood by people, it could become a major means by which property is acquired in this country. When the complications are taken out of such transactions, because the principals deal directly with each other, and, as mentioned above, they are free of all the middlemen described above, then, this is a very desirable way to acquire what one wants or needs. The real salient position beyond this is that no one has to expend any funds out of pocket to obtain what he wants or needs. The same application can be used to acquire virtually anything in this country, provided the parties are willing, act in good faith, are fair, just, honest, capable, and trade or exchange in equal value.

For instance, if one party has a truck worth $10,000.00, he can trade that for a lot of land worth $10,000.00. If one wants to trade a boat worth $40,000.00 for a classic Lincoln worth $40,000.00, this can be done. Someone might want to trade a small office building worth $500,000.00 for a small apartment building of equal value. All of these trades can be done without any money exchanging hands, as was done "back in the day". A vast number of items, services, skills, crafts, etc. can be traded by people, either with equal value, or unequal value. What we have presented above are trades of equal value. In the paragraphs below, we shall give examples of unequal value trades and show how to equalize their value.

All of the types of trades listed above have three characteristics in common: (1) each party wants the other party's property or service and each is willing to trade for it; (2) the property of each party is free of debt and liens; (3) the value of each property is the same. When such a trade occurs between principals, then, an even trade or equal balance trade takes place. In other situations, principals would like to trade, but own properties of unequal value, and could do so, provided the values could be equalized to accommodate the trade. For example, one principal has an antique automobile collection worth $2,500,000.00, without any debt on it. Another principal would like to own this collection and is willing to trade for it. He owns an excellent beach house, free and clear, in an exclusive area with a value of $2,200,000.00 and offers this to the antique car collector. The antique car collector is willing to trade his collection for the beach house, but there is a $300,000.00 differential in value which he, of course, does not want to lose. If the owner of the beach house were to trade his property and give a note of $300,000.00 to the antique car collector, secured by a mortgage, on terms the principals arrange themselves, then, an even trade or zero balance trade can take place. This premise covers possibilities that can include almost all goods and services, whether they are of equal value or unequal value. The note and mortgage position can balance and equalize the value of any trade. All that is necessary to accomplish this are two willing, capable, honorable parties, and the security for the party who receives the note is the property that is secured by the note.

When debt is present on items of trade, trade can still occur by each principal assuming the other principal's debt *obligation* and making adjustments to reach a zero balance or equal value trade through executing notes and mortgages. An example of this could be the following. The first principal owns a thoroughbred horse farm with a value of $10,000,000 which has a current bank loan balance of $3,000,000.00. Another party owns an office building in the same area which has a value of $8,500,000.00 with a current bank debt of $2,000,000. The building's owner wants to trade his building for the horse farm. If we subtract the $3,000,000 debt on the horse farm, from the $10,000,000.00 value, the horse farm owner has equity value of $7,000,000. Since the office building is worth $8,500,000, with $2,000,000 in debt, the building owner has equity value of $6,500,000 in his building.

The principals discuss terms and draw up a contract which contains their mutually agreed-upon terms of the swap. The horse farm owner assumes the *obligation* for the building owner's $2,000,000.00 debt, while the owner of the building assumes the $3,000,000.00 debt of the owner of the horse farm. Since there is a difference of $500,000 in equity between the horse farm equity value of $7,000,000.00 and the building equity value of $6,500,000.00, the owner of the building gives a $500,000.00 note and mortgage to the horse farm owner, which brings the trade to an equal value or zero balance trade. The mortgage is filed against the horse farm, now owned by the former building owner. Should the former building owner, now the new horse farm owner, default on the mortgage, then the new building owner can foreclose and retake his former property. The former building owner can also place a note and mortgage upon his former building to assure that his debt obligation to the bank, assumed by the new owner, gets paid on a timely basis. A secured note arranged by and between two capable, honorable principals, any type of trade transaction involving products, real estate, property, land, items, goods, services, etc. can take place among willing participants.

In the early days of trade, barter and swaps, what was traded was not restricted to items traded among individuals, only. Products and items worth much more than those traded by individuals were routinely traded. One man may have 10 wagon loads of oats that he wanted to trade for 5 wagon loads of pigs. Another might have 100 head of horses he might want to trade for 75 head of cattle. Trading was expansive and was part of commercial exchanges, thus, encompassed many different items, products and services. In the same vein as those days, trading involving major commercial products could also take place today, without the use of brokers, middlemen, bank financing and/or out of pocket money spent by principals. This type of trading does not exist anymore in America, but does take place in various third world and undeveloped countries. However, this type of trading could come back to America, if those who desire the trade understand the simplicity involved and the ease with which such trades could be accomplished, then decide to do so.

Just as one willing principal could trade a signature office building in a major city that is worth $200,000,000.00 for a manufacturing company of the same value, trades in other large- ticket commodities can take place. As stated, this is not part of business-as-usual in America at this time, but there is no good reason why this type of trade could not be part of business in America. For instance, a million barrels of crude oil that meet certain specifications could be traded for agricultural products, livestock or other manufactured products for equal value to that of the million barrels of oil. At present, this does not seem possible, because business is conditioned to working within the money-driven control of the economic, banking and governmental systems. However, shifts may take place in the society by which, in the near future, trades of this nature could reemerge and become commonplace. In the current marketplace, if a corporation were to contract to sell a million barrels of oil, that corporation would likely enlist the services of brokers, other middlemen and bankers, as well as bear transport costs in order to do so. All of these costs can be considerable for such a transaction, take away from the profit, and, of course, there will be a tax on the profit. If the astute businessman were to realize that he could trade that oil for other products of similar value, and the corporate principals were to deal directly with each other, without brokers, middlemen and/or bankers, then, a trade of equal value products can occur, without any gain or profit for the taxman to come after.

Many advantages exist in such trades, whether the trades are of a large or small nature. We shall list a few that have already been mentioned: (1) the principals obtain what they want at no monetary cost to them, since the trade was for something of equal value or balanced out by secured notes; (2) no brokers are involved, therefore, no brokerage fees are incurred. All negotiations occur directly between the principals; (3) no bank financing means no bank note, liens, fees and restrictions; (4) no gain or profit made on the equal exchange, therefore, no reason for any tax to be imposed. Nothing was sold, therefore, no profit was made that could be taxed.

It is pretty obvious that when a corporation or a business sells a large volume of products of a certain value with the intention of buying another large volume of products of equal value from another corporation or business, the usual conditions apply, namely, some type of brokerage or banking involvement is required to procure the products along with the usual costs and fees and complications. Further, the sales involve the typical machinations and complexities needed to effectuate the sales, and, of course, the profits derived from the sales are "taxable". When the corporation or business buys the desired products from the other corporation or business, if we are looking at equal value here, then the corporation can defer or eliminate its "taxes" on profits. However, if these corporations or businesses were to enter into an equal trade to exchange the desired products, then the usual requirements of any type of sale and purchase can be eliminated or drastically reduced. All of this falls within the notion of common sense and operating under the best business practices.

In a similar vein, countries that are well known for producing certain products can barter those products for other desired products produced by another country in the same simple direct manner. An even barter between nations makes a lot of economic sense, principally because no funds are expended, except for transport costs, yet both countries get exactly what they want. The same process can be used by states, counties, cities and towns, executed by the respective public servants of those entities. Just imagine how simple, yet beneficial, this could be, and how many local farmers, ranchers, manufacturers and businesses could have ready, easy markets for their products and services and how thrifty these trades and swaps could be for the people who support the cost of government at all levels!

For example, let us speculate that Corporation A deals in the purchase and sale of crude oil on a contractual basis. At the present time, the purchase contract calls for more barrels than the company can actually sell to its clients and/or on the open market. Let us say that this amounts to 100,000 barrels per month for a three year period. Under contractual conditions the corporation is obliged to purchase this amount, but has no ready market for that specific amount. Let us speculate that Corporation B is an agri-business that also deals in the development, purchase and sale of agricultural products. Like Corporation A, Corporation B has a contractual obligation to buy various agricultural products for which it has an insufficient market. However, Corporation B does have interest in crude oil, because one of its subsidiaries has an existing need for crude oil over a three year period. One of the subsidiaries of Corporation A has an existing need for certain agricultural products. If these corporations were creative in their approaches and were open to a trade of products on an equal value basis, then, they could enter into contracts providing for the trade.

Let us say that another corporation deals in timber and has a percentage excess which it cannot currently sell, so would have to store it at great expense. This corporation would be willing to trade its excess timber on an equal value basis for a product that one of its subsidiary operations needs. Another corporation has an excess supply of various roofing materials and other materials, that a subsidiary of the timber corporation would like to acquire. Instead of both corporations buying the other corporation's product, which in many instances would require bank funding and other complexities, the two corporations enter into a contract for an equal value trade with each other, since what is swapped between them is of equal value.

As we have said throughout this book, system's ways can stymie creativity to the extent that the same type of business operations in the same type of manner are conducted over and over again, without much thought or due consideration. If we, individually, collectively, corporately, etc. begin to think outside of the proverbial box and come up with solutions that are not only creative, but enterprising and extremely profitable, then, it makes sense to put those solutions and ideas into practical action. America has millions of companies and corporations that produce all sorts of products which have value, which value is essentially a "commodity" that can be used to obtain other products of equal value. Businesses of any size, whether large, medium or small, and corporations of any size, may find that there is a great advantage in swapping some of the products they produce for some other products they need on a regular basis for business operations. What this really takes is a few enterprising businesses, companies and corporations to engage in such activities. Once this simple concept has been put into action, and others see how successfully such swaps and trades work, then, they may see the rationale within it and start engaging in their own swaps and trades.

The same principles which apply to corporate and business swaps and trades can definitely apply to country, state, county, city and town swaps. Some countries produce excesses of products and have little to no use for those products in that country. However, other countries may have a definite need for those products, and since countries all over the world produce hundreds of thousands of products, there is a wealth of opportunity for successful, productive swaps and trades among the countries of this world.

CHAPTER FIFTY EIGHT

CORPORATE AND COUNTRY
SWAPS AND TRADES

several CHAPTERs in this SECTION described in detail how people could swap and trade real estate with each other, either with equal or unequal value and whether free and clear or with existing bank debt. Swapping and trading has been part of the human condition since the very beginning of time and, as we explained in the beginning of this SECTION, there is every reason for like-minded people with common interests to swap and trade with each other, whether it be property or something else.

Swapping and trading takes place directly between the principals, without the involvement of brokers, bankers or other third parties. The best way to conduct business is for serious principals to deal directly with one another. One of the most significant benefits of engaging in this type of activity is that there is no need for any bank funding, as described in the relevant CHAPTERs of this SECTION. As previously explained, if properties or whatever is to be traded are of equal value, then, the trade for each other's property or object is an equal value trade. Since no one had to engage a broker, no fees were incurred, and in this case, since there were two parties, that saves two brokerage fees.

If the properties are of unequal value, the trade can still be made by which the party who has the lesser value property or object makes up the difference with a secured note in favor of the other party. If both properties have existing bank debt, the swap can still be made as described in CHAPTER 56 and other relevant CHAPTERs of this SECTION, by which each party assumes the obligation of the other party, but not the note itself. Any difference is made up with a secured note from the party who owes more debt to the party who owes less debt. As we always say and as many people are beginning to realize, there are always better ways to do almost anything. What is required for this is an enterprising person, group or organization with a creative mindset and the ability to think outside the box and create new ideas and approaches not in current use that can obtain the bottom line objective for the person, group or organization.

Since people, groups and organizations can trade and swap whatever they want, then, it is reasonable for corporations and nations to do the same thing. As discussed above and more fully detailed in the referenced relevant CHAPTERs of this SECTION, there are many benefits to swaps and trades, whether of equal value, unequal value and with or without existing bank debt. Further, neither the use of brokers nor bank funding is required, which save the corporations or nations effectuating the trades significant financial sums and time. For example, let us say that another corporation deals in timber and has a percentage excess which it cannot currently sell, so would have to store it at great expense. This corporation would be willing to trade its excess timber on an equal value basis for a product that one of its subsidiaries' needs. Another corporation has an excess supply of various roofing materials, such steel and other materials, that a subsidiary of the timber corporation would like to acquire. Instead of both corporations buying the other corporation's product, which in many instances would require bank funding, the two corporations enter into a contract for an equal value trade with each other, since what is swapped between them is of equal value.

Many countries throughout the world produce products unique to that nation as well as a long list of products and goods that are needed by other nations. Imagine all the nations producing virtually everything that is needed by all other nations. If all such producing nations were to make their production available to other countries for products that the first nation wants, through swaps and trades, then the challenges of supply and demand can be quickly solved. One nation produces what another nation wants, and the first nation produces what the other nation wants. This amounts to a simple supply and demand position, with no monies expended for the exchanged products, no banks, no brokers. Sometimes the best way to do things is the simple way, and the entire world needs to return to simple, effective ways of doing business rather than deal in excessive complications and involving banks and middlemen.

One nation, such as America, may have an abundance of cars, trucks, tractors, farm equipment, machinery, machine parts, and so on. Another nation may have other products American people want, such as clothing, agricultural products, wood products, cell phones, computers, etc. Each country has its own work force and production apparatus that produced the products, and for a healthy economy, that work force in each nation needs to be kept working to produce the nation's products. An overabundance of products not sold in the nation indicates that the market in that nation is weak for those products. However, the market for the products in another nation is strong, and vice versa. When the two nations evenly trade for products needed by the other, both parties receive what they want. One of the important points here is that the work forces in swapping nations keep their economies up because of constant swaps and trades, with new markets opening up for their products.

The above scenario is far better than the practice in some nations, and mainly America, to bury agricultural products in the ground, destroy livestock and livestock products, discard milk, cheese, butter and a host of other products TO ARTIFICIALLY KEEP THE PRICES UP, DEMAND UP AND THE SUPPLY LOW. This practice amounts to a fraudulent, contrived and manipulated market that is totally opposed to legitimate, true market-based supply and demand. This practice hurts the market and damages the American people. It would be far better for all if such lunacy stops immediately and those products discarded are instead swapped by America for products needed and desired by Americans. The ridiculous destruction of goods to keep prices up directly opposes fair market supply and demand. However, if those products were swapped for other products of equal value, then those producers in both nations would have continuous markets for their products, keep their businesses operating, their workers working and keep their respective nations economically healthy. There are always better ways to do things *better*. However, if we do not accept this strong reality, then things will be done as they are continually done to suit the government, banks, vested interests and power forces, and all to the detriment of the American people.

SECTION SEVEN

EPILOGUE

CHAPTER FIFTY NINE

SPECULATION

Speculation and speculators have been part of human society upon this planet from the very beginning. Numerous forms of speculation exist in all areas of business, banking, the economy, the stock and all other markets–housing, farming, food, oil, raw materials, futures markets and on and on. All types of speculators are present within these markets, and the vast majority of speculation is detrimental and harmful to people and their societies because it drives up prices, but it is very lucrative for the handful of speculators at the top who manipulate and profit greatly from this.

Throughout human history, speculators of all types have created economic and other booms within societies, then, brought the booms to a crashing halt and destroyed those societies for the benefit of the self-interest of the speculators. Different speculator types and classifications permeate all markets. These could extend from extremely powerful, insider and informed government, market, banking and elite business speculators down to the small home-buying speculator. The former are ruthless, thus, dangerous, while the latter is just trying to advance his interests without harming the general society. However, when the small speculator joins forces with other speculators for the same product in the same market, thereby creating a *cartel*, then this cartel also becomes dangerous to the economic well-being of the general public which deals in that particular market. As stated, speculation consistently drives prices upward, creates an unnatural artificial value and harms the general public. Just like water, real values should seek their own level and never be artificially stimulated. Unfortunately, in human society, thanks to the greed factor, this is not how matters typically work.

There is a huge difference between the creation and manipulation of a market and speculation within that market. The extremely powerful forces referenced above usually participate in both positions, which create no risk for them, while the average speculator participates only in the latter. If he is wrong, he can lose. However, those who create, manipulate and speculate in markets *they* create and *manipulate* seldom ever lose, but their deceived victims almost always do. This is an extremely sad fact that the American people have not grasped yet and, because of the immense propaganda and public relations machinery present in this country that favors the big business speculators, likely never will. For many years, Margy and I, along with countless others, have said: "If something is not broken, then, don't fix it!" This is logical and conforms to common sense. To the opposite extreme, when something is broken and adversely affects the entire society, then, it is the responsibility of that society to expose and correct the cause of that problem. When the problem is not corrected, then, obviously, it flourishes unabated and continues to rob the society upon which it feeds.

The purpose of this book is multifold, but, specifically, it intends to clearly demonstrate how average sellers can sell their properties in tough times and how average buyers can purchase property in tough times. One may not think that speculation has any effect, whatsoever, on individuals buying and selling property, yet it does. Earlier in this book, we referred to the mortgage debacle in which banks, mortgage companies and other institutional lenders were making "loans" as quickly as they could on homes, then, bundling the notes and mortgages and selling them as "mortgage backed securities". There were and still are many different levels to this scheme and speculation exists within each one of them.

When enormous amounts of funds became available for real estate purchases, this was both a form of market creation and speculation, which resulted in a rapid, inflated rise in real estate prices that were totally unjustified, and would never have been achieved except for the market-created conditions. Obviously, this market creation and/or conditions created within an existing market followed by speculation, created a "bubble" in many, if not most, real estate markets across the country, all of which harmed to some degree the average owners of real estate and definitely the average buyers for real estate. This is how contrived and well-planned schemes by extremely well-entrenched, well-financed and well-protected vested interests can harm an entire nation.

Some people may believe that the owners of real estate were not harmed by the "bubble", but we disagree. History has proven throughout the ages that most people deal in a "rich like a drunken sailor's" mentality. As soon as money is available or on the table, unfortunately, most people in this country will spend it well beyond their means and, further, even spend what they do not have. This, sadly, creates enormous debt which most people cannot meet, but which is exactly what the banks and the government wants because this creates dependence upon them, which translates to more control over the people. There was always and still always is a percentage of the general public that can benefit from speculation and increased prices, by knowing when to sell and when to get out of a market. However, this percentage is very small.

History demonstrates that over time, when home values are high and consistently climbing higher all the time, many people will refinance their properties and/or take out second or third mortgages, deceptively called "home equity loans", and use the funds to buy extra cars, boats, vacation homes, travel abroad, "toys", pay college costs, etc., etc. When the boom finally busts, which all of them eventually do, people who put themselves into extensive debt can no longer afford to pay the debt and usually go into foreclosure which often results in the loss of their properties and, many times, other assets as well. This is a huge societal problem, as we mentioned before, which has happened many times in America, and as we also mentioned, unless the people become aware of the problem, the problem will continue and the society will be damaged.

As a result of these market speculations, "booms" and the inevitable "busts", home prices and real estate values in many markets have fallen dramatically from the artificially inflated highs they once attained. Many people in America now have mortgage debt that is higher than the value of their homes. Tremendous losses have taken place right across the board, and home prices have fallen so dramatically that in many areas hordes of speculators and investors have come in and are coming in to buy for very low, wholesale prices properties upon which the banks foreclosed. The previous owners of these properties virtually lost everything. Of course, the exceptions to this whole economic situation are found in the so-called "star cities", such as Boston, New York, Los Angeles, San Francisco and others akin to these.

Although one can purchase these referenced properties from banks at very low prices, we would never suggest that anyone buy foreclosed properties, primarily because there is an ethical question involved, and, further, because buyers can never be assured that they have valid title to the bought properties. As we referenced earlier, when the vast majority of banks foreclosed on properties, most were not in possession of the ORIGINAL wet-ink-signed promissory notes and mortgages. The notes and mortgages had been conveyed upon sale in the after-market to investors for so-called mortgage backed securities. A lawful requirement for foreclosure is that the foreclosing party must be the owner and possessor of the original note and mortgage prior to initiating foreclosure. Since many of these foreclosures were conducted absent these lawful requirements, then, if these foreclosures are eventually judged to be invalid, for fraud, many people who bought foreclosed properties could be in trouble, because the original owner can rightfully reclaim his property. A Massachusetts Supreme Court case, namely, *Bevilacqua v. Rodriguez*, (460 Mass. 762), ruled in favor of the former owner who lost his house to foreclosure, because the foreclosure was improper.

Market speculation that results in decline in market values can create opportunities for sellers, buyers and investors of real estate. Now, and for the past many years, low-priced properties are available in virtually all markets across the country, with the exception, of course, of properties located in some areas of the referenced "star" markets. In life, what goes up eventually comes down, as we have seen. However, what goes down also eventually comes up, and for those interested in purchasing properties, this is a very good time to buy. Aside from foreclosed properties, there are some excellent buys for good, decent, stable homes. Although buyers may be plentiful for these properties, unfortunately, the banks are not lending to average buyers as easily as they have in the past and the banks' qualifications for buyers have become much more restrictive as have some government policies. Obviously, there are many sellers who are willing to sell their properties at reasonable prices, but since banks are not as eager to lend to average buyers as they once were, and since most homes are purchased through bank mortgages, this creates a dilemma for both buyers and sellers. As you have seen, the *ByPass* programs can readily resolve this dilemma for both buyers and sellers, as fully described throughout this book.

Just as home prices can fluctuate over time, so can conditions and appearances of many neighborhoods in the nation's various housing markets. When properties are new and occupied by long-term, caring, responsible homeowners, pleasant, desirable neighborhoods develop, become stable, usually improve due to homeowners' pride in their properties, and this benefits the entire area. However, if properties in a neighborhood are not properly tended by live-in homeowners, or if a lot of properties eventually become rentals, even the nicest neighborhoods can go downhill. This decline can escalate rapidly, especially if renters are slovenly, irresponsible and neglect or abuse the properties they rent. In such scenarios, live-in homeowners will likely be unwilling to remain in a neighborhood that is becoming unkempt, unattractive and possibly unsafe, and eventually, they will sell or lease their properties until the neighborhood is comprised of more rentals than homes occupied by live-in owners.

At this time, there are a lot of neighborhoods all throughout America which have fallen into the latter category. It is undeniably sad to see a once-lovely area of fine homes with pretty yards devolve into a dilapidated ghetto of run-down structures surrounded by dirt, weeds, junk cars and trash. You likely have seen this kind of decline occurring in some areas in or near your own communities and, like us, have probably lamented this aloud and wondered what can be done to stop and reverse it. While there are no "quick fixes" in life, there are approaches that can be taken to turn a downward trend around and, hopefully, start a renaissance of positive change in nearly any community.

One way to begin such a change is the purchase of older, distressed, but still sound, properties in neighborhoods that are either in decline or are marginal, at best. While this course of action may not be for everyone, it can be a good way for young couples to achieve home ownership, at more affordable costs, often in areas that offer the benefit of convenience to public transportation, workplaces, schools, libraries, restaurants, shopping, recreation and other needed services and amenities. With the changeability and uncertainty of gasoline prices, living in a neighborhood that offers such proximity could be a sound financial move.

It has been shown that when people buy homes in such areas and make an effort to improve them with fresh paint, tidied-up yards, new lighting and other improvements that can turn old neglected houses into updated, comfortable homes, a new spirit takes root in these neighborhoods, and before long, other people buy homes in them, existing homeowners spruce up their properties and, thanks to the influx of new people, a rebirth of the entire area takes place. More people living in a neighborhood will bring more trade to local shops, benefiting "mom and pop" grocery stores, dry cleaners, luncheonettes, thrift shops, beauty and barber shops, other businesses, movie theaters, etc. Obviously, this would be a win-win situation for everyone involved and can be a major force in transforming decaying and dying neighborhoods into very desirable places to live, work, shop and have fun.

When neighborhoods experience rebirths in this manner, people bond in a special way. Their efforts and accomplishments give them a sense of healthy pride which fosters a spirit of renewal and optimism where dejection and despair once existed. Often, they will form neighborhood associations in which they volunteer to work with others to beautify the area, creating parks and green spaces with walking trails and play equipment for children, planting trees and flowers in public spaces, and possibly adding period lighting for aesthetics and safety. Neighborhood groups like this can encourage new businesses to locate in vacant storefronts and help existing businesses, who may be struggling to survive, improve their appearances to attract new trade. When like-minded, well intentioned people have a stake in a neighborhood, they are usually motivated to make it nice and keep it that way. They may have friends and relatives in the arts and music whom they can persuade to open galleries or night spots or do neighborhood art fairs and outdoor concerts. There is no end to the positive things that can come out of a group of caring, committed people.

America is facing a severe crisis of the soul, as well as crises in virtually every important aspect of life. Just as it is impossible to eat a chocolate layer cake in one bite, it is impossible to fix America in one fell swoop. In Jack's and my view, the way to fix this nation is one neighborhood, one community, one city or town, one county, one state at a time. To do this, requires the sincere, dedicated efforts of ordinary, regular people who, want a better life for them and their families, and will work both hard and smart to achieve this. And by "better life", we don't mean accumulating more "stuff". We mean restoring, returning to and appreciating good old-fashioned values that stand the test of time–the kinds of things that are real and mean something at the end of the day or the end of one's life. Things like a loving family, a happy home, a job well done, helping others, creating new opportunities in all areas and restoring pride in our neighborhoods and communities. These are the real things which once used to define us, as a people, made us special and made this country great. Our nation sorely needs to get back to basics. It also needs more genuine entrepreneurship and can-do community spirit. To us, this can only begin at the local level, neighborhood by neighborhood, community by community, until it exponentially grows and spreads throughout every state in these United States of America.

CHAPTER SIXTY

FUTURE FORECAST

Imagine a future America in which people choose their own destinies, make their own decisions and acquire real estate and other commodities directly from other principal parties, without the interference of bankers, lawyers, brokers and other middlemen. This future could be a real one, provided the people recognize the value in simplicity and directness, by accepting and utilizing the concepts set forth in this book. Unfortunately, at the present time, for the vast majority of Americans, these new, different concepts are not known, thus, "not on their radar". The only traditional concept that is in use to some degree is the purchasing of debt-free property through owner financing. Sadly, even this time-tested method does not happen very much anymore, primarily because of banker involvement and the way that people have essentially been brainwashed into thinking that getting a loan from banks is the only way they can afford to buy real estate.

The other innovative concepts we present are not now in use because of the fact that people do not know of them, since they have not yet been introduced to the public. This book introduces new possibilities to the American people for the buying, selling, financing, investing and developing of real estate which could possibly change the dynamics of all of these activities for the explicit benefit of the people of America.

Real estate ownership *should* be available to almost all Americans in any financial category. Unfortunately, the way the traditional system operates in this country makes it very difficult for regular people to afford to buy property. The system is very convoluted, contrived and rigged to perpetrate cycles of ups and downs that impact the entire economy and financial matters which adversely affect the real estate markets and virtually everything else throughout America. Because the people have mistakenly given their power away to the "experts" of all stripes, largely because they are overwhelmed by the contrived complexities mentioned above, so think they need the help of these so-called "experts", they are unfortunately suffering the consequences of not exercising their natural inherent powers, especially when it comes to real estate and banking matters. How many of these "experts" have been right in their prognostications and forecasts about America's economy and financial markets? Not many, if any! You might want to think about that and how their wrong predictions and assessments have adversely affected you and this country.

For over a hundred years, the banks have made unnatural, unjustified profits off the backs of people who came to them seeking mortgages to buy property. As we mentioned earlier in this book, America's central bank, aka, the Federal Reserve Bank, so tightly controls the economy that it can create booms or busts at will, and does so. Neither of these extremes is good for the average American, yet the banks have consistently created booms and busts over the years to the detriment of the society in general and to the individual homeowner in particular, and at the same time providing the banks additional profits and control over more assets. As we mentioned earlier in this book, when people, businesses and industries obtain loans from banks, they put up collateral for the loans, which collateral was *earned* through the work efforts of the borrowers. What collateral do banks put up? The answer is: *nothing*, because as explained previously, the banks bundle the "loans", receive that amount plus a factor times that amount from the Federal Reserve Bank for the funds to make the "loans". In other words, the banks use none of their own assets to make the loans, nor depositors' money to make the loans, but simply borrow the funds from the Fed, based upon the signatures of the borrowers. In the case of default, the banks have no risk because they have nothing in the venture to begin with, but upon default, they take all of the hard-earned assets of the borrowers. Our rational, objective observers, True and Reality, strenuously object to this type of chicanery! The Federal Reserve Bank is a private bank that creates and issues fiat currency, at will, with no backing for the currency, whatsoever, and its decisions, which are all secretly private, vastly impact the lives and fortunes of all Americans each and every day. It is astounding how few Americans know anything at all about this private central bank and its lending machinations.

This bank is not Constitutionally authorized, thus, has no lawful authority to exist or to exert the overreaching massive control it has over America, her people and her economy. Unfortunately, mostly through their own ignorance, the American people have permitted this bank to operate, with impunity, and control the economy of the entire nation at the expense of the people and America, herself. As we said before, controls like these should not be upheld by government when they work to the detriment of the people, while enriching the very few. As we also said before, freedom is not free. Nothing is free. Someone or some group must "pay" to achieve freedom. Independence cannot be gained if people allow controls to be placed upon them which prohibit freedom and independence of any kind. Since we all live in a society that is highly controlled, if that society does not lawfully remove those controls, then, courageous individuals within that society must seek out viable ways and methods to be as independent as possible within the constraints placed upon the people. The new methods and approaches in this book can do just that, if the American people want financial independence and control over their own lives. As many of us know, America is presently at a crossroads, and the future is not yet written. However, if the American society, at least in some significant percentage, seeks freedom and independence and the people are willing to use creative approaches to achieve them, then, the new concepts and methods outlined in this book could be the wave of the future. In fact, it could be monumental to the extent that it actually changes the way business is done in this country, and the real benefactors of this change would be the American people, themselves, instead of private, for-profit, government favored vested interests.

Some people have minimal funds that will allow them only low cost housing, but to those people, their homes are invaluable. Houses come in all sorts of sizes, designs and prices, and people should have a ready, easy access to ownership, as their means permit and access should not be denied to anyone, if the financial ability to make a home purchase exists. This book has outlined numerous methods and approaches by which people can buy all types of property, whether those properties are free of debt, have debt, and whether people want to swap properties, invest in properties or develop properties as a business.

The *ByPass* programs outlined are exclusively for the principals involved, and those principals make their own decisions in all areas of the purchase. If the approaches and methods discussed become accepted and utilized by many people throughout America, then, these methods could become commonplace in the purchase, sale, financing of and investment in real estate. The ideas, methods and approaches discussed in this book are sound, realistic, and workable for the entire American society. Whether that society readily accepts and acts upon what is presented in this book remains to be seen. Initially, some adventurous, independent people will employ these methods in their buying, selling, financing and investing in real estate. If this initial acceptance becomes well known and integrated within the American society, then, many others may see and understand the very basic, simple wisdom of our methods which recommends their widespread use.

New ideas, procedures, creations and inventions sometimes spring up overnight, in terms of acceptance by society. Others take time for the people to understand, accept and utilize, but once that acceptance begins, it tends to grow rapidly. While our methods can apply to virtually all people, they were essentially written for the American people who have been unfairly disenfranchised by the collusive political, governmental and financial systems. No sane society should hold the welfare of the elite, powerful, political and money interests above the welfare of the entire population of any nation. Unfortunately, in today's world and in today's America, this is exactly what occurs and can be readily confirmed by one's observations of the actions of government, big banks, vested market interests and the power forces. The people have been given short shrift and are expected to quietly abide by the unfair treatment imposed upon them, while favorable treatment is routinely given to powerful, wealthy, controlling interests. This book clearly demonstrates how average Americans can benefit themselves, by and through their own efforts, in buying, selling, financing and investing in homes and other property without new institutional funding and institutional systems' approaches. It also demonstrates how one can purchase, sell or swap real estate with existing financing debt by accepting the obligation of that debt, but not the actual note, itself. Any contract entered into by and between a buying principal and a selling principal cannot *lawfully* be abrogated by government. People have the right to make their own choices, decisions, contracts and obligations of contracts without government interference and this right is enshrined in Article I, Section 10 of the 1787 *Constitution for the united states of America as amended in 1791 with the Bill of Rights.*

If America accepts and utilizes the methods presented in this book, then, the entire nature of institutional financing and systems' approaches typically used in the buying, selling, financing and investing in real estate will drastically change for the benefit of the people and to the detriment of the rigged system. People need change that will benefit *them*, and not vested, powerful interests that have controlled America for a very long time. If no one had supported Marconi, Edison, Tesla, Steinmetz and other inventors and innovators, then, their benefits to society might never have been realized. The ideas and programs specified in this book are intended to benefit the American people, should they choose to utilize them. We hope they do!

The worlds' governments and their partner power forces united behind this COVID-19 scam, and, as usual, the people reacted exactly as the governments wanted. However, growing elements within our American society are waking up. If this awakening increases throughout the nation, then America can again become the beacon of freedom she was intended to be long ago. The future is all up to the people, as it has been all along. Let us expect that they will choose wisely and courageously, for the benefit of a truly free people and truly free Nation.

CHAPTER SIXTY ONE

SOME FINAL THOUGHTS

In this book, we have attempted to demonstrate that the actions of government are not necessarily done in the very best interests of the people, which interests governments are sworn to uphold, yet, in fact, in most instances, governments actually *deliberately* oppose and betray the best interests of the people. Our rational observer and analytical computer have not only determined this sad fact, but have also determined that government and the power forces which exert control over and through government are solely vested in their own self-serving interests, power and positions, and only use the people as cogs in the never-ending machinery of control that maintains and increases those power positions by co-opting and bribing the machinery of government at every level. As we have said millions of times over the years, *Power ruthlessly uses its power against the powerless to bring everyone and everything within the control of that Power.* As previously referenced, many years ago, Lord Acton astutely said that power corrupts, and absolute power corrupts absolutely. The real unadulterated history of the world has undeniably proven that both of these positions are absolutely correct. The American people would do themselves and America a great service by keeping these two proven factual positions not only uppermost in their minds, but also by being fully aware of them as they go about their daily lives, in all aspects, viewing what they observe through the lens of these pernicious controlling positions.

Our objective observer, True, and his companion, the analytical computer, Reality, make their conclusions based solely upon information observed and received—the truth, the facts and the relevance of any matter. In this way, they reach the bottom-line position, predicated only in the truth and the relevant facts. They are not swayed by wishful thinking or blinded by previously conceived notions and opinions. There is no bias here. As we have mentioned on several occasions in this book, the bottom line is the most important position if one is going to accurately judge and objectively evaluate any matter or situation. The bottom line is always there and always observable, that is, if one knows that it exists and truly seeks it.

As previously discussed, there are many "covers", distractions and subterfuges used by the power forces to take people's focus away from the bottom line, to obscure it and/or to provide their own "justifications" for that bottom line. Our two analysts are not concerned with rationales, excuses, distractions, subterfuges, propaganda, etc.—but simply bypass all that nonsense and proceed directly to the bottom line, factually determine what it is, and then assess by what methods, actions, motives and objectives that bottom line was reached. Anyone can do the same thing they do, and it is very direct, simple, extremely telling and quite revealing. Our two, objective analysts **measure Constitutional requirements placed upon government officers by and through their oaths, then measure the actions committed by those government officers against those requirements**. In virtually every case, the actions of government officers, in all phases and facets of government activities—federal, state, county and local—directly oppose the Constitutional mandates imposed upon them by and through their oaths, fail their duties and requirements, exceed their limited delegated authority and perjure their Constitutional oaths. This in itself is a stark revelation to any truth seeker as to what is really blatantly and egregiously wrong with how government operates in this nation. When one looks at this in this way, without rose-colored glasses, nothing can be sugar coated. It is what it is. When government officers, throughout the entire nation, consistently and constantly, each and every day, violate their oaths by their own actions and directly oppose the Constitutional mandates imposed upon them, fail their duties and responsibilities, usurp authority not lawfully delegated to them, and routinely violate the inherent secured Rights and Due Process Constitutionally *guaranteed* to American Citizens, then the only logical conclusion our analysts can possibly derive is that something is radically and dangerously wrong and flagrantly criminal with how governments of all types operate in America.

If one does not believe this, we previously mentioned a test that the doubter can take to determine just where the allegiance of the federal, state and local governments actually lies. Place our Constitution on a wall and the communist manifesto next to it. The federal, state and local governments do not follow the Constitution and do not uphold Rights and due process Constitutionally guaranteed to all Americans, but do follow, uphold, implement and enforce the principals of the communist manifesto. This is treason against our Republic!

A little description of what is and what constitutes a "bottom line" is probably warranted here. Whenever an action is taken, there is always a result of that action, which we and many other people call the "bottom line". This basically amounts to "cause and effect". Some type of cause occurs which manifests some type of effect, which effect has been generated by the initial cause. The cause can be nearly anything. It can be an act or action of some type, or a plan, a program, an intention, a promise, a contract, a political platform, a political promise and so on. Each of these causes, actions and promises produce a bottom line position that can accurately be measured in one way or another. For instance, if one makes a promise to another, the bottom line position of that promise is whether it was fulfilled, or not. When a politician makes a political campaign promise, the bottom line position that can be measured is whether that campaign promise was fulfilled, or not. Most of you are fully aware of the bottom line results of these political candidate promises which, with very few exceptions, remain unfulfilled, which means the candidates *lied* to the people. As we have asked before, once you know someone to be a liar, can you ever trust him again?

Years ago a political "war on poverty" was initiated, with much fanfare and bravado, theoretically intended to end poverty in this nation, especially within inner city black communities. The purported intentions never materialized and, unfortunately, inner city black communities now experience more poverty than they did when the "war" began. The bottom line of this "war on poverty" proved, beyond doubt, that this "war" failed miserably and harmed those it theoretically intended to help. Of those entities that really need help in this country, the inner city black communities certainly qualify and definitely deserve sincere, committed, pragmatic help, yet despite the promises and the so-called "war" on poverty, this never happened. Many have called this program a total and complete fraud. The measured and assessed bottom line proves that they are correct.

Because of the drug problem in the inner cities and throughout America, another "war" was initiated by the government. This time it was and still is called a "war on drugs". Most people who are aware of this problem fully realize that this "war" was and is a complete failure. They determine this by observing and measuring the bottom line of the ongoing enormous and insidious drug problems all over this country – and not just in the inner cities. In these two situations, the bottom line of each one clearly proves that these "wars" proved to be total failures that never accomplished their objectives and only exacerbated the problems, while creating enormous bureaucracies and making lots of money for those operating them. If people were to measure the bottom line of promises made by political candidates, politicians, government officers, unelected bureaucrats, political parties and governments of any type in this country, they could quickly and factually determine that in most, if not all of these situations, the bottom- line results do not match the promises made.

Politicians and governments lie continuously and consistently to their own people, yet, in America, the people never hold the politicians and governments lawfully responsible for their lies. In fact, the American people support and *reelect* these liars and, in so doing, apparently condone, aid and abet their continuous ability to lie. In a rational, sensible situation, this makes no logical sense whatsoever, but, unfortunately, by the actions and *inactions* of the American people, this is the ongoing standard practice in America. The old adage of "Fool me once, shame on you. Fool me twice, shame on me", as demonstrated by the bottom-line actions and inactions of the people, does not apply to the American people with respect to their politicians and governments. As we see it, when anyone lies once, and we know that he lied, we never believe anything else he says. A proven liar *lies*. He may tell the truth on occasion, but how does anyone know when he tells the truth and when he lies? When people believe and put trust in proven liars to tell the truth, then they do so at their own risk. A growing number of Americans are finally beginning to see the outright lies and ongoing fraud our politicians and governments routinely perpetrate upon the American people. This leads to the question: What, if anything, will the American people do about this? We are all responsible to uphold our duty as Americans to oppose domestic enemies ruling in governments, but so far, the American people have never banded together to take lawful actions against these domestic enemies, which is why these domestic enemies continue their treason.

The bottom-line position is also very telling to any truth seeker, since that bottom-line position can be observed, measured and assessed in the reality in which it exists. Our analysts determine through actions and objectives committed by governments how they reached these bottom-line positions. In virtually every instance, the actions of the government officers, which resulted in that bottom line, were directly opposed to the Constitutional mandates imposed upon them by Law. Earlier we mentioned that the power forces "cover", "mask", "rationalize", "justify" and try to explain away the bottom-line position and their actions committed in reaching it, that is, if anyone even questions this entire situation. The glaring fact is that very, very few Americans question anything that government does, even fewer challenge anything, and still fewer know the real truth regarding the activities that culminated in the bottom-line position. The very miniscule few who engage in any such questioning activity are so few in number, compared to the total population, that, unfortunately, they do not count on any measurement scale and their opposition is usually quickly ignored, trivialized, minimized and/or dismissed. Unfortunately, the miniscule few who challenge the reality of anything never use the correct Constitutionally based authority that would support their challenges. This is all too present throughout the entire country, which is why, to a great extent, government and the power forces do whatever they want to do to anyone they want, at any time they want. Without lawful and competent opposition, all actions are open and readily available to them. If two football teams entered the field and began a game, and Team A received the kickoff and marched right down the field, without any opposition from Team B, Team A would easily score. When Team A subsequently kicked off to Team B, and Team B did not field the kick or even try to do so, then, Team A recovered the ball and scored again. The same thing occurred on the next Team A kickoff. This may be an absurdly ridiculous example, but it gets the point across. **Without any meaningful, effective lawful opposition from the people, government will do exactly what it wants, in spite of oaths taken to the Constitutions and the mandates imposed by and through those oaths.**

In earlier CHAPTERs, we spoke of the Preamble to the Constitution, the Constitution, itself, and the rights and due process guarantees to the American people contained therein. Our American Constitution is the Supreme Law of the Land, thus it is *the highest* **authority** *of Law in America* and is the document to which all public officers and employees have sworn or affirmed their oaths of office. State public officers and employees have also sworn or affirmed oaths to their state Constitutions, as well. No oath taker has the Constitutional authority—or any other form of valid authority—to oppose the very documents to which he or she swore or affirmed his/her oath. Any act by any legislature, and any action by any oath taker either supports and upholds the Constitution(s), or opposes and violates them. It is this simple, and these simple, powerful facts can quickly reveal Constitutional compliance or Constitutional defiance.

The Preamble to our national Constitution sets forth the intentions and requirements of that Constitution and the mandates of that Constitution imposed upon all government officers, as do all state Preambles to the state Constitutions. When public officers, federal, state, county and local, swear or affirm oaths to these Constitutions, these oaths are, in part, given in exchange for the **Public Trust**. This basically means that the public should be able to lawfully *trust* those public officers/ employees to abide by their oaths in the performance of their official duties. Further, by and through Constitutional guarantees, in addition to trust, the public should be able to lawfully *expect* that all government officers/employees will uphold their oaths in the performance of their official duties, thus uphold all inherent secured rights and due process of law Constitutionally guaranteed to the American people. To this end, most state Constitutions required public officers to purchase surety bonds, also called faithful performance bonds, to ensure that public officers did in fact uphold their oaths. Yet, if one attempts to call public officers' bonds, due to their errant actions, he will likely find that individual surety bonds are not in place for these officers, as Constitutionally required. Further, he will likely find that the state unlawfully created Risk Management Divisions or Departments which purchased blanket bonds, not individual bonds, using public funds, thereby defeated the very reason that public officers are supposed to have such bonds—individual responsibility and financial risk for poor performance! Still further, these bond, along with public officers' oaths, are Constitutionally required to be kept in the office of the secretary of state or of the county clerk to be available for public scrutiny, yet how many people know of these requirements or ever think to exercise their right and duty to ensure that these Constitutional mandates are being honored and upheld? These are simple, but *powerful*, Constitutional requirements which the people should know, test and lawfully enforce and which all public officers and forms of government should uphold and obey. However, as previously stated, when our analysts or any other interested, objective, rational observer assesses these Constitutional requirements against the actions of government officers/ employees, then, they can quickly determine that the actions committed by public officers and governments violate virtually all of these Constitutional requirements. Such actions are criminal.

For instance, our national Preamble to our Constitution speaks of the <u>government's duty to insure</u> *domestic tranquility*, when in reality the actions of governments across the country are conducted in opposition to domestic tranquility. Of course, governments will provide excuses and a "rationale" for their actions and inaction, intended to cover or mask those actions or inaction, but the fact is that by and through their own unlawful actions and failure to act, governments have not upheld their duties to insure domestic tranquility throughout this entire nation. This is so commonplace throughout America that even the most die-hard government supporter could not fail to notice it. Earlier, we referred to the massive drug problems permeating America, the pernicious influence of the drug cartels upon all levels of government and society, the ongoing crimes happening throughout the country harming the American people, the escalating violence, murders and climates of fear pervading major American cities and other communities, the unprecedented fraud and political corruption on the part of governments, at all levels, and much more which does <u>not</u> insure domestic tranquility. In fact, government seems to work in the opposite direction, which as previously mentioned was echoed by the former Democratic mayor of Chicago and former chief of staff to Obama, when he said, "Never let a good crisis go to waste!"

Further, the Preamble requires government to *promote the general welfare*, which essentially means upholding the well-being of the people of the nation. Yet, by the routine activities of all governments, this Constitutional objective is consistently violated by government. The Preamble also requires the *establishment of justice*, yet the average American is beginning to realize that there are two distinct forms of justice in this country. One is for government, the power forces, their "elite" friends and associates, with a second, entirely different form of "justice" for average Americans. All forms of government and all courts are lawfully mandated to uphold Rights and Due Process guaranteed to the people in the Constitution(s), but as our analysts have determined, based upon the *actions* of these governments and courts, these public bodies routinely violate and oppose these Constitutional objectives; therefore, decimate the rights of the people as the apparent, but unwritten and unacknowledged custom, practice and policy of governments and courts. As a result, justice only exists for the ones in the "just-us club" and for those who can afford to pay for "justice", which certainly does not include the average American.

The Preamble requires that government secure the *blessings of liberty*, but when governments of all types across the nation consistently oppose Constitutional mandates pretty much in everything they do, then it should be painfully obvious to any observer that government not only fails to secure the blessings of liberty for the people, but in fact, directly opposes and suppresses that liberty. If people read and understand the Bill of Rights, they, like our analysts, can quickly determine that governments by and through their standard operations, each and every day, oppose each and every one of the Rights guaranteed in the Bill of Rights. Again, this is a simple measurement process by which the Constitutional requirements imposed upon governments are listed in one column and the activities of government are listed in another column. Any truthful observer who looks at this comparison can quickly and easily determine that governments throughout America flagrantly violate these Constitutional requirements all the time. Are these the types of governments operated by government officers/employees that have earned your trust? Can you respect and uphold their actions taken against and in opposition to their sworn Constitutional requirements? Would you trust these government officers and the governments for whom they speak and act to properly represent you and make laws, rules and regulations that govern you and restrict your freedoms, your right to earn a living, your right to express yourself and many other inherent rights that the Constitution(s) recognize and guarantee to you and your family? Our analysts have determined that a truly sane, objective and rational American would never support any such unlawful, criminal governments.

Beyond government, there are the *power forces* operating throughout the country and these forces exert tremendous influence and control throughout the entire nation. They have their own methods of operation, all bent on maintaining and increasing the control and influence of these particular power forces. These include, but are not limited to, the private central bank that owns and controls our entire economy, the member banks; all major financial institutions and investment firms; all major corporations, all major markets, all major producers, all forms of industry, including the massive defense manufacturing and contracting industry in all areas; all forms of media, including "entertainment" through television and films; all of academia, scientific institutions, and most, if not all, "think tanks"; the entire scope of modern allopathic medicine, including pharmaceuticals, hospitals, medical schools, testing centers, laboratories, research facilities; the chemical cartel, the corporate food and agriculture cartel and many, many more, much too extensive in number to list here.

Virtually all of these enterprises have been given "life" by and through government and are supported by the central bank and its member banks in this country. Something that many people do not think about or even consider is the fact that what has been given "life" by government and the private banking system, owes allegiance to that government and that banking system. Thus, government has massive control over these enterprises, and these enterprises subject themselves to government controls, in part, in order to operate, continue in existence and earn profits. When people consider all of these factors, then they can quickly comprehend, as do our two analysts, that there is a huge, incestuous interconnectedness between and among all of these various enterprises and the government, the private central bank and its member banks. All of these interrelationships, combined, wreak enormous control and influence over the entire society, the economy, the successes or failures inherent therein, the people, themselves, and everything that affects their lives and their nation, including their ability or inability to earn a living.

America is supposed to be a "free enterprise" nation, which is one in which people, companies and businesses can deal freely in this country in fair and open competition. In reality, only a very small percentage of enterprises can deal in this manner. **What is truly free has no impediments.** When restrictions and conditions are placed upon freedom, then there is no true freedom but only the *appearance* of freedom. When our two analysts review the contractual associations between government and all the related enterprises mentioned above, they can readily ascertain that the amount of these contractual interrelationships is absolutely enormous and affects every aspect of life. The American people who work in these enterprises are working for corporations of various types that all have ongoing contractual relationships with government. Again, when people consider the vast extent of these contractual relationships and financial entanglements across the total spectrum, then they can see that the vast majority of people who work in this nation either work directly for government, in one form or another—federal, state or local—or for corporations and enterprises under contractual obligations to and financial dependence upon government. This equates to a network of insidious control that has a stranglehold upon virtually all enterprises in this country and in turn upon the people.

The word "control" is monumentally important when one considers all the manifestations of how such control is orchestrated and enforced. When the entire, or nearly the entire, enterprise factors of any nation are given "birth" by the governments of that nation, therefore, owe obligations to those governments, are in contractual relationship with those governments, thus financially depend upon them, the ultimate control exerted upon the society is clearly in the hands of those governments. What governments do with their control can be readily observed in the bottom-line events which affect the entire society! Anyone seriously interested can seek, review and understand these bottom-line positions. With the observation of the *deliberately* manufactured creation of continuous cycles of depressions, recessions, slow-downs, economic booms and busts, foreclosure crises, wholesale exportation of industries to other nations, massive drug problems, escalating criminality, contrived military interventions throughout the world, increasing banking controls and restrictions, one can get a better understanding of how that ultimate control is ruthlessly imposed upon the general American society in virtually all areas of life. Although the overt control is manifested through governments, there is a symbiotic partnership among governments and the power forces to the extent that each works in a cooperative effort for mutual gain and further control of the people and the nation. The question then becomes the following: "Is this government control in compliance with or opposed to the Constitution(s) and the Rights and Due Process guaranteed to the American people in every state?" The measurement scale referred to above can quickly determine the answer for any truly objective, rational observer.

Pursuant to the foregoing, the phrase "free enterprise" would appear to have a different meaning than what its words imply. While some free enterprise does exist in this nation, it is entirely limited in scope, activity, success and influence. The general overall interrelated controls exerted by governments and the power forces determine who and what succeeds and who and what do not succeed. Since most people either work for government in one form or another—federal, state, county and local—or within enterprises in contractual relationship with government, then, whether they realize it or not, they essentially work within a *non*-free enterprise organization that has both in-house and external controls exerted upon it, while that enterprise exerts its own inner controls upon its workers, its operations and the markets. Since there is both an inner and outer controlling power structure directing these enterprises, then those who work in these enterprises are subject to, thus, at the mercy of, these power forces whether they realize this or not. The connecting web of control is absolutely staggering! There is growing evidence revealing that two huge corporations, Black Rock and Vanguard, are the owners, thus, the ultimate controllers, of virtually all other corporations and large enterprises in this country. How many Americans know anything about these two corporate behemoths?

Unfortunately, most people realize very little that is outside of their narrow purview and usual frame of reference, so this grave fact of absolute control eludes them, but unfortunately, many are quickly finding out due to this COVID-19 scam. The bottom line here is that there is a power structure with power forces that are both internal and external to virtually every enterprise. The workers, whether in management, on the factory floor or elsewhere in the enterprise, are not part of those power structures, have no knowledge of their machinations, yet, are entirely dependent upon and subject to those internal and external power structures for their livelihoods. It matters not whether a worker earns three million dollars a year or fifty thousand dollars a year. The bottom-line position for the worker is controlled by and subject to those power structures.

This extensive network of control, whether internal or external, is unknown by most people, largely because they are more concerned with the challenges of surviving every-day life. However, the survival of this nation, as a free Constitutional republic, *should* be important to everyone living in this nation. Yes, people are fully aware that they work for some type of corporation or company, and within that working environment, they work for a section of the company and within that section, they have a boss to whom they are responsible who also has a boss, under a hierarchy of bosses all the way up to the top level. This is a just a common sense acknowledgement which almost anyone has, but the vast elements of internal and external control remain virtually unknown to them. For instance, the company for which Willy Worker works just received a ten billion dollar contract from the federal government which is going to keep Willy on the job for another 15 to 20 years. Jim Jobber works for a company that just lost a ten billion dollar contract with the federal government, so Jim Jobber is out of a job next week, with few prospects for finding another comparable job. Free enterprise has little to do with awarding or withdrawing contracts from various enterprises. However, in the alternative, the operating enterprise depends almost entirely upon the whim and will exerted by the power-force control outside of that enterprise, with possible other controls exerted by other enterprises within that field of operation. In other words, this is basically the law of the jungle in which the strongest survive in an extremely corrupt system driven by the will to control, survival of the fittest, profit and greed. In this system which pervades our society in all aspects, the sad truth is that good guys, who want to do the right thing, based upon merit, finish last! Many more Americans are beginning to realize this sobering, soul crushing fact each and every day.

When these controlling factors are present, as they exist in virtually all areas of life, there is no such thing as "free enterprise", and this greatly impacts any free choice the people believe they have. Even if a boss somewhere in the chain of command *wants* to do the right thing for the right reason, if what he wants to do is opposed by the referenced controlling elements, he quickly realizes that either he sets aside his ethical concerns and does what he is told to do, or he is out of a job. As we have said many times throughout this book, economic violence is the most insidious control element in human society, because it governs every aspect of life. People are suffering under economic violence right now because of this un-Constitutional national economic shutdown. Our two analysts have determined that such control and the systematic operations of this extensive control network, within and without these enterprises, do not work in the best interests of the American people, do not promote the general welfare, do not insure domestic tranquility, certainly do not establish justice and in no way secure the blessings of liberty to the people.

When an entire society is subject to these very powerful controlling forces, then, obviously, the society operates as *decreed* by these power forces. When the two components of these power forces, namely, governments in all forms and the banking/corporate cartel, work hand in hand to achieve their unified objectives throughout society, and in so doing harm that society in myriad ways, there is not much the people can do about this. Or is there? Whenever governments and government controlled entities operate outside the lawful scope of their *limited* delegated duties and authorities, their actions are un-Constitutional, unlawful, thus without lawful force and effect upon the people, and render the perpetrators of these actions criminal traitors. The power forces will never change their modus operandi. The only ones who can stop and correct the massive problems created and allowed by governments and their corporate allies in this country are the American people, themselves. There are no heroes in white hats or white knights or some magical or spiritual force that will sweep down from the sky to get rid of all the evil in this world and create a just, peaceful planet for the people. The primary reason for this is that this responsibility was given to the people and so far, the people have failed miserably.

The word "freedom" signifies exactly that, as does the word "control", the word "authority" and so many other words unthinkingly bandied about each day. Words have direct bottom-line meanings, as do the three words just mentioned. Above, we have spoken of "free enterprise", how that so-called "free enterprise" is not really *free* at all and how the constraints on that enterprise can and do affect the entire society, typically for the benefit of the controllers and usually to the detriment of the people. When we speak of individual freedom, in the theoretically "freest" of all nations, America, is that so-called freedom truly free, without constraints, or does it have restrictions upon it as does the so-called "free enterprise system"? Most Americans *believe* that they are free, because they have been conditioned since birth to think they are free people living in a free country. In the same vein, most people in the so-called "free enterprise system" also believe that this system is free. We have mentioned before that there is a major difference between *thinking* one knows and *knowing* one knows. If the average American sincerely believes that he is free, then he might want to test that freedom against the constraints placed upon him by governmental and power forces. If and when he does this, he will quickly discover that he has been living under a false premise all his life. Of course, people who believe they are free, when in fact they are not, are very easily controlled, which, obviously, is the objective of the power forces and government. This speaks volumes as to why the power forces and government continue their hypocritical hype about freedom and free enterprise.

The saying "Freedom is not free" tells it all. Although this saying arose in a different context, these words apply here. If freedom is not free, then, obviously, there must be some type of restriction, limitation, cost, control or obligation associated with and imposed upon that freedom. A very real, but disturbing, picture is beginning to form in people's minds revealing that what they thought was freedom is an illusion, a façade, and not the reality they were led to believe it was. Previously, we have spoken about the bottom line and stated that if people really want to understand the reality of any particular situation, and not accept the hype and propaganda around that situation, then they would be best served by seeking and observing the bottom-line position. Once they understand that bottom-line position, then they can assess the actions, motives, objectives and positions taken by the controllers to create and reach that bottom-line position. When people live their entire lives in an *illusion*, then, essentially they are delusional and not immersed in the reality in which they truly exist. This is the tragic case for Americans in America. Unfortunately, the people have not comprehended that the illusion was insidiously created for them intentionally by the referenced controlling power forces, in virtually all aspects of life. The people's failure to recognize this overarching control resulted in the grand delusion intended by the power forces to keep the people on the plantation, down on the farm, or in the factory, quietly keeping all the cogs in the machinery going full tilt, without asking "troublesome" questions, and without any threat to the evil agenda of the controlling elements.

As we have said before, fortunately, some people in America are beginning to awaken to these ugly realities and beginning to understand that for most of their lives they have not recognized the existing operating realities that are all around them every day, governing everything they do. They are also beginning to understand that, when restriction, limitation and control are put upon their personal freedom, then, that so-called freedom does not exist. What may exist are benefits, privileges or a certain amount of liberty, dispensed by the power forces under certain conditions, which can also be withdrawn by those power forces if the people do not comply with the controls exerted upon them. These conditions are certainly not the marks of a free people in a free society in a free nation. In order to achieve the freedom that was originally intended, at the cost of a very bloody Revolution, and as embodied within our Constitution(s), it is really incumbent upon the American people to come to a very quick understanding of the realities operating and controlling America, and then reach a further understanding that these realities do not serve the noble objectives of our Constitutional republic, our Constitution, the American people and America, herself.

The most important reality is the fact that our Constitution is the Supreme Law of this land, thus supersedes all lesser law. **What is written in the Constitution is valid and authorized, thus enforceable. What is not written in the Constitution is prohibited by the Constitution, thus unenforceable.** This basic Constitutional position is vitally important and should be fully understood by the people. Think of how many "laws", statutes, codes, rules, regulations, programs, "authorities", policies, "guidelines", agencies, departments of government and so much more exist that interfere with, limit and control our daily lives, but are not authorized in the Constitution! For instance, the Constitution does not authorize taxation on labor, on compensation received for labor, and on rights and property. Yet, Americans are being unlawfully taxed on all of these. As we mentioned previously, a law must be valid, that is, *Constitutionally compliant,* to exist and must exist to be enforced. This is simple common sense, yet the IRS has never stated the exact law, duly enacted by Congress, and entered into the Statutes-at-Large, that makes Americans <u>subject to, thus, liable for</u> paying income taxes to the IRS, *because no such law exists.* During a press conference in 2003, Mark Everson, then IRS Commissioner, when repeatedly asked what law required Americans to pay taxes to the IRS, repeatedly did not answer and completely evaded and avoided the questions. Steven T. Miller, Acting IRS Director, from November 10, 2012 to May 21, 2013, appeared before Congress and admitted that the income tax is *voluntary,* <u>not</u> mandatory. Others in government and those who truly understand this **fraud** perpetrated upon the people by their own government, openly stated that income taxes are not necessary because money is simply printed, at will, with no assets backing it, thus, money can be printed to pay the expenses used to "justify" imposing taxes. If this were done, then the American people would not be burdened and America would truly be a land of perpetual prosperity. However, if this were to happen, then, the government would lose the enormous control it has fraudulently exerted over the people of this entire country. While common sense sees this as an excellent solution, truth be told, our governments rarely deal in common sense.

For instance, banks fund debt from funds banks receive from the central bank, the so-called Federal Reserve Bank. Further, the Fed also funds banks up to nine times the amount of their total bundled debt. Americans have the Constitutional right to earn a living and to receive compensation for their labor, skill and time. Yet, they are duped into to paying income taxes on their labor, which is totally un-Constitutional. In contrast, under the current financial system, banks do not labor for their funds, since they receive funds from the Fed based upon their bundled loans, and receive interest from the borrowers upon funds the bank received from the Fed. The banks do not labor for their compensation, except efforts expended to make loans. Banks are close to government and receive favorable treatment, while average Americans are used by government and treated very, very differently. Common sense sees vast injustice here. Do you agree?

Despite these facts, the reader is well aware that governments unlawfully impose taxes on these inherent rights secured in the Constitution(s). When the people do not enforce Constitutional mandates imposed upon governments and their officers, then in the absence of lawful opposition, those governments and officers impose whatever they want upon the compliant people. This monumental outrage does not comply with the intent and objectives clearly established by our truly courageous Founding Fathers. It would be best for America and her government-compliant people if groups of courageous, competent and committed Americans, in accord with the Founding Fathers, initiate lawful, effective actions against errant governments and agencies all over this nation, and begin the desperately needed journey back to restoration of Constitutional governance in America. For those who are truly concerned about America and her future, please review our Constitutional Methods listed in CHAPTER EIGHT.

As we said above, understanding is important, but what is even more vitally important is the necessity for the people to take lawful, effective action based upon that understanding. To do this, the people must really begin to think for themselves again, and not let someone else think for them, as do the politicians, the talking heads in the media, the celebrities in the so-called "entertainment" industries, the academic theoreticians, the think tanks, the so-called experts, the systematic controlling power forces, all with their own selfish agendas. All people are part of the societies in which they dwell, but all people are also individuals, possessing individual opinions, tastes, viewpoints, positions, abilities, needs and all manner of expression on all subjects. Individuality is vital to the well-being of a particular person as well as to the society in which that person lives. Good thoughts generate good ideas, expressed by individuals and creative people within society, which can generate even further good thoughts and ideas and expand upon the original ideas expressed. For that society to be well-adjusted and healthy, it must function as an expression of all the individuals within it, and not as directed by external power forces bent upon their own self-serving agendas and objectives. For far too long, people have gotten very lax about thinking for themselves and thus have allowed others, some referenced above, to do their thinking for them. This type of universal position does not bode well for any healthy society, primarily because the people have given their own individual, thus collective, power away to others. These powerful others, such as the various power forces, impose their thinking upon the people, make decisions for them, establish public policies to control them and/or "politically correct", (P.C.), positions that are mandated as "normal", institute policies and programs to achieve agenda adverse to freedom, independence and the best interests of the people. We call "P.C." pure communism and pure corruption. Americans have carelessly given away both their political and thinking powers to the system controlled by these very same power forces. However, if the people begin to take back their rightful powers, then it is possible to make proper lawful changes to initiate Constitutional control over criminal, un-Constitutional government and its partner power forces and lawfully remove them from office, pursuant to the self-executing Sections 3 & 4 of the 14th Amendment, as well as for other reasons. The alternative will give us more of the insidious evil effects routinely inflicted upon all of us each and every day. Please note that the governments, the power forces and the controlling elements have over time stolen the consciousness of the people. From a human pragmatic view and from a spiritual view, this is the worst crime against humanity that any government can ever institute upon its own people. Please be aware of this and take back your own power and never surrender it again.

Fake news has been with us forever, though unknown to most people, who naively believed what was presented, because it was in the newspaper, somewhere in print or on radio or television. Based upon the enormous amount of lies, misinformation, disinformation, partial or slanted truth, propaganda, position pieces and outright fraud in the print and broadcast media, some people have learned to distrust these once trusted sources. The enormous increase in "newsprint" fraud is staggering. To a great extent, we not only now have "fake news" but also deliberately deceptive news, blatantly fraudulent news and "no fact-check" news. At one time, and not that long ago, the news media would not print or broadcast anything unless the facts were checked and verified. Apparently, fact-checking is now obsolete and dismissed as a memento of past *true* journalism. It is very difficult for anyone who wants the truth to believe anything said in news programs or anywhere in the media. The words "truth" and "honor" do not seem to have any place in the media, in government, in many institutions or even in the home, within this American society. The troubling fact that the American society is degenerating is pretty obvious to many awakening people. Our analysts have already recognized this. We and all aware Americans give sincere thanks to those in America who still possess these fine qualities. Once the people have duly thought about and really considered all of the positions mentioned herein, then they must question, object and lawfully challenge the fraudulent media and, more importantly, so-called "authority", which in reality is not *lawful* authority at all. Unlawful government feigning authority, making un-Constitutional "laws" and performing un-Constitutional actions which harm the American people is an absolute abomination to our Constitutional Republic and everything for which it stands.

This abomination and media fraud should never be tolerated by the American people. A similar abomination was both arduously and courageously dispatched by a very small percentage of the American patriots in the bloody but courageous war that separated us from that putrid, festering cesspool "across the pond". For the sake of America and all Americans, this time, only lawful, effective action, and not violence, should be taken by a committed people to restore our nation back to her proper status as *our* Constitutional Republic. In fact, if the people of this nation ever hope to be truly free, they must set aside all of the false information, belief systems and programming which they have blindly accepted all of their lives, and refuse to live and act under any and all of it. Instead, they must make their own assessments of situations and circumstances, as our two analysts do, then predicate their decisions, positions and actions on the facts they discover, exercising critical thinking, using common sense and listening to that "still small voice" that dwells in all of us, lighting the way to discernment of right and wrong, truth or falsehood, good or evil.

As of this writing, the government of Virginia is leading the way in the ominous escalating threat being made by government(s) in this country to un-Constitutionally seize arms from law abiding Citizens. Obviously, the legislators, the governor and the public officers of Virginia have sworn or affirmed oaths to support and defend the Constitutions, national and state. However, their actions in this regard are directly opposed to, violate and perjure their oaths and deny rights and due process guaranteed to the Virginia Citizens. In so doing, they have revealed themselves as domestic enemies by their own un-Constitutional actions, and ironically, the term "domestic enemies" was used by another famous Virginian, Thomas Jefferson, in the Declaration of Independence. Jefferson stated that it is the duty of all American Citizens to oppose all enemies of this republic, both foreign and domestic. As we have said many times before, the American people are beginning to realize that there are far more domestic enemies in government, media and the power forces, who want to destroy America, than there are foreign enemies. How this un-Constitutional, treasonous government position is handled by the people of Virginia remains to be seen. While many are calling for armed resistance, this is not a sane, wise and correct choice against the actions of a government committed to evil which uses tyrannical force against the Citizens. Of course, that force will be carried out by other Virginia Citizens, who work for and are paid by government, who are just as evil as the hidden masters who really control government. Apparently they have forgotten or never knew that an unlawful order does not have to be followed. The Constitution is the Supreme Law of the Land and as such the people of Virginia can lawfully enforce the Constitution upon their treasonous government and in so doing, lawfully remove the traitors from office and begin the road back to Constitutional governance. Since this has never happened in America—ever—whether this occurs, or not, will likely determine the fate of the people of Virginia and in fact the whole nation. Engaging in armed resistance or lawfully enforcing the Constitution. Which choice would our objective analytical observers make?

Good, both knowingly and unknowingly, has been supporting Evil for so long that many people are beginning to realize, based upon existing realities, that Evil essentially rules this entire world. Recognition of this undisputable fact by the people and their willingness to rectify past mistakes could begin the process by which Good stops its support of Evil, then begins to support only Good. No human is perfect. We all make mistakes. We are all, at one point or another, deceived by other humans, by governments, by the system, by power forces. Tragically, this is part and has been part of the human condition for millennia. Recognition of this condition and the admission that we have been "taken over the coals" by people and institutions we mistakenly thought we could trust is essential if we, as a people, are to lawfully retake our own powers, both individually and collectively. This is our first step back to sanity. While we share some blame for our actions or inactions, we cannot beat ourselves up and take full blame for deceptions perpetrated upon us by others, especially those *duty bound by oaths* to represent and uphold our best interests, who have so cruelly and wantonly deceived us, but we can certainly do something about it. This is what is needed now.

SOME POSITIONS TO CONSIDER
AND REMEMBER

Any sound society or nation needs some basic ethical and moral governing rules or behavioral codes established by the people for the benefit of the people and the healthy, efficient operation of that society. Such a fundamental undertaking is simply common sense. If no common rules or behavioral codes are adopted by the people for that society, given the lower aspects nature of mankind and enough time, then chaos, confusion, disruption, the "law of the jungle" and "survival of the fittest" would likely manifest. For good, proper order that benefits all within that society, some universally agreeable behavioral codes of conduct and actions must be established by all within that society. However, if the objective is to establish an egalitarian society, this effort must involve all people and not just certain people. All must be given their voices and consensus must be reached. Unfortunately, the non-egalitarian history of mankind has clearly proven that the few within that society, and not the many—not the people themselves—write the rules, establish the order and take control. Even in those societies in which the people jointly participate in formulating their own founding documents or codes, eventually, the few take control over the many, because the many abdicate their responsibilities to participate and oversee. When this occurs, as it always unfortunately has, the many give away their power to the few and those few control the many, as the few exclusively decree and dictate. The people are totally left out of the process.

America was and is no exception. Although America was initiated as a nation of freedom in which all people were to participate in the Rights and due process of law guaranteed in our Constitution, it was the few, and not the many, who formulated this nation. Only a small percentage of the population supported the Revolution, and only a miniscule percentage of that comprised the governing body that established our Constitution and America, as a nation. The total population had no input or voice, whatsoever. This is not unusual, but, in fact, is what usually takes place when any new peoples' movement, action, revolution or nation is being formed. The many give away their power to the few. Nothing has changed over the millennia. What was present in the distant past is present now. The remarkable difference is the fact that many of those who founded this nation were well intended, courageous, intelligent beings, who established the most egalitarian document ever created for the governance of a nation by the people of that nation. Unfortunately for America, the people did not understand our Constitution then, and even more tragically, the overwhelming majority of Americans does not understand it now, or even have any interest in it. At that time, the people did not accept and enforce their power over government granted to them in the Constitution(s), as they do not accept and enforce that power now. Because of this massive systemic failure by the people, America is operated by out-of-control machineries of government—federal, state, county and local—corrupt and un-Constitutional, beyond measure. Again, nothing has changed regarding the many giving their power away to the few and nothing has changed regarding the few controlling the many. As we said above, but as bears repeating, America is no exception to this historical and universal "rule" of control and domination.

Earlier, we discussed the intent of our Founding Fathers, embodied in the Preamble to the Constitution—the Supreme Law—in the Bill of Rights, which guarantees numerous inherent Rights and Due Process of law to the people, and the Constitutional mandates imposed upon governments, by and through oaths taken by public officers/employees. The taking of oaths is not *optional*, but mandatory and a requirement before any public officer can assume office and execute any duties thereof. We have shown that all forms of government in this country, at all levels, by their own actions, have consistently opposed and violated the Constitutions, national and state, at will. These are factual positions that any reasonable, rational, objective observer can easily determine, as have our two analysts. If people were to truly analyze what governing "rules" the federal, state and local governments follow, then they could quickly see and realize that these governments do not follow the Constitutions and protect Rights and Due Process guaranteed therein, but, as we have said repeatedly for decades, they do follow, implement and enforce the principles of the Communist Manifesto and the worldwide communist movement. This may be shocking to many people, but then again, the truth is rather shocking, especially when people have predicated their beliefs and world views on lies and propaganda all of their lives. If you doubt this, take a good look at the policies of the U.S. government from at least the War of Northern Aggression and more especially during the past thirty years.

Additionally, governments have routinely "lost" or misappropriated enormous amounts of public funds, are corrupt, favor the power forces over the people, operate governmental administrative agencies, not even authorized in the Constitution, which routinely violate the Constitutions and deny peoples' inherent, secured Rights, do not uphold Due Process of law, do not dispense justice, instead impose economic and financial violence upon the people, create un-Constitutional "laws", subject the people to physical violence through governments' lax immigration and border policies, hold people to those un-Constitutional "laws", and routinely commit heinous crimes against the people by committing actions not Constitutionally authorized. As we have stressed, economic violence is one of the worst crimes that governments can perpetrate upon the people. Some people would say that those operating our governments are stupid, incompetent, and lazy, while others may say they are criminal thieves. In both cases, their actions harm and threaten the people, thus, they are evil and perpetuate evil.

Most awakening or aware Americans would agree that many, if not all of these insidious designations apply to governments in America. Our two analysts have concluded that no sane Americans want such deplorable, insidious governments operated by criminals to rule them and their families, make "laws" and policies that control most of their lives and activities, perpetrate economic and financial violence upon them, routinely violate their Constitutionally guaranteed Rights and Due Process of law, and so much more. These governments DO NOT uphold the Constitutions, Rights and due process guaranteed therein, DO NOT provide domestic tranquility, DO NOT uphold the general welfare, and the common defense, justice and the blessings of liberty to all. Such government operations oppose all of the sacred Rights and guarantees made to the people. These governments will never remove themselves, as no evil government ever does. As it was, when necessity compelled opposition to the tyranny of King George III, a small group of Americans did the work that the others refused to do despite how difficult it was to share news at that time. Now, in this age of instant communication via internet, it is up to the mass of the American people to recognize and *END* the evil ruling America, and this time, instead of using violence to stop the tyranny, LAWFULLY ***USE THE SUPREME LAW OF THE LAND, AS OUR FOUNDING FATHERS INTENDED***—TO REMOVE THIS OPPRESSIVE BLIGHT FROM THE PEOPLE, AND FROM AMERICA, PERMANENTLY.

The ongoing COVID-19 scam and the utterly unnecessary economic shutdown of America should make it plainly obvious to the people of America that government is not our friend; therefore, the people must control the government, as our founders intended, and not be controlled by the government. As we mentioned earlier, Lord Acton astutely said that power corrupts and absolute power corrupts absolutely. The American government in practice and in reality has usurped absolute power over the American people, because the American people have allowed this by foolishly surrendering their power to government, with the usual few exceptions here and there.

Those few are akin to the few in the American Revolution who fought a gigantic bully in order to establish a sovereign, egalitarian nation. Those few paid a heavy price, while the vast majority received the benefits provided to them by the sacrifices of the few, but took no action whatsoever to create the nation. In a similar, but convoluted vein, the few in America who speak of freedom and attempt to establish and maintain that freedom for the rest of the people get nowhere because the overwhelming majority of the people support and defend whatever the government wants, no matter how heinous or dictatorial. It is obvious that those who fought the Revolution created benefit for all, including those who opposed the Revolution. In the reversed position to the two elements within that Revolution, the few who have seen the truth, know the truth, comprehend its gravitas, can unfortunately be overcome by the overwhelming majority of Americans who either cannot or refuse to see truth or simply go along to get along, follow government dictates without question, support all the evil the government creates and in so doing allow the enslavement of a whole nation under the yoke of absolute tyranny. Will the few prevail again, as they did during the Revolution, or will they be swept under by the actions and inaction of those who just don't give a damn? Are the American people going to squander what those brave Revolutionaries fought for, or are they going to finally find their backbones, become true Americans and take back their country? We have also mentioned that Thomas Jefferson, the truly enlightened third president of this country, stated that it is the duty of all Americans to oppose all enemies of our republic, both foreign and domestic. It should be glaringly obvious now that those who rule us, pretty much across the board, are the domestic enemies of whom Jefferson spoke. Will the American people accept and exercise their duty to lawfully stop and remove these domestic enemies or submit to total slavery? The next few years will tell the story.

NARRATIVE EXPLANATIONS FOR *BYPASS* BUY/SELL PROGRAMS

INTRODUCTION TO PROJECTIONS

As many Americans have experienced and observed, today's society, in virtually all aspects, is very volatile, changeable, unpredictable and uncertain. What works successfully today may not work well eighteen months from now, or might be replaced by something totally different. Technology is rapidly changing our society in many different aspects. Prices, products, services, terms, governments' edicts and policies change quickly and often without notice. Understandably, a large segment of Americans are uncertain about the near future. Who know what may happen six months from now let alone what will happen in twenty years or so? Will the society still function along the same lines that it functions now, or will it be totally changed through governments' rules, regulations and restrictions, advanced technology, the AI culture, business and international considerations and myriad other uncertainties? Most Americans worry whether they will receive social security benefits when they retire, or their pensions, 401K accounts and other retirement programs in which they have invested, have been promised and expect. A lot of expectations have been altered by interfering forces, including government, of course. Uncertainty and change are rampant and constant. It seems that very little in today's world is safe and secure. In such a volatile society and economic climate, large numbers of people look ahead with concern to the uncertain future and those who are able want to invest now to achieve a substantial retirement in twenty years or so. Others may want to invest in something that may be safe and secure over a short term period with a reasonable return upon investment. The programs contained in this section address both situations.

The eternal consideration that always arises in the minds of investors is: where can they invest their money so that it is safe, secure and provides a reasonable return on investment over a long time period? If the investor wants that long term investment which meets these needs, pickings are slim and the field is limited. Some typical examples follow: (1) the stock market; (2) mutual funds; (3) existing businesses; (4) new businesses; (5) metals, such as gold or silver; (6) new ventures and speculation; (7) long term bank certificates of deposit; (8) corporate bonds and commercial paper; (9) rental properties. In the following paragraphs, we will take a look at each of these positions.

Throughout this book we have shown how government exerts so much control, so many restrictions and regulations upon the American society and businesses that it has become difficult to accomplish what one truly wants, without government interference. If people invest in the traditional ways, investing for either short term or long term gain can be adversely affected and limited by government, governmental control edicts and/or manipulated markets creating booms and busts. Choices can become very tight. The so-called American "free enterprise system" is not as free as people believe it is and certainly not as free as it was one hundred years ago. People who invest in a rigged, controlled, manipulated system, whatever that investment type may be, are at risk and could lose everything they invested. Our idea is to control our own money, in our own hands, under our own direction, and not place our money in the hands of others who could lose it overnight, or in the very rare alternative, make us a fortune. We prefer a safe, secure, largely unregulated, unrestricted form of enterprise that can provide a reasonable return upon investment, with minimal risks. Investments made in a rigged stock market are similar to making bets in a gambling casino. The difference between these two is that the casino gives better odds! The stock market is so manipulated and restricted that we do not consider it a safe place for long or even short term investment funds. The volatility is enormous and the institutional bank trading deals result in the transfer of millions upon millions of stocks in a matter of seconds. What chance do millions of small-time investors have in such scenarios? That type of manipulation combined with everything else we have discussed in this book keeps us very far away from the stock market.

Investing in mutual funds is just as risky as investing directly in the stock market for the reasons discussed and for the fact that the investor does not control his own funds and has no idea what will happen to them. Investments made in an existing business again place the control of the investor's money in the hands of others and for us this is not a safe, secure way to invest. Investments in new businesses are a gamble that could either produce great returns or the total loss of the investment, plus the possibility of incurring liabilities due to business losses. Unfortunately, in today's America many new businesses fold within three to five years. Gold and silver are safe and secure investments for a short time period, but if one expects great returns in twenty years, he could be very disappointed, or perhaps quite delighted. These investments can be a major risk. The precious metal markets, like virtually all other markets, are manipulated by the power forces. We would not invest any sum in markets that we know are manipulated, and those who do so, take a great risk. Gold has increased enormously in value over the past twenty or more years, as has silver. However, the history of the U.S. government puts a cloud over precious metal investing, as this shameful history clearly demonstrates that gold was confiscated from the people by the government and could be confiscated again. The people foolishly did not complain when their gold was unjustifiably and un-Constitutionally taken from them in 1933 by FDR's Executive Order 6102 that forced them to sell at rates well below market and will likely not complain again, if and when it happens again. Since the government likes non-complainers, because they are easy to control, the chances of confiscation occurring again are high, in our opinion. Further, gold is a passive investment and its value depends upon what occurs in the markets, which, of course, as we said above, are greatly manipulated, and on what government decrees and decides to do with the assets of the people. We do not consider this a safe investment at all. Silver at one time had a very high value and groups who owned large amounts of silver wanted to coin that metal into a currency. The government quickly stepped in and stopped this enterprise before it began and the price of silver essentially fell through the floor. We do not consider this a safe, secure investment.

There are always new ventures and speculative projects into which people can invest. However, the risks can be very high and the rewards either disastrous or excellent. For instance, land speculation in certain areas provided enormous profits for the speculators, but in some instances, it took forty to fifty years for the property to produce high returns. In other situations, it took less time, depending upon locations, proximities to population centers, population and business movement trends. In still other situations, the land proved to be valueless entirely. It takes real understanding and know-how to make safe, secure investments in land speculation. There are many other projects, ideas, schemes and inventions in which people can invest, but the vast majority of these are extremely risky, while the small minority may possibly provide enormous wealth. It is truly a crap shoot.

The American people are either already well aware or are becoming well aware of the monumental bank fraud perpetrated upon them, fully sanctioned by government. Long term investment in bank certificates of deposit is something we would never do, under any circumstances, no matter what promises or guarantees are made by the banks. We consider such guarantees worthless, based upon the actions of the banks. The interest that one would likely receive over the long term is so negligible that over twenty years the total return would be worth less than the original investment, given factors such as inflation, market and currency manipulations and God only knows what else.

Corporate bonds and commercial paper may seem like good investments, but over a twenty year time period, anything, and we mean *anything*, can happen to those bonds and that paper. Corporations could continue to grow and expand in power and market share, or they could go out of business, as so many have. If the latter case occurs, then those who own the corporate bonds or the commercial paper may have to settle for a mere percentage of their value, or worse, nothing at all. A twenty year bet on the success of the corporation or business has so many different variables that this investment is much too speculative for us.

Rental property usually at least maintains its market value and historically has increased in value over time, with the added benefit that the tenants who occupy the property pay for all expenses incurred by the property and leave a profit for the investor. This type of investment may not be considered glamorous or cutting edge, but it is usually safe, secure, protects wealth, builds wealth and provides a long term excellent return to the investor. This type of investment may be the safest of all—the most secure—and provide the most value to investors seeking these sound, prudent objectives.

BACKGROUND DATA AND PERSPECTIVE FOR PROJECTIONS

E ven people who are usually unaware of current situations and events occurring before them can now see that many events and matters in America have gotten way out of hand and vastly out of the control of the people within the American society. These mostly unaware people comprise a very large percentage of the American population. When this factor is combined with other more aware segments of our society, then an even larger percentage of our population is now aware on some level that something is very wrong. Throughout this book, we have demonstrated how the power forces have and continue to squeeze the people in order to reach the objectives these forces established long ago. Control, restrictions, manipulations, fraud, dependence upon the system for virtually everything, including food and shelter, are part of what the "swamp", to quote President Trump, has in store for most people in our American society. As we have said many times, because it bears repeating, economic, financial and monetary violence comprise the most insidious forms of violence that can be perpetrated upon a people by the governing body of a nation. When the people begin to recognize these factors and attempt to stop and eliminate these forms of violence, through making grievances to the system, then, instead of helping the people, this system employs systems' violence to protect those who created, fostered and benefit from the economic, financial and monetary violence. Anyone in America who has gone through the catastrophes of foreclosure and job loss is well aware of what the system does to protect the wrongdoing of the system. None of this is how the United States of America was designed, but this is now the ugly reality existing throughout our once great Constitutional republic.

When these factors are combined with climate control, weather manipulation, secret government actions kept from the people by government, the implementation of 5G, GWEN towers, HAARP, manipulations and obfuscations of solar and other cosmic cycles, and many other disturbing situations, such as the rapid deployment of AI, then people should be aware that they cannot put their faith and trust in government and its systems. It would be far better for the American people to place their trust in themselves, become as independent as possible, resourceful, responsible, creative, inventive, and look to themselves to care and provide for themselves and their families. The investments stated within these projections may be one way for the resourceful, independent-minded investor to invest in his own wisdom and not in others who take his money, his control, power and investment funds from him. Wise, aware people might want to have a home they own, without bank debt, and a monetary stream that cannot lawfully be stopped, restricted or controlled by government edict, intervention, administrative regulations—or some other form of draconian control that spells destruction of the people's liberty, ownership and right to engage in and earn an independent living. We all, as human beings, and especially as American Citizens, have the natural *inherent* right to earn a living and provide for ourselves and our families independently from restrictive government policies.

Hardworking Americans who have done the right thing most of their lives and worked diligently to support themselves and their families have been thrown out of their own homes, while illegal immigrants, indigents, druggies, bums and ne'er do well criminals and deviants are given Section 8 housing and other government subsidized housing arrangements, travel accommodations, food and clothing, cash vouchers, transportation and medical care by the U.S. government that is Constitutionally required to maintain the "general welfare" of *all* the Americans the government was put into place to serve and protect. The only "welfare" this government upholds is financial welfare for the referenced reprobates, while the average American worker gets screwed into the ground by the same government that gives everything to the lowest, non-productive, parasitical elements in society, at the expense of the productive members of society. Of course, on the other end, the government provides tremendous welfare, in the form of subsidies, grants, tax breaks and other benefits, to the wealthiest corporations and banks in this nation, again, at the expense of the average hard-working, productive American. All this amounts to gross economic violence committed by the government upon the resourceful, productive, well-meaning and well-intended working people, and financial largess for the derelict, destructive elements of society, and the richest elements. Most Americans are very good people and most Americans have absolutely no problem with providing financial welfare to those within our society who are in genuine need of that assistance. Americans are among the most generous people in this world and have proven this over and over again, but these generous American people do not deserve to be deceived, used and abused by their own government. Despite all of this, the people are still unaware that they live in a covert communist country, ruled by a government that purposefully drives the nation, the people, small businesses and small corporations and virtually the entire society into economic and social desperation, poverty and ruin. Our deceptive government does this to gain and maintain total control over the people, the economy, businesses and industries of America to pave the way for overt communism.

It may sound very strange, but in this very insane world, sometimes what appears to be "strange" is the exact reality that our controllers and power forces have planned for a very long time, want firmly established in America, but don't want Americans to recognize. As stated earlier, more and more Americans are realizing every day that many things are very wrong in this nation. What most people still do not realize, however, is that the real root of what is wrong is the rule of the domestic-enemy-traitors and governments that control this nation to achieve only the sinister objectives that these power forces want—and not to uphold the will and best interests of the people. If America were truly a free and open society, with a government that had the best interests of the people in mind and in practice and truly wanted to uphold the "general welfare", then the restrictive present governmental controls would never exist. The fact that massive controls exist throughout American society conclusively proves that America is not a free nation and the will of the people is not upheld by their own governments. These governments and power forces have long planned for people and businesses to fail so that government will gain more power through these failures. Those people who failed in life and those who work for businesses and corporations that failed became dependent upon government in one way or another. Through these machinations the governments become more powerful by providing welfare to these people and thus controlling them in virtually all economic, political and social aspects. If those who receive government benefits display independence or opposition, they lose their benefits. This destroys any ambition among the people, any "outside the box" thinking and keeps people under the control of the system, which, of course, was the power forces' original design.

If governments truly wanted business and personal success within America, then it is pretty obvious to any logical American that governments would work diligently *with* the people and businesses to achieve that objective. The fact that they do not proves this position. Even the most non-aware people are beginning to see this. At present, few understand it and the reasons for it, but at least they are becoming aware of it. Becoming aware is the necessary first step to bring about beneficial changes. When governments place massive restrictions, regulations, controls, license and permit requirements, burdensome costs and fees, never-ending and ever-increasing taxes and numerous other controlling devices upon existing and new businesses—especially those that are not huge corporations—then eventually most of those businesses and small corporations fail. People can see this happening everywhere across America and definitely within their own communities. Of course, the so-called "star" city areas, with lucrative and plentiful government contracts, such as Boston, New York, Los Angeles, Denver, San Francisco, etc., do extremely well, but average America outside of these "star" cities fares much less well in varying degrees. If governments wanted businesses and small corporations to succeed, then obviously governments would not have imposed such harsh restrictive conditions which greatly contributed to their failures.

In the alternative, governments would not have imposed restrictive conditions and taxes upon businesses, but instead would have aided and abetted the viability of the businesses in many constructive ways so that the chances for real success and long standing operation would be assured. Policies such as these would be implemented by governments that encourage and want personal and business successes throughout the nation, and not the current draconian measures imposed by governments to essentially ruin small businesses and corporations. The backbone of American commerce—small businesses and small corporations—have been largely decimated by governments' policies and restrictions. Previously we mentioned that the federal government encouraged corporations and entire industries to abandon America and set up their operations in third world countries. Our government instituted trade policies with other nations that further damaged existing American businesses, industries and manufacturing. None of these trade policies did nor do now benefit the average American and average American business, but in fact hurt people, businesses and, as a result, whole communities and the entire nation.

Another factor that most people do not realize is that inflation is a monetary killer, a wealth killer, a gain killer and of course makes virtually everything more expensive for all parties. All of this saps funds from the people and businesses by making them pay more for less in terms of products, goods and services and a never-ending price escalation cycle. The more funds people and businesses spend because of inflation, the less they have to spend on necessities and the usual expenditures required for them to live a normal, healthy, happy life. Higher costs for products that should never cost more force people to buy less and/or stop buying certain items altogether. Reduced spending for fewer products and services can cause some businesses and suppliers to reduce their business activities or to eliminate them entirely. Some things are just too expensive for a large segment of the population.

Obviously, to the objective, rational observer, inflation is not necessary and certainly not good for businesses or industries at all. When one really wants to find out who benefits from such a situation, then a good step forward is to follow the money. The real question is who controls, causes and implements inflation? That can be answered by naming the entity that controls, owns and issues the money supply—namely, America's central bank, the private, for-profit Federal Reserve Bank, acting as if it were owned and operated by the government. No matter what this bank and government may say to the contrary, inflation works in their favor to reach their objectives. If this were not true, then inflation would either be non-existent or minor, at best. Another factor regarding inflation is the gigantic corporations and those who own and control them. If people were to do some research on this subject, they would discover that virtually all of the major large corporations, businesses, industries and banks are owned and controlled by a very small elite power force, many of which are interconnected. Inflation advances their agenda, their control and their objectives. In the alternative, it is clear that inflation does not work well for average Americans or average American small businesses. Inflation is a key element in achieving the evil results that the power forces want.

As we have said earlier, and as the people have begun to see, when average Americans lose their jobs, exhaust unemployment benefits, cannot get another comparable job, paying a comparable salary, lose their homes, wind up in small rental properties, or with relatives, friends or even on the street, it is beyond doubt that the systems' policies put them there and put the businesses for which they worked out of business or out of the country. There is no help for them from the same government whose policies destroyed them and the company for which they worked. However, there is major help for the people who do not work, choose not to work, have not worked for a long time, for the welfare kings and queens, for the degenerates or druggies or bums who get everything they need and want from the same government that destroyed the average American workers and the companies for which they worked. Obviously, to anyone with a modicum of common sense there is something awfully wrong with this scenario in the so-called "land of the free". When large numbers of productive, capable workers in our American society suffer economic violence from their own government and the power forces, while the unproductive, the lazy, the dependent, druggies, degenerates, criminals, bums, welfare frauds and immigrants, whether legal or illegal, are given vast funds and massive benefits from that same government, then it is clearly evident that those policies are *intentional,* and not accidental.

Can any American who understands this and other truths that government has hidden from the people ever trust that government and that system again? Logic would say "NO!" Just because those who do not see this now are so blind, because it does not affect them now, does not mean that they themselves will not be affected at some future time. We are all Americans and when our fellow Americans get damaged, we get damaged. Injustice against the productive must be halted, and quickly, while institutional welfare for the unworthy must immediately cease. Government will never do this, because government never stops its own programs, especially when the real motive behind these programs is to get the people totally dependent upon government, in virtually all areas of life.

As it has always been, it is now up to the people to hold governments accountable, responsible and liable for their actions and to right the wrongs governments have committed forever against the good, worthy, industrious, hard-working, decent American people who are the backbone of our nation. The people must learn that they have the political power *guaranteed* to them in the Constitution and must take and lawfully use this power so that they can begin to restore Constitutional governance to America. This will not happen all at once, but can begin one community, one town, one city, one county, one state at a time. President Trump has stated many times that he wants to return the political power back to the people. However, if the American people fail to retake and lawfully assert that power, then the people will get more of the same ill treatment from the un-Constitutional governments that control them in so many ways and can bring economic and other forms of devastation upon them at will.

All this is just common sense and thankfully people are beginning to develop common sensibilities again. To truly understand what occurs in this country, all people really have to do is open their eyes, open their minds and objectively look at the existing realities operating in this nation. People do not have to be students of history or of human behavior or of government to understand what is going on directly before them. As many of us have known, when the bully has no opposition, and is not stopped in his tracks, he does exactly what he wants to anyone he wants at any time he wants. If the American people fail to take back and lawfully exercise their political power, then things will become even more difficult for Americans. For those of you who realize that you must be as independent from government and the system, as possible, both within your home and family and with an independent, continuous financial stream, the projections in this book could be of immense value and help to you.

CHAPTER SIXTY FIVE

PROJECTIONS – A NARRATIVE EXPLANATION

L ater in this CHAPTER, we will present projections regarding the buying and selling and then the buying and renting of houses, both of which may be of interest to investors. These financial projections are quite sound, safe, secure and doable in today's real estate market. Before we get into the substance of the projections, we want to provide a little background material.

The buying and selling of homes, as presented in this book, is rather unique and quite beneficial to both the buyer and the seller. As referenced previously, obtaining bank mortgages has been a major obstacle and hurdle for both buyers and sellers. Unfortunately, these mortgage obstacles have prevented many sales that were scheduled to close from taking place, much to the detriment and disappointment of both buyers and sellers. The buying/selling/mortgage approaches discussed in this book are very easy, direct and conducted between the principals, with no third parties or banks involved, as things of this nature should be. In the typical conventional markets approaches, a variety of entities which are not parties to the contract, not principals, impose contractual terms which bind the principals. This is certainly not a free market position for principals, because they get obligated by conditions dictated by others. Many buyers and sellers would have avid interest in property transactions accomplished on our simple, common sense basis, and some of them may want to become investors using these methods. For those who do, we have developed six different sets of projections for the buying and selling of homes, as well as for the buying and renting of homes.

As discussed earlier, under our methods, homes can be purchased whether they are debt free or have existing mortgages. Since the buyer-investor of a home under these methods can resell the home and then carry the note for the new buyer, the investor's buyer does not need to obtain a bank mortgage. This is a major advantage and attraction for most buyers. Because the seller-investor will carry the note, this puts his home in a uniquely desirable position in comparison to homes being sold via system's methods and could help it sell very quickly. Largely because of the disastrous mortgage debacle, in which millions of people lost their homes through foreclosure, thus, created huge numbers of renters, the rental market is strong now in most areas of the country, which, obviously, is a major advantage to any investor who purchases homes with the intent of renting them. The projections referenced deal in both the buying/selling and renting of homes.

All of our projections contain two *hypothetical* house examples. One example is a house purchased for $100,000.00, with 15% down ($15,000.00), namely 15% of the purchase price, and the $85,000.00 balance is carried by the seller at 5% for 15 years. The second example is a house purchased for $60,000.00, with 15% down, ($9,000.00), with a balance of $51,000.00 carried by the seller at 5% for 15 years. **These are examples only**, since investors will purchase houses in various different price ranges, with different mutually agreed upon terms. We use these two examples because the greater need for seller-carried mortgages typically exists in these lower price ranges. Of course, the need for seller-carried mortgages exists in virtually all price ranges, but from the investors' position, the lower price ranges should provide them with many more buyers and sellers.

Previously, we discussed how the contrived and disastrous mortgage crisis damaged millions of American families throughout this country, causing them to lose their homes and move into less desirable apartments or rental homes, or tragically, even live in cars, in boxes, under bridges or roam the streets. America was not designed in such a way and the American people should never be subject to conditions such as these through the intentional criminal actions of governments and banks. If Americans were much more cognizant of the Constitution, the declared Supreme Law of the Land, they would know that the Preamble to this Constitution, as well as the document itself, prohibit such activities being conducted by the government which inflict such disastrous results upon the people. In many cases, the rentals occupied by people who lost their homes cost more per month than the mortgage payments had been on the homes that were lost. Since most of these people who are working and thus capable of purchasing another home would not qualify for a bank mortgage, many of them would be very willing and eager buyers for lower priced houses with notes carried by the seller. When sellers are willing to accept a down payment and ready to carry the balance for a 15 year period, at reasonable interest, then they should have many capable buyers eager to make that purchase.

In previous CHAPTERs which described the down payment and mortgage arrangements for these two examples, we mentioned that the amount of the 180 monthly note payments—15 years—for the $85,000.00 note on the $100,000.00 house is projected to be $650.29 per month. For the $51,000.00 note on the $60,000.00 house, the amount of the 180 monthly note payments—15 years—is projected to be $390.10 per month. Obviously, figures will vary for different priced houses on different terms and interest rates. As previously mentioned, of the $650.29 projected monthly mortgage payment for the $100,000.00 house, $472.22 is paid to principal and $177.78 is paid to interest. Of the projected $390.10 mortgage payment for the $60,000.00 house, $283.33 is paid to principal and $106.67 is paid to interest. An extremely favorable feature of this type of mortgage arrangement is that the buyer can accrue equity quickly because of the equal and standardized distribution of principal and interest payments over the life of the mortgage. Buyers pay their standard monthly payments to secure their positions, and the sellers' receipt of these payments, through the mortgage on their own former home, provides them with excellent security. Should the buyer default, the seller-investor could call the note, take over the property, keep the down payment and all mortgage payments received, then sell the house again. The second buyer could sell the house he purchases, provided he guarantees the monthly mortgage payment to the original seller-investor. The best way to do this is for the second seller, or in this case, the investor, to take a small second mortgage on the house when he sells it. Again, should his buyer default, then the seller-investor can call the note, take over the house and sell it again. This method of buying/selling/financing houses is very straightforward, safe, secure and equally favorable to both buyer and seller.

This type of buying/selling/financing can work in any price range, since many capable buyers in any price range would have avid interest in a property whose seller will accept a down payment and carry the note. In the higher price ranges, some factors to consider are the higher down payment requirements and the higher note amount, because of the higher purchase price. For example, if an investor were to purchase a home for $500,000.00 and make a 15% down payment, that amounts to $75,000.00. The seller would carry a note of $425,000.00. If we remain within the same projection percentage range of the lower priced properties, then the investor would resell his home for $575,000.00. Since the investor, who is now the seller will carry the note of $425,000.00 and possibly a second note, so that the buyer can make a lesser down payment up front, the buyer is not required to obtain bank financing and deal with the usual bank qualifications, processes, requirements, inspections, lawyers, high closing costs and, of course, the never-ending points and additional fees.

The return to the investor would be excellent, if he wants to deal in higher priced homes and has the means to do so. However, the number of homes and the turnover rate would likely not be in the same range as would be those of the lower priced houses. Each market is different, but all markets have the same appeal for a capable buyer with a seller who will accept a down payment and carry the balance. In whatever price range the investor chooses, it would be best to start slowly, conservatively, and test the market. When investors have seen and appreciated the results and know the success rate, then moving forward quickly to make other purchases would be in their best interests. Keep in mind that many sellers with existing mortgages on their homes in any price range have difficulties selling their homes in the conventional market approach because of those mortgages. We have discussed this at length in previous CHAPTERs. In the lower price ranges, many capable buyers cannot pass bank scrutiny, cannot qualify to assume an existing mortgage or obtain a new mortgage. As a result, a home that should easily sell on the open market does not sell. This is also true, but in fewer numbers, for both buyers and sellers in the higher price ranges.

Other reasons exist for buying/selling/financing lower priced houses. As mentioned several times, millions of families lost their homes through the economic disaster and the massive foreclosure crisis that began in earnest in 2007. Some of those people lost everything. As also mentioned, some were forced to take apartments or rental houses in less desirable areas that cost more per month than their prior mortgage payments on the homes they lost. A very large segment of these families should have avid interest in purchasing lower priced houses, and especially when the seller is willing to carry the note. Few of these people could qualify for bank financing, but have the financial capability to purchase and pay for a home in the lower price ranges. As discussed earlier, many sellers with existing mortgages have difficulty selling, because the bank usually wants to be paid off at closing and/or will not allow the new buyer to assume the note. Our type of buying/selling/financing arrangement can satisfy the needs of multitudes of buyers and sellers and allow for home purchases that never would have taken place, had banks dictated the terms and/or denied the financing.

As many people now know, even though the economy nationwide is still weak, despite glowing reports from government, prices of just about everything across the board are steadily rising, with no end in sight. Electric rates are rapidly going up. Fuel oil prices are increasing, as are coal, natural gas and wood. Water and sewer bills are on the rise. Gasoline prices, food, medicines, health care, prescriptions, plumbing, electrical work, carpentry and other skilled service costs are skyrocketing. Property taxes are rapidly increasing in many areas of the country, even though a large part of America is still in economic turmoil and many people are struggling just to stay afloat.

Because of these and other factors, it may serve the best interests of most families to purchase homes in the lower price ranges.

If one were to compare all operating costs for homes in the range of $60,000.00 to $100,000.00 to all operating costs for homes in the $600,000.00 range, there is a vast difference in all areas. The upkeep and repair costs, alone, would be vastly different. The electric, heating and air conditioning costs would be substantially higher. Property taxes for the $600,000.00 home would be much higher than for the lower priced homes. Water and sewer rates would be much higher. Government restrictions and codes could likely be more severe and restrictive for the $600,000.00 home in a higher priced neighborhood. Even though some can afford it, rather than spend a considerable amount of funds to purchase a $600,000.00 home, meet the high mortgage payments, pay the high operational and maintenance costs, it may better serve a family to purchase a lower priced home, then invest the extra funds they would have paid for the higher priced house in additional properties that would produce a steady income and/or quick returns that would put them in a secure position and then possibly put them into a better position to buy a higher priced home in the future.

The American people are slowly beginning to realize that the "American Dream" is definitely not what it was and may not even be achievable for most people. In earlier CHAPTERs we referred to economic violence perpetrated upon the people, which is the most insidious of all forms of violence. When people want to remove themselves from the clutches of economic violence and go to the system for relief, that system exerts more violence upon them in terms of judicial/court violence, governmental violence and system violence. At present, our so-called justice system is improperly named, because the only "justice" it typically dispenses is to the criminal, treasonous element, and not to the average, hard-working, decent, well-meaning American. If we, as an American society, continue to allow our governments and courts to restrict our Rights, to deny our Rights, to deny our guaranteed Due Process of law, to prevent us from achieving economic parity or success, and to essentially rob us blind, in association with their greedy corporate partners, especially the banking partners, then the evil that has enslaved America for so long will expand and escalate exponentially.

Another major consideration is the state of the economy which, as we have indicated and as we fully believe, is egregiously manipulated, controlled by extremely powerful forces who cruelly determine the fate of the American people. We have seen that in other financial disasters many people who had high-paying jobs lost them overnight. However, the bills continue to pour in, even though there is no money to pay them. Most people in America not only live within their means, but live way beyond their means, which means that many of them go deeply into bank and other debt. When a financial crisis happens, as they regularly do in this nation, and large amounts of such people lose their jobs, with little to no prospects of other similar jobs, then they are essentially two to three paychecks away from disaster. Living within one's means is very important, and taking on unnecessary bank and other debt is something people should never do, because they become beholden to and controlled by the system. The material and the projections in this book show a way out for many Americans, who, otherwise, could be caught in an economic catastrophe. Please look over the projections very closely and see if something along these lines will suit the best interests of you, your family, your home and your future earning ability. It is vitally important today that people become as independent from the system and from government as they possibly can. We all live in a highly controlled society, but engaging in an enterprise that has great potential and fewer controls is the best way to free yourself and live the life you want. Investing in real estate in the manner we describe is the best way to fulfill that objective, in our opinion.

CHAPTER SIXTY SIX

PROJECTIONS EXPLAINED

The following pages contain three (3) sets of projections which we designed for an investor or investors who want to place a relatively small sum into a down payment for purchase of a house, then sell that house at a higher price through our mortgage program. The first set of projections deals with a buy/sell with a $15,000.00 investment. As we have mentioned before, and as is well known in today's society, conventional approach mortgage problems hinder many buyers and sellers, thus have prevented them from closing purchase transactions. As we have seen, many sellers cannot sell their houses with an existing mortgage, since the bank holding the mortgage wants to be paid cash upon sale or will not allow the potential buyer to assume the mortgage. On the other side, many buyers are prevented from purchasing houses with existing mortgages because of this restriction or because they cannot qualify to assume the existing mortgage or obtain a new one. This amounts to a basic "catch 22" in which many different people on both sides are prevented from either buying or selling. Large numbers of both buyers and sellers who are willing to transact a sale are unable to do so because of these restrictive mortgage considerations. If a seller could offer his home for sale and also offer to accept a 15% or so down payment then carry the remaining balance through a note on the property, he could likely sell his house very quickly. It is pretty obvious that large numbers of capable buyers would be very willing to buy a home if the seller would do this. In this type of purchase, no new bank financing is necessary, which means no bank paperwork, no bank points and fees, no bank demands, no bank restrictions, no bank inspections and no costly closings. The transaction would be conducted between the principals, only—the buyer and the seller—with no outside third party requirements and no interference.

In earlier CHAPTERs, we specified how a financially capable buyer with a down payment and steady work so that he has the ability to pay a monthly mortgage payment could purchase a home with the balance carried by the seller. One approach would be the purchase from a home seller who owns his home debt-free—with no mortgage—willing to carry the balance. Another is from a seller who has an existing mortgage on his home and is willing to sell it on the basis we described earlier. You might want to review those sections for more clarification. Our prospective investor buys a house from a seller, based upon one of the above scenarios, then, offers the house for resale and states that he will accept a down payment and carry the balance on reasonable terms. Since obtaining a conventional mortgage is a major obstacle for many buyers, being able to purchase a home from the seller who will carry the balance should quickly attract serious attention from many serious, sincere and capable buyers.

We call these types of transactions **buy/sell sales** and we present three different sets of projections regarding this type of investment. The first set of projections is for an investor or group of investors who purchases a home from a seller for $100,000.00. The seller either owns the home, free and clear, with no mortgage debt, or has an existing mortgage on the property. In the first case, the seller accepts a down payment of $15,000.00 and carries the $85,000.00 balance at 5% for 15 years. In the second case, the seller contracts the sale with the buyer, accepts the $15,000.00 down payment and the buyer purchases 50% of the house, takes possession of it, accepts the *obligation* of the existing mortgage, but does not assume the mortgage and note. The difference between the down payment and the existing mortgage is carried by the seller on terms mutually agreed upon between buyer and seller. The purchase contract and note permit the buyer to sell the house, provided the buyer maintains a financial interest in the house and guarantees the original seller that the monthly mortgage note will be timely paid. The original buyer's financial interest in the house is a small second mortgage. Our buyer now becomes a seller and offers the house for sale at $115,000.00, with the balance carried by him. Again, there is no new bank financing and all that this would entail in this scenario, therefore, no bank qualification constraints, whatsoever. The new buyer will have to demonstrate to our seller that he has the down payment amount and the financial capability to pay both the original seller's existing monthly mortgage payment and the second mortgage note amount to the secondary seller. Many buyers can do this, but, sadly, many of them have been excluded from doing so, because they cannot qualify for a bank mortgage. The seller's willingness to carry the note is what makes the transaction possible.

In the first set of projections, the seller buys the house for $100,000.00. He made a $15,000.00 down payment and has an $85,000.00 note at 5% interest for a 15 year term. Our seller-investor sells the house for $115,000.00, accepts a down payment of $25,000.00, carries the

$85,000.00 note, and takes a second or third mortgage on the house for $5,000.00. The $25,000.00 down payment, plus the $85,000.00 note and the second or third mortgage for $5,000.00 total the purchase price of $115,000.00. The $25,000.00 down payment amounts to 21.7% of the purchase price, which is quite reasonable for buying a house from a seller who is willing to carry the balance. As we have discussed in previous CHAPTERs, down payment amounts can be handled in different, creative ways, if there is sincere interest in consummating a sale. For instance, if the buyer cannot meet the $25,000.00 down payment at the time of the sale, other arrangements can be made. The seller could accept $20,000.00 down, 17.3% of the purchase price, with the other $5,000.00 paid over 24 months to meet the $25,000.00 down payment amount. Further, with $20,000.00 down, the other $5,000.00 could be added to the second or third mortgage, now making that mortgage amount $10,000.00.

We project that, on this basis, our seller can sell that house for $115,000.00 within a two month period. The major component that makes this sale possible very quickly is that the seller carries the note and the buyer does not need to seek financing from a bank with all of the usual restrictive requirements. Logically, many financially capable buyers would be very interested. In this case, the sale could happen more quickly than within a two month period. However, we project seller's carrying costs until the house sells for the two month period, which include principal and interest payments, taxes and insurance. These costs approximately amount to the following: (1) mortgage payments--$650.29 x 2 = $1,300.58; (2) taxes: $233.33; (3) insurance--$150.00; (4) home inspection--$350.00. These carrying costs total $2,033.91 for the two month period which we round up to $2,050.00. When our seller-investor sells the house, we project that he receives a $25,000.00 down payment, as stated above, thus he recaptures his original $15,000.00, paid when he bought the property, plus whatever profit he makes on the sale. We project a reasonable $12,950.00 profit, as follows: $10,000.00 cash gross profit, minus $2,050.00 two-month carrying costs, for a cash return of $12,950.00 plus $7,950.00, for a total of $22,950.00. The other $5,000.00 of the $15,000.00 profit is in a $5,000.00 second or third mortgage which secures our seller-investor's financial interest in the property. As stated, our seller-investor guarantees his original seller that the payments on the original seller's existing mortgage will be timely made. Should our seller-investor's buyer default, then our seller-investor can foreclose, take over the property and sell it again. We project an interest rate of 10% on all second and third mortgages, payable yearly on the anniversary of the sale, principal balance due in 15 years. The second or third mortgage, in any amount, is extremely important, since that mortgage, as stated above, maintains our seller-investor's financial interest in the property as a mortgage holder. Should his buyer default, then, pursuant to the second or third mortgage position our seller-investor holds, he can repossess the house and sell it again.

Our projections call for six phases per year, two months per phase. For the second phase, our seller-investor has $22,950.00 available to buy other properties for resale. In phase two, we project the investor will buy two houses priced at $60,000.00 each, with $9,000.00 down payments per house—15% of the purchase price—totaling $18,000.00. The two-month carrying expenses amount to $1,330.00 per house, a total of $2,660.00 for both houses. These costs per house are broken down as follows: (1) mortgage payments--$390.17 x two = $780.34; (2) taxes--$83.33; (3) insurance--$87.50; (4) house inspection $350, for a total cost of $1,301.17. We round this off to $1,330.00 per house for phase two costs, times two houses, totaling $2,660.00. The investor offers the houses for resale at $70,000.00 each, and states that he will carry the balance through 15 year notes, which, again, should attract many capable buyers, since the buyer is not required to qualify for and obtain a bank mortgage by jumping through the usual hoops.

Our seller-investor sells the houses at $70,000.00 each and receives the $17,000.00 down payment per house, which is 24% of the purchase price, totaling $34,000.00. Our seller-investor invested $18,000.00 in down payments when he bought the two houses, $9,000.00 each, receives $34,000.00 from down payments when he sells the houses, minus $2,660.00 for the two-month carrying expenses, for a cash profit of $13,340.00. Added to this profit are his initial $18,000.00 down payments amount, recaptured upon sale, and the $4,950.00 cash overage from phase one, for a cash return of $36,290.00. The $51,000.00 note on each house is assumed by the buyers. Our seller-investor places a $2,000.00 second or third mortgage on each property. As a mortgage holder, he can take over the property should the buyer default and thus maintain the first mortgage payment contract with the original seller. The $70,000.00 selling price per house consists of: (1) $17,000.00 down payment; (2) note of $51,000.00; (3) second mortgage of $2,000.00, for a total of $70,000.00.

From the $36,290.00 cash available to our seller-investor, in phase three, he buys four houses for $60,000.00 each, with a 15% down payment of $9,000.00 per house, which amounts to $36,000.00 invested. The six columns in our projections spell out the financials for each of the six phases. Column one spells out the cash amount available for house purchases. Column two spells out the number of houses bought and the down payment amount paid, which indicates the house price. 9T is for a $60,000.00 house; 15T is for a $100,000.00 house. Column three specifies cash profit for a house, minus carrying costs and sales expenses.

Column four states total cash returned, consisting of investment, plus profit. Column five specifies second or third mortgage amounts. Column six states cash overage, meaning the available cash amount remaining after house purchases.

The projections are listed by year and by phase. As stated, each phase is two months, six phases per year. The first page of projections is Year One, Phase One, followed on the next pages with Phase Two, up to Phase Six. Each page and phase has six columns, as follows: (1) column one—AVAILABLE CASH; (2) column two—INVESTMENT AMOUNT; (3) column three—CASH PROFIT; (4) column four—CASH RETURN; (5) column five—SECOND AND THIRD MORTGAGES; (6) column six—CASH OVERAGE. These phases are more fully described above. Each year of projections follows the same format. Funds flow from phase to phase and year to year. For instance, we will explain the investment figures in columns in Year One, Phase One. In Year One, Phase One, the investor begins with a $15,000.00 investment, which is listed in column one under AVAILABLE CASH. The $15,000.00 investment is used as a down payment to purchase a house for $100,000.00, and the seller carries the $85,000.00 balance. One house with a $15,000.00 down payment is listed in column two, INVESTMENTS. The investor sells the house for $115,000.00 with a $25,000.00 down payment (21.7%), $85,000.00 carried by the seller, and a $5,000.00 second or third mortgage totals $115,000.00. $10,000.00 of the profit is listed in column three, CASH PROFIT. The other $5,000.00 is listed in SECOND MORTGAGES in column five. From this $10,000.00 profit, $2,050.00 in carrying costs, explained previously, is deducted as sales expenses, leaving net cash profit of $7,950.00 listed in column three. Upon sale, the total return to seller-investor is listed in column four, CASH RETURN. These returns are: (1) $15,000.00, investor's down payment; (2) $7,950.00, investor's profit, for a cash return of $22,950.00. Column five, SECOND MORTGAGES, spells out one second or third mortgage of $5,000.00 payable to the seller-investor. Column six, CASH OVERAGE, specifies cash amounts remaining after the investments are made in each phase. These cash amounts can be added to available cash in the next phase for additional house purchases. As stated, the CASH RETURN, column four, flows from phase to phase and year to year.

At the end of the first year projections, we will provide a brief recap and a further explanation.

SECTION NINE

BYPASS BUY/SELL PROGRAMS PROJECTIONS

PROJECTIONS – BUY/SELL $15,000 PROGRAM – YEAR ONE, PHASE ONE

Available Cash	Investment	Cash Profit	Cash Return	Second Mortgages	Cash Overage
$15,000	1 House down payment for $15,000 = $15,000	1 x $10,000 Less sales expenses of $2,050 For	$15,000 investment Combined with $7,950 profit For	1 x $5,000 = $5,000	$0
		Net profit of $7950	Total cash return of $22,950		
TOTALS					
$15,000	$15,000 outlay for 1 house	$7,950 53% on investment	$22,950 153% return	$5,000	$0

PROJECTIONS – BUY/SELL $15,000 PROGRAM – YEAR ONE, PHASE TWO

Available Cash	Investment	Cash Profit	Cash Return	Second Mortgages	Cash Overage
$22,950	2 house down payments for $9,000 each = $18,000	2 x $8,000 = $16,000 Less sales expenses: 2 x $1,330 = $2,660 = $13,340 net, + $ 4,950 cash overage for	$18,000 investment Combined with $18,290 profit FOR	2 x $2,000 = $4,000	$4,950 Less $4,950 to profit = $0
		Net profit of: $18,290	Total cash return of: $36,290		
TOTALS					
$22,950	$18,000 outlay for 2 houses	$18,290 101.61% on investment	$36,290 206.61% return	$4,000	$0
CUMULATIVE TOTALS					
$37,950	$33,000 outlay for 3 houses	$26,240 79.51% profit	$59,240 179.51% R	$9,000	$0

PROJECTIONS – BUY/SELL $15,000 PROGRAM – YEAR ONE, PHASE THREE

Available Cash	Investment	Cash Profit	Cash Return	Second Mortgages	Cash Overage
$36,290	4house down payments for $9,000 each= $36,000	4 x $8,000 = $32,000 Less sales expenses: 4 x $1,330 = $5,320 FOR	$36,000 investment Combined with $26,680 PROFIT FOR	4 x $2,000 = $8,000	$290
		$26,680 Net profit	$62,680 Total cash return		
TOTALS					
$36,290	$36,000 outlay for 4 houses	$26,680 74.11 % Profit	$62,680 174.11% R	$8,000	$290
CUMULATIVE TOTALS					
$74,240	$69,000 outlay for 7 houses	$52,920 76.69% profit	$121,920 176.69% R	$17,000	$290

PROJECTIONS – BUY/SELL $15,000 PROGRAM – YEAR ONE, PHASE FOUR

Available Cash	Investment	Cash Profit	Cash Return	Second Mortgages	Cash Overage
$62,680	7 house down payments of $9,000 each = $63,000	7 x $8,000 = $56,000 Less sales expenses: 7 x $1,330 = $9,310 FOR	$63,000 investment Combined with $46,690 PROFIT FOR	7 x $2,000 = $14,000	$(30)
		$46,690 Net profit	$109,690l cash return		
TOTALS					
$62,680	$63,000 outlay for 7 houses	$46,690 74.11% profit	$109,690 174.11% R	$14,000	$(30)
CUMULATIVE TOTALS					
$255,690	$132,000 outlay for 14 houses	$99,610 75.46% profit	$231,610 175.46% R	$31,000	$260

PROJECTIONS – BUY/SELL $15,000 PROGRAM – YEAR ONE, PHASE FIVE

Available Cash	Investment	Cash Profit	Cash Return	Second Mortgages	Cash Overage
$109,690	12 house down payments of $9,000 each = $108,000	12 x $8,000 = $96,000 Less sales expenses: 12 x $1,330 = $15,960 FOR	$108,000 investment Combined with $80,040 profit FOR	12 x $2,000 = $24,000	$1,690 less ($30) = $1,660
		$80,040 Net Profit	$188,040 cash return		
TOTALS					
$109,370	$108,000 outlay for 12 houses	$80,040 74.11% PROFIT	$188,040 174.11 RETURN	$24,000	$1,660
CUMULATIVE TOTALS					
$365,360	$240,000 outlay for 26 houses	$179,650 74.85% PROFIT	$419,640 174.85% RE-TURN	$55,000	$1,920

PROJECTIONS – BUY/SELL $15,000 PROGRAM – YEAR ONE, PHASE SIX

Available Cash	Investment	Cash Profit	Cash Return	Second Mortgages	Cash Overage
$188,040	21 house down payments of $9,000 each = $189,000	21 x $8,000 = $168,000 Less sales expenses: 21 x $1,330 = $27,930 for	$189,000 investment Combined with $140,070 profit for	21 x $2,000 = $42,000	$1,660 - 960 $ 700
		Net profit of $140,070	Total cash return of $329,070		
TOTALS					
$188,040	$189,000 for 21 houses	$140,070 74.11% profit	$329,070 174.11% R	$42,000	$700
CUMULATIVE TOTALS					
$434,330	$429,000 for 47 houses	$319,720 74.52% profit	$748,710 174.52% R	$97,000	$2,620

ANALYSIS OF YEAR ONE PROJECTIONS

IMPORTANT POINTS – YEAR ONE PROJECTIONS

All projections in this section of this book are intended for profit derived through the buying and selling of houses. HOWEVER, THERE ARE ADDITIONAL SUBSTANTIAL PROFITS THAT WE DID NOT INCLUDE IN THESE PROJECTIONS—AND THEY ARE EXTENSIVE.

These additional projected profit categories are listed below:

1. Retained earnings;
2. Recaptured earnings;
3. Profit derived from interest paid on second and third mortgages;
4. Principal balance of second and third mortgages.

Retained earnings and recaptured earnings are projections that will likely occur in Year One through Year Three, or to the end of the investment program. These projected profits will be included as additional profit to short-term Year One profits as an example. Although they will occur, these projected profits will not be added beyond year one projections, since we want to be very conservative so that the yearly projections will stand on their own merits. Additional profits are a bonus. We did not add the projected profits from interest and from the principal balance of second and third mortgages to the buy/sell profits, because we wanted to specify the profits from Year One as short-term profits derived from purchases and sales from that year. Interest paid is done on a year to year basis, and principal balances of second and third mortgages are paid in 15 years. Therefore, these profits we consider long-term profits.

An explanation of the above four categories is included below.

RETAINED EARNINGS

As you have seen from Year One Projections, we project that sales of houses will occur within two months of the closing contract between our investor and his buyer; thus, each phase lasts two months and each year contains six phases. Since the investor-seller carries the mortgage notes, and since the buyer need not obtain a mortgage loan from a bank and go through all of the usual entanglements associated with that process, it is highly likely that many capable buyers will want to purchase these houses quickly. Because of this key factor, there could be many financially capable buyers wanting to purchase the same house. As a result of this, many, if not most, house sales to buyers could take place rather quickly, such as within two to three weeks, or less, from their first viewing and/or the signing of the house sales contract. As stated earlier, our investor-seller pays the two month carrying cost expenses associated with each house he is selling and these expenses are stated in the projections. However, when the buyer purchases the home within one month or less, the investor-seller will pay the expenses for one month but not the two month carrying cost expenses, with the exception of the $350.00 professional home inspection fee. Those carrying costs are as follows and are stated in the projections: (1) for the $70,000.00 house--$1,330.00; (2) for the $115,000.00 house--$2,050.00. The break-down of these expenses is listed in the section just prior to Year One Projections. For each $70,000.00 sale, the investor will retain approximately $192.25, broken down, as follows: (1) mortgage interest, $106.84; (2) taxes, $41.65; (3) insurance, $43.75. For the $115,000.00 sale, the investor will retain approximately $369.72, broken down, as follows:

(1) mortgage interest, $178.07; (2) taxes, $116.65; (3) insurance, $75.00. The recaptured mortgage principal is listed below. The mortgage interest retained above is for the one month's expenses our investor does not pay.

RECAPTURED EARNINGS

As stated above, we expect that many buyers will purchase their homes quickly because the seller will carry the note and mortgage and several qualified buyers may be interested in purchasing the same house. Despite this likelihood, we project a two month time period from the time the investor-seller purchases a house until the time he sells that house. As stated, each phase is for two months and each year has six phases. As we also stated, the investor-seller pays the carrying cost expenses for each house for these two months and the expenses are listed in the projections. In some cases, a buyer could contract to purchase the $115,000.00 house and close on that house two months later. Since the investor-seller pays all of the carrying costs until the closing, then at closing, the investor will recapture from the buyer the equity amounts the investor paid when he made the two month's mortgage payments, but not the interest. For instance, for the $115,000.00 house, we project our standard payment of $650.29 per month, of which $472.22 is paid to the principal balance and $178.07 to interest. When the investor made these payments, he paid $472.22 per month for two months or $944.44 to principal. The investor contracted with the buyer to purchase the house for $115,000.00 and by the time of the closing two months later, the investor, in paying the mortgage notes, reduced the principal balance by $944.44. At closing, the buyer pays this $944.44 to the investor-seller, which is the amount the investor-seller recaptures upon sale.

We project the monthly mortgage payment for the $70,000.00 house will be $390.17 or $780.34 for the two months. $283.33 of the $390.17 payment is paid to reduce the principal balance and $106.84 is paid to interest. At closing, our investor recaptures $283.33 times 2 for a total of $566.66. If, for some reason, the buyer prefers to pay these amounts over the next 12 months, instead of at closing, this could be done, if the seller is agreeable, which is highly likely.

PROFIT RECEIVED FROM INTEREST PAID ON 2ND & 3RD MORTGAGES

The second and third mortgages are necessary for the investor-seller so that he has a financial position or stake in the house. The investor's agreement with the entity who sold him the house allows him to sell, provided the investor-seller guarantees that the monthly payments to *his* seller will be made. Should the investor's buyer default, then the investor can take over the house, pursuant to his second or third mortgage position, maintain his agreement with his seller and make the monthly payments. The investor can then sell the house again and, of course, keep all the funds paid by his original buyer who defaulted and the investor receives the benefits of the principal payments his buyer made to him, which could be considerable.

We project 10% interest, paid annually, on the anniversary of the closing date. These payments are always one year in arrears, so the payments will be made the following year on the anniversary of the closing date. The interest payments the investor receives are placed in the long-term 15 year return, although they will be made each year for 15 years.

PRINCIPAL BALANCE OF 2ND AND 3RD MORTGAGES

Since each house sold by the investor-seller also carries a mortgage in favor of this seller, the aggregate principal balance amounts can be very considerable. These principal balance amounts are due and payable on the 15th anniversary of the house closing. These amounts are added to the interest payments and included in the long-term return.

POTENTIAL OF INCREASED SALES

As anyone can plainly see, when a seller is willing to carry the note and mortgage, he should attract many serious, capable buyers, rather quickly. We offer some suggestions here as to how to attract large amounts of potential clients.

BILLBOARDS, NEWSPAPERS AND RADIO ADVERTISING

People read billboards, newspapers and listen to the radio, all of which keeps these enterprises in business through advertising. Large numbers of people travel on highways and city thoroughfares that have billboards and local people see them constantly. If our investor-seller were to place an ad on key billboards in his geographic and sales areas, he would likely attract quite a bit of attention, depending upon the language of the ad. For instance, if an ad were to read:

"We Buy houses from Sellers who meet our reasonable buying criteria and Sell houses, carry notes and mortgages for Buyers who meet our commonsense selling criteria."

An ad like this on several highly visible billboards should produce large numbers of very interested potential buyers and sellers. If the same simple ad were put into local newspapers and advertised on local radio, we expect that these would attract large numbers of both capable, interested sellers and buyers. One can also make up colorful, attractive flyers with the same verbiage and post them in highly visible locations, such as bulletin boards available in various retail businesses, supermarkets, coffee shops, restaurants, etc. The Internet is also a good option for ads in any designated area.

As we have discussed on several previous occasions, many people are unable to sell their homes because of existing mortgages, this should comprise a very large market in any given area. If the seller of such a property contracts to sell his property to the investor, the investor might inquire as to the seller's intentions after the house is sold. Does he intend to remain in the area? Does he intend to move away? Does he intend to retire? If the seller intends to remain in the area and wants to purchase another house, but is concerned that he may have trouble obtaining a mortgage for the new house he wants to buy, then the seller becomes a prime candidate to buy a house from the investor's housing inventory and the investor will of course carry the mortgage. In this way, the investor contracts two sales with the same person and helps him achieve both objectives which he likely could not easily achieve otherwise.

There are many creative ways in which an astute investor-seller can attract clients and, of course, the entire key to his success is the fact that he will carry the note and mortgage. Having a good rapport with both sellers and buyers is important to the investor and to his clients. Working in harmony and with honor is something that must be restored to the American public. The investor could offer his client, whether the client is one who has bought a house from the investor or sold a house to the investor, a bonus, such as $200.00, for introducing the investor to potential clients who either buy from or sell a house to the investor. Given the ease by which the buying and selling process can be conducted, it is highly likely that both buyers and sellers will be very happy with their results and thus will be eager to tell their friends about their successful experiences with the investor. It is also highly likely that some of the clients' associates could become additional clients, and as additional clients who purchase from or sell property to the investor, they also have friends and family who could also be interested. In this way, our investor has and can further develop a natural, word-of-mouth clientele that can repeat and keep repeating.

You have just seen the Year One Projections and by now you likely realize the ongoing enormous potential afforded by these methods. New ideas sometimes take a while to develop and catch on, but as people gain success through them, others see that success and will want to mimic it. In the first year of buys and sells, the example projects 47 houses which were bought and sold. We project that one investor can easily handle the business operations for 47 houses on his own, because nothing is complicated about these transactions. If there are multiple investors, then they can share the responsibilities. In fact, the lack of complication and confusion is an added bonus to these types of investments. In Year One, the investor started with $15,000.00 and at the end of the first year, earned a total return and a projected profit of $329,070, which is extremely substantial in anyone's estimation. This amounts to a short-term projected return of 2,193.8%, which is phenomenally outstanding and not readily achievable in any other type of safe, secure investment. The investment in real estate is solid, tangible, real wealth, as opposed to other intangible investments, where the security to the investor is in paper, such as stocks, bonds, commercial paper, etc. In a market crash, that paper could be worth little to nothing in comparison to what the investor paid for it. In real estate, there is always a willing market for an investor who will carry the note.

If the investor is to continue in Year Two and invest his profit, then you can imagine the expected projected profit to be derived from Year Two. As a result of the increased business activity, we project that the investor will likely need professional help, such as secretaries, office workers and professional in-house buyers and sellers. It is also possible for the investor to work with real estate sales people in both buying and selling properties. When the in-house personnel and the real estate people see the success of these buy/sell programs, some of them will want to emulate the methods the investor used to gain such success. Other investors will also see the success of these methods and want to invest on their own. At first, some of these investors may invest small amounts, such as the original $15,000.00 investment made by our original investor. However, some of these investments could be considerably larger. Success attracts a lot of attention very quickly and huge success attracts enormous interest. Some major investors or institutional investors may also adopt these methods, which, frankly, would be good for everyone in this entire nation. However, with this possibility, the creative, inventive investor, who likes what he sees and realizes the huge potential within these projections, might not want to wait too long before he decides to invest. He could start small, as does our $15,000.00 investor, and test out the market for one year to ascertain if this type of investment program would work for him. If it does, then it might well be to his advantage to jump in with both feet, before the rest of the world does!

YEAR ONE PROJECTION REVIEW

1. Our investor-seller began with an investment of $15,000.00 as a down payment to purchase a $100,000.00 house.

2. The investor-seller sold this house for $115,000.00, by and through the *ByPass* methods, and through taking the profits from sales and investing them our investor-seller bought and sold 47 houses during this one year period.

3. The projected short-term return, one year profit for the first year is $329,070 plus $27,010.00 the investor recaptures upon sale on equity payments he made during this two month sales period, for a projected total of $356,080.00 During this two month period, our investor pays all carrying costs expenses on the houses. When the investor sells the houses, he will recapture from the buyer the equity mortgage amounts upon sales. For the $115,000.00 house, this equity is $944.44, per house. For the $70,000.00 house, this equity is $566.66, per house. 47 houses were sold—1 at $115,000.00 and 46 at $70,000.00.

        1 at $115,000.00 x $944.44 = $ 944.44
        <u>46 at $70,000.00 x $566.66 = $26,066.36</u>
        Total = $27,010.80

4. The above projections assume that our investor will contract with his buyer for the purchase of a house and then consummate the sale at closing in two months' time. Since the sales price has been established, during the two month period, before closing, the investor makes the mortgage payments; thus, upon sale, recaptures the principal amount he paid on the mortgage for these two months, but not the interest.

5. One of the main reasons why this sale is so attractive to a buyer is because the seller carries the note and mortgage. Since this factor is vital to many buyers, it is very possible that most sales will take place within a few weeks, and not over two months. In such situations, the investor would not be required to pay carrying costs expenses for two months, but we project he will pay expenses for one month. These savings to our investor would be

considerable and amount to approximately $1,314.16 for the $115,000.00 priced house and $758.90 for the $70,000.00 house. For Year One Projections, in order to be very conservative, we projected that some houses would be sold within one month, but most would be sold within two months. Because of the projected and expected success in Year One, we fully expect that most of the houses will sell very quickly, as in within three weeks, and not take the full two months.

6. The projected total return and profit of $329,070, as stated in paragraph 3, above, combined with the $27,010.80, also cited in the referenced paragraph 3, totals $356,080, the projected total return and Year One short-term profit. Please note that the original investment was $15,000. Everything earned after that is profit, which profit is reinvested in more purchases and creates additional profits. The projected one year profit amounts to a projected profit of $7,576 per house.

7. The projected short-term profit and return of $356,080 is a 2,373.8% return on the $15,000.00 investment. This extremely high percentage return on investment is virtually impossible with the usual, traditional types of investments, therefore another sound and sensible reason for engaging in our investment programs. In the high risk/high return rare types of investments, they usually require very large amounts of money to be invested. Our types of investments do not so require, as can be easily seen in Year One Projections. Further, these high risk/high return investments do not return 2,373% on investment, but in fact, much, much less. Still further, high risk means exactly that. The investor could lose all investment capital, or in the rare alternative, make a fortune. With our investments, the investor always owns solid, tangible and substantial assets, namely houses, with a marketable value that can be sold at any time, especially since the investor carries the note and mortgage.

8. When the long-term second and third mortgage totals and interest are added to the projected profit, then the projected and combined total short-term and long-term returns are much higher. Second and third mortgages principal total $97,000.00 for the first year. When $97,000.00 is added to the projected short-term profit of $356,080, this amounts to $453,080, which is a projected 3,020% return on investment. The long-term interest projected for the second and third mortgages is 10% per year on $9,700.00 for 15 years. For $97,000.00 in second and/or third mortgages payments, this amount to $145,500.00 over 15 years. Added to the $453,080, cited above, this amounts to $598,580, a projected 3,990% total short and long term return on the original $15,000 investment. Most investors and most professionals would consider such a return as absolutely phenomenal, and we agree.

Although $242,500.00, namely, $97,000 in principal mortgage amounts and $145,500 in interest over 15 years, are long term returns, the total projected percentage return of 3,990% is based on the original $15,000.00 investment. It would be virtually impossible to find either a short term or long term *safe and secure* investment that would pay such an enormously high return on the original investment.

9. As stated above, the projected short-term profit per house is $7,576. The projected short and long term profit is $12,735 per house. These are rather remarkable returns for an original $15,000.00 investment. That investment began a one year program that returned a short-term projected profit of $356,080, which begins the second year projections. $356,080 amounts to a projected 2,373% return on the $15,000 investment. Instead of a $15,000.00 investment that returned a projected short term profit of $356,080, imagine if that original investment had been ten times that amount, namely $150,000.00. With the same projected 2,373% return on investment, that would amount to a projected short-term one year profit and return of approximately $3,559,500. When the second and third mortgage projected principal and interest amounts are considered, combined with recaptured earnings and retained earnings, then the amount increases significantly.

10. This projected buy/sell program with an investment of $15,000 makes it highly possible for small investors to enter a program that could make them a very sizeable fortune. Such investment opportunities are very rare for that investment amount, which opens up possibilities that, otherwise, would likely not be available to that small investor. If an investor or investment group were to begin with a $150,000 investment instead of $15,000, then the $3,559,500 PLUS one year, short term returns and profit could be achieved provided the investor or investment group were totally serious and dedicated to the objective. As long as our investor carries the notes, secondary buyers should be plentiful throughout this nation. This is a rare opportunity for those who see the wisdom in this and the other methods contained in this book and are willing to set aside the standard system created by others, and work for themselves in their own, creative enterprises for their own benefit and self-interest.

Since 47 houses were projected for Year One, the business operations can easily be managed by the investor. However, higher investment amounts and Year Two Projections involve a much larger number of purchases and sales, so we have projected costs for professionals under the hire of our investor who would operate and manage the investment programs on a day to day basis, such as managers, sales people, office staff, etc. The Year One sales amount to less than one house per week, which as stated above, the investor should easily be able to manage on his own. Year Two Projections indicate that 528 houses will be bought and sold during the year. With such a volume, our investor will likely require a professional staff who could work under his direction and management. Year Two projected expenses for staff are listed in AVAILABLE CASH, COLUMN ONE. Staff can expand from phase to phase, based upon the increase in house purchases and sales. These expenses are listed in COLUMN ONE of each phase. Following the Year Two Projections is a Projection Review that will list staff personnel, expenses and salaries. After staff expenses, the Phase One investment amount for Year Two is $306,380.00. Projected profit for Year Two is $3,496,400.00 and $1,699,000.00 in second and third mortgages, a total of $5,195,400.00, for a 1,695.7% short and long term return upon investment. Interest paid on $1,699,000.00 over 15 years, amounts to $2,548,500.00. This amount added to $5,195,400.00 cited above, is $7,743,900.00, a 2,527.5% long and short term projected return upon a $306,380.00 investment. The Review at the end of Year Two Projections will recap all details.

PROJECTIONS – BUY/SELL $15,000 PROGRAM – YEAR TWO, PHASE ONE

Available Cash	Investment	Cash Profit	Cash Return	Second Mortgages	Cash Overage
$329,070 + $27,010 recaptured _____ $356,080 - 49,700 Op. Exp. _____ $306,380	19 house down payments x $9,000 each = $171,000 PLUS 9 house down payments x $15,000 each = $135,000 = $306,000	19 x $8,000 each = $152,000 PLUS 9 x $10T = $90,000 = $242,000 PROFIT Less sales expenses: 19 x $1,330 = $25,270 + 9 x $2,050 = $18,450 43,720 expenses = $242,000 Gross Profit - 43,720 EXP $198,280	$306,380 Investment PLUS $198,280 PROFIT= $504,280	19 x $2T = $38,000 +9 x $5T = $45,000 = $83,000	-$380 –
TOTALS $306,380	$306,000 outlay for 28 houses	$198,280 64.79% Profit	$504,280 164.79% Return	$83,000	-$380-
CUMULATIVE TOTALS					
$740,710	$735,000 for 75 houses	$518,000 70.47% Profit	1,252,990 170.47% Rtn	$180,000	$3,000

PROJECTIONS – BUY/SELL $15,000 PROGRAM – YEAR TWO, PHASE TWO

Available Cash	Investment	Cash Profit	Cash Return	Second Mortgages	Cash Overage
$504,280 - $74,700 OPER-ATING EXPENS-ES = $429,580	26 house down payments of $9,000 each = $234,000 PLUS 13 house down payments of $15,000 each = $195,000 = $429,000	26 x $8,000 = $208,000 PLUS 13 x $10T = $130,000 $338,000 Less sales expens-es: 26 x $1,330 = $34,580 + 13 x $2,050=$26,650- $61,230 EXP $338,000 GP - $61,230 exp $276,770	$429,000 in-vestment + $276,770 Profit = $705,770	26 x $2T = $52,000 +13 x $5T = $65,000 = $117,000	-$580 –
TOTALS $429,580	$429,000 outlay for 39 houses	$276,770 64.51% profit	$705,770 164.51% Rt	$117,000	-$580-
CUMULATIVE TOTALS					
$1,170,290	$1,164,000 for 114 houses	$794,770 68.27% Profit	$1,958,760 168.27% Rt	$297,000	$3,580

PROJECTIONS – BUY/SELL $15,000 PROGRAM – YEAR TWO, PHASE THREE

Available Cash	Investment	Cash Profit	Cash Return	Second Mortgages	Cash Overage
$705,770 - 74,700 OPER-ATING EXPENS-ES = $631,070	38 hose down payments of $9,000 each = $342,000 PLUS 19 house down payments of $15,000 each = $285,000 $627,000	38 x $8,000 = $304,000 PLUS 19 x $10,000 = $190,000 $494,000 Less sales expenses: 38 x $1,330 = $50,540 PLUS 19 x $2,050 = $38,950 $89,490 EXP $494,000 GP --89,490 EXP $404,510	$627,000 investment PLUS $404,510 Profit = $1,031,510	38 x $2,000 = $76,000 PLUS 19 x $5,000 =$95,000 $171,000	$4,070
TOTALS $631,070	$627,00 outlay for 57 houses	$404,510 64.51% profit	$1,031,510 164.51% Rtn	$171,000	$4,07045
CUMULATIVE TOTAS					
$1,801,360	$1,791,000 for 171 houses	$1,199,280 66.96% Profit	$2,990,270 166.96% Rtn	$468,000	$7.650

PROJECTIONS – BUY/SELL $15,000 PROGRAM – YEAR TWO, PHASE FOUR

Available Cash	Investment	Cash Profit	Cash Return	Second Mortgages	Cash Overage
$1,031,510 - $74,700 OP EX $ 956,810	56 house down payments x $9,000 each = $504,000 PLUS 30 house down payments x $15,000 each = $450,000 $954,000	56 x $8,000 = $448,000 PLUS 30 x $10,000 =$300,000 $748,000 Less sales expenses: 56 x $1,330 = $74,480 PLUS 30 x $2,050 = $ 61,500 $135,980 EXP = $748,000 GP -135,980 EXP $612,020	$954,000 investment + $612,020 Profit=____ $1,566,020	56 x $2T = $112,000 +30 x $5T = $150,000 = $262,000	$2,810
TOTALS $956,810	$954,000 outlay for 86 houses	$612,020 64.15% profit	$1,566,020 164.15% Rt	$262,000	$2,810
CUMULATIVE TOTALS					
$2,758,170	$2,745,000 for 257 houses	$1,811,300 65.98% Profit	$4,556,290 165.98% Rt.	$730,000	$10,460

PROJECTIONS – BUY/SELL $15,000 PROGRAM – YEAR TWO, PHASE FIVE

Available Cash	Investment	Cash Profit	Cash Return	Second Mortgages	Cash Overage
$1,566,020 - $161,400 OP EX $ 1,404,620	82 house down payments x $9,000 each = $738,000 PLUS 44 house down payments x $15,000 each = $660,000 $1,398,000	82 x $8,000 = $656,000 PLUS 44 x $10,000 = $440,000 $1,096,000 Less sales expenses: 82 x $1,330 =_ $109,060 PLUS 44 x $2,050 = $ 90,200 $199,260 EXP $1,096,000 GP_ - 199,260 EXP $896,740	$1,398,000 investment PLUS $ 896,740 Profit =____ $2,294,740	82 x $2T = $164,000 +44 x $5T = $220,000 = $384,000	$6,620
TOTALS: $1,404,620	$1,398,000 outlay for 126 houses	$896,740 64.14% profit	$2,294,740 164.14 % Rt	$384,000	$6,620
CUMULATIVE TOTALS					
$4,162,790	$4,143,000 for 383 houses	$2,708,040 65.35% Profit	$6,851,030 165.35% Rtn	$1,114,000	$17,080

PROJECTIONS – BUY/SELL $15,000 PROGRAM – YEAR TWO, PHASE SIX

Available Cash	Investment	Cash Profit	Cash Return	Second Mortgages	Cash Overage
$2,294,740 - $161,400 OP EX $2,133,340	125 house down payments x $9,000 each = $1,125,000 PLUS 67 house down payments x $15,000 each = $1,005,000 $2,130,000	125 x $8,000 each = $1,000,000 PLUS 67 house down payments x $10,000 =$670,000 $1,670,000 Less sales expenses: 125 x $1,330 = $166,250 PLUS 67 x $2,050 = $ 137,350 $303,600 EXP $1,670,000 GP_ - 303,600 $1,366,400	$2,130,000 investment PLUS $1,366,400 Profit = ____ $3,496,400	125 x $2T = $250,000 +67 x $5T = $335,000 = $585,000	$3,340
TOTALS: $2,133,340	$2,130,000 outlay for 192 houses	$1,366,400 64.15% Profit	$3,496,400 164.15%	$585,000	$3,340
CUMULATIVE	**TOTALS**				
$6,296.130	$6,273,000 for 575 houses	$4,074,440 64.95% Profit	$10,347,430 164.95% Rtn.	$1,699,000	$20,420

ANALYSIS OF YEAR TWO PROJECTIONS

YEAR TWO PROJECTION REVIEW-- $15,000.00 INVESTMENT

1. Our investor made a short-term profit in Year One of $356,080.00, plus the interest and second and third mortgages principal long-term profit referenced earlier.

2. Minus Phase One, Year Two operating expenses of $49,700.00, our investor made a $306,380.00 investment in the buying and selling of houses, as stated in Phase One of Year Two Projections.

3. 528 houses were projected to be bought and sold in Year Two.

4. Year Two projected short-term profit is $3,496,400.00, plus $9,700.00 in second and third mortgage interest, payable in Year Two, plus return of equity payments to investor and retention of funds not spent during the two month sales period. These are called RETAINED EARNINGS and RECAPTURED EARNINGS, as further explained previously in the Year One Projection Review.

5. Of the projected 528 house sales for Year Two, 346 were sold for $70,000.00 and 182 were sold for $115,000.00.

6. Because of the investor's willingness to carry the mortgage notes, we project that: (1) 50% of the buyers will purchase homes very quickly, such as within 2 to 3 weeks, as previously explained in RETAINED EARNINGS; (2) for these buyers, we project that our investor will pay carrying costs for one month; (3) the other 50% will contract to purchase houses and then close within two months, as explained previously in RECAPTURED EARNINGS; (4) for these buyers, we project that our investor our will pay two months' carrying charges.

7. Two month's carrying costs, as stated previously in Year One Projection Review, for the $115,000.00 house are $2,050.00, and $1,330.00 for a $70,000.00 house. Based upon these projections, the following figures apply:

    (1) 50% of 346 houses priced at $70,000.00 = 173 houses

    (2) 50% of 182 houses priced at $115,000.00 = 91 houses

    (3) $1,330.00 two month's carrying cost expenses for the $70,000.00 house:

    Mortgage payments…$780.34; one month, $390.17

    Tax:…………………$ 83.33; one month, $ 41.65

    House insurance…….$ 87.50; one month, $ 43.75

    House inspection…....$350.00; one month, $350.00

    Totals: two months: 1,301.17; one month: $825.57

(4) $2,050 two months carrying costs for the $115,000 house:

Mortgage payments…$1,300.58; one month, $650.29

Tax…..................…$ 233.33; one month, $116.65

 House insurance…….$ 150.00; one month, $ 75.00

 House inspection……$ 350.00; one month, $350.00

Totals: two months….$2,033.97; one month, $1,191.94

346 houses priced at $70,000 each are projected to be sold by the investor in Year Two. 50% of these house sales (173) are projected to be sold within one month of the investor's purchase of that house. 182 houses priced at $115,000 are projected to be sold by the investor in Year Two. 50% of these house sales (91) are projected to be sold within one month of the investor's purchase of that house.

For houses sold by our investor in one month or less after he purchased the house, the following figures are his carrying costs:

173 (50%) houses priced at $70,000.00 x $ 825.57 = $142,824

91 (50%) houses priced at $115,000.00 x $1,191.94 = $106,466

The figures below are the investor's projected carrying costs for houses he sold after one month, but within two months.

173 (50%) houses priced at $70,000 x $1,301.17 = $225,102

 91 (50%) houses priced at $115,000 x $2,033.97 = $185,091

Total projected investor's carrying costs for 346 houses priced at $70,000………$367,926

Total projected investor's carrying costs for 182 houses priced at $115,000……..$291,557

TOTAL…………………………………………………………………………….$659,843

In the yearly projections, the projected carrying costs for the $70,000 house are $1,330.00

For the $115,000 house…………………………………………………………………..$2,050.00

346 houses priced at $70,000 x $1,330 = $460,180

Above carrying costs for $70,000 house = $367,926 ($142,824 + $225,102)

> **$ 92,254 – projected amount RETAINED by Investor,
> thus the category, RETAINED EARNINGS**

182 houses priced at $115,000 x $2,050   = $373,100

Above carrying costs for $115,000 house = <u>-$291,557</u>

> **$ 81,543 - projected amount RETAINDED by
> Investor in RETAINED EARNINGS**

TOTAL PROJECTED RETAINDED EARNINGS…………..$173,797 ($92,254 + $81,543)

RECAPTURED EARNINGS (EQUITY)

As mentioned previously, when our investor contracts to sell houses within two months of his purchase, he pays all carrying costs until the closing takes place. Part of his carrying costs will be the mortgage payments he pays, until the houses are sold. When the closings occur, the investor recaptures the EQUITY of the mortgage payments from the buyer, since the investor's payments lowered the price by that amount, thus he RECAPTUREs the equity from buyer upon the sale.

Equity for the $70,000 house is projected at $283.33 per month, and $473.22 per month for the $115,000 house

346 houses priced at $70,000 each x $566.66 (two months' equity) = $196,064

182 houses priced at $115,000 each x $944.44 (two months' equity) = <u>$171,888</u>

TOTAL RECAPTURED EQUITY…………………………..……………$367,952

PROJECTED RETAINED EARNINGS……………..$173,797

PROJECTED RECAPTURED EQUITY……………..$367,952

TOTAL…………………………………………….$541,749

For Year Two, based upon the above logical, common-sense projections, the investor will retain and recover $541,749 if he sells the 528 homes within one or two months after he purchased them. The short-term profit level for Year Two is projected to increase by $541,749, but, as said earlier, we did not add this amount to the Year Two projections. When a seller carries the mortgage, many capable buyers are expected to act quickly, so all houses are expected to be sold by the investor within two months, or less. The $541,749 can be considered a bonus to be used at the discretion of the investor(s).

When the Retained Earnings and Recaptured Equity are combined for the $70,000 house, that average amount is $833.28 per house.

When the Retained Earnings and Recaptured Equity are combined for the $115,000 house, that average amount is $1,392.48 per house.

346 $70,000 houses x $833.28   = $288,314

182 $115,000 houses x $1,392.48 = $253,431

TOTAL.................................. $541,745

These averages per each priced house will be used in our projections.

The projected total of $541,745 cited above is <u>additional</u> profit <u>not</u> <u>specified</u> in the Year Two Projections. In addition, the second and third mortgage principal balance from Year One totals $97,000.00, which pays 10% interest, namely, $9,700.00, due in Year Two, for a further projected one year short-term profit of $551,445.00. As stated, these additional projections were <u>not calculated</u> in the yearly phase to phase projections. $551,445 added to the short-term projected profit of $3,496,400.00 totals $4,047,845. This is a projected return of 1,321% return on the $306,380.00 Year Two investment listed in Available Cash, COLUMN ONE. Since the initial investment that began these investments was $15,000, which was the means to create all future profits, then the projected profit of $4,047,845 is a return of 2,699% on that $15,000 investment.

8. When the long-term investment amounts and returns are added to the one year short-term amounts and returns, the figures are much higher. Year Two Projections indicate a second and third mortgage principal amount of $1,699,000.00. Interest is projected at 10% per year for 15 years. $169,900.00 per year x 15 years is $2,548,500.00. This interest amount added to the principal amount of $1,699,000.00 totals $4,247,500.00, a 1,386% long-term return on Year Two investment of $306,380.

9. The short-term projected profit of $4,047,845 added to the long-term projected profit of $4,247,500.00 is $8,295,534, a combined short and long term return of 2,707% on the Year Two investment of $306,380.00, and a 55,303% return on the initial $15,000 investment.

10. Projections demonstrate that 528 houses were bought and sold by the investor during Year Two. Year Two total projected short-term profit of approximately $4,047,845 is a projected profit of approximately $7,666 per house. Combined projected short and long term profit of approximately $8,295,534 indicates a projected profit of approximately $15,711 per house. Any sensible, rational, realistic man and woman, or any such qualified professional, would consider these returns on safe, secure investments as phenomenally high and not possible or attainable with any other types of traditional investments. Please note that these investments began with a $15,000.00 amount; thus, as mentioned above, the projected total short and long term returns on $15,000.00 would be approximately 55,303%.

11. If our investor continues with this Buy/Sell investment program over many years, then purchases and sales of houses increase in number and continue to do so. Larger market areas that will accommodate the very substantial amount of buying and selling will be needed to rapidly expand the program. According to some sources, on average, nationally, one house is sold for approximately every 40 people, depending upon the location and density. More populated areas naturally have a higher density, so the average is much lower than one house sold per every 40 people. Since more houses will be sold in more populated areas, then the average decreases below 40. If the investor wants to continue his investments, he will need to expand to more areas or larger market areas that will accommodate his increasing volume. The absolute key to most sales is the rare fact that the investor will carry the note and mortgage, and as we have repeatedly mentioned, since it is one of the most important factors, this, alone, will attract many capable buyers very quickly.

12. Because major increases in buys and sells will occur, beginning in Year Two, we project that operational staff expenses will be needed to service the increased business. For Year Two, Phase One, we project operational and staff costs for Phase One at $49,700.00, broken down as follows. Please note these are *projected* Phase One expenses only:

PHASE ONE PROJECTED OFFICE EXPENSES:
   (1) $11,700.00 for two office workers
   (2) $20,000.00—cash reserves
   (3) $ 3,000.00—office expenses
   (4) $15,000.00—office $49,700.00

For each successive phase, staff and operational expenses are projected to increase, based upon increased business activity. The $11,700.00 (number 1, above) is the Phase One expenses for two office workers each of whom earns $35,100.00 per year. The $20,000.00 (number 2, above) and the $3,000.00 office expenses (number 3, above) continue from phase to phase and increase in amounts due to increased business activity. These funds are budgeted each phase and are available for use whether they are employed or not. As stated, the $15,000.00 for an office facility will increase in amount when business expansion requires additional offices. We project that one or more of the houses the investor purchases could easily be converted into an office. Thus, the home/office(s) would be owned by the investor, which would save him the expense of renting office space. For instance, a house could be purchased somewhere within the sales area or on the periphery of this area, which would be an ideal location for an office. Please note that the $20,000.00 cash reserves, the $15,000.00 office fund and $3,000.00 office expenses are allocated for *each* of the following phases, whether the funds are expended or not. If not expended, they are available for expenditure when needed to be applied where necessary.

13. In Phase Two, five more staff people were hired to assist in office work and begin training in the buying and selling of property, each at $30,000.00 per year. Our investor is the trainer and the manager for all operations, unless, of course, he wants to allocate this position to someone else. This hiring added $25,000.00 more to Phase Two costs for a new operating cost of $74,700.00 per phase. In Phase Five, five more staff people, two more office workers, and five professionals were hired for buying and selling operations. The professionals were hired at $60,000.00, each, per year, the office workers at $35,100.00, each, per year, the staff at $30,000.00, each, per year, and trained in the buying and selling of property.

The buying and selling within these methods is simple, easy, uncomplicated, therefore, anyone with a certain amount of common sense can be trained to easily buy and sell property. The staff is hired at $30,000.00, each, and trained to become proficient in the business operations of buying and selling. As they learn and become professionally competent, that salary can be increased to the $60,000.00 level rather quickly. The professionals that were hired are those who are already well adept in the buying and selling of property and in business operations, therefore, can easily facilitate the buying and selling expeditiously.

The ultimate keynote to the success of these methods is the willingness of the investor-seller to carry the note and mortgage, as we think we all can agree. Therefore, the potential market is absolutely enormous. When potential clients understand the ease of conducting either a sale or a purchase by and through these *ByPass* methods, that factor, alone, should increase business activities, because, as we all know, word of mouth is one of the best ways to do that.

As a rough gauge of potential business activity in appropriate areas, meaning areas that are not the New York City metro area, the greater Boston metro area, greater Los Angeles and other so-called "Star Cities", which most of this country is not, we estimate that a significant percentage of all houses in non Star Cities on the market for sale are priced at $100,000.00 or less. Because of the factors mentioned above, namely the seller carrying the note, and the absolute ease of the buying and selling transaction, combined with the fact that those who still have existing mortgages on their houses have trouble selling because of this, and the fact that many financially capable buyers cannot meet bank qualifications to obtain mortgages, we estimate that a significant number of owners of houses in this category could become clients of the investor. There is obvious, enormous potential for everyone involved in these operations, whether they are buyers, sellers or investors.

When these factors are added to the suggestions in Year One Projection notes, such as the billboards, the bonuses, etc., the already enormous potential can rapidly increase. Common sense would tell us that a seller who wants to sell his house, but has a mortgage that makes this impossible, is going to respond to that billboard ad. Any financially capable buyer, who cannot pass muster to obtain a bank mortgage, possibly because he went through foreclosure, will most likely eagerly respond to the ad on that billboard. When all factors are combined, the enormous potential can be quickly calculated. Phrases like, "Fast Track Home Path, Your Road to the Future" and/or "Fast Track Housing Supermarket" could likely interest quite a few people. When buyers realize that the seller will carry the note and then see the simplicity in the purchase process, many financially capable buyers should be eager to participate.

PROJECTIONS – BUY/SELL $15,000 PROGRAM – YEAR THREE, PHASE ONE

Available Cash	Investment	Cash Profit	Cash Return	Second Mortgages	Cash Overage
$3,496,400 - $161,400 OP EXP $3,335,000	195 house down payments x $9,000 each = $1,755,000 PLUS 105 house down payments x $15,000 each = $1,575,000 $3,330,000	195 x $8,000 = $1,560,000 PLUS 105 x $10T = $1,050,000 $2,610,000 Less sales expenses: 195 x $1,330 = $259,350 PLUS 105 x $2,050 = $215,250 $474,600 EXP $2,610,000 GP -$474,600 = ____ $2,135,400	$3,330,000 investment PLUS $2,135,400 Profit= ____ $5,465,400	195 x $2T = $390,000 + 105 x $5T = $525,000 = $915,000	$5,000
TOTALS: $3,335,000	$3,330,000 outlay for 300 houses	$2,135,400 64.12% Profit	$5,465,400 164.12% Rtn.	$915,000	$5,000
CUMULATIVE TOTALS					
$9,631,100	$9,603,000 for 875 houses	$6,209,840 64.66% Profit	$15,812,830 164.66% Rtn.	$2,614,000	$23,360

PROJECTIONS – BUY/SELL $15,000 PROGRAM – YEAR THREE, PHASE TWO

Available Cash	Investment	Cash Profit	Cash Return	Second Mortgages	Cash Overage
$5,465,400 - 211,400 OP EXP $5,254,000	307 house down payments x $9,000 each = $2,763,000 PLUS 166 house down payments x $15,000 each_ $2,490,000 = $5,253,000	307 x $8,000 = $2,456,000 PLUS 166 x $10,000 = $1,660,000 $4,116,000 Less sales expenses: 307 x $1,330 = $408,310 PLUS 166 x $2,050 = $340,300 $748,610 EXP $4,116,000 GP -$748,610= $3,367,390	$5,253,000 investment PLUS $3,367,390 Profit = $8,620,390	307 x $2T = $614,000 + 166 x $5T = $830,000 = $1,444,000	$1,000
TOTALS: $5,254,000	$5,253,000 outlay for 473 houses	$3,367,390 64.10% Profit	$8,620,390 164.10% Rtn	$1,444,000	$1,000
CUMULATIVE TOTALS	$14,856,000 for 1,348 houses	$9,577,230 64.46% Profit	$24,433,220 164.46% Rtn	$4,058,000	$24,360
$14,885,100				$4,058,000	$24,360

PROJECTIONS – BUY/SELL $15,000 PROGRAM – YEAR THREE, PHASE THREE

Available Cash	Investment	Cash Profit	Cash Return	Second Mortgages	Cash Overage
$8,620,390 - 383,066 OP EXP $8,237,324	480 house down payments x $9,000 each = $4,320,000 PLUS 261 house down payments x $15,000 each=_ $3,915,000 $8,235,000	480 house down payments x $8,000 each = $3,840,000 PLUS 261 x $10,000 = $2,610,000 $6,450,000 Less sales expenses: 480 x $1,330 =_ $638,400 PLUS 261 x $2,050 = $535,050 $1,173,450 EXP $6,450,00 GP $1,173,450 $5,276,550	$8,235,000 investment PLUS $5,276,550 Profit___ $13,511,550	480 x $2T = $960,000 PLUS 261 x $5T = $1,305,000 = $2,265,000	$2,324
TOTALS: $8,237,324	$8,235,000 outlay for 741 houses	$5,276,550 64.07% Profit	$13,511,550 164.07% Rtn	$2,265,000	$2,324
CUMULATIVE TOTALS	$23,091,000 for 2,089 houses	$14,853,780 64.32% Profit	$37,944,770 164.32% Rtn	$6,323,000	$26,684
$23,122,424	2,089 houses			$6,323,000	$26,684

PROJECTIONS – BUY/SELL $15,000 PROGRAM – YEAR THREE, PHASE FOUR

Available Cash	Investment	Cash Profit	Cash Return	Second Mortgages	Cash Overage
$13,511,550 - 553,066 OP EXP $12,958,484	756 house down payments x $9,000 each= $6,804,000 PLUS 410 house down payments x $15,000 each = $6,150,000 $12,954,000	756 x $8,000 = $6,048,000 PLUS 410 x $10,000= $4,100,000 $10,148,000 Less sales expenses: 756 x $1,330 = $1,005,480 PLUS 410 x $2,050 = $840,500 $1,845.980 EXP $10,148,000 GP 1,845,980 $ 8,302,020	$12,954,000 investment PLUS $8,302,020 Profit = $21,256,020	756 x $2T = $1,512,000 + 410 x $5T = $2,050,000 = $3,562,000	$4,484
TOTALS: $12,958,484	$12,954,000 outlay for 1166 houses	$8,302,020 64.08% Profit	$21,256,020 164.08% Rtn	$3,562,000	$4,484
CUMULATIVE TOTALS					
$36,080,908	$36,045,000 for 3,255 houses	$23,155,800 64.24% Profit	$59,200,790 164.24%	$9,885,000	$31,168

PROJECTIONS – BUY/SELL $15,000 PROGRAM – YEAR THREE, PHASE FIVE

Available Cash	Investment	Cash Profit	Cash Return	Second Mortgages	Cash Overage
$21,256,020 - 1,020,000 OP EX $20,236,020	1,180 house down payments x $9,000 each = $10,620,000 PLUS 641 house down payments x $15,000 each = $9.615,000 $20,235,000	1,180 x $8,000 = $9,440,000 PLUS 641 x $10,000= $6,410,000 $15,850,000 Less sales expenses: 1180 x $1,330 = $1,569,400 PLUS 641 x $2,050= $1,315,050 $2,883,450 ex $15,850,000 p - 2,883,450 $12,966,550	$20,235,000 investment PLUS $12,966,550 Profit = $33,201,550	1180 x $2T = $2,360,000 + 641 x $5T = $3,205,000 = $5,565,000	$1,020
TOTALS: $20,236,020	$20,235,000 outlay for 1821 houses	$12,966,550 64.07% Profit	$33,201,550 164.07%	$5,565,000	$1,020
CUMULATIVE TOTALS					
$56,316,928	$56,280,000 for 5,076 houses	$36,122,350 64.18% Profit	$92,402,340 164.18% Rtn	$15,450,000	$32,188

PROJECTIONS – BUY/SELL $15,000 PROGRAM – YEAR THREE, PHASE SIX

Available Cash	Investment	Cash Profit	Cash Return	Second Mortgages	Cash Overage
$33,201,550 - 1,940,000 OP EX $31,261,550	1,875 house down payments x $9,000 each = $16,875,000 PLUS 959 house down payments x $15,000 each = $14,385,000 $31,260,000	1,875 x $8,000 = $15,000,000 PLUS 959 x $10,000= $9,590,000 $24,590,000 Less sales expenses: 1875 x $1,330 = $2,493,750 PLUS 959 x $2,050 = $1,965,950 $4,459,700 ex $24,590,000 P_ - $4,459,700 $20,130,300	$31,260,000 investment PLUS $20,130,300 Profit = $51,390,300	1875 x $2T= $3,750,000 PLUS 959 x $5T = $4,795,000 $8,545,000	$1,550
TOTALS: $31,261,550	$31,260,000 outlay for 2834 houses	$20,130,300 64.39% Profit	$51,390,300 164.39% Rtn	$8,545,000	$1,550
CUMULATIVE TOTALS					
$87,578,478	$87,540,000 for 7,910 houses	$56,252,650 64.25% Profit	$143,792,640 164.25% Retn	$23,995,000	$33,738

YEAR THREE PROJECTION ANALYSIS

YEAR THREE PROJECTIONS REVIEW
--$15,000.00 INVESTMENT

1. Our investor is projected to have made a short-term projected profit in Year Two of approximately $3,496,400, plus the long-term projected profit referenced previously and, again, in this review. The RETAINED EARNINGS, the RECOVERED EARNINGS, second and third mortgage interest, and second and third mortgage principal were additional profits, but not added to Year Two Projections and, as you can see, were not added to Year Three Projections.

2. The $3,496,400 return at the end of Year Two, Phase Six, was invested in Year Three, Phase One. At the conclusion of Year Three, Phase Six, the Total cash return is projected to be $51,390,300. This is a projected one year return of 1,469.8% on the Year Three $3,496,400 investment. It is also a 342,602% return on the original $15,000 investment.

   Both these projected returns on investment are extremely high and rather phenomenal for an original $15,000 investment.

3. The main advantage to buyers is the fact that the investor/owner will carry the mortgage. This is a powerful incentive for many buyers, so, as mentioned earlier, many may want to purchase the same house. The main advantage to most homeowners who sell their homes to the investor is the fact that they can sell to him whether they have an existing mortgages on their homes, or not. This frees many sellers who have been restricted before. When several or more capable buyers want to purchase the same home, then it is likely that the sale can take place quickly. We projected a two month sales period, or about nine weeks, from the owner's purchase. However, with multiple buyers for the same property, the sale could occur much more quickly.

4. The projections call for profits to be reinvested in the purchase of more homes for resale during the duration of the program. If the investor(s) want funds over the duration, rather than take from profit from the program, it would be better to take an active participation in the program and receive a salary(ies) from the operating expenses budget. This allows the profits to be reinvested and provides funds for the investor(s) to live on.

5. Minus PHASE ONE, YEAR THREE, OPERATING EXPENSES, our investor invested $3,335,000.00 in Year Three, Phase One for the buying and selling of houses. 7,335 houses were projected to be bought and sold in Year Three, for a total of 7,910 houses over the three year projection period. The projected three year cash return of $51,390,300 is a projected profit of approximately $6,500 per house.

6. The projected Year Three short-term profit of $51,390,300.00 is a monumental figure that began with a $15,000.00 investment three years earlier. In addition to the short-term profit stated in the projections is the projected long-term profit that we describe below. Additionally, interest payments on second and third mortgages from Year One and Year Two are due and payable in Year Three. Further, RETAINED EARNINGS, plus RECAPTURED EARNINGS, will be described below.

7. Of the 7,335 houses projected to be sold in Year Three, 4,793 were projected to sell for $70,000.00, each, and 2,542 projected to sell for $115,000.00, each.

RETAINED EARNINGS

As we did in Year Two Projections, we project that 50% of all sales will occur quickly, such as within two to three weeks, but within one month of investor's purchase of that property. The other 50% is projected to close after one month, and within the second month after the investor purchased the property.

In the Year Two review, combined Retained Earnings and Recaptured Equity averages were established for the $70,000 priced house and the $115,000 priced house, as stated below.

$ 70,000 priced house - average of $833.28 per house

$115,000 priced house - average of $1,392.48 per house

4,793 $ 70,000 priced houses x $833.28 = $3,993,911

2,542 $115,000 priced houses x $1,392.48 = $3,539,684

TOTAL...$7,533,595

Please note that the projections for these RETAINED EARNINGS <u>were not</u> included in Year Three Projections, as they were not included in Year Two Projections, for the reasons mentioned. To be very conservative, we separate the actual phase to phase buying and selling projections from the projected RETAINED EARNINGS, the RECAPTURED EARNINGS, the interest paid on the second and third mortgages, and the second and third mortgage principal. When these projections are added to Year Three Projections, the actual profit amount is much, much higher.

$51,390,300 – PROJECTED Year Three PROFIT

+ $ 7,533,595 – PROJECTED RETAINED & RECAPTURED EARNINGS

$58,923,895 – PROJECTED ACTUAL THREE YEAR SHORT-TERM PROFIT

THIS IS A RETURN ON THE $3,335,000.00 YEAR THREE INVESTMENT OF APPROXIMATELY 1,766%, and 3,928% on the original Year One $15,000 investment.

As we have noted before, this is a remarkable, extremely high return for such a safe, secure investment. Obviously, all investments bear *some* risk, which the aware and astute investor acknowledges. As mentioned, successful high risk/high return investments are extremely rare, and bear the risk of costing the investor his investment funds or, in the alternative, can pay a high return, but certainly not 1,766% in one year. The safety in this investment program is found in the physical, tangible assets, namely, the houses that have a saleable market value and can be quickly sold through the *ByPass* mortgage methods specified in this book. However, other returns have not yet been factored in, such as the principal on the second and third mortgages and the interest they bear. By the end of Year Three, second and third mortgage projections total $23,995,000.00 in principal amounts. Interest projections are 10%, paid yearly on the anniversary of the sale. At the end of Year Two, second and third mortgage principal amount is $1,699,000.00, due and payable in Year Three. This amounts to $169,900.00 interest, and added to actual Year Three projected profit, that total is $59,093,795, a 1,771% short-term return on the Year Three investment of $3,335,000.00, as stated in COLUMN ONE, AVAILABLE CASH.

When the long-term returns are included, then the total short and long term return amount more than doubles. As stated above, the projected second and third mortgage principal balance at end of Year Three is $23,995,000.00. Interest is projected at 10%, paid annually upon the anniversary of the sale, for 15 years. Principal balance is due in 15 years. Interest for one year = $2,399,500.00 x 15 years = $35,992,500.00, minus $169,900.00 paid in Year Three = $35,822,600.00. The mortgage principal added to the interest totals $59,987,500.

LONG TERM PRINCIPAL = $23,995,000.00

LONG TERM INTEREST = $35,992,500.00

$59,987,500.00 – TOTAL PROJECTED

LONG-TERM PRINCIPAL& INTEREST

YEAR THREE SHORT TERM PROJECTED PROFIT..........$58,923,895

LONG TERM PROJECTED PROFIT............................$59,987,500

TOTAL...$118,911,395

$59,987,500 long-term profit added to the short-term one year profit of $58,923,895 in Year Three amounts to $118,911,395, an approximate 3,565% projected short and long term return on Year Three, Phase One $3,335,000 investment. This is a projected approximate total profit of $15,033 per house. Most aware, knowledgeable and astute people, and like-minded investors and business people, would likely conclude that these types of safe and solid investments are extremely rare and would be of major value to any forward thinking, creative investor. As we mentioned earlier in this book, we want to provide an extremely logical method and means to the American people to purchase their own homes, sell their own homes and deal in investment methods that most likely would provide excellent returns to the investors, whether the investments are small or large. Finding and purchasing a home without bank debt or without incurring new bank debt will become extremely important to the American people in the near future. Finding safe, secure, sound and profitable investments, *outside of the box,* with as few governmental and system's controls, as possible, will also become very important to the people in the very near future. If you have thoroughly read this book, then you understand why. Margy and I hope that we may have provided some suggestions, solutions and methods that will be very helpful to you and your family.

ANALYSIS OF YEAR THREE EXPENSES

In Year Three, Phase Two, five more professionals were hired at $60,000.00, each, per year. In Year Three, Phase Three, ten more professionals were hired at $60,000.00, each, per year, two more secretaries at $35,100.00, each, per year; $20,000.00 more is allocated to cash reserves; $30,000.00 more is allocated for offices and $10,000.00 more for office expenses. Please note that these expenses are allocated for each and every phase, whether the funds are used or not. In Phase Four, fifteen more professionals were hired at $60,000.00, each, and $20,000.00 more is allocated to cash reserves.

Purposefully, we *overestimated* expenses for each phase of the year so that the projections would be conservative. In actual operations, the expenses would not likely be this high. Expenses for Year Three are projected to be $4,268,932.00 for all staff and all operational expenses. Both these operational expenses and sales expenses are listed in the yearly projections. As we mentioned previously, if multiple investors are involved, then these investors, family members, relatives and friends, could be hired to staff the operation and receive salaries. Year Three projected operational and staff expenses of $4,268,932.00 could be paid to family, relatives and friends rather than to outside workers. This would keep the funds "in house". $4,268,932.00 can go a very long way within the investors' "structure" and keep loved ones, relatives and friends well paid for their work.

In all projections in COLUMN ONE, AVAILABLE CASH, the projected expenses are immediately taken from the available cash, which is scheduled for investment. In Year Three, AVAILABLE CASH is $3,496,400.00, minus $161,400.00 staff and operational expenses, which leaves $3,335,000.00 for investments. The $161,400.00 in projected expenses is for the two months of Phase One and is taken immediately, but will not be spent immediately. Obviously, the subtraction of all expenses at the very inception of a phase greatly reduces the amount available for investment. Those expense funds will be spent in increments over two months, and not all at once. Again, we did this to be quite conservative. In actual operations, these funds would be spent weekly, and not monthly. They would likely be spent in equal amounts over an 8 to 9 week period. On this basis, total first week expenses would be $161,400.00, divided by 8.5 weeks = $18,988.23, which would be the projected first week expenses for Year Three, Phase One, week one. $161,400.00, minus

$18,988.23 = $142,411.77, which amount could be invested into buying and selling rather than sitting in a safe somewhere. It is always good to keep funds active, and not passive.

In a similar vein, the $4,268,932.00 Year Three projected operational expenses, divided by 52 weeks = $82,095.00, per week. $4,268,932.00, minus $82,095.00 = $4,186,837.00. This $4,186,837.00, on a phase to phase operational average, would be added to the AVAILABLE CASH in each phase to be invested. It will be invested by percentage in each phase and not all at once. This total amount, using our purchasing methods, and allocating 75% to the purchase of $60,000.00 homes and the rest to the purchase of $100,000.00 homes could produce an additional $3 million or more to Year Three total returns. These profits would be derived from sales in each phase, which phase profits could also be added to AVAILABLE CASH in the following phase. Obviously, the more funds invested, the higher the profits. These additional projected profits are <u>not contained</u> in our projections, but are presented to you for your consideration in your business operations. If the same procedure were started in Year Two, then that year's profit projection would increase.

POSSIBLE EXPANSION INTO YEAR FOUR

If our investor(s) wants to continue his investments into Year Four and beyond, the investor(s) would have to establish and expand operations in many different areas to accommodate the expected large volume of increased business. If the investor were to invest the projected short term profit at the end of Year Three, that would be approximately $59,093,795, including mortgage interest. Year Three short term projected return of $58,923,895 is 1,770% of Year Three, Phase One investment of $3,335,000. If the same projected Year Three short-term return of 1,770% is taken on Year Three profits of $58,923,895, then the Year Four one year short-term projected return would be approximately $1,042,952,941. Projected Year Three short and long term profits are 3,570% of the Year Three, Phase One investment of $3,335,000. Year Three short profits of $58,923,895 times 1.01805 % equal long term projected returns of $59,987,500. Projected Year Four short term profits of $1,042,952,941 times 1.01805% indicate long term projected returns of approximately $1,061,778,241. The total Year Four projected profits are **$2,104,731,182**.

PROJECTED YEAR FOUR SHORT TERM PROFITS………$1,042,952,941

PROJECTED YEAR FOUR LONG TERM PROFITS………..$<u>1,061,778,241</u>

TOTAL YEAR FOUR PROJECTED PROFITS……………$2,104,731,182

The possibilities are literally endless, since capable buyers will always be very eager to purchase property with mortgages carried by the seller. If our investor stopped his operations at the end of Year Three and retired, his total projected short term profit from the three years of operation would be approximately $59,093,795. To give you an idea as to the enormous profit that is possible, this amounts to an approximate return of 393,958% on the first year initial investment of $15,000.00. Further, he would have a projected $23,995,000.00 in second and third mortgages, paying a projected 10% per year, approximately $2,995,000 per year. Mortgage principal of $23,995,000 combined with mortgage interest of $35,992,500 over 15 years, plus three year short term profit of $58,923,895, make his total short and long term projected returns approximately $118,911,395. This is a staggering return for a $15,000.00 original investment, but doable and achievable for the aware, astute, capable and dedicated investor.

As we have stated, we wrote this book to inform the American people of the existing realities present in our society and to show them how they can provide a home and investment possibilities for themselves and their families. Some people who do not have $15,000.00 to invest may want to do this program, but since they lack the funds, have no idea how they could proceed. In a previous CHAPTER, we wrote of how it may be possible for such a potential investor to option a property, then, sell it to a buyer at a profit through the use of the *ByPass* methods. This profit, or working several options that result in sales to buyers, could provide the seed capital to the investor for his own investment(s).

Because there is so much potential profit in these investments, we want to offer other suggestions for those who want to invest, but lack the needed capital to do so. The initial $15,000.00 investment could be made by two people who invest $7,500.00, each; or by three people who invest $5,000.00, each; or by five people who invest $3,000.00, each, – or even by ten people who invest $1,500.00, each, or even by twenty people who invest $750.00, each. Again, the possibilities are unlimited, but for many people in this very tight economy the funds to invest may well be limited. Combining efforts and funds could prove to be extremely profitable, provided the participating investors are serious, dedicated, capable, responsible, honorable and willing to work cooperatively together to accomplish their common objective(s).

When considering investments with other people, it is best that all participants are like-minded, have the same understanding, the same objective(s), and share a common work ethic to accomplish their goals. Working together with people one knows and trusts is probably best, such as family members, other relatives, friends, close neighbors, coworkers, club members, team members, etc. There is enough potential in these investment programs for all participants and the more participants, the lower the amount of capital needed from each investor. Everyone who wants to invest in such sound programs should be able to do so, which is why we have spelled out these combined investment possibilities. To this end, below we provide some projected returns for investors based upon Year Three combined short and long term projected profits and break it down for different numbers of investors who made their combined $15,000.00 investment in Year One, Phase One.

Year Three Projected Short-term Profit	= $ 58,923,895
Year Three Projected Long-term Profit	= $ 59,987,500
Year Three Combined Short and Long term Projected Profit	= $118,911,395

No. of Investors	Amount	Short-term Profit	Long-term Profit	Combined Profit
1	$15,000.00	$58,923,895	$59,987,500	$118,911,395
2	$7,500.00 Each	$29,461,947 Each	$29,993,750 Each	$59,455,697 Each
3	$5,000.00 Each	$19,641,283 Each	$19,995,833 Each	$39,637,116 Each
5	$3,000.00 Each	$11,784,779 Each	$11,997,500 Each	$23,782,279 Each
10	$1,500.00 Each	$5,892,389 Each	$5,998,750 Each	$11,891,139 Each
20	$750.00 Each	$2,946,194 Each	$2,999,375 Each	$5,945,569 Each

As you can see, these projections for investors in the above categories, investing anywhere from $7,500.00 down to $750.00, could receive fabulous wealth for their investments, both short and long term. Of course, if it is only one investor, investing the $15,000, then his total return is projected to be $118,911,395. The short-term projected profit is the approximate cash profit that the investor(s) would receive at the end of Year Three, if the investors decide to stop operations and go no further. For all investors in all categories, the short-term profit is projected to be approximately 3,928% of the original investment amount. The combined short and long term projected profit is approximately 7,927% of the *original* investment amount. As we mentioned earlier, we wrote this book for *everyone* and there is something in it for everyone. We want to show that even an investor with a small amount of funds could combine those funds with other like-minded, honorable investors and reach goals that they thought were the stuff of dreams and never obtainable for them in this life. Everyone can benefit, if everyone participates. The opportunity is there for those who want it and are willing to work for and earn it.

From Year Two through Year Three and beyond, office staff and sales staff will be needed to service the expected increased business volume. Year One will not require any staff, since the investors can easily handle the business operations. However, since multiple numbers of investors may be involved, then they, or at least some of them, could fulfill paid positions instead of hiring outside of the investment group. In this case, with 10 or 20 investors, various husbands, wives, other family members and relatives could take many of the paid positions. In this way, investors will not only be actively involved in day to day business operations, but also get paid for their involvement—and who better to do a good job than those with vested interests in the success of the operation!

Success begets more success, and sometimes encourages people to pursue further success. Some groups of investors may want to continue into Year Four and beyond, while others are perfectly happy to take their profits and retire, or pursue something else, since they will have the funds available for those pursuits. Whatever those pursuits may be, the projected profits derived from the *ByPass* investments programs can financially aid any further enterprise(s). Some investment groups may want to distribute a percentage of the short-term profits to investors, then, invest the rest in Year Four operations. Some also may want to follow up on that success by investing all of Year Three profits into Year Four operations. Below we list projected profits for Year Four with projected returns to each participant, depending upon his original investment amount.

No. of Investors	Amount	S̲hort-term Profit	Long-term Profit	Combined Profit
1	**$15,000.00**	**$1,042,952,941**	**$1,061,778,241**	**$2,104,731,182**
2	$7,500.00 Each	$521,476,470 Each	$530,089,120 Each	$1,052,365,591 Each
3	$5,000.00 Each	$347,650,980 Each	$353,926,000 Each	$701,577,060 Each
5	$3,000.00 Each	$208,590,588 Each	$212,355,000 Each	$420,946,000 Each
10	$1,500.00 Each	$104,295,294 Each	$106,177,842 Each	$210,473,118 Each
20	$750.00, Each	$51,147,647Each	$53,088,912 Each	$105,236,559 Each

The above projected returns likely seem fantastic to the average man or woman, but are very doable and realistic. People have three basic necessities—sustenance, shelter and clothing. Every day people buy food and clothing and millions of homes are bought and sold each and every year. Because of the plandemic Covid 19 fraud, projections on national sales are uncertain. Originally, national sales projections for 2020 called for approximately 5,900,000, plus, sales of existing homes. Projections for Year Four involve sales of approximately 122,700 houses which is approximately 2% of national existing home sales projections. The total projected sales of 122,700 homes may seem very high, but in comparison to national sales amounts, this figure is quite small. All of this means that there is enormous room for extensive investments through the *ByPass* programs from capable and willing investors.

It is a sad fact that most business operations in America are driven by profits, *only*, while customers and clients are considered merely assets to be used and abused, a means to an end, that contribute to those all-important profits, with no other considerations extended by the businesses. There is nothing inherently wrong with capitalism and nothing wrong with profits, since these keep businesses in business and provide the incentive to people and companies to create businesses. However, the type of capitalism conducted and how profits are derived are either just or unjust— right or wrong. Everything is *right* about an honest profit received from an honest business operation providing a useful, beneficial product or service to the client at a reasonable, competitive price. Everything is *wrong* with the type of capitalism that provides for unjust, avaricious, greedy profits extracted forcibly from the people in one way or another and driven by the power forces that encourage and support this type of ruthless capitalism. Sound familiar?

The American people are beginning to see the adverse effects this type of ruthless capitalism wreaks upon their lives, how pervasive it has been for *centuries*, how "cozy" the relationship among government, banking and big business is and how intertwined are the corporate structures in and among each other, with interlocking boards of directors, owners and controllers. All of these factors contribute to an overreaching control dominating virtually every form of activity necessary for human life. Unfortunately for humans, pernicious "crony-capitalism" has to a great extent ruled this world and this country as far as human memory can reach. While pockets of beneficial capitalism have existed and do exist, eventually these safe havens for the people are bought up, controlled or driven out of business by the power forces, which consider businesses that derive *just* profits anathema to their way of doing business. John D. Rockefeller was fond of saying that competition is a sin. When the power forces wreak this economic havoc upon the people, they manipulate and control a great deal, if not most or all, of the various markets that exist—right across the board. These "legal" pirates can extract virtually anything they want from the people, anytime, because they are "in bed with" the government, and as most of you now realize, the government serves the interests of the power forces, and not the interests and rights of the people, despite the pandering rhetoric and hollow promises professional politicians make to the people during every election cycle! As a result, the unjust, excessive profits stolen from the American people further add to the economic slavery that has existed in this nation and this world for eons. Anyone with common sense and a rational, reasonable mind can easily see the overarching connections and interconnections between governments and these "legal" pirates, otherwise known as bankers and corporate magnates. In situations such as these, social justice and economic justice go right out the window.

Throughout America's history, there have been many devastating economic "downturns" which have harmed millions upon millions of people. You are aware of the devastating market crashes and foreclosures that occurred *en masse* beginning in 2007 and 2008. Many of you are familiar with the other economic downturns this nation has had over the decades, and some of you may be familiar with the crash that took place in 1929. Prior to 1929, there were numerous other crashes that took place in America and all of these devastated millions of people who in some cases lost everything and were left absolutely penniless. The real question is how and why, these crashes occurred, who orchestrated them, and for what purpose? The simple answer leads to an age old maxim: Cui bono? In other words, who and what benefits and who and what control the monetary system? FDR was quoted as saying that anything that happens in politics doesn't happen by accident. The same is true for economics, especially when the private central bank has usurped the authority of the Constitution, with the criminal approval of congress, therefore controls and manipulates every possible aspect of the American economy. If you own the dice in a casino, you can rig the dice to come up with any number you want. As President Trump said early in his campaign, "The system is rigged." It is well past time for the American people to be well aware of this fact.

The government and the monetary system benefit from these crashes, since the government gains additional power, and the monetary system gains additional wealth and control over businesses, industries and from those who lost everything in the crashes. Please remember that when someone loses something, someone else gains those losses. If one investor lost two million shares in a triple A rated company because of the economic crash, then, obviously, someone else gained those two million shares, and you have a pretty good idea as to who that is. All markets are manipulated and have been for a very long time, which is something that most people do not understand or even want to consider. The rational, reasonable observer, exhibiting common sense, could easily conclude that the one who controls and gains through market destructions is certainly in a position to manipulate and cause those market destructions. Since governments at all levels work very closely with the power forces and money forces, who orchestrate these market disasters to their benefit, no one, except a rare throwaway lower level scapegoat from time to time, is ever held accountable for these economic disasters that ruin massive amounts of people and devastate America's economy, all of which has a direct impact upon the average American.

The Preamble to our Constitution predicates and is vital to the positions set forth in the Constitution, and all politicians and government officers have sworn or affirmed oaths to uphold and support the federal and state Constitutions. The Preamble requires government *"to establish Justice, ensure domestic Tranquility, provide for the common defence, promote the general Welfare, and secure the Blessings of Liberty to ourselves and our Posterity"*. Thomas Jefferson strongly urged the people to bind government in the chains of the Constitution and knew well that government which is not bound under the control of the people will control and eventually destroy the people and the nation in which they live. All of these "public officers" are bound by the Constitutional mandates imposed upon them, not only those in the Preamble, but also those in the body of the Constitution and the Amendments. Unfortunately, the American people, as a society, have never held government to any Constitutional standard whatsoever. As a result, the federal, state and local governments do whatever they want, and it is clear that governments, by and through their own actions, want to and have supported and continue to support the power forces and the money interests over the rights and well-being of the people. The present COVID-19 scam is a classic example. Can anyone actually claim that when governments covertly permit and, in collaboration with the power forces, *engineer* devastating financial collapses that the government is "promoting the general Welfare, ensuring domestic Tranquility, establishing Justice and securing the Blessings of Liberty for ourselves and our Posterity"? Our rational, objective observer and his analytical computer would say, with conviction, that, by its actions, the governments are the **domestic enemies** of which Jefferson spoke in the Declaration of Independence.

Given the fact that such a government-sanctioned, overreaching business climate exists in and dominates America, we believe, that in the best interests of the American people, a more honorable, honest, human win-win approach can benefit both businesses and their clients/customers to the extent that each faction functions in a cooperative, reciprocal effort for mutual beneficial objectives and purposes. This type of business benefits all those involved. Sadly, in today's ever-increasingly materialistic America this is not the case, except in rare instances of some small business operations. In the investment enterprises we are proposing, profit is definitely an objective, but when one considers the other implications involved, these programs go well beyond profit. Since the investors will not only make a substantial profit, but will also help others fulfill their objectives, then, the investors' actions result in far more than mere profits. For sellers facing difficulties selling their homes through usual systems approaches in a tough sellers' market, and for buyers whose only ability to buy a home is by and through these "outside the box" programs, the investors provide avenues unavailable elsewhere in America.

Whether the investors originally intended it or not, when they engage in these programs, they provide valuable social and economic benefits to their clients—true win-win situations—tangible benefits denied them by the very system that is supposed to protect them. When our investors can both realize their own profits and, in the process, help others who would have few to no other alternatives—then, the investors are providing a very real, needed avenue to their clients that was not accessible before, and further provide true social and economic benefits to the entire community. Many of their clients would basically be system's rejects and throwaways with little or no chance of regaining what they lost because of system's restrictions imposed upon them. Such economic and social violence should <u>not</u> exist in a so-called free nation controlled by a government that is required to "promote the general Welfare" for the people. Economic machinations and system's restrictions do not promote the general Welfare! In essence, what our potential investors would do is create social and economic justice denied by the system and raise social and economic consciousness for the people and community that they helped. As we said and as most people know, success begets success, and others will copy successful methods. In this way, one investor's efforts in one particular area could literally reverberate around the entire country.

Consider the family that lost its home through foreclosure. As you know, there are millions of them across the country. Consider the workers, whether blue, gray or white collar, who lost jobs because their companies moved to a third world nation and others who lost their jobs through no fault of their own, due to a disastrous economy made possible by a government that is required to promote the general welfare. For the most part, these people have no place to go, as we have said previously. They are the true victims of economic violence. Since most of these people have been productive throughout their lives, most of them will not give up, but will try something else in some other enterprise, so they can work, be productive and provide for their families. Over time, some of these people have been able to put some money aside, but are not able to purchase homes because their "poor credit" prohibits them from passing bank restrictions, as mentioned throughout this book. We mention this over and over because such policies resulted in a continuing disaster that should not have taken place and still exists in a so-called "free America, with opportunity for all". Conditions imposed by the government/power forces caused most of these people to be placed in terrible positions, and they will remain there unless something else emerges that can help them help themselves. Our *ByPass* Programs can provide that opportunity for many of these people. Since these *ByPass* Programs were not available before, most of these potential home buyers simply could not and would not qualify at all. However, the *ByPass* Programs open up ways and means for them to do so, all made possible by the investor(s). On the other side, the seller who could not sell his home in a very down market in the conventional manner, or the seller who had a mortgage on his home which prevented him from selling, can now do so by and through these programs, again, all made possible by and through the investor(s). Our investors may not be aware of this factor, but they are definitely providing otherwise unavailable benefits to both buyers and sellers which were not possible without their involvement; therefore providing social and economic benefits for many others and to the community, at large.

In a previous section of this book, we mentioned that professionals in the legal arena, who attended our seminars, told us that our Constitutional methods should be taught in law schools, because they are extremely effective and work quite well against the corrupt, rigged systems operating in this country. As mentioned, we said that for these very reasons, our Constitutional methods would *never* be taught in law schools. Upholding the fraud and avoiding Constitutional solutions that win against that fraud is the *business* of law schools, so it does not take a genius to figure out that these law schools would never teach or advocate anything that would cut into the business and profits of the system to which they are all indebted and for which they would do virtually anything to maintain the status quo control of that system to which they are beholden. In a similar vein, our investment methods would likely never be taught or advocated in business schools, because these methods empower average human beings to separate themselves from insidiously corrupt financial, economic and governmental systems, which separation could provide economic security and freedom for them and their families. No matter how loudly the American governmental and business systems *claim* they love freedom, the exact opposite is the true reality. Again, the COVID-19 fraudulent shutdown is a prime example. The deceptive American system wants the average American subservient to and dependent upon that system and all its subsystems. Freedom, especially economic freedom, is absolutely anathema to the system. Although most colleges and universities in this country, if not all of them, provide business courses as majors to many of their undergraduate students, these institutions will likely never teach our methods.

In addition to this, there are graduate level business schools, especially in the Ivies and other "top tier" schools, which usually attract intelligent students, often with means, who want to quickly advance in the business world. That said, we propose what many may think of as an unrealistic possibility, but which in reality is quite possible. These various schools which would likely never teach our methods, because they benefit the people of the nation, and not the controlling systems of the nation, may have students who could quickly understand the economic viability of these *ByPass* methods and, in fact, engage in them. Systems' institutions protect systems' institutions across the board, and when it comes to a choice between protecting the people or the systems, systems' organizations always decide in favor of the systems, and against the interests of the people. This has been apparent for a very long time and thankfully the American people are finally beginning to recognize this fact and the enormous impact of this ugly, but true, reality.

Let us say that a group of college students attending the same school, either in an undergraduate or graduate business program, read this book, truly understand the potential of the methods and projections presented, and want to invest as spelled out in our methods and projections. However, these students, being young, eager and ambitious, do not want to wait until they graduate. They want to invest now—while still in school. This scenario may not be as far-fetched as it may seem at first glance. Creative, inventive, ambitious, forward-thinking and industrious students can produce wonders! Let us speculate that ten of them decide to invest jointly in the $15,000.00 program, with each participant investing $1,500.00. As long as there is a mutual understanding and agreement among all participants, set forth in writing, in a written contract entered into and agreed to by all parties, the investment can begin. As we said before, the first year of investment is a test case that determines whether the investors want to proceed further, or take their profits and disband.

Let us say that these business-student-investors are very pleased with their first year and proceed into the second year. A definite further benefit to these business students is the fact that their investments provide very unique, rare on-the-job practical, hands-on business experience which can prove to be invaluable. Rather than deal with business "theory" and tedious, repetitive teachings, boring statistics and business philosophy, these students are actually invested in and working within an actual business operation that is producing results, profits and valuable experience not available in any business schools. By the end of Year Three, pursuant to the projections, each one of the ten student investors has amassed $5,892,389 in projected short-term profits, $5,998,758 in projected long-term profits and $11,891,139 in combined short and long term projected profits. For each of these ten students to invest $1,500 each and to receive a projected short and long term profit of approximately $11,891,139 after just three years of safe, sound investing, would conclusively prove to any rational man, woman or business professors that these students have definitely demonstrated their abilities and worth in the business world.

Their business professors might agree, but since many of these professors think that they have far superior expertise over their students, they might not publicly express their agreement. Hopefully, some of these educators would congratulate and be quite proud of their students for doing so well, so quickly. Many, if not most or all, parents of our student investors would be deliriously happy and excited by what their children accomplished in just three years, while still attending college or business school. Further, since our projections call for business expenses beginning in Year Two, then each and every one of the ten students could perform a needed business function and get paid for it while still in school. This would reduce the need for hiring outside workers and keep our hypothetical student investors well-funded during their school years and relieve their parents of their financial burdens, which, with today's high college tuitions and other costs, are extremely heavy.

When college students major in business, then go to graduate business schools, they could be in school for six years, or more. If our ten investors decided to roll the projected profits into Year Four, projections indicate that short-term returns for each investor would be approximately $104,295,296. Long-term projected returns would be approximately $106,177,842. Combined short and long term projected profits are approximately $210,473,118, <u>PER STUDENT INVESTOR.</u> Such returns, based upon an initial $1,500 investment per student, would financially enable these students to pursue whatever business interests, other interests and lifestyles they choose. The obvious question that most people would likely ask is: "Is all of this fabulous wealth possible for a $1,500.00 investment?" If the ten students are truly dedicated, have the same common objectives, are willing to work together in a cooperative effort to achieve their collective goals, display honor, personal and collective responsibility, and deal ethically and honestly, then the answer is "Yes, this is possible." The success of these hypothetical students would likely become a topic of conversation on campus and it is quite possible that other students would be eager to try to emulate their success. Students within various fraternities, young women in sororities, athletes on various school teams, and diverse students within clubs, associations and organizations within the school might be very interested in building a very large nest egg to be cashed in upon graduation, and at the same time, get paid for building that nest egg. As we have said before, and as society has seen repeatedly, success begets success, and most people would like to be successful.

The students could be so successful that they could pay off any and all school debts and loans, any funds advanced to them by parents, and still maintain abundant wealth. It is a sad fact that the only way most students can afford college is by taking out student loans, which loans place these students under the yoke of crushing debt as soon as they graduate. Years ago, there was a period of grace time allotted so students could obtain jobs and then begin paying back their loans. Those days are gone, and now the student debt burden has become excessive to the point that many loans are in default, which poses another financial crisis for those who are so indebted, the numbers of which are massive and growing. For our student investors, cash-in takes two forms, namely, short-term profit, which is taken all at once, and long-term profit, which is paid each and every year for the next 15 years. As previously stated, such funds would allow the students to pursue virtually any course of action, any enterprise, fulfill any dream or ambition and live any lifestyle he or she chooses, without the need to incur any debt and give them the ability to pay off any and all prior student loans.

The students may be so grateful and appreciative of the wealth their success has brought them and respectful of the fact that their parents funded their educations to the extent that they not only repay what their parents have expended, but also possibly pay off their parents' mortgages, or provide other funds to assist in other ways. Some may be so grateful that they would like to help others in areas of life where need arises, such as the homeless, animal shelters and other authentic charities. When people becomes so successful so quickly, it is always very good and honorable to remember the ones who helped them along the way. Payback is part of the honor system, and this country desperately needs to return to honor in virtually all aspects of life and society. Some parents may be so enthralled with their children's success that those parents may want to make the same types of investments as their children did. Again, in this vein, the possibilities are endless. It could be anywhere from one or two parents, who would likely invest much more than $15,000.00

to begin the program, up to multiple family members getting on board as investors in a cooperative effort, just as their children did.

When people who are friends, neighbors, extended family members, fellow workers, church, business and club associates of these parents see the success the parents have garnered, then the "success bug" may bite these others, and they might want to invest in the same way. Families all over the nation fall into several categories–doing well, not doing well, or just getting by, and some of them may be seeking other methods to better their lives and improve their lifestyles. While one or two investors can be quite successful using these methods, sometimes there is safety in numbers, especially with like-minded people sharing the same objectives and goals. If large numbers of people across the nation were to begin these affordable investments in a cooperative effort, and gain the success that can be achieved through diligence, consistency and common sense-wisdom, then new trends can be established and these types of buying, selling and financing methods would become a new way of realizing *true* independence and wealth for the people. In fact, all of this could be the new wave of the future.

Consider how many clubs, organizations, associations, fraternal groups and societies, as well as adult league sports teams exist throughout America. There are thousands of them and countless numbers of people in them. Just as the success of the original business students could easily become known to other students at school, and some other students could start using the *ByPass* investment programs, too, information regarding that success could spread to other colleges and universities throughout the country. Again, success begets success, and when new ideas and trends gain popularity, that popularity spreads like wildfire. New methods that work soon become the norm and there could be thousands upon thousands of students across the nation engaging in such investment programs. Similarly, people in various clubs, social organizations, professional societies, charitable enterprises, grant organizations, etc. will likely hear of the successes of other adults who have successfully invested using the *ByPass* programs and methods and may want to delve into this type of investing on their own, or with family members and friends, or with club and association members.

As most Americans know, a large number of college students graduate each year and cannot find suitable work commensurate with their educations, so quite a few of these unfortunates either take low paying jobs, or none at all. Many of them live with their parents, which, for the most part, is not what either expected and not usually a preferable arrangement. If some of these students or their parents were to read this book, then they may have a solution that could greatly improve their mutual circumstances. Those parents able to do so could provide the $15,000 investment seed money to their children to begin the *ByPass* $15,000 buy/sell Investment Program, and take a financial interest in it, such as 50%. With serious, capable students, unable to find work, this could be a panacea for both them and their parents. If the parents and their children are serious, but $15,000 is a bit high, then they might think of other parents and students who might want to also participate. Parents have friends and relatives, and their sons or daughters likely know other students in similar conditions. Three investors could put in $5,000, each, or five, $3,000 each. Again, the possibilities are endless for creative, independent, serious people willing to do something new that could help them, and many others. This solution could provide confidence, financial and emotional independence for the students, and comfort, relief and welcomed financial benefits for the parents.

As we mentioned previously, Margy and I wrote this book to help the American people and show them a new way to buy, sell and invest in property that could be significantly important to them and their families in the near future. The first part of this book spelled out the existing governmental, political, judicial and banking controlling realities existent in this country and the need for the American people to not only be aware of these very severe, contrived restrictions and limitations upon the people, but also to make them understand that they must take lawful action on their own and collectively to stop these problems, before the problems overtake and destroy the entire country, with no way back. As we see it, there is a definite, crying need for the people to be as independent and free as they possibly can in a very tightly controlled, antagonistic, adversarial system that is getting tighter and more restrictive in many ways by the week.

In prior CHAPTERs we pointed out the various created/controlled financial disasters that destroyed many millions of Americans and, further, cost many millions their homes, their livelihoods and their assets. *The American people must learn from history, or they are doomed to repeat it*, so they must learn to provide for themselves and their families as they best can, and not depend upon the system or any of its parts to "have their backs". Millions of Americans who had bank mortgages on their homes lost those homes even though most did nothing wrong. What happened in the past will happen in the future, unless the people learn from the past and do not repeat their mistakes in the future. The people must realize that these *deliberate* assaults on the people's wealth were systematically planned long ago, just as this COVID-19 fraud was, and the economic violence that the planners of these assaults continuously use against the people is by no means over. Thus, it would be far better if no American is indebted in any way whatsoever to the banks, to the government or to the corporations. Anyone with a bank or corporate mortgage on his house, business, assets, car, or possessions of any kind, can be vulnerable, just as were the millions of Americans who lost their homes, businesses, cars, other possessions, their livelihoods, their dreams and their self-respect.

The whole conceptual idea behind the *ByPass* methods and programs is to *ByPass* the banks, the government and the power forces as the controlling factors over the people and place the economic power and control, usurped by these entities, back into the hands of the people, themselves. Additionally, since there has been so much negativity ascribed to "capitalism", especially in recent years with the insane and ill-advised push to "socialism" being foisted upon Americans, in particular, young Americans, it is time to clear the air about this very important topic. Capitalism, at its best, is what built America. Capitalism, at its worst, is what is now ruining America. How can this be? Capitalism practiced by decent, honorable, hard-working, responsible and reasonable people in a just and fair system is unequivocally a path to success. However, when capitalism is practiced by greedy, dishonorable, ruthless, manipulative people, in an unjust rigged system, it becomes a path to fabulous wealth for the *very* few and the road to poverty or outright ruin for the many. The *ByPass* programs of which we speak in this book reflect capitalism at its best, practiced by people with righteous intentions, reasonable ambitions, aspirations and responsible applications. This type of common sense, *compassionate capitalism* is the best way to eliminate the pernicious form of capitalism being conducted by the banks, large corporations and virtually all forms of government on this planet, and to put economic independence, freedom and control right back into the hands of the people, where it rightfully belongs.

It should be clear to most anyone by now that the way the system conducts capitalism poses so many restrictions and obstacles in the path of the average human being that most people never dare dream of engaging in successful independent ventures. The system, by its abuses and greed, has vilified the very idea of capitalism so that many people are loath to even admit to wanting to reach for economic success. This is exactly how the system wants it. The system wants the people to be disempowered and never believe that they can do and have more than the crumbs the system allows them. The system wants the people to believe that being successful and wealthy are bad traits to emulate. The system wants the people to hate capitalists and shun any attempts at exercising capitalism. The system wants the people to so hate capitalism that they will run blindly into the insidious embrace of communism. Tragically, the system has done a masterful job of deceiving the people into "throwing out the baby with the bathwater." Instead of Americans blindly hating capitalism, Americans need to concentrate their scorn on the ruthless greedy entities of all stripes that have abused the capitalistic system, made enormous fortunes for themselves in the process, and turned it into an economic nightmare for the vast majority of people on this Earth. It is these greedy, evil people who should be held accountable for their heinous crimes and utter disregard for human life, not capitalism.

To be free of such adverse mental conditioning and controls, the people need to reclaim their personal ambitions, and one very good way to do this is through the *ByPass* methods. Taking the middle men out of the equation is beneficial, improves the portents for success, thus the buying, selling and funding of property should be between principals, only, and on a personal basis, as described in the *ByPass* methods. This provides safety to the people and extricates them from the claustrophobic umbrella of overreaching banking, governmental and corporate controls all operating within the system's box created for and crippling the people. When the next financial disaster happens and people lose their jobs, if they are mortgaged to a bank, they could be in serious trouble. If they are mortgaged to a fellow American, however, that fellow American is more likely to have compassion and empathy, thus, is not likely going to apply the same strong-arm, loan-shark tactics that a bank would against a homeowner. Further, if the homeowner is involved in a successful business operation that is somewhat out of the system, he has a far better chance of escaping the contrived financial crisis unscathed and likely will do very well on his own. The *ByPass* investment programs described in this book can help nearly any willing American embark upon the road to real personal and financial success and security.

Economic disasters will be triggered again, for the reasons discussed. In fact, given the economic shutdown imposed upon America due to the COVID-19 scamdemic, the Mother of All Disasters is waiting in the wings to swallow up the wealth and prosperity of many of the American people. It would be far better for the average American to be safe, own his or her own home, with no bank, corporate or government debt, and to have no systems loans on anything, including cars and assets. Instead of relying on credit cards to make purchases, it would be far better to have funds set aside so that purchases could be made using cash or debit cards. It would also be best if the average American could have his or her own source of ongoing funds to make it easier to do this, as would be the case through the *ByPass* investment programs described herein. When people are involved in successful investment programs, and others are losing their homes, jobs, assets, with no funds coming in, the successful investors and their families could be very safe and secure despite the chaos around them. Further, through these investment programs, the investors could help others whom the system essentially discarded and threw away.

If people began to engage in these *ByPass* Programs, they would quickly empower themselves. When people are successful, they feel good about themselves, and those good feelings carry over into every aspect of their lives and the lives of their families, friends, coworkers, associates, teammates, etc. They can not only see their productivity garnered through their creation, but can actually measure that productivity. The investors took responsibility and can recognize the fruits they derive from exercising that responsibility. Such activities create self-confidence and could possibly lead to other types of creativity and inventions that would be helpful to society as a whole. Perpetual success has no boundaries, except those we create ourselves. Let success continue as long as there is the will to achieve it. For successful investors to get out of the restrictive control "box" established for them by the system is not only good for those who escape the box, but also good for the others they help, because they, themselves, will have escaped that control.

Unfortunately, the great mass of American people has not fully understood the dangers of debt in all its myriad forms, both public and private. Debt is seductive, extensive and is promoted and encouraged almost everywhere, therefore the temptations are high to get into debt and stay in debt. It seems "normal" to most Americans to be in continuous debt. Most Americans have been accustomed to debt through propaganda, conditioning, and advertising to the extent that being in debt is considered routine, therefore they want to buy whatever they want, whenever they want it, provided the means for financing their purchases are available. However, following the last couple of severe financial crises, some people have realized that there is a big price associated with debt, and when that price cannot be paid, then, those people could lose everything. We say that it is far better to buy through profits made and not through debt incurred. The system wants virtually everyone loaded down with debt, because that debt puts the assets of the people under the control of the system. When disasters happen, such as the COVID-19 scam, and since they are deliberately planned, they *do* happen, then those Americans with debt, and without jobs or the ability to service the debt, will lose whatever they pledged for that debt, including homes, businesses, cars, boats, second homes, and any other pledged assets. The banks and their allies are the only ones who benefit, while, tragically, many people are ruined.

Wise humans learn from the past and try to avoid bank and system's debt like the plague. They know what will happen to their holdings if they are debt heavy when the economy crashes, or even just hits a "speed bump". However, if they buy their homes through our *ByPass* methods, and make investments as described in this book, either alone or with others, then, their homes should be safe and the funds they earn through the investments should keep them and their families safe, secure and financially well off even if others around them are not doing well. In fact, the worse the economy is, the better the investment possibilities can be for our investors. Tragically, people will lose jobs and homes again, but since people always need shelter and since there are always those who can make the mortgage payments to the investors, they can expect to have ample buyers and sellers. Remember, when the financial disasters hit people unexpectedly before, most of them had no way out, because they had no way to pay their bank mortgages and no way to sell their bank-mortgaged homes. With the *ByPass* methods, even with a bank mortgage, owners can sell their properties, and not lose them, as millions of unfortunate victims of the banking system did. No one wants to be a victim, but unfortunately, so many people are so unaware of the existing realities operative in this nation that they become victims to a debt system and lose everything for which they have worked so hard and for so long. As we stated, wise people learn from history and learn from the mistakes made by others, so they can avoid making those same mistakes; thus avoid catastrophe, while at the same time, investing in a profitable, secure enterprise that will keep them financially safe and independent.

Because of the reasonableness, substance, methodologies and the problems the *ByPass* methods would solve, it is very possible that these buying/selling and investing approaches could not only be the wave of the future, but, in fact, may be the leading edge into the future by which properties are routinely bought and sold. In this way, the financial control remains in the hands of the buying/selling principals, and not under the control of the banks and the government. This would be a major benefit, not only to the principals, but to America, herself. If these approaches develop and spread as expected, then within anywhere from five to fifteen years, any and all existing bank debt would have been paid off by those using the *ByPass* methods. Further, virtually all debt carried by sellers will have been paid off. Buyers would own their homes, free and clear of all debt, which is an absolutely wonderful feeling. However, with the standard banking and system's approaches, house debt is rarely paid off. Banks and the system encourage refinancing and urge people to obtain loans against their equity to buy "toys", vacation homes, take trips, etc. Obviously, this keeps people in perpetual debt, which is the lenders' objective. Property without debt is far superior to property with debt. Most people who sell homes buy another home. Sellers who own their homes free and clear can sell their homes by and through our *ByPass* methods and then buy other homes also through the *ByPass* methods—without any bank financing whatsoever. When a sizable percentage of homeowners in the country have no bank debt on their homes, and own them free and clear, this would wrest an enormous amount of control from the banks and the system and put financial control back into the hands of the people, where it properly belongs.

As we have mentioned, in the early days of humanity, barter was the main form of commerce among people. In some societies, barter may still exist, but it is no longer the major way of buying and selling because banks have interceded and are the "third man" in any contract. As we have noted, when parties deal with banks, they must deal with restrictions and limitations, some of which can be quite burdensome and severe, and they are usually required to pay fees, points and subject themselves to outside control. When people barter with each other, the contractual arrangement and the financing is directly between the principals, with no other outside involvement whatsoever, unless, of course, the principals want that involvement. Homes are bought and sold all the time throughout America, every day, in all price ranges. Let us say that a fellow who owns a home worth $100,000.00—free and clear—in Waterville, Maine, sells his home to a buyer through the use of the *ByPass* methods. The buyer pays $15,000.00 down and the seller carries $85,000.00 for 15 years at 5%, with a principal and interest payment of $650.29, per month. The seller now purchases a home in another city or another state for $100,000.00, by and through our *ByPass* methods, and pays to his seller the same $15,000.00 he received as a down payment for his home and also pays the seller $650.29, per month, for the $85,000.00 mortgage his seller carries for 15 years at 5%. What we have here is an even trade for equal value, at no cost to the seller. He simply traded his home for another home, by and through the *ByPass* methods.

In all of our work over the years, Margy and I have tried to make things as simple, as easy and as direct as possible. When people realize what they can do, buying, selling and investing through these *ByPass* methods, understand the ease with which these methods can work, and understand the benefits to selling their own homes and buying others, then it is possible that more and more people will be interested in these approaches and, as a result, will ByPass the banks. In life, sometimes debt is unavoidable and we have all seen conditions that require debt. However, to perpetually remain in debt to a rigged, corrupt, ruthless banking system does not benefit anyone except the rigged system. Escaping the box, getting out of debt and beginning the road to freedom and independence are the only things that can and will bring Americans back to life, restore a value-based economy and bring America back from the brink of the looming financial abyss. We hope you join us in reestablishing freedom, independence and real opportunity within the American people, and through these processes, make America great again and the true Constitutional Republic she was created to be!

ByPass $48,000 BUY/SELL PROGRAM
PROJECTIONS PHASES

PROJECTIONS – BUY/SELL $48,000 PROGRAM – YEAR ONE, PHASE ONE

Available Cash	Investment	Cash Profit	Cash Return	Second Mortgages	Cash Overage
$48,000	2 house down payments of $9,000 each = $18,000	2 x $8,000 = $16,000	$48,000 investment Combined w/	2 at $2,000 = $4,000	- 0 -
	2 house down payments of $15,00 each = $30,000	2 x $10,000 = $20,000 FOR	$29,240 profit FOR	2 at $5,000 = $10,000	
	Total: 4 house down payments for $48,000	Combined cash profit: $36,000	Total cash return: $77,240	Combined total: $14,000	
Sales expenses deducted from profits: ▶▶▶▶▶▶ ▶		Less: Sales expenses 2 x $1,330 = $2,660, PLUS 2 x $2,050 = $4,100 Total expenses = $6,760 FOR Net profit of $29,240			
TOTALS					
$48,000	$48,000 outlay for 4 houses	$29,240 60.91%Profit	$77,240 160.91%Return	$14,000	- 0 -

PROJECTIONS – BUY/SELL $48,000 PROGRAM – YEAR ONE, PHASE TWO

Available Cash	Investment	Cash Profit	Cash Return	Second Mortgages	Cash Overage
$77,240	5 house down payments of $9,000 = $45,000	5 x $8,000 = $40,000 PLUS	$75,000 investment COMBINED WITH	5 at $2,000 = $10,000	$2,240
	2 house down payments of $15,000 = $30,000	2 x $10,000 = $20,000 FOR	$49,250 profit FOR	2 at $5,000 = $10,000 FOR	
	Total: 7 house down payments for $75,000	Combined cash profit of $60,000	Total cash return of $124,250	Combined total of $20,000	
Sales expenses deducted from profits:		Less: 5 x $1,330 = $6,650 PLUS 2 x $2,050 = $4,100, TOTAL EXPENSES $10,750 FOR Net profit of $49,250			
TOTALS					
$77,240	$75,000 outlay for 7 houses	$49,250 65.66% Profit	$124,250 165.66% Retn	$20,000	$2,240
CUMULATIVE TOTALS					
$125,240	$123,000 outlay for total of 11 houses	$78,490 63.81% Profit	$201,490 163.81% Return	$34,000	$2,240

PROJECTIONS – BUY/SELL $48,000 PROGRAM – YEAR ONE, PHASE THREE

Available Cash	Investment	Cash Profit	Cash Return	Second Mortgages	Cash Overage
$124,250	5 house down payments of $9,000 each = $45,000 PLUS	5 x $8,000 = $40,000 PLUS	$120,000 invest-ment COMBINED WITH	5 x $2,000 = $10,000	$4,250
	5 house down payments of $15,000 = $75,000	5 x $10,000 = $50,000 FOR	$ 73,100 PROFIT FOR	5 x $5,000 = $25,000 FOR	
	Total: 10 house down pay-ments for $120,000	Combined cash profit of $90,000	Total cash return of $193,100	Combined total of $35,000	
Sales expenses deducted from profits:	▶▶▶▶▶▶▶	Less Sales ex-penses: 5 x $1,330 = $6,650 PLUS 5 x $2,050 = $10,250 Total Expenses = $16,900 FOR Net Profit of $73,100			
TOTALS					
$124,250	$120,000 outlay for total of 10 houses	$73,100 60.91% Profit	$193,100 160.91 Return	$35,000	$4,250
CUMULATIVE TOTALS					
$249,490	$243,000 outlay for total of 21 houses	$151,590 62.36% Profit	$394,590 162.36% Return	$69,000	$6,490

PROJECTIONS – BUY/SELL $48,000 PROGRAM – YEAR ONE, PHASE FOUR

Available Cash	Investment	Cash Profit	Cash Return	Second Mortgages	Cash Overage
$193,100	8 house down payments of $9,000 = $72,000 PLUS	8 x $8,000 = $64,000 PLUS	$192,000 investment COMBINED WITH	8 at $2,000 = $16,000 PLUS	$1,100
	8 house down payments of $15,000 = $120,000	8 x $10,000 = $80,000 FOR	$116,960 profit FOR	8 at $5,000 = $40,000 FOR	
	Total: 16 house down payments for $192,000	Combined cash profit: $144,000	Total cash return: $308,960	Combined total: $56,000	
Sales expenses deducted from profits:	►►►►►►►	Less: Sales expenses 8 x $1,330 = $10,640 PLUS 8 x $2,050 = $16,400 Total expenses = $27,040 FOR Net profit: $116,960			
TOTALS					
$193,100	$192,000 outlay for 16 houses	$116,960 60.91% Profit	$308,960 160.91% Return	$56,000	$1,100
CUMULATIVE TOTALS					
$442,590	$435,000 outlay for 37 houses	$268,550 61.73% Profit	$703,550 161.73% Return	$125,000	$7,590

PROJECTIONS – BUY/SELL PROGRAM - $48,000 – YEAR ONE, PHASE FIVE

Available Cash	Investment	Cash Profit	Cash Return	Second Mortgages	Cash Overage
$308,960	16 house down payments of $9,000 each= $144,000	16 x $8,000 = $128,000 PLUS	$309,000 Investment COMBINED WITH	16 x $2,000 = $32,000 PLUS	($40)
	11 house down Payments of $15,000 = $165,000	11 x $10,000 = $110,000 FOR	$194,170 PROFIT FOR	11 x $5,000 = $55,000 FOR	
	Total: 27 house down payments for $309,000	Combined cash profit: $238,000	Total cash return: $503,170	Combined total: $87,000	
Sales expenses deducted from profits:		Less: Sales expenses: 16 x $1,330 = $21,280 PLUS 11 x $2,050 =$22,550 Total expenses = $43,830 FOR Net profit of $194,170			
TOTALS					
$308,960	$309,000 outlay for 27 houses	$194,170 62.83% Profit	$503,170 162.83% Return	$87,000	($40)
CUMULATIVE TO-TALS					
$751,550	$744,000 outlay for 64 houses	$462,720 62.19% Profit	$1,206,720 162.19% Return	$212,000	$7,550

PROJECTIONS – BUY/SELL PROGRAM - $48,000 – YEAR ONE, PHASE SIX

Available Cash	Investment	Cash Profit	Cash Return	Second Mortgages	Cash Overage
$503,170	44 house down payments of $9,000 each = $396,000 PLUS	44 x $8,000 each = $352,000 PLUS	$501,000 Investment COMBINED WITH	44 x $2,000 = $88,000 PLUS	$2,170
	7 house down payments of $15,000 each = $105,000	7 x $10,00 each = $70,000 FOR	$339,820 PROFIT = TOTAL cash For	7 x $5,000 = $35,000 FOR	
	Total: 51 house down payments for $501,000	Combined cash profit: $422,000	Total cash return: $840,820	Combined total: $123,000	
Sales expenses deducted from profits:	► ► ► ► ► ► ►	51 x $1,330 = $67,830 PLUS 7 x $2,050 =$14,350 Total expenses = $82,180 For Net profit of $339,820			
TOTALS					
$503,170	$501,000 outlay for 51 houses	$339,820 67.82% Profit	$840,820 167.82% Return	$123,000	$2,170
CUMULATIVE TOTALS					
$1,254,720	$1,245,000 outlay for 115 houses	$802,540 64.46% Profit	$2,047,540 164.46% Return	$335,000	$9,720

-

$48,000 INVESTMENT PROGRAM
- YEAR ONE PROJECTION ANALYSIS

Year One, Phase One began with a $48,000 investment and ended in Phase Six with a return of $840,820. This is a projected 1,751.7% return on the $48,000 investment. No further investments beyond the initial $48,000 were required to reach the projected $840,820 return. Throughout investment circles, rational, objective observers would see this as a phenomenal return for a safe secure investment based in marketable real estate.

Everything we present in this book is based in and founded upon common sense, reason, soundness, direct positions and simple, uncomplicated approaches. As we mentioned previously, common sense would indicate that it is entirely reasonable to understand that many capable buyers would have avid interest in purchasing a home with the mortgage carried by the seller, and especially those who have been restricted from purchasing a home through traditional bank funding. Common sense would also indicate that homeowners who could not previously sell their homes because of existing mortgages that prevented a sale would have strong interest in selling to our investors. Further, many other homeowners suffering from a depressed market and bad economy would find a way out through our *ByPass* programs. Still further, those homeowners in foreclosure or about to face foreclosure would have strong interest in selling to our investors. Those homeowners who would prefer a straight cash sale could always sell their first mortgages on a discounted basis to investors who deal in such acquisitions. Since the seller is not paying a real estate commission to a broker, this kind of discounted sale is entirely reasonable.

In addition to the short term return referenced above, projections indicate that additional returns will come from Retained Earnings and Recaptured Earnings explained in the analysis after completion of the $15,000 Investment Program. Average projected returns were established for both priced homes. These returns are $833.28 for the $60,000 purchased house and $1,392.48 for the $100,000 priced house. Projections called for the investor to purchase 115 homes in Year One, of which 80 are purchased for $60,000 and 35 for $100,000.

60 x $ 833.28 = $49,996.80
35 x $1,392.48 = $48,736.80
Total..............$98,733.60

As mentioned before, the amounts derived from Retained Earnings and Recaptured earnings are not added to Returns and not invested into the Programs. These amounts can be distributed to investors or invested into the Programs, as investors decide. As more houses are purchased and sold over the life of the Program, these funds substantially increase.

Beyond the above, there is also a long term return emanating from principal and interest amounts on second and/or third mortgages. Interest payments are due one year after purchase and principal amounts are paid on the 15th anniversary of purchase. Interest from Year One is received and credited to Year Two figures.

Year Two Projections follow.

PROJECTIONS – BUY/SELL PROGRAM - $48,000 – YEAR TWO, PHASE ONE

Available Cash	Investment	Cash Profit	Cash Return	Second Mortgages	Cash Overage
$840,820	70 house down payments of $9,000 each = $630,000	70 x $8,000 = $560,000	$840,000 Investment	70 x $2,000 = $140,000	$820
	PLUS	PLUS	COMBINED WITH	PLUS	
	14 house down payments of $15,000 each= $210,000	14 x $10,000 = $140,000 For	$578,200 PROFIT FOR	14 x $5,000 = $70,000 FOR	
	Total 84 house down payments for $840,000	Combined cash profit: $700,000	Total cash return of	Combined total: $210,000	
Sales expenses deducted from profits:	▶ ▶ ▶ ▶ ▶ ▶	LESS: 70 x $1,330 = $93,100 PLUS 14 x $2,050 = $28,700 Total Expenses: $121,800 FOR Net profit of $578,200			
TOTALS					
$840,820	$840,000 outlay for 84 houses	$578.200 68.83%	$1,418,200 $168.33%	$210,000	$820,000
CUMULATIVE TOTALS					
$2,095,540	$2,085,000 outlay for 199 houses	$1,380,740 66.22%	$3,465,740 166.22%	$545,000	$17,730

PROJECTIONS – BUY/SELL PROGRAM - $48,000 – YEAR TWO, PHASE TWO

Available Cash	Investment	Cash Profit	Cash Return	Second Mortgages	Cash Overage
$1,418,200 Less Operating Expenses of $112,000 = $1,306,200 Available Cash	108 house down payments of $9,000 each= $972,000 PLUS	108 x $8,000 = $864,000 PLUS	$1,302,000 Investment COMBINED WITHJ	108 $2,000 = $216,000 PLUS	$4,200
	22 house down payments of $15,000 each = $330,000 FOR	22 x $10,000 = $220,000 For	$895,260 PROFIT FOR	22 x $5,000 = $110,000 For	
	Total130 house down payments for $1,302,000	Combined cash profit: $1,084,000	Total cash return of: $2,197,260	Combined total: $326,000	
Sales expenses deducted from profits: ►►►►►►►		LESS: 108 x $1,330 = $143,640 PLUS 22 x $2,050 = $45,100 Total Expenses: $188,740 FOR Net profit of: $895,260			
TOTALS					
$1,306,200	$1,302,000 outlay for 130 houses	$895,260 68.76%	$2,197,260 168.76%	$326,000	$4,200
CUMULATIVE TOTALS					
$3,401,740	$3,387,000 outlay for 329 houses	$2,276,000	$5,663,000	$1,106,000	$21,930

PROJECTIONS – BUY/SELL PROGRAM - $48,000 – YEAR TWO, PHASE THREE

Available Cash	Investment	Cash Profit	Cash Return	Second Mortgages	Cash Overage
$2,197,260 Less Operating Expenses of $174,000 = $2,023,260 Available Cash	168 house down payments of $9,000 each = $1,512,000 PLUS	168 x $8,000 = $1,344,000 PLUS	$2,022,000 Investment COMBINED WITH	168 x $2,000 = $336,000 PLUS	$1,260
	34 house down payments of $15,000 each = $510,000	34 x $10,000 = $340,000 FOR	$1,390,860 PROFIT FOR	34 x $5,000 = $170,000 FOR	
	Total 202 house down payments for $2,022,000	Combined cash profit: $1,684,000	Total cash return of $3,412,860	Combined total: $506,000	
Sales expenses deducted from profits:	►►►►►►	Less: x 168 $1,330 = $223,440 PLUS 34 x $2,050 = $69,700 Total Expenses: $293,140 For net profit of: $1,390,860			
TOTALS					
$2,023,260	$2,022,,000 outlay for202 houses	$1,390,860 68.78%	$3,412,860 168.78%	$506,000	$1,260
CUMULATIVE TOTALS					
$5,425,000	$5,409,000 outlay for 531 houses	$3,666,860 67.79%	$9,075,860 167.79%	$1,612,000	$23,190

PROJECTIONS – BUY/SELL PROGRAM - $48,000 – YEAR TWO, PHASE FOUR

Available Cash	Investment	Cash Profit	Cash Return	Second Mortgages	Cash Overage
$3,412,860 Less Operating Expenses of $270,000 = $3,142,860 Available Cash	262 house down payments of $9,000 each = $2,358,000 PLUS	262 x $8,000 = $2,096,000 PLUS	$3,138,000 Investment COMBINED WITH	262 x $2,000 = $524,000 PLUS	$4,860
	52 house down payments of $15,000 each = $780,000 FOR	52 x $10,000 = $520,000 FOR	$2,160,940 PROFIT FOR	52 x $5,000 = $260,000 FOR	
	Total:314 house down payments for $3,138,000	Combined cash profit: $2,616,000	Total cash return of $5,298,940	Combined total: $784,000	
Sales expenses deducted from profits: ▶▶▶▶▶▶▶		LESS:262 x $ 1,330 = $348,460 PLUS 52 x $2,050 = $106,600 Total Expenses: $455,060 For Net Profit of: $2,160,940			
TOTALS					
$3,142,860	$3,138,000 outlay for 314 houses	$2,160,940 68.86%	$5,298,940 168.86%	$1,340,000	$4,860
CUMULATIVE TOTALS					
$8,567,860	$8,547,000 outlay for 845 houses	$5,827,800 68.18%	$14,374,800 168.18%	$2,396,000	$28,050

PROJECTIONS – BUY/SELL PROGRAM - $48,000 – YEAR TWO, PHASE FIVE

Available Cash	Investment	Cash Profit	Cash Return	Second Mortgages	Cash Overage
$5,298,940 Less Operating Expenses of $407,000= $4,891,940 Available Cash	407 house down payments of $9,000 each =$3,663,000 PLUS	407 x $8,000 = $3,256,000 PLUS	$4,893,000 investment Combined with	407 x $2,000 = $814,000 PLUS	$(1,060)
	82 house down payments of $15,000 each = $1,230,000	82 x $10,000 = $820,000 FOR	$3,366,590 PROFIT FOR	82 x 5,000 =$410,000 FOR	
	Total 489 house down payments for $4,893,000	Combined cash profit: $4,076,000	Total cash return of $	Combined total: $1,224,000	
Sales expenses deducted from profits: ▶▶▶▶▶▶▶		Less: 407 x $1,330 = $541,310 PLUS: 82 x $2,050 = $168,100 Total Expenses: $709,410 For Net profit of: $3,366,590			
TOTALS					
$4,891,940	$4,893,000 outlay for 489 houses	$3,366,590 68,80%	$8,259,590 168.80%	$1,224,000	$-1,060
CUMULATIVE TOTALS					
$13,459,800	$13,440,000 outlay for 1,334 houses	$9,194,390 68.41%	$22,634,390 168.41%	$3,620,000	$26,990

PROJECTIONS – BUY/SELL PROGRAM - $48,000 – YEAR TWO, PHASE SIX

Available Cash	Investment	Cash Profit	Cash Return	Second Mortgages	Cash Overage
$8,259,590 Less Operating Expenses of $635,000 = $7,624,590 Available Cash	635 house down payments of $9,000 each = $5,715,000 PLUS	635 x $8,000 each = $5,080,000 PLUS	$7,620,000 Investment COMBINED WITH	635 x $2,000 = $1,270,000 PLUS	$4,590
	127 house down payments of $15,000 each = $1,905,000 FOR	127 x $10,000 each = 1,270,000 $ FOR	$5,245,100 PROFIT FOR	127 x $5,000 = $635,000 FOR	
	Total 762 house down payments of $7,620,000	Combined cash profit: $6,350,000	Total cash return of $12,865,100	Combined total: $1,905,000	
Sales expenses deducted from profits:	► ► ► ► ► ► ►	Less: 635 x $1,330 = $844,550 PLUS 127 x $2,050 = $260,350 Total Expenses: $1,104,900 Net profit of $5,245,100			
TOTALS					
$7,624,590	$7,620,000 outlay for 762 houses	$5,245,100 68.83%	$12,865,100 168.83%	$1,905,000	$4,590
CUMULATIVE TOTALS					
$21,084,390	$21,060,000 outlay for 2,096 houses	$14,439,490 68.56%	$35,499,490 168.56%	$8,082,000	$36,440

$48,000 INVESTMENT PROGRAM
- YEAR TWO PROJECTION ANALYSIS

At the end of Year One, Phase Six, cash return was projected to be $840,820, which is invested in Year Two, Phase One. At the end of Year Two, Phase Six, total cash return is projected to be $12,865,100. This is a 1,530.06% return on the $840,820 investment. As mentioned earlier, the rational, impartial and objective observer would consider this return remarkable for a safe, secure investment based in marketable real estate.

In order to provide the outstanding qualities of these programs and the benefit to all involved in them, Year Two return is projected at 26,802.29% of the original $48,000 investment. It would be extremely difficult to find a very safe, secure investment that would provide the same returns.

In addition to the above cash return, funds are returned from Retained Earnings and Recaptured Earnings. These average $833.28 for the $60,000 house and $1,392.48 for the $100,000 house. In Year Two, 1,981 houses were projected to be bought and sold by our investor(s), of which 1,650 are $60,000 homes and 331 are $100,000 homes.

$$1,650 \times \$\ 833.28 = \$1,374,912$$
$$331 \times \$1,392.48 = \underline{\$\ 460,910}$$
Total……………$1,835,822

These funds are projected to be received throughout Year Two, but we did not project them as Profit to be added to total returns and reinvested into the Program. The investor(s) can decide whether to distribute these funds amongst themselves, retained as profit or reinvested into the Program.

In addition to the above, Year One second mortgage interest is due in Year Two. The Principal amount is $423,000 at 10% interest, which amounts to $42,300. We did not project these amounts as Profit added to return. Our investor(s) can decide whether to retain this as Profit, or invest it into the Program.

Year Three projections follow.

PROJECTIONS – BUY/SELL PROGRAM - $48,000 – YEAR THREE, PHASE ONE

Available Cash	Investment	Cash Profit	Cash Return	Second Mort-gages	Cash Overage
$12,865,100 Less Operating Expenses of $990,000= $11,875,100 Available Cash	923 house down payments of $9,000 each = $8,307,000 PLUS	923 x $8,000 = $7,384,000 PLUS	$11,877,000 Investment COMBINED WITH	923 x $2,000 = $1,846,000 PLUS	$(1,900)
	238 house down payments of $15,000 each= $3,570,000	238 x $10,000 = $2,380,000 FOR	$7,563,610 PROFIT FOR	238 x $5,000 = $1,190,000 FOR	
	Total 1,161 house down payments for $11,877,000	Combined cash profit: $9,764,000	Total cash return of $19,440,610	Combined total: $30,360,000	
		LESS sales expenses: 923 x $1,330 = $1,227,590 PLUS 238 x $2,050 = $487,900 Total expenses= $2,203,390 FOR Net profit of $7,563,610			
TOTALS					
$11,875,100	$11,877,000 outlay for 1,161 houses	$7,563,610 63.68%	$19,440,610 163.68%	$30,360,000	$(1,900)
CUMULATIVE TOTALS					
$35,777,320	$32,937,000 outlay for 3,257 houses	$22,003,100 66.80%	$54,940,100 166,80%	$35,885,000	$29,680

PROJECTIONS – BUY/SELL PROGRAM - $48,000 – YEAR THREE, PHASE TWO

Available Cash	Investment	Cash Profit	Cash Return	Second Mortgages	Cash Overage
$19,440,610 Less Operating Expenses of: $ 1,475,000= $17,965,610 Available Cash	1,537 house down payments of $9,000 each = $13,833,000 PLUS	1,537 x $8,000 each = $12,296,000 PLUS	$17,958,000 investment COMBINED WITH	1,537 x $2,000 = $3,074,000 PLUS	$7,610
	275 house down payments of $15,000 each = $4,125,000 FOR	275 x $10,000 = $2,750,000 FOR	$12,438,040 PROFIT FOR	275 x $5,000 = $1,375,000 FOR	
	Total 1,812 house down payments for $17,958,000	Combined cash profit: $15,046,000	Total cash return of $30,396,040	Combined total: $4,449,000	
		LESS sales expenses: 1,537 x $1,330 = $2,044,210 PLUS x $2,050 = $563,750 Total Expenses: $2,607,960 FOR Net profit of $12,438,040			
TOTALS					
$17,965,610	$17,958,000 outlay for 1,812 houses	$12,438,040 69.26%	$30,396,040 169.26%	$13,122,000	$7,610
CUMULATIVE TOTALS $50,925,100	$50,895,000 Outlay for 5,069 houses	$34,441,140 67.67%	$85,336,140 167.67%	$51,564,000	$37,290

PROJECTIONS – BUY/SELL PROGRAM - $48,000 – YEAR THREE, PHASE THREE

Available Cash	Investment	Cash Profit	Cash Return	Second Mortgages	Cash Overage
$30,396,040 Less Operating Expenses of $2,250,000 = _____ $28,146,040 Available Cash	2,190 house down payments of $9,000 each= $19,710,000 PLUS	2,190 x $8,000 = $17,520,000 PLUS	$28,140,000 Investment COMBINED WITH	2,190 x $2,000 = $4,380,000 PLUS	$6,040
	562 house down payments of $15,000 each= $8,430,000	562 x $10,000 =$5,620,000 FOR	$19,075,200 PROFIT FOR	562 x $5,000 =$2,810,000 FOR	
	Total 2,752 house down payments for $28,140,000	Combined cash profit: $23,140,000	Total cash return of $47,215,200	Combined TOTAL $7,190,000	
		LESS sales expenses: 2,190 x $1,330 = $2,912,700 PLUS 562 x $2,050 = 1,152,100 _____ Total Expenses: _____ $4,064,800 FOR Net profit of: $19,075,200			
TOTALS					
$28,146,040	$28,140,000 outlay for 2,752 houses	$19,075,200 67.78%	$47,215,200 167,78%	$7,190,000	$6,040
CUMULATIVE TOTALS					
$79,071,140	$79,035,000 Outlay For 7,871 houses	$53,516,340 67.71%	$132,551,340 167.71%	$47,524,000	$43,330

PROJECTIONS – BUY/SELL PROGRAM - $48,000 – YEAR THREE, PHASE FOUR

Available Cash	Investment	Cash Profit	Cash Return	Second Mortgages	Cash Overage
$47,215,200 Less Operating Expenses of $3,300,000 = _____ $43,915,200 Available Cash	3,660 house down payments of $9,000 each =$32,400,000 PLUS	3,660 x $8,000 each = $29,280,000 PLUS	$122,940,000 Investment COMBINED WITH	3,660 x $2,000 each= $7,320,000 PLUS	$10,200
	767 house down payments of $15,000 each = $11,505,000	767 x $10,000 each = $7,670,000 FOR	$84,026,190 PROFIT FOR	767 x $5,000 each = $3,835,000 FOR	
	Total 4,427 house down payments for $43,905,000	Combined cash profit: $36,950,000	Total cash return of $80,855,000	Combined total: $11,155,000	
		LESS sales expenses: 3,660 x $1,330 each =$4,867,800 PLUS 767 x $2,050 each= 1,572,350 Total expenses $6,440,150 For Net profit of: $30,509,850			
TOTALS					
$43,915,200	$43,905,000 outlay for 4,427 houses	$30,509,850 69.49%	$74,414,850 169.49%	$11,155,000	$10,200
CUMULATIVE TOTALS					
$91,493,200	$122,940,000 for 12,298 houses	$84,026,190 68.34%	$206,966,190 168.34%	$58,694,000	$53,530

PROJECTIONS – BUY/SELL PROGRAM - $48,000 – YEAR THREE, PHASE FIVE

Available Cash	Investment	Cash Profit	Cash Return	Second Mortgages	Cash Overage
$74,414,850 Less Operating Expenses of $ =4,688,000 $69,726,850 Available Cash	5,810 house down payments of $9,000 each = 52,290,000 PLUS	5,810 x $8,000 = $46,480,000 PLUS	$69,720,000 investment COMBINED WITH	5,810 x $2,000 = $11,620,000 PLUS	$6,850
	1,162 house down payments of $15,000 each= $17,430,000	1,162 x $10,000 = $11,620,000 FOR	$47,990,600 PROFIT FOR	1,162 x $5,000 = $5,810,000 FOR	
	Total 6,972 house down payments for $69,720,000	Combined cash profit: $58,100,000	Total cash return of $117,710,600	Combined total: $17,430,000	
		LESS sales expenses: 5,810 x $1,330 = $7,727,300 PLUS 1,162 x $2,050 = $2,382,100 Total Expenses: $10,109,400 FOR Net profit of $47,990,600			
TOTALS					
$69,726,850	$69,720,000 outlay for 6,972 houses	$47,990,600 68.83%	$117,710,600 168,83%	$17,430,000	$6,850
CUMULATIVE TOTALS					
$161,166,050	$192,660,000 for 19,270 houses	$132,016,790 68.52%	$324,676,790 168.52	$76,124,000	$60,380

PROJECTIONS – BUY/SELL PROGRAM - $48,000 – YEAR THREE, PHASE SIX

Available Cash	Investment	Cash Profit	Cash Return	Second Mortgages	Cash Overage
$117,710,600 Less Operating Expenses of $7,100,000 = _____ $110,610,600 Available Cash	9,218 house down payments of $9,000 each = $82,962,000 PLUS	9,218 x $8,000 each = $73,744,000 PLUS	$110,607,000 Investment COMBINED WITH	9,218 x $2,000 = $18,436,000 PLUS	$3,600
	1,843 house down payments of $15,000 each =$27,645,000	1,843 x $10,000 = $18,430,000 FOR	$76,135,910 PROFIT FOR	1,843 x $5,000 = $9,215,000 FOR	
	Total 11,061 house down payments for $110,607,000	Combined cash profit: $92,174,000	Total cash return of $186,742,910	Combined total: $27,651,000	
		LESS sales expenses: 9,218 x $1,330each = $12,259,940 PLUS 1,843 x $2,050 each = $3,778,150 $ 16,038,090 Total Expenses: FOR Net profit of $76,135,910			
TOTALS					
$110,610,600	$110,607,000 outlay for 11,061 houses	$76,135,910 68.83%	$186,742,910 168.83%	$27,651,000	$3,580
CUMULATIVE TOTALS					
$271,776,650	$303,267,000 for 30,331 Houses	$208,152,700 68.63%	$511,419,700 168.63%	$115,005,000	$68,820

$48,000 INVESTMENT PROGRAM – YEAR THREE ANALYSIS

Year Two Return was $12,865,820, which is invested in Year Three, Phase One. At the end of Year Three, Phase Six, the projected return is $186,742,910, which is a 1,451.54% return on the $12,865,820 Year Three investment. This $186,742,910 is also a 389,047.72% return on the original Year One investment of $48,000. Upon the conclusion of Year Three, our investor(s) has turned $48,000 into $186,742,910 cash.

Projected averages for Retained Earnings and Recaptured Earnings cited are below:

23,338 x $ 833.28 = $19,447,088
 4,847 x $1,392.48= $ 6,749,350
 Total......................$26,196,438

As in previous years, the total amounts projected for Retained Earnings and Recaptured Earnings were not added to Profit for further investment in the Program. The investor(s) can either distribute these funds to investor(s) as profit or invest the funds into the next year buy/sell Program.

Year One and Year Two second/third mortgage interest is due in Year Three. Principal amount for Year One is $423,000. Principal amount for Year Two is $8,082,000.

$ 423,000
$ 8,082,000
$ 8,505,000 Total x 10% = $850,500.
$10,377,500 Year Three Second Mortgage Interest is Due in Year Four

As in previous years, mortgage interest paid is not added to Profit, thus not invested into the Program for additional buys and sells. The interest and principal balances are part of the long term profit and then added to short term profit for the total combined short and long term returns. These are cited below and on the following return chart for investor(s). The investor(s) will determine if these funds will be distributed to investor(s) as profit, or invested into the following year's buy/sells Program.

Short term Profit = Profit + retained/recaptured earnings = ... $215,144,730
Lone term Returns – Mortgage Principal + Interest =...........$259,437,500

$48,000 PROGRAM – PROJECTED RETURNS TO INVESTOR(S)

Investors	Amount	Short term Profit	Long term Profit	Combined Profit	%Rtn
1	$48,000	$212,939,348	$259,437,500	$472,376,848	984,118%
2	$24,000 Each	$106,469,674 Each	$129,718,750 Each	236,188,424 Each	984,118% Each
4	$12,000 Each	$ 53,234,837 Each	$64,859,375 Each	$118,094,212 Each	984,118% Each
8	$ 6,000 Each	$ 26,617,418 Each	$ 32,429,687 Each	$ 59,047,105 Each	984,118% Each
10	$ 4,800 Each	$ 21,293,934 Each	$ 25,943,750 Each	$ 47,237,684 Each	984,118% Each
16	$ 3,000 Each	$ 13,308,709 Each	$ 16,214,843 Each	$ 29,523,552 Each	984,118% Each
24	$ 2,000	$ 8,872,472	$ 10,809,895	$ 19,682,367	984,118%

ByPass $48,000 BORROW BUY/SELL INVESTMENT PROGRAM

YEAR ONE OF THE $48,000 BORROW PROGRAM IS THE SAME AS YEAR ONE OF THE REGULAR $48,000 BUY/SELL PROGRAM. REFER TO YEAR ONE OF THE REGULAR PROGRAM.

BORROWING STARTS WITH YEAR TWO OF THE BORROW PROGRAM.

PROJECTIONS–BUY/SELL $48,000 BORROW PROGRAM–YR 2, PH 1

Available Cash	Investment	Cash Profit	Cash Return	Second Mortgages	Cash Overage
$840,820 +_ $380,000 Loan $1,220,82 0 - $94,00 0 Operational expenses $1,126,820	95 house down payments x $9,000 each = $855,000 PLUS	95 x $8,000 = $760,000	$1,125,000 investment COMBINED WITH	95 x $2,000 = $190,000 PLUS	$ 1,820
	18 house down payments x $15,000 each = $270,000	18 x $10,00 = $180,000 FOR	$776,750 FOR	18 x $5,000 = $90,000 FOR	
	Total: 113 house down payments for $1,125,000	Combined cash profit: $940,000 LESS Sales expenses of	Total cash return: $1,901,750	Combined total: $280,000	
		95 x $1,330 = $126,350 PLUS 18 x $2,050 =$36,900 Total expens- es: $163,250 = Net profit of $776,750			
TOTALS	$1,125,000	$776,750	$1,901,750	$280,000	$1,820

$1,126,820	$1,125,000 outlay for 113 houses	$776,750 69.04% Profit	$1,901,750 169.04% Return	$280,000	$ 1,820
CUMULATIVE TOTALS					
$2,381,540	$2,370,000 outlay for 228 houses	$1,579,290 66.63% Profit	$3,949,290 166.63% Return	$615,000	$11,540

PROJECTIONS–BUY/SELL PROGRAM–$48,000 BORROW PROGRAM–YR 2, PH 2

Available Cash	Investment	Cash Profit	Cash Return	Second Mortgages	Cash Overage
$1,901,750 + $290,000 Loan $2,191,750 -$170,000 Op. expenses $1,731,750	134 house down payments x $9,000 each = $1,206,000 PLUS	134 x $8,000 = $1,072,000 PLUS	$1,731,000 Investment COMBINED WITH	134 x $2,000 = $268,000 PLUS	$750
	35 house down payments x $15,000 each= $525,000	35 x $10,000 = $350,000 FOR	$1,114,280 PROFIT FOR	35 x $5,000 =$175,000 FOR	
	Total: 169 house down payments for $1,731,000	Combined cash profit: $1,422,000 Less sales expenses of	Total cash return: $2,845,280	Combined total: $443,000	
		134 x $1,330 = $178,220 PLUS 35 x $2,050 =$71,750 Total expenses of $307,720 Net profit of $1,114,280			
TOTALS					
$1,731,750	$1,731,000 outlay for 169 houses	$1,114,280 64.37% Profit	$2,845,280 164.37% Return	$443,000	$750
CUMULATIVE TOTALS					
$4,113,290	$4,101,000 outlay for 397 houses	$2,693,570 65.68%	$6,794,570 165.68%	$1,146,000	$12,290

PROJECTIONS–BUY/SELL PROGRAM–$48,000 BORROW PROGRAM–YR 2, PH 3

Available Cash	Investment	Cash Profit	Cash Return	Second Mortgages	Cash Overage
$2,845,280 + $550,000 Loan $3,395,280 -$261,000 Op expense $3,134,280	261house down payments x $9,000 each =$2,349,000 PLUS	261 x $8,000 = $2,088,000 PLUS	$3,129,000 Investment COMBINED WITH	261 x $2,000 = $522,000 PLUS	$5,280
	52 house down payments x $15,000 each = $780,000 FOR	52 x $10,000 =$520,000 FOR	$2,154,270 PROFIT FOR	52 x $5,000 =$260,000 FOR	
	Total: $3,129,000 for 313 houses	Combined cash profit: $2,608,000 LESS sales expenses of	Total cash return: $5,283,270	Combined total: $782,000	
		261 x $1,330 = $347,130 PLUS 52 x $2,050 = $106,600 expenses of $453,730 Net profit of $2,154,270			
TOTALS					
$3,134,280	$3,129,000 outlay for 313 houses	$2,154,270 68.84% Profit	$5,283,270 168.84% Return	$782,000*	$5,280
CUMULATIVE TOTALS					
$7,247,570	$7,230,000 outlay for 710 houses	$4,847,840 67.05 % Profit	$12,077,840 1167.05% Return	$1,928,000	$17,570

PROJECTIONS–BUY/SELL PROGRAM-$48,000 BORROW PROGRAM–YR 2, PH 4

Available Cash	Investment	Cash Profit	Cash Return	Second Mortgages	Cash Overage
$5,283,270 + $2,650,000 Loan $7,933,270 -$615,000 Op expense $7,318,270	610 house down payments x $9,000 each = $5,490,000 PLUS	610 x $8,000 = $4,880,,000 PLUS	$7,320,000 Investment Combined with	610 x $2,000 = $1,220,000 Plus	Minus $1,730
	122 house down payments x $15,000 each =$1,830,000	122 x $10,000 = $1,220,000 FOR	$5,038,600 PROFIT FOR	122 x $5,000 = $610,000 FOR	
	Total: $7,320,000 for 732 house down payments	Combined cash profit: $6,100,000 LESS sales expenses of	Total cash return: $12,358,600	Combined total: $1,830,000	
		610 x $1,330 = $811,300 PLUS 122 x $2,050 =$250,100 $475,000, for Total expenses of: $1,061,400 = Net profit of $5,038,600			
TOTALS					
$7,318,270	$7,320,000 outlay for 732 houses	$5,038,600 68.83% Profit	$12,358,600 168.83% Rtn	$1,830,000	($1,730)
CUMULATIVE TOTALS					
$14,565,840	$14,550,000 outlay for 1,442 houses	$9,886,440 67.94% Profit	$24,436,440 167.94% Return	$3,670,000	$11,500

PROJECTIONS–BUY/SELL PROGRAM-$48,000 BORROW PROGRAM–YR 2, PH 5

Available Cash	Investment	Cash Profit	Cash Return	Second Mort-gages	Cash Overage
$12,358,600 + $6,200,000 Loan $18,558,600 -$1,470,000 Op exp $17,088,600	1,424 house down payments x $9,000 each = $12,816,000 PLUS	1,424 x $8,000 = $11,392,000 PLUS	$17,076,000 Investment COMBINED WITH	1,424 x $2,000 = $2,848,000 PLUS	$12,600
	284 house down pay-ments x $15,000 each = $4,260,000	284 x $10,000 = $2,840,000 FOR	$11,808,630	284 x $5,000 = $1,420,000 FOR	
	Total: $17,076,000 for 1,708 house down payments	Combined cash profit: $14,232,000 LESS sales expenses of	Total cash return: $28,884,630	Combined total: $4,268,000	
		1,424 x $1,330 = $1,893,920 PLUS 289 x $2,050 =$529,450 Total expenses of:$2,423,370 Net profit of $11,808,630			
TOTALS					
$17,088,600	$17,076,000 outlay for 1,708 houses	$11,808,630 169.15% Profit	$28,884,630 169.15% Return	$4,268,000	$12,600
CUMULATIVE TOTALS					
$31,654,440	$31,626,000 outlay for 3,150 houses	$21,695,070 68.59% Profit	$53,321,070 168.59% Return	$7,938,000	$24,100

PROJECTIONS–BUY/SELL PROGRAM–$48,000 BORROW PROGRAM–YR 2, PH 6

Available Cash	Investment	Cash Profit	Cash Return	Second Mortgages	Cash Overage
$28,884,630 + $14,440,000 Loan $43,324,630 — $3,465,000 op ex _ $39,859,630	3,322 house down payments x $9,000 each = $29,898,000 PLUS	3,322 x $8,000 = $26,576,000 PLUS	$39,858,000 Investment COMBINED WITH	3,322 x $2,000 = $6,644,000 PLUS	$1,630
	664 house down payments x $15,000 each = $9,960,000	664 x $10,00 = $6,640,000 FOR	$27,436,540 PROFIT FOR	664 x $5,000 = $3,320,000 FOR	
	Total: $39,858,000 for 3,986 house down payments	Combined cash profit: $33,216,000 LESS sales expenses of	Total cash return: $67,294,540	Combined total: $9,964,000	
		3,322 x $1,330 = $4,418,260 PLUS 664 x $2,050 =$1,361,200 Total expenses of $5,779,460 = Net profit of $27,436,540			
TOTALS					
$39,859,630	$39,858,000 outlay for 3,986 houses	$27,436,540 68.83% Profit	$67,294,540 168.83%	$9,964,000	$1,630
CUMULATIVE TOTALS					
$71,514,070	$71,484,000 for 7,136 houses	$49,131,610 - 68.76% Profit	$120,615,610 168.76% Return	$17,902,000	$30,070

$48,000 BORROW PROGRAM
– YEAR TWO PROJECTION ANALYSIS

At the end of Year One of the $48,000 Borrow Program, $840,820 is projected as the return upon the $48,000 investment. This $840,820 is invested in Year Two, Phase One to buy and sell houses, plus loans, and produced a projected return of $67,294,540 at the end of the year. This amounts to a return on investment of 8,003.44%. To provide a further perspective, this amounts to a return of 140,197% on the *original* $48,000 investment. As referenced earlier, the rational, objective observer imbued with common sense would consider this a staggering return for safe, secure and readily marketable real estate products.

No loans occurred in Year One, for the reasons mentioned below. During Year Two, a total of $24,510,000 was borrowed throughout the year for the purchase and sale of houses. Funds are borrowed in stages based upon contractual buys and sells between our investor(s), his sellers and his buyers. Security for the lender is a lien on second/third mortgages and the business assets of the investor(s). The loans allows our investor(s) to increase his number of buy/sells, thereby significantly increases his returns.

As mentioned in prior projections, two financial returns to the investor exist in these programs. One is the short term profit and the other, long term profit. Short term profits are returns upon investment, and long term are interest and principal returns on the second or third mortgages. Part of short term returns are sums which emanate from Retained Earnings and Recaptured Earnings. As referenced earlier, these sums are short term profits which we did not project as profits or returns to be invested into the programs. These funds are spent or distributed as the investor(s) decides. Also referenced previously, the investor(s) will want to receive funds from the investment, but it is better to let the investment roll from phase to phase and year to year to increase profits and returns. Funds for the investor(s) can come from Retained and Recaptured Earnings and from interest paid on the second or third mortgages. This choice allows the investment funds to remain in the program, and grow.

Retained and Recaptured Earnings

Projections call for 7,021 houses to be bought and sold during Year Two, of which 5,846 will be sold for $70,000 and 1,175 for $115,000. Projected average returns for Retained and Recaptured Earnings are $833.28 for the $70,000 house and $1,392.48 for the $115,000 house.

5,846 x $833.28   = $4,869,746
1,175 x $1,392.48 = $1,636,164

$6,505,910 Projected Return

Our investor(s) is expected to receive these above funds for Retained and Recaptured Earnings upon the sale of every house sold within two months of his purchase of that house. Earlier we acknowledged that our investor(s) want to earn funds from the buy/sell programs, which is obvious. Rather than take funds from the investment amounts, it would be better to take them in two different ways, which will allow the investment funds to roll over and produce more profits and returns. One way is to assign a salary(ies) from the operational expense funds, which are plentiful. The other way is to receive and distribute the funds returned throughout the year from Retained/Recaptured earnings and from yearly interest payments. As you can see from the above figures, the amounts of these funds are quite considerable.

Second Mortgage Principal and Interest

Year One interest is due in Year Two. The principal outstanding balance is projected at $423,000 x 10% = $42,300. Added to the $6,505,910 cited above amounts to $6,548,210, which is a very large amount for payments to investor(s) rather than to be taken from investment funds.

Borrowing greatly increases the amount of houses bought and sold, thus dramatically increases the profits and returns. Borrowed funds permit this increase, and without those funds, figures would be much lower. Until the principal amounts of these funds are repaid, they are used on a roll-over basis to increase the number of houses bought and sold. In Year Two of this Borrow Program, 7,021 houses are projected to be bought and sold. Total Return is projected at $67,294,540. In the regular Year Two Program 2,096 houses are projected to be bought and sold, with a projected Return of $12,865,100. There is an obvious substantial difference in favor of borrowing, with an approximate 523% increase in Return and an approximate 335% increase in houses bought and sold. Recaptured/Retained Earnings of $6,509,910 are approximately 356% higher than Year Two regular Returns of $1,825,822. This roll-over use of borrowed funds for the purchase and sale of more houses is invaluable.

Private investors who loan funds for businesses, projects and developments make certain that the business to which they loan funds is stable, financially sound, has capable management, can repay loaned amounts, plus interest, and provide solid collateral. Our investor(s) operated the first year of the buy/sell program to comply with these requirements and demonstrated that this buy/sell business operation is very solid with a strong, growing market. No loans were taken in Year One to demonstrate that the program can stand on its own merits, without loan funds.

During Year Two, a projected total of $24,510,000 was borrowed. This borrowing is projected to occur on a need basis depending upon the number of houses our investor contracts to purchase. This position protects the lender as well as our investor(s). The lender does not loan lump sums based upon possible future business, but, instead, loans smaller amounts based upon contracts to buy and sell large numbers of houses. Our investor(s) does not borrow large sums and pay interest based upon possibilities, but does so only when he has executed purchase and sale contracts. Collateral for the lender is based in two positions. First, the lender receives the assignment of all second and third mortgages. Second, he has a lien on the operating business.

Projections indicate that six percent (6%) interest is payable on the anniversary of the loan, and principal due on the third anniversary of the loan, plus interest owing. Extensions, loan amounts, terms, interest and repayment will be decided by the lender and our investor(s). These projections provide an example of arrangements that would serve the interest and objectives of both parties.

YEAR THREE *ByPass* BUY/SELL
$48,000 BORROW PROGRAM

PROJECTIONS–BUY/SELL PROGRAM-$48,000 BORROW PROGRAM–YR 3, PH 1

Available Cash	Investment	Cash Profit	Cash Return	Second Mortgages	Cash Overage
$67,295,534 + $37,000,000 loan $104,295,534 - $8,343,650op ex $95,951,884 -$17,400 loan interest = $95,934,484	7,995 house down payments x $9,000 each = $71,955,000 PLUS	7,995x $8,000 = $63,960,000 PLUS	$95,925,000 Investment COMBINED WITH	7,995 x $2,000 = $15,990,000 PLUS	$9,484
	1,598 house down payments x $15,000 each= $23,970,000	1,598 x $10,000 = $15,980,000 FOR	$61,316,640 PROFIT FOR	1,598 x $5,000 = $7,990,000 FOR	
	Total: $95,925,000 house down payments for 9,593 houses	Combined cash profit: $79,940,000 Gross profit LESS	Total cash return: $157,241,640	Combined total: $23,980,000	
		7,995 x $1,330 = $10,633,360 PLUS 1,598 x $2,050 = $7,990,000 Total expenses = $18,623,360 Net profit of $61,316,640			
TOTALS					
$95,934,484	$95,925,000 outlay for 9,593 houses	$61,316,640 63.92% Profit	$157,241,640 163.92% Return	$23,980,000	$9,484
CUMULATIVE TOTALS					
$167,448,554	$167,409,000 16,729 houses	$110,448,250 66.52% Profit	$277,857,250 166.52% Return	$41,882,000	$38,560

PROJECTIONS–BUY/SELL PROGRAM-$48,000 BORROW PROGRAM–YR 3, PH 2

Available Cash	Investment	Cash Profit	Cash Return	Second Mort-gages	Cash Overage
$157,241,640 + <u>$78,000,000 loan</u> $235,241,640　　　- $18,819,000op ex $216,422,640 -$22,800 loan inter-est on $380,000 loan =$216,399,840	15,628 house down payments x $9,000 each = $140,652,000 PLUS	15,628 x $8,000 = $125,024,000 PLUS	$216,387,000 Investment COM-BINED WITH	15,628 x $2,000 = $31,256,000 Plus	$12,840
	5,049 house down payments x of $15,000 each= $75,735,000	5,049 x $10,000 = $50,190,000 FOR	$144,078,310 PROFIT FOR	5,049 x $5,000 = $25,245,000 FOR	
	Total: $216,387,000 house down pay-ments for 20,677 houses	Combined cash profit: $175,214,000 LESS sales expenses of	Total cash return: $360,465,310	Combined total: $56,501,000	
		15,628 x $1,330 = $20,785,240 PLUS 5,049 x $2,050 =$10,350,450 Total expenses $3 1,135,690 Net profit of $144,078,310			
TOTALS					
$216,399,840	$216,387,000 outlay for 20,677 houses	$144,078,310 66.58%　Profit	$360,465,310 166.58% Return	$56,501,000	$12,840
CUMULATIVE TOTALS					
$383,848,399	$423,665,988 37,406 houses	$254,526,560 66.55% Profit	$638,322,560 166.55%	$98,383,000	$51,4,00

PROJECTIONS–BUY/SELL PROGRAM-$48,000 BORROW PROGRAM–YR 3, PH 3

Available Cash	Investment	Cash Profit	Cash Return	Second Mortgages	Cash Overage
$360,465,310 + $180,000,000 loan $540,465,310 - $43,000,000op ex $497,465,310 -$33,300 interest on $550,000 Loan = $497,432,010	35,925 house down payments x $9,000 each =$323,325,000 PLUS	35,925 x $8,000 = $287,400,000 PLUS	$497,415,000 Investment COMBINED WITH	35,925 x $2,000 = $71,850,000 PLUS	$17,010
	11,606 house down payments x $15,000 each $174,090,000	11,606 x $10,000 = $116,060,000 For	$331,887,450 PROFIT FOR	11,606 x $5,000 = $58,030,000 FOR	
	Total: $497,415,000 house down payments for 47,531 houses	Combined cash profit: $403,460,000 LESS sales expenses of	Total cash return: $829,302,450	Combined total: $129,880,000	
		35,925 x $1,330 = $47,780,250 PLUS 11,606 x $2,050 = $23,792,300 Total expenses =$71,572,550 Net profit of $331,887,450			
TOTALS					
$497,432,010	$497,415,000 outlay for 47,531 houses	$331,887,450 66.72% Profit	$829,302,450 166.72% Return	$129,880,000	$17,010
CUMULATIVE TOTALS					
$881,280,409	$921,080,988 for 84,937 houses	$586,414,010 66.64% Profit	$1,467,625,010 166.64% Return	$228,263,000	$68,410

PROJECTIONS–BUY/SELL PROGRAM-$48,000 BORROW PROGRAM–YR 3, PH 4

Available Cash	Investment	Cash Profit	Cash Return	Second Mortgages	Cash Overage
$829,302,450 + $414,000,000 Loan = $1,243,302,450 -$95,000,000 operational exps. $1,148,302,450 -$159,000 interest on $2,650,000 loan $1,148,143,450	79,094 house down payments x $9,000 each= $711,846,000 PLUS	79,094 x $8,000 = $632,752,000 PLUS	$1,148,136,000 Investment COMBINED WITH	79,094 x $2,000 = $158,188,000 PLUS	$7,450
	29,086 house down payments x of $15,000 each= $436,290,000	29,086 x $10,000 = $290,860,000 FOR	$758,790,680 FOR	29,086 x $5,000 = $145,430,000 FOR	
	Total: $1,148,136,000 house down payments for 108,180 houses	Combined cash profit: $923,612,000 LESS sales expenses of 79,094 x	Total cash return: $1,906,926,680	Combined total: $303,618,000	
		$1,330 = $105,195,020 PLUS 29,086 x $2,050 = $59,626,300 Total sales expenses = $164,821,320 Net profit = $758,790,680			
TOTALS					
$1,148,143,450	$1,148,136,000 outlay for 108,180 houses	$758,790,680 66.08% Profit	$1,906,926,680 166.08% Return	$303,618,000	$7,450
CUMULATIVE TOTALS					
$2,029,271,490	$2,069,216,988 for 193,117 houses	$1,345,204,690 66.33% Profit	$3,374,551,690 166.33% Return	$531,881,000	$75,860

PROJECTIONS–BUY/SELL PROGRAM-$48,000 BORROW PROGRAM–YR 3, PH 5

Available Cash	Investment	Cash Profit	Cash Return	Second Mortgages	Cash Overage
$1,906,926,680 +$900,000,000 LOAN $2,806,926,680 -$24,000,000 exp $2,782,926,680 -$372,000 interest on$6,200,000 loan: <u>$2,782,554,680</u>	185,500 houses down payments x $9,000 each = $1,669,500,000 PLUS	185,500 houses x $8,000 each= $1,484,000,000 PLUS	$2,782,500,000 Investment COMBINED WITH	185,500 x $2,000 each = $371,000,000 PLUS	$34,680
	74,200 house down payments x $15,000 each $1,113,000,000	74,200 x $10,000each = $742,000,000 FOR	$1,827,175,000 FOR	74,200 x $5,000 = $371,000,000 FOR	
	Total: $2,782,500,000 house down payments for 259,700 houses	Combined cash profit: $2,226,000,000 LESS sales expenses of	Total cash return: $4,609,675,000	Combined total: $742,000,000	
		185,500 x $1,330 = $246,715,000 PLUS 74,200 x $2,050 =$152,110,000 <u>$398,825,000</u> Total expenses Net profit: $1,827,175,000			
TOTALS					
$2,782,534,680	$2,782,500,000 outlay for 259,700 houses	$1,827,175,000 65.66% Profit	$4,609,675,000 165.66% Return	$742,000,000	$34,680
CUMULATIVE TOTALS					
$4,811,826,170	$4,851,716,988 – 452,817 houses	$3,172,379,690 65.95% Profit	$7,984,226,690 165.95% Return	$1,273,881,000	$110,540

PROJECTIONS–BUY/SELL PROGRAM-$48,000 BORROW PROGRAM–YR 3, PH 6

Available Cash	Investment	Cash Profit	Cash Return	Second Mortgages	Cash Overage
$4,609,675,000 +$2,300,000,000 LOAN $6,909,675,000 -$552,750,000 Operational ex -$866,400 interest on: $14,440,000 loan: $6,356,058,600	423,725 house down payments x $9,000 each= $3,813,525,000 PLUS	423,725 x $8,000 each= $3,389,800,000 PLUS	$6,355,950,000 Investment COMBINED WITH	423,725 x $2,000 each= $847,450,000 PLUS	$108,600
	169,495 house down payments x $15,000 each $2,542,425,000	169,495 x $10,000 each = $1,694,950,000	$4,173,731,000 For	169,495 x $5,000 each = $847,475,000 FOR	
	Total: $6,355,950,000 for 593,220 house down payments	Combined cash profit: $5,084,750,000 LESS sales expenses of	Total cash return: $1,797,903,100	Combined total: $1,694,925,000	
		423,725 x $1,330 = $563,554,250 PLUS $347,464,750 169,495 x $2,050 = $347,464,750 Total expenses $911,019,000 Net profit: $4,173,731,000			
TOTALS					
$6,356,058,600	$6,355,950,000 outlay for 593,220 houses	$4,173,731,000 65.66% Profit	$10,529,681,000 165.66% Return	$1,694,925,000	$108,600
CUMULATIVE TOTALS					
$11,167,884,770	$11,207,666,988 – 1,046,037 houses	$7,346,110,690 65.79% Profit	$18,513,907,690 165.79% Return	$2,968,806,000	$219,140

$48,000 BORROW PROGRAM
– YEAR THREE PROJECTION ANALYSIS

Returns to Investor(s)

In earlier CHAPTERs we mentioned that as the investments grow, the investor(s) must grow with their investments and expand into other markets. Year Three shows this need for expansion into many other areas and states, while maintaining existing markets.

Year Two Returns are projected to be $157,241,640, which is invested into Year Three, Phase One, buys and sells. Year Two Returns are projected at $67,295,534. Year Three returns are projected at $10,529,681,000, which are approximately 15,646.9% higher than Year Two Returns.

During Year Two, 7,021 houses are projected to be bought and sold. At the end of Year Three, 1,046,037 houses are projected to be bought and sold over those three years. This house amount is approximately 14,898.6% higher than the Year Two amount of 7,021.

These percentage increase figures are very substantial, as our rational, reasonable objective observer/analyst and any other authentic analyst would agree for safe, secure investments based in marketable real estate. These substantial percentage increases are made possible through loan amounts based only on contracted buys/sells throughout Years Two and Three. Therefore, loans are not loaned indiscriminately, but made only on secured positions with secured collateral. This protects the lender as well as the investor(s).

Retained Earnings & Recaptured Earnings

Retained Earnings and Recaptured Earnings are part of the short-term profit, but, as noted all along, are not included in profits for reinvestment into the Programs. Our investor(s) decide whether to distribute these funds to the investor(s) or reinvest them into the program. 1,038,901 houses were projected to be bought and sold during Year Three. Total loan amounts for Year Three are projected at $3,909,000,000. This may seem to be a staggering amount, but please note that all loans made throughout Year Two and Year Three are based upon contractual buys and sells. Since loans are made solely upon this basis, there is little to no risk for the lender and our investor(s).

Average returns for Retained and Recaptured Earnings are projected at $833.28 for the $70,000 house and $1,392.48 for the $115,000 house. During Year Three sales period, 1,038,901 houses were sold. 747,867 were sold for $70,000 and 291,034 sold for $115,000.

$$747,867 \times \$833.28 = \$623,182,613$$

$$291,034 \times \$1,392.48 = \underline{\$405,259,024}$$

$$\mathbf{\$1,028,441,637}$$

Year Three Totals + Years One & Two Totals = $1,035,068,539

As has been our position from the start, we did not project these funds to be used in the Programs, but to be used as the investor(s) decide. These funds are very substantial, as are the mortgage interest and principal returns. The investor(s) could distribute them to the investor(s) as profit, invest them into the programs or pay interest and principal loan amounts on loans taken for the Program.

Mortgage Interest

Mortgage interest from Year Two and Year One are due and payable in Year Three, which amounts to 7,136 house interest payments. Of this, 5,926 are $70,000 houses, paying $200 each and 1,210 paying $500 each on the $115,000 houses.

$$5,926 \times \$200 = \$1,185,200$$

$$1,210 \times \$500 = \underline{\$ \ \ 605,000}$$

TOTAL......$1,790,200

Retained/Recaptured Earnings: $1,028,441,637

Mortgage Interest: $\underline{\$ \ \ \ \ 1,790,200}$

GRAND TOTAL............$1,030,231,837

The above projected amounts are for buys/sells made throughout the Year Three sales period. As you can see, they are extremely large and provide the investor(s) substantial sums, for their own use, beyond the Program returns. The second mortgage principal totals and the retained and recaptured earnings for Years One, Two & Three are projected, as follows:

$2,968,806,000 – Second & Third Mortgage Principal

$\underline{\$1,035,068,539}$ – Retained & Recaptured Earnings

$4,003,874,539 – Total Projections

As referenced previously, our *ByPass* programs are based upon common sense, reason, rationality, simple, uncomplicated procedures and the need for housing by a large segment of the population excluded from the housing market, which segment wants private, non-bank financing. It is reasonable to understand that many people who are financially capable of purchasing a house but who have been prevented from buying because of job loss, poor credit, bad economy, foreclosure, or some other reason, would be very interested in buying a house with non-bank, private financing. Further, many other buyers who usually finance through banks would likely be quite interested in purchasing a house with private financing. Given the complications and hidden requirements with bank financing, compared to the ease and simplicity of our methods, who would not?

Enough people are now aware that banks are not trustworthy and have harmed large segments of the American population, at public expense, through their cozy, close relationships with government. Earlier in this book we spoke of the vast bailouts of the banks by government, largely because, in part, the banks loaned mortgage funds to financially incapable people on overpriced property, fully realizing that these people could not make their mortgage payments. Such borrowers, for the most part, were equally irresponsible and are also to blame. Although no one seems to know the exact figures, it has been reported that government bailouts to banks and corporations were estimated at THIRTY EIGHT TRILLION DOLLARS. Let this sink in. The banks and lenders which essentially created the problem so they could sell mortgage backed securities, caused a massive depression, crushed the housing and other markets, caused people to lose their jobs and millions more to lose their homes through foreclosure, were exonerated by the government and "bailed out" for their "losses". This is bad enough, and done at the peoples' expense, but, given the relationship among banks and our government, did actual losses exist, especially at the bailout amounts? Obtaining the actual figures on the "losses" and the genuine bailout figures from the perpetrators is difficult, for obvious reasons. Full disclosure of the actual amounts would clearly demonstrate to the American people the absurdity and corruption between the government and the banking cartel. Thirty eight trillion is massive and the real figure is gigantic and incomprehensible for most Americans. These funds could have been used to bail out THE PEOPLE and allow them to repay the government rather than lose their homes by the millions. Given these duplicitous actions and government largess, common sense indicates that it is very reasonable to expect that a massive amount of capable people would have avid interest in purchasing a home with private, non-bank financing.

When our investor(s) seriously consider these positions, they should expect very strong interest from a large, capable segment of our American population in property purchases offering private, non-bank financing. Homeowners who want to sell to our investor(s) based upon our mortgage programs should also be plentiful. Many reasons exist for this and we have covered some of them in prior CHAPTERs. For those sellers who want cash for their homes, our investor(s) can show them how to sell their first mortgages to other investors or investment groups whose business is to purchase first mortgages, usually at discount. Since the seller does not contract with and pay a real estate broker five or six percent to sell his house, then he should easily be able to sell his first mortgage at discount and forfeit little to nothing.

These programs can solve a multitude of all too common, serious problems for many people and, further, create vast wealth for investors who see and understand why and how these programs will find much success among average Americans. The entire premise is based in common sense, reason, logic, direct and easy methods that can act as an alternative to a pernicious, controlling, complicated, avaricious money and control-driven system joined at the proverbial hip with our government. The real question is whether that government is yours or theirs. Actions speak much louder than words and the usual assortment of propaganda distributed to the American people by government to protect protected vested interests. Information about these detrimental bank actions that have harmed so many Americans, so many businesses and so many markets for so long is readily available for those who want to know, and then act accordingly, in cautious, vested but fair-minded self-interest. What has happened in the past can and will happen again. Self-interest is vital if one wants to protect himself, his family, their future and their possessions.

Loan Repayment

During Year Two, a total of $24,510,000 is projected to be borrowed for investment into the Program. Loans are made in increments throughout the year based upon buy/sell contracts our investor(s) have made with their sellers and buyers. To be conservative, we have scheduled the full loan amounts to begin at the start of each Phase, which will cause interest payments to be higher than if they were borrowed throughout the Phase. Interest is projected at six percent (6%), payable upon the yearly anniversary of the loan. Principal is payable on the anniversary of the second year, or as contracted between lender and investor(s).

These are projections only, since actual amounts, terms and conditions will be decided and arranged by and between the lender and our investor(s). Since the lender makes loans based upon contractual buys and sells, his risk is low, if any, at all. Lender's collateral is assignment of all second and third mortgages, which will prove to be very substantial, plus a lien on the business, until all loans are paid in full. As we mentioned earlier, our investor(s) did not borrow during Year One. That year was the test case for the Program to demonstrate to lenders that the Program is financially viable and provides much needed housing to large numbers of financially capable people who have been restricted from the housing market. Further, many other buyers who employ the normal financing standard may have avid interest in non-bank, private funding, without the usual complications and problems.

LOAN SCHEDULE FOR YEAR TWO

	Loan Amount	6% Interest
Phase One	$ 380,000	$ 22,800
Phase Two	$ 290,000	$ 17,400
Phase Three	$ 550,000	$ 33,000
Phase Four	$ 2,650,000	$ 159,000
Phase Five	$ 6,200,000	$ 372,000
Phase Six	$ 14,440,000	$ 866,400
Totals	**$ 24,510,000**	**$1,470,000**

LOAN SCHEDULE FOR YEAR THREE

	Loan Amount	6% Interest
Phase One	$ 37,000,000	$ 2,220,000
Phase Two	$ 78,000,000	$ 3,900,000
Phase Three	$ 180,000,000	$ 7,200,000
Phase Four	$ 414,000,000	$ 12,420,000
Phase Five	$ 900,000,000	$ 18,000,000
Phase Six	$2,300,000,000	$ 23,000,000
TOTALS	**$3,909,000000**	**$ 66,740,000**
Years 2 & 3 Totals	**$3,933,510,000**	**$ 68,210,000**

All borrowed funds, plus interest owing, are scheduled to be repaid on the second anniversary of the loan, or as decided between principals. In the above second year loan schedule, not all loans will run the full year since the Program will end upon the completion of Year Two. Phase One loan of $37,000,000 will cover twelve (12) months, but Phase Two loan of $78,000,000 will extend only ten (10) months since the Program will end at the end of Year Two. The loan duration for Phase Three will extend for eight months, and other Phases for fewer months. Six percent (6%) interest per year is charged for the months that the loans are outstanding. As mentioned, to be conservative, loans are scheduled to be made at the beginning of any phase, when in reality, loans are made throughout the phase based upon the numbers of contracted buys/sells. If there are no contracted buys/sells, there are no loans needed. Interest is charged based upon actual loan duration, which would be less time when loans are made throughout the phase rather than at the start of the phase.

In the Year Two Phase Projections, loan interest is due twelve (12) months from the date of the loan. We listed probable interest charges for Phase Two loans based upon actual one year time duration. As referenced, we charged interest on all loans from the start of all phases.

$68,210,000 is the projected interest payments amounts for Years Two and Three, minus $1,470,000 already made in Year Two Projections. This amounts to Year Two and Three interest payments of approximately **$66,740,000**.

Interest for Year Two loans is paid off in Year Two, but these loans extend into Year Three and interest is charged for the loan time duration, which amounts to $407,200. Added to $66,740,000 above, total approximate projected interest charges amount to **$67,147,200**. This interest amount will be deducted from the total returns, as will the principal balance of **$3,933,510,000** listed above.

Projected Returns to Investor(s)

Year Three Projections for the $48,000 Borrow Program project a short term, three year return of $10,529,681,000 to investor(s). Such a return for an investment of $48,000 is absolutely remarkable, as virtually all prognosticators, investors and analysts would agree. This is short term only, since there are both short and long term returns to our investor(s). All costs and expenses have been paid over the three years, as provided for in the Projections, with the exception of the final interest and principal balance of the loans.

Year Three Projected Returns: $10,529,681,000

Minus Principal loan Balance.....$ 3,933,510,000

Minus loan interest...............$ 67,147,200

Projected short term Return to Investor(s) $ 6,529,023,800

Total Projected Retained & Recaptured Earnings

Projected Retained & Recaptured Earnings: $1,035,068,539

Projected Returns...................................$6,529,023,800

Projected Retained/Recaptured Earnings $1,035,068,539

Total Projected Short term Returns...........$7,564,092,339

Projected Long Term Returns

Long term returns are interest on second and third mortgages and the principal balance of those mortgages. Projections show that a house sold for $70,000 has a second mortgage of $2,000. The house sold for $115,000 has a $5,000 second mortgage. Principal balances are due on the 15th anniversary of the sale. Interest is 10% payable on the yearly anniversary of the sale. This is $200 per year for the $70,000 house and $500 per year for the $115,000 house. Second mortgages to our investor(s) are important since these allow the investor(s) to take over the house and house payments should buyers default.

At the end of Year Three, projections show that 1,046,037 houses have been bought and sold through the $48,000 Borrow Program. Second mortgages total $2,968,806,000, due in 15 years, plus interest of $296,880,600 due yearly.

Second Mortgage Principal......................$2,968,806,000

Second Mortgage Interest Payments............$4,453,209,000

TOTAL LONG TERM RETURNS............$7,422,015,000

PROJECTED SHORT TERM RETURNS............$7,564,092,339

PROJECTED LONG TERM RETURNS......,,,......$7,442,015,000

TOTAL SHORT AND LONG TERM RETURNS - $15,006,107,339

Projected Number of houses bought & sold over 3 years………1,046,037

Average short term profit per house……………$7,226.56

Average long term profit per house…………….<u>$7,114.48</u>

<u>TOTAL AVERAGE PER HOUSE…………$14,341.05</u>

<u>COLLATERAL FOR LENDER</u>

As mentioned, our investor(s) operated the first year of the buy/sell Program as a test case for both prospective lenders and themselves. The lender oversaw the results of the first year buy/sell operation and could see that there is a large demand for these programs. Loans are made based upon contracts our investor(s) have with their sellers and buyers, thus, the lender has little risk, if any. Loans are <u>not</u> front-loaded. They are secure when made. Collateral for the lender is contained in the assignment of all second and third mortgages, plus a lien-hold on the business pending repayment of all loans, plus interest.

Over Years Two and Three, $3,933,510,000 in loans were made, with interest of approximately $68,210,000. These were short term loans, all repaid within two years, and in Year Two, the heavier borrow year, most loan terms were only for months, and not a full year. The principal second mortgage collateral to the lender, at the end of Year Three, is $2,968,806,000 in second and third mortgages for $3,933,510,000 in loans, plus $296,880,600 in mortgage interest payments per year for 15 years. This amounts to $7,125,134,400 in collateral for $3,933,510,000 in loans. Further, if the lender were to lend $3,933,510,000 at six (6%) interest per year, that amount would be $236,010,600 per year as opposed to $296,880,600 paid on the second mortgages. Still further, the lender has a lien-hold on the business, pending repayment of all loans, plus interest.

This type of business operation between the lender and our investor(s) is highly beneficial to the two principal parties, and allows the investor(s) to greatly increase their number of buys and sells. In turn, this permits more people to purchase homes that they, for the most part, would, otherwise, not be able to buy. In short, these Programs are a Win-Win-Win for all involved. Different parties in different positions are present in all markets, all of which make those markets both functional and successful. Each has his own position in the market. When all positions are in harmony with each other, then that market can be healthy and even flourish.

In prior CHAPTERs we have spoken of arranged economic downturns, rigged markets, depressions, bank bail outs, massive foreclosure losses, and much more. In times like these it is extremely difficult for investors to find the right investment for their investment funds, let alone a safe, secure one that will pay a massive return and benefit people and communities all over the country. As we were finishing this book, the corona virus scare put many people into a state of not only concern, but panic. The government actions closed many businesses across the country, which, of course, caused many people to lose their jobs, possibly temporarily, but maybe not. Many small business owners are worried that they may lose their businesses, depending upon the severity of government actions. The markets are depressed, then rise, then drop again, and continue in that manner, just as they did before the 1929 crash, and many others, as well. In such dire times, private lenders also seek financially trustworthy businesses for their loans, and the choices can be risky and very limited. Our *ByPass* Programs can work well during any financial climate, whether strong or weak, but even better in a weak one. These programs offer unique opportunities to those who have the vision to see, the ability to understand, the way to expand, and possibly, become extremely wealthy during any type of financial market.

If our investor(s) stop the Program at the end of Year Three, they have $2,968,806,000 in second and third mortgages paying $296,880,600 each year for the next twelve years. This is a monumental retirement fund for anyone. However, success breeds success, so continuing into Year Four could dramatically increase that success and provide many homes for people who need them, and who could likely not get homes through the regular institutional channels.

Year Four Possibilities

Year Three projected total for houses bought and sold over three years numbers 1,046,037 houses. Current figures indicate that approximately 5,800,000 houses are projected to be sold in 2020. Over three years this amounts to approximately 17,400,000 houses. Our 1,046,037 houses amount to approximately 6.011% of this total, over a three year period.

Within America, the overwhelming majority of houses are bought, sold and bank financed through the usual, normal, standard traditional customs and practices in which homes are bought, sold and financed. As we have repeatedly mentioned, many financially capable home buyers are excluded from this market for various reasons stated previously. If approximately 5,800,000 homes are sold annually through normal procedures, how many millions of homes could be bought and sold through the *ByPass* programs contained in this book? Before the planned foreclosure crisis devastated the housing market, 7,080,000 homes were sold in 2005 and 6,520,000 were sold in 2006. The 5,800,000 homes sales forecasted for 2020 is still way behind those earlier figures, so many more homes could be bought and sold to reach or surpass 2005 and 2006 sales.

   Millions of people lost their homes through foreclosure, and many more lost because of an orchestrated bad economy, job loss, depressed markets, bank restrictions, and other reasons. Most of these people lost their family homes through no fault of their own. Some were at fault because they contracted for loans they never could repay, let alone make mortgage payments. This type of buyer should never affect those who lost through other externally created factors over which they had no control. The *ByPass* Programs could help these people and /or people in similar circumstances to get back into home purchases and not be dependent upon banks and the system.

   The large majority of these people are good, decent, working people, but most without homes. Many of them have funds for a down payment, but, as mentioned before, cannot qualify for a bank mortgage. Sellers of homes with bank mortgages cannot sell to a buyer who cannot assume the mortgage since most banks do not allow this. These *ByPass* programs make it possible for these people to buy and sell in an easy, non-bank, non-complicated program. How many millions would do this? Our book is meant to help average Americans buy or sell a home even though they have been damaged by a pernicious system. The investment programs can play a major role to this end. If investors all over America were to engage in the buy/sell Programs, they could help themselves financially and possibly gain a fortune in the doing. Each house an investor buys and sells provides a home for a family and/or a sale where none was possible before. This may not seem remarkable to the investor(s), but is indeed remarkable to the buyers or sellers they helped. Helping oneself through fair-minded self-interest, while at the same time helping others, promotes a growing consciousness of mutual self-benefit and cooperation for all involved, rather than selfish greed and ruthless competition which helps the very few, while it hurts the very many. The more this occurs, the better for our American society in general.

   The American people have been damaged enough by governmental forces which are Constitutionally mandated to protect their Rights and interests, as well as by corporate entities which are required by law to treat them fairly, justly and without deceit. Sadly, what is Constitutionally mandated and required by law in this country simply does not happen as it should, so the people must become as independent and as free as they can, as quickly as they can. Isn't about time that the tables on these injustices get turned? Isn't it about time for the people to look beyond the system to other, better ways of doing business which will actually help them and their families, rather than harm them and put them further into debt and financial and emotional insecurity?

All this really takes is a conscious awareness that the present system is detrimental to the people, by design, is a rigged game, and one from which they need to extricate themselves. Once this is realized and accepted, then they can seek other, better ways of doing business that lead to freedom and independence instead of control and repression.

As of this writing, the governments of America have essentially shut down the nation, prevented people from working their jobs, closed businesses all over this country, greatly harmed the economy and put many people on the financial breaking point. All this has been done for what appears to be another government sham and fraud – the "novel" corona virus. Since virtually every other nation has done the same thing, the obvious conclusion is that this is a world-wide closure by governments. It may be possible that draconian measures are forthcoming. The aftermath could be a major increase in foreclosures and more bailouts for the banks. In addition to the major bank bailouts mentioned earlier, the Fed bails out banks on a regular basis for foreclosures. The next round could be massive, unless the American people awaken to how they have been duped, then, take lawful effective actions to stop and correct the unlawful actions by government and banks that have severely damaged them. They might also awaken to the strong possibility that more repressive controls will be imposed upon the people, **unless the people lawfully put a stop to them.** Those who are able to purchase homes now may be better off to do so now rather than wait. The future is unknown and can be difficult to predict, but if we know the past we can fairly accurately predict the future based upon that past. The "Now" is a good time to do anything worthwhile and important.

As we mentioned at the very beginning, and many other times throughout this book, we wrote this book for everyone, because every individual has individual needs, desires and dreams and deserves real opportunities to achieve them. We have tried to offer as many realistic positions as possible to accommodate those needs, desires and dreams. If one person wants to buy a house through these *ByPass* methods and one wants to sell a house through these methods and that is all, then we are overjoyed that we could be of assistance. If another person or a group wants to deal in these methods to make a fortune, we are glad that we could instigate this. However, there may be others who simply want to use the investment programs on a smaller, more limited basis, such as the original $15,000 Year One investment program, earn approximately $356,000 every year and build up a solid second mortgage portfolio. Still others may want to buy and sell five or six houses a year and be satisfied with the profit they make on those sales. Each of us look at things very differently and no established system-driven institutional program can suit individual needs. Our *ByPass* programs try to do this as much as possible so that there is truly real opportunity for virtually everyone who has interest in creating their paths to a better future for them and their families. Margy and I wish you well in whatever you decide works best for you and yours.

Following are the projected Year Three Returns for all levels of investors and their investment amounts. Year Three Total Returns are considerably higher than those of Year Two. Imagine what levels Year Four could reach! Also imagine how many millions of capable buyers would purchase homes with seller carried financing and without the need to obtain new bank financing. We mentioned before that investors can make it possible for large numbers of buyers to purchase homes the easy way, and do financially quite well in the process. With the *ByPass* methods, it may be possible to not only reach the aforementioned 7,080,000 house sales figure from 2005, but surpass it. *ByPass* methods could provide a whole new and expansive way for many millions of people to get back into homes, and stay there, without complications and the usual problems. The only limits for the American people are those we place upon ourselves, and, of course, we allow no one or anything to place limits upon us. Americans are free and independent, so we live it.

$48,000 BORROW PROJECTED RETURNS TO INVESTOR(S) YEAR THREE

Short term Returns to Investor(s) …………………….. **$7,564,092,339**

Long term Return to Investor(s) ………………………**$7,442,015,000**

Total……………………………………………………..**$15,006,107,339**

Investors	Amount	Short term Profit	Long term Profit	Combined Profit	% return
1	$48,000	$7,564,092,339	$7,442,015,000	$15,006,107,339	31,262,723%
2	$24,000 Each	$3,782,046,169 Each	$3,721,007,500 Each	$ 7,503,053,669 Each	31,262,723% Each
3	$16,000 Each	$2,521,364,113 Each	$2,480,671,666 Each	$ 5,002,035,779 Each	31,262,723% Each
8	$ 6,000 Each	$ 945,511,542 Each	$ 930,251,875 Each	$ 1,875,763,417 Each	31,262,723% Each
16	$ 3,000 Each	$ 472,755,771 Each	$ 465,125,937 Each	$ 937,881,703 Each	31,262,723% Each
24	$ 2,000 Each	$ 315,170,514 Each	$ 310,083,958 Each	$ 625,254,472 Each	31,262,723% Each

ByPass PROGRAMS – BUY/RENT/SALE OF HOUSES

BYPASS PROJECTIONS – BUY, RENT & SALE OF HOUSES

Introduction to Projections

The following pages of this Section contain three different ByPass Programs which provide for three different approaches for the purchase, rental and sale of houses at the end of Year Twenty or Year Twenty One. The three sets are as follows:

1. Twenty Year Standard Projections – 9,457 houses
2. Year Twenty Alternative Projections – 15,308 houses
3. Year Twenty One Alternative Projections – 15,308 houses

In addition to the above Programs are three additional Programs based upon and adapted from the original Programs. Each Program has several Projections and they indicated different financial positions. Year Twenty Standard Projections are predicated upon house purchases made at the end of any year based upon projected profit made during that year. From Year Five forward, we allowed more projected profit for the owner, rather than investing that projected retained profit into the purchase of additional houses. Had this projected retained profit been directed to house purchases, then the number of houses owned at the end of Year Twenty would be considerably higher than 9,457.

If we take the same percentage increase in house purchases from Year Twenty Standard Projections to Year Twenty Alternative Projections, namely, 9,457 houses, in Twenty Standard, to 15,308 in Year Twenty Alternative, an increase of 61.86%, and apply this buying method through Year Twenty, the total houses owned is projected to be 433,798. We have been conservative in all our projections. The real upside is much greater than we projected. If the owner/investor were to employ monthly house purchases, from projected monthly profit, and use the same percentage buying ratio, then by Year Eleven, projections indicate that the owner would have 20,819 houses.

Year Twenty Alternative Projections demonstrate the amount of additional houses that can be purchased when projected monthly profits purchase houses on a monthly basis during the year, rather than only once a year at year end. It is common business practice to spend profits when they are derived for items necessary for that business, rather than wait to the end of the year and then buy necessary items from profits derived over the year. In the following projections, please note that we started this process only in Year Nineteen when we took Year Nineteen projected profits to purchase houses for Year Twenty. Then, in Year Twenty Alternative, we took projected monthly profits to purchase houses monthly throughout Year Twenty. On this basis, we projected a total purchase of 15,308 houses, 5,851 more houses than at the end of Year Twenty Standard Projections. As stated, this amounts to 61.86% more houses purchased. Had we started monthly purchases earlier, such as in Year Five, instead of making purchases at the end of the year, the number of houses owned by the end of Year Twenty would be much higher than 15,308. More houses owned mean more rentals, more profit and much more profit when the housing inventory is sold.

In each of the three Programs, you will find three separate sales projections for each category. These are projections for (1) sales to a buyer/investor, based upon sales price increases of 3% per year, plus projected profits received over twenty years; (2) sales to current renters and other house buyers; (3) sales to a buyer/investor, based upon a projected return in relation to the sales price. Other projections are listed for each Program.

All sales prices are based upon the original sales price, plus a 3% value increase per year. To ascertain this price, we took the original price and added 3% for each year owned. Existing house debt was determined upon the amount owed for each house at the time of sale. This can be either $3,400, per house, per year owned, or $283.33 per month, per house, for each month owned remaining after sale.

TWENTY YEAR STANDARD PROJECTIONS

EQUITY BUY - INVESTMENT PROGRAM – 20 YEARS
TWENTY YEAR RENTAL PROJECTIONS

$600,000 investment buys 65 houses priced at $60,000 each.

15% down payment = $9,000 x 65 houses = $585,000.

The remaining $15,000 is used to purchase one (1) home to convert into office space.

Seller carries a $51,000 note, per house, for 15 years, principal and interest monthly payments of $390.17.

Rents start at $750 per month, per house.

YEAR ONE

RENT: $750 x 12 x 65 houses..$585,000

EXPENSES: Mortgage notes = $390.17 x 12 x 65.............................$304,332

                Taxes...............$500.00 x 65.................................$ 32,500

                Insurance...........$525.00 x 65................................$ 34,125

                Vacancies and repairs – 10%...............................$ 58,500

                Manager...$ 45,000

                Secretary..$ 30,000

                Miscellaneous..$ 3,000

                                    $507,457....................$ 507,457

                    Projected Profit End of Year One .... $ 77,543

Costs for purchase of 8 houses @ $9,000 DP each in Year Two .... $ 72,000

                            Net Profit Year One ....$ 5,543

          Total houses owned going into Year Two: 65 + 8 = 73 houses

YEAR TWO

73 houses owned at start of Year Two

RENT: $765 x 12 x 73 houses..$ 670,140

EXPENSES: Mortgage notes = $390.17 x 12 x 73............................$341,788

                Taxes...............$500.00 x 73...................................$ 36,500

                Insurance...........$525.00 x 73................................ $ 38,325

                Vacancies and repairs – 10% .... $ 67,014

                Manager...$ 45,000

                Secretary.. $ 30,000

                Miscellaneous..$ 3,000

                                   $561,627....................$ 561,627

                    Projected Profit End of Year Two $108,513

Costs for purchase of 11 houses @ $9,000 DP each – Year Three ....$ 99,000

                            Net Profit Year Two .... $ 9,513

         Total houses owned going into Year Three: 73 + 11 = 84 houses

YEAR THREE

84 houses owned at start of Year Three

RENT: $780 x 12 x 84 houses.. $ 786,240

EXPENSES: Mortgage notes = $390.17 x 12 x 84................................. $ 393,291

               Taxes..............$500.00 x 84... $ 42,000

               Insurance..........$525.00 x 84..................................... $ 44,100

               Vacancies and repairs – 10% ....$ 78,624

               Manager...$ 45,000

               Secretary..$ 30,000

               Miscellaneous..$ 3,000

                                $ 636,015.................... $ 636,015

                Projected Profit End of Year Three $150,225

Costs for purchase of 15 houses @ $9,000 DP each for Year Four ....$ 135,000

                       Net Profit Year Three...............................$ 15,225

               Total houses owned going into Year Four: 84 + 15 = 99 houses

---

YEAR FOUR

99 houses owned at start of Year Three

RENT: $780 x 12 x 99 houses..$938,520

EXPENSES: Mortgage notes = $390.17 x 12 x 99................................. $ 463,521

               Taxes..............$500.00 x 99...$ 49,500

               Insurance..........$525.00 x 99.....................................$ 51,975

               Vacancies and repairs – 10% ....$ 93,852

               Manager...$ 45,000

               Secretary.. $ 30,000

               Miscellaneous..$ 3,000

                               $766,848..................... $ 736,848

                Projected Profit End of Year Four ....$ 201,672

Costs for purchase of 22 houses @ $9,000 DP each for Year Five ....$ 198,000

                       Net Profit Year Four................................$ 3,672

               Total houses owned going into Year Five: 99 + 22 = 121 houses

YEAR FIVE

121 houses owned at start of Year Five

RENT: $805 x 12 x 121 houses...$1,168,860

EXPENSES: Mortgage notes = $390.17 x 12 x 121..............................$566,526

                Taxes...............$575.00 x 121.......................................$ 69,575

                Insurance..........$600.00 x 121.....................................$ 72,600

                Vacancies and repairs – 10% $116,886

                Manager..$ 45,000

                Secretary...$ 30,000

                Miscellaneous...$ 3,000

                                      $903,587.....................$ 903,587

                  Projected Profit End of Year Five ....$ 265,273

Costs for purchase of 28 houses @ $9,000 DP each for Year Six.... ....$ 252,000

                        Net Profit Year Five ....$ 13,273

                Total houses owned going into Year Six: 121 + 28 = 149 houses

---

YEAR SIX

149 houses owned at start of Year Six

RENT: $815 x 12 x 149 houses...$1,457,220

EXPENSES: Mortgage notes = $390.17 x 12 x 149................................$697,623

                Taxes...............$575.00 x 149.......................................$ 85,675

                Insurance..........$600.00 x 149.....................................$ 89,400

                Vacancies and repairs – 10% $145,722

                Manager..$ 45,000

                Secretary...$ 30,000

                Miscellaneous...$ 5,000

                                   $1,098,420.....................$1,098,420

                  Projected Profit End of Year Six ....$ 358,850

Costs for purchase of 38 houses @ $9,000 DP each for Year Seven......................$ 342,000

                        Net Profit Year Six ....$ 16,850

                Total houses owned going into Year Seven: 149 + 38 = 187 houses

YEAR SEVEN

187 houses owned at start of Year Seven

RENT: $830 x 12 x 187 houses...$1,457,220*

*$405,300 paid to gen. exp

EXPENSES: Mortgage notes = $390.17 x 12 x 187................................$875,541

Taxes..............$575.00 x 187......................................$107,525

Insurance..........$600.00 x 187....................................$112,200

Vacancies and repairs – 10% $186,252

Manager...$ 50,000

Secretary..$ 35,000

Clerk...$ 25,000

Buyer..$ 45,000

Miscellaneous..$ 20,000

$1,456,518.................$1,456,518

Projected Profit End of Year Seven ....$ 406,002

Costs for purchase of 44 houses @ $9,000 DP each for Year Eight....................$ 396,006

Net Profit Year Seven ....…....$ 10,002

Total houses owned going into Year Eight: 187 + 44 = 231 houses

---

YEAR EIGHT

231 houses owned at start of Year Eight

RENT: $845 x 12 x 231 houses...$2,342,340*

*$100,000 paid to gen. exp.

EXPENSES: Mortgage notes = $390.17 x 12 x 231................................$1,081,551

Taxes..............$575.00 x 231......................................$ 132,825

Insurance..........$600.00 x 231....................................$ 138,600

Vacancies and repairs – 10% ....$ 234,234

Manager...$ 50,000

Secretary..$ 35,000

Clerk...$ 30,000

Buyer..$ 45,000

Miscellaneous...$ 20,000

$1,867,210...................... $1,867,210

Projected Profit End of Year Eight ....$ 475,130

Costs for purchase of 51 houses @ $9,000 DP each for Year Nine...........................$ 459,000

Net Profit Year Eight ....$ 16,130

Total houses owned going into Year Nine: 231 + 51 = 282 houses

---

YEAR NINE

282 houses owned at start of Year Nine

RENT: $860 x 12 x 282 houses..$2,910,240

EXPENSES: Mortgage notes = $390.17 x 12 x 282.............................$1,320,335

Taxes...............$575.00 x 282......................................$ 162,150

Insurance...........$600.00 x 282......................................$ 169,200

Vacancies and repairs – 10%.......................................$ 291,024

Manager...$ 50,000

Secretary...$ 35,000

Clerk...$ 30,000

Buyer...$ 45,000

Two Maintenance People...$ 70,000

Miscellaneous..$ 35,000

$2,207,709.................... $2,207,709

Projected Profit End of Year Nine ....$ 702,531

Costs for purchase of 77 houses @ $9,000 DP each for Year Ten.........................$ 693,000

Net Profit Year Nine ....$ 9,531

Total houses owned going into Year Ten: 282 + 77 = 359 houses

YEAR TEN

359 houses owned at start of Year Ten

RENT: $875 x 12 x 359 houses..$3,769,500

EXPENSES: Mortgage notes = $390.17 x 12 x 359..............................$1,680,852

Taxes..............$625.00 x 359.....................................$ 224,375

Insurance..........$650.00 x 359.....................................$ 233,350

Vacancies and repairs – 10% ....$ 376,950

Manager...$ 50,000

Secretary..$ 35,000

Clerk...$ 30,000

Buyer..$ 45,000

Two Maintenance People...$ 70,000

Miscellaneous...$ 35,000

$2,780,527.....................$2,780,527

Projected Profit End of Year Ten ....$ 988,973

Costs for purchase of 107 houses @ $9,000 DP each –Year Eleven.......................$ 963,000

Net Profit Year Ten....................................$ 25,973

Total houses owned going into Year Eleven: 359 + 107 = 466 houses

---

YEAR ELEVEN

466 houses owned at start of Year Eleven

RENT: $890 x 12 x 466 houses..$4,976,808

EXPENSES: Mortgage notes = $390.17 x 12 x 466..............................$2,181,830

Taxes..............$625.00 x 466.....................................$ 291,250

Insurance..........$650.00 x 466.....................................$ 302,900

Vacancies and repairs – 10% ....$ 497,688

Manager...$ 55,000

Secretary..$ 40,000

Clerk...$ 30,000

Buyer..$ 90,000

Two Maintenance People..............................$ 70,000

Miscellaneous..$ __50,000__

$3,608,668...............$3,608,668

Projected Profit End of Year   Eleven $1,368,132

Costs for purchase of 149 houses @ $9,000 DP each for Year Twelve...............$1,341,000

Net Profit Year Eleven..........................$ 27,132

Total houses owned going into Year Twelve: 466 + 149 = 615 houses

___

YEAR TWELVE

615 houses owned at start of Year Twelve

RENT: $900 x 12 x 615 houses...$6,642,000

EXPENSES: Mortgage notes = $390.17 x 12 x 615...................$2,879,454

Taxes...............$625.00 x 615..........................$ 384,375

Insurance..........$650.00 x 615........................$ 399,750

Vacancies and repairs – 10%............................$ 664,200

Manager...…..$ 55,000

Secretary...…... $ 40,000

Two Clerks...…..…$ 60,000

Two Buyers..…..…$ 90,000

Two Maintenance People...........................…..$ 70,000

Miscellaneous..…$ __60,000__

$4,702,779...............$4,702,779

Projected Profit End of Year   Twelve $1,939,221

Costs for purchase of 212 houses @ $9,000 DP each – Year Thirteen...............$1,908,000

Net Profit Year Twelve..........................$ 31,221

Total houses owned going into Year Thirteen: 615 + 212 = 827 houses

YEAR THIRTEEN

827 houses owned at start of Year Thirteen

RENT: $915 x 12 x 827 houses...$9,080,460

EXPENSES: Mortgage notes = $390.17 x 12 x 827...........................$3,872,047

       Taxes...............$625.00 x 827................................$ 516,875

       Insurance...........$650.00 x 827..............................$ 537,550

       Vacancies and repairs – 10% ....$ 908,046

       Manager...$ 55,000

       Secretary...$ 40,000

       Two Clerks...$ 60,000

       Three Buyers...$ 135,000

       Three Maintenance People......................................$ 105,000

       Miscellaneous..$ 75,000

                  $6,304,518....................$6,304,518

           Projected Profit End of Year   Thirteen....................$2,775,942

Costs for purchase of 305 houses @ $9,000 DP each – Year Fourteen..........................$2,745,000

               Net Profit Year Thirteen................................$ 30,942

      Total houses owned going into Year Fourteen: 827 + 305 = 1,132 houses

---

YEAR FOURTEEN

1,132 + 425 houses owned at start of Year Fourteen

RENT: $925 x 12 x 1,132 houses...$12,565,200

EXPENSES: Mortgage notes = $390.17 x 12 x 1,132...........................$5,300,069

       Taxes...............$625.00 x 1,132...............................$ 707,500

       Insurance...........$650.00 x 1,132.............................$ 735,800

       Vacancies and repairs – 10% ....$ 1,256,520

       Manager...$ 100,000

       Asst. Manager...$ 50,000

       Two Secretaries..$ 80,000

       Three Clerks..$ 105,000

Three Buyers..$ 135,000

Three Maintenance People....................................$ 105,000

Miscellaneous...$ 125,000

$8,699,889..................$8,699,889

Projected Profit End of Year   Fourteen................ $3,865,311

Costs for purchase of 425 houses @ $9,000 DP each for Year Fifteen.................$3,825,000

Net Profit Year Fourteen........................$ 40,311

Total houses owned going into Year Fifteen: 1,132 + 305 = 1,557 houses

---

YEAR FIFTEEN

1,557 + 600 houses owned at start of Year Fifteen

RENT: $940 x 12 x 1,557 houses.....................................$17,562,960

EXPENSES: Mortgage notes = $390.17 x 12 x 1,557.................$7,289,936

Taxes..............$700.00 x 1,557.......................$1,089,900

Insurance..........$725.00 x 1,557.......................$1,128,825

Vacancies and repairs – 10%............................$1,756,296

Manager...$ 125,000

Asst. Manager...$ 60,000

Two Secretaries.. $ 80,000

Three Clerks...$ 105,000

Three Buyers..$ 135,000

Four Maintenance People...............................$ 160,000

Miscellaneous...$ 155,000

$12,079,957..................$12,079,957

Projected Profit End of Year   Fifteen.................$ 5,483,003

Costs for purchase of 600 houses @ $9,000 DP each for Year Sixteen.................$ 5,400,000

Net Profit Year Fifteen.............................$ 83,003

Total houses owned going into Year Sixteen: 1,557 + 400 = 2,157 houses

---

YEAR SIXTEEN

2,157 houses owned at start of Year Sixteen

RENT: $955 x 12 x 2,157 houses……………………………………………$24,719,220

EXPENSES: Mortgage notes* = $390.17 x 12 x 2,092……………$9,794,827

            *65 houses paid off (2,157 – 65 = 2,092)

            Taxes……………$700.00 x 2,157……………………$1,509,900

            Insurance………..$725.00 x 2,157……………………...$1,563,825

            Vacancies and repairs – 10% …………………………...$2,471,922

            Manager…………………………………………………$ 200,000

            Asst. Manager………………………………………..$ 75,000

            Two Secretaries……………………………………$ 80,000

            Four Clerks…………………………………………...$ 140,000

            Three Buyers…………………………………………...$ 135,000

            Four Maintenance People…………………………….$ 160,000

            Miscellaneous……………………………………...$ 200,000

                             $16,330,474……………….$16,330,474

                   Projected Profit End of Year   Sixteen………………$ 8,388,746

Costs for purchase of 925 houses @ $9,000 DP each for Year Seventeen…………..$ 8,325,000

                          Net Profit Year Sixteen………………………...$ 63,746

        Total houses owned going into Year Seventeen: 2,157 + 925 = 3,082 houses

---

YEAR SEVENTEEN

3,082 houses owned at start of Year Seventeen

RENT: $970 x 12 x 3,082 houses……………………………………………$35,874,480

EXPENSES: Mortgage notes* = $390.17 x 12 x 3,009……………...$14,088,258

            *73 houses paid off (3,082 – 73 = 3,009)

            Taxes……………$700.00 x 3,082……………………$ 2,157,400

            Insurance………..$725.00 x 3,082……………………...$ 2,234,450

             Vacancies and repairs – 10%…………………………$ 3,578,448

            Manager……………………………………………$ 225,000

Two Asst. Managers…………………………………$ 150,000

Four Secretaries…………………………………...$ 160,000

Five Clerks…………………………………….…...$ 175,000

Three Buyers.…………………………………….....$ 135,000

Four Maintenance People..……………………….......$ 160,000

Miscellaneous…………………………………..….$ 250,000

$23,322,556……………$23,322,556

Projected Profit End of Year   Seventeen……………$12,551,924

Costs for purchase of 1375 houses @ $9,000 DP each for Year Eighteen……………$12,375,000

Net Profit Year Seventeen…………………......…$ 176,924

Total houses owned going into Year Eighteen: 3,082 + 1,375 = 4,457 houses

---

YEAR EIGHTEEN

4,457 houses owned at start of Year Eighteen

RENT: $985 x 12 x 4,457 houses…………………………………………$52,681,740

EXPENSES: Mortgage notes* = $390.17 x 12 x 4,373……………$20,474,560

*84 houses paid off (4,457 – 84 = 4,373)

Taxes……………$700.00 x 4,457…………………$ 3,119,900

Insurance………..$725.00 x 4,457…………………$ 3,231,325

Vacancies and repairs – 10%………………………$ 5,268,174

Manager.…………………………………………..$ 275,000

Two Asst. Managers.………………………………...$ 150,000

Four Secretaries………………………………………$ 160,000

Five Clerks…………………………………….…...$ 175,000

Six Buyers.…………………………………………. $ 270,000

Eight Maintenance People.………………………… $ 320,000

Equipment.…………………………………………..$ 100,000

Miscellaneous.……………………………………….$ 500,000

Contingency.…………………………………………$ 500,000

$34,543,959…………$34,543,959

Projected Profit End of Year   Eighteen…………….$18,137,783

Costs for purchase of 2,000 houses @ $9,000 DP each for Year Nineteen..........$18,000,000

Net Profit Year Eighteen........................$ 137,783

Total houses owned going into Year Nineteen: 4,457 + 2,000 = 6,457 houses

---

YEAR NINETEEN

6,457 houses owned at start of Year Nineteen

RENT: $1,000 x 12 x 6,358 houses...$77,484,000

EXPENSES: Mortgage notes* = $390.17 x 12 x 4,373...............$29,768,410

*99 houses paid off (6,457 – 99 = 6,358)

Taxes...............$700.00 x 6,457.......................$ 4,519,900

Insurance..........$725.00 x 4,457.....................$ 4,681,325

Vacancies and repairs – 10%............................$ 7,748,400

Manager...$ 300,000

Two Asst. Managers.......................................$ 150,000

Four Secretaries..$ 160,000

Five Clerks...$ 175,000

Ten Buyers...$ 450,000

Eight Maintenance People................................$ 320,000

Equipment...$ 100,000

Miscellaneous...$ 750,000

Contingency...$ 750,000

$49,773,035...........$49,773,035

Projected Profit End of Year   Nineteen...............$27,710,965

Costs for purchase of 3,000 houses @ $9,000 DP each for Year Twenty................$27,000,000

Net Profit Year Nineteen..........................$ 710,965

Total houses owned going into Year Nineteen: 6,457 + 3,000 = 9,457 houses

---

YEAR TWENTY

9,457 houses owned at start of Year Twenty

RENT: $1,015 x 12 x 9,457 houses...$115,186,260

EXPENSES: Mortgage notes* = $390.17 x 12 x 9,336...............$43,711,524

         *121 houses paid off (9,457 – 121 = 9,336)

         Taxes..............$700.00 x 9,457.....................$ 6,619,900

         Insurance..........$725.00 x 9,457.....................$ 6,856,325

         Vacancies and repairs – 10% $11,518,626

         Manager...$ 400,000

         Two Asst. Managers....................................$ 170,000

         Four Secretaries......................................$ 160,000

         Five Clerks...$ 175,000

         Twelve Buyers...$ 540,000

         Eight Maintenance People..............................$ 320,000

         Equipment...$ 100,000

         Miscellaneous...$ 750,000

         Contingency...$ 1,500,000

                                         $72,721,375.........$72,721,375

       Projected Profit End of Year   Twenty...........…..…………...$42,464,885*

           *$4,490.31 profit per house

YEAR TWENTY PROJECTED SALES AND PROFITS

     $ 629,739,760 – Sales Prices of 9,457 houses 3% yearly appreciation

    - $ 375,496,800 – Debt on houses

     $ 254,242,960 – Buyer pays at closing &Cash Sales Profit to Seller

    + $ 43,892,624 – Year to Year Profits

     $298,135,584 – Year Twenty Total Cash Sales & Rental Profits

$298,135,584 divided by 9,457 houses = $31,525 profit per house

HOUSE SALES TO BUYER WHO ASSUMES DEBT

The projection following indicates the sale of the 9,457 house inventory for cash at closing of $254,242,960, and assumption of $375,496,800 in existing house debt, to an individual buyer/investor or group of buyer/investors, hereinafter: Buyer. All yearly profits plus Year Twenty profits are projected at $43,892,624, which is a 17.26% return on buyer's $254,242,960 investment. Total price is $629,739,760. Tenants pay the debt service on the existing debt through their rents.

Sales prices for the 9,457 houses are determined by taking the original price paid by our owner, plus an appreciation value increase of 3% per year for each year owned. Existing house debt amount is calculated at $3,400, per year, per house, or $283.33 per month, owed for each year or month, after sales closing to buyer takes place.

$\quad$ $ 629,739,760 – Houses sales price at closing at 3% yearly appreciation

$\quad$ - $\quad$ 375,496,800 – House debt remaining….assumed by Buyer

$\quad$ $ 254,242,960 – Cash paid by Buyer and received by Seller at closing

$\quad$ + $\quad$ 43,892,624 – Year Twenty Standard Profit

$\quad$ **$ 298,135,584 – Total Projected Profit to Owner/Investor(s)**

The projected sales price of $629,739,760 is based only on the appreciated value and <u>not the business value</u>. Therefore, the net to Seller is also lower than if the price were based on the appreciated value plus the business value. On the projected sales price of $629,739,760, Buyer's projected return of $254,242,960 is 17.264% return on his investment. A lower return on Buyer's investment would increase profit to Owner/Investor(s).

For instance, a projected Buyer's investment of $400,000,000, instead of $254,242,960, provides a 10.973% return to Buyer. A $450,000,000 investment produces a 9.755% return; an investment of $500,000.000, produces an 8.778% return; an investment of $550,000,000, a 7.98% return to Buyer.

Buyer buys not only the 9,457 housing inventory, but also buys the business and the business models structured by the Owner/Investor(s). This business model built the business and the enormous profits earned through that model. Our Owner/Investor(s)/Seller, depending upon the sales price he determines, can receive, upon sale, a projected profit from $298,135,584 to $550,000,000. This is a monumental return for a $600,000 investment in safe, secure, solid and marketable properties.

Buyer also receives yearly value appreciation of houses, projected at 3% per year, and equity appreciation of existing debt paid through tenants' rents. The average house value appreciation is about $2,480, per year, per house. $2,480 x 9,457 houses = $23,453,360. Equity appreciation is $3,400, per house, per year, or $283.33, per month, per house. $3,400 x 9,457 houses = $32,153,800.

$43,892,624 – Projected Yearly Net Profit, plus increases

$23,453,360 – Projected House Value Appreciation

$32,153,800 – Loan Balance Reduction

$99,499,784 - Total Gain

Buyer could realize his cash investment of $254,242,960 in approximately two and one half years. Definitive financial gains, returns and benefits accrue to the principal seller and buyer in this projected transaction example.

In the following pages are projections that specify the projected cash profit received by seller of $298,135,584, which includes Year Twenty projected profit of $43,892,624. These projections indicate the return that one investor or multiple investors would receive. Four columns are listed in these projections: (1) Investors; (2) Amount Invested; (3) Cash Profit; (4) Percentage Return.

Each column specifies the number of investors, their investment amounts, their cash profits, and percentage return on investment. For example, the first line specifies one investor who invests $600,000, receives a cash profit of $298,135,584 and a 49,689% return on investment.

The fourth line specifies eight investors who invest $75,000 each, receive a cash profit of $37,266,948 each, with a 49,689% return on investment.

The sixth line specifies 15 investors who invest $40,000 each, receive a cash profit of $19,875,705 each, with a 49,689% return on investment.

Most aware, astute and objective investors would readily agree that these projected returns are extremely remarkable for a safe, secure investment, with profits purchasing additional properties that can be rented or sold at any time. Most would likely agree that such returns are very rare and almost non-existent in investment circles.

Projected return to buyer for his $254,242,960 cash investment is 17.26%, which is very respectable on any sale basis. As stated, the total sales price was arrived at by taking the original price paid by the buyer/investor and adding 3%, per year, for each year owned. This is when the owner/seller establishes a price that provides the buyer with a strong return, but not one as high as 17.26%. If the present buyer were to pay a cash price of $300,000,000 and assume existing debt, then his projected return on his $300,000,000 cash investment would be 14.63%, which is still very strong. In this situation, our owner/seller would obtain a total cash profit of $343,892,624, rather than $298,235,584, a difference of $45,657,040 in favor of the seller.

In projections that follow, you will see percentage returns that our seller/investor(s) receive upon sale, which is 49,689% on the $600,000 investment. As referenced earlier, most astute, objective investors would agree that this is a highly unusual, remarkable return for such a safe, sound investment and quite rare for investment returns, especially when the security is financially solid. However, when you read the following projections, you will find the projected returns to be considerably higher because of other projected sales practices and increased profit levels for the same safe, secure investment. Thus, before we present this, we want to demonstrate what the Buyer can expect if he were to sell the entire 9,457 house inventory in seven years after his purchase from our owner/investor. On the above figures, the Buyer invested $254,242,960 at closing when he purchased the 9,457 houses. The price he paid was $629,739,760, including assumption of $375,496,800 in house debt. When we enter the house value appreciation, the mortgage note appreciation and profits, with moderate rent increases, total projected sales price in seven years is $965,795,100. The Buyer paid $254,242,960 at closing and received a projected return of $965,795,100 in seven years, which is a total return of 379.8% on the $254,242,960 investment in seven years. When owner/investors want to sell to a Buyer, it is best to consider what options that Buyer has for profits and short and long term sales. These figures are below.

PROJECTED SEVEN YEAR SALES & RENTAL PROFITS FOR BUYER WHO PURCHASED 9,457 HOUSE INVENTORY FROM OUR SELLER/INVESTOR(S)

BUYER PAID $629,739,760 SEVEN YEARS EARLIER.

$774,500,000 – Sales price = original price + 3% yearly appreciation

-$150,420,200 - House Debt

$624,079,800 – Sales Profit

+$317,376,815 - Yearly Profits

$941,456,615 - Total Projected Profit to Seller

This is a projected 370.29% Return on Buyer's $254,242,960 cash investment paid to our owner/investor(s) at closing.

On the following page are the Year Twenty Sales Projections for Owner/investor(s)

Year Twenty Sales, Profits and Returns

OWNER/INVESTOR(S) YEAR TWENTY PROJECTED SALES AND RENTAL PROFIT

$ 629,739,760.........Sale of 9,457 houses

-_375,496,800_   ...…...Existing house debt

$ 254,242,960.…....... Sales Profits

+__43,892,624_ ....Yearly and Year 20 Profits

$298,135,584   Year Twenty Total Profits

YEAR TWENTY PROJECTED PROFITS AND PROJECTED RETURNS TO INVESTORS

Investors	Amount Invested	Projected Profit	Percentage Return
1	$ 600,000	$ 298,135,584	496,892%
2	$ 300,000 each	$ 149,067,792 each	496,892%
5	$ 120,000 each	$ 59,627,117 each	496,892%
8	$ 75,000 each	$ 37,266,948 each	496,892%
10	$ 60,000 each	$ 29,813,558 each	496,892%
15	$ 40,000 each	$ 19,875,705 each	496,892%
20	$ 30,000 each	$ 14,906,779 each	496,892%
25	$ 24,000 each	$ 11,925,424 each	496,892%

The previous projection indicated a projected profit to our seller/investor(s) of $298,135,584 for the sale of 9,457 houses to buyer/investors. This amounts to a projected profit of $31,525 per house and a projected 496,892% return on the original $600,000 investment. These amazing profits and returns are enormously high for a safe, secure investment in which yearly profits purchase rental properties over a twenty year period. As previously stated, we project the sales value of the houses to increase by a conservative 3% per year. The projected sales price of $298,135,584 to the buyer was calculated on this yearly 3% increase in house value. Actual sales prices could be considerably higher.

Following are two sets of additional projections. One pertains to house sales by our seller/investor(s) to their current house renters and other house buyers. The second pertains to sales to a buyer/investor(s), based upon a sales price which provides the buyer with a substantial return upon his investment in the 9,457 houses.

Throughout this book, we discussed the fact that millions of Americans have unfortunately lost their homes through foreclosure and many of these people were not at fault because economic conditions severely harmed them and their ability to financially maintain their homes. Many of these people are still unable to purchase homes because of restrictive banking requirements and conditions as we have previously mentioned. As a result of this, most of these people rent. Whenever a seller is willing to accept a down payment and carry the balance of the purchase price, without the usual systems requirements, financially capable people are definitely eager to purchase. These buyers can include some of those who lost their homes and now currently must rent. Since the seller accepts a down payment and carries the balance, and since the buyer's monthly service costs are usually less than the rent he pays, capable renters become willing buyers. Sales are available to not only renters but to anyone who may want to take advantage of such an opportunity. As stated in the Buy/Sell Projections, $10,000 is added to the price since the seller carries the balance.

The projected average sales price per house is $76,590 which is derived as follows.

$ 629,739,760 – 9,457 house sales, plus

+   94,570,000 -- $10,000 bonus per house

House Sales……………....$ 724,309,760, ÷ by 9,457 houses = $76,590

House Debt……………. $ 375,496,800, ÷ by 9,457 houses = $39,706 average house debt

Projected down payment is $22,000 (28.7% per house). Existing house debt, namely, first mortgage, averages $39,706 per house, and second mortgage is projected at $14,884. These are averages only and will change depending upon years remaining on first mortgage, which will change the amount of the second mortgage. Averages follow:

$76,590 – Projected Selling Price

$39,706 – Existing Debt (first mortgage)

$22,000 – Down Payment

+ $14,884 – Second Mortgage

$76,590 – Projected House Sales Price

9,457 houses x $76,590 = $724,311,630 Total Sales Prices

As stated above, these figures are averages. The projected sales price does not change, but the amounts of the first and second mortgages do change depending upon years remaining on the first mortgage when the sale occurs. Those remaining years change the years remaining and principal amount due on the first mortgage, which began with a 15 year maturity. Yearly payments on the first mortgage do not change. The second mortgage maturity is also 15 years. Second mortgage principal and yearly payments will change based upon years remaining on first mortgage when closing takes place. For instance, let us say that a sale takes place with a first mortgage balance of $45,900 remaining, and 13.5 years remain until maturity. Price is $76,590 minus balance of $45,900, plus down payment of $22,000, which leaves a second mortgage of $8,690. First mortgage payment remains the same, and now second mortgage payment is $869 per year for 15 years. Mortgage amounts change depending upon remaining first mortgage balance when sale occurs.

Buyer's average monthly debt service: $39,706 First Mortgage   = $4,682 per year

$14,884 Second Mortgage = <u>$1,488</u> per year

$6,170 Total per year

<u>**$6,170, divided by 12 = $514.16, per month, projected monthly payments**</u>

If some financially capable buyers do not have the $22,000 for down payment, but do have $10,000 or $15,000, then the seller could accept the $10,000 or $15,000 down and carry the difference ($7,000 to $12,000) on the second mortgage. The seller could also accept a monthly payment for these amounts over three to five years. When these amounts are fully paid, the monthly payment returns to the projected $514.16. This one of many ways that buyers and sellers can work out methods to achieve a successful transaction for the benefit of both parties.

SALES TO RENTERS AND OTHER BUYERS

$724,311,630 – Average sales price of $76,590 x 9,457 houses

- <u>$375,499,642</u> – Average first mortgage debt of $39,706 x 9,457 houses

$348,811,988

+ $140,757,988 – Average Second Mortgage

+ $140,757,988 – Average Second Mortgage Interest

$+\ \$\ \ 43,892,624$ - Previous Year to Year Rental Profits

$\underline{+\ \$\ \ \ \ \ \ 188,012}$ - Misc. Bonus Sales Amount

$\ \ \ \ \ \$674,408,600$ – Total Profits to Owner/Investor(s) upon Sale

Our Owner/Investor(s) receive projected $14,075,798 yearly for Second Mortgage Interest Payments until the entire principal debt remaining has been paid off and retired. Second Mortgage maturity per house can range from 15 years for recently purchased houses, down to one year for originally purchased houses. A projected average of 10 years per mortgage provides an additional profit of $140,757,988, for a total projected profit of $674,408,600. This amounts to projected return of 112,370% on the $600,000 investment. Such a return is truly remarkable for a safe, secure, solid investment. It would be extremely difficult, if not impossible, to find this type of return for even the most speculative and risky investments.

YEAR TWENTY PROJECTED PROFITS ON SALES TO RENTERS/HOUSE BUYERS

Projected Return to Investors

Investors	Amount	Cash @ Closing	Note Principal	Note Interest	Total Return	% Return
1	$600,000	$392,892,624	$140,757,988	$140,757,988	$674,408,600	112,401%
2	$300,000 Each	$196,446,312 Each	$ 70,378,994 Each	$70,378,994 Each	$337,204,300 Each	112,401% Each
5	$120,000 Each	$ 78,578,524 Each	$ 28,151,597 Each	$ 28,151,597 Each	$134,881,718 Each	112,401% Each
8	$ 75,000 Each	$ 49,111,576 Each	$ 17,594,485 Each	$ 17,594,485 Each	$ 84,301,075 Each	112,401% Each
10	$ 60,000 Each	$ 39,289,262 Each	$ 14,075,798 Each	$ 14,075,798 Each	$ 67,440,860 Each	112,401% Each
15	$ 40,000 Each	$ 26,192,841 Each	$ 9,383,865 Each	$ 9,383,865 Each	$ 44,960,573 Each	112,401% Each
20	$ 30,000 Each	$ 19,644,631 Each	$ 7,037,899 Each	$ 7,037,899 Each	$ 33,720,430 Each	112,401% Each
25	$ 24,000 Each	$ 15,715,692 Each	$ 5,630,319 Each	$ 5,630,319 Each	$ 26,976,310 Each	112,401% Each

First mortgage maturity, as previously noted, is 15 years. Second mortgage term is also for 15 years. However, because of sales of all homes purchased over 15 years, second mortgage maturities could be anywhere from 1 to 15 years. We averaged the term of second mortgages at 10 years. Obviously, if the second mortgage were to be carried for 15 years, the total interest on that second mortgage would increase by approximately $20,000,000, total.

Projections on the next page indicate Year Twenty second mortgage note payments and note payment amounts received by each investor over a ten (10) year period. As mentioned throughout this book, the projected interest for second mortgages is 10%, per year, with the principal balance due on the anniversary of the closing on the final year.

There are seven columns in the projection: (1) Investors; (2) Note Amount; (3) Yearly Payments; (4) Interest Total; (5) Note Principal; (6) Total Principal & Interest; (7) Yearly Average Payment.

These projections follow the same lines as the previous projections. For instance, the first line indicates one investor who has a second mortgage note amount of $140,758,960. Yearly payments are projected at $14,075,896. The total interest over 10 years is $140,758,960. The note principal is $140,758,960. Total principal and interest is $281,517,920. Yearly average payment is $28,151,792. Since there is only one investor, he receives all of this.

In line 5, we have 10 investors, with note amounts of $14,075,896, each. Yearly payments to investors are $1,407,589 each. Interest total is $14,075,896 each. Note principal is $14,075,896 each. Total principal and interest is $28,151,792 each, and yearly average payment is $2,815,179 each.

In line 8, we have 25 investors, with note amounts of $5,630,358 each. Yearly payments are $563,035 each. Interest total is $5,630,358 each. Note principal is $5,630,358 each. Total principal and interest is $11,260,716 each and yearly average payment is $1,126,071 each.

Each investor receives cash at closing, as indicated in the previous set of projections, plus the note amounts specified here. Because the seller/investor(s) are willing to carry notes over a 10 year period, their total return is much more than it would have been in an all cash sale. The yearly average payment amount contains the average of both principal and interest for the year. The way in which interest payments are structured is that 10% interest is paid per year on the anniversary of the closing and the principal amount is due in full on the 10th anniversary of the closing. Buyer and seller can arrange any type of reasonable payment structure that is acceptable to each one and suits both of them.

Previous projections showed a 15 year term.
Below projections show a 10 year term.

YEAR TWENTY NOTE PAYMENTS

Note Payments Received by Investors Over Ten Years

Investors	Note Amt.	Yearly Pmt.	Int. Total	Note Principal	Total P & I	Yearly Avg. Pmt.
1	$140,758,960	$14,075,896	$140,758,960	$140,758,960	$281,517,920	$ 28,151,792
2	70,379,480	7,037,948	70,379,480	70,379,480	140,750,960	14,075,090
5	28,151,792	2,815,179	28,151,792	28,151,792	56,303,584	5,630,358
8	17,594,890	1,759,489	17,594,890	17,594,890	35,189,780	3,518,978
10	14,075,896	1,407,589	14,075,896	14,075,896	28,151,792	2,815,179
15	9,383,930	938,393	9,383,930	9,383,930	18,767,860	1,876,786
20	7,037,948	703,794	7,037,948	7,037,948	14,075,896	1,407,589
25	5,630,358	563,035	5,630,358	5,630,358	11,260,716	1,126,071

The next projections provide a breakdown of returns to our seller/investor(s) for the sale of house inventory to a single buyer/investor or investor group, hereinafter: Buyer, for $300,000,000 cash at closing and assumption of $375,496,800 in existing house debt. Total price is $675,496,800. Year Twenty profit is projected at $43,892,624, which is a projected 14.63% return on buyer's $300,000,000 investment. As previously stated, Buyer purchases the entire property portfolio, but also buys the successful business established by Owner/Investor(s). If Buyer continues the business model, then, his returns will soar. A lesser return on Buyer's investment will provide greater profit for Owner/Investor(s). An investment of $400,000,000 will provide Buyer a projected 10.979% return on investment. An investment of $500,000,000 projects an 8.778% return on investment. Our Owner/Investor(s) could sell the portfolio at a price from $675,496,800 to $875,496,800. Moderate yearly rent increases, at $10 to $15 per month, will slightly increase the net profit. Tenants pay debt service on the $375,496,800 existing house debt through their rents.

In addition to net profits, Buyer benefits through yearly appreciation of the houses projected at 3% per year, and equity appreciation, or reduction, of existing debt paid through tenants' rents. Average value appreciation is approximately $2,480, per house, per year. $2,480 x 9,457 houses = $23,453,360. Equity appreciation is $3,400, per year, or $283.33, per month, per house. $3,400 x 9,457 houses = $32,153,800.

$ 43,892,624 – Projected Net Profit
23,453,360 – Projected Value Appreciation
+ 32,153,800 – Loan Balance Reduction
$ 99,499,784 – Total Projected Yearly Gain

On this basis, the Buyer could realize his $300,000,000 cash investment in approximately three years. If a transaction or sale is to be successful, there must be definite benefits and financial gain for both the principal buyer and seller. Projected profit within this projected sale demonstrates solid gains, benefits and excellent returns to both parties.

PROJECTED SALE TO BUYER OR INVESTMENT GROUP
$ 675,496,800 - Sales Price
- $ 375,496,800 - House debt
$ 300,000,000 - Buyer pays at closing
+$ 43, 892,624 – Yearly Profits
$ 343,892,624 – Seller's Cash Profit

The following projection specifies the projected cash sale price of $300,000,000 and Year Twenty profits of $43,892,624.

Four columns are listed: (1) Investors; (2) Amount Invested; (3) Profit; (4) Percentage Return. Each column specifies the number of investors, their investment amount, their returns and the percentage return on investment. For example, the first line specifies one investor who invested

$600,000, receives a profit of $343,892,624 and a 57,315% on investment.

The third line specifies five investors who invested $120,000 each, receive a profit of $68,778,525 each, a 57,315% return on investment.

The seventh line specifies twenty investors who invested $30,000 each, receive a profit of $17,194,631 each, a 57,315% return on investment.

YEAR TWENTY PROJECTED PROFITS
ON SALES TO BUYER/INVESTOR

Projection: Buyer/Investor pays $300,000,000 cash (14.63% projected return) at closing and assumes $375,496,800 in house debt. Total price--$675,496,800

Cash Return to Seller--$300,000,000 + $43,892,624 Year Twenty Profit = $343,892,624

PROJECTED CASH RETURNS TO INVESTORS

Investors	Amount Invested	Cash Profit	Percentage Return
1	$600,000	$343,892,624	57,315%
2	$300,000 each	$171,946,312 each	57,315%
5	$120,000 each	$ 68,778,525 each	57,315%
8	$ 75,000 each	$ 42,986,578 each	57,315%
10	$ 60,000 each	$ 34,389,262 each	57,315%
20	$ 30,000 each	$ 17,194,631 each	57,315%
25	$ 24,000 each	$ 13,755,705 each	57,315%

As stated previously, Owner/Investor(s) could sell the inventory for another $100,000,000 to $200,000,000 and substantially increase profits from $343,896,624 up to $543,896,624.

YEAR TWENTY ALTERNATIVE PROJECTIONS

Following are Year Twenty Alternative Projections, in which houses are purchased in Year Twenty on a monthly basis from profits made instead of purchases made at the end of the year from aggregate yearly profits. In normal business situations, purchases are made monthly or when needed, and not at year's end. Monthly purchases allow for many more houses to be purchased and added to house inventory. Had this purchasing been done from the very inception, then a much larger number of houses would be bought and sold within the housing inventory. This added number would provide additional rents, profits and vastly increase sales amounts. We took the conservative position in our projections, which is very profitable, but monthly purchases are far more profitable.

Year Twenty Alternative

YEAR TWENTY ALTERNATIVE PURCHASES —MONTH TO MONTHRENTAL PROJECTIONS

YEAR TWENTY ALTERNATIVE -- MONTH ONE

Profit for Years One to Nineteen	=	$1,425,419
At end of Year Nineteen, 158 houses bought x $9,000	= -	$1,422,000
	Profit	$ 3,419

In this Year Twenty Alternative Purchases Projection, during Year Twenty, houses are bought on a month-to-month basis throughout Year Twenty, with funds derived from monthly profits. Houses are not bought at end of the year, as shown in prior Projections.

9,457 houses plus 158 houses purchased in Month One = 9,615 houses

RENT: $1,015 x 9,615 houses………......………………………………$9,759,225

EXPENSES:
Mortgages 9,615 – 121 = 9494 x $390.17……………….$ 3,704,274

Taxes 9,615 x $700 divided by 12..………………….....$ 560,875

Insurance 9,615 x $725 divided by 12…………………....$ 580,906

Vacancies and repairs @ 10%.……………………….….$ 975,922

Staff...$ 152,673

Miscellaneous...$ 63,750

Contingency...$ 127,083

Total Expenses $6,165,483.......................$6,165,483

Profit $3,593,742

Profit ....$ 3,593,742

Buy 399 houses x $9,000 DP..........................$ 3,591,000

$ 2,742 Profit – Month One

9,615 houses + 399 = 10,014 houses for Month Two

YEAR TWENTY ALTERNATIVE – MONTH TWO

9,615 + 399 = 10,014 houses for Month Two

RENT: $1,015 x 10,014 houses..$10,164,210

EXPENSES: Mortgages 10,014 – 121 = 9893 x $390.17......................$ 3,859,952

Taxes 10,014 x $700 divided by 12..............................$ 584,150

Insurance 10,014 x $725 divided by 12.........................$ 605,012

Vacancies and repairs – 10%.......................................$ 1,016,421

Staff...$ 160,000

Miscellaneous...$ 75,000

Contingency...$ 135,000

$ 6,435,535...... - $ 6,435,535

Profit..................$ 3,728,675

Profit $3,728,675

Buy 414 houses x $9,000 DP......................... $3,726,000

$ 2,675 Profit – Month Two

****

10,014 houses + 414 = 10,428 houses for Month Three

YEAR TWENTY ALTERNATIVE – MONTH THREE

10,014 + 414 = 10,428 houses for Month Three

RENT: $1,015 x 10,428 houses…………....………………………………….…$10,584,420

EXPENSES: Mortgages 10,428 – 121 = 10,307 x $390.17…………$4,021,428

                  Taxes 10,428 x $700 divided by 12…………….……$ 608,300

                  Insurance 10,428 x $725 divided by 12………………$ 630,025

                  Vacancies and repairs – 10%…………………………$1,058,442

                  Staff…………………………………………....……$ 190,000

                  Miscellaneous……………………………………....…$ 85,500

                  Contingency…………………………………….…....$ 150,000

                                    $ 6,743,249…… - $ 6,743,249

                                    Profit…………….. $ 3,841,171

        Profit …………………………………$ 3,841,171

        Buy 426 houses x $9,000 DP………....$ 3,834,000

                         $ 7,171 Profit – Month Three

****

10,428 houses + 426 = 10,854 houses for Month Four

YEAR TWENTY ALTERNATIVE – MONTH FOUR

10,428 houses + 426 = 10,854 houses for Month Four

RENT: $1,015 x 10,854 houses…………....………………………………….…$11,016,810

EXPENSES: Mortgages 10,854 – 121 = 10,733 x $390.17…………$ 4,187,695

                  Taxes 10,854 x $700 divided by 12……………..……$ 633,150

                  Insurance 10,854 x $725 divided by 12………………$ 655,762

                  Vacancies and repairs – 10%…………………………$ 1,101,681

                  Staff…………………………………………………$ 225,000

                    Miscellaneous…………………………………………$ 100,000

                  Contingency…………………………………………$ 175,000

                                      $ 7,078,288……. - $ 7,078,288

                                    Profit…………….... $ 3,938,522

Profit ……………………………....$ 3,938,522

Buy 437 houses x $9,000 DP……...…$ <u>3,933,000</u>

$ 5,522 Profit – Month Four

****

10,854 houses + 437 = 11,291 houses for Month Five

YEAR TWENTY ALTERNATIVE – MONTH FIVE

10,854 houses + 437 = 11,291 houses for Month Five

RENT: $1,015 x 11,291 houses…………....……………………………………$11,460,365

EXPENSES: Mortgages 11,291 – 121 = 11,170 x $390.17……………$4,358,199

Taxes 11,291 x $700 divided by 12..………………….$ 658,641

Insurance 11,291 x $725 divided by 12……...........……$ 682,164

Vacancies and repairs – 10%……………………………$1,146,036

Staff……………………………………………………...$ 240,000

Miscellaneous………………………………….….……$ 120,000

Contingency……………………………………………$ <u>195,000</u>

$7,400,040…….. - $ 7,400,040

Profit…………….....$ 4,060,325

Profit ………………………………$ 4,060,325

Buy 451 houses x $9,000 DP………$ <u>4,059,000</u>

$ 1,325 Profit – Month Five

****

11,291 houses + 451 = 11,742 houses for Month Six

YEAR TWENTY ALTERNATIVE – MONTH SIX

11,291 houses + 451 = 11,742 houses for Month Six

RENT: $1,015 x 11,742 houses…………....……………………………….……….$11,918,130

EXPENSES: Mortgages 11,742 – 121 = 11,621 x $390.17……………$4,534,165

Taxes 11,742 x $700 divided by 12..............................$ 684,940

Insurance 11,742 x $725 divided by 12.....................$ 709,412

Vacancies and repairs – 10%...............................$1,191,813

Staff...$ 260,000

Miscellaneous...$ 135,000

Contingency...$ 210,000

$ 7,725,340…... - $ 7,725,340

Profit...................$ 4,192,790

Profit .... $ 4,192,790

Buy 465 houses x $9,000 DP.........$ 4,185,000

$ 7,790 Profit – Month Six

****

11,742 houses + 465 = 12,207 houses for Month Seven

YEAR TWENTY ALTERNATIVE – MONTH SEVEN

11,742 houses + 465 = 12,207 houses for Month Seven

RENT: $1,015 x 12,207 houses………......................................$12,390,010

EXPENSES: Mortgages 12,207 – 121 = 12,086 x $390.17......$ 4,715,595

Taxes 12,207 x $700 divided by 12.................$ 712,075

Insurance 12,207 x $725 divided by 12……........$ 737,506

Vacancies and repairs – 10%......................$ 1,239,001

Staff..$ 300,000

Miscellaneous.......................................$ 150,000

Contingency...$ 230,000

$ 8,084,177…… - $8,084,177

Profit...................$4,305,833

Profit ....$ 4,305,833

Buy 478 houses x $9,000 DP........$ 4,302,000

$ 3,833 Profit – Month Seven

12,207 houses + 478 = 12,685 houses for Month Eight

YEAR TWENTY ALTERNATIVE – MONTH EIGHT

12,207 houses + 478 = 12,685 houses for Month Eight

RENT: $1,015 x 12,685 houses…………......………………….……………$12,875,275

EXPENSES: Mortgages 12,685 – 121 = 12,564 x $390.17…………$ 4,902,095

Taxes 12,685 x $700 divided by 12…………….…….$ 739,958

Insurance 12,685 x $725 divided by 12……………….$ 766,385

Vacancies and repairs – 10% ………………………....$ 1,287,527

Staff…………………………………………….…..$ 325,000

Miscellaneous…………………………………....…..$ 175,000

Contingency…………………………………….………$ 260,000

$ 8,455,965….. - $ 8,455,965

Profit……………..... $ 4,419,310

Profit ………………………………….$ 4,419,310

Buy 491 houses x $9,000 DP……………$ 4,419,000

$ 310 Profit – Month Eight

****

12,685 houses + 491 = 13,176 houses for Month Nine

YEAR TWENTY ALTERNATIVE – MONTH NINE

12,685 houses + 491 = 13,176 houses for Month Nine

RENT: $1,015 x 13,176 houses…………......……………………….………………$13,373,640

EXPENSES: Mortgages 13,176 – 121 = 13,055 x $390.17…………$ 5,093,669

Taxes 13,176 x $700 divided by 12…………….…….$ 768,600

Insurance 13,176 x $725 divided by 12……………….$ 796,050

Vacancies and repairs – 10%…………………………$ 1,337,364

Staff…………………………………………………….$ 350,000

Miscellaneous..$ 195,000

Contingency..$ 275,000

$ 8,815,683... - $ 8,815,683

Profit.................$ 4,557,957

Profit ....$ 4,557,957

Buy 506 houses x $9,000 DP............$ 4,554,000

$ 3,957 Profit – Month Nine

****

13,176 houses + 506 = 13,682 houses for Month Ten

YEAR TWENTY ALTERNATIVE – MONTH TEN

13,176 houses + 506 = 13,682 houses for Month Ten

RENT: $1,015 x 13,682 houses………..$13,887,230

EXPENSES: Mortgages 13,682 – 121 = 13,561 x $390.17............$ 5,291,095

Taxes 13,682 x $700 divided by 12........................$ 798,117

Insurance 13,682 x $725 divided by 12..................$ 826,621

Vacancies and repairs – 10%............................$ 1,388,723

Staff...$ 375,000

Miscellaneous...$ 205,000

Contingency...$ 285,000

$ 9,169,556..... - $ 9,169,556

Profit...............$ 4,717,680

Profit ....$ 4,717,680

Buy 524 houses x $9,000 DP............$ 4,716,000

$ 1,680 Profit – Month Ten

****

13,682 houses + 524 = 14,206 houses for Month Eleven

YEAR TWENTY ALTERNATIVE – MONTH ELEVEN

13,682 houses + 524 = 14,206 houses for Month Eleven

RENT: $1,015 x 14,206 houses…………...……………………….……………$14,419,090

EXPENSES:

Mortgages 14,206 – 121 = 14,085 x $390.17…………$ 5,495,544		
Taxes 14,206 x $700 divided by 12…..……………..……$ 828,683		
Insurance 14,206 x $725 divided by 12……………....$ 858,279		
Vacancies and repairs – 10%…………………………$ 1,441,909		
Staff……………………………………………………....$ 400,000		
Miscellaneous………………………………………....$ 215,000		
Contingency…………………………………………$ 300,000		
	$ 9,539,415……. $ 9,539,415	
	Profit…………....$ 4,879,675	

Profit ………………………………$ 4,879,685

Buy 542 houses x $9,000 DP………$ 4,878,000

$ 1,685 Profit – Month Eleven

****

14,206 houses + 542 = 14,748 houses for Month Twelve

YEAR TWENTY ALTERNATIVE – MONTH TWELVE

14,206 houses + 542 = 14,748 houses for Month Twelve

RENT: $1,015 x 14,748 houses…………...……………………….……………$14,969,220

EXPENSES:

Mortgages 14,748– 121 = 14,627 x $390.17…………$ 5,707,017	
Taxes 14,748 x $700 divided by 12…..……………….$ 860,300	
Insurance 14,748 x $725 divided by 12……………....$ 891,025	
Vacancies and repairs – 10%…………………………....$ 1,496,922	
Staff……………………………………………………....$ 430,000	
Miscellaneous………………………………………....$ 225,000	
Contingency……………………………………………$ 315,000	

$ 9,925,264..................... - $ 9,925,264
                              Profit................. $ 5,043,956

    Profit ....$ 5,043,956
    Buy 560 houses x $9,000 DP............$ 5,040,000
                                $ 3,956 Profit – Month Twelve

****

14,748 houses + 560 = 15,308 houses

YEAR TWENTY ALTERNATIVE ANALYSIS

These Year Twenty Alternative Projections demonstrate how additional houses can be purchased DURING Year Twenty when monthly profits are used to purchase houses, each month, rather than at the end of the year. All prior Projections in this Section project that houses are purchased at the end of the year, and not each month. In this approach, the seller/investor(s) has 15,308 houses, as opposed to 9,457, when buys were made once a year. The difference between the two approaches is substantial, which, in this case, amounts to 5,851 more houses or an additional 61.86%. In the Year Twenty Standard Projections, please note that houses are purchased at the end of the year from profits derived during that year. In these Year Twenty Alternative Projections, ongoing purchases of houses are made from monthly profits. If houses were purchased monthly from Year One forward, instead of at the end of the year, then far more than 15,308 houses would have been purchased.

If the same percentages and ratios were used from Year One through Year Twenty, then the projected houses purchased by the end of Year Twenty would be over 1,113,000. This may seem very high, but the buys are made over twenty (20) years, an average of about $55,650 per year. Yearly house sales amount to 6,000,000 houses or more, so the yearly average on these projections is about 9.27% of yearly house sales.

Our projections are conservative and indicate what gains can be achieved over a twenty year period by a serious, dedicated investor(s) who want to accumulate true wealth in a safe, secure manner, based upon property that can always be rented or sold. In actual business operations, property purchases would be made monthly, when profits are made, rather than at the end of the year, from accumulated profits. If this had been done every month from Year One, then the actual houses bought and owned during the twenty year operation would be considerably higher than

9,457, as we conservatively projected. More house purchases gain more monthly rents, additional profit and much more profit when the housing inventory is sold. Further, from Year Six of the Standard Projections we began to leave increasing profit for the owner, rather than spend it for additional house purchases. Had this profit been spent on buying additional houses, then at the end of the twenty years, the projected actual houses owned would be substantially higher.

The following projection specifies the cash sales price of $348,181,565, plus debt assumption to an individual buyer/investor or group of investors, and the returns breakdown to each of our seller/investor(s) based upon the amount s/he invested.

The $348,226,211 projected cash profit is derived as follows:

$1,002,185,165 – Projected house inventory sales price - 3% appreciation

- 654,003,600 – Projected house debt assumed

$ 348,181,565 – Cash profit

+ $ 44,646 – Year Twenty month to month profit

$ 348,226,211 – Total Year Twenty Alternative Projected Profit

Through their rents, tenants pay debt service on buyer's debt assumption of $654,003,600. In addition to profits, the Buyer receives the benefit of house value appreciation, projected at 3%, per year, per house, plus equity appreciation through debt service paid by tenants. Average house value appreciation is projected at 3% per year, about $2,480 x 15,308 houses = $37,963,840. Equity appreciation through debt reduction is projected at $3,400, per year, per house x 15,308 houses = $52,047,200, which reduces the buyer's debt principal amount. In one year of operation, the buyer is projected to make $71,447,248 in profits from rent, $37,963,840 in house value appreciation, and $52,047,200 in equity appreciation, a total of $161,458,288. In a little over two years, the buyer could realize his cash investment. Said in a different way, the buyer can realize about 46.37% per year on his investment. Although the sales appreciation and debt principal reduction will not be realized until the property is sold, these asset values are intrinsic within the property owned.

YEAR TWENTY ALTERNATIVE PROJECTED SALES AND PROFITS

$348,226,211 Profit Returns to Investors:

Investors	Amount Invested	Profit	Percentage Return
1	$ 600,000	$ 348,226,211	58,037.7%
2	$ 300,000	$ 174,113,105	58,037.7%
5	$ 120,000	$ 69,645,242	58,037.7%
8	$ 75,000	$ 43,528,276	58,037.7%
10	$ 60,000	$ 34,822,621	58,037.7%
15	$ 40,000	$ 23,215,080	58,037.7%
20	$ 30,000	$ 17,411,310	58,037.7%
25	$ 24,000	$ 13,929,048	58,037.7%

In Year Twenty Standard Projections, we projected other means to sell the housing inventory. As indicated, one of these is to sell the houses to the current renters or to other financially capable house buyers. In these Year Twenty Alternative Projections, our seller/investor(s) now have 15,308 houses to sell, as opposed to 9,457 in Year Twenty Standard Projections. The projected sale prices for the 15,308 houses and mortgage costs to individual buyers follow:

PROJECTED SALES TO RENTERS & OTHER BUYERS

$ 1,002,185,165 – Sales Prices at 3% appreciated value per year per house

+ $ 153,080,000 -- $10,000 bonus per house

$ 1,155,265,165 – Sales Prices, divided by 15,308.......$75,470 average price per house

- $ 654,003,600 – House Debt, divided by 15,308....$42,723 average debt per house

$ 501,261,565 – **Sales Profit**

+$ 44,646 – Year Twenty Month to Month Profits

$ **501,306,211 – Year Twenty Alternative Cash Profits from Sales to Renters**

PLUS: Second mortgages principals and balances

The average projected sales price of $75,470 and mortgage costs of a house buyer are outlined below.

$75,470 – Average Sales Price

$42,723 – Existing Debt – First Mortgage

22,000 – Down Payment – 29.15%

10,747 – Second Mortgage

$75,470 – Average Sales Price

Projected Mortgage Payments:

$42,723 -- $4,682 per year

$10,747 -- $1,074 per year

$5,756, divided by 12 = $479.66 – Projected Monthly Payment

As we have mentioned before, if a financially capable and willing buyer is unable to make the $22,000 down payment, but can pay anywhere from $10,000 to $15,000, the seller could add the difference to his second mortgage, or take payments for the difference over three to five years. Thereafter, the projected monthly payment is returned to $479.66 per month. Whenever willing principals come together for common purpose, a reasonable structured arrangement can be worked out between them for mutual benefit.

This projected $501,261,565 profit to owner/investor(s) from sales to renters and other house buyers is considerably higher than the projected profit of $348,226,211 to a single buyer/investor or group of investors. A beneficial increase of $153,035,354 accrues to our seller/investor(s). However, since our seller/investor(s) carry note balances, with interest payments on the second mortgages, the total projected return is $665,836,422, which is $317,610,211 higher than a sale to a buyer/investor or investor group.

-

YEAR TWENTY ALTERNATIVE PROJECTED PROFITS FROM YEAR TWENTY-ONE SALES TO RENTERS AND HOUSE-BUYERS

$665,836,422 Projected Profit Returns to Investors:

Investors	Amt. Invested	Cash @ Closing	Note Principal	Note Interest	Profit	% Return
1	$600,000	$336,776,000	$164,530,211	$164,530,211	$665,836,422	110,972%
2	$300,000	$168,388,000	$ 82,265,105	$ 82,265,105	$332,918,210	110,972%
5	$120,000	$ 67,355,200	$ 32,906,042	$ 32,906,042	$133,167,284	110,972%
8	$ 75,000	$ 42,097,000	$ 20,566,276	$20,566,276	$ 83,229,552	110,972%
10	$ 60,000	$ 33,677,600	$ 16,453,021	$ 16,453,021	$ 66,583,642	110,972%
15	$ 40,000	$ 22,451,733	$ 10,968,680	$ 10,968,680	$ 44,389,094	110,972%
20	$ 30,000	$ 16,838,800	$ 8,226,510	$ 8,226,510	$ 33,291,821	110,972%
25	$ 24,000	$ 13,471,040	$ 6,581,208	$ 6,581,208	$ 26,633,456	110,972%

YEAR TWENTY ALTERNATIVE -- PROJECTED YEARLY NOTE PAYMENTS RECEIVED BY INVESTORS OVER TEN YEARS

Investors	Note Amount	Yearly Payments	Interest Total	Note Principal	Average Total P & I	Yrly Pymt
1	$164,530,211	$16, 453,041	$164,530,211	$164,530,211	$329,060,422	$32,906,042
2	$ 82,265,105 Each	$ 8,226,510 Each	$ 82,265,105 Each	$ 82,265,105 Each	$164,530,211 Each	$16,453,021 Each
5	$ 32,906,042 Each	$ 3,290,604 Each	$ 32,906,042 Each	$ 32,906,042 Each	$ 65,812,084 Each	$ 6,581,208 Each
8	$ 20,566,276 Each	$ 2,056,627 Each	$ 20,566,276 Each	$ 20,566,276 Each	$ 41,132,552 Each	$ 4,113,255 Each
10	$ 16,453,021 Each	$ 1,645,302 Each	$ 16,453,021 Each	$ 16,453,021 Each	$ 32,906,042 Each	$ 3,290,604 Each
15	$ 10,968,680 Each	$ 1,096,868 Each	$ 10,968,680 Each	$ 10,968,680 Each	$ 21,937,360 Each	$ 2,193,736 Each
20	$ 8,226,510 Each	$ 822,651 Each	$ 8, 226,510 Each	$ 8,226,510 Each	$ 16,453,020 Each	$ 1, 645,302 Each
25	$ 6,581,208 Each	$ 658,120 Each	$ 6,581,208 Each	$ 6,581,208 Each	$ 13,162,416 Each	$ 1,316,241 Each

The projection on the next page is a sale to an individual investor or group of investors who want a favorable return on their investment funds. Projected profits for Year Twenty One Alternative Projections are approximately $71,447,248 for 15,308 houses, which is the same number of houses for Year Twenty Alternative Projections. We used the same profit figure for Year Twenty Alternative. A buyer/investor or investor group which pays $500,000,000 cash at closing and assumes $654,003,600 in existing house debt is projected to receive $71,447,248, 14.2894% on the $500,000,000 cash investment. Cost for the house debt of $654,003,600 is absorbed by and paid for by the renters.

In addition to profit derived from his investment, the buyer receives the benefits of house appreciation and debt reduction appreciation, paid for by his renters. At 3% value increase per year, the average projected house appreciation is approximately $2,480 per year, per house, times 15,308 houses, which equals $37,963,840, per year value appreciation to the buyer. When the renters pay their rents, the rents paid pay for the owner(s)' debt service. For each month's payment, $283.33 of that payment amount reduces the principal amount of existing house debt. On a year's basis, this amounts to $3,400, per house, times 15,308 houses, equaling $52,047,200, which reduces the principal amount owed by the owner(s). In one year of operation, the buyer is projected to make $71,447,248 in rental profits, $37,963,840 in value appreciation, and $52,047,200 in equity appreciation for a projected one year total of $161,458,288. On this basis, our buyer/investor(s) could expect to realize the $500,000,000 cash investment in approximately three years. When value appreciation and equity appreciation are added to projected profit, the buyer/investor(s) could realize a return of approximately 32.29% per year on the investment.

If our seller/investor(s) did not sell the 15,308 housing inventory for $348,226,221, pursuant to sales and profit projections seen earlier, but rather sold for $500,000,000 cash to a single buyer or group of investors, then it is obvious that our seller/investor(s) would gain an additional extremely large return on the original investment. This is where negotiation comes into play. Our seller/investor(s) sell(s) property that has value and the buyer wants a favorable rate of return on investment. A price favorable and beneficial to both parties can consummate the transaction. If our owner sells for $500,000,000 cash, he gains an additional $151,773,789 upon the sale.

YEAR TWENTY ALTERNATIVE -- PROJECTED PROFITS FROM SALE TO BUYER/INVESTOR IN YEAR TWENTY ONE

Projection: Buyer/Investor pays $500,000,000 cash (14.289% return) at closing to our Owner/investor(s) and assumes $654,003,600 in existing house debt.

Total Projected Price: $1,002,185,165

Projected Return to Seller: $500,000,000 + $44,646 in month to month profits = $500,044,646

Investors Projected Return

Investors	Amount Invested	Profit	Percentage Return
1	$600,000	$500,044,646	83,340%
2	$300,000 Each	$250,022,100 Each	83,340% Each
5	$120,000 Each	$100,008,929 Each	83,340% Each
8	$ 75,000 Each	$ 62,505,580 Each	83,340% Each
10	$ 60,000 Each	$ 50,004,464 Each	83,340% Each
15	$ 40,000 Each	$ 33,336,309 Each	83,340% Each
20	$ 30,000 Each	$ 25,002,232 Each	83,340% Each
25	$ 24,000 Each	$ 20,001,785 Each	83,340% Each

In the following Projections, Year Twenty Alternative is carried forward to Year Twenty One. No houses are purchased during Year 21 Alternative; therefore the Profit is very substantial. This, plus housing inventory, provides excellent bases for sales prices.

YEAR TWENTY ONE ALTERNATIVE – PROJECTED PROFITS

RENTS: 15,308 houses x $1,030 x 12 ....$189,206,880

Mortgages: 15,308 – 149 = 15,159 x 390.17 x 12....................$70,975,044

Taxes: 15,308 x $700..$10,715,600

Insurance: 15,308 x $725..$11,098,300

Vacancies and Repairs..$18,920,688

Manager...$ 500,000

Staff..$ 2,750,000

Miscellaneous.. $ 1,000,000

Contingency...$ 1,800,000

$118,259,623 $118,259,632

Profit... $ 71,447,248

YEAR TWENTY ONE ALTERNATIVE PROJECTED PROFIT: $71,447,248

YEAR TWENTY ONE ALTERNATIVE – PROJECTED YEAR 21 SALES AND PROFITS ANALYSIS

$ 648,634,380 – Projected Sales of 9,457 houses – Standard buys

$ 372,445,405 – Projected Sales of 5,851 houses – Alternative buys

$ 1,021,079,785   15,308 houses

+$ 71,447,248 – Year Twenty One Alternative Projected Profit

+$ 44,646 – Year Twenty Alternative Projected Profit

+$ 1,092,571,679 – Gross Projected Profit

-$ 602,463,000 – Existing House Debt - Assumed by Buyer

$ 490,108,679 – **Buyer pays at closing - Seller's Projected Cash Profit**

Year Twenty One Alternative Projected Cash Profit:

$490,108,679

YEAR TWENTY ONE ALTERNATIVE – PROJECTED YEAR 21 SALES AND PROJECTED TOTAL PROFITS PROFIT
$490,108,679 Projected Profit

PROJECTED RETURNS TO INVESTORS:

Investors	Amount Invested	Profit	Percentage Return
1	$600,000	$490,108,679	81,684%
2	$300,000 Each	$245,054,340 Each	81,684%
5	$120,000 Each	$ 98,021,735 Each	81,864%
8	$ 75,000 Each	$ 61,263,585 Each	81,864%
10	$ 60,000 Each	$ 49,010,868 Each	81,864%
15	$ 40,000 Each	$ 32,673,912 Each	81,864%
20	$ 30,000 Each	$ 24,505,434 Each	81,864%
25	$ 24,000 Each	$19,604,347 Each	81,864%

These pages provide a background to the next set of projections and projected profits for our Seller/Investors when they sell the 15,308 houses to existing renters and other house buyers. These sales provide additional benefits to both the selling investors and their buyers. As stated in the BUY/SELL PROJECTIONS, a $10,000 bonus is added to the sales price of each house, since the Seller/Investor will accept a down payment and carry the balance. As mentioned throughout this book, many potential and financially capable buyers are unable to purchase a home because of restrictive banking and mortgage lending requirements and qualifying criteria, no matter the financial capability of the buyer. To us, these restrictions are a form of economic violence perpetrated by the in-the-box system upon far too many Americans and their families. As quite a few of us know by now, millions of families lost their homes due to the foreclosure crisis and most of those losses were not the fault of the homeowner. It is unknown at this time how many Americans will lose their homes and more due to the economic shutdown unlawfully forced upon this country on the premise of a phony health crisis. This book might help many of them save their homes or enable to sell their homes prior to actual foreclosure.

Since the Seller/Investor accepts a down payment and carries the balance, the $10,000 bonus serves both the interests of the seller and the buyer. The projected sales price for 15,308 houses is $1,021,079,788, to which is added $153,080,000 for a total of $1,174,159,788. From this figure, the existing house debt of $602,463 is subtracted, which leaves a profit of $571,696,788 from house sales. To this is added the Year Twenty One Alternative Projected Profit of $71,447,248 and the Year Twenty Alternative Projected Profit of $44,646 for a projected profit total of $643,188,682 from sales to renters and other house buyers. The following figures will illustrate this.

$1,021,079,788 – **Projected Sales Prices for 15,308 houses**

+ $ 153,080,000 – **$10,000 bonus per house**

$ 1,174,159,788 – **Projected Total Sales to renters and other house buyers**
An average price of $76,700 per house

- $ 602,463,000 – **Existing House Debt - Assumed by Buyer**

$ 571,696,788 – **Buyer pays at closing - Seller's Projected Profit**

The Seller/Investor sells to the renters/house buyers, accepts a down payment and carries mortgage notes for the buyers. When sellers carry notes for the balance of the purchase price for buyers, this provides many of these buyers with opportunities they would not have received through the usual system's banking requirements. The average sales price is projected to be $76,700, as indicated above. The projected down payment per house is $22,000, 28.6% of the selling price. $76,700 - $22,000 = $54,700 carried for buyer by seller. At $22,000 down payment per house, times 15,308 houses, that amount is $336,776,000, which, subtracted from projected profit of $571,696,788, leaves $234,920,788 in mortgage notes seller will carry. As projected in the BUY/ SELL PROJECTIONS, the second mortgage note is carried by the seller at 10% per year, paid over ten years, with principal balance due on the anniversary of closing in ten years. At 10% per year, total interest is $234,920,788. The down payment amount is projected at $336,776,000, plus note principal of $234,920,788, plus note interest of $234,920,788, plus Year Twenty One Alternative Profit of $71,447,248, plus $44,646 Year Twenty Alternative Profit, which totals a projected Total Profit of $878,109,470.

Figures follow below:

$336,776,000 – **$22,000 x 15,308 houses – down payments**

$234,920,788 – **Principal Notes Amount**

$234,920,788 – **Notes Total Interest**

+ $ 71,447,248 – **Year Twenty One Alternative Projected Profit**

+ $ 44,646 – **Year Twenty Alternative Projected Profit**

$878,109,470 – **Projected Profit**

Year Twenty One Alternative Projected Profit from Sales to Renters and Other House Buyers

$878,109,470

Buyer's Average House Price and Mortgage Expenses

As stated in the last projection, the average house price paid by the buyer is $76,700. This is derived, as follows:

$1,021,079,788 – Projected Sales Price for 15,308 houses
+ $ 153,080,000 – $10,000 bonus price per house
$1,174,159,788, divided by 15,308 houses = **$76,702**

$602,463,000 – Assumed existing house debt, divided by 15,308 houses = $39,356 per house

Projected House Price, Down Payment and Mortgage Expenses

$76,700 – Projected Sales Price
- $39,356 – Assumed Existing Debt
$37,344 – Balance
- $22,000 – Down Payment
$15,344 – Second Mortgage

Projected Debt Service for First and Second Mortgages

$39,356 – First Mortgage at $390.17 x 12   = $4,682 per year
$15,344 – Second Mortgage at 10% per year = $1,534 per year
$6,216, divided by 12, = **$518 per month**

Average Monthly Payment: $518

In earlier CHAPTERs, we presented possible solutions for down payment concerns. A $22,000 down payment for a house, when the seller carries the balance of the purchase price in notes is quite reasonable. This amounts to 28.6% of the projected selling price. However, in some situations, an interested financially capable buyer may be unable to make the $22,000 down payment, but could easily make a lesser payment, such as $12,000 or $15,000. A willing seller can add the difference to the second mortgage amount, in this case, $7,000 to $10,000, or carry these amounts over three to five years in added monthly payments. This amounts to $116.66 per month, plus interest, for $7,000, carried over 60 months, and $194.44, plus interest, carried for 36 months. For $10,000, that cost is $166.66, plus interest, per month for 60 months and $277.77, plus interest, for 36 months. After these payments have been made, the debt service returns to the projected $518 per month. This type of personalized purchase and willingness on the seller's part to help the buyer buy the house greatly benefits the buyer who would not have had the ability to purchase a home in the system's way.

YEAR TWENTY ONE ALTERNATIVE — PROJECTED
YEAR 21 SALES AND PROFITS TO RENTERS AND HOUSE BUYERS
$878,109,470 – Projected Profit

Projected Returns to Investors:

Investors	Amt. Invested	Cash @ Closing	Note Principal	Note Interest	Profit	% Return
1	$600,000	$408,267,894	$234,920,788	$234,920,788	$878,109,470	146,351%
2	$300,000	$204,133,947	$117,460,394	$117,460,394	$439,059,735	146,351%
	Each	Each	Each	Each	Each	Each
5	$120,000	$ 81,653,579	$ 46,984,158	$ 46,984,158	$175,621,985	146,351%
	Each	Each	Each	Each	Each	Each
8	$ 75,000	$ 51,033,487	$ 29,365,099	$ 29,365,099	$109,763,685	146,351%
	Each	Each	Each	Each	Each	Each
10	$ 60,000	$ 40,826,789	$ 23,492,078	$ 23,492,078	$ 87,810,945	146,351%
	Each	Each	Each	Each	Each	Each
15	$ 40,000	$ 27,217,859	$ 15,661,385	$ 15,661,385	$ 58,540,629	146,351%
	Each	Each	Each	Each	Each	Each
20	$ 30,000	$ 20,413,399	$ 11,746,039	$ 11,746,039	$ 43,905,472	146,351%
	Each	Each	Each	Each	Each	Each
25	$ 24,000	$ 16,330,715	$ 9,396,832	$ 9,396,832	$ 35,124,379	146,351%
	Each	Each	Each	Each	Each	Each

YEAR TWENTY ONE ALTERNATIVE – PROJECTED YEARLY NOTE PAYMENTS RECEIVED BY INVESTORS OVER TEN YEARS

Projected Returns to Investors:

Investors	Note Amt.	Yearly Paymt.	Interest Total	Note Principal	Total P & I	Avg. Yearly Paymt.
1	$234,920,788	$23,492,078	$234,920,788	$23,492,078	$469,841,576	$46,984,157
2	$117,460,394	$11,746,039	$117,460,394	$117,460,394	$234,920,788	$23,492,078
	Each	Each	Each	Each	Each	Each
5	$ 46,984,158	$ 4,698,415	$ 46,984,158	$ 46,984,158	$ 93,968,316	$ 9,396,831
	Each	Each	Each	Each	Each	Each
8	$ 29,365,099	$ 2,936,500	$ 29,365,099	$ 29,365,099	$ 58,730,198	$ 5,873,019
	Each	Each	Each	Each	Each	Each
10	$ 23,492,078	$ 2,349,207	$ 23,492,078	$ 23,492,078	$ 46,984,156	$ 4,698,415
	Each	Each	Each	Each	Each	Each
15	$ 15,661,385	$ 1,566,613	$ 15,661,385	$ 15,661,385	$ 31,322,770	$ 3,132,277
	Each	Each	Each	Each	Each	Each
20	$ 11,746,039	$1,174,603	$ 11,746,039	$ 11,746,039	$ 23,492,078	$ 2,349,207
	Each	Each	Each	Each	Each	Each
25	$ 9,396,832	$ 939,683	$ 9,396,832	$ 9,396,832	$ 18,793,664	$ 1,879,366
	Each	Each	Each	Each	Each	Each

The last projection in this series follows, and projects a house inventory sale to a Buyer for $600,000,000 cash at closing, plus debt assumption and returns to our Seller/Investor(s) based upon their respective investment amounts. $600,000,000 cash paid by Buyer and received at closing by our Owner/investor(s) provides a projected 11.907% return to the Buyer. The existing debt service assumed by the Buyer is paid through the tenants' rents.

Previous projections provide additional financial benefits which accrue to the Buyer. These are a 3% per year house value appreciation, which amounts to $37,963,840 per year. Equity appreciation through debt reduction is projected at $52,047,200 per year. When the projected profit of $71,447,248 is added to these, this amounts to $161,458,288. In approximately three and a half years, the Buyer can realize his $600,000,000 cash investment.

YEAR TWENTY ONE ALTERNATIVE
– PROJECTED SALES AND PROFITS TO BUYER/INVESTOR

Projection: Buyer/Investor pays $600,000 cash (11.907% return) at closing and assumes $602,463,000 in existing house debt.

Projected Sales Price: $1,202,463,000
Projected Returns to Investors:

Investors	Amount Invested	Profit	Percentage Return
1	$600,000	$600,000,000	100,000%
2	$300,000	$300,000,000 Each	100,000%
5	$120,000	$120,000,000 Each	100,000%
8	$ 75,000	$ 75,000,000 Each	100,000%
10	$ 60,000	$ 60,000,000 Each	100,000%
15	$ 40,000	$ 40,000,000 Each	100,000%
20	$ 30,000	$ 30,000,000 Each	100,000%
25	$ 24,000	$ 24,000,000 Each	100,000%

YEAR TWENTY ALTERNATIVE PROJECTED PROFITS AND PROJECTED RETURNS TO INVESTORS

$348,226,211 Profit

Investors	Amount Invested	Profit	Percentage Return
1	$600,000	$348,226,211	58,037%
2	$300,000 each	$174,113,105 each	58,037%
5	$120,000 each	$ 69,645,242 each	58,037%
8	$ 75,000 each	$ 43,528,276 each	58,037%

10	$ 60,000 each	$ 34,822,621 each	58,037%
15	$ 40,000 each	$ 23,215,080 each	58,037%
20	$ 30,000 each	$ 17,411,310 each	58,037%
25	$ 24,000 each	$ 13,929,048 each	58,037%

<u>R1-BORROW-RENT – SELL – EQUITY INVESTMENT PROGRAM PROJECTIONS - 20 YEARS</u>

$600,000 investment buys 65 houses priced at $60,000 each.

15% down payment = $9,000 x 65 houses = $585,000.

The remaining $15,000 is used to purchase one (1) home to convert into office space.

Seller carries $51,000 note, per house, for 15 years, principal and interest monthly payments of $390.17. Rents start at $750 per month, per house. Funds are borrowed in these Projection for houses purchases, combined with purchases from Profits.

<u>YEAR ONE</u>

RENT: $750 x 12 x 65 houses...$585,000

EXPENSES: Mortgage notes = $390.17 x 12 x 65.....................$304,332

Taxes..............$500.00 x 65...........................$ 32,500

Insurance..........$525.00 x 65.........................$ 34,125

Vacancies and repairs – 10%...........................$ 58,500

Manager...$ 45,000

Secretary ....$ 30,000

Miscellaneous...$ 3,000

$507,457............$507,457

Projected Profit End of Year One .... $ 77,543

Costs for purchase of 8 houses @ $9,000 in Year Two ....$ 72,000

Net Profit Year One ....$ 5,543

Total houses owned going into Year Two: 65 + 8 = 73 houses

YEAR TWO

73 houses owned at start of Year Two

RENT: $765 x 12 x 73 houses...$670,140

EXPENSES:

Mortgage notes = $390.17 x 12 x 73....................	$341,788	
Taxes...............$500.00 x 73...........................	$ 36,500	
Insurance..........$525.00 x 73.........................	$ 38,325	
Vacancies and repairs – 10%	$ 67,014	
Manager..	$ 45,000	
Secretary..	$ 30,000	
Miscellaneous...	$ 3,000	

$561,627......$561,627

Projected Profit End of Year Two $108,513

Costs for purchase of 11 houses @ $9,000 for Year Three .... $ 99,000

Net Profit Year Two ....$ 9,513

Total houses owned going into Year Three: 73 + 11 = 84 houses

YEAR THREE

84 houses owned at start of Year Three

RENT: $780 x 12 x 84 houses..$786,240

EXPENSES:

Mortgage notes = $390.17 x 12 x 84....................	$393,291	
Taxes...............$500.00 x 84...........................	$ 42,000	
Insurance..........$525.00 x 84.........................	$ 44,100	
Vacancies and repairs – 10%...........................	$ 78,624	
Manager..	$ 45,000	
Secretary..	$ 30,000	
Miscellaneous...	$ 3,000	

$636,015......$636,015

Projected Profit End of Year Three $150,225

Costs for purchase of 15 houses @ $9,000 for Year Four ....$ 135,000

Net Profit Year Three............................ $ 15,225

Total houses owned going into Year Four: 84 + 15 = 99 houses

YEAR FOUR

99 houses owned at start of Year Three

RENT: $780 x 12 x 99 houses...$938,520

EXPENSES:	Mortgage notes = $390.17 x 12 x 99.................	$463,521	
	Taxes...............$500.00 x 99.......................	$ 49,500	
	Insurance..........$525.00 x 99.......................	$ 51,975	
	Vacancies and repairs – 10%..........................	$ 93,852	
	Manager...	$ 45,000	
	Secretary...	$ 30,000	
	Miscellaneous..	$ 3,000	
		$736,848......$736,848	

Projected Profit End of Year Four $201,672

Costs for purchase of 22 houses @ $9,000 for Year Five ....$ 198,000

Net Profit Year Four.......................... $ 3,672

Total houses owned going into Year Five: 99 + 22 = 121 houses

YEAR FIVE

121 houses owned at start of Year Five.   First Loan is taken in Year Five.

RENT: $805 x 12 x 121 houses..$1,168,860

EXPENSES:	Mortgage notes = $390.17 x 12 x 121...............	$566,526	
	Taxes...............$575.00 x 121....................	$ 69,575	
	Insurance..........$600.00 x 121....................	$ 72,600	
	Vacancies and repairs – 10%..........................	$116,886	
	Manager...	$ 45,000	
	Secretary...	$ 30,000	
	Miscellaneous..	$ 3,000	
		$903,587........$903,587	

Projected Profit End of Year Five $265,273

First Loan -- $3,000,000, at 7% interest, paid on anniversary of loan, principal carried through Year 20

      $3,265, 273 – funds to buy houses from the $265,273 profit and the $3,000,000 loan

     - $1,980,000 purchases 220 houses at $9,000 down payment, each

     <u>- $1,275,000</u> **purchases 85 houses at $15,000 down payment, each**

     $ 10,273 cash available

Total houses owned going into Year Six: 121 9K houses, previously, + 220 at 9K = 341 9K houses

85 houses for 15K = 85 15K houses

Total houses for Year Six = 426

YEAR SIX

426 houses owned at start of Year Six

RENT: 9K -- 341 x $815 x 12.. $3,334,980

15K – 85 x $1,100 x 12 ....   <u>$1,122,000</u>

                                                     $4,456,980

EXPENSES:	Mortgage: 341 x $390.17 x 12	$1,596,575
	85 x 650.29 x 12	$ 663,295
	Taxes: 341 x $575	$ 196,075
	85 x $1,100	$ 93,500
	Insurance: 341 x $600	$ 204,600
	85 x $1,000	$ 85,000
	Vacancies and repairs – 10%.................	$ 445,698
	Manager...	$ 55,000
	Secretary..	$ 35,000
	Clerk	$ 30,000
	Miscellaneous.....................................	$<u> 5,000 </u>

                                           $3,409,743...... <u>$3,409,743</u>

                    Projected Net Profit End of Year Six............ $1,047,237

$1,047,237 – Year Six Projected Profit

-   210,000 – interest payment on $3,000,000 loan

$ 837,237 – funds to buy houses

- $450,000 -- 50 houses at $9,000 down payment, each

- $345,000 -- 23 houses at $15,000 down payment, each

$ **42,237 – available cash**

Total houses owned going into Year Seven: 341 9K houses, previously, + 50 for 9K = 391 9K houses

85 houses for 15K, previously, + 23 = 108 15K houses = Total houses for Year Seven = 499

YEAR SEVEN

499 houses owned at start of Year Five

RENT: 391 x $830 x 12 .... $3,894,360

108 x $1,115 x 12 .... $1,445,040

$5,339,400

EXPENSES:		
Mortgages = 391 x $390.17 x 12	$ 1,830,677	
108 x $650.29 x 12	$ 842,775	
Taxes...............$575.00 x 391.....................	$ 224,825	
$1,100 x 108	$ 118,800	
Insurance..........$600.00 x 391.....................	$ 234,600	
$1,000 x 108	$ 108,800	
Vacancies and repairs – 10%..............................	$ 533,940	
Manager..	$ 65,000	
Secretary..	$ 40,000	
Clerk	$ 30,000	
Two Buyers, Closers & Closing Costs	$ 90,000	
Two Maintenance Men & Equipment	$ 95,000	
Miscellaneous..	$ 50,000	
	$ 4,263,617........$4,263,617	
Projected Profit End of Year Seven $1,075,783		

Loan and Profit Figures Follow

$1,075,783 Year Seven Projected Profit

- $ 210,000 interest on $3,000,000 loan

 $ 865,703 – funds to buy houses

- $ 495,000 – 55 houses at 9K

- $ 330,000 – 22 houses at 15K

 $ 40,783 – available cash

Total houses owned going into Year Eight: 391 9K houses, previously, + 55 for 9K = 446 9K houses

108 houses for 15K, previously, + 22 = 130 15K houses

Total houses for Year Eight= 576

YEAR EIGHT

576 houses owned at start of Year Eight

RENT: 446 x $845 x 12		$4,522,440
130 x $1,130 x 12		$1,762,800
		$6,285,240
EXPENSES: Mortgages = 446 x $390.17 x 12	$ 2,088,189	
130 x $650.29 x 12	$ 1,014,452	
Taxes..............$575.00 x 446........................	$ 256,450	
$1,100 x 130	$ 143,000	
Insurance..........$600.00 x 446........................	$ 267,600	
$1,000 x 130	$ 130,000	
Vacancies and repairs – 10%...........................	$ 628,524	
Manager...	$ 65,000	
Secretary...	$ 40,000	
Two Clerks	$ 60,000	
Four Buyers, Closers & Closing Costs	$ 180,000	
Three Maintenance Men & Equipment	$ 130,000	
Miscellaneous..	$ 75,000	
	$5,078,215...	$5,078,215
Projected Profit End of Year Eight		$1,207,025

Second Loan -- $7,000,000, at 7% interest, paid on anniversary of loan, principal carried through Year 20

$1,207,025 – Year Eight Projected Profit

$7,000,000 loan

$8,207,025 – Total of the $1,207,025 profit and the $7,000,000 loan

- $ 210,000 interest on $3,000,000 loan

$ 7,997,025 – funds to buy houses

-$4,410,000 – 490 houses at $9,000 down payment, each

- $3,540,000 – 236 houses at $15,000 down payment, each

$ 47,025 – available cash

Total houses owned going into Year Nine: 446 9K houses, previously, + 490 for 9K = 936 -9K houses

130 houses for 15K, previously, + 236 = 366 - 15K houses

Total houses for Year Nine = 1,302

YEAR NINE

1,302 houses owned at start of Year Nine, 936 at 9K and 366 at 15K

RENT: 936 x $860 x 12		$ 9,659,520
366 x $1,145 x 12		$ 5,028,840
Total Rent		**$14,688,360**
EXPENSES: Mortgages = 936 x $390.17 x 12	$ 4,382,389	
366 x $650.29 x 12.........................	$ 2,856,074	
Taxes...............$575.00 x 936........................	$ 538,200	
$1,100 x 366	$ 402,600	
Insurance...... .....$600.00 x 936.....................	$ 561,600	
$1,000 x 366	$ 366,000	
Vacancies and repairs – 10%..........................	$ 1,290,216	
Manager...	$ 80,000	
Assistant Manager......................................	$ 45,000	
Two Secretaries...	$ 80,000	
Two Clerks..	$ 60,000	

Six Buyers, Closers & Closing Costs	$ 270,000	
Four Maintenance Men & Equipment ....….	$ 140,000	
Miscellaneous..….....	$ 125,000	
Contingency.......................................…........	$ 250,000	
	$11,447,079...	$11,447,079
Projected Profit End of Year Nine		**$ 3,241,281**

Loan and Profit Figures Follow

$3,241,281 -- Year Nine Projected Profit

- $ 210,000 -- interest on $3,000,000 loan

- $ 490,000 -- interest on $7,000,000 loan

$ 2,541,841 – funds to buy houses

- $ 468,000 – 52 houses at 9K

- $ 420,000 – 28 houses at 15K

$ 1,653,841 – available cash

Total houses owned going into Year Ten: 936 9K houses, previously, + 52 for 9K = 988 9K houses

366 houses for 15K, previously, + 28 = 394 15K houses

Total houses for Year Ten= 1,382

YEAR TEN

1,382 houses owned at start of Year Ten, 988 at 9K and 394 at 15K

RENT: 988 x $875 x 12		$10,374,000
394 x $1,160 x 12		$ 5,484,480
Total Rent ....….....		**$15,858,480**
EXPENSES: Mortgages = 988 x $390.17 x 12	$ 4,625,855	
394 x $650.29 x 12 ....….....	$ 3,074,571	
Taxes..............$625.00 x 988....................	$ 617,500	
$1,150 x 394	$ 453,100	
Insurance..........$650.00 x 988....................	$ 642,200	
$1,050 x 394	$ 413,700	

Vacancies and repairs – 10%............................	$ 1,585,848
Manager...	$ 100,000
Assistant Manager..	$ 50,000
Two Secretaries...	$ 80,000
Two Clerks..	$ 60,000
Six Buyers, Closers & Closing Costs	$ 270,000
Maintenance Crew & Equipment	$ 140,000
Miscellaneous.......................................….....	$ 125,000
Contingency ………………………………………..	$ 250,000

$12,487,774... $12,487,774

Projected Profit End of Year Ten **$3,370,706**

Loan and Profit Figures Follow

$3,370,706 -- Year Ten Projected Profit

- **$ 210,000 -- interest on $3,000,000 loan**

- **$ 490,000 – interest on $7,000,000 loan**

$2,670,706 – funds to buy houses

- **$1,413,000 – 157 houses at 9K**

- **$1,155,000 -- 77 houses at 15K**

$ 102,706 – available cash

Total houses owned going into Year Eleven: 988-9K houses, previously, + 157 for 9K = 1,145-9K houses

394 houses for 15K, previously, + 77 = 471-15K houses

Total houses for Year Eleven= 1,606

YEAR ELEVEN

1,606 houses owned at start of Year Eleven, 1,145 at 9K and 471 at 15K

RENT: 1,145 x $890 x 12		$12,228,600
471 x $1,175 x 12		$ 6,641,100
Total Rent		**$18,869,700**

EXPENSES: Mortgages = 1,145 x $390.17 x 12	$ 5,360,935	
471 x $650.29 x 12	$ 3,675,439	
Taxes..............$625.00 x 1,145....................	$ 715,625	
$1,150 x 471	$ 541,650	
Insurance..........$650.00 x 1,145....................	$ 744,250	
$1,050 x 471	$ 494,550	
Vacancies and repairs – 10%................................	$ 1,889,970	
Manager...	$ 125,000	
Assistant Manager.......................................	$ 50,000	
Two Secretaries..	$ 80,000	
Three Clerks..	$ 90,000	
Eight Buyers, Closers & Closing Costs	$ 360,000	
Maintenance Crew & Equipment	$ 140,000	
Miscellaneous...	$ 150,000	
Contingency	$ 250,000	
	$14,664,419...	$14,66,419
Projected Profit End of Year Eleven......................		$ 4,205,281

Loan and Profit Figures Follow on the Next Page

Third Loan -- $12,000,000, at 7% interest, paid on anniversary of loan, principal carried through Year 20

$ 4,205,281 – **Year Eleven Projected Profit**

+$ 12,000,000 **loan**

$ 16,205,281 – **Total of the $4,205,281 profit and the $12,000,000 loan**

- $ 210,000 -- **interest on $3,000,000 loan**

- $ 490,000 – **interest on $7,000,000 loan**

$ 15,505,281 – **funds to buy houses**

-$ 8,505,000 – **945 houses at $9,000 down payment, each**

- $ 6,915,000 – **461 houses at $15,000 down payment, each**

$ 85,281 – **available cash**

Total houses owned going into Year Twelve: 1,145 - 9K houses, previously, + 945 for 9K = 2,090 9K houses

471 houses for 15K, previously, + 461 = 932 - 15K houses

Total houses for Year Twelve = 3,022

YEAR TWELVE

3,022 houses owned at start of Year Ten, 2,090 at 9K and 932 at 15K

RENT: 2,090 x $900 x 12 ……………………………………………..		$22,572,000
932 x $1,190 x 12 ………………………………………..		$13,085,280
Total Rent ……………………………………................		**$35,657,280**
EXPENSES: Mortgages = 2,090 x $390.17 x 12 ………………	$ 9,785,463	
932 x $650.29 x 12 …………….......	$ 7,272,843	
Taxes…………….$625.00 x 2,090………………..	$ 1,306,250	
$1,150 x 932 …………………...	$ 1,071,800	
Insurance………..$650.00 x 2,090………………..	$ 1,358,500	
$1,050 x 932 …………………...	$ 978,600	
Vacancies and repairs – 10%.................................	$ 3,565,728	
CFO…………………………………………….…	$ 150,000	
Manager…………………………………………….	$ 150,000	
Two Assistant Managers…………………………....	$ 120,000	
Four Secretaries…………………………………..	$ 160,000	
Five Clerks………………………………………..	$ 150,000	
Twelve Buyers, Closers & Closing Costs …………	$ 720,000	
Maintenance Crew & Equipment …………………	$ 200,000	
Administrative……………………………………..	$ 1,000,000	
Miscellaneous……………………………………....	$ 250,000	
Contingency …………………………………..…	$ 400,000	
Total Expenses………..	$28,639,184…	$28,639,184
Projected Profit End of Year Twelve……………		**$ 7,018,096**

$7,018,096 -- Year Twelve Projected Profit

- $ 210,000 -- interest on $3,000,000 loan

-$ 490,000 – interest on $7,000,000 loan

-$ 840,000 – interest on $12,000,000 loan

 $ 5,478,096 – funds to buy houses

- $3,150,000 – 350 houses at 9K

- $2,100,000 -- 140 houses at 15K

 $ 228,096 – available cash

Total houses owned going into Year Thirteen: 2,090 - 9K houses, previously, + 350 for 9K = 2,440 9K houses

932 houses for 15K, previously, + 140 = 1,072 - 15K houses

Total houses for Year Thirteen = 3,512

YEAR THIRTEEN

3,512 houses owned at start of Year Thirteen, 2,440 at 9K and 1,072 at 15K

RENT: 2,440 x $915 x 12 ………………………………………………		$ 26,791,200
1,072 x $1,200 x 12 ………………………………………..		$ 15,436,800
Total Rent ………………………………………………….		**$ 42,228,000**
EXPENSES: Mortgages = 2,440 x $390.17 x 12 ………………..	$ 11,424,177	
1,072 x $650.29 x 12 ……………….....	$ 8,365,330	
Taxes…………….$625.00 x 2,440……………….….	$ 1,525,000	
$1,150 x 1,072 ……………….….	$ 1,232,800	
Insurance………..$650.00 x 2,440……………….…...	$ 1,586,000	
$1,050 x 1,072 …………………..	$ 1,125,600	
Vacancies and repairs – 10%………………………….	$ 4,222,800	
CFO ……………………………………………………....	$ 175,000	
Manager………………………………………………..	$ 175,000	
Two Assistant Managers……………………………..	$ 120,000	
Four Secretaries……………………………………….	$ 160,000	
Five Clerks……………………………………………..	$ 150,000	
Twelve Buyers, Closers & Closing Costs ………….	$ 720,000	

Maintenance Crew & Equipment .... $ 200,000

Administrative .... $ 500,000

Miscellaneous... $ 250,000

Contingency .... $ 400,000

Total Expenses .... $32,331,707... $32,331,707

Projected Profit End of Year Thirteen........... **$ 9,896,293**

Loan and Profit Figures Follow on the Next Page

$9,896,293 -- Year Thirteen Projected Profit

- $ 210,000 -- interest on $3,000,000 loan

-$ 490,000 – interest on $7,000,000 loan

- $ 840,000 – interest on $12,000,000 loan

$ 8,356,293 – funds to buy houses

- $4,905,000 – 545 houses at 9K

- $3,225,000 -- 215 houses at 15K

$ 226,293 – available cash

Total houses owned going into Year Fourteen: 2,440 - 9K houses, previously, + 545 for 9K = 2,985 - 9K houses

1,072 houses for 15K, previously, + 215 = 1,287 - 15K houses

Total houses for Year Fourteen = 4,272

YEAR FOURTEEN

4,272 houses owned at start of Year Fourteen, 2,985 at 9K and 1,287 at 15K

RENT: 2,985 x $925 x 12 .... $ 33,133,500

1,287 x $1,215 x 12 .... $ 18,764,460

Total Rent .... **$ 51,897,960**

EXPENSES: Mortgages = 2,985 x $390.17 x 12 .... $ 13,975,889

1,287 x $650.29 x 12 ....…..... $ 10,043,078

Taxes..............$625.00 x 2,985.................... $ 1,865,625

$1,150 x 1,287 .... $ 1,480,050

Insurance...........$650.00 x 2,985.................... $ 1,940,250

$1,050 x 1,287 .... $ 1,351,350

Vacancies and repairs – 10%................................. $ 5,189,796

CFO .... $ 200,000

Two Managers…...….......................….….. $ 400,000

Four Assistant Managers….….......................….. $ 240,000

Eight Secretaries….. $ 320,000

Seven Clerks…... $ 245,000

Twelve Buyers, Closers & Closing Costs .... $ 720,000

Maintenance Crew & Equipment .... $ 250,000

Administrative .... $ 300,000

Miscellaneous….............................…........... $ 250,000

Contingency .... $ 400,000

Total Expenses .... $39,171,038... $39,171,038

Projected Profit End of Year Fourteen................... **$ 12,726,922**

Loan and Profit Figures Follow

Fourth Loan -- $100,000,000, at 7% interest, paid on anniversary of loan, principal carried through Year 20

$ 12,726,922 -- Year Fourteen Projected Profit

- $ 210,000 -- interest on $3,000,000 loan

-$ 490,000 – interest on $7,000,000 loan

- $ 840,000 – interest on $12,000,000 loan

$ 11,186,922 – net profit

+$100,000,000 – fourth loan

$111,186,922 – funds to buy houses

- $ 71,640,000 – 7,960 houses at 9K

- $ 39,315,000 – 2,621 houses at 15K

$ 231,922 – available cash

Total houses owned going into Year Fifteen: 2,985 - 9K houses, previously, + 7,960 for 9K = 10,945 - 9K houses

1,287 houses for 15K, previously, + 2,621 = 3,908 - 15K houses

Total houses for Year Fifteen = 14,853

YEAR FIFTEEN

14,853 houses owned at start of Year Fifteen, 10,945 at 9K and 3,908 at 15K

RENT: 10,945 x $940 x 12 ………………………………………… $ 123,459,600

3,908 x $1,215 x 12 …………………………………….. $ 57,682,080

Total Rent …………………………………………….. **$ 181,141,680**

EXPENSES: Mortgages = 10,945 x $390.17 x 12 ……………… $ 51,244,927

3,908 x $650.29 x 12 ………………...... $ 30,495,999

Taxes…………..$700.00 x 10,945………………….. $ 7,661,500

$1,100 x 3,908 ………………… $ 4,298,800

Insurance………..$725.00 x 10,945……………….. $ 7,935,125

$1,200 x 3,908 ………………… $ 4,689,600

Vacancies and repairs – 10%................................ $ 18,141,680

CFO ……………………………………………….. $ 300,000

Management…....………………………………... $ 1,650,000

Office Staff …………………………………….… $ 1,400,000

Buyers, Closers & Closing Costs …………………. $ 1,850,000

Maintenance Crew & Equipment ………………… $ 650,000

Administrative ……………………………………... $ 1,000,000

Miscellaneous………………………………….......... $ 650,000

Contingency …………………………………….… $ 950,000

Total Expenses ………. $132,917,631…$132,917,631

Projected Profit End of Year Fifteen……………….. **$ 48,224,049**

Loan and Profit Figures Follow on the Next Page

$ 48,224,049 -- **Year Fifteen Projected Profit**

- $ 210,000 -- **interest on $3,000,000 loan**

- $ 490,000 – **interest on $7,000,000 loan**

- $ 840,000 – **interest on $12,000,000 loan**

- $ 7,000,000 – **interest on $100,000,000 loan**

$ 39,684,049 – **funds to buy houses**

- $ 25,875,000 – **2,875 houses at 9K**

- **$ 13,890,000** -- **926 houses at 15K**

$ (80,951) – available cash, borrowed from Year 14 Profit

Total houses owned going into Year Sixteen: 10,945 9K houses, previously, + 2,875 at 9K = 13,820 - 9K houses

3,908 houses for 15K, previously, + 926 = 4,834 - 15K houses

Total houses for Year Sixteen = 18,654

YEAR SIXTEEN

18,654 houses owned at start of Year Sixteen, 13,820 at 9K and 4,834 at 15K

RENT: 13,820 x $955 x 12		$ 158,377,200
4,834 x $1,245 x 12		$ 72,219,960
Total Rent		**$ 230,597,160**
EXPENSES: Mortgages = 13,820 – 65 x $390.17 x 12	$ 64,401,460	
4,834 x $650.29 x 12	$ 37,722,022	
Taxes...............$700.00 x 13,820...................	$ 9,674,000	
$1,100 x 4,834	$ 5,317,400	
Insurance..........$725.00 x 13,820.................	$ 10,019,500	
$1,200 x 4,834	$ 5,800,800	
Vacancies and repairs – 10%................................	$ 23,059,716	
CFO	$ 350,000	
Management.....................................…...	$ 2,775,000	
Office Staff	$ 2,350,000	
Buyers, Closers & Closing Costs	$ 3,100,000	
Maintenance Crew & Equipment	$ 1,200,000	
Administrative	$ 1,700,000	
Miscellaneous.................................……........	$ 1,100,000	
Contingency	$ 1,600,000	
Total Expenses ....……	$170,169,898...$170,169,898	
Projected Profit End of Year Sixteen.......................…...		**$ 60,427,262**

Loan and Profit Figures Follow

Fifth Loan -- $246,000,000, at 7% interest, paid on anniversary of loan, principal carried through Year 20

$ 246,000,000 -- Loan

$ 60,427,262 -- Year Sixteen Projected Profit- $ 210,000 -- interest on $3,000,000 loan

-$ 490,000 – interest on $7,000,000 loan- $ 840,000 – interest on $12,000,000 loan

-$ 7,000,000 – interest on $100,000,000 loan

-$ 189,720,000 – 21,080 houses at 9K

-$ 108,075,000 – 7,205 houses at 15K

$ 92,262 – available cash

Total houses owned going into Year Seventeen: 13,820 - 9K houses, previously, + 21,080 = 34,900 - 9K houses

4,834 houses for 15K, previously, + 7,205 = 12,039 - 15K houses

Total houses for Year Seventeen = 46,939

YEAR SEVENTEEN

46,939 houses owned at start of Year Seventeen, 34,900 at 9K and 12,039 at 15K

RENT: 34,900 x $970 x 12		$ 406,236,000
12,039 x $1,260 x 12		$ 182,029,680
Total Rent		**$ 588,265,680**
EXPENSES: Mortgages = 34,900 – 73 x $390.17 x 12 ....….	$ 163,061,407	
12,039 x $650.29 x 12 ....….	$ 93,946,096	
Taxes..............$700.00 x 34,900...................	$ 24,430,000	
$1,100 x 12,039 ....…...	$ 13,242,900	
Insurance..........$725.00 x 34,900.................	$ 25,302,500	
$1,200 x 12,039	$ 14,446,800	
Vacancies and repairs – 10%..............................	$ 58,826,568	
CFO ………………………………………………....	$ 400,000	
Management…....………………………………....	$ 7,000,000	
Office Staff …………………………………….…	$ 6,000,000	

Buyers, Closers & Closing Costs	$ 9,000,000	
Maintenance Crew & Equipment	$ 2,000,000	
Administrative	$ 8,000,000	
Miscellaneous..	$ 2,500,000	
Contingency	$ 3,000,000	
Total Expenses	$ 431,156,271....$431,156,271	
Projected Profit End of Year Seventeen..............	**$ 157,109,409**	

Loan and Profit Figures Follow on the Next Page

$ 157,109,409 -- **Year Seventeen Projected Profit**

-$ 210,000 -- **interest on $3,000,000 loan**

-$ 490,000 – **interest on $7,000,000 loan**

-$ 840,000 – **interest on $12,000,000 loan**

-$ 7,000,000 – **interest on $100,000,000 loan**

-$ 16,800,000 – **interest on $246,000,000 loan**

-$ 85,545,000 – **9,505 houses at 9K**

-$ 46,050,000 – **3,070 houses at 15K**

$ 174,409 – **available cash**

Total houses owned going into Year Eighteen: 34,900 - 9K houses, previously, + 9,505 = 44,405 - 9K houses

12,039 houses for 15K, previously, + 3,070 = 15,109 - 15K houses

Total houses for Year Eighteen = 59,514 houses

YEAR EIGHTEEN

59,514 houses owned at start of Year Eighteen, 44,405 at 9K and 15,109 at 15K

RENT: 44,405 x $985 x 12	$ 524,867,100	
15,109 x $1,275 x 12	$ 231,167,700	
Total Rent	**$ 756,034,800**	
EXPENSES: Mortgages = 44,405 – 84 x $390.17 x 12	$ 207,508,012	
15,105 x $650.29 x 12 ....…...	$ 117,902,779	
Taxes..............$700.00 x 44,405...................…..$ 31,083,500		
$1,100 x 15,109	$ 16,619,900	

Insurance………..$725.00 x 44,405………………	$	32,193,625
$1,200 x 15,109 ………………..	$	18,130,800
Vacancies and repairs – 10%………………………..	$	75,603,480
CFO ………………………………………………	$	500,000
Management…..………………………………….....	$	8,900,000
Office Staff ………………………………………….	$	7,700,000
Buyers, Closers & Closing Costs …………………..	$	9,000,000
Maintenance Crew & Equipment …………………..	$	2,550,000
Administrative ………………………………………	$	8,000,000
Miscellaneous……………………………………...........	$	3,000,000
Contingency …………………………………………$		5,000,000

Total Expenses ………. $ 543,696,096...$ 543,696,096

Projected Profit End of Year Eighteen…………...   **$ 212,338,704**

Loan and Profit Figures Follow on the Next Page

Sixth Loan -- $500,000,000 at 6% interest, paid on anniversary of loan, principal carried through Year 20

$ 500,000,000 -- Loan

$ 212,338,704 -- Year Eighteen Projected Profit

$ 712,338,704   Total

-$ 210,000 -- interest on $3,000,000 loan

-$ 490,000 – interest on $7,000,000 loan

-$ 840,000 – interest on $12,000,000 loan

-$ 7,000,000 – interest on $100,000,000 loan

-$ 16,800,000 – interest $246,000,000 loan

-$ 447,300,000 – 49,700 houses at 9K

-$ 239,520,000 – 15,968 houses at 15K

$ 178,704 – available cash

Total houses owned going into Year Nineteen: 44,405 - 9K houses, previously, + 49,700 = 94,105 - 9K houses

15,109 houses for 15K, previously, + 15,698 = 31,077 - 15K houses

Total houses for Year Nineteen = 125,182

YEAR NINETEEN

125,182 houses owned at start of Year Nineteen, 94,105 at 9K and 31,077 at 15K

RENT: 94,105 x $1,000 x 12 .... $ 1,129,260,000

31,077 x $1,290 x 12 .... $ 481,071,960

Total Rent **$1,610,331,960**

EXPENSES: Mortgages = 94,105 – 99 x $390.17 x 12 .... $ 440,139,852

31,077 x $650.29 x 12 .... $ 242,508,747

Taxes..............$700.00 x 94,105.................... $ 65,873,500

$1,100 x 31,077 .... $ 34,184,700

Insurance..........$725.00 x 94,105................ $ 68,226,125

$1,200 x 31,077 .... $ 37,292,400

Vacancies and repairs – 10%............................. $ 112,926,000

CFO .... $ 500,000

Management....................................... $ 18,750,000

Office Staff .... $ 16,200,000

Buyers, Closers & Closing Costs .... $ 15,000,000

Maintenance Crew & Equipment .... $ 5,500,000

Administrative .... $ 8,000,000

Miscellaneous....................................... $ 3,500,000

Total Expenses .... $1,068,601,324.....$1,068,601,324

Projected Profit End of Year Nineteen...............$ 541,730,636

Loan and Profit Figure

$ 1,025,000000 **Loan – 7th Loan**

$ 541,771,908 -- **Year Nineteen Projected Profit**

-$ 210,000 -- **interest on $3,000,000 loan**

-$ 490,000 – **interest on $7,000,000 loan**

-$ 840,000 – **interest on $12,000,000 loan**

-$ 7,000,000 – **interest on $100,000,000 loan**

-$ 16,800,000 – **interest on $246,000,000 loan**

-$ 30,000,000 – interest on $500,000,000 loan

-$ 312,975,000 – 34,775 houses at 9K

-$ <u>168,255,000</u> – 11,217 houses at 15K

 $ 5,394,741 – available cash

Total houses owned going into Year Twenty: 94,105 - 9K houses, previously, + 35,152 = 129,257 - 9K houses

31,077 houses for 15K, previously, + 11,339 = 42,416 - 15K houses

Total houses for Year Twenty = 171,673 houses

Year 19 Loan -

YEAR TWENTY

171,673 houses owned at start of Year Twenty, 129,257 at 9K and 42,416 at 15K

RENT: 129,257 x $1,020 x 12		$ 1,582,105,680
42,416 x $1,315 x 12		$ 669,324,480
Total Rent		**$ 2,251,430,160**
EXPENSES: Mortgages = 129,257 – 341 x $390.17 x 12	$ 603,589,869	
42,416 x $650.29 x 12	$ 330,992,407	
Taxes...............$700.00 x 129,257	$ 90,479,900	
$1,100 x 42,416	$ 46,657,600	
Insurance..........$725.00 x 129,257..................	$ 930,711,325	
$1,200 x 42,416	$ 50,899,200	
Vacancies and repairs – 10%...	$ 225,143,016	
CFO	$ 750,000	
Management.....……….............................	$ 37,500,000	
Office Staff	$ 32,000,000	
Buyers, Closers & Closing Costs	$ 25,000,000	
Maintenance Crew & Equipment	$ 12,000,000	
Administrative Contingency............................	$ 10,000,000	
Miscellaneous...	$ <u>7,000,000</u>	
Total Expenses .... $1,565,723,318...............		<u>$1,565,723,318</u>
Projected Profit – Year Twenty……………..		**$ 685,706,842**

Loan and Profit Figures Follow

$ 685,706,842 – Year Twenty Projected Profit

+$ 8,640,078 – Years One to Nineteen Profit

$ 694,346,920 -- Total

$868,000,000 was borrowed for this program, and the interest on the outstanding debt was paid each and every year. $694,346,920, Net Profit Years One to Twenty, was paid at the end of Year Twenty and reduced the principal balance to $173,653,080, which will be paid, plus interest, from the proceeds of the upcoming house sales at the end of Year Twenty.

R-3 YEAR TWENTY REGULAR - BORROW-EQUITY INVESTMENT PROGRAM

Projected House Sales, Total Debt and Profit

$ 13,781,621,465 – 171,673 House sales by 3% yearly appreciation

- $ 8,396,901,478 – House debt remaining – assumed by Buyer

- $ 173,653,080 – Borrowed debt remaining – Seller pays at closing

$ 5,211,066,907 – Seller's Profit / Buyer Pays

$ 5,211,066,907 – Profit – 868,511% Return on $600,000 Investment

$685,706,842 – Year Twenty Profit -- divided by $5,211,066,907– Buyer's Investment = 13.158% Return on Buyer's Investment

171,673 houses comprise the housing inventory, of which 129,257 are less expensive and 42,416 are more expensive. When we add in the note reduction and note appreciation of $679,830,000 per year, and the 3% yearly projected house value appreciation of approximately $413,448,644, this amounts to approximately $1,093,278,644. Yearly projected profit of $685,706,842, plus moderate rent increases of $180 per house, total $716,607,982. Combined with the figures above, the total amounts to $1,809,886,626. The Buyer can realize his investment of $5,211,066,907 in approximately 2.87 years. These asset values are intrinsic within the Program and will be paid upon Buyer's sale of the housing inventory. Please note that the appreciation value further increases by 3% per year of operationr, as does the moderate rent increases, which increase well beyond the figures provided for the first year of operation.

NOTE: $868,000,000 was borrowed for this program and interest was paid on the outstanding debt each year. The $868,000,000 principal amount remaining was paid down from Years One to Twenty Total Profits amount of $694,346,920, leaving a balance of $173,653,080, which was paid off from proceeds of house sales closings.

R-3 YEAR TWENTY REGULAR - BORROW -EQUITY INVESTMENT PROGRAM

SALE TO INSTITUTIONAL INVESTOR

This sales price of $15,000,000,000 was reached by calculating the Buyer's projected net profit, which is projected at 10.665%. This does NOT INCLUDE the projected moderate yearly rent increase of $180, per house, which would be an approximate 11.145% return on the Buyer's $6,429,445,442 investment.

Projected House Sales, Total Debt and Profit

$15,000,000,000 – Sales by Net Return to Buyer

- $ 8,396,901,478 – House debt remaining – assumed by Buyer

- $ 173,653,080 – Borrowed debt remaining – Paid by Seller

$6,429,445,442 – Seller's Profit / Buyer Pays

1,071,574% -- Return on $600,000 Investment

$685,706,842 – Year Twenty Profit -- divided by $6,429,445,442 – Buyer's Investment = 10.665% Return on Buyer's Investment.

171,673 houses comprise the housing inventory, of which 129,257 are less expensive and 42,416 are more expensive. When we add in the note reduction and note appreciation of $679,830,000 per year, and the 3% yearly projected house value appreciation of approximately $413,448,644, this amounts to approximately $1,093,278,644. Yearly projected profit of $685,706,842, plus moderate rent increases of $180 per house, total $716,607,982. When combined with the figures above, the total amounts to $1,809,886,626. The Buyer can realize his investment of $6,429,445,442 in approximately 3.552 years. These asset values are intrinsic within the Program and will be paid upon Buyer's sale of the housing inventory. Again, please note that appreciation values increase by 3% per year of operation, as do moderate rent increases,

R-3 YEAR TWENTY REGULAR - BORROW-EQUITY INVESTMENT PROGRAM

The $15,500,000,000 price was determined by calculating Buyer's return on his $6,929,443,442 investment, which is projected at 9.895%. When yearly rent increases of $180 per house are added, then the return on Buyer's $6,929,443,442 investment is projected at 10.34%.

Projected House Sales, Total Debt and Profit

$ 15,500,000,000 – Sales by Net Return

- $ 8,396,901,478 – House debt remaining – assumed by Buyer

- $ 173,653,080 – Borrowed debt remaining – paid by Seller

$6,929,445,442 – Seller's Profit / Buyer Pays

115,490% Return on $600,000 Investment

$685,706,842 – Year Twenty Profit -- divided by $6,929,445,442 – Buyer's Investment = 9.895% Return on Buyer's Investment. When the moderate projected yearly rent increase of $180 per house is added, then the projected return to Buyer is 10.34%.

171,673 houses comprise the housing inventory, of which 129,257 are less expensive and 42,416 are more expensive. When we add in the note reduction and note appreciation of $679,830,000 per year, and the 3% yearly projected house value appreciation of approximately $413,448,644, this amounts to approximately $1,093,278,644. Yearly projected profit of $685,706,842, plus moderate rent increases of $180 per house, total $716,607,982. When combined with the figures above, the total amounts to $1,809,886,626.

The Buyer can realize his investment of $6,929,445,442 in approximately 3.829 years. These asset values are intrinsic within the Program and will be paid upon Buyer's sale of the housing inventory.

YEAR TWENTY-ONE – PROFIT AND EXPENSE SHEET

The following Projections follow Year Twenty Borrow Program into Year Twenty One. No houses are purchased during Year Twenty One, therefore, the Profit is very substantial and provides an excellent basis, along with housing inventory, for excellent house inventory sales prices.

R-3 YEAR TWENTY ONE-REGULAR - BORROW -EQUITY INVESTMENT PROGRAM

Profit and Expense Sheet

YEAR TWENTY-ONE

129,257 + 42,416 = 171,673 houses owned at start of Year Twenty-One,

RENT: 129,257 x $1,040 x 12		$ 1,613,127,360
42,416 x $1,340 x 12		$ 682,049,280
Total Rent		**$ 2,295,176,640**
EXPENSES: Mortgages = 129,257 – 391 x $390.17 x 12		$ 603,355,767
42,416 - 85 x $650.29 x 12		$ 330,329,112
Taxes............$700.00 x 129,257		$ 90,479,900
$1,100 x 42,416		$ 46,657,600
Insurance.........$725.00 x 129,257		$ 93,711,325
$1,200 x 42,416		$ 50,899,200
Vacancies and repairs – 10%		$ 229,517,664
CFO		$ 750,000

Management…..………………………………......$ 31,875,000

Office Staff …………………………………………..$ 25,600,000

Maintenance Crew & Equipment …………………..$ 12,000,000

Administrative Contingency…………………………$ 5,000,000

Miscellaneous…………………………………...........$ 5,000,000

Total Expenses … $1,525,175,568……$1,525,175,568

Projected Profit End of Year Twenty.……………$ 770,001,072

R-3 YEAR TWENTY ONE REGULAR - BORROW -EQUITY INVESTMENT PROGRAM

Projected House Sales In Year 21, Total Debt and Profit

$ 14,204,428,660 – House sales by 3% House Appreciation

- $ 7,718,712,538 – House debt remaining – assumed by Buyer

 - $ 184,072,265 – Borrowed debt remaining – paid by Seller

 $ 6,301,643,857 – Buyer Pays/Seller's house sales Profit

+ $ 770,001,072 – Year Twenty-One Projected Profit

$ 7,071,644,429 –Projected Seller's Total Profit – 117,860% return on $600,000 inveswtment

---

$ 770,001,072 – Year Twenty-One Profit -- divided by $6,301,643,857– Buyer's Investment = 12.219% Return on Buyer's Investment. When projected rent increase of $180 per house per year is added, the projected return is 12.71% on Buyer's $6,301,643,857 investment.

NOTE: $868,000,000 was borrowed for this program and interest was paid on the outstanding debt each year. The $868,000,000 principal amount remaining was paid down from Years One to Twenty Total Profits amount of $694,346,920, leaving a balance of $173,653,080, plus interest, totaling $184,072,265 which was paid from proceeds of house sales closings.

171,673 houses comprise the housing inventory, of which 129,257 are less expensive and 42,416 are more expensive. When we add in the note reduction and note appreciation of $679,830,000 per year, and the 3% yearly projected house value appreciation of approximately $413,448,644, this amounts to approximately $1,093,278,644.   Yearly projected profit of $685,706,842, plus moderate rent increases of $180 per house, total $716,607,982. When combined with figures above, the total amounts to $1,809,886,626. The Buyer can realize his investment of $6,301,643,857 in approximately 3.481 years. These asset values are intrinsic within the Program and will be paid upon Buyer's sale of the housing inventory.

R-3 YEAR TWENTY ONE REGULAR - BORROW -EQUITY INVESTMENT PROGRAM

The $15,500,000,000 price was determined by assessing a fair and reasonable return to Buyer, which is 10.135% on his $7,597,215,197 investment. When moderate yearly rent increases of $180 per house per year are added to $770,001,072 projected profit, then the total return on investment is projected at 10.54%

Projected House Sales, Total Debt and Profit

$ 15,500,000,000	– House sales by Net Profit
- $ 7,718,712,538	– House debt remaining – assumed by Buyer
- $ 184,072,265	– Borrowed debt remaining – Paid by Seller
$ 7,597,215,197	– Buyer Pays/Seller's House Sales Profit
+$ 770,001,072	– Year Twenty-One Projected Profit
$ 8,367,216,269	– Seller's Total Profit

$ 770,001,072 – Year Twenty-One Profit -- divided by $7,597,215,197– Buyer's Investment = 10.135% Return on Buyer's Investment

171,673 houses comprise the housing inventory, of which 129,257 are less expensive and 42,416 are more expensive. When we add in the note reduction and note appreciation of $679,830,000 per year, and the 3% yearly projected house value appreciation of approximately $413,448,644, this amounts to approximately $1,093,278,644. Yearly projected profit of $685,706,842, plus moderate rent increases of $180 per house, total $716,607,982. When combined with the figures above, the total amounts to $1,809,886,626. The Buyer can realize his investment of $7,597,215,197 in approximately 4.197 years. These asset values are intrinsic within the Program and will be paid upon Buyer's sale of the housing inventory.

Year TWENTY ONE BORROW and Related Projections

YEAR TWENTY ONE REGULAR - BORROW-EQUITY INVESTMENT PROGRAM

The $16,000,000,000 price was determined by assessing a fair and reasonable return on Buyer's $8,097,215,197 investment, which is projected at 9.509%. When rent increases of $180 per house per year are added, then the projected return on Buyer's investment is 9.89%

Projected House Sales, Total Debt and Profit

$ 16,000,000,000	– House sales by Net Profit
- $ 7,718,712,538	– House debt remaining
- $ 184,072,265	– Borrowed debt remaining
$ 8,097,215,197	– Buyer Pays
+ $ 770,001,072	– Year Twenty-One Projected Profit
$ 8,867,216,269	– Seller's Total Profit

$ 770,001,072 – Year Twenty-One Profit -- divided by $8,097,215,197– Buyer's Investment = 9.509% Return on Buyer's Investment

171,673 houses comprise the housing inventory, of which 129,257 are less expensive and 42,416 are more expensive. When we add in the note reduction and note appreciation of $679,830,000 per year, and the 3% yearly projected house value appreciation of approximately $413,448,644, this amounts to approximately $1,093,278,644. Yearly projected profit of $685,706,842, plus moderate rent increases of $180 per house, total $716,607,982. When combined with figures above, the total amounts to $1,809,886,626 The Buyer can realize his investment of $8,097,215,197 in approximately 4.473 years. These asset values are intrinsic within the Program and will be paid upon Buyer's sale of the housing inventory.

YEAR TWENTY ALTERNATIVE and Related PROJECTIONS

The following Projections, Year Twenty Alternative, follow the same procedure as prior Year Twenty Alternatives. A commitment for a $1,025,000,000 loan was taken in Year Nineteen for purchase of houses in Year 20 Alternative, namely, 97,944 houses, 74,027 with a $9,000 down payment each and 23,917 with a $15,000 down payment each. Nineteen years of successful business operations clearly indicate that this and other subsequent loans are warranted. Additional loans will be taken on a monthly basis throughout Year Twenty Alternative. Collateral for the loans are the usual liens on the second and third mortgages and the entire business operation until all loans, plus interest, are fully paid. Since loans are made based upon sales contracts between owner/borrower and his buyers and not upon speculative purchases, the lender has little to no risk.

R-3 YEAR TWENTY ALTERNATIVE
Profit and Expense Sheet

MONTH ONE

Houses Owned:	$ 60,000	$100,000	
	129,257	42,416	
	74,027	23,917	-- Purchased from $1,025,000,000 Loan
	203,284 +	66,333 = 269,617	

RENTS:	203,284 x $1,020...	$ 207,349,680
	66,333 x $1,315...	$ 87,227,895
	Total Rents	$ 294,577,575
EXPENSES:	Mortgages 203,284 - 341 x $390.17...............	$79,182,270

66,333 x $650.29............................	$43,135,687
Taxes..............$700.00 x 203,284 / 12	$11,858,233
$1,100 x 66,333 / 12.....................	$ 6,080,525
Insurance..........$725.00 x 203,284 / 12..................	$12,281,742
$1,200 x 66,333 / 12.................	$ 6,633,300
Vacancies and repairs – 10%..	$29,457,757
CEO & Staff..	$ 125,000
Management & Staff..	$10,000,000
Office Staff	$ 8,825,000
Buyers, Closers, Closing Costs................................	$ 9,500,000
Maintenance & Staff....................................... .	$ 2,050,000
Administrative Contingency...............................	$ 2,950,000
Miscellaneous...	$ 2,350,000
Total Expenses	$244,429,514.......$244,429,514
Projected Profit End of Month One	....$ 70,148,061

Houses Purchased from Profit and Loan Proceeds

$70,148,061- Profit x 70% = $49,103,642 ÷ $9,000 = 5,454 houses   Plus $17,642

$70,148,061- Profit x 30% = $21,044,418 ÷ $15,000 = 1,402 houses   Plus $14,418

Loan = $820,000,000

x 70% = $574,000,000 ÷ $9,000 = 63,777 houses   Plus $ 7,000

x 30% = $246,000,000 ÷ $15,000 = 16,400 houses   Even...

Month One Incidental Profit................................ $39,060

Houses for Month Two:

$60,000	$100,000
5,454 -- From Profit	1,402 -- From Profit
63,777 -- From Loan	16,400 -- From Loan
203,284 -- Existing	66,333 -- Existing
272,515 -- Total	**84,135 -- Total**

R-3 YEAR TWENTY ALTERNATIVE
Profit and Expense Sheet

MONTH TWO

Houses Owned: $ 60,000 $100,000

5454 -- From Profit	1,402 -- From Profit
63,777 -- From Loan	16,400 -- From Loan
203,284 -- Existing	66,333 -- Existing
272,515	**84,135**

RENTS: 272,515 x $1,020……………………………………….. $ 277,965,300

                     84,135 x $1,315……………………………………….. $ 110,637,525

                 Total Rents ……………………………………………..... **$ 388,602,825**

EXPENSES: Mortgages   272,515 x $390.17………………..…….. $106,327,177

                            84,135 x $650.29…………………..…….. $ 54,712,149

                 Taxes…………..$700.00 x 272,515 / 12 ……………... $ 15,896,708

                          $1,100 x 84,135 / 12……………...……. $ 7,712,375

                 Insurance………..$725.00 x 272,515 / 12……………..…. $ 16,464,448

                          $1,200 x 84,135 / 12……………..…. $ 8,413,500

                 Vacancies and repairs – 10%………………………........…. $ 38,860,282

                 CEO & Staff……………………………………………… $ 250,000

                 Management & Staff……..…………………….....……. $ 12,950,000

                 Office Staff ………………………………………….…. $ 11,000,000

                 Buyers, Closers, Closing Costs………………….…....……. $ 12,500,000

                 Maintenance & Staff…………………………………….$ 2,750,000

                 Administrative Contingency…………………………… $ 3,886,000

                 Miscellaneous……………………………...............…. $ 3,350,000

                 Total Expenses $286,659,139……..$286,659,139

                 Projected Profit End of Month Two ……….…………………………….....**$101,943,686**

Houses Purchased from Profit and Loan Proceeds

$101,943,686-Profit x 70% = $71,360,580 ÷ $9,000 = 7,289 houses Plus $5,759,580

$101,943,686 -Profitx 30% = $30,583,106 ÷ $15,000 = 1,874 houses Plus $2,473,106

$8,232,686

Loan = $770,000,000

x 65% = $500,500,000 ÷ $9,000 = 55,611 houses   Plus $ 1,000

x 35% = $269,500,000 ÷ $15,000 = 17,966 houses   Plus $10,000

$11,000

Month Two Incidental Profit……………………………………..$8,243,686

Houses for Month Three:

$60,000	$100,000
7,289 -- From Profit	1,874 -- From Profit
55,611 -- From Loan	17,966 -- From Loan
272,515 -- Existing	84,135 -- Existing
335,415 -- Total	103,975 -- Total

R-3 YEAR TWENTY ALTERNATIVE
Profit and Expense Sheet

MONTH THREE

Houses Owned:	$ 60,000	$100,000
	7,289 -- From Profit	1,874 -- From Profit
	55,611 -- From Loan	17,966 -- From Loan
	272,515 -- Existing	84,135 -- Existing
	335,415 -- Total	103,975 -- Total

RENTS:	335,415 x $1,020	....	$342,123,300
	103,975 x $1,315	....	$136,727,125
	Total Rents	....	**$478,850,425**
EXPENSES:	Mortgages	335,415 x $390.17.........................	$130,868,871
		103,975 x $650.29...........................	$ 67,613,903
	Taxes..............$700.00 x 335,415 / 12		$ 19,565,875
		$1,100 x 103,975 / 12.....................	$ 9,531,042
	Insurance..........$725.00 x 335,415 / 12...................		$ 20,264,656
		$1,200 x 103,975 / 12...................	$ 10,397,500
	Vacancies and repairs – 10%..		$ 47,885,042
	CEO & Staff..		$ 300,000
	Management & Staff..		$ 16,000,000
	Office Staff		$ 14,000,000
	Buyers, Closers, Closing Costs.............................		$ 15,000,000
	Maintenance & Staff...		$ 3,500,000
	Administrative Contingency....................................		$ 4,500,000
	Miscellaneous...		$ 3,800,000
	Total Expenses	$363,226,889........$363,226,889
	Projected Profit End of Month Three...$115,623,536

Houses Purchased from Profit and Loan Proceeds

$115,623,536 x 70% = $80,936,475 ÷ $9,000   = 9,007 houses   **Minus $126,525**

$115,623,536 x 30% = $34,687,061 ÷ $15,000 = 2,316 houses   **Minus $ 52,939**

                                                  Minus Total $179,464

Loan = $965,000,000

x 65% = $627,250,000 / $9,000   = 69,694 houses   **Plus $ 4,000**

x 35% = $337,750,000 / $15,000 = 22,516 houses   **Plus $10,000**

                                                      $14,000

Month Three Incidental -- ....Minus ($165,464)

Houses for Month Four:

$60,000	$100,000
9,007 -- From Profit	2,316 -- From Profit
69,694 -- From Loan	22,516 -- From Loan
335,415 -- Existing	103,975 -- Existing
414,116 -- Total	**128,807 -- Total**

R-3 YEAR TWENTY ALTERNATIVE
Profit and Expense Sheet

MONTH FOUR

Houses Owned: $ 60,000 $100,000

78,701 – New Purchase	24,832 – New Purchase
335,415 -- Existing	103,975 -- Existing
414,116 -- Total	**128,807 -- Total**

RENTS:

414,116 x $1020... $ 422,398,320

128,807 x $1315... $ 169,381,205

Total Rents **$591,779,525**

EXPENSES:

Mortgages   514,116 x $390.17........................... $161,575,639

128,807 x $650.29............................. $ 83,761,904

Taxes ....$700.00 x 414,116 / 12 .... $ 24,156,767

$1,100 x 128,807 / 12..................... $ 11,807,308

Insurance..........$725.00 x 414,116 / 12.................... $ 25,019,508

$1,200 x 128,807 / 12.................... $ 12,880,700

Vacancies and repairs – 10%............................... $ 59,078,275

CEO & Staff.. $ 400,000

Management & Staff…….………….………….............	$ 16,250,000
Office Staff ……………………………………………	$ 14,250,000
Buyers, Closers, Closing Costs…………….………........	$ 15,000,000
Maintenance & Staff….………….………………………	$ 3,750,000
Administrative Contingency.…………………………	$ 5,000,000
Miscellaneous.……………………………..…...............	$ 4,000,000
Total Expenses	$436,930,101……436,930,101
Projected Profit End of Month Four..………………………………………...**$154,849,424**	

Houses Purchased from Profit and Loan Proceeds

$154,849,424 x 70% = $108,394,597 ÷ $9,000 = 12,016 houses   + $250,597

$154,849 x 30% = $46,454,827 ÷ $15,000 = 3,090 houses   + $104,827

Profit Total: **$355,424**

<u>**Loan = $1,220,154,000**</u>

x 70% = $854,107,800 ÷ $9,000   = 94,900 houses   + $ 7,800

x 30% = $360,046,200 ÷ $15,000 = 24,003 houses   + $ 1,200

$ 9,000

Month Four Incidental Profit…………………………………………$364,424

Houses for Month Five:

<u>$60,000</u>	<u>$100,000</u>
12,016 -- From Profit	3,090 -- From Profit
94,900 -- From Loan	24,003 -- From Loan
<u>414,116</u> -- Existing	<u>128,807</u> -- Existing
521,032 -- Total	**155,900 – Total**

676,932 Houses for Month Five

R-3 YEAR TWENTY ALTERNATIVE
Profit and Expense Sheet

MONTH FIVE

Houses Owned: $ 60,000 $100,000

106,916 – New Purchase	27,093 – New Purchase
414,116 -- Existing	128,807 -- Existing
521,032 -- Total	**155,900 -- Total**

RENTS:

521,032 x $1020..	$ 531,452,640
155,900 x $1315..	$205,008,500
Total Rents	**$736,461,140**

EXPENSES:

Mortgages	521,032 x $390.17......................	$203,291,055
	155,900 x $650.29.......................	$101,380,211
Taxes..............$700.00 x 521,032 / 12		$ 30,393,533
	$1,100 x 155,900 / 12.................	$ 14,290,833
Insurance..........$725.00 x 521,032 / 12................		$ 31,479,017
	$1,200 x 155,900 / 12...............	$ 15,590,000
Vacancies and repairs – 10%........................		$ 73,456,437
CEO & Staff..		$ 400,000
Management & Staff....................................		$ 16,500,000
Office Staff		$ 14,500,000
Buyers, Closers, Closing Costs...........................		$ 15,000,000
Administrative Contingency...............................		$ 6,300,000
Miscellaneous...		$ 4,500,000
Total Expenses	$527,171,086.........$527,171,086	
Projected Profit End of Month Five...**$209,290,054**		

Houses Purchased from Profit and Loan Proceeds

$209,290,054 x 65% = $136,038,535 ÷ $9,000 = 15,090 houses   + $228,535

$209,290,054 x 35% = $73,126,020 ÷ $15,000 = 4,875 houses   + $ 1,020

                           Profit Total: $229,555

Loan = $1,485,000,000

x 65% = $965,250,000 ÷ $9,000 = 107,250 houses   Even

x 35% = $519,750,000 ÷ $15,000 = 34,650 houses   Even

Month Five Incidental Profit...$229,555

Houses for Month Six:

$60,000	$100,000
15,090 -- From Profit	4,875 -- From Profit
107,250 -- From Loan	34,650 -- From Loan
521,032-- Existing	155,900 -- Existing
643,372 -- Total	**195,425 – Total**

838,797 Houses for Month Six

R-3 YEAR TWENTY ALTERNATIVE
Profit and Expense Sheet

MONTH SIX

Houses Owned:	$ 60,000	$100,000
	122,340 – New Purchase	39,525 – New Purchase
	521,032 -- Existing	155,900 -- Existing
	643,372 -- Total	**195,425 -- Total**

RENTS:	643,372 x $1020..	$656,239,440
	195,425 x $1315..	$256,983,875
	Total Rents	**$913,223,315**

EXPENSES:	Mortgages	643,372 x $390.17........................	$251,024,453
		195,425 x $650.29........................	$127,082,923
	Taxes..............$700.00 x 643,372 / 12		$ 37,530,033
		$1,100 x 195,425 / 12...................	$ 17,913,958
	Insurance..........$725.00 x 643,372 / 12................		$ 38,870,392
		$1,200 x 195,425 / 12..............	$ 19,542,500
	Vacancies and repairs – 10%..		$ 91,222,654
	CEO & Staff...		$ 475,000
	Management & Staff...		$ 20,000,000
	Office Staff		$ 17,500,000
	Buyers, Closers, Closing Costs............................		$ 15,000,000
	Maintenance and Staff.....................................		$ 6,000,000
	Administrative Contingency................................		$ 8,000,000
	Miscellaneous..		$ 5,750,000
	Total Expenses	$655,911,913..........$655,911,913

Projected Profit End of Month Six..$257,311,402

Houses Purchased from Profit and Loan Proceeds

$257,311,402 x 65% = $167,252,411 ÷ $9,000 = 18,583 houses   + $ 5,411

$257,311,402 x 35% = $ 90,058,990 ÷ $15,000 = 6,003 houses   + $ 13,990

                                                    Profit Total: $ 19,401

Loan = $1,875,000,000

x 70% = $1,312,500,000 ÷ $9,000 = 145,833 houses   + $ 3,000

 x 30% = $562,000,000 ÷ $15,000 = 37,500 houses   Even

Month Six Incidental Profit..$22,401

Houses for Month Seven:

$60,000	$100,000
18,583 -- From Profit	6,003 -- From Profit
145,833 -- From Loan	37,500 -- From Loan
643,372 -- Existing	195,425 -- Existing
807,788 -- Total	**238,928 – Total**

1,046,716 Houses for Month Seven

R-3 YEAR TWENTY ALTERNATIVE
Profit and Expense Sheet

MONTH SEVEN

Houses Owned:

$ 60,000	$100,000
164,416 – New Purchase	43,503 – New Purchase
643,372 -- Existing	195,425 -- Existing
807,788 -- Total	**238,928 -- Total**

RENTS:

807,788 x $1020.. $ 823,943,760

238,928 x $1315.. $ 314,190,320

Total Rents **$1,138,134,080**

EXPENSES:

Mortgages   807,788 x $390.17.......................... $315,174,643

238,928 x $650.29............................. $155,372,489

Taxes..............$700.00 x 807,788 / 12 .... $ 47,120,966

$1,100 x 238,928 / 12.................... $ 12,947,707

Insurance..........$725.00 x 807,788 / 12...............…..... $ 48,803,858

$1,200 x 238,928 / 12.................. $ 23,892,800

Vacancies and repairs – 10%........................….... $113,813,400

CEO & Staff..…..…..... $ 600,000

Management & Staff…..........................…..…..... $ 35,000,000

Office Staff	$ 30,000,000
Buyers, Closers, Closing Costs....................................	$ 25,000,000
Maintenance and Staff..	$ 7,900,000
Administrative Contingency.......................................	$ 11,000,000
Miscellaneous...	$ 8,500,000
Total Expenses	$835,125,877..........$835,125,877
Projected Profit End of Month Seven....................................$303,008,203

Houses Purchased from Profit and Loan Proceeds

$303,008,203 x 65% = $196,955,332 ÷ $9,000 = 21,883 houses   + $ 8,332

$303,008,203 x 35% = $106,052,871 ÷ $15,000 = 7,070 houses   + $ 2,871

Profit Total: $ 11,203

Loan = $2,420,859,000

x 65% = $1,573,558,350 ÷ $9,000 = 174,840 houses   - $ 1,650

x 35% = $847,300,650 ÷ $15,000 = 56,846 houses   +$ 10,650

Month Seven Incidental Profit..$20,203

Houses for Month Eight:

$60,000	$100,000
21,883 -- From Profit	2,871 -- From Profit
174,840 -- From Loan	56,486 -- From Loan
807,788-- Existing	238,928 -- Existing
1,004,511 -- Total	**298,285 – Total**

1,302,796 Houses for Month Eight

R-3 YEAR TWENTY ALTERNATIVE
Profit and Expense Sheet

MONTH EIGHT

Houses Owned: $ 60,000 $100,000

	$60,000	$100,000
	196,723 – New Purchase	59,357, – New Purchase
	807,788 -- Existing	238,928 -- Existing
	1,004,511 -- Total	**298,285 -- Total**

RENTS:

1,004,511 x $1020…………………………………………………………… $ 1,024,601,220

298,285 x $1315………………………………………….....…….... $ 392,244,775

Total Rents …………………………………………………............. **$1,416,845,995**

EXPENSES: Mortgages

	1,004,511 x $390.17…………………..……	$ 391,942,932
	298,285 x $650.29………………..……	$ 193,971,752
Taxes……………$700.00 x 1,004,511 / 12 ……………		$ 58,596,475
	$1,100 x 298,285 / 12……………..…	$ 27,342,791
Insurance………..$725.00 x 1,004,511 / 12……………		$ 60,689,206
	$1,200 x 298,285 / 12…………….…	$ 29,828,500
Vacancies and repairs – 10%…………………………….……		$141,684,599
CEO & Staff……………………………………………		$ 1,000,000
Management & Staff……...…………………..……		$ 42,000,000
Office Staff …………………………………………		$ 37,000,000
Buyers, Closers, Closing Costs…………………………		$ 30,000,000
Maintenance and Staff…………………………………		$ 11,000,000
Administrative Contingency…………………….…		$ 12,950,000
Miscellaneous………………………………...………..		$ 9,500,000

Total Expenses $1,047,506,250……1,047,506,250

Projected Profit End of Month Eight..……………………………...............**$ 369,339,745**

Houses Purchased from Profit and Loan Proceeds

$369,339,745 x 70% = $258,537,821 ÷ $9,000 = 28,726 houses   + $ 3,821

$369,339,745 x 30% = $110,801,924 ÷ $15,000 = 7,386 houses   + $ 11,924

Profit Total: $ 15,745

Loan = $3,080,052,000

x 70% = $2,156,036,400 ÷ $9,000 = 239,560 houses   - $ 3,600

x 30% = $924,015,600 ÷ $15,000 = 61,601 houses   +$ 600

Month Eight Incidental Profit…………………………………..$12,745

Houses for Month Nine:

$60,000	$100,000
28,726 -- From Profit	7,386 -- From Profit
239,560 -- From Loan	61,601 -- From Loan
1,004,511-- Existing	298,285 -- Existing
1,272,797 -- Total	367,272 – Total

1,640,069 Houses for Month Nine

R-3 YEAR TWENTY ALTERNATIVE
Profit and Expense Sheet

MONTH NINE

Houses Owned:	$ 60,000	$100,000
	268,286 – New Purchase	68,987 – New Purchase
	1,004,511 -- Existing	298,285 -- Existing
	1,272,797 -- Total	367,272 -- Total

RENTS:	1,272,797 x $1020	....	$ 1,298,252,940
	367,272 x $1315	....	$ 482,962,680
	Total Rents	....	**$1,781,215,620**

EXPENSES:	Mortgages	1,272,797 x $390.17	.....................................$ 496,607,205
		367,272 x $650.29	....................................$ 238,833,308
	Taxes...............$ 700.00 x 1,272,797 / 12	....	$ 74,246,491
	$1,100 x 367,272 / 12	....	$ 33,666,600
	Insurance...........$725.00 x 1,272,797 / 12	....	$ 76,898,152
	$1,200 x 367,272 / 12	....	$ 36,727,200
	Vacancies and repairs – 10%	....	$ 178,121,562
	CEO & Staff	....	$ 1,250,000
	Management & Staff	....	$ 50,000,000
	Office Staff	....	$ 45,000,000
	Buyers, Closers, Closing Costs	....	$ 42,000,000
	Maintenance and Staff	....	$ 12,500,000
	Administrative Contingency	....	$ 16,000,000
	Miscellaneous	....	$ 12,500,000
	Total Expenses	$1,314,350,518	......$1,314,350,518
	Projected Profit End of Month Nine	....	..........$ 466,865,102

Houses Purchased from Profit and Loan Proceeds

$466,865,102 x 70% = $326,805,571 ÷ $9,000 = 36,311 houses   + $ 6,571

$466,865,102 x 30% = $140,059,530 ÷ $15,000 = 9,337 houses   + $ 4,530

                                            Profit Total: $ 11,101

Loan = $3,915,555,000

x 70% = $2,740,888,500 ÷ $9,000 = 304,543 houses   + $ 1,500

x 30% = $1,174,666,500 ÷ $15,000 = 78,311 houses   + $ 1,500

        Month Nine Incidental Profit...$14,101

Houses for Month Ten:

$60,000	$100,000
36,311 -- From Profit	9,337 -- From Profit
304,545 -- From Loan	78,311 -- From Loan
1,272,797 -- Existing	367,272 -- Existing
1,613,653 -- Total	**454,920 – Total**

2,068,573 Houses for Month Ten

R-3 YEAR TWENTY ALTERNATIVE
Profit and Expense Sheet

MONTH TEN

Houses Owned:

$ 60,000	$100,000
340,856 – New Purchase	87,648 – New Purchase
1,272,797 -- Existing	367,272 -- Existing
1,613,653 -- Total	**454,920 -- Total**

RENTS:	1,613,653 x $1,020..	$ 1,645,926,060
	454,920 x $1,315..	$ 598,219,800
	Total Rents	**$ 2,244,145,860**
EXPENSES:	Mortgages	1,613,653 x $390.17........................	$ 629,598,991
		454,920 x $650.29...........................	$ 295,829,926
	Taxes...............$700.00 x 1,613,653 / 12	$ 94,129,758
		$1,100 x 454,920 / 12.....................	$ 41,701,000
	Insurance..........$725.00 x 1,613,653 / 12.................	$ 97,491,535
		$1,200 x 454,920 / 12...................	$ 45,492,000
	Vacancies and repairs – 10%...............................	$ 224,414,586

CEO & Staff.. $ 1,500,000

Management & Staff…..................................... $ 50,000,000

Office Staff .... $ 45,000,000

Buyers, Closers, Closing Costs......................... $ 52,000,000

Maintenance and Staff...................................... $ 16,000,000

Administrative Contingency............................... $ 20,000,000

Miscellaneous... $ 17,000,000

Total Expenses $1,630,157,796…$1,630,157,796

Projected Profit End of Month Ten...…………………...............$ 613,988,064

Houses Purchased from Profit and Loan Proceeds

$613,988,064 x 70% = $429,791,644 ÷ $9,000 = 47,754 houses   + $ 5,644

$613,988,064 x 30% = $184,196,419 ÷ $15,000 = 12,279 houses   + $ 11,419

                                            Profit Total: **$ 17,063**

Loan = $4,990,000,000

x 65% = $3,243,500,000 ÷ $9,000 = 360,388 houses   + $ 8,000

x 35% = $1,746,500,000 ÷ $15,000 = 116,433 houses   + $ 5,000

Month Ten Incidental Profit……………………………………...$30,063

Houses for Month Eleven:

<u>$60,000</u>   <u>$100,000</u>

47,754 -- From Profit   12,279 -- From Profit

360,388 -- From Loan   116,433 -- From Loan

1,613,653-- Existing   454,920 -- Existing

2,021,795 -- Total   **583,632 – Total**

2,605,427 Houses for Month Eleven

R-3 YEAR TWENTY ALTERNATIVE
Profit and Expense Sheet
MONTH ELEVEN

Houses Owned: $ 60,000 $100,000

408,142 – New Purchase   128,712 – New Purchase
1,613,653-- Existing   454,920 -- Existing
2,021,795 -- Total   **583,632 -- Total**

RENTS:	2,021,795 x $1,020…………………………………………...	$ 2,062,230,900
	583,632 x $1,315………………………………………..........	$ 767,476,080
	Total Rents ……………………………………………..........	**$ 2,829,706,980**
EXPENSES:	Mortgages 2,021,795 x $390.17…………………..... $ 788,843,755	
	583,632 x $650.29…………………........... $ 379,530,053	
	Taxes…………..$700.00 x 2,021,795 / 12 …………… $ 117,938,042	
	$1,100 x 583,632 / 12………………..... $ 53,499,600	
	Insurance………..$725.00 x 2,021,795 / 12…………..… $ 122,150,115	
	$1,200 x 583,632 / 12……………….... $ 58,363,200	
	Vacancies and repairs – 10%…………………………….. $ 282,970,698	
	CEO & Staff……………………………………….....… $ 2,000,000	
	Management & Staff……...……………………........… $ 70,000,000	
	Office Staff ……………………………………….…… $ 58,000,000	
	Buyers, Closers, Closing Costs………………….............. $ 64,000,000	
	Maintenance and Staff………………………………… $ 22,000,000	
	Administrative Contingency…………………………. $ 27,000,000	
	Miscellaneous………………………………….............…. $ 23,000,000	
	Total Expenses $2,069,295,463…$2,069,295,463	
	Projected Profit End of Month Eleven……...…………….......................…$ 760,411, 517	

Houses Purchased from Profit and Loan Proceeds

$760,411,517 x 70% = $532,288,062 ÷ $9,000 = 59,143 houses   + $ 1,062

$760,411,517 x 30% = $228,123,455 ÷ $15,000 = 15,208 houses   + $ 3,455

Profit Total: $ 4,517

Loan = $5,602,000,000

x 70% = $3,921,400,000 ÷ $9,000 = 435,711 houses   + $ 1,000

x 30% = $1,680,600,000 ÷ $15,000 = 112,040 houses   Even

Month Eleven Incidental Profit………………………………$5,517

Houses for Month Twelve:

$60,000	$100,000
59,143 -- From Profit	15,208 -- From Profit
435,711 -- From Loan	112,040 -- From Loan
2,021,795-- Existing	583,632 -- Existing
2,516,649 -- Total	710,880 – Total

3,227,529 Houses for Month Twelve

R-3 YEAR TWENTY ALTERNATIVE
Profit and Expense Sheet

MONTH TWELVE

Houses Owned:	$ 60,000	$100,000
	494,854 – New Purchase	127,248 – New Purchase
	2,021,795-- Existing	583,632 -- Existing
	2,516,649 -- Total	710,880 -- Total

RENTS:	2,516,649 x $1,020..	$ 2,566,981,980
	710,880 x $1,315...	$ 934,807,200
	Total Rents	**$ 3,501,789,180**
EXPENSES:	Mortgages 2,516,649 x $390.17........................	$ 981,920,940
	710,880 x $650.29...............................	$ 462,278,155
	Taxes..............$700.00 x 2,516,649 / 12	$ 146,804,525
	$1,100 x 710,880 / 12....................	$ 65,164,000
	Insurance..........$725.00 x 2,516,649 / 12................	$ 152,047,543
	$1,200 x 718,880 / 12...................	$ 71,088,000
	Vacancies and repairs – 10%...........................	$ 350,178,918
	CEO & Staff..	$ 3,000,000
	Management & Staff..	$ 137,000,000
	Office Staff	$ 122,000,000
	Buyers, Closers, Closing Costs................................	$ 87,000,000
	Maintenance and Staff.......................................	$ 31,000,000
	Administrative Contingency................................	$ 37,000,000
	Miscellaneous...	$ 32,000,000
	Total Expenses $2,678,482,081...$2,678,482,081
	Projected Profit End of Month Twelve...$ 823,307,099

Houses Purchased from Profit and Loan Proceeds

$823,307,099 x 70% = $576,314,969 ÷ $9,000 = 64,034 houses   + $ 8,969

$823,307,099 x 30% = $246,992,129 ÷ $15,000 = 16,466 houses   + $ 2,129

Profit Total: $11,098

Loan = $5,700,000,000

x 70% = $3,990,000,000 ÷ $9,000 = 443,333 houses   + $ 3,000

x 30% = $1,710,000,000 ÷ $15,000 = 114,000 houses   Even

Month Twelve Incidental Profit.......................................$14,098

Houses for Year Twenty One:

$60,000	$100,000
64,034 -- From Profit	16,466 -- From Profit
443,333 -- From Loan	114,000 -- From Loan
2,516,649 -- Existing	710,880 -- Existing
3,024,016 -- Total	**841,346 – Total**

3,865,362 Houses for Year Twenty One

R-3 TWENTY YEAR ALTERNATIVE BORROW—INVESTMENT PROGRAM – YEAR TWENTY ONE

Projected Year Twenty One Receipts and Expenses

Rents: 3,024,016 x $1,060 x 12 .... $38,465,483,520
841,346 x $1,360 x 12 .... $13,730,766,720
Total Rents.............. **$52,196,250,240**

Expenses:

Mortgages: 3,024,016 – 446 x $390.17 x 12 .... $14,156,475,683
841,346 – 130 x $650.29 x 12 ....…......... $ 6,564,412,231
Taxes: 3,024,016 x $770 .... $ 2,328,492,320
841,346 x $1,100 .... $ 925,480,600
Insurance: 3,024,016 x $775 .... $ 2,343,612,400
841,346 x $1,200 .... $ 1,009,615,200
Vacancies & Repairs .... $ 5,219,625,024
CEO & Staff .... $ 30,000,000
Management & Staff .... $ 800,000,000
Office Staff .... $ 775,000,000

House Closers & Closing Costs	$ 400,000,000	
Maintenance	$ 360,000,000	
Administrative Contingencies	$ 175,000,000	
Miscellaneous	$ 175,000,000	
Expenses	$35,262,713,458	$35,262,713,458

Profit $16,933,536,782

R-3 TWENTY YEAR ALTERNATIVE

BORROW—INVESTMENT PROGRAM – YEAR TWENTY ONE

PROJECTED HOUSE SALES – YEAR TWENTY-ONE

$297,441,214,463	– Sales by 3% House Appreciation
- $195,119,560,949	– House Debt – Assumed by Buyer
$102,321,653,514	– Buyer Pays at Closing
- $ 34,765,250,106	– P & I Borrowed Debt Seller Pays at Closing
$ 67,556,403,408	– Seller's Sale Proceeds
+ $ 16,933,536,782	– Year Twenty One Profit
+ $ 8,830,389	– Year Twenty Alt Incidental Profit
$ 84,498,770,579	– Seller's Projected Sale Proceeds & Profits
$ 84,498,770,579	– Seller's Projected Sales & Profit Proceeds
	14,083,128% Return on $600,000 Investment

$ 16,933,536,782 – Year Twenty One Projected Profit divided by Buyer's Investment of $102,321,653,514 = 16.549% Return on Buyer's Cash Investment. Yearly moderate rent increases of $180 per house per year added to projected profit of $16,933,536,782 amounts to $17,629,301,942 projected for Buyer's first year of operation, which is projected to be a return of 17.22% of Buyer's $102,321,653,514 investment.

House debt reduction is $15,049,259,297 per year. 3,024,016 houses x $3,400 = $10,281,654,400; 841,346 houses x $5,666.64 per year = $4,767,604,897. Total house debt paid off in Buyer's first year = $15,049,259,297

Yearly rent increase = $695,747,160 plus projected profit of $16,933,536,782 = $17,629,301,942. Added to the $15,049,259,297 yearly house debt reduction = $32,678,561,239. House appreciation is projected at 3% per year, which is $8,923,236,433. This adds up to $41,601,797,672. In approximately 2.459 years, Buyer is projected to realize his $102,321,653,514 investment.

R-3 TWENTY YEAR ALTERNATIVE
BORROW--INVESTMENT PROGRAM – YEAR TWENTY ONE
Projected Returns to Investors from House Sales & Profit in Year 21

Investors	Amount Invested	Return on Investment	Percentage Return
1	$600,000	$84,498,770,579	14,083,128%
2	$300,000, each	$ 42,244,385,528, each	14,083,128%
3	$200,000, each	$ 28,166,256,859, each	14,083,128%
5	$120,000, each	$ 16,899,541,158, each	14,083,128%
8	$ 75,000, each	$ 10,562,346,322, each	14,083,128%
10	$ 60,000, each	$ 84,498,770,579 each	14,083,128%
15	$ 40,000, each	$ 5,633,251,371, each	14,083,128%
20	$ 30,000, each	$ 4,224,938,528, each	14,083,128%
25	$ 24,000, each	$ 3,379950,823, each	14,083,128%
30	$ 20,000, each	$ 2,816,625,685 each	14083,128%

R-3 TWENTY YEAR ALTERNATIVE
BORROW—INVESTMENT PROGRAM – YEAR TWENTY ONE

PROJECTED HOUSE SALES – YEAR TWENTY ONE

The $315,000,000,000 price was determined by calculating a fair and reasonable yearly profit to Buyer, which is 14.459% on Buyer's $119,880,439,051 investment.

$315,000,000,000	– Sales by Net Profit Factor
- $195,119,560,949	– House Debt – Assumed by Buyer
$119,880,439,051	– Buyer Pays at Closing
- $ 34,765,250,106	– P & I Borrowed Debt Seller Pays at Closing
$ 85,115,188,945	– Seller's Sale Proceeds
+ $ 16,933,536,782	– Year Twenty One Profit
+ $ 8,839,389	– Year Twenty Alt Incidental Profit
$ 102,057,556,116	– **Seller's Projected Sale & Proceeds Profits**
	17,009,592% Return on $600,000 Investment

$102,057,556,116 – Seller's Projected Sales & Profit Proceeds

$16,933,536,782 – Year Twenty One Projected Profits divided by Buyer's Investment of $119,880,439,051 = 14.125% Return on Buyer's Cash Investment. When $180 yearly rent increase per house is added to the projected Profit, the projected Profit is 14.7% on the Buyer's $119,880,439,051 investment.

As stated previously, projected Profit, house debt reduction and yearly house appreciation amounts total $41,601,814,499 for one year. Buyer can expect to realize his $119,880,439,051 investment in approximately 2.881 years.

R-3 TWENTY YEAR ALTERNATIVE
BORROW—INVESTMENT PROGRAM – YEAR TWENTY ONE

PROJECTIONS – SALES IN YEAR TWENTY-ONE

Projected Returns to Investors from House Sales & Profit in Year 21

Investors	Amount Invested	Return on Investment	Percentage Return
1	$600,000	$102,057,556,116	17,009,592%
2	$300,000, each	$ 51,028,778,058 each	17,009,592%
3	$200,000, each	$ 34,019,185,372, each	17,009,592%
5	$120,000, each	$ 20,411,511,223, each	17,009,592%
8	$ 75,000, each	$ 12,757,194,514, each	17,009,592%
10	$ 60,000, each	$ 10,057,556,116, each	17,009,592%
15	$ 40,000, each	$ 6,803,837,074, each	17,009,592%
20	$ 30,000, each	$ 5,102,877,805, each	17,009,592%
25	$ 24,000, each	$ 4,082,230,224, each	17,009,592%
30	$ 20,000, each	$ 3,401,918,537, each	17,009,592%

The 3,865,362 houses produced a projected rental profit of $16,942,367,171 at completion of year Twenty One Alternative. This amounts to a 2,823,727% return on the $600,000 investment over twenty one years. 65 houses were purchased in Year One. Projections now number houses at 3,865,362, an increase of 5,946,710% over twenty one years. This would be an extremely remarkable accomplishment for anyone or any group of investors. After twenty one years of operation, the Owners/Investors could continue with the buying, renting of houses, cease buying and maintaining the housing inventory, or sell the entire portfolio to other buyers. If sold to other buyers, since the inventory is so large, then, it would be best to have blocks of houses that can be sold to separate buyers. Blocks could contain 100 houses, 500 houses, 1,000 houses, 3,000 houses, 5,000 houses, 10,000 houses, 25,000 and 50,000 houses. This selling of blocks of houses would permit many diverse investors to purchase them.

If the Owners/Investors were to cease buying operations and maintain the houses as rentals, then, expenses can be reduced considerably and house closer and closing expenses eliminated. This would provide a projected profit, including 3% rent increases, of $19,356,534,678 or more in the following year of operation. This projected profit is enormous for a safe, solid and secure investment consisting of valuable and marketable properties. If the Owners/Investors were to maintain and continue to rent the houses, each and every year, an approximate $15,049,276,124 reduction in debt would occur. At a 3% appreciation rate, the following year, the housing portfolio would increase approximately $8,923,236,433 in value, and 3% of total value for each additional year. Maintaining property that can produce such enormous profits, returns and values is extremely good business.

If the Owners/Investors decide to sell their portfolio to other buyers or investors, allocating houses in blocks for sale, as mentioned previously, provides opportunity for many buyers. 3,865,362 houses could be bought by a few extremely wealthy buyers. However, it may be better to stagger the sales in blocks. Sales projections follow, and they are very beneficial to both sellers and buyers. Buyers have the choice to continue the buying/renting operation, cease buying other houses, but continue the rental operations, or, within a few years, sell the entire operation to other buyers. Yearly profit, appreciated value, rent increases and debt reduction of $15,049,276,124 per year ensure a substantial profit for a safe and solid investment. Debt reduction per year of operation goes directly to profit when the entire operation is sold.

YEAR TWENTY-ONE SALES PROJECTIONS TO RENTERS

The following projection shows figures for house sales to renters and other buyers. If renters have been occupying the house for several years, and if financially qualified, then they likely would be very interested in purchasing the property, and more, since the owner will carry. Renters can have the first purchase option, but if they are not interested, then other buyers will be, since the owner will carry paper.

Projections show that 3,865,362 homes were purchased over a twenty year period, beginning with a $600,000 investment. Seller(s)/Owner(s) projected Profits for sales to renters and other buyers are projected at $216,523,369,537, which is a projected 36,087,228% return on the original $600,000 investment. In any investment circles, this would be considered an almost unreachable return. Had purchases and loans started within the first few years of operation, then the housing inventory, profits and sales prices would be much, much higher. Although we took the conservative approach, no investor need do this.

Projected sales price is $75,470 for 3,024,016 houses, with projections of $17,800 down, $42,723 remaining first mortgage and $14,947, second mortgage.

$17,800 – Down payment   (23.5%)

$42,723 - First Mortgage

$14,947 – Second Mortgage

$75,470 - Projected Sales Price

Projected Mortgage costs: $4,682 - First mortgage

$1,494 - Second Mortgage

$6,176 - Per Year; $514.67 per month, average

Projected sales price for 841,346 houses is $118,311, with projections of $27,200 down, $51,157 remaining first mortgage, and $39,954, second mortgage.

$ 27,200 – Down Payment   (23%)

$ 51,157 – First Mortgage

$ 39,954 – Second Mortgage

$118,311 – Projected Sales Price

Projected Mortgage costs: $ 7,843.48 – First Mortgage

$ 3,995.40 - Second Mortgage

$11,838.88 - Per Year; $986.67 per month, average

The above are projections only, which the investor(s) can employ or use their own methods to arrive at their own costs, profits and projections.

TWENTY YEAR ALTERNATIVE
BORROW—INVESTMENT PROGRAM – *YEAR TWENTY ONE*
PROJECTIONS BASED UPON SALES IN YEAR 21
Projected House Sales – In Year Twenty One - to Renters & Other Buyers

$ 327,762,947,126	– House Sales to Renters
- $ 172,233,772,890	– House Debt Assumed by Renters
$ 155,529,174,236	– Balance
- $ 76,712,096,000	– Down Payment Amounts
$ 78,817,078,236	– Projected Second Mortgages Total

+ $ 76,712,096,000	– Down Payment Amounts
- $ 6,976,174,565	– Borrowed Debt – Seller Pays at Closing
$ 155,529,174,236	– Balance
- $ 34,765,250,106	– P & I Borrowed Debt Seller Pays at Closing
$ 120,763,924,130	– Balance
+ $ 16,933,536,782	– Year Twenty One Projected Profits
+ $ 8,839,389	– Year Twenty Alt- m- to- m Profits
$ 137,706,291,301	– Projected Cash Sale Proceeds & Profit to Seller
+ $ 78,817,078,236	– Second Mortgages Interest Over 10 Years
$ 216,523,369,537	– **Seller's Profit Over 10 Years**

$216,523,369,537 – Seller's Projected Sales & Profit Proceeds
36,087,228% Return on $600,000 Investment

If the maturity of the second mortgages were for 15 years instead of 10, then the investors would receive an additional $39,408,539,118 in interest.

The Owners/Investors can sell their 3,865,362 house inventory to an institutional buyer(s) or cartel and make an enormous fortune, or they could sell individual houses to the current renters or other buyers and make an even larger enormous fortune. In the first situation, the Owners/Investors sell rental houses to buyer(s) who will likely maintain and operate the rental houses as a business. This real estate portfolio of 3,865,362 houses, purchased over 21 years, could be sold to an extremely wealthy organization. However, it would be better to break up the inventory into smaller blocks, ranging anywhere from 100 houses, 500 houses, 1,000 houses or other amounts up to 100,000 houses. This will give pension funds, retirement funds and other capable buyers the ability to purchase the inventory in smaller amounts.

In the second situation, the Owners/Investors sell the houses to the current renters and other likely individual buyers/homeowners. By doing this, the Owners/Investors make it possible for 3,865,362 families to purchase homes through owner financing, thereby *bypassing the banks*. This would be an excellent and profitable arrangement for our Owners/Investors and their individual buyers, many of whom may have been otherwise unable to purchase houses through the usual purchase and bank methods. As we mentioned previously, the Owners/Investors, whether they are aware of it or not, can enable millions of families to buy homes, when, for many of them, it would not be possible through normal system's channels.

R-3 TWENTY YEAR ALTERNATIVE
BORROW—INVESTMENT PROGRAM – *YEAR TWENTY ONE*
PROJECTIONS - HOUSE SALES TO RENTERS
Projected Returns to Investors from House Sales & Profit in Year 21

Investors	Amount Invested	Return on Investment	Percentage Return
1	$600,000	$216,523,369,537	36,087,228%
2	$300,000, each	$108,261,684,768, each	36,087,228%
3	$200,000, each	$ 72,174,456,512, each	36,087,228%
5	$120,000, each	$ 43,304,673,907, each	36,087,228%
8	$ 75,000, each	$ 27,065,421,192, each	36,087,228%
10	$ 60,000, each	$ 21,652,336,953, each	36,087,228%
15	$ 40,000, each	$ 14,434,891,302, each	36,087,228%
20	$ 30,000, each	$ 10,826,168,477, each	36,087,228%
25	$ 24,000, each	$ 8,660,934,781, each	36,087,228%
30	$ 20,000, each	$ 7,217,445,651, each	36,087,228%

If the second mortgages maturities were for 15 years instead of 10, the investor(s) would have received $39,408,539,118 additional interest.

R-3 TWENTY YEAR ALTERNATIVE
BORROW—INVESTMENT PROGRAM – *YEAR TWENTY ONE*
Projected Breakdown of Returns to Investors
From House Sales & Profit in Year 21

Investors	Cash at Closing	Int. Pymts/10 Years	Princ. Pymt/10 Years	Total Payments
1	$58,889,213,065	$ 7,881,707,823 = $78,817,078,236	$78,817,078,236	$216,523,369,537
2	$29,444,606,532 Each	$ 3,940,853,911 x 10 = $39,408,539,118, Each	$39,408,539,118, Each	$108,261,684,768 Each
3	$19,629,737,688 Each	$ 2,627,235,941 x 10 = $26,272,359,410, Each	$26,272,359,410, Each	$ 72,174,456,512 Each
5	$11,777,842,613 Each	$ 1,576,341,564 x 10 = $15,763,415,640, Each	$15,763,415,640, Each	$ 43,304,673,907 Each
8	$7,361,151,633 Each	$ 985,213,477 x 10 = $9,852,134,770, Each	$ 9,852,134,770, Each	$ 27,065,421,192 Each
10	$ 5,888,421,306 Each	$ 788,170,782 x 10 = $7,881,707,820, Each	$ 7,881,707,820, Each	$ 21,652,336,953 Each
15	$ 3,925,947,537 Each	$ 525,447,188 x 10 = $5,254,471,880, Each	$ 5,254,471,880, Each	$ 14,434,891,302 Each
20	$ 2,944,460,653 Each	$ 394,085,391 x 10 = $3,940,853,910, Each	$ 3,940,853,910, Each	$ 10,826,168,476 Each
25	$ 2,355,568,522 Each	$ 315,268,312 x 10 = $3,152,683,120, Each	$ 3,152,683,120, Each	$ 8,660,934,781 Each
30	$ 1,962,973,768 Each	$ 262,723,594 x 10 = $2,627,235,940, Each	$ 2,627,235,940, Each	$ 7,217,445,651 Each

If the second mortgages maturities were for 15 years instead of 10, the investor(s) would have received $39,408,539,118 additional interest.

CHAPTER SIXTY SEVEN

PROJECTIONS OVERVIEW

The extensive projections in this book offer programs for virtually everyone. These extend from very simple, basic investments, beginning with $15,000, up to investments of $600,000. All of the projections for any investment in this book indicate that vast fortunes can be made, no matter how much the investment, provided the projections are followed. The projections are accurate, but some minor mathematical errors may have occurred. Figures were rounded up to the nearest dollar or hundred dollars. These projections are examples to show you what can be accomplished by using these methods. They can also be used as a basis for you to do your own projections according to your means and to satisfy your needs.

Documents for buying, selling, offers, financing, and other transactions will be made available for interested parties. For more information, call 207-404-9093 or email us at takebackourrights@yahoo.com or mdflynn2003@yahoo.com.

These projections may appear incredible and the work of fantasy, but enormous trees grow from tiny acorns and miniscule seeds. Sometimes, what appears to be utterly fantastic and simply fiction, manifests in reality. Most of us, at some point in our lives, have seen and experienced actual, real events that seem impossible, but there they are, right in front of us. Reality can be stranger than fiction. Real things are accomplished by real people who have dedicated work ethics and the ability to carry through until their objectives are accomplished. A small investment made by a conscientious investor(s) diligently following the *ByPass* Buy/Sell Programs can produce an extremely large profit within three to four years. A larger investment of $600,000 can purchase a very large number of houses over 20 or 21 years, with staggering profits derived from the sale of inventory, plus profits, over the years of operation.

A review of the very last projection in this book is an example. With a $600,000 investment, our projections indicate that our mythical investor(s) purchased 3,865,362 houses over a twenty-one year period. Purchases were made over that time from profits received and private loans taken. These purchases were made at the end of each year, rather than on a monthly basis, from profits and loans taken out each month based upon the number of houses contracted. Therefore, risks to private investors are minimal. Had monthly purchases been made over the life of the Program, then, a significantly higher number of houses could have been purchased, providing a much larger housing inventory, increased rental profits and much higher sales profits. We were conservative, but investors will choose as best serves their objectives. Total projected profit for the sale of the 3,865,362 housing inventory to renters and individual house buyers, plus rental profits, is a projected $216,523,369,537, which is an amazing 36,087,228% return on the $600,000 investment. In some circles, our mythical investor could be called an investment genius, but it is really all common sense, knowing the markets, working diligently, knowing supply and demand, and fully realizing that many capable buyers will be very interested in purchasing seller-financed houses. On the other side, sellers prohibited from selling because of market, economic and other conditions, such as bank restrictions on assumptions of mortgages and tight lending requirements, should be very receptive to our Buyer/Investor. If the seller wants cash, he can always sell his note at discount, and since no realtor was involved, the seller could be very pleased with the sale.

While the projected purchase of 3,865,362 houses over 21 years may seem unrealistic, the reality is quite evident when the facts are considered. An average of approximately 6,000,000 single family houses are sold each year. As years pass and populations increase, this 6,000,000 average will likely increase yearly. It could reach 7,000,000, 8,000,000 or more, as years pass. When we take the present 6,000,000 average, over 21 years, the projected sales amount to 126,000,000. The projected 3,865,362 houses purchased amount to 3.067% of 126,000,000, which is extremely realistic. Further, as these programs continue to grow over time, because of direct seller financing, the very straightforward and easy, low cost closing, the lack of legalese, no broker involvement and many other factors cited throughout this book, it is possible that the *ByPass* Programs could be the buying wave of the future. If this occurs, then for the capable buyers, sellers, investors and financers, it is highly likely that both ample numbers of house sellers and buyers will be extremely eager to engage with you.

The purchase and sale of 3,865,362 houses over 21 years begins with a much lower number of purchases, but the number of purchases grows as years pass. As purchases increase, then, obviously, new market areas must be sought to accommodate additional house purchases. As the numbers grow, then, markets in multiple states and in various locations within those states will likely be needed to accommodate the growing number of house purchases. Previously in this book we suggested certain marketing strategies and those can be reviewed. One of the best mediums for this purpose is the Internet by which the Owner(s)/Investor(s) seek to buy properties and specify the terms on which they are prepared to buy the properties. The Internet can be an amazing marketing tool for such projects. Since the Internet reaches everywhere, then it would be possible to reach sellers willing to sell their properties on the terms mentioned who are located in other states. In such situations, the Owner(s)/Investor(s) could have consultants in those states to view the properties, assess them, and then, report their findings on the properties to the Owner(s)/Investor(s). If a purchase is consummated through these consultants, then, they can receive pre-agreed upon fees for their services.

Many combined factors exist which can produce these results, the most important of which is common sense, an extremely important quality and a major asset to any investor. While the so-called "experts" are wrong most of the time, true common sense is rarely wrong and those with the wisdom to heed it usually succeed. A prime example follows. If the experts were correct, then the outrageous, harmful and massive problems that now exist in America would not exist. Those people and investors with common sense who did not listen to the "experts", but, instead, listened to themselves and made their own assessments, did well. Common sense sets us apart from the herd that follows the leaders' directions which will take them over the cliff. Common sense allows us to see, envision, invent, and establish what others will not, primarily because they lack the understanding and the vision. It gives us a keen insight and perspective which others lack. Common sense provides us with discernment, understanding and an immediate grasp of nearly all situations. It allows us to know when politicians lie, to discern when what government and the "system" presents is false, when something does not feel right, no matter how lavishly and bountifully it is presented. Relying upon ourselves, our own intuition and our common sense separates us from those who rarely notice, object, challenge and question, and simply follow the systems' directions to their self-imposed boxes.

People constantly buy and sell houses, and common sense would indicate that many of those buyers would prefer to purchase houses with the ease of seller carried financing. This should be very obvious for anyone to understand, and what is obvious should be recognized and accepted as obvious. As we have mentioned throughout this book, millions of people lost their homes during the last foreclosure debacle and common sense tells us that many of them who are financially able would eagerly purchase homes with seller financing. Common sense also tells us that some people who have purchased homes through bank financing may be very interested in purchasing their next home through seller financing. Sellers who want cash at closing but are hindered by tough market conditions, depressed economy, banker restrictions on buyers, and many other factors may relish selling their homes through the *ByPass* methods, then, discount their notes for cash. Since no real estate salesperson was involved and no commission had to be paid, a discounted note should provide what the seller wants, or close to it.

Common sense also clearly indicates that what the government has done before to the people, the government will do again to the people. This goes back to the old, sage position that, unfortunately, societies do not learn through experience, but fortunately some individuals do. America has suffered many orchestrated recessions and depressions in which millions of people lost nearly everything. As we previously mentioned, during the devastating depression of 2007 – 2008, many millions of people lost their homes through unlawful foreclosures. Further, both gold and silver have previously been un-Constitutionally, thus, unlawfully, debased in value and confiscated by the government. What the government has done before, the government will do again, and, unfortunately, people can expect a massive depression will occur again. As a result, another massive foreclosure assault on the people will likely also begin again. However, those who have read this book and understand the positions and protections discussed within it can persevere by selling their own properties and others can do so by buying their properties through seller financing.

Common sense allows us to realize that many people throughout America are unhappy with their work, uncertain about their jobs, changing conditions, overreaching government regulations, and would be very happy to pursue investment opportunities that make real sense in the real marketplace. When investor(s) invest into these *ByPass* Programs and realize they can create ongoing, continuous profits from these programs, then the investor(s) can effectuate their dreams of getting "out of the box". Providing for one's family through programs that can provide a continuous and growing cash stream is an excellent way to separate from an overbearing, controlling system. If you know the derivation of the word system, it came from the word Greek word for sewer. America has experienced many economic downturns, and one of the worst was deliberately orchestrated to defraud millions of Americans in 2007 and 2008. Since then, large numbers of Americans are much more concerned about financial, economic, banking and government controlled and imposed conditions that could severely impact them. Many of those feared conditions emerged during the COVID-19 Plandemic, so those concerned Americans were correct in their assessments. If the American people do not awaken to the massive fraud continuously perpetrated upon them by their own governments, then the fraud will continue, thus, common sense indicates distancing from the system, at least as much as possible, is the proper, wise and sane way to proceed. Those who do not do so will be even more totally controlled by the system and absolutely dependent upon it.

In the near future, it would be best if the people were secure in their own homes, papers and assets, without bank or any other type of institutional debt. Because of restrictive government controls, which have harmed and likely will further harm our economy, both small and large investors will seek safe, solid and stable investments, backed by ready marketable assets. Private lenders will have difficulty finding such uncontrolled investments and markets for their funds. Thus, they will eagerly seek the safe, secure investments for their lending dollars, provided by *ByPass* Programs, which are about as safe, secure and marketable as any investment can get.

The sellers who understand the uncomplicated approach and ease of these methods, combined with their many benefits, should have avid interest. Sellers can take a 15%, or so, down payment and carry a first mortgage on their own former homes. When sellers realize that various investors routinely purchase first and second mortgages, those sellers can sell their mortgages, receive cash for the sale, and in so doing, *bypass the banks*. When sellers do this successfully, their success will be noticed by others who will want to mimic that success. If large numbers participate, then this movement could grow quickly and *ByPass* methods could become the new selling, buying and financing wave of the future, without banks. People can work directly, principal to principal, achieve their objectives, and totally *bypass the banks*.

As we have mentioned before in this book, all government officers and public officials in this country, federal, state and local, are Constitutionally mandated to abide by their oaths in the performance of their official duties, are bound by oath to the Constitution, pursuant to Article VI, Clauses 2 & 3, and must uphold the Constitution as the supreme Law over and above any other form of law. These same government officers and officials are required to uphold the Preamble to the Constitution, as well. Tragically, few, if any, in this entire country abide by these requirements and the overwhelming vast majority of them shred the Constitution and rights guaranteed therein to the people millions of times each day. Governments operated by such domestic enemies will never do the right thing for the American people. An example follows.

The last projection in this book demonstrated how nearly four million houses were bought over a twenty-one year period and could be sold to individual investors or to approximately four million families who desperately need their own homes. If the investors who own these properties were to sell the properties to existing renters and to other buyers, then, they could make more profits than if they were to sell them to individual large investors. This is where **social consciousness** can benefit both the buyer and the seller. If our governments were concerned about the people of America and wanted to help them and the general economy, instead of destroying everything in sight, then, those governments could devise programs similar to *ByPass* programs in which a helping hand is rendered to the people, not a handout, which helping hand would allow people to purchase and own their own properties, instead of living in apartments, many of which are substandard, located in dangerous neighborhoods, surrounded by squalor, yet the rents are high. If governments wanted the people to have access to and the ability to retain private property, rather than have many lose it to the banks, then, government would devise programs similar to the one discussed. Instead, government is waging war against its own people, discouraging many and making it impossible for them to ever own private property. When the government attacks the people, jeopardizes their livelihoods, destroys their economy, then, obviously, the government is not working in the best interest of the people, not upholding their oaths, not upholding the Constitution and certainly not upholding its Preamble. The American people have long suffered under this form of pernicious government and growing numbers of people are realizing this ugly truth daily. Now, they must truly realize that it is *only* the people who can lawfully stop the egregious, un-Constitutional, pernicious actions of government.

The banking system in America was un-Constitutionally established by **traitors in government** over one hundred years ago and maintained by traitors in government ever since. This banking system is un-Constitutional and definitely unfriendly to average Americans. In the alternative, these institutions are extremely friendly to entities of vast wealth and to government. If this were not the case with both government and the banking system, then, there would be a combined or individual effort by these entities to promote the general welfare and secure the blessings of liberty to the people by actually helping the people purchase and keep private property. These entities will never do this, because they openly defy and disparage the Constitution, hate our Constitutional Republic and look at the people as chattel for them to use to make money and increase the control of the system. Such entities care nothing about the people and will never truly support the rights and due process of law Constitutionally guaranteed to the American people, including the right to own, maintain and enjoy private property. If it were otherwise, then, these two powerful institutions, which essentially are "joined at the hip" —government and banking— would long ago have devised programs similar to the ones presented in this book and would have made it possible for many millions of people to secure their own homes, and not handouts, which would have secured the blessings of liberty so long denied to them. **It is very important that the people truly comprehend the evil nature of their real enemy.** Without seeing this truth, they will continue to live in the fraudulent system that has abused and misused them for so long, instead of living in the true Constitutional Republic that our forefathers designed, fought and died for, to benefit their posterity and their creation.

THE PRESENT VERSUS THE FUTURE

The present exists because of the past and the future will exist because of the present. This is how life and human societies exist, progress or digress. If we, as Americans, are not happy with our present, then we must look at our past actions or inactions that created the problems now present in our present. As a society, if we fail to do this, we are bound to repeat the same mistakes over and over again, until we finally learn. Our present will create our future since what we do or not do now will determine that future, just as the past determined our present. If we have not learned from the past, and, unfortunately, most people and most societies do not, America is doomed to have a very bleak future.

Throughout this book, we have spoken of the massive controls that all governments in this nation, federal, state and local, combined with the power forces, have and still exert upon the American people. America was designed as a Paradise, an egalitarian Constitutional Republic and a beacon of Freedom and Light for all the peoples of this world. Tragically, the original design and intentions never manifested because the American people failed their responsibility of self-governance, thus, never held governments to the strict Constitutional mandates imposed upon all government officers. We have mentioned this before, but it is so important that we mention this again. Without Constitutional controls exerted by the people upon their governments, federal, state and local, the governments did and do whatever they want, therefore routinely harm the people and America, herself, by vast numbers of un-Constitutional acts and actions. If the American society takes stock of this fact and does not want to continue its failure, then that society must awaken to its failure and resolve to correct it. CHAPTER Eight provides some methods for those who are interested in maintaining what is left of our Constitutional Republic.

As we mentioned earlier in this book, the American Constitution is the finest egalitarian document ever created by mankind for the governance of a nation by the people of that nation.

Tragically, the American people have never once, as a society, ever taken the responsibility entrusted to them by the Constitution, thus, as stated above, have never held governments to the Constitutional mandates imposed upon them. As a result of this societal failure, governments do whatever they so choose, without serious, Constitutional challenge, objection or comment from the people. The recent COVID-19 scam is a prime and present example, but in American history, there are *thousands* more. However, the magnitude of governments' blatantly criminal violations of Constitutional mandates imposed upon them—their abject refusal to honor and uphold Constitutional guarantees made to the people!—should be a clarion call to we the people that **there is no legitimate, lawful, constitutional governance anywhere in America!**

Though governments' fraudulent "justifications" of their un-Constitutional, unlawful tyranny under the cover of COVID-19 may have initially seemed rational to many who believed the alleged "pandemic" was real, by now, most Americans have realized that this alleged "pandemic" was in fact a scam deliberately created to harm them. This realization should be a dire warning to all Americans of the impending despotic slavery these traitors intend to impose upon every freedom-loving American. If we, the American people, as individuals and as a society, allow this ruthless criminal tyranny to stand unopposed, then, a free America is doomed. If we lack the *courage* to exercise our inherent political power, enforce our lawful rights, uphold our duties to expose and stop this genocidal scam, holding those orchestrating and imposing it fully accountable for their treason, then we fail ourselves and America so monumentally that the darkest, cruelest tyrannies in known history will be repeated and exceeded in a bleak dystopian existence. I include here a relevant quote from a July 7th, 1775 letter written by one of Jack's most famous maternal ancestors, John Adams, to his beloved wife, Abigail: *"Your Description of the Distresses of the worthy Inhabitants of Boston, and the other Sea Port Towns, is enough to melt an Heart of Stone. Our Consolation must be this, my dear, that Cities may be rebuilt, and a People reduced to Poverty, may acquire fresh Property: But a Constitution of Government once changed from Freedom, can never be restored. Liberty once lost is lost forever. When the People once surrender their share in the Legislature, and their Right of defending the Limitations upon the Government, and of resisting every Encroachment upon them, they can never regain it..."*

In the face of the threats to our freedoms, one of the things Americans must quickly do is to get as **independent** as possible, away from stifling, overbearing government restrictions and controls, away from corporate and banking controls, and out of the restrictive box that the system has established for the American society. Independence in all aspects of life is the only thing that can protect Americans from the adverse effects caused by the actions, and inactions, of despotic governments and their collaborating power forces, in all forms. When people are dependent upon anyone or any system, other than themselves, they are at the mercy of and beholden to the will and the whim of those others. In a fair and just world, where the playing fields are level, perhaps this would not present too much of a challenge or obstacle. However, in a world where virtually everything is rigged in favor of greedy, power hungry, ruthlessly controlling people in governments and throughout the entire controlling system, which governments and the power forces enforce, then, any form of dependency upon this evil system these miscreants have created and rule is dangerous to the extreme. The need for independence has never been greater than it is right now! Just as the brave people who came to America before our nation was founded showed independent spirits, courageously living challenging lives just to survive, then, eventually thrive, the people of today's America must possess and demonstrate independence of spirit, of mind, and knowledge of practical skills in order for them to survive and thrive.

No one who is dependent upon others will fare well in the chaos that is threatening America, so it is imperative that Americans realize this and do everything they possibly can to strike out on their own, earn their own way, and make the best lives they can for themselves and their families. The system, as it is now, is wicked, and will likely become even wickeder, unless the people of this nation lawfully rise up against it and stop the frightening progress of evil in America. Our Constitution demands this of us! This may or may not happen, and it is impossible to predict with certainty how events will manifest in our nation, given the blatant communist takeover which has just shown its ugly head after many decades lurking in the shadows. However, it is clear to most rational, reasonable observers that *unless someone does something to change the system*, the system will continue on its repressive, regressive path until nothing that used to be "American" is recognizable, and everything that epitomizes communism will be shoved in our faces, 24/7/365. Jack and I hate to have to say this, but only the truth can set us free and empower us to make lasting changes for the better.

If Americans have any chance to avoid the horrific fate that awaits them under life in an overtly communist nation, then they must recognize who, what, how and why communism is now openly breathing down our collective necks. This terrible reality did not just happen suddenly, overnight. No, this communist takeover has been brewing, insidiously, patiently, stealthily and steadfastly since around the time of the War of Northern Aggression. You might ask yourself how it is possible that no one in America saw this communism insinuating itself into our nation in every possible way. The answer to this query is that some people did see this; did speak and write and warn of it, but in the way that so many Americans do today, the people, the society, to whom these prescient few people tried to speak just could not fathom this ugly concept in any manner whatsoever. One of the main reasons for this is that Americans are among the most brainwashed, programmed, propagandized and falsely conditioned people on this Earth, but they have no idea that this is so.

From cradle to grave, Americans are told that our nation is the strongest, grandest, most capable nation on Earth, one that holds freedom and justice above all, that would never submit to or support tyranny in any form. Yet, in reality, in the operations of day to day life, it is painfully clear that America *has* submitted to tyranny at the hands of communists who have infiltrated American life by inserting themselves into key positions of influence and power in virtually every institution, industry, corporation, think tank, academic arena, politics, government, religion, "new age" pursuits, media broadcasting, entertainment and other necessary operations and activities of modern life. These communists have created, polished and pushed their sick ideology upon Americans of all stripes, but especially upon the young and vulnerable minds of our children, who have been fed a steady diet of communist propaganda, disguised under various innocuous and benefic sounding names like "socialism, progressivism, liberalism", etc., which, theoretically were "necessary" responses to the alleged "threat of dirty, rotten capitalism", "white privilege", racism, sexism, and other falsely exaggerated narratives invented and implemented by these communist psychopaths.

This more recent, exaggerated form of communism launched its vicious assault on America in earnest sometime around the late '60's, during a time of social unrest that arose from opposition to the ongoing warmongering of the U.S. government, and although the chaos seemed to die down, the relentless provocateurs were always at work, in the shadows, behind the scenes, stirring the pot, working their agenda, creating non-existent problems over minor issues they made up into artificially big problems to keep the people divided and at odds with one another. In reality, communism has been present in America since before the War of Northern Aggression and even earlier, lying in wait to fulfill its diabolical objective—*the total elimination of any form of freedom on this Earth*—which requires the destruction of the American Republic. Tragically, the American people did not realize that they were being played, being used to foment dissidence, division and disenchantment among themselves. The scenario has worked spectacularly well for the communists who have managed in about three generations to turn intelligent, concerned, caring Americans into mindless, apathetic idiots who cannot tell truth from fiction, good from bad, sanity from insanity, friend from foe. The communist agenda which engineered the epic degradation of American society is the real pandemic infecting and threatening all of humanity on Earth!

As you all know, the phony COVID-19 Plandemic was perpetrated upon the entire world, not only America. Communism is bent upon world domination and control in all sectors of government, business, industry, banking, monetary policy, institutions, academia, media and society. For a very small group of people to be able to pull this scam off on the entire world within a two to three week period speaks volumes about the depth, width and breadth of the hold used by those who direct the communist agenda and ruthlessly use it to expand their wealth, power and control. For such a small segment of society to wield such enormous power and control clearly indicates that this power base has a total lock on the entire world. If this were not true, then, obviously, the COVID-19 Plandemic would never have materialized in the first place. The fact that it did clearly demonstrates the massive power and influence within this small controlling group. When every leader of every nation and every corporation, bank, scholastic, medical, religious, media and other institution bend their knees to this power and follow the tyrannical dictates presented to them, what chance does the average guy or gal have against this enormous power force? Unfortunately, as we have said right along, average people are not very aware of reality at all, and if they were and if they exhibited some basic intelligence and common sense, then the diabolical tyranny now ruling us would never have been allowed to arise. The fact that it did further reinforces the massive power held by that small group, and illuminates the dire cost of the people's ignorance.

Basic common sense is very important, if we as a people are to ever escape the clutches of this diabolical power manifest in every country of the world, especially right here in America. Common sense gives us the ability to recognize this evil, but the system has drummed out common sense in the people, has vilified it to the point that most people will only consider what is spoken by the "experts" on television, on radio and in newsprint, whether these are politicians, bureaucrats, doctors, lawyers, movie stars, sports figures or some other form of "authority". The people will swallow the musings of unqualified celebrities, but will not think for themselves, because they have been programmed not to. It is very unfortunate that most people do not exhibit even a modicum of basic intelligence and common sense, and simply follow orders, do as they are told, do not question, object or challenge, but simply remain in their little boxes throughout their entire existences. While Margy and I would welcome and love to see a genuine spiritual epiphany take place overnight to awaken these people to the horrific realities playing out throughout the world, it is very doubtful that Spirit even wants to deal with such ridiculous people. It is a well-founded position that Spirit provided humans with an opportunity to learn, to grow, to make mistakes, recognize and correct them, and solve their own problems, but humans, as societies, have never been able to do this in the entire history of this world. Individuals have. Small groups have, but entire societies never have, so the problems persist and increase exponentially, because the people fail to recognize their errors, do anything differently and never learn from their past.

If *you* do not want to be subject to the conditions that will impact the unquestioning herd in the near future, unless by some miracle the evil is stopped in its tracks, then separation from the herd is absolutely imperative. For those who are sane enough to understand the true reality as it exists, and not as it is propagandized to be, getting as far away from the herd, the box and from system's controls is absolutely requisite. Margy and I would obviously love to see the American people and the people of the world awaken and take the proper lawful measures to stop this manifest evil. However, based upon the past, which, unfortunately influences and controls the present, the people have never so acted, which is why these past problems persist in the present. The present problems are not being resolved by the world's societies; therefore, absent mindful, lawful actions by the people to stop and correct them, the present problems will carry into the future. If you want a viable future for yourself and your family, then what you do now can help ensure that *your* future will be as good as it can be in a totally insane world. Hopefully, this book has provided you with the methodology to help you do exactly that and we wish you much success in your future endeavors.

Jack and Margy Flynn
Cherokee Village, Arkansas

September 17th, 2021

JACK AND MARGY FLYNN

Jack and Margy were both born in Boston, Massachusetts, the birthplace of the American Revolution and once the cradle of liberty for America. Sadly, it is now one of the seats of communism in this country. Throughout their lives, they have lived in many different states in this country and traveled extensively in Europe. Both have been involved in many different professions over the years, but their main focus has always been justice, truth, the Constitution and the quest to restore true Constitutional governance to America.

Since they were very young children, Jack and Margy did not see the world and its societies as their parents, relatives, friends, schoolmates and others did and do. They quickly learned that the overwhelming majority of society saw things, events and actions as they were falsely programmed to see them, not as they actually were. From an early age, Jack and Margy decided to walk their own paths, and speak direct truth in the most straightforward manner possible. Over the decades, they have met countless people who opposed this directness and especially this truth. When they met in 1991, it was love at first sight and they soon found out that they had been traveling the same paths for years and were kindred spirits who love their country, but could see a terrible future stealthily unfolding for America and this world through the insidious infiltration of communism in government and every American institution.

Their combined intent was to restore Constitutional governance to America by awakening the people to the unadulterated truth that their governments have been usurped by traitors and to the existing realities imposed by the ruthless beings who malevolently control societies worldwide. The Flynn's did this in lectures, seminars, workshops, on radio, television and in films. However, of all the people they have reached over the years, amounting to many millions, only a very minuscule percentage of those people actually used Jack and Margy's Constitutional Methods and court procedures to stop errant governments and gain victories for the people, in and out of court. Had the percentages been reversed, then, their Constitutional Methods would have established tremendous traction in America, the errant, un-Constitutional governments would have been held accountable for their crimes and treason, and, possibly, the problems now crushing America and her people would never have occurred.

Because the message which Jack and Margy have tried to convey to the American people is so disturbing to the minds of those who have been conditioned to blindly obey "authorities", no matter how senselessly they act and how ineffectively and despotically they govern, it has been very difficult for most Americans to accept the truths Jack and Margy have shared, and almost impossible for the people to fathom that they have the inherent right and duty to demand good government and to lawfully enforce the mandates of the Constitution upon any and all forms of governance in this nation. The propaganda and programming is so deep, so effective and so controlling that most people cannot envision themselves ever challenging "the powers that be", so they never do so. This ignorance is profoundly tragic in a country that is supposed to be a self-governing nation. Jack and Margy emphasize that self-governing people willingly and enthusiastically oversee and direct their governments, realize that they must be vigilant, persistent and consistent in their oversight, and must take all lawful means available to them to rein in errant governments by holding those who operate them to the strict mandates of our Constitution. As Margy taught during seminars and workshops, "Self-governance is not a spectator sport!" and "Freedom and Responsibility are two sides of the same coin." If Americans want to be truly free, then, they must willingly accept the responsibility which truly self-governing people routinely exercise to hold their governments accountable for their actions.

Jack and Margy stress the fact that since the Constitution is the supreme Law of the Land, and since all government officers take oaths to the Constitution, then, no one in any government has any lawful authority or excuse to disobey, deny, defy, oppose and violate the Constitution, and if public officers so act, then, they exceed their limited authority delegated to them by the people through the Constitution, therefore are unfit to hold office, prohibited to receive public funds, so must be immediately removed, pursuant to the mandates of Sections 3 & 4 of the 14th Amendment. In essence, government officers, once challenged on their un-Constitutional actions, have absolutely no comeback for the Constitution and their sworn duties to uphold it over and above any other form of law. Period! The Constitution is the governments' kryptonite! However, it is up to the people to use it against these miscreants in public office. It is Jack and Margy's fondest wish that the American people, who now appear to be waking up in ever-growing numbers, due to the tyranny they have endured during the Covid-19 Scamdemic, will finally claim their inherent political power as the legitimate, lawful, *de jure* government of this nation, recognize that the only way to save America is the restoration of Constitutional governance, comprehend that *they* are the ones who must do this, en masse, and then use Jack and Margy's Constitutional Methods to lawfully take back their precious country—our Constitutional Republic.

In early spring, 2022, Jack and Margy announced their fourth retirement from active work with the Constitution. Both are very disappointed that, in the nearly seven decades in which they have been active in not only teaching the Constitution, but also showing the people how to *apply* it against errant governments, the great masses of the American people have had no interest in methods that would restore Constitutional governance to America and bring justice, prosperity and sanity back to their lives. From this point forward, they will devote their time to writing books, both non-fiction and fiction, which they hope may rekindle in the American people the courageous spirit and love of freedom shared by our amazing forefathers who founded this great nation. If, by some miracle, this should happen, the future could be bright for us all, something which both Jack and Margy would truly love to see manifest. Until then, the Flynns live peaceably and quietly in Cherokee Village, Arkansas, with their three beautiful dogs, four lovely cats and the various wild wood creatures and birds that grace them with their visits from time to time.

CPSIA information can be obtained
at www.ICGtesting.com
Printed in the USA
LVHW051329070123
736454LV00006B/518